The Wealth of a Nation

The Wealth of a Nation

A History of Trade Politics in America

C. DONALD JOHNSON

OXFORD
UNIVERSITY PRESS

Oxford University Press is a department of the University of Oxford. It furthers
the University's objective of excellence in research, scholarship, and education
by publishing worldwide. Oxford is a registered trade mark of Oxford University
Press in the UK and certain other countries.

Published in the United States of America by Oxford University Press
198 Madison Avenue, New York, NY 10016, United States of America.

Library of Congress Cataloging-in-Publication Data
Names: Johnson, Don, 1948– author.
Title: The wealth of a nation : a history of trade politics in America / C. Donald Johnson.
Description: New York, NY : Oxford University Press, [2018] | Includes bibliographical references.
Identifiers: LCCN 2017033348 | ISBN 9780190865917 (hardcover) | ISBN 9780190865931 (epub)
Subjects: LCSH: Free trade—United States—History. | United States—Commercial policy—History. |
United States—Commerce—History. | United States—Economic policy.
Classification: LCC HF1753.J64 2018 | DDC 382/.710973—dc23
LC record available at https://lccn.loc.gov/2017033348

9 8 7 6 5 4 3 2

Printed by Sheridan Books, Inc., United States of America

To Suzanne Spratlin Johnson, Anna Johnson Barnett,
and the memory of Eugenia Hailey Johnson
—the strong, loving, wise, and stabilizing
women in my life.

Contents

List of Figures   ix

Preface   xiii

Acknowledgments   xix

Introduction: The Battle in Seattle and Adam Smith   1

**PART ONE: FROM HAMILTON TO SMOOT-HAWLEY: THE RISE
              AND FALL OF THE US PROTECTIONIST SYSTEM**

1 "A Genuine American System"   35

2 Crisis, Compromise, and Free Trade in the
  Jacksonian Democracy   61

3 Civil War and Robber Barons   85

4 The Gilded Age of Protectionism   108

5 Trade Reform in the Progressive Era   136

6 The Roaring Twenties and the Path to
  Smoot-Hawley   176

PART TWO: TRANSFORMATION: THE CREATION OF
            THE LIBERAL ECONOMIC ORDER

 7 FDR and Cordell Hull   207

 8 The Brain Trust   225

 9 The Dawn of the Multilateral Trading System   256

10 The Anglo-American Special Relationship   284

11 The Postwar Atlantic Alliance   314

12 The Birth of GATT   343

13 The Havana Charter   377

PART THREE: THE SURVIVAL OF THE SYSTEM

14 A New Economic Order?   405

15 Labor's Love Is Lost   440

16 Advancing Worker Rights beyond the WTO   486

Conclusion: Donald Trump, the Forgotten Man, and
the Liberal Economic Order   528

Notes   565

Bibliography   607

About the Author   617

Index   619

Figures

I.1 Adam Smith, John Kay 1790 engraving (Library of Congress)   10

1.1 Alexander Hamilton, John Trumbull 1805 painting
(Library of Congress)   40

1.2 Thomas Jefferson, Charles Balthazar Julien Fevret de
Saint-Mémin 1805 engraving (Library of Congress)   46

1.3 Henry Clay, John Neagle 1843 painting (Library of Congress)   54

2.1 John C. Calhoun, A. H. Richie 1852 engraving
(Library of Congress)   70

2.2 Andrew Jackson in Lafayette Square inscribed with
his anti-nullification toast: "Our Federal Union—it
must be preserved"   75

3.1 Ida Tarbell, muckraking journalist and author of *The Tariff
in Our Times* depicting the corruption in trade politics
after the Civil War (Library of Congress)   107

4.1 *Puck*'s late nineteenth-century satirical depiction of
collusion among Congress and the corporate monopolies
to rob taxpayers through protectionist tariffs: "Our Robber
Barons" (in author's collection)   125

5.1 Presidents Theodore Roosevelt and William Howard Taft
c.1909 (Library of Congress)   139

5.2 *Puck*'s portrayal of ex–robber baron Andrew Carnegie as
"Brutus" turning against protection for the steel industry
after he sold his interest: "Et tu, Andy!" (Library of Congress)   143

5.3 Woodrow Wilson and William Jennings Bryan as a team
     in 1912 (Library of Congress)   158
5.4 AFL president Samuel Gompers at Democratic National
     Convention 1912 (Library of Congress)   161
5.5 President Wilson was the first president to address
     Congress since John Adams when he called a special
     session for tariff reform in 1913 (Library of Congress)   162
6.1 Representative Willis Hawley (left) and Senator Reed Smoot
     in 1929, authors of the Smoot-Hawley Tariff Act of 1930
     (Library of Congress)   191
7.1 Representative Cordell Hull as chairman of the Democratic
     National Committee in 1924 (Library of Congress)   216
8.1 President Hoover and FDR on the way to the US Capitol
     for Roosevelt's inauguration March 4, 1933
     (Library of Congress)   234
9.1 Secretary of State Hull signs the first trade agreement
     under the RTAA with Brazil in the Oval Office in
     the presence of President Roosevelt with
     the Brazilian minister of finance Arthur Souza Costa
     and Brazilian ambassador Oswaldo Aranha
     (Library of Congress)   271
10.1 FDR presents to Secretary Hull the pen he used to
     extend the RTAA program in 1940 for three more years
     in the presence of (L to R) Secretary of Agriculture
     (and soon to be vice president) Henry Wallace; Senator Pat
     Harrison, chairman of the Senate Finance Committee; and
     Rep. Robert Doughton, chairman of the House Ways
     and Means Committee (Library of Congress)   286
10.2 Senators Robert Taft and Arthur Vandenberg, leaders of
     the GOP isolationists until after Pearl Harbor, when
     Vandenberg became a pro-trade internationalist often
     at odds with the Taft wing of the party (Library of Congress)   289
10.3 FDR and Prime Minister Winston Churchill
     aboard the battleship HMS *Prince of Wales* on
     August 10, 1941, during the Atlantic
     Conference (Associated Press)   298

11.1 Lord John Maynard Keynes and Lady Keynes, Lydia
      Lopokova, at the first meeting of the IMF in Savannah,
      Georgia, March 10, 1946, one month before his death
      (Associated Press)   335
12.1 President Truman (right) confers with his former Senate
      colleagues, Secretary of State James Byrnes (left) and
      Senator Arthur Vandenberg (center) (Harry S. Truman
      Presidential Library)   349
12.2 British foreign secretary Earnest Bevin and Chancellor
      of the Exchequer Sir Stafford Cripps (1949) (Library of
      Congress)   374
13.1 Will Clayton with Clair Wilcox signing the ITO Charter
      in Havana on March 24, 1948 (Harry S. Truman
      Presidential Library)   401
15.1 President Eisenhower, Senate Majority Leader Lyndon
      Johnson, and Secretary of State John Foster Dulles at a
      bipartisan White House luncheon seeking a more
      receptive political environment for trade (1955) (Library
      of Congress)   449
15.2 President-elect John F. Kennedy with Arthur Goldberg,
      special counsel to AFL-CIO to become Secretary of Labor,
      and AFL-CIO president George Meany at Kennedy's
      Georgetown home (1960) (Associated Press)   453
15.3 Representative Wilbur Mills, the powerful chairman
      of the Ways and Means Committee (1971) (Library
      of Congress)   459
16.1 The author and Cambodian commerce minister Cham
      Prasidh sign the US–Cambodia Textile Agreement
      in Phnom Penh (January 1999)   503
16.2 Chairman of the House Ways and Means Committee
      Charlie Rangel (left) and Subcommittee on Trade
      chairman Sander Levin, authors of the May 10th
      Agreement (Associated Press)   515
C.1   President Trump, with then chief of staff Reince Preibus
      (center) and trade adviser Peter Navarro (right), displays
      Executive Order directing USTR to exit TPP and move
      to bilateral from multilateral negotiations (Getty Images) 530

Preface

As the seasons change from summer to fall from the vantage point of my office on our family farm in rural north Georgia, I am struck by the tumult and turbulence the world is facing in the early months of the Trump era. In this particular setting—in an old house that has seen so many seasons of American history since before the Civil War, surrounded by old trees outside and even older books inside—and at this particular moment—with the liberal geopolitical and economic institutions created to avoid another Depression and the world wars of the twentieth century facing perhaps the greatest existential threats since they were created—I review the final edits of the manuscript for this book taking the long view of the politics of trade in America.

Centuries before President Donald Trump withdrew from the Trans Pacific Partnership and other international leadership roles, while promising to build a "big, beautiful wall"—indeed, centuries before Adam Smith wrote the seminal treatise that is the foundational reference for this book—there was another great global power that chose to withdraw from engagement with the world and its markets and to retire behind a Great Wall.

Since I began traveling to East Asia as a trade negotiator in the late 1990s and began reading Chinese history, one of the more fascinating periods that I have come across—a period that has particular relevance to the politics of trade today—takes place during the reign of Zhu Di, who became Yongle, the third emperor of the Ming Dynasty, in 1402. Zhu Di moved the capital to Beijing from Nanjing and expanded the sphere of Chinese culture and influence far beyond its territories. He repaired and reopened the 2,000-mile Grand Canal to transport grain from the fertile Yangtze River valley in the south to Beijing and built majestic monuments known to most tourists visiting China today, including the imperial palace of the Forbidden City and the Temple of Heaven, and he established the Ming Tombs with his own. Zhu Di personally led five successful military campaigns north of the Great Wall against the Mongols, who had ruled China for the century preceding Ming rule under the Yuan Dynasty beginning under Kublai Khan. Zhu Di fought the Mongols his entire life as they continued to be the greatest threat to Ming rule. Although Zhu Di's tactics were often ruthless, his reign is considered one of the most brilliant in Chinese history.

One of the premier achievements of the reign of emperor Yongle was the expansion of the Ming naval fleet under the admiral Zheng He and the historic maritime empire created through Zheng's expeditions. Zheng He was the son of a devout Muslim of Mongol extraction who fought with Mongol rebels against the Ming army and was killed in battle. The Ming soldiers captured the ten-year-old Zheng, castrated him, and gave him as a servant to Zhu Di, a prince and prominent young army officer at the time. Though during the reigns of Zhu Di's predecessors, eunuchs were not trusted with political or significant administrative assignments, Zheng became a valued adviser and confidant to Zhu Di throughout his military campaigns, including the rebellion Zhu Di led to take the throne from his nephew not long after the death of Zhu Di's father, emperor Hong Wu. Shortly after becoming emperor, Zhu Di placed Zheng in charge of his naval fleet.

Chinese vessels and sea charts had led the world for several centuries, but Zheng He expanded the capacity and reach of China's navy exponentially. His lead ships, called "treasure ships," were estimated to be between 400 and 600 feet long and over 150 feet wide (at least five times the size of the vessels sailed by Christopher Columbus ninety years later). Each of these ships, which numbered more than sixty on the first voyage with nine masts and twelve sails, carried at least 500 sailors and treasures of Chinese porcelain, silk goods, iron implements, and silver coins. The entire fleet of over 300 assorted ships carried horses, weaponry, grain, and a crew of around 28,000 men. From 1405 to 1433, Zheng led seven voyages, lasting two years each, to more than thirty countries throughout Asia, the Middle East, and Africa. His plan under Zhu Di's direction was to chart the entire world, carrying thousands of tons of treasure and a military force to promote the power and influence of the Ming dynasty and build a great empire through gifts, trade, and foreign domination. Using his military and diplomatic skills, Zheng founded numerous colonies during these voyages and brought many of the kingdoms he visited within the Chinese tribute system. Zheng spread Chinese culture and influence throughout the regions he traveled, which can be traced centuries after his expeditions ended, and temples were constructed in his honor.

After Zhu Di died in 1424 from an illness acquired during his last expedition against the Mongols, however, the imperial power and influence of the Chinese navy soon came to an end. The two succeeding emperors found Zheng's expeditions too extravagant at a time when Mongols continued to be the greatest threat to the dynasty. Unlike Zhu Di and Zheng He, they saw little value in interaction with the outside world. Zhu Di's grandson, emperor Xuande, permitted only one last voyage during which Zheng traveled to Mecca and died at sea on the return home.

From this time forward, the dynasty allowed its oceangoing vessels to deteriorate without repair and withdrew behind the Great Wall in the grand sanctity of the "Middle Kingdom." The kingdom closed its ports to foreign ships, which the powers believed only carried barbarians, in xenophobic resistance to the outside world. This policy continued into the Qing dynasty and ultimately led to disastrous and humiliating consequences in the last century of the empire and beyond. The Opium Wars, the territorial concessions taken by the Western powers, and the ravaging abuses inflicted by Japanese militarism have all instilled a lasting national resentment that impacts Chinese policy to this day.

The current leader of the Chinese Communist Party, Xi Jinping, who has become the most powerful Chinese ruler at least since Deng Xiaoping, invoked the slogan the "Chinese Dream" as the guiding creed for his regime soon after he became president of the People's Republic of China in 2012. At first, many observers likened the phrase to a meaning similar to the "American dream" of individual economic prosperity, especially in view of the rising wealth of China as much of its population emerged from poverty under the economic reforms implemented during Deng's rule. But Xi's use of the slogan offered a much broader theme. The dream he proposed was a nationalistic call for "a great rejuvenation of the Chinese nation." Frankly, the message sounds something like a call very similar to one that we often see on baseball caps in America, "Make China Great Again," but with a true reference point to a time when China really was the single most powerful nation on Earth.

President Xi cited the Chinese dream for a national rejuvenation in a speech given at the National Museum of China commending an exhibition called "Road to Revival," which juxtaposed the achievements of ancient imperial China in the permanent exhibit against the spectacle of national humiliation that followed the penetration of European imperialists into the isolated Middle Kingdom and ended with the Second Sino-Japanese War from 1931 to 1945. The exhibition presented a sanitized version of the progress made since the communist "liberation" of China in 1949 on the road to the current "socialist market economy," or what Deng Xiaoping called "socialism with Chinese characteristics." Of course, the exhibits gave no hint of the 1989 massacre that occurred in front of the museum on Tiananmen Square, downplayed the chaotic destruction of the Cultural Revolution, and largely ignored China's other self-inflicted disasters occurring during the rule of the charismatic Mao Zedong. It was against this backdrop that Xi urged national unity in the effort to revive the pride and greatness of China.

The legacy of the eunuch admiral Zheng He's maritime exploits was almost lost when after his death the Mandarin elites, who were competing with the eunuchs for important ranks in the imperial court, destroyed most of the records of his voyages and diplomatic accomplishments. Yet as the new Chinese republic began building a navy to defend against the imperial Japanese incursions in the early twentieth century, the memory of Zheng's powerful navy was revived for a time. More recently in the present century his diplomatic successes are being honored by recalling his exploits as a national hero and by imitation, especially in the use of soft power to extend Chinese influence. As China has risen to become the second largest economy in the world behind the United States, it has taken its modern version of treasure ships abroad to welcoming countries and invested in infrastructure and established trade relationships.

I spent eight summers teaching American and Chinese law students at Tsinghua University Law School in Beijing a course on U.S.-China Trade Issues under the WTO, which included seminars with the Chinese Ministry of Commerce and the American Embassy in Beijing hearing each complain about the other's trade violations. One thing that my students learned from this experience, if nothing else, is that the rules-based liberal trade system now embodied in the World Trade Organization is critical to the economic stability vital to the national interests of these two economic powers. It may even help them become "great" again.

As an American who has been involved with trade policy as a congressional staffer, practitioner, policymaker, negotiator, and academic for over four decades, I freely admit to being a partisan for the liberal economic institutions that the generation of our fathers and grandfathers created. Their effort was the culmination of a struggle that began at the time Adam Smith published *An Inquiry into the Nature and Causes of the Wealth of Nations*. Smith's seminal treatise declared itself to the world in the same year that our founding fathers declared the existence of the United States of America. The world-changing history that followed 1776, I believe, is no coincidence. While we owe a multitude of different factors for our growth as the most powerful and prosperous nation in world history, certainly one of the most influential is that we have led the world in applying the liberal insights of both Adam Smith and our own founders in structures and institutions that support broad prosperity, particularly for the working class. This book tells the practical political story of how that happened, in all its fits and starts.

Today, the United States and most societies of the world are in a period of profound technological, economic, social, and political transition that threatens to undermine the liberal economic order that we created—indeed, threatens to undermine liberalism itself. The wealth of our nation depends on whether we can learn a new lesson from our own history.

Don Johnson
Royston, Georgia
September 2017

Acknowledgments

The first debt I acknowledge concerning this work is for the interest in politics that I inherited from my family. This interest came to me from my father, Clete Johnson, as well as my grandfather, and great-grandfather—all lawyers who served honorably in elected public office. Without this driving curiosity, I would likely not have experienced political office myself nor have been able to finish the research and writing for the book. I am also indebted to my primary professor and mentor in law school, Dean Rusk, who arranged a scholarship for me to study international law at The Hague. Secretary Rusk and Lord Lionel Robbins, whose lectures on economic history during graduate school at LSE, inspired my interest in the liberal postwar international order that both men played a role in creating.

I am also grateful to Congressman Phil Landrum (D-GA) for giving me my first job after law school and later for making sure that I was hired on the staff of the House Ways and Means Committee as it began consideration of the legislation that became the Trade Act of 1974. It was there, under the wise and tolerant tutelage of Harry Lamar, that I began to learn the real lessons of trade politics by watching such committee members as Chairman Wilbur Mills (D-AR), Sam Gibbons (D-FL), Charlie Vanik (D-OH), James Burke (D-MA), Herman Schneebeli (R-PA), and Barber Conable (R-NY) as they represented their diverse interests. Twenty years later, as a member of Congress during consideration of NAFTA and the WTO, I absorbed more intense lessons in trade politics from my constituents in the 10th District of Georgia and from Democratic colleagues on both sides of the issue, including congressmen Bill Richardson (D-NM) and Bob Matsui (D-CA) on the pro-side and Dick Gephardt (D-MO), Dave Bonior (D-MI), and my fresh-man friend Sherrod Brown (D-OH) on the opposition. With most of the favorable votes coming from the GOP by this time, I learned new lessons about how a bipartisan coalition can achieve pro-trade victories.

I thank President Bill Clinton for the opportunity to serve as ambassador and chief textile negotiator in the Office of the United States Trade Representative (USTR) under the effective leadership of Ambassador Charlene Barshefsky. I am grateful for the support and counsel given me in that job by Congressman John Spratt (D-SC), leader of the Textile Caucus. Anyone who has worked in the comparatively small agency of USTR comes away impressed, if not overwhelmed, by the diligence and high quality of public servants employed in the Winder Building. My deputy, Caroyl Miller, knew more about the history and technical aspects of textile trade negotiations than I ever thought possible, and my lawyer, Demetrios Marantis, later became the chief trade counsel for the Senate Finance Committee before becoming deputy USTR under President Barack Obama. My experience at USTR was invaluable in the formulation of this book, and my colleagues on the interagency negotiating delegation, especially Troy Cribb at Commerce, were critical to the narrative.

After leaving the Clinton administration and joining the Patton Boggs law firm in Washington, DC, I began researching and writing the introductory section of the book. I am thankful to my partners there, including especially the late Tom Boggs, Frank Samolis, and Tim Chorba (among many others) for supporting this effort and for the pleasure of working with them on trade policy issues for several years.

I wrote most of this book over the past decade while serving as director of the Dean Rusk Center for International Law and Policy and teaching courses in international trade law at the University of Georgia School of Law. I am extremely grateful to Dean Rebecca H. White for the support she gave to me and to the Rusk Center during my tenure there. Without Dean White's commitment we could not have attained the record of scholarship; high-profile conferences; study abroad programs in China, Brussels, and Geneva; international judicial training programs; and foreign internships for students. Above all, I am quite sure that I owe the completion of this work to my presence on the Georgia Law campus for eleven years.

I am very grateful to my colleagues at the Rusk Center in assisting with the book. The late international law professor Gabriel Wilner read and provided valuable comments on some of the early drafts of the first part of the book, and we shared countless conversations about its theme, a subject he had taught for decades. He was always an important resource for me and a close friend. I was very fortunate to have two excellent writers to serve as assistant directors at the Center during my time there—Andre Barbic and Laura Kagel. As "light" editors they dutifully came along behind me and turned some of my long sentences into short ones and awkward passive statements into readable active ones. I was especially grateful that they were not afraid to tell me when something I had written made no sense to them. One of the great benefits of academic life is the opportunity to work with bright, diligent students and, of course, to profit from their research. I am especially thankful to the following student research assistants who worked with me over a number of years on this book: the late Richard Houston, Nate Hunt, Jackson Harris, Kelly Pierce, Matthew Bennett, Daniel Olds, Jared Hegberg, Mitch O'Hara, and Eric Heath.

Another vital advantage to a project of this breadth is the library resources available at a great research university. The staff at the main and law school libraries of the University of Georgia have been extraordinary in ensuring that I had all the necessary tools and materials for this research. Likewise, I am most grateful for the superb assistance provided to me by the staff at the Library of Congress, the Congressional Research Service, and the presidential libraries of Franklin D. Roosevelt, Harry S. Truman, John F. Kennedy, and Lyndon B. Johnson.

I give a special word of thanks to my close friend at the University of Georgia School of Public and International Affairs, Professor Loch Johnson. An expert in many fields—foremost in national security intelligence—Loch has been a faithful counselor to me in the long process of completing this book. He has been willing to share, without complaint, much of his valuable time to read chapters and provide important insights and critical recommendations that have been enormously helpful.

Finally, and most important, I thank my family for all their help and inspiration in completing this work. My two sons, Clete and Alex—both lawyers, excellent writers, and US Senate committee staffers for much of the time I was writing the book—were extremely helpful with research and editing. But their most valuable contribution came in the same form as that rendered by my wife and best friend (also a careful editor), Suzanne, and daughter, Anna. It is the unconditional love, support, and encouragement from my family that have made finishing this book possible for me.

The Wealth of a Nation

Introduction

The Battle in Seattle and Adam Smith

Political economy, considered as a branch of the
science of a statesman or legislator, proposes two
distinct objects: . . . to enrich both the people and the
sovereign.

To promote the little interest of one little order of men
in one country, it hurts the interest of all other orders
of men in that country, and of all men in all other
countries.[1]

—Adam Smith

The idea for this book came to me on a rainy day in Seattle at the end of
November 1999, as 40,000 anti-globalization protesters effectively trapped
me and the other delegates representing 134 different countries inside our
hotels blocking our participation in a ministerial meeting of the World
Trade Organization (WTO).

The demonstrators were a colorful lot—dressed nonthreateningly
as sea turtles, butterflies, dolphins, trees, and vegetables—as they took to
the streets determined to shut down the wicked activities in which they
presumed we were engaged. Many of the foreign delegates stared in puz-
zled amusement, and later bemused annoyance, as they seemed to be trying to figure out the connection between the costumes and the issues that
they, the delegates themselves, were there to negotiate. In most cases there
was some trade-based connection to the protests, but the event attracted

many of society's discontents who just seemed to be longing for an opportunity to bring back the 1960s. There were, to name a few among the oddly allied opponents, the "Vegan Dykes" marching topless along with electrical workers, right-wing militiamen, anti-nuclear activists, communists, free Burma and free Tibet demonstrators, the Bicycle Alliance of Washington, and defenders of the long-deceased singer/actor/activist Paul Robeson and Mumia Abu-Jamal, a former journalist and Black Panther on death row in Philadelphia for killing a policeman in 1981. "It has sort of become a grab bag of people unhappy with capitalism . . . a little bit carnival like," admitted Mike Dolan, a field director for Global Trade Watch, one of the principal organizers of the demonstrations. A message scribbled on a store window attempted to sum up their collective message: "I don't know what a WTO is, but I fucking hate rich people."[2]

This broad message, which, along with countless more focused ones, had been promoted effectively by the myriad of protest organizers on the World Wide Web of free-market technology, had a broad international following. There were complementary outbursts of the protest as far away as London and Manila, and in more remote and unlikely corners of the world, such as Nashville, Tennessee, at the presidential campaign headquarters of Vice President Al Gore. In Seattle, there were strong protest contingents from all parts of Latin America, Asia, and Europe.

The most prominent of the foreign participants was José Bové, the French sheep farmer and activist who was protesting the retaliatory 100 percent US tariffs imposed on his Roquefort cheese after the European Union refused to comply with a WTO decision against a ban on American hormone-treated beef. Bové spent much of his early childhood in America while his parents studied at the University of California–Berkeley. He became an international celebrity and a national hero in France for bull-dozing a McDonald's restaurant under construction in a French city only a few months before coming to Seattle. His contribution to the protest came in the form of serving 484 pounds of Roquefort cheese, along with French baguettes and Bordeaux wine, in front of a McDonald's while denouncing "*la mal-bouffe*," the lousy "food of the WTO," as he called it, under a sign reading, "Resist McDonaldization."[3]

If there had been a mascot to symbolize the Seattle demonstrations, it no doubt would have been the turtle. It was certainly the predominant costume of the environmental protesters. Appearing like an invasion of teenage mutant ninja turtles, an estimated 250 of the cardboard amphibians pranced through Seattle with signs reading, "Free trade = dead sea turtles." If overwrought for rhetorical impact, they at least had a complaint connected to the WTO. In 1998, the WTO ruled that certain US regulations banning the importation of shrimp from countries that did not require the use of turtle protection devices were inconsistent with WTO obligations.[4] Based upon this decision, Patricia Forkan, the director of the US Humane Society, charged, "The road to Seattle is littered with sea turtle carcasses."

An objective review of this decision, however, leads to a less dramatic conclusion. The US law upon which the regulation was based had two principal objectives. The law fostered the environmentalist objective of forcing governments to adopt stronger protections for the endangered sea turtles. It was also designed to equalize the costs of operation between US fishermen, who were required to use turtle excluder devices in their trawling nets, and their foreign competitors. The Louisiana senators sponsoring the legislation readily acknowledged that they did so to help "our shrimpers in Louisiana."

A large number of shrimp-exporting countries saw it as a discriminatory protectionist measure and initiated the case against the United States in the WTO dispute settlement system. Supported by briefs filed by eleven international environmental organizations, the United States argued that its shrimp-turtle restrictions were sanctioned under Article XX of the General Agreement on Tariffs and Trade (GATT). This provision permits trade restrictions that are "necessary to protect human, animal or plant life or health," or relate to "the conservation of exhaustible natural resources," if they are not arbitrary or discriminatory, nor simply "a disguised restriction on international trade." At the first stage of the dispute settlement process, a WTO panel refused even to consider the amicus curiae briefs of the environmental groups and summarily rejected the American defense of its measures under Article XX. The panel concluded that the restrictions were a clear "threat to the multilateral trading system."

If the panel decision had prevailed on appeal, the environmentalists' protest in Seattle would have been on firmer ground. However, the decision of the Appellate Body was far more balanced. In the first place, it said the panel should have considered the briefs filed by the environmental organizations and sharply criticized the panel's excessive reach in extending a categorical superiority to its view of the purpose of the WTO obligations— that is, to develop a "durable multilateral trading system," which the US shrimp-turtle measure was "undermining." Importantly, the Appellate Body found that the US measures were in fact related "to the protection of exhaustible natural resources" and therefore within the purview of Article XX. It was in the application of these measures that it found fault with the US position. Essentially, it held that the manner in which the measure was being implemented was arbitrary and discriminatory in its application to the WTO member states. The final WTO decision did not attempt to "overturn" the basic restriction, which the ruling found to have sufficient inherent flexibility to be enforced consistently with WTO obligations.[5]

Indeed, well before the Seattle Ministerial, the United States accepted the decision without changing the underlying law and simply revised its regulatory guidelines so as to continue requiring foreign shrimpers to use turtle-excluding devices in order to export to the American market. As in most cases with balanced decisions, however, neither the advocacy groups nor the complaining countries were pleased. The Earth Island Institute, the principal environmental group behind the broad application of the restrictions, called it "a death blow for sea turtles," while the complaining foreign countries decried it as "dangerous," predicting that it "will result in explosive growth in unilateral, discriminatory, trade-related environmental measures."[6]

While the turtle may have become the symbol of the protest, the clear leader of its mobilization was the American labor movement. The most widely perceived victim, and correspondingly the most attractive underdog, of trade liberalization is the American worker. It is a perception that has created a formidable bond among the vast majority of those associated with the blue-collar job market, union and non-union alike. This bond is not limited to workers impacted by trade, such as those in textile and steel jobs; counterintuitively, it even includes workers whose jobs depend on trade for survival. The local Seattle Machinists Union at Boeing—the nation's largest exporter, deriving nearly half its revenues from foreign sales—supplied 900 marshals for the Seattle protest. An estimated 9,600 dockworkers from the International Longshore and Warehouse Union took part in the protest by temporarily shutting down not only the Seattle port but dozens of others all along the West Coast, including the country's largest in Los Angeles and Long Beach, California. Viewing the WTO as the pinnacle of the corporate-dominated world marketplace created "by the corporations, of the corporations and for the corporations," in the words of the American Federation of Labor and Congress of Industrial Organizations (AFL-CIO) president John Sweeney,[7] tens of thousands of workers converged upon Seattle demanding to be heard. According to a handout distributed by the AFL-CIO, "Fast

Facts on Mobilization," union members were to arrive from more than fifty unions, twenty-five states, and 144 countries in car caravans, more than 185 buses, nine planes, and two trains.

On the conference's scheduled start date, November 30, the protesters ruled. The front line surrounded the convention hall with little or no interference by Seattle police. Most of the officials in the trade delegations were pinned in their hotels for much of the day, afraid or unable to venture out. The opening ceremonies were canceled, and any trade negotiations that took place were carried on in hotel rooms and by telephone. In the largest labor protest in American history, 25,000 trade unionists joined forces with at least 10,000 environmentalists and other assorted protesters to take over the streets of Seattle in a rain-soaked march and rally with thunderous anti-trade speeches from the all-star luminaries of American labor. Jay Mazur, president of the Union of Needle Trades Industrial and Textile Employees (UNITE), declared: "The rules of this new global economy have been rigged against workers and we're not going to play by them anymore."[8] United Steelworkers president, George Becker, promised to lead an effort that would force the US Congress to abandon the WTO. "Either they fix the goddamn thing," he said, "or we're going to get out." Teamsters president James P. ("Jimmy") Hoffa declared, "We want the message to go out that the WTO is in trouble; the citizens are re-voting," and proclaimed the event the beginning of a worldwide revolt against "corporate greed."[9]

By late afternoon, the largely peaceful labor protest was followed by a rash of violent acts by a small contingent of "anarchists" wearing black clothing, masks, and, in some cases, Nike sneakers. The anarchists ran through the streets smashing windows and spray painting graffiti on the downtown retail outlets of establishments they considered to be the culprits of trade evils—Niketown, Starbucks, the Gap, and a McDonald's restaurant that had been the site of Jose Bové's protest earlier in the day. As bonfires of trash and police barricades were being ignited on the street corners, the Seattle police with full riot gear finally moved in and shut down the protest with tear gas, rubber bullets, and pepper spray, creating the frightful appearance of an urban war zone in a week that came to be known as the "Battle in Seattle." A Hollywood film of the same name, starring Charlize Theron and Woody Harrelson, later celebrated the triumph of the protest over the alleged nefarious intentions of the WTO.

The first reaction to the demonstrations from free-trade proponents was sublime disdain. The popular liberal economist Paul Krugman offered this explanation of the "urban legend" spurring the anticipated protests in the Internet publication, *Slate,* the week before they began:

> The WTO has become to leftist mythology what the United Nations is to the militia movement: the center of a global conspiracy against all that is good and decent. According to the myth, the "ultra-secretive" WTO has become a sort of super-governmental body that forces nations to bow to the wishes of multinational corporations. It destroys local cultures . . . it despoils the environment; and it rides roughshod over democracy, forcing governments to remove laws that conflict with its sinister purposes.[10]

The *Economist* called the protesters "militant dunces," parading "their ignorance through the streets of Seattle."[11] Jerry Jasinowski, president of the National Association of Manufacturers, called them "loopy . . . dancing in the streets, pushing people, acting crazy."[12] Thomas Friedman, the foreign affairs columnist for the *New York Times,* called them "a Noah's ark of flat-earth advocates, protectionist trade unions and yuppies looking for their 1960s fix."[13] In short, they were a silly and obnoxious hindrance, not to be taken seriously.

But many Western (and, according to the *Economist,* "lame-brained") politicians took them quite seriously.[14] Of the eighty-eight members of the US Congress who attended the Seattle conference, at least one-third had come in sympathy with one or more of the protest groups and some even joined in the opening day march. In a speech to a labor rally, the House Democratic Whip, Congressman David Bonior (D-MI), called the WTO "a battering ram against a century of social progress from clean air and water to consumer safety and workers' rights."[15] While most of the visiting foreign officials from developing countries were critical of the demonstrators and the lack of police control, a member of the European Parliament sympathetic to the protests criticized the police crackdown. "They dress in very strange sort of Star Wars outfits, had tear gas, and I think it was quite a draconian response to the demonstration," she said to a British television reporter.[16] WTO director general Mike Moore, a savvy politician who had risen from a labor organization to become briefly prime minister of New Zealand, condemned the violence but acknowledged that "peaceful protest has often led to important social reforms . . . [and] our critics are not always wrong."[17]

Leaders of both the European Union (EU) and US delegations saw the protests as an opportunity to promote their respective negotiating positions. The French trade minister welcomed them as evidence that economics and politics are inseparable in the fight to limit the negative effects of uncontrolled agricultural trade and genetically modified food imports. Pascal Lamy, the EU trade commissioner, noted with undisguised delight, "What's happening outside is having an effect on the negotiations." In particular, he pointed to the farmers' protest as making it "less possible" for the negotiations to eliminate government subsidies for agricultural exports. On the US side, Sue Esserman, a deputy United States trade representative, chose to comment on the labor demonstrations. "A clear expression of concern by ordinary workers has to be taken into consideration," she declared in explanation of the priority of the US labor rights working group proposal.[18]

The preeminent official sympathizer, however, was US president Bill Clinton. "We should open the process up to all those people who are now demonstrating on the outside," he told reporters as he left for Seattle. "They ought to be a part of it."[19] In a telephone interview with the *Seattle Post-Intelligencer*, he said that while deploring the violent conduct of some of the protesters, he believed that most of the demonstrators were making a valuable contribution to the WTO meeting. From San Francisco, where he was attending a fundraising event for Democratic congressional candidates, he told the reporter that the WTO process must be opened up "so that the voices of labor, the environment and the developing countries can be heard, and so that the decisions are transparent, the records are open, and the consequences are clear." While arguing that, on balance, "the world is much better off because we've expanded trade over the last fifty years," he insisted "we've got to make a better case down deeper into society."[20]

Personally, I viewed the Seattle protest with mixed emotions. As one who had participated in and supported the anti-war and civil rights protests of the late sixties and early seventies, I had sympathy for the protest message but found it misguided as to the effects of the WTO trade regime upon the working class, the environment, and Third World development. Many protesters, longing for a return to the glory days of the protest movement of thirty years before, seemed to have simply latched on to the anti-globalization attack on the WTO and presented it as a tool for the evil purposes of multinational corporations. They could not, I thought, have been aware of the long history in American politics of progressive support for liberal trade policies in a struggle against the corporate special interests seeking protection from market forces that lowered the cost of living for most workers. On the other hand, it was certainly true that many of the labor and environmental issues affected by trade needed to be addressed more effectively and the protesters deserved to be heard.

I will come back to Seattle in chapter 16 of the book, but for now I readily concede that the governmental responses to the demands of labor and environmental organizations to date had been seriously inadequate. In the interest of full disclosure, I am a pro-trade Democrat, which, like the sea turtle, is a political breed currently on the endangered species list. Like President Clinton, I believe that the "world is better off" with "expanded trade," but society deserves a better explanation as to why that is so. Society also deserves to know what is being done to ensure that the system governing international trade will benefit ordinary working families. My own perspective on these issues as a congressional staffer, practitioner, and policymaker since the 1970s has contributed to the theme that runs through the narrative of this book. In contrast to the current conventional view of trade politics, protectionism has historically, more often than not, been a tool of big business to entrench moneyed interests at the expense of the working class.

The purpose of this book is to review the political path leading to the adoption of liberal trade policies in America, the creation of a liberal world trading system, and the current threats to those policies and the system. Political clashes between progressive and conservative forces fighting over free trade and protectionism have raged since 1776, the year Adam Smith published *The Wealth of Nations* and America declared its independence from Great Britain. Smith's enlightened perspectives have remained relevant throughout every period in our history and offer lessons that apply today. This story is far more than a tale of competing economic interests over tariffs; in many ways, the development of American trade policy and the political fights over trade have been a driving force of American history. Often they have contributed substantially to matters of war and peace. This analysis of the evolution of American trade policy will be viewed through the lens of the central political struggle over the wealth of the nation between business and the working class from the birth of the nation to the creation of the global multilateral trading regime.

This book is about the politics, personalities, and political forces— the visible hands—that have narrowly shaped trade policy and broadly influenced American history. It is not a book focused on the pure economics of trade. In the formulation of American trade policy, politics has nearly always trumped economics. In a classic illustration of this point, President Herbert Hoover signed into law the infamous Tariff Act of 1930 (commonly known as the Smoot-Hawley Tariff) after receiving a letter signed by over a thousand of the most prominent economists and business leaders from all over the United States urging him to veto it. This is not to say that good politics is always in conflict with good economics in the making of trade decisions—they often lead to the same policy. After all, American politicians always profess to be acting in the best interest of the country or at least the best interest of their particular constituency. My effort here may often question the sincerity of such claims while attempting to discern and reveal true motivations, but I will not attempt with statistics and graphs to prove or refute whether an action taken was truly in the best economic interest of the country or even the politician's constituency as a whole. That is the job of economists to sort out; mine is to weigh the interests that motivate the policy decision, whether it is driven by a pure conscience regarding the public good, political self-preservation, or some form of bribery.

ADAM SMITH: PHILOSOPHICAL PATRON OF THE WORKING CLASS

A common, if not obligatory, point of reference for any historical discussion of the politics of international trade is Adam Smith's masterpiece, *An Inquiry into the Nature and Causes of the Wealth of Nations*. While the interests affected by trade have evolved since its publication in 1776, many of the core issues in the bitter debates that characterize trade politics today remain essentially unchanged, and an informed discussion about the politics of trade in today's global economy requires a closer look at the principal themes of Smith's seminal work. His simple yet powerful arguments favoring free trade unencumbered by government-imposed protective restrictions have been profound and enduring, yet conventional political wisdom surrounding the book is often misleading. *The Wealth of Nations* is frequently heralded as the gospel authority for the eternal and absolute virtues of free-market economics, and Smith is viewed by many as the intellectual father of self-regulated capitalism—even the godfather of Ayn Rand's crusade for individualism over collectivism. That perspective is, however,

The Author of the Wealth of Nations

FIGURE I.1   Adam Smith, John Kay 1790 engraving (Library of Congress)

an oversimplified and distorted view of Smith's work and his legacy in the world economy over the past two and a half centuries. Most important, it ignores the social, philosophical, and political context in which Smith introduced his theories of political economy.

On one level, Adam Smith's work represents the scientific efforts of an objective scholar determined to explain how the economic system works and how it could be improved. But *The Wealth of Nations* is also fundamentally a political essay. Some of its most moving passages condemn the exploitation by moneyed special interests of mercantilism, the prevailing economic system in eighteenth-century Europe. Smith eloquently championed the workingman whom he felt to be the principal victim of this inefficient and corrupt system. His pro-market arguments were grounded in a belief that a sound economy ensures a fair wage for the laboring classes and allows them to purchase material necessities at a fair price. A broadly based system for creating national wealth that would allow workers to earn and spend more money was his antidote to the inequities of the mercantilist system, which only promoted the wealth of protected vested interests.

THE POLITICAL CONTEXT: MERCANTILISM IN THE AGE OF ENLIGHTENMENT

Although considered the father of classical economics, Adam Smith wrote and taught as a moral and social philosopher, and his major work prior to *The Wealth of Nations* was published under the title *The Theory of Moral Sentiments*. Economics was not considered a distinct discipline in eighteenth-century Britain. Smith and his close friend David Hume, along with other philosophers of the Scottish Enlightenment, focused primarily on the study of human relations. Among Hume's brilliant works were *A Treatise of Human Nature* and *Inquiries Concerning Human Understanding*. Smith's lectures at the University of Glasgow concentrated on ethics, logic, and jurisprudence, drawing from history and social anthropology, as he analyzed the progress of social institutions and the role of law and government in society.

Smith's conclusions in his famous treatise on commercial relations and public prosperity derived from studies of social behavior. His central thesis recognized "a certain propensity in human nature . . . to truck, barter, and exchange one thing for another."[21] This propensity, he determined, is unique to humans: "Nobody ever saw a dog make a fair and deliberate exchange of one bone for another with another dog."[22] Although didactic in style, his simple illustrations about the profound effects of human nature on national wealth were not recounted as part of a purely academic dissertation. Rather, by the time he wrote *The Wealth of Nations*, the professor of moral philosophy's principal intent was to influence policy, not to educate students. The book's lengthy analysis of economic concepts, such as the role of the division of labor in enhancing productivity, no doubt laid the foundation for the independent science of economics. Yet, the analysis was only ancillary to his polemic against mercantilism, which he viewed as a conspiracy against the public good, if not an assault upon nature itself.

Even though prosperity increased for many as the industrial revolution emerged in the post-feudal era of the late 1700s, the masses continued to live in hopelessly miserable conditions. Smith believed, with ample justification, that such conditions were largely the product of misguided government policies embedded in the mercantile system that had dominated the economy of Britain and most of Europe for the two centuries prior to the publication of *The Wealth of Nations*. Under its classical definition, mercantilism demanded a favorable balance of trade—that is, more exports than imports—in order to accumulate national wealth in specie, or coined money, and precious metals. One method of accomplishing this goal was limiting imports; another was imposing severe limitations on the rising cost of domestic labor.

Smith reached his innovative insights about basic economic incentives in the context of a British labor environment that would seem as foreign and nonsensical to us today as leeches are to modern medicine. Since Elizabethan times, prosperity had been denied to laborers by employment restrictions imposed through a strict guild system that prevented competition and kept wages low. Not only were workers coerced into selected trades and prohibited from entering others; instead of the minimum wage and maximum working hour requirements that protect workers today, British laws in Smith's day actually imposed *maximum* wages and *minimum* work days to ensure only subsistence living conditions for the working class and only a few leisure hours.

For instance, in order to prevent "the Encouragement of Idleness," a 1720 law forbade journeymen tailors from being paid more than two shillings per day and required them to work from six in the morning until eight at night with one hour for dinner.[23] In 1768, Parliament increased their *maximum* wage to two shillings and seven pence halfpenny per day and reduced their *minimum* workday from thirteen to twelve hours—not much improvement in a forty-eight-year interval. Under this law, employers convicted for paying their workers too much were fined five pounds, while the recipients of excessive wages were subject to two months at hard labor in the House of Correction.[24]

In addition to the statutory restrictions against improving wages and hours for workers, employers conspired to ensure that the cost of labor did not infringe upon their profits. "Masters," Smith observed, "are always and everywhere in a sort of tacit, but constant and uniform combination, not to raise the wages of labour."[25] In fact, they engaged in what would today be illegal collusion practices:

> To violate this combination is everywhere a most unpopular
> action, and a sort of reproach to a master among his neighbors
> and equals. We seldom, indeed, hear of this combination, because
> it is the usual, and one may say, the natural state of things, which
> nobody ever hears of. Masters, too, sometimes enter into particu-
> lar combinations to sink the wages of labour even [lower]. These

are always done in the utmost silence and secrecy, till the moment of execution.[26]

While employers were free to collude with each other to restrict workers' wages, workers themselves were statutorily prohibited from forming "combinations" or unions of their own to demand better wages or other improved working conditions.[27] Supporters of these restrictive laws argued that higher than subsistence wages and more free time only led to laziness and an unseemly aspiration to luxury. The restrictions, however, not only prevented these undesirable aspirations but also the consumption of many basic necessities. Cloth, for example, was so expensive that most people could afford only a few garments in a lifetime. The Tower Hill area in London became known infamously as "Rag Fair" where the poor trafficked in "dilapidated garments."[28] Even the apparel of plague victims was often scavenged by survivors.

Smith's revolutionary prescription for this problem was to set the market free from these constraints in order to determine the proper level of wages: "The money price of labour is necessarily regulated by two circumstances; the demand for labour, and the price of the necessities and conveniences of life."[29] The "fluctuations" in the price for basic goods aggravated the situation, since wages remained stagnant regardless of a laborer's actual purchasing power.[30] In effect, if a laborer bought food one year at an affordable price, he conceivably would not be able to buy as much the following year. Smith's keen insight into the wage issue demonstrated how this set of circumstances stifled a country's overall wealth and prosperity, not just that of the common worker. Sounding very much the student of human nature, Smith wrote, "The wages of labour are the encouragement of industry, which, like every other human quality, improves in proportion to the encouragement it receives."[31] Far from fostering idleness, Smith believed wage increases would stimulate worker productivity and the whole nation would reap financial rewards.

Smith cited North America as a practical example where no restraints existed on the wages a worker could earn with his labor. While England was then a much richer country than any part of North America, wages were higher in the American colonies than in any part of England. "It is not the actual greatness of national wealth, but its continual increase," Smith contended, "which occasions a rise in the wages of labour." It is not in the richest countries "but in the most thriving, or in those which are growing

rich the fastest, that the wages of labour are highest." Smith presciently inti-
mated that while Great Britain was richer at that point than North America,
this might not always be the case. "Though North America is not yet so rich
as England, it is much more thriving, and advancing with much greater
rapidity to the further acquisitions of riches."[32] After reviewing the circumstances in several other countries, he drew this conclusion:

> The liberal reward of labour, therefore, as it is the necessary effect,
> so it is the natural symptom of increasing national wealth. The
> scanty maintenance of the labouring poor, on the other hand, is
> the natural symptom that things are at a stand, and their starving
> condition that they are going fast backwards.[33]

These oppressive restrictions on laborers were not the only hindrances
to general prosperity imposed by the mercantile system. Book IV of *The
Wealth of Nations* is a polemical attack upon the entire British commercial
system and the monopolist interests controlling it. In this book, Smith popularized "mercantilism" as a pejorative term for the ages. Based essentially
upon the belief that a nation's wealth is measured by its accumulation of
gold and silver, the system was born in the Age of Discovery, and the necessity of funding the expensive navies of the rising maritime nation-states led
to its perpetuation. The government treasury alone could not sustain the
costly wars of the sixteenth and seventeenth centuries, which often arose
as sovereigns competed for economic plunder. Privateers were licensed to
engage in their own conquests against competing nations and to feast on
the spoils of "discovery" in foreign lands. For example, the British crown
granted the intrepid pursuer of El Dorado, Sir Walter Raleigh, a monopoly
on the wine trade for his piracies against Portuguese vessels. The British
East India Company was given not only the spoils of its territory in India
but also the authority to maintain a system of government and defense to
secure its bounty.

To further encourage the enrichment of their country's wealth in gold
and silver, Parliament made trade policy fundamental to the mercantilist system. In order to enhance the national balance of trade, according
to Smith,

> it necessarily became the great object of political economy to
> diminish as much as possible the importation of foreign goods for

home consumption, and to increase as much as possible the exportation of the produce of domestic industry. Its two great engines for enriching the country, therefore, were restraints upon importation, and encouragements to exportation.[34]

This was accomplished through a strict system of export subsidies and export duty refunds, called drawbacks, and import controls, including high import duties and absolute prohibitions of certain sensitive imports. Special interests were also granted import protection and export encouragement through the establishment of foreign colonies and treaties of commerce with other countries, which discriminated against goods from third countries.

By the end of seventeenth century, however, the mercantilist concept of private production of sovereign wealth through conquest had been turned on its head. Instead of enhancing the national treasury, the mercantilists depleted national resources in battles over foreign acquisitions. The enormous cost of Britain's dominion over its colonies—established principally, if not solely, for the purpose of maintaining private monopolies—could not be justified morally or economically. Sovereign wealth was being depleted, and the English people were being forced to pay high prices to cover the excessive profits and fraud in the management of such monopolies as the East India Company. In Smith's view, the mercantilist system sacrificed overall public prosperity in favor of special interests who, with the help of the government, carved out monopolies for themselves.

Smith conceded that import protection had helped create jobs and capital in certain British monopolies but noted, "Whether it tends either to increase the general industry of the society, or to give it the most advantageous direction, is not, perhaps, altogether so evident."[35] Indeed, he later went to great lengths to show "that the single advantage which the monopoly procures to a single order of men is in many different ways hurtful to the general interest of the country."[36] He saw the regulation of commerce through protection of domestic monopolies as an "artificial" diversion of finite national resources for the benefit of a few at the expense of the whole population in defiance of natural liberty in the Age of Enlightenment. In book V, Smith offers a broader condemnation of a system that maintains "inequality of fortune" by securing to the rich "possession of their own advantages." "Civil government, so far as it is instituted for the security of property," Smith contends, "is in reality instituted for the defence of the rich against the poor, or of those who have some property against those who have none at all."[37]

THE INVISIBLE HAND: NATURAL JUSTICE AND ECONOMICS

Smith viewed the restrictions on trade and labor imposed by the mercantile system as both uneconomical and unethical. The benefits of trade should not be measured in the accumulation of gold and silver, he argued, but rather by the exchangeable value of the annual produce of the land and labor of the country. "It would," he wrote, "be too ridiculous to go about seriously to prove that wealth does not consist in money, or gold and silver; but in what money purchases."[38] This point about the true nature of wealth, however, was lost on the mercantilists. The hoarding of precious metals, which resulted from an obsession with an excessively favorable balance of trade, only increased the prices of other commodities in the home market, causing a decrease in wealth. This economic system inhibited consumption, which Smith believed was the sole and self-evident purpose of all production. Rather than measuring wealth by profits directed to protected monopolies and trade guilds, Smith proposed that the abundance of necessities available to its entire people determined a nation's prosperity. "It is but equity besides that they who feed, clothe, and lodge the whole body of the people should have such a share of the produce of their own labour as to be themselves tolerably well-fed, clothed, and lodged."[39]

A principal concern of Smith and his colleagues of the Scottish Enlightenment derived from the idea of natural justice. Smith followed John Locke's belief that

> though the Earth, and all inferior creatures be common to all men, yet every man has a property in his person. This no Body has any right to but himself. The Labour of his body, and the work of his hands, we may say, are properly his. Whatsoever then he removes out of the state of that Nature hath provided, and left it in, he hath mixed his Labour with, and joined to something that is his own, and thereby makes it his property.[40]

Maximum wage laws and monopolistic prices, which infringed upon the rights of man to the products of his own labor, violated this Lockean view of natural law and justice. Moreover, Smith contended, the frustration of the natural motivation of "every man to better his condition" is bad economics.[41] Smith, the moral philosopher, was concerned with the natural rights and social conditions of mankind, but the strength of his argument came not from a moral appeal to the better angels of his audience. The monumental influence of his work arose from the eloquent and sound simplicity of his appeal to the self-interest of his audience. He sought to persuade eighteenth-century policymakers that the mercantile system, whose purpose was to enhance national wealth, actually debased a country's overall security and prosperity. Pointing out "the mean rapacity . . . of the merchants and manufacturers, who neither are nor ought to be the rulers of mankind," he observed that "the capricious ambition of kings and ministers has not during the present and preceding century been more fatal to the repose of Europe than the impertinent jealousy of merchants and manufacturers."[42]

These special interests had had their way in keeping wages low, as well as prices and profits high, by restricting competition—both foreign and domestic—all the while arguing the national advantages of these effects. Smith viewed as pure sophistry such mercantilist pamphlets as Thomas Munn's *England's Treasure by Foreign Trade*, published in 1664, which touted the benefits to the general public of trade restrictions and a favorable balance of trade, thus strengthening the special-interest influence on public policy. "I have never known," he wrote, "much good done by those who affected to trade for the public good."[43] After all, Munn, a director of the British East India Company for twenty-six years, was hardly a neutral observer.

Smith, too, based his argument on the broader public benefits of his free-trade philosophy, but if he had a motivating bias, it was a compassion for the "lower orders" of mankind. In a mock review of the book in the "millennium issue" of the *Economist* magazine in 1999, the editors observed:

"Wealth of Nations" is animated, to a striking, even alarming degree, by concern for the welfare of the common labourer. Mr. Smith endlessly deplores the idleness and cupidity of the rich, their remorseless seeking after preference that weighs on the people at large. He favours the marketplace partly—nay, mainly, it often seems—because of the curbs it places on the mighty.[44]

Smith advanced an approach "which occasions, in a well-governed society, that universal opulence which extends itself to the lowest ranks of the people."[45] He maintained, "No society can surely be flourishing and happy of which the far greater part of the numbers are poor and miserable."[46] When a person is allowed to enjoy the fruits of his labors, he will strive to enhance his own revenues and unintentionally those of his nation simultaneously. This point is made over and over again in the body of his work but most poignantly in the following famous quotation:

> It is not from the benevolence of the butcher, the brewer, or the baker that we expect our dinner, but from their regard to their own interest. We address ourselves, not to their humanity but to their self-love, and never talk to them of our own necessities but of their advantages.[47]

This is the context of the most celebrated—and perhaps most misunderstood—evocation of Smith's masterpiece. In an effort to enhance his own gain and economic security, man is "led by an invisible hand to promote an end [i.e., public prosperity] which was no part of his intention."[48] The economy is thus the creation of thousands of individual human wills, thousands of efforts to improve individual standing, thousands of butchers, brewers, bakers, and others promoting their own self-interest—all the while unconscious of the spontaneous beneficial economic order they are producing. In contrast to the conventional wisdom of today, Smith's free-trade argument was far deeper and broader than a mere argument against regulations on business; instead, it was an argument for taking the shackles of special interests off individual workers so that they could collectively promote the public good through their individual efforts to enhance their own well-being.

No legislator decreed the specialization of division of labor to enhance productivity or the creation of money to facilitate trade. Rather, these economic advances evolved slowly but instinctively from the general disposition of men "to truck, barter, and exchange" the products of their labor in a free market. To impose mercantilist limitations upon this sacred right of mankind denied prosperity to the lowest ranks of the people and, consequently, shackled the wealth of the entire nation.

Smith's emphasis on the benefits of a spontaneous economic order driven by the invisible hand of unfettered self-interest in the marketplace was complemented by a direct attack on the interloping role of the more visible hand of government in managing commerce to hoard wealth favoring a selected class. "It is the highest impertinence and presumption . . . in kings and ministers to pretend to watch over the economy of private people. . . . They are themselves always and without any exception the greatest spendthrifts in the society. Let them look well after their own expense and they may safely trust private people with theirs."[49]

THE GOVERNMENT'S ROLE

Smith's well-known disdain for government oversight of "the economy of private people" arose in the context of the mercantilist system that awarded special interests at the expense of society in general and working people in particular. Given the artificial distortions that government-enabled special interests brought to the economy, Smith generally recognized a role for government in performing only three principal duties: providing a common defense, maintaining a system of justice, and erecting public works. It would follow, then, that Smith's prescription for international trade would be simply to get government out of the way altogether. This is certainly the conventional view of what Smith's free-trade ideas brought to international economics.

The truth, however, is more nuanced than this, as Smith's free-market philosophy derived from his antipathy for the damage that privileged special interests did to the public good through their restraints on labor and popular consumption. These special-interest distortions were often, but not always, synonymous with government restrictions on international trade. In fact, Smith noted at least four situations where import restrictions were justifiable for the public good.

First, he conceded that trade restrictions may be justified to protect a domestic industry necessary for national defense. Inasmuch as the defense of Great Britain depended vitally upon the strength of its navy, a British shipping monopoly was properly supported by heavy burdens upon the shipping of foreign countries, and absolute bans in some cases. Smith acknowledged that Parliament may have been motivated solely by national animosity toward the Dutch when it passed the Act of Navigation that imposed these burdens. The act certainly "was not favourable to foreign commerce, or to the growth of that opulence which can arise from it."[50]

Regardless of the motivation behind it, however, the result is the same as if it had been the product of the most deliberate wisdom. Even considering its negative economic impact, national security "is of much more importance than opulence."[51]

Second, Smith supported imposing a tariff on foreign imports when a domestic tax is imposed upon a similar product of a home industry. The import tax should be equal to the tax on the domestic product so as to "leave the competition between foreign and domestic industry, after the tax, as nearly as possible upon the same footing as before it."[52] Care should be taken to avoid the temptation of laying a much heavier tax on competitive foreign products, Smith noted, "in order to stop the clamorous complaints of our merchants and manufacturers that they will be undersold at home."[53]

The third case in which he suggested that restrictions on imports might be justified involved retaliation against the products of foreign nations that used high duties or prohibitions to restrain the importation of goods that competed with its domestic products. Smith singled out the French as being "particularly forward to favour their own manufactures" and blamed French protectionism for inciting war with the Dutch on at least one occasion and provoking an enduring "spirit of hostility" with the English.[54] "Revenge in this case naturally dictates retaliation" when there is a probability that the retaliatory restrictions will prompt the foreign nation to eliminate its barriers.[55] Unfortunately, he observed, the judgment as to whether the retaliation is likely to have that effect is left to "that insidious and crafty animal, vulgarly called a statesman or politician," who may fall under the influence of "momentary fluctuations of affairs,"[56] meaning presumably petty politics or perhaps a loathing for all things French. The inherent risk of retaliation, he noted, is that it nearly always injures citizens who had not been harmed by the foreign restraints.

Finally, Smith took the position that some trade restrictions should remain in place and only gradually be eliminated when high trade barriers had protected an industry for an extended period of time. Freedom of trade should be restored in this case with "reserve and circumspection" due to the requirements of "humanity." For if the protective restrictions were taken away all at once, the cheaper foreign imports might flood the home market and "deprive all at once many thousands of our people of their ordinary employment and means of subsistence."[57] Here again, Smith's bias toward the working class apparently outweighed his preference for pure free-market economic policies. It is this exception from his free-trade views that provides support for the slow-staged removal of US textile import protection at the end of the twentieth century.

SMITH'S LEGACY IN NINETEENTH-CENTURY BRITAIN

The underlying message of *The Wealth of Nations* is that the interests of merchants, manufacturers, landowners, wage earners, and others affected by commerce are forever subject to the varying influences of market forces and government policies. Based upon principles of equity and sound economics, according to Smith, market forces should be favored over government intervention to balance these interests, except in the limited circumstances he outlined. This was especially obvious in Smith's day. Government-imposed mercantilism stunted national economic growth and encroached upon tenets of natural justice by granting exclusive privileges to "merchants and manufacturers" at the expense of the "poor workman" and discharged soldiers who had defended their country "with their blood" and were looking for work in the restricted system.[58]

Yet Smith was also a realist who understood the political process. Powerful monopoly interests had corrupted government policymakers and "like an overgrown standing army . . . have become formidable to the government, and upon many occasions intimidate the legislature."[59] Members of Parliament who supported the monopoly interests received not only "the reputation of understanding trade, but great popularity and influence with an order of men whose numbers and wealth render them of great importance." On the other hand, those who opposed them could not avoid "the most infamous abuse . . . personal insults, nor sometimes real danger, arising from the insolent outrage of furious and disappointed monopolists." Consequently, he harbored little hope about the success of his appeal for more free trade.

> To expect, indeed, that the freedom of trade should ever be entirely restored in Great Britain is as absurd as to expect that an Oceana or Utopia should ever be established in it. Not only the prejudices of the public, but what is much more unconquerable, the private interests of many individuals, irresistibly oppose it.[60]

Smith was correct in assuming that Britain was not likely to become a free-trade Utopia, but the impact of his message took effect sooner than he expected. In 1784, eight years after the publication of *The Wealth of Nations*, the bold, reform-oriented William Pitt the Younger became prime minister at the age of twenty-four and, as an avowed Smith follower, initiated several trade liberalization policies. He began by slashing the heavy import duties on tea, which by the eighteenth century was a key part of the English cultural diet, from 119 to 12.5 percent. While this action drew strong opposition in Parliament, as well as from the smugglers who operated a thriving business in a highly developed black market, it was very well received by the lower classes who were now able to afford a beverage that had been considered a luxury. With the resulting increased volume of imported tea, the lower tariff yielded nearly the same amount of revenue for the treasury as had the high duties.

Pitt's next free-trade venture, however, was not as successful. Long suffering under oppressive British trade policies, Ireland was in a state of economic depression and political rebellion when Pitt assumed office. Not wanting to repeat the mistakes that his predecessors had made in the American colonies, Pitt sought a solution that would give Ireland some commercial advantages, yet maintain security and economic benefits "to the common exigencies of the empire."[61] Under the influence of Smith, he proposed, in effect, a free-trade agreement with Ireland, which would reduce tariffs on manufactured and agricultural products to the lowest levels in each country for each other's products. In his speech to Parliament, Pitt spoke of the "cruel and abominable" treatment of Ireland over the past century, observing how it had been denied "the enjoyment and uses of her own resources; to make [Ireland] subservient to the interests and opulence of this country, without suffering her to share in the bounties of nature, in the industry of her citizens," and he called for "a system of equality and fairness" in a new trade relationship that would "seek the aggregate interests of the empire."[62] But as Smith had predicted, leaders of the opposition bench wasted no time in denouncing this proposal for free trade. Members representing domestic manufacturers forced Pitt to abandon the effort with overwhelming arguments against the damage that would ensue from cheap Irish labor.

In 1786, Pitt took another bold step by concluding a reciprocal trade agreement with France, which offered unprecedented mutual trade concessions following decades of tariff wars and military conflicts between the two countries. Having learned from his experience with his Irish proposal, Pitt had been careful in monitoring the negotiations of the agreement with the French to ensure that the tariff concessions favored British manufacturers, and he was not shy about making this point in his speech promoting its passage. British woolens, cottons, porcelain, and other products of the new industrial age would have better access to the French market with its 24 million inhabitants, and French brandy, wine, and oil could be imported instead of smuggled across the English Channel. Despite protests by the opposition that France was "the natural political enemy of Great Britain,"[63] Parliament approved the treaty by better than a 2-to-1 vote. The trade advantages brought to the two countries did not survive for long; they disintegrated with the commencement of war between Britain and France in 1793. Pitt's trade liberalization efforts were sidelined as the rise of Napoleon necessitated war-related tariff revenue.

The fall of Napoleon at Waterloo in 1815 brought peace but also a fear among the landed interests controlling Parliament of being flooded with grain imports. As a result, the government enacted the infamous Corn Laws prohibiting the importation of wheat until the domestic grain price reached a certain high level. While these laws were never effective in stabilizing the market for British farmers, they were maintained for decades to the detriment of the nutritional needs of the "inferior classes" who sometimes rioted against them.

Demands for change beginning in the 1820s led to greater trade liberalization and to the removal of some of the labor restrictions that Smith had railed against. Under the leadership of William Huskisson, a Tory Member of Parliament (MP) serving as president of the Board of Trade, Parliament reduced the prohibitively high tariffs on silk, wool, cotton goods, and numerous other products with great fiscal success and to popular acclaim. Conservative Tory forces and strong business interest groups, as might have been expected, raised loud opposition to these modifications. Yet in the years since Smith had written his gloomy predictions for free-trade proposals in 1776, the country had gone through periods of economic distress and political and social upheaval following the war with France, all of which led to a demand for reform. In 1824, Parliament repealed the Combination Acts, which had prohibited workers from forming unions, and Huskisson's trade reforms were similarly successful as measures easing the burdens of workers and helpful to the growing middle class.

The 1840s, however, brought the most dramatic round of trade reforms when Sir Robert Peel became prime minister. Although Peel's Tory Party was known to be more protectionist than the opposition Whigs, he and William Gladstone, his brilliant young vice president of the Board of Trade, proposed a budget in 1842 that reduced or abolished 750 tariffs out of nearly 1,200 total items then included in the tariff system. His proposal removed prohibitively high tariffs, reduced duties on most raw materials to 5 percent, and reduced duties on manufactured goods to between 10 percent and 20 percent. He paid for any loss of revenue with a 3 percent income tax that affected only the upper-income population for a four-year period. Gladstone promoted the tariff cuts in an article propounding the thesis that the measure would stimulate trade, increase consumption, and increase customs revenue. When he was able to prove this thesis with the results of trade statistics the following year, he and Peel began to push ahead with further cuts in 1844, 1845, and 1846. According to nineteenth-century financial historian Sydney Buxton, "the total number of duties reduced by him was 1,035, the total number entirely repealed 605—duties for the most part on articles which concerned the food, the clothing, and the comfort of the people, or which, as levied on the raw material of manufacture, affected employment."[64]

The Corn Laws, firmly defended by both the landed aristocrats of the Tory Party and Peel when he took over the leadership, presented a much tougher issue for trade reformers. After a period of poor harvests drove food prices up, a group of middle-class discontents in the industrial town of Manchester founded the Anti-Corn Law League in 1838 under the leadership of Richard Cobden, who, along with John Bright, would become a seminal figure in the promotion of free-trade economics and social reform, under what became known as the "Manchester School" of liberal economics. Though not formally well educated, Cobden was a voracious reader, absorbing works by Adam Smith, David Hume, and Benjamin Franklin. Cobden's passion for free trade derived from his belief that protective tariffs deprived people of affordable food and maintained the old feudal system of order that denied individual freedom, responsibility, and enterprise, and his belief that free trade was linked with peace, while protectionism was linked with war.

Cobden, who had begun work as a warehouse clerk and traveling salesman, understood that the landlord interests controlled Parliament and that the laws protecting these interests would not be repealed solely as a result of persuasive speeches in the House of Commons. He and Bright organized the Anti-Corn Law League to perform the role of an outside pressure group. From the date of its founding, it published thousands of pamphlets, organized innumerable meetings and lectures all across the country, and inundated Parliament with petitions demanding "freedom of commerce, national justice, and the mutual goodwill of mankind."[65]

In 1841, Cobden was elected to Parliament and began his fight for repeal from within the House of Commons, as he and the League maintained outside pressure through a network of affiliated societies around the nation. Year after year, while proposing resolutions to abolish the Corn Laws, the League's leader railed against his colleagues for "maintaining a law which restricts the supply of food to be obtained by the people" and for supporting a law that raised the price of grain for the benefit of agricultural interests. Even during the "time when prices were highest under this law," he declared, "the condition of the agricultural labourers was at the worst."[66] He did not mince words when condemning the beneficiary landlords, noting that they "had the absolute command of the legislature of the country." He argued, "Let the farmer perfectly understand that his prosperity depends upon that of his customers—that the insane policy of this House has been to ruin his customers, and that Acts of Parliament to keep up prices are mere frauds to put rents into landlords' pockets, and to juggle his tenants."[67] Although Cobden seemed to be getting the better of the argument in 1843, in agriculture much depends upon the weather. When 1844 brought a good harvest, reform stagnated.

In the autumn of 1845, however, not only was the rainfall the heaviest in memory, but disease struck Ireland's potato crop, leading to the historic famine. By December of that year, Peel had decided that it was time to repeal the Corn Laws, but a majority of his cabinet remained opposed. When they did not side with him, he resigned for a brief period, but was recalled by Queen Victoria to form a new government and begin the repeal process anew. The debates of the 1846 session of Parliament have been called some of the most dramatic in history, with Peel in the paradoxical position of receiving broad support from all except members of his own party.

The Tory protectionists found in Benjamin Disraeli a brilliant new orator, who attacked Peel as a traitor to his country with unsparing taunts and the virulent personal attacks predicted by Adam Smith. But with support from free-traders and the Whig opposition, Peel was able to secure a majority vote of 327 to 229 to pass the repeal in May. His personal success was short-lived. The following month, on the very day that the repeal passed the House of Lords, Peel was defeated on an unrelated measure in the Commons by a combination of his Tory opponents out for revenge and the Whig opposition seeking to bring down the government for their own advancement. He was thus forced to resign, never to return to office.

In his resignation speech, Peel made a special, selfless effort to give credit to the person he considered most responsible for ending the Corn Laws, his former opponent Richard Cobden. He commended Cobden for his "pure and disinterested motives" and his "appeals to reason, enforced by an eloquence the more to be admired because it was unaffected and una-dorned." He concluded with the following aspiration for his own final effort in Parliament that had caused his political demise:

> It may be that I shall leave a name sometimes remembered with expressions of good will in the abodes of those whose lot it is to labour and to earn their daily bread by the sweat of their brow, when they shall recruit their exhausted strength with abundant and untaxed food, the sweeter because it is no longer leavened by a sense of injustice.[68]

The battle for free trade in Britain was now practically won. In 1849, a Whig-controlled government repealed the Navigation Acts, which since 1660 had required most trade through British ports to be on British ships. The fallout from the Corn Law debate had ended the long period of con-trol of Parliament by the Tories, who were mortally divided into factions of old-line protectionists and Peel supporters, now known as Peelites. By 1852, a new coalition of Whigs and Peelites—an early stage of what later became the Liberal Party—formed a new government with Peel's free-trade disci-ple William Gladstone serving as chancellor of the Exchequer. In a series of budgets from 1853–55 and 1859–65, with the Crimean War causing the interruption of the late 1850s, Gladstone effectively brought free trade to Britain by eliminating all protective duties. In 1860, Britain entered into a commercial treaty with France, which Richard Cobden personally negoti-ated with Emperor Napoleon III, allowing duty-free importation of French manufactured goods and reduced tariffs for wines in exchange for lower tariffs on British exports to France.

With the bad harvest and potato famine in 1846, Mother Nature had added a critical boost in bringing down the Corn Laws, but the rise of the middle class and the pressures manifested in the Anti-Corn Law League in the years that followed made laissez-faire economic policies not only politically acceptable but imperative. Classical economist John Stuart Mill effectively brought Adam Smith up to date with his *Principles of Political Economy*, which was first published in 1848 and served as the dominant economics textbook in the English language for the next forty years. He put it this way: "*Laisser-faire* [*sic*], in short, should be the general practice: every departure from it, unless required by some great good, is a certain evil."[69]

By the 1860s, free trade was accepted orthodoxy in British politics among all parties hoping to win elections. Even Disraeli, the raging protectionist of the 1840s, accepted the reality that protection was "not only dead but damned."[70] When the Tories finally returned to power in 1874 with Disraeli as prime minister, they made no effort to reverse the political and economic reforms enacted during the previous Liberal Party governments—especially not the free-trade system.

Except for its trade relationship with France during the period when the "Cobden Treaty" was in effect, Britain maintained its free-trade policies unilaterally with respect to its major trading partners. After the Franco-Prussian War, France followed Germany under Bismarck's protectionist trade practices in the late 1870s. With few exceptions, most other European states also had protective trade policies by this time. The United States had become increasingly more protectionist during its first decades of existence until a period of gradual liberalization under the Jacksonian Democratic administrations prevailed in the antebellum years, but American protectionism returned with a vengeance during and after the Civil War. Britain was virtually alone as a proponent of liberal international trade policies among the major economies in the second half of the nineteenth century.

By the early 1880s, a generation after the repeal of the Corn Laws and during a depression and a period of bad harvests, a protectionist movement arose again and formed a "Fair Trade League" that essentially called for "Reciprocity and Retaliation" in dealing with other nations' protectionist trade practices. The Liberals under Gladstone, however, were able to defeat efforts to change the system. They scornfully refused to return to the past miseries that had been inflicted on the working classes in order to keep up the rents of landlords. In 1903, following the Boer War, the Conservatives attempted another move at tariff protection prompted by a group of domestic manufacturers who claimed they were being harmed by cheap American and European imports being "dumped" in British ports.

Conservative colonial secretary Joseph Chamberlain led a major move-ment to adopt a system of "imperial preferences" to promote trade within the British Empire to the exclusion of exports from the "dumping" nations. Chamberlain's efforts provoked the anger of a rising young Member of Parliament, Winston S. Churchill. Churchill railed against abandoning the "system of free trade and cheap food" under which the British people "had thriven so long,"[71] and he dramatically switched political parties over the issue, leaving the Tories for the Liberals for two decades. Chamberlain's campaign failed in the face of opposition not only from the Liberal Party, but also the Irish Nationalist Party, and the newly formed Labor Party, which feared that wage earners would lose purchasing power with higher tariffs.

It was not until 1915, during the first year of World War I, that the era of free trade began to come to an end in Great Britain. After the first ten months of conspicuous failures in prosecuting the war, the Liberal govern-ment formed a coalition with the Conservatives to secure national unity. As one of its first acts, the coalition government introduced a new budget with 33.3 percent tariffs for the purported purposes of limiting luxury imports and saving space on ships. Although the government made promises that the duties would be lifted at the end of the war, the weakness of the Liberal Party and the economic uncertainties in the aftermath of the war made such promises difficult to fulfill. In the turbulent postwar Europe of the 1920s, the British free-traders simply no longer had the political capital to impose their will in Parliament. When the Great Depression began tak-ing its disastrous toll on employment around the world and nations began enacting unprecedented protectionist policies globally, Britain joined in the trade wars, enacting higher import tariffs in 1931 and adopting the imperial preference system within the Commonwealth in 1932.

IMPACT OF THE BRITISH FREE-TRADE ERA

By all measures, the six-decade period in which free-trade policies pre-vailed in Britain was an unqualified success story. By the mid-1880s Britain dominated the world trade markets in all the major sectors and London had become the financial capital of the world, even as the United States began to eclipse British industrial supremacy. Britain's total trade volume doubled four times following the tariff reductions imposed by Peel and Gladstone beginning in 1842, which brought average duties down from 35 percent to about 8 percent in 1870. At a time when national income was increasing sevenfold, the index of wholesale commodity prices was falling by nearly 60 percent, thus increasing the British consumer's purchasing power sixteen times in the nineteenth century.[72] For the laboring classes, the standard of living, which had been stagnant in the first half of the century, rose sharply between 1850 and 1914. Even though there were difficult periods, such as the "cotton famine" of the 1860s during the American Civil War, a "great depression" that lasted twenty years, and several years of bad harvests, the boom periods created significant boosts in wages as prices continued to fall gradually. With this combination enhancing purchasing power and providing a little surplus available for more than the essentials of food, clothing, and housing, the average workweek also fell from fifty-six to fifty hours between 1860 and 1900, and the working classes began for the first time to have some leisure time.

As working classes grew in prosperity and benefited from political reforms, they joined trade unions to protect their gains and negotiate for better wages and working conditions in the latter part of the century. Most of the union leadership remained firmly supportive of Gladstone politically, as they resisted the socialist ideas that were beginning to take hold in some working-class circles in continental Europe. Even after the formation of the Labour Party, organized labor remained in alliance with the Liberals on free-trade policies to maintain the cost of living gains of the working classes.

This is not to suggest that free trade alone made Britain into a superpower and its working classes well off. Many factors were at play in the development of Britain's industrial and financial strength in the nineteenth century. One must also acknowledge that the improvements in the quality of life seen by the British laborer in this period did not eliminate poverty but only enhanced working conditions above the levels of misery depicted so graphically in the novels of Charles Dickens.

The point here is to illustrate Adam Smith's thesis that protectionist policies for the benefit of special interests deny the working class its natural right to earn a fair wage and access the necessities of life while at the same time inhibiting the wealth of the nation as a whole. The political, social, and economic reforms that evolved in mid-nineteenth-century Britain were in a broad sense associated with liberal trade policies and shared economic progress. The growth of the middle class as a political force came about simultaneously with the formation of the Anti-Corn Law League and effectively ended the political dominance of landed aristocrats. With the tariff reforms of Peel and Gladstone and the repeal of the Corn Laws and the consequential lowering of commodity prices, the living costs of the working classes went down as their wages increased.

IMPACT ON AMERICAN TRADE POLICY

This brief review of Adam Smith's great work and the impact it had on nineteenth-century British trade policy is also important as an introduction to the ensuing chapters, which review the history of the politics of trade in the United States. *The Wealth of Nations* was published in 1776, not inconsequentially the year Thomas Jefferson wrote the Declaration of Independence. Not only had British trade restrictions on the American colonies been one of the causes of the American Revolution, but Jefferson and the other American founding fathers also had much in common intellectually with Smith. They were steeped in the Enlightenment movement, as well as Smith's Lockean views of natural law, and many were committed to putting its ideas to work in their new nation.

Smith's call for a "simple system of natural liberty," where "every man, as long as he does not violate the laws of justice, is left perfectly free to pursue his own interest his own way, and to bring both his industry and capital into competition with those of any other man, or order of men,"[73] could, with just a bit more flourish, have come from Jefferson's pen. Benjamin Franklin met and became friendly with Smith and Hume in Scotland when he was Pennsylvania's agent in Britain in 1759[74] and is said to have reviewed and commented on parts of the manuscript of *The Wealth of Nations* in meetings with Smith in the early 1770s.[75] Franklin, Jefferson, James Madison, or John Adams could have each written Smith's condemnation of British trade and industrial restrictions on the American colonies—such as the absolute prohibition upon the erection of steel furnaces:

> To prohibit a great people . . . from making all that they can of every part of their own produce, or from employing their stock and industry in the way that they judge most advantageous to themselves, is a manifest violation of the most sacred rights of mankind.[76]

Despite the natural sympathy of views between Smith and many of the American founding fathers, other factors intervened and often limited the influence of Smith in the development of trade policy in the young nation. One important factor was the negative legacy of antipathy toward Great Britain following the American Revolution, reinforced by the British invasion of Washington and the burning of the US Capitol and executive mansion during the War of 1812. For much of the nineteenth century, Britain was a domineering political and economic rival whose policies were viewed with contempt in most US political circles. While the classical economists who followed Smith—David Ricardo, James Mill, John Stuart Mill, and others—strengthened the case for free trade in Britain, in America there was a strong move toward protectionism and economic nationalism based upon the economic arguments of men such as Friedrich List and Henry Carey, combined with a political aversion to Britain. Nevertheless, America contained strong free-trade supporters, especially among the merchants and shippers of New England and in the agrarian southern states, who often quoted passages from Smith's book.

The debates in the United States over trade during the development period were almost always two-sided, except during and for an extended time after the American Civil War. Through its classical economists, its economic strength, and its long experiment with free trade, Britain had an important influence on US trade policy in the nineteenth century—though often in the negative. With the elections of Woodrow Wilson in 1912 and Franklin Roosevelt (FDR) in 1932, however, this same British influence—reflected in the legacy of Smith, Gladstone, Bright, and Cobden, so admired by Wilson and Roosevelt's secretary of state, Cordell Hull—laid the foundation for the dominant twentieth-century American trade policy.

As will be seen, the Anglo-American alliance—which Churchill and FDR fostered during the Second World War to fulfill their mutual goals of winning the war and achieving postwar security, prosperity, and full employment—ultimately bore fruit. This relationship was not without serious conflict that could have been fatal to the partnership on several occasions. Nevertheless, the alliance proved critical to the birth of the liberal world economic order embodied in the postwar multilateral trading system.

PART ONE

From Hamilton to Smoot-Hawley

The Rise and Fall of the US Protectionist System

1

"A Genuine American System"

There are some, who maintain, that trade will
regulate itself, and is not to be benefitted by the
encouragements, or restraints of government. . . . This
is one of those wild speculative paradoxes, which
have grown into credit among us, contrary to the
uniform practice and sense of the most enlightened
nations. . . . To preserve the ballance of trade in favour
of a nation ought to be a leading aim of its policy.[1]
—Alexander Hamilton, 1782

When asked to compare multilateral trade negotiations during the period
before the creation of the World Trade Organization in 1994 and those of
the twenty-first-century Doha Round, a frustrated senior US trade official points to the growing impact of new members from developing countries. He notes the difficulty in reaching a consensus when, in his view, the
developing countries expect all of the market concessions to come from
developed countries. "Frankly, you ask yourself," he says, "Why did they
join? Didn't anyone tell them that the purpose of the WTO is to liberalize trade?"[2] Representatives of the developing countries commonly reply,
"Why do the rich countries expect us to open our markets now, when their
markets were effectively closed during their development stage?" And,
indeed, they do have a point. Current critics of the United States in the
developing world are exactly right when they note that the US economy
industrialized in the nineteenth century under the same protectionist trade

policies that American negotiators are now seeking to dismantle in developing countries.

In fact, for much of the period from George Washington's first administration in 1789 until the first Franklin Roosevelt administration in 1933, economic nationalism and protective tariffs largely dominated the trade policy of the United States. Protectionism in early America developed very deliberately through high-profile conflicts among a pantheon of prominent figures of the day: Hamilton, Jefferson, Madison, Clay, Jackson, Calhoun, and Webster. Their free trade versus protectionism debates, central to this history, raged in the late eighteenth and early nineteenth centuries; they roiled relations between the regions of the fledgling country, with tariff policy not only playing a large role in economic policy but also driving a wedge between the largely protectionist North and the free-trade South. This wedge, fatally driven by the slavery issue, would eventually lead to the Civil War.

It is no exaggeration to say that tariff and trade policy helped determine the early political and economic course of the United States. Thus, it is no surprise that developing countries would look to those early American trade policies to rationalize protectionist practices in their own development. After all, America's present status as the world's only superpower might suggest to some developing countries that the United States must have done something right in those early years. However, the critical lesson for developing countries—and for the United States—is not that protectionism works, or that it is necessary for development or economic success. Instead, what early American history teaches us is a more basic point: The interests that drive trade policy, on all sides of the debate, are so powerful that they can determine the course of a new nation—and can even drive it toward war.

TRADE OPPRESSION IN THE COLONIES AND CHAOS IN THE NEW CONFEDERATION

Indeed, British industrial and trade restrictions imposed on the American colonies, which bore an evil kinship with "taxation without representation," were a leading cause of the American Revolution. As noted in the Introduction, Adam Smith was highly critical of the prohibition on steel furnaces in the colonies, but the British Parliament also criminalized the manufacture and export in the colonies of most products made in the mother country, including *hats*. In fact, hats could not even "be loaded on a horse, cart, or other carriage, for transportation from one plantation to another [within the colonies]."[3] It is no wonder that three of the most famous American political writers of the period—Benjamin Franklin, Thomas Paine, and Thomas Jefferson—all took up the cause of free trade in the pre-revolutionary period.[4]

The most notorious and momentous example of British excesses in commercial trade oppression of the colonies are the actions leading up to the Tea Act Crisis in 1773. The British East India Company's monopoly of all trade between India and the rest of the empire gave it control of the tea market in America, except for smuggled Dutch tea, but a boycott by the colonists protesting a hefty tax on the tea had caused a glut in its warehouses in England. The new prime minister, Lord North, addressed the problem by reducing the tax and cutting out the English and American middlemen, thus allowing the East India Company to cut its price and compete with the Dutch smugglers. Although the lower cost was tempting, the colonists had had their fill of British-imposed monopolies and refused to unload the shipments in New York and Philadelphia and sent the ships back to England. At the famous "Tea Party" in Boston a band of patriots, thinly disguised as painted Indians, boarded the ships carrying the tea and dumped it into the harbor, as thousands of Bostonians cheered them on. This action naturally infuriated the British, who retaliated the following spring of 1774 by passing the Coercive Acts, one of which closed Boston Harbor to all commerce until the colonists paid for the sabotaged tea.

These Coercive Acts, renamed the "Intolerable Acts" by the Americans, prompted the Massachusetts colonists to call for a meeting of delegates from all the colonies to take joint action to defend themselves against British colonial actions. This call led to the First Continental Congress in Philadelphia in September 1774, where the delegates organized a "Continental Association" to ban exports to Britain and boycott British goods. They also passed a resolution condemning British actions since 1763, and endorsed taking up arms to defend their rights. Although not many colonists were ready to declare independence, the revolution was effectively under way. Two years later, Thomas Jefferson included King George III's assent to Parliament's "cutting off our Trade with all parts of the world" prominently among the list of grievances justifying the Declaration of Independence.

The Revolutionary War interrupted most international commerce and out of necessity forced the birth of American domestic manufacturing. At the end of the war in 1783, however, new complexities arose as foreign trade resumed. Under the Articles of Confederation, which governed the United States from 1781 until 1789, Congress had no authority to regulate trade; rather, each state regulated its own trade, imposing such duties as it desired—not only on foreign products but also on those of its sister states. There was no uniformity of rates of duties. States with new industries considered vulnerable to imports erected high tariff barriers. States with commercial or export interests enacted few or no tariffs. Savvy foreign traders and importers simply brought their products into the country through the ports of states with low tariffs. Some states also enacted their own navigation laws, requiring shipments through their ports to be on vessels built in their state. At the same time, foreign governments, especially the British, imposed strict barriers to US products and shipping, thus leaving the states to fight trade wars among themselves with no tariff revenues available for national debt requirements. Adding to the confusion, a postwar import surge exacerbated the severe economic conditions and intensified the interstate rivalries.

There were many reasons motivating Congress to organize the 1787 Constitutional Convention in Philadelphia for the "express purpose of revising the Articles of Confederation," but clearly a principal reason was to resolve the fiscal questions plaguing the country, foremost among them trade issues. One of the primary authors of the Constitution, James Madison, explained in a letter to Thomas Jefferson: "Most of our political evils may be traced to our commercial ones."[5] Madison had attempted to convene a meeting of state delegations to address problems of trade and commerce in the Confederation at Annapolis the year before but failed to attract a quorum. The delegates who made it to Annapolis adopted a resolution, drafted by Alexander Hamilton of New York, calling for the Constitutional Convention at Philadelphia the next year.

Richard Henry Lee, later an arch Anti-Federalist leader in the fight against ratification of the Constitution in Virginia, observed on the second day of the Philadelphia convention:

The present causes of complaint seem to be, that Congress cannot command the money necessary for the just purposes of paying debts, or for supporting the federal government, and that they cannot make treaties of commerce, unless power unlimited, of regulating trade be given.[6]

One of the strongest arguments for the new Constitution at the convention and during the ratification process was the need to centralize trade regulation with Congress in order to deal effectively with the oppressive European trading powers and to generate public revenue. It was no surprise when the framers of the Constitution proposed that Congress have the power to collect taxes and duties and to regulate commerce with foreign nations, and among the several states. Following ratification in 1788 by a sufficient number of states, Congress wasted no time in exercising its new powers.

The first legislative measure passed by the United States Congress, the Tariff Act of 1789, had as its purpose not only the generation of revenue, but also "the encouragement and protection of manufactures."[7] It incorporated into federal law some of the protective duties previously imposed independently by the states under the Articles of Confederation. But, subject to compromise among the conflicting state interests, the rates, ranging from 5 to 15 percent with an 8.5 percent average duty, were actually quite moderate by most protectionist standards. The northern and middle states preferred higher protection for their struggling industries, while the southern states wanted low tariffs to avoid retaliation against their agricultural exports. Pennsylvania sought high iron and steel tariffs, which were opposed by New Englanders needing these metals for shipbuilding, as well as by southerners who used them for agricultural implements. While this first tariff act reflected a degree of protectionist spirit and intent, it largely favored the prevailing agrarian and commercial interests that thrived on European trade in the late eighteenth century.

ALEXANDER HAMILTON: FOUNDING FATHER OF AMERICAN PROTECTIONISM

Moderate trade policies, however, were not the prevailing philosophy of President George Washington's top economic cabinet officer. Treasury Secretary Alexander Hamilton, in fact, established himself as the founding father of American protectionism when he submitted to Congress his *Report*

FIGURE 1.1 Alexander Hamilton, John Trumbull 1805 painting (Library of Congress)

on Manufactures—a plan advocating government support for American industry—on December 5, 1791.[8] Hamilton, brilliant and highly educated in the literature of his age, was well versed in the arguments for free trade in Adam Smith's treatise, *The Wealth of Nations*, first published only fifteen years prior to Hamilton's *Report*. From a purely comparative cost and advantage standpoint, he conceded that the United States could more efficiently produce agricultural products than industrial products. "If the system of perfect liberty to industry and commerce were the prevailing system of nations," and a "free exchange, mutually beneficial" could be concluded, the United States might indeed be better off trading farm exports for manufactured imports from other nations with better industrial capabilities and efficiencies and refraining from pursuing its own manufacturing industries. This was a reference to the prescription of his bitter political rival, Secretary of State Thomas Jefferson, who led a partisan faction opposed to industrialization in what Jefferson considered the American agrarian utopia.

The problem in Hamilton's view was that such a world of free exchange did not exist and, according to him, the "regulations of several countries, with which we have most extensive intercourse, throw serious obstructions in the way of the principal staples of the United States."[9] Under these conditions, Hamilton argued that the United States could not trade with Europe on equal terms and, consequently, it was necessary to have an economy based in both manufacturing and agriculture in the competitive and unfair trading world that then existed. Further, he concluded, "If Europe will not take from us the products of our soil, upon terms consistent with our interest, the natural remedy is to contract as fast as possible our wants of her."[10]

The *Report* also made a direct attack on Smith's invisible hand doctrine, which Hamilton paraphrased as "the proposition, that Industry, if left to itself, will naturally find its way to the most useful and profitable employment: whence it is inferred that manufactures without the aid of government will grow up as soon and as fast, as the natural state of things and the interest of the community may require."[11] Hamilton held this proposition to be unrealistic in the case of start-up enterprises, which "have to contend not only with the natural disadvantages of a new undertaking, but with the gratuities and remunerations which other governments bestow [upon its industries]."[12] In the real world, mercantilist trade practices still prevailed. Agricultural exporters and infant industries of America were up against well-seasoned European traders. Therefore, according to Hamilton, government aid and interference would be indispensable.

After completing his analysis refuting the free-trade principles of Adam Smith as they might apply in the developing American economy, Hamilton offered a litany of proposals "of the Means proper to be resorted to by the United [S]tates . . . which have been employed with success in other Countries."[13] His list included items that are very familiar to modern trade lawyers and negotiators who are still trying to eliminate them as unfair trade practices in the twenty-first century.

First, he proposed setting tariffs sufficiently high on imports of products competitive with domestic products to allow the domestic manufacturers to "undersell" the foreign producers and to generate revenue. On some products, where the domestic market was sufficiently competitive and domestic manufacturers provided an adequate supply "on reasonable terms," he would set duties at prohibitively high levels, or ban their imports outright in order to create a domestic monopoly for United States citizens. This policy, according to Hamilton, was "dictated, it might almost be said,

by the principles of distributive justice," considering that it was "the reign-
ing policy of manufacturing Nations" to give a monopoly of the domestic market to its own manufacturers. Surely, he thought, it was the duty
of the United States to endeavor to secure to its citizens "a reciprocity of
advantages."[14]

Second, Hamilton proposed a low tariff rate for raw materials required
for domestic manufacturing and sought a prohibition on the exportation
of materials used by domestic manufacturers to ensure a "cheap and plen-
tiful supply" of materials—of a special quality or limited quantity—needed
in particular industries. In addition, tariffs imposed on imported inputs
needed for American manufacturers would be rebated with the producer's
exports. According to Hamilton's reasoning, these measures would enable the young nation to develop a manufacturing base. Without them, he
believed that American industry would not have the wherewithal to compete with other countries, and consequently would be smothered by foreign
imports.

Third, Hamilton offered a long, strained justification for "pecuniary
bounties" or subsidies. He said these various forms of government payments to private businesses were "the most efficacious means of encouraging manufactures, and, is in some views, the best."[15] He admitted that
there was a prejudice against them because of the "appearance of giving
away public money without an immediate consideration, and from a sup-
position that they serve to enrich particular classes, at the expense of the
Community." In the case of new or "infant" industries, he argued, the subsidies were justifiable and often necessary, and, therefore, validated under
a broad and controversial definition of the authority given to Congress to
"provide for the common defense and *general welfare*" in the Constitution.[16]

Fourth, Hamilton advocated government payments to manufacturing societies to reward excellence, skill, and superiority in production. He
was, in effect, arguing that subsidies would encourage the entrepreneur-
ship of American manufacturers. Without them, Hamilton contended, the
American manufacturer would have less incentive to expand his means of
production. Consequently, the United States would lag behind the industrialized nations of Europe and never be able to compete with them. Unlike
Adam Smith, he was arguing for a *helping hand*, since he believed an "invisible hand" only worked when a nation had reached a level equivalent to the
richer nations of the earth "where there is great private wealth." But, "in a
community situated like that of the United States, the public purse must

supply the deficiency of private resource."[17] Otherwise, the United States would be at the mercy of countries seeking to take unfair advantage of the young nation's infant industries.

Finally, he urged the government to actively encourage new inventions and the introduction into the United States of those that already had been made in other countries. This would involve rewards and some limited and, admittedly, ineffective intellectual property protection. An effort would be made to prohibit the exportation of implements and machines invented in the United States.[18] In this proposal Hamilton displayed the Machiavellian nature of his approach, as he sought to protect American inventors from being pickpocketed in the same fashion that he was attempting to steal technology from Europe.

Hamilton's efforts to establish a manufacturing base in the developing American economy of which he had taken charge were not limited to his written *Report* to Congress. He found time in his frenetic schedule early in 1791 to begin setting in motion his own manufacturing experiment. This experiment essentially involved stealing British textile industry technology—including patented machinery—and duplicating it in new factories created at an undeveloped site near a river and waterfalls in what was to become Paterson, New Jersey. According to biographer Ron Chernow, "Hamilton put the full authority of the Treasury behind the piracy of British trade secrets."[19] With the treasury secretary's imprimatur fully embossed, the plan was designed as a manufacturing society run by private sources but blessed by the government as an industrial incubator, dubbed innocently the Society for Establishing Useful Manufactures (SEUM). Its prospectus promised "to procure from Europe skilful workmen and such machines and implements as cannot be had here in sufficient perfection."[20] This was at a time when British technical innovations in the fabrication of textiles were at the forefront of the industrial revolution. In order to protect these innovations, Britain had enacted severe criminal laws against exporting machinery and tools used in the textile manufacturing process as well as prohibiting the emigration of skilled factory workers.

In the end, it was not the lack of tested European technology or skilled workmen that prevented the Society's success. Unfortunately for Hamilton, he made some bad leadership choices, and his daring experiment was the victim of bad timing. As governor of the Society he chose William Duer, formerly his assistant secretary of the treasury and in 1791 a highly leveraged financial speculator. In 1792, the financial markets in New York suffered a severe panic, which led to Duer's financial ruin and his being sent to debtors' prison. Duer refused to resign as governor of the SEUM or to account for the Society's funds. It was soon learned that Duer had used a large portion of these funds for his own purposes. Nevertheless, Hamilton was able to come up with new financing, including some of his own money, to salvage the experiment and get a basic textile manufacturing process up and running. Due to bad design, weak financing, and further poor management, however, the project struggled and factory operations were shut down within four years.[21]

Hamilton's *Report on Manufactures* suffered a similar fate. Except for some moderate tariff increases adopted in 1792, the proposals were ignored by the House of Representatives with no follow-up legislative action on his recommendations. Unlike his previous masterful reports to Congress on financial issues—all of which had spurred specific legislative actions—this report effectively bombed. Congress seemed to be growing a bit weary of him, and his political capital was diminishing. Hamilton's broad interpretation of the "general welfare" clause of the Constitution, which he said allowed the government to pay subsidies or "bounties" to private companies, horrified Thomas Jefferson and Congressman James Madison, Hamilton's former principal partner in the drafting of *The Federalist Papers*. Madison and Jefferson, leaders of the political faction favoring limited government, states' rights, and an agrarian economy, saw this *Report* as proposing unconstitutional powers to Congress and the federal government to promote private industries. In a letter to President Washington, Jefferson wrote that Hamilton's proposal "flowed from principles adverse to liberty, and was calculated to undermine and demolish the republic."[22]

While astutely deferring to the Jeffersonian faction on the predominance of the agrarian economy, the *Report*, in essence, represented the exposition of Hamilton's industrial philosophy for America and made the crucial arguments for governmental encouragement and protection of industry. Some of these arguments are similar to those still being raised by developing countries more than two centuries later. The most obvious example is the infant industry theory, which Hamilton practically invented to protect new domestic industries with subsidies and high tariffs until they are able to withstand foreign competition. Like developing countries today, Hamilton also spoke positively about providing diverse employment opportunities for the underemployed, citing the example of Britain, where most of the textile workers were women and children—"many of them of a very tender age."[23] Hamilton's protectionist arguments in favor of the rich and jobs for tender-aged children offer an ironic contrast to some of the anti-globalization arguments of today, which attack free trade for benefiting rich multinationals without concern for labor standards, including child labor prohibitions.

While the *Report* generated no immediate implementing legislation on its major themes, it served as an inspiration to legislators supporting American business and protectionism for more than a century and is a classic footprint in American economic history. Chernow declares it "a prescient statement of American nationalism";[24] historian Arthur Schlesinger Jr. calls the *Report* "the first great expression of the industrial vision of the American future." In Schlesinger's view, "Alexander Hamilton . . . gave the new industrialism its political philosophy. The precarious days of the Revolution had convinced him that social stability rested on the firm alliance of government and business."[25] Hamilton believed that by giving the wealthy class "a distinct, permanent share in the government," it would be in their interest to "maintain good government."[26] Referring to his plan for a National Bank, Hamilton argued that "it links the interest of the State in an intimate connection with those of the rich individuals belonging to it; . . . it turns wealth and influence of both into a commercial channel, for mutual benefit."[27] This concept of linking the interests of the rich with those of the government marked a fundamental contrast to the approach of Adam Smith, who denounced the corruption that he saw flowing from the ties of the special interests of merchants and manufacturers to the government. Smith's arguments appear particularly prescient in view of the post–Civil War period of American history, when Hamilton's approach was adopted as the prevailing philosophy of the Republican governments during the era of the robber barons.[28]

THOMAS JEFFERSON AND ECONOMIC NATIONALISM

Thomas Jefferson, Hamilton's principal rival in Washington's cabinet, had an entirely different view of how America's economy should work. In his *Notes on the State of Virginia* composed during the years 1781–82, Jefferson wrote dreamily of the attributes of an agricultural economy and

FIGURE 1.2 Thomas Jefferson, Charles Balthazar Julien Fevret de Saint-Mémin 1805 engraving (Library of Congress)

portentously of the corruption that industry would bring upon American society:

> Those who labour in the earth are the chosen people of God, if ever he had a chosen people, whose breasts he has made his peculiar deposit for substantial and genuine virtue. . . . While we have land to labour then, let us never wish to see our citizens occupied at a work-bench, or twirling a distaff. . . . [F]or the general operations of manufacture, let our workshops remain in Europe.

He envisioned industrialization bringing to America the "mobs of great cities" with their less than desirable "manners and principles" creating a "canker" on the republic which would eat "the heart of its laws and constitution."[29] In 1774, he wrote a blistering indictment of the "unjust incroachment" by the British Parliament upon "the exercise of a free trade with all parts of the world, possessed by the American colonists, as of a natural right, and which no law of their own had taken away or abridged."[30]

Consistency, however, was not one of Jefferson's virtues, and over time he mellowed his stance against encouraging the development of industry in America and on his view of free trade as a natural right that should not be diminished. As secretary of state, in 1793, he submitted a *Report on Commerce* to Congress that outlined the restrictions that foreign countries placed on American exports and shipping. By far, the largest trading partner of the United States was Britain, which, according to the report, maintained an overwhelming trade surplus: $15.3 million in imports from Britain compared to $9.4 million in US exports to Britain. Jefferson's list of trade restrictions imposed by all countries on US exports was daunting and frustrated his lingering belief in free trade. He offered this observation, echoing Adam Smith, whose work he had read and admired:[31]

> Instead of embarrassing commerce under piles of regulating laws, duties, and prohibitions, could it be relieved from all its shackles in all parts of the world, could every country be employed in producing that which nature has best fitted it to produce, and each be free to exchange with others mutual surpluses for mutual wants, the greatest mass possible would then be produced of those things which contribute to human life and human happiness; the numbers of mankind would be increased, and their condition bettered.[32]

In order to combat the offensive restrictions of other countries, Jefferson recommended that Congress impose retaliatory restrictions based upon reciprocity and on nearly a tit-for-tat basis. Where a nation imposed high or prohibitive tariffs on American products, Jefferson proposed to burden that nation with similar high tariffs or to exclude such of its products as were in competition with US products. His proposal was to impose lighter duties at first, but heavier ones over time, as alternative supply sources from third countries opened to fill domestic needs. Ironically, he mentioned a motivation in conflict with his vision of an agrarian utopia expressed a decade earlier in *Notes on Virginia*. "Such duties having the effect of indirect encouragement to domestic manufactures of the same kind," Jefferson said, "may induce the manufacturer to come himself into these States, where cheaper subsistence, equal laws, and a vent of his wares, free of duty, may ensure him the highest profits from his skill and industry."[33] He was careful to distinguish this encouragement from that described in Hamilton's *Report on Manufactures*, however, by proposing state subsidies rather than federal subsidies. He stressed that "it would be in the power of the State governments to co-operate essentially, by opening the sources of encouragement which are under their control," and he emphasized fostering the progress of "*household* manufactures" [his emphasis] rather than public factories. Later, in February 1801, only two weeks before assuming the presidency, he offered a rebuttal to his critics among the manufacturing and financial class who considered him "an enemy to commerce." "They admit me a friend to agriculture," Jefferson wrote to a correspondent, "and suppose me an enemy to the only means of disposing of its produce."[34]

Jefferson's report to Congress on trade was one of his last official acts as secretary of state before resigning from Washington's cabinet. As in the case of Hamilton's report, Congress failed to act on his recommendations. Yet the report was influential nevertheless, particularly its blatant anti-British sentiments. While it catalogued the transgressions of all nations against the United States, those of Great Britain were dominantly highlighted. For example, Jefferson urged the negotiation of commercial agreements with other nations based on reciprocity in order to eliminate trade restrictions. He pointed out that France, a beneficiary of his well-known bias, had proposed such negotiations but was presently prevented from pursuing them by "her internal disturbances,"[35] an understated reference to the Reign of Terror period of the French Revolution, during which tens of thousands, including many of Jefferson's friends, were then being guillotined. On the other hand, he observed, the British had snubbed proposals by the United States for such negotiations. Thus, not only did Britain prohibit American grain, fish, and whale oil imports; impose heavy duties on rice and tobaccos; and deny American vessels entry into English ports, but the British refused even to discuss these issues. Anti-British economic nationalism was the principal message of Jefferson's final report as he retired to Monticello.

A few months later, in 1793, after the commencement of Britain's epic wars with post-revolutionary France, as the British began seizing American ships in the course of enforcing its naval blockade of France, Congressman James Madison proposed an embargo on trade with both France and Britain in order to force each of them to honor the neutrality of the United States as the two countries engaged in war. Since Britain consumed more than 75 percent of US trade, the measure was regarded as anti-British. More important, it was economically suicidal—as Hamilton, with an Anglophile bias, was quick to point out—because nearly all of the government's revenues were funded by import duties mostly imposed on British products. Although the debate strengthened the anti-British nationalism of the new Democratic-Republican Party that Madison and Jefferson were creating to counter the Hamiltonian Federalists, the measure died in the Senate.

This was the second time Hamilton had been able to block a joint effort by Jefferson and Madison to restrict British trade; they had made a similar proposal in 1791. Writing to a friend, Hamilton had then complained of his opponents: "They have a womanish attachment to France and a womanish resentment against Great Britain. . . . Various circumstances prove to me that if these gentlemen were left to pursue their own course, there would be in less than six months, an open war between the United States and Great Britain."[36] Without regard to the Freudian aspects of his analysis, Hamilton correctly foresaw the risks that Jefferson and Madison's anti-British stance posed. The War of 1812 eventually proved his point.

THE EMBARGO ACT AND THE WAR OF 1812

Thomas Jefferson's nationalistic approach to trade policy during his service as Washington's secretary of state presaged his actions on trade upon becoming president. When the Anglo-French forces resumed combat in the Napoleonic Wars in 1803, as the combatants' hostile seizures of American vessels on the high seas intensified, Europe again threatened to draw the United States into battle. By 1807, Napoleon had seized more than 200 American ships and the British had seized more than 500. Jefferson had previously dry docked all but thirteen frigates in the American Navy to save money, and he was not inclined, nor at all prepared, to go to war with either of the European powers. On the advice of Madison, then serving as his secretary of state, he proposed the Embargo Act in 1807, which forbade all international trade to and from American ports, essentially in order to safeguard the country's ships, goods, and sailors. He and Madison hoped that this action would prevent war and move the British and the French to accept American neutrality. Treasury Secretary Albert Gallatin, however, opposed the embargo, declaring that in view of the embargo's "privations, suffering, revenue, effect on the enemy, politics at home, etc.," he preferred war. Sounding as if he were quoting from Adam Smith, Gallatin prophetically advised Jefferson: "Governmental prohibitions do always more mischief than had been calculated; and it is not without much hesitation that a statesman should hazard to regulate the concerns of individuals as if he could do it better than themselves."[37] Jefferson was obviously troubled by Gallatin's opinion, writing a few months later, "For a certain length of time I think the embargo is a less evil than war. But after a time it will not be so."[38]

In a highly favorable biography, which attempts to explain rather than simply gloss over the inconsistencies between the third president's philosophical principles and his political actions, Jon Meacham offers a rationale for Jefferson's decision to expand executive authority during his presidency while espousing limited government. "Like the Louisiana Purchase—which was, to say the very least, vastly more successful," Meacham writes, "the embargo illustrated Jefferson's flexibility and capacity to adapt his professed ideology to present realities."[39]

The Embargo Act, which passed quickly through Congress, had little impact upon the huge economies of the two European adversaries, but it had a calamitous effect upon the American economy. While enforcement was difficult and smuggling became widespread, exports fell from $108 million in 1807 to $22 million in 1808. Harbors filled with idle ships, merchants depending on imports were bankrupted, and 30,000 sailors lost their employment.

Despite its immediate stress on the economy, the embargo had the unintended consequence of nourishing America's budding industries during its fourteen months' duration, a development Jefferson found to be favorable despite his earlier pronouncements against manufacturing. "Our embargo, which has been a very trying measure, has produced one very happy, and permanent effect," Jefferson wrote to his friend the Marquis de Lafayette. "It has set us all on domestic manufacture, and will I verily believe reduce our future demands on England fully one half."[40] Years later, he admitted, "Experience has taught me that manufactures are now as necessary to our independence as to our comfort."[41] This was definitely an acquired taste for Jefferson, who was known to enjoy the finer apparel and furnishings imported from Europe, even when his personal budget could ill-afford them. In *Notes on Virginia*, he had described the wool fabric manufactured in America at the time as "very coarse, unsightly, and unpleasant" in comparison with European manufactured fabrics.[42] Biographer Dumas Malone relates that at the end of his presidency, during the debate over repealing the Embargo Act and the corresponding struggle between the commercial and manufacturing interests, Jefferson was apprised of a Connecticut factory that made fine cloth. He promptly ordered enough of it to make a coat. Sounding much like Mahatma Gandhi in his struggles against the British in a later age, Jefferson commented, "Homespun is become the spirit of the times. I think it an useful one, and therefore that it is a duty to encourage it by example."[43]

The embargo expired at the end of Jefferson's presidency but was replaced in 1809 with the Non-Intercourse Act, which allowed trade to resume with all countries except Britain and France. This measure proved as ineffective and controversial as the general embargo and was abandoned after a year. Britain continued to interfere with American shipping and trade, however, and this harassment was one of the causes of the War of 1812. It is estimated that more than 5,000 sailors were impressed into service in the Royal Navy after being pirated off American vessels on the high seas from 1803 to 1812.

Although most of the trade woes befalling Americans in 1812 came from Jefferson and Madison's trade restrictions, the "war hawks" laid the problems squarely on the British restrictions and ship seizures prior to the Embargo Act. In fact, "Free Trade and Sailors' Rights" became an early battle cry for the Americans in the war. Early in his administration, President James Madison, Jefferson's successor, recommended prohibitively high tariffs to Congress to protect American manufacturers from European imports, but he was unsuccessful until war broke out; at that time all rates were doubled to raise revenue for the country's defense, and trade with Britain was again prohibited. In any event, Britain maintained a blockade on the Atlantic shore that effectively dried up all foreign trade during the war. While the increased duties were imposed for the purpose of increasing revenue, their protectionist effects were quite appealing to the emerging industries and their political champions.

As might be expected, the restrictive trade policies of Jefferson and Madison did not enjoy universal approval throughout the country. Opposition was especially strong among the merchants and shippers in the Northeast, particularly in New England. Some Federalists charged that Napoleon had dictated the embargo as a precondition for an alliance with France against the British, and that war was declared in 1812 to aid the French. In the early days of the Democratic-Republican Party, Jefferson and Madison painted the Federalists as monarchists. However, after the Louisiana Purchase, which heralded Jefferson's unprecedented expansion of executive power, and his enforcement of the embargo, the tables were turned. His opponents dubbed him "Thomas the First." When the war began and Madison called for troops from state militias to be put under the command of the War Department, some northeastern states refused to respond, and their citizens also refused to pay taxes and boycotted war loans. The Massachusetts governor Caleb Strong even sent emissaries on a covert mission to seek an independent peace settlement with Britain.

By 1814, many New England radicals, and indeed most leading Federalist newspapers in the region, were talking of secession. In December, at the call of the Massachusetts state legislature, delegates from Rhode Island, Connecticut, Massachusetts, Vermont, and New Hampshire convened in Hartford, Connecticut, to discuss actions they might take to protect New England's trading interests. The convention, which lasted for three weeks, was closed, and no records were made of the discussions or of the votes taken. Contemporary correspondence indicates that Federalists made efforts to convince the delegates to move for New England's secession, but that was not the outcome. With some irony, the Hartford Convention's report proclaimed that New England had a duty to assert its authority over federal unconstitutional infringements on its sovereignty—a principle consistent with the Kentucky and Virginia Resolutions written by Jefferson and Madison in 1798 to counter Federalist John Adams's Alien and Sedition Act. As will be discussed in Chapter 2, the "nullifiers" of South Carolina would assert this same principle against strong opposition from New England in the "Tariff of Abominations" crisis that divided the nation some fifteen years later.

The Hartford report proposed seven amendments to the US Constitution, designed to make it more difficult to impose trade embargos, declare war, and elect a president from Virginia.[44] It is not likely that any of the delegates to the Hartford Convention expected that the Democratic-Republican–controlled Congress would give their proposals any hope for passage. Yet even if they only wanted to embarrass the president and gain some partisan advantage, their hopes were upended early in 1815. When Massachusetts sent three commissioners to Washington to present the Hartford proposals, they were met unexpectedly with the celebration of General Andrew Jackson's miraculous victory in the Battle of New Orleans and the peace settlement with Britain. The embarrassment was theirs, as news and rumors about the Hartford Convention were turned against the Federalists. The war and the Federalists' reaction to it effectively ended the party's existence on the national stage, but the trade isolation imposed on

New England may have been a blessing in disguise. Without the British imports, the traders had been forced to form their own manufacturing base and did so very successfully. In the postwar years, trade politics in New England began to reflect this changing interest.

THE EMERGENCE OF THE "AMERICAN SYSTEM"

Following the Treaty of Ghent, which ended the war with Great Britain in 1815 in a stalemate, an economic boom and a surge in nationalism were unleashed across the United States. The plantations in the South began to maximize their production, particularly of cotton; in the North, industrialization engendered spectacular employment growth in the cotton mills of New England. Although, as Hamilton predicted, these mill jobs involved predominantly women and children, they were in "paternalistic environments" away from urban locations, and thus dodged some of the worst social corruptions afflicting the European factories that Jefferson had foretold as America's fate.[45]

Among the new political champions of emerging industries and the protectionist system that developed during the war, the young speaker of the House of Representatives, Henry Clay of Kentucky, soon became the lead spokesman. Clay's initial interest in trade emanated from his parochial Kentucky concern with protecting domestic hemp production. He did his best to make sure that the US Navy gave preference to Kentucky's dew-rotted hemp over the better-quality water-rotted imported hemp in its procurement for rope and sailcloth production. But Clay's interests went beyond those of his home-based constituency. He was a strong Jeffersonian Democratic-Republican partisan when he arrived in Washington in 1807 to fill an unexpired Senate term and became an economic nationalist of the first order. But he soon began to sing from the Alexander Hamilton *Report on Manufactures* hymnal and picked up Hamilton's baton in encouraging government assistance to American industry, especially with regard to infant industries, in competing against foreign imports.

Being a westerner, Clay saw a certain need for public assistance for economic development of the West, thus leading him to combine the government-business partnership approach of Hamilton with the economic nationalism of Jefferson and Madison. While new industry seemed to be thriving in New England without public help, the trade

FIGURE 1.3   Henry Clay, John Neagle 1843 painting (Library of Congress)

practices of Britain at the time were politically provocative and economically threatening. This was exacerbated in a nationalistic period
when British troops had only recently sacked Washington and burned
the Capitol as well as the new executive mansion of the president. In
1816, the second year after trade was permitted again after the war,
British exports to the United States nearly doubled to $151 million, from
$85 million in 1815.

The British tactics in dealing with American competition lacked sub-
tlety. In a widely quoted remark in Parliament, Lord Henry Brougham substantiated the complaint that this import surge was the result of a "dumping"
attack to destroy American industry with underpriced goods:

It was well worth while to incur a loss upon the first exportation, in order by the glut, to stifle in the cradle, those rising manufactures, in the United States, which the war had forced into existence, contrary to the natural course of things.[46]

Clay's efforts to impose protective tariffs received support from President Madison, who recommended that Congress consider "means to preserve and promote the manufactures which have sprung into existence, and attained an unparalleled maturity throughout the United States, during the period of the European Wars."[47] Madison's treasury secretary, Alexander Dallas, recommended three levels of duties: (1) prohibitively high rates on products manufactured in the United States in quantities that fulfilled domestic demand; (2) protectively high rates on products that had not yet been, but could potentially be, produced in such quantities; and (3) lower rates, for revenue purposes, on products not manufactured in America. For example, under level (2) Clay and his allies in Congress attempted to raise the ad valorem duties on textiles to 33 1/3 percent, but they were effectively opposed by Daniel Webster, then a promising young Massachusetts congressman representing New England merchant and shipping interests who opposed protectionist tariffs. The final compromises resulting in the Tariff Act of 1816 did not provide the degree of protection Clay had desired. The duties on textiles were set at 25 percent for three years and then were scheduled to fall to 20 percent. Interestingly, however, Webster supported placing a prohibitive tariff on cotton sheeting to protect Massachusetts manufacturers from cheap imports from British India as a result of some astute lobbying from constituent and textile magnate Francis Lowell. According to historian Maurice G. Baxter, this provision "would be the favorite target of antiprotectionist complaint."[48]

As time passed, momentum grew in support of Clay's efforts to promote domestic manufacturing and curb imports. The scheduled reduction in textile tariffs was postponed to 1826, and duties on other sensitive products were increased. In 1820, another protectionist bill was debated that again proposed increasing textile tariffs to 33 percent and placing specific duties on forged iron and other import-threatened products. Southern agrarians objected, with references to the free-trade arguments of Adam Smith against subsidizing industry and burdening the consumer and agricultural interests. Clay countered, expounding upon the benefits and importance of developing national independence and pointing out the hypocrisy of

Britain's trade practices, especially its Corn Laws, which denied American grain exports access to the British market. In the end, the bill was tabled in the Senate by two votes. Predictably, the agrarian South went against the protectionist measure, the manufacturing North and Mid-Atlantic states were for it, and New England, representing both manufacturing and shipping interests, was split. These regional divisions on trade would become deeper and more portentous as the young nation matured.

The next major effort to increase tariffs to higher protective levels was in 1824, at a time when Speaker Clay had been dealt a much more favorable hand. First, American business was suffering from a lingering economic depression and had sought the help of an army of Washington lobbyists. Second, recent congressional reapportionment had caused an increase in votes in the House of Representatives from the protectionist section of the country—Pennsylvania, Ohio, and New York. And finally, not only were President James Monroe and Treasury Secretary William Crawford both southerners—from Virginia and Georgia, respectively—supportive of protective rates as economic nationalists in the Jefferson-Madison vein, but all of the major presidential contenders in the pending 1824 election, including Clay, Crawford, John Quincy Adams, and General Andrew Jackson, also saw protective rates as desirable.

Despite this favorable climate, there remained strong opposition to further protectionism, which came most prominently from the southern cotton representatives and members representing the New England shipping and commercial interests.

Clay responded forcefully on the House floor, however, with a historic speech blending elements of Jeffersonian nationalism and Hamilton's infant industry protectionism. His speech went on for two days and established the framework for the US trade debate for decades to come. He began by describing the general distress then pervading "every part of the Union," citing diminished exports and commerce, "unthreshed crops of grain, perishing in our barns and barn-yards for the want of a market," numerous bankruptcies among all orders of society, unemployment and reduced wages, and a precipitous 50 percent drop in property values.[49] For these "unhappy" conditions "of this widespreading distress, of this deep depression," he laid the blame squarely on European trade policies, such as the British Corn Laws, which had resulted in a decline in markets for American products for which there was no hope of reversal. He noted that the trade statistics in the twenty-eight-year period from 1795 to 1823 showed less than a 15 percent increase in American exports. Moreover, nearly two-thirds of these exports were of three products—cotton, rice, and tobacco—all of which were produced in the South where only one-fifth of the population resided. Cotton was the only product whose exports had been increasing substantially, but cotton prices had been declining, thus reducing the value even of that export.

Clay's solution was to create a home market for the encouragement and consumption of American production. The concept was to provide not only a stable market for American agricultural produce but also to create a domestic supply of manufactured goods for the home market that had, until then, been supplied almost exclusively by foreigners. He noted that about four-fifths of the population "makes nothing that foreigners will buy"; and if they could not sell, they could not buy. A protected home market, Clay believed, would result in steady and comparative certainty in the market, creation of reciprocity of interests between suppliers and merchants, greater economic security, and increased quantity and lower prices. It could, however, only be assured by protective legislation:

> Let us counteract the policy of foreigners, and withdraw the sup-
> port we now give to their industry, and stimulate that of our own
> country. It should be a prominent object with wise legislators, to
> multiply the vocations and extend the business of society, as far as
> it can be done, by the protection of our interests at home, against
> the injurious effects of foreign legislation.[50]

Clay called for the creation of "a genuine American System," based upon the development of the domestic market through the aid of government resources and restrictions, with limited exceptions, on foreign trade. He urged protection through tariffs against the "overwhelming influence of foreigners," the sole object of which was "to tax the produce of foreign industry, with the view of promoting American industry."[51] Passage of this bill, the Tariff Act of 1824, Clay argued, would mark an essential first step in developing the home market of the American System. The United States would be modeling its economy after Britain, which, after all, had clearly not yet adopted the principles of Adam Smith. Much of Clay's speech described the experiences of other nations in developing and conducting their trade and industrial policies. He especially seemed to glory in describing the wealth and power of archvillain, Great Britain, which Clay declared to have eleven times the productive power of the United States at that time. Emphatically and unequivocally, Clay mocked Smith's arguments, declaring that protection, not free trade, was the key to achieving wealth as a nation—including, most pointedly, for Smith's own Great Britain:

> The measure of the wealth of a nation is indicated by the measure of its protection of its industry; and . . . the measure of the poverty of a nation is marked by that of the degree in which it neglects and abandons the care of its own industry, leaving it exposed to the action of foreign powers. Great Britain protects most her industry, and the wealth of Great Britain is consequently the greatest.[52]

He also attributed the wealth of France to its protective system and noted that the "calamities" that had befallen Spain were due to its abandonment of the care of its own internal industry. Finally, he quoted the emperor of Russia in describing the results of his country's two-year trial of a free-trade system in a world of protective nations: "Events have proved that our Agriculture and our Commerce, as well as our Manufacturing Industry, are not only paralyzed, but brought to the brink of ruin."[53]

The strongest opposition Clay faced came from southern representatives who saw little promise for manufacturing in their section of the country. Representative Philip P. Barbour of Virginia, an agrarian Democratic-Republican, asked, "What hope is there in the career of competition [in regard to manufacturing], between two sections of the country, in one of which there is a combination of the three great advantages of large capital, dense population, and free labor; and in the other of which there is a combination of the three great disadvantages of a deficient capital, sparse population, and slave labor?"[54] Clay had little patience with this argument, observing that, surely, these circumstances did not disqualify the South from all branches of manufacturing. But so what if they did, Clay argued! "Can it be expected that the interests of the greater part of our population should be made to bend to the condition of the servile part of our population? That, in effect, would be to make us the slaves of slaves."[55] What he offered the cotton growers was a more stable domestic market for their products, which certainly, he reasoned, would be better in the long run for them than being forever subject to the sole discretion of the British market.

Once again, Clay's chief adversary in the debate was the rising New England orator, Massachusetts congressman Daniel Webster, who also spoke for two days. Webster refuted Clay's gloomy picture of the American economy and expounded upon the positive effects of free "commercial intercourse" and "unrestrained individual action" in his version of the American System. According to biographer Robert Remini, Webster was of the opinion that "Great Britain and other European nations were moving away from the mercantilism that had helped trigger the American Revolution and toward a policy of free trade."[56] In his speech Webster opined, "I think it is clear, that, if we now embrace the system of prohibitions and restrictions, we shall show an affection for what others have discarded, and be attempting to ornament ourselves with cast-off apparel."[57] He cited the example of American shipping's excellent performance on the world stage. "How, sir, do the ship-owners and navigators accomplish this?" Webster asked. "It is not by protection and bounties: but by unwearied exertion . . . by that manly and resolute spirit which relies on itself to protect itself."[58] Further, following the moral philosophy of Adam Smith, Webster questioned the fairness of protection:

> I know it would be very easy to promote manufactures . . . if we might act in disregard of other interests. We could cause a sudden transfer of capital, and a violent change in the pursuits of men. We could exceedingly benefit some classes by these means. But what then becomes of the interests of others? . . . For my part, I see very little relief for those who are likely to be deprived of their employments, or who find the prices of their commodities which they need raised.[59]

However, Webster's lofty rhetoric about the "manly and resolute spirit" of New England shipowners eschewing government protection and subsidies, and the unfairness of promoting or protecting manufacturing interests, was undermined by his continued support for protective tariffs for his woolen and cotton manufacturing constituents.[60] And it would not be long before he would broaden his protectionist support even further, as the influence of New England's textile interests began to eclipse that of its commercial and shipping interests in the politics of Daniel Webster.

Over the course of the legislative process there were compromising amendments, but thanks largely to Speaker Clay's tactical skills, the bill passed the House narrowly by a vote of 107 to 102. Again, the midwestern and northwestern states voted solidly in favor; New England was split,

23 to 15 against; the South, 70 to 6 heavily against the measure.[61] It passed the Senate by a four-vote margin. Although the final product was not as protectionist as Clay would have liked, he was satisfied that Congress had endorsed his concept of the American System. Clearly the forces of the Mid-Atlantic and Western states had gained in their economic battle with New England and the South on the free-trade issue. As for New England, free trade was becoming less important as the region moved more and more into textile manufacturing. Daniel Webster would come to personify his region's political-economic evolution.

In the southern states, however, the issue was leading inexorably to crisis. With their primary product, cotton, now exposed to an unprotected world market where prices were spiraling downward, those states were forced to pay protective tariffs on manufactured imports or purchase inferior products at higher prices from a protected market. Moreover, the revenues from these duties were expected to be spent on internal improvements outside of their region, which the southerners considered to be an unconstitutional abuse of congressional power. They saw the protective tariff on imported manufactured goods as an oppressive measure destined to enrich other sections of the country at the South's expense. It would prove to be an ominous debate.

2

Crisis, Compromise, and Free Trade in the Jacksonian Democracy

A protective tariff is a question regarding the enhancement of the profits of capital. That is the object, and not to augment the wages of labor, which would reduce those profits. . . . It discriminates in favor of the rich and against the poor.[1]

—Robert J. Walker,
US Secretary of the Treasury, 1845

One might wonder why politicians have always gotten so agitated over tariffs, an issue that appears dull on its face; it is just a matter of taxes on imports after all. Yet trade issues provided one of the principal grievances that sparked both the American Revolution and the War of 1812. In the first half century after the ratification of the US Constitution, tariffs provoked fierce debates in Congress year after year, and, as will be reviewed in this chapter, led the country to the brink of domestic armed conflict in the Nullification Crisis in a preview of the American Civil War. As the main source of revenue for the fledgling government, tariffs had an obviously critical function in the political economy. But, perhaps more important, due to the corresponding function of setting revenue policy in the distribution of economic resources among the competing interests, economic classes, and geographical sections of the young republic, tariffs also played a fundamental role in the development of political parties in the late eighteenth and early nineteenth centuries.

From the incubation of Thomas Jefferson's Democratic-Republican Party, economic issues stood at the center of its differences with the Federalists under the leadership of Alexander Hamilton. Jefferson and James Madison charged their new political opponents with being monarchists conspiring to impose a British-style parliamentary empire over the state governments. During the debates at the Constitutional Convention, Hamilton had, in fact, declared that the centralized, aristocratic British government dominated by a strong monarchy was the best form of government. But it was Hamilton's financial plan of 1790–91 that stirred the decisive debate. The narrow passage of the bill proposed by Hamilton to create the Bank of the United States was the defining moment separating the merchant class led by Hamilton from the Jeffersonian agrarians. Underlying the arguments of monarchical versus republican politics was a power struggle between the financial elites of New York and New England and the Virginia planter class, who often represented their faction as underdog yeomen farmers and workingmen.

Hamilton rejected Adam Smith's free-trade, anti-mercantilist approach and viewed a close partnership between business and government as vital to the development and survival of the young nation. He argued that the bank and this partnership were necessary to provide stability in the face of great national debt following the Revolution. If private parties were benefited by public investments in the bank, so be it; where was the evil in it? Jefferson and Madison took a different view. They saw corruption in the efforts of the bank's private investors to enrich themselves using public resources. To them, according to historian Joseph Ellis, "It was like the biblical scene when the money changers took over the temple."[2] Perhaps more important, they feared that these new moneyed interests would become the power aristocracy behind the Federalist throne. The Virginia planters had suffered under the oppressive practices of British creditors and did not want to be under the political and financial thumb of northern financiers. Again, according to Ellis, "The fiscal program of Hamilton, most graphically embodied in the bank, surely did conjure up the dreaded menace of a northern commercial elite as vampires sucking the blood out of the agrarian south."[3]

Jefferson's views on Hamilton and his wealthy benefactors are portrayed by Lin-Manuel Miranda's exceptional Broadway musical, *Hamilton*, in hip-hop verse:

Jefferson:
Our poorest citizens, our farmers, live ration to ration
As Wall Street robs 'em blind in search of chips to cash in.

. . .

Jefferson, Madison, Burr:
Let's follow the money and see where it goes.
Because every second the Treasury grows.
If we follow the money and see where it leads,
Get in the weeds, look for the seeds of
Hamilton's misdeeds.[4]

As discussed in Chapter 1, the economic chasm between Jefferson and
Hamilton finds further illustration in their respective reports to Congress
on trade policy. Hamilton's *Report on Manufactures*, submitted in 1791,
called for linking government to business with subsidies and protectionist tariffs to assist new industries attempting to compete with European
imports. Jefferson abhorred this linkage as a threat to the republic, especially its government subsidies. In his own report to Congress on foreign
commerce of 1793, Jefferson outlined and condemned the litany of trade
restrictions imposed by other nations on American shipping and exports,
emphasizing those of Britain. While expressing a preference for free trade
in the language of Adam Smith, he recommended raising tariffs against
offending nations in retaliation—also consistent with Smith's principles—
and recommended entering into negotiations to lower them based on reciprocity. He noted that such negotiations were not likely to be successful
with the arrogant British regime, thus leaving his proposals for tariff retaliation as simply a token of economic nationalism had they been adopted.

Actually, until the 1820s, economic nationalism promoted by the leadership of the Jeffersonian Democratic-Republican Party was the principal
motivating force behind United States trade policy. Hamilton's scheming in
1800 to undermine his fellow Federalist, President John Adams, helped not
only to prevent Adams from gaining a second term but also weakened his
party and led to the beginning of a Virginia Democratic-Republican dynasty
that lasted twenty-four years. By the end of the War of 1812—which most of
the few remaining Federalists had opposed—Hamilton's former party had
effectively dissolved. Although Hamilton's life ended prematurely in a duel
with Vice President Aaron Burr in 1804, his influence on protectionist trade

policy extended well beyond his demise and that of his party. The development of new industry during Jefferson's embargo, the War of 1812, and the
renewed onslaught of British imports after the war led to a new call for protection based upon Hamilton's business-government partnership.

While Congress was effectively all Democratic-Republican in the postwar years, some members—especially among the southern agrarians—were
not pleased with the nationalistic trade policy espoused by Jefferson and
Madison, calling it "neo-Federalism."[5] The Madison administration "out-
Hamiltons Alexander Hamilton,"[6] wrote John Randolph, a Virginia agrarian Democratic-Republican who became a sharp critic of James Madison's
protectionist agenda and approval of the second Bank of the United
States. Indeed, US trade policies over the next decade began evolving in a
Hamiltonian direction. Henry Clay's persistent rhetoric and efforts to legis-
late his "American System" of protective tariffs and internal improvements
merged Jefferson's anti-British economic nationalism with Hamilton's
infant industry and government-business partnership ideas.

Without partisan divisions, the debates were largely sectional, with
the commercial shipping interests in New England and the agrarian South
offering the strongest opposition to protectionist measures. In the years
immediately following the War of 1812, however, the fervor for nationalism
remained high and the southern "war hawks" who had favored declaring
war with Britain were not ready to disarm economically. In 1816, this group
even included John C. Calhoun, who would soon become a leader of the
southern free-traders. As the rise in cotton production began to explode in
the postwar years, however, few southerners remained in this economic war
hawk camp into the 1820s. Southern representatives, quoting Adam Smith,
insisted that protective tariffs were oppressive taxes that unfairly raised
consumer prices and encouraged retaliatory tariffs on their products. Some
of them also argued, like Smith, that protectionism impoverished workers,
laying the groundwork for future populist anti-protectionist arguments.

In the North, where manufacturing was taking off, the cry for protection was based on Hamilton's infant industry argument, as well as economic nationalism against the British Leviathan. British trade reformers,
led by William Huskisson, had initiated tariff reductions in Parliament;
yet Britain, with its Corn Laws, remained a highly restricted market that
prohibited American grain imports and maintained other import restrictions that gave Britain a highly favorable balance of trade. In the West,
where economic development was new, politicians generally followed

Kentuckian Clay's lead in supporting the protectionist American System because high tariffs financed internal improvements, such as roads and canals.

THE INCONCLUSIVE ELECTION OF 1824

The controversial presidential election of 1824 left the country in a confusing and leaderless state for the next four years. The dominant candidate going into the election, Secretary of the Treasury William Crawford of Georgia, suffered a paralytic stroke just before the campaign began, but he remained in the race. Secretary of State John Quincy Adams and Speaker Clay were also strong contenders representing New England and the West. Secretary of War John C. Calhoun from South Carolina had been in the race but later moved his candidacy to the more certain vice-presidential ballot. The wild card in the race was the immensely popular General Andrew Jackson, the hero of the Battle of New Orleans, who had been elected to the Senate in 1823. All of the candidates more or less came from the same political party, the Jeffersonian Democratic-Republicans, since Adams had abandoned the now moribund Federalist Party. They had all supported protective tariffs, although Jackson had been on both sides of the issue and Crawford had become the candidate most against the American System.

In the end, the election, which largely turned on sectionalism and personality, was inconclusive. Jackson won a plurality, but not a majority, of the popular and electoral vote, with Adams coming in second, and the decision was thrown to the House of Representatives. In that chamber Clay prevailed to swing the election to Adams. Within a matter of days the president-elect offered Clay the post of secretary of state in his new government—an appointment that Jackson supporters concluded was Clay's payoff in what was thereafter dubbed the "corrupt bargain."

The inconclusiveness of the election and the attacks surrounding the "corrupt bargain," together with the weak leadership emanating from the president, resulted in very little progress for the American System during the Adams administration. Adams, who was scholarly and principled, had received his early training from two original founding fathers of the republic; his father, John Adams, and Thomas Jefferson had served together as ministers in Paris. John Quincy Adams had been an able diplomat in several administrations and, as secretary of state under President James

Monroe, he was credited with formulating the Monroe Doctrine. As president, however, he was lackluster at best and politically inept.

In the period of the fallout from the controversial election, Jackson resigned his seat in the Senate and returned home to Tennessee to begin plotting his campaign for the presidency in 1828. Though outwardly Jackson took his defeat in stride, he revealed bitterness along with intent for revenge in private correspondence. "The *Judas* of the West has closed the contract and will receive the thirty pieces of silver," he wrote. "His end will be the same."[7] Soon a pro-Jackson group formed in Congress to block any significant legislative initiative by the new president, and it was largely successful. By 1827, this faction had taken over majority control of both houses of Congress in opposition to the Adams administration.

THE TARIFF OF ABOMINATIONS

While Clay was mainly preoccupied with his foreign affairs portfolio, he kept a keen eye on economic policy. With the administration stymied on most of its agenda, protective tariffs again became the major issue of the developing parties surrounding the competing Adams-Clay and pro-Jackson factions. Early in 1827, the House passed a bill to raise the tariffs on raw wool and woolen textiles by 50 percent. When it got to the Senate, the measure was stalled until Vice President John C. Calhoun broke a tie vote and tabled the bill, effectively killing it. This action marked a strong signal from Calhoun, who had been a supporter of economic nationalism since the Tariff Act of 1816. It was now clear that he could not be counted on to support the Adams-Clay tariff policy. Calhoun knew that his vote would be offensive at the national level, but it was more important that he maintain his influence among southerners and particularly his preeminence in South Carolina politics. For Clay and other protectionists it now became crucial to begin plotting immediately for tariff protection for the next session, which could be their last.

The Adams-Clay forces held a convention in Harrisburg, Pennsylvania, with more than 100 delegates from thirteen northeastern and western states in the summer of 1827 and adopted a legislative proposal to increase rates on a broad range of imports. In his speeches that summer Clay hailed the benefits of the American System and the dangers posed to them by the

Jacksonians. Naturally, the pro-Jackson forces viewed the Pennsylvania convention as a political maneuver leading up to the 1828 election and were drawn into the battle. Although Jackson was himself a southern cotton planter and slaveholder, he had voted for the protectionist Tariff Act of 1824. Since that time, however, he had clouded his position on tariffs as much as possible. His supporters presented him as a free-trader to southerners and as a protectionist in the North.

Both Clay and Adams anticipated that the Jacksonians in Congress would oppose the American System in the tariff debate—a move they believed would inure to Adams's political advantage. They misjudged their opponents.

Rather than opposing the high duties proposed at the Pennsylvania convention, Adams's opponents came up with their own protectionist bill in the 1828 session that added, rather inconsistently, even more excessive duties. In the words of historian Robert V. Remini, "It was the most lopsided and unequal piece of legislation imaginable. Virtually every item in it contained marks of political favoritism."[8] The bill was plainly designed with the 1828 election in mind; tariffs that helped interests in support of Jackson were favored whereas tariff interests that supported Adams were disfavored. For example, 50 percent tariffs would ultimately be imposed on raw wool, but the rate for manufactured wool products was set too low to help New England factories compete with British imports, especially if they had to pay higher duties on imported raw wool. Products of the western and Mid-Atlantic states, such as iron, hemp, and flax, were favored with high rates because they came from regions dominated by Jackson supporters, and products of New England like woolen manufactures were not, because likely Adams voters produced them.

In the South, there was no support for Adams and vehement opposition to any protective tariff, so the Jackson supporters needed a delicate strategy. The Jacksonian congressional leaders managing the bill convinced the southern representatives to accept the measure in the House with the understanding that the New Englanders would defeat the bill in the Senate, thus causing Adams embarrassment. The strategy failed, however, when after the House passed the bill by eleven votes, it went on to gain passage in the Senate with tariffs on woolens amended by Senator Daniel Webster and other New Englanders to a higher, more satisfactory level. President Adams promptly signed it, increasing tariffs generally from around 30 to 50 percent.

Believing the Jacksonian managers had deceived them, the southerners were outraged and named the new act the "Tariff of Abominations."

The hope for Adams's reelection was now slim. Clay had worked hard to build a party of support based largely on a broad field of state organizations advocating protective tariffs and economic nationalism embodied in the American System, but he was up against several critical impediments: His candidate was not popular and adamantly refused to campaign, while his opponent, Jackson, enjoyed enormous popularity and had a well-organized campaign. Jackson won in a landslide.

THE SEEDS OF THE NULLIFICATION CRISIS

The other victor in the election, Vice President John C. Calhoun, had switched his allegiance from Adams to Jackson. Responding to South Carolina politics, he wanted no part of the American System's high tariffs. He was also motivated by the opportunity that he might have to succeed Jackson as president. In November 1828, on his plantation before taking office in the new administration the next year, Calhoun solidified his stance on the Tariff of Abominations by drafting a long report to a special committee of the South Carolina House of Representatives appointed to prepare a protest against the tariff. The draft, which was unsigned but well known to be Calhoun's work, was published as the *South Carolina Exposition and Protest* and widely disseminated. His report began with a refined restatement of the southern position on protectionism and free trade, pointing out that the southern economy could not survive selling only to the home market in America. He argued that the protective American System was impoverishing South Carolina workers and that it would soon do the same for northern workers, as similar systems had harmed European workers:

> To understand its ultimate tendency in distributing the wealth of society among the several classes, we must turn our eyes to Europe, where it has been in action for centuries, and has been among the efficient causes of that great inequality of property, which prevails in most European countries. No system can be more efficient to rear up a monied aristocracy. Its tendency is to make the poor, poorer, and the rich, richer. Heretofore in our country this tendency has displayed itself principally in its effects as regards the

different sections, but the time will come, when it will produce the same result between classes in the manufacturing states. . . . Under operation of the system wages will sink much more rapidly than the prices of the necessaries of life, till the operatives will be reduced to the lowest point, where the portion of the products of their labour left to them, will be barely necessary to preserve existence.[9]

The adoption of the Tariff of Abominations, according to Calhoun, represented an abuse of majority power that was a threat to the Republic. The founding fathers had foreseen this problem and addressed it with the separation of powers, not only among the three branches of government but also between the powers of the states and federal government. Citing arguments of Madison and Jefferson in their Virginia and Kentucky Resolutions for nullification of the Alien and Sedition Acts of 1798, he asserted the rights of states to contest the authority of the federal government. Moreover, he believed each state had the right to decide how the issue was to be resolved within its borders through a state convention chosen to determine whether a particular federal law was unconstitutional and should be vetoed or "nullified" within the state.

Having thus laid claim to the most radical position of the southern free-traders, Calhoun softened the sting of his report with a word of caution. He said that while calling a convention at this time on the issue of the tariff would be fully justified, it should be delayed pending "the great political revolution" imminent with Jackson's election, "which may be followed up under his influence with a complete restoration of the pure principles of our Government."[10] Many southerners expected Jackson, a fellow planter, to reduce tariffs, and Calhoun's *Exposition* offered more than a little encouragement on the issue.

Unfortunately for Calhoun, the new president was not anxious to move on the tariff issue upon taking office. Jackson understood the political risks involved in opening up the tariff debate again so soon after the previous controversy and wanted to take a slow, moderate approach at least until retiring the national debt still lingering from the War of 1812. While his personal sympathies seemed to lie with his agrarian, free-trade section of the country, his comments revealed a degree of Jeffersonian nationalism that may not have warranted Calhoun's hopes for a restoration of "pure principles." In his first message to Congress in December 1829, he admonished the politicians that "local feelings and prejudices [on

FIGURE 2.1 John C. Calhoun, A. H. Richie 1852 engraving (Library of Congress)

tariff issues] should be merged in the patriotic determination to promote the great interests as a whole . . . [d]iscarding all calculations of political ascendancy." As a general rule, Jackson said, duties on foreign manufactures should be graduated so as to "place our own in fair competition with those of other countries."[11]

The legislative activity affecting tariffs in the first two years of Jackson's administration was insignificant, but the debates continued. The most famous of these was the Senate debate between Webster of Massachusetts and Robert Y. Hayne of South Carolina in January 1830. As Vice President Calhoun sat silently presiding over the Senate in his ex officio role, Hayne argued from Calhoun's *Exposition* that the North, through its majority control of the government, had pushed the South to the brink of destruction and the country would suffer for its actions:

> Do gentlemen estimate the value of the Union at so low a price that they will not even make one effort to bind the States together with cords of affection? . . . If so, let me tell gentlemen the seeds of dissolution are already sown, and our children will reap the bitter fruit.[12]

Webster, who in the 1824 debates was a free-trader—albeit a free-trader who made parochial exceptions for good political cause—had metamorphosed into an arch-protectionist by this time. He underpinned his two-day response with a nationalistic rationalization. While bitterly chastising Hayne and his South Carolina friends for being willing to risk the breakup of the Union for a pittance in import tariffs, his own reasoning for changing from free-trader to protectionist reflected more political expediency than policy rationale.

> With a great majority of the Representatives of Massachusetts, I voted against the tariff of 1824. My reasons were then given, and I will not now repeat them. But, not withstanding our dissent, the great states of New York, Pennsylvania, Ohio, and Kentucky went for the bill, in almost unbroken column, and it passed. Congress and the President sanctioned it, and it became the law of the land. What, then, were we to do? Our only option was, either, to fall in with the settled course of public policy, and accommodate ourselves to it as well as we could, or to embrace the South Carolina doctrine, and talk of nullifying the statute by State interference. . . . I had voted against the tariff of 1824, but it passed; and in 1827 and 1828 I voted to amend it, in a point essential to the interest of my constituents. Where is the inconsistency?[13]

Webster used the extreme stances of Calhoun and Hayne to obscure his radical change of position on the trade issue. However wrong Hayne may have been to argue for nullification, he had been correct that Webster had "erected to free trade a beautiful and enduring monument" in 1824 and was now singing an entirely different tune.[14] The Massachusetts senator overstated his constituents' concerns, reflected in his stark change from a free-trade advocate to a protectionist. He had a few constituents to whom he listened more than others. One in particular was wealthy businessman Abbott Lawrence, who had been an importer until moving into the textile manufacturing business in the 1820s, at which time he began to see the advantages import tariff protection provided to his ledgers. According to the memoirs of John Quincy Adams, Lawrence was "devoted to Webster" and was his main pillar of support, "both pecuniary and political" in 1828 when he advised Webster to vote for the controversial Tariff of Abominations.[15] After this vote Webster never looked back.

Nevertheless, Webster's patriotic eloquence on the importance of the Union was what is best remembered from the debate with Hayne, and indeed it became legendary. Hayne had posed the question, "What interest has South Carolina in a canal to the Ohio?" Webster responded, "According to [Hayne's] doctrine, Ohio is one country, and South Carolina is another country. . . . I look upon Ohio and South Carolina to be parts of one whole—parts of the same country—and that country is my country. . . . I hope that I may not see the flag of my Country, with its stars separated or obliterated, torn by commotion, smoking with the blood of civil war." He derided the motto of "Liberty first, and Union afterwards," as "words of delusion and folly," preferring "that other sentiment, dear to every true American heart: Liberty *and* Union, now and forever, one and inseparable!"[16]

Soon after the Hayne-Webster debate, on the occasion of the annual political celebration dinner of Jefferson's birthday, President Jackson and Vice President Calhoun had their own famous debate—albeit in the form of concise but gauntlet-tossing toasts. Prior to the dinner, the president had learned that a number of nullification sympathizers were scheduled to give toasts, and they were expected to tie the doctrine to Jefferson as its father. In fact, Jackson concluded "that the celebration was to be a nullification affair altogether," and, accordingly, he plotted a preemptive response—in the form of a toast. As the audience, eagerly anticipating the unfolding political drama, sat quietly straining to hear how he would react to the challenge of South Carolina, the state of his birth, Jackson stood at the head table and, while staring down at Calhoun, said simply, "Our Federal Union—it must be preserved." Interestingly, this toast is inscribed on Jackson's statue erected across from the White House in Lafayette Square and dedicated by Senator Stephen Douglas just eight years before the Civil War.

Calhoun, who spoke next, chose not to deliver a moderate toast for the sake of harmony with his president and to foster his own chances to

succeed Jackson in the presidency; instead, he threw down his own rhetorical gauntlet. "The Union," Calhoun responded, "next to our liberty the
most dear; may we all remember that it can only be preserved by respecting
the rights of the states and distributing equally the benefits and burdens of
the Union."[17] The breach between Jackson and Calhoun, which had been
developing over a number of largely personal issues, was now public and
beyond repair.

Although it had been no secret that Calhoun had drafted the *South
Carolina Exposition and Protest,* which had ignited the nullification debate,
he sought to refine—and publicly amplify—his position in the summer of
1831 with his widely disseminated *Fort Hill Address.* He argued that the protectionist tariffs were unconstitutional violations of the congressional revenue and commerce powers, resulting in southerners being unfairly taxed
to benefit northern manufacturers. Quoting again from Thomas Jefferson's
and James Madison's Kentucky and Virginia Resolutions, he contended
that the doctrine of "interposition" was the traditionally accepted remedy
for states in this situation. That is, the Constitution grants certain specified
powers to the federal government and reserves all other powers to the states
to be exercised respectively within their geographic boundaries. Thus,
when a state decides that the federal government has exceeded its authority
with a federal act, the state can *interpose* its authority and prevent the act
from being implemented within that state. According to biographer Irving
H. Bartlett, "The constitutional path toward peaceful resolution of such
conflicts in the United States was interposition by the aggrieved state, and
every sentence that Calhoun wrote in what became famous as the *Fort Hill
Address* was intended to show that there was nothing to fear in the Carolina
doctrine; it was profoundly conservative."[18] Regardless of his intentions, its
calming effect was negligible, and the nullifiers in South Carolina continued to grow.

By December 1831, a new Congress had been elected which now
included former secretary of state Henry Clay in the Senate and former
president John Quincy Adams in the House, and a new tariff debate began.
Adding to the intensity of the debate, 1832 was an election year, and the
new National Republican Party had nominated Clay to head the ticket on
a platform based on the American System and critical of Jackson's tariff
positions. The president, with a view toward reelection, also got off the
sidelines of the tariff battle and proposed a duty reduction. In doing so, he
cited the diminishing national debt, but the free-trade element of his party

was probably also on his mind. Jackson's party affiliation remained formally under the Jeffersonian Democratic-Republican title, but the Jacksonians had since the 1828 election begun calling themselves simply Democrats—a name once deployed by Federalists against Jeffersonians to imply a party of mob rule. Indeed, from 1828 to 1836 the Jacksonian democracy became the populist antithesis to Hamiltonian Federalism, with free trade as a key party principle.

The trade debate raged on for months, replete with vitriolic ad hominem attacks. For example, Clay, after invoking the names of Washington, Hamilton, and Jefferson as supporters of protective legislation since 1789, launched into a bitter assault on Albert Gallatin, who served for thirteen years as the acclaimed treasury secretary under both Jefferson and Madison. Clay, Gallatin, and John Quincy Adams had worked together in the delegation that negotiated the Treaty of Ghent with the British ending the War of 1812. Gallatin had just presented to Congress the results of a free-trade convention attended by several state delegations, attacking protectionism, "setting forth the evils of the existing tariff of duties," and calling for the modification of the Tariff of Abominations.[19] "Go home to your native Europe," Clay said to Gallatin, "and there inculcate upon her sovereigns your Utopian doctrines of free trade, and when you have prevailed upon them to unseal their ports, and freely admit the produce of Pennsylvania and other States, come back, and we shall be prepared to become converts, and to adopt your faith."[20] According to an entry in Adams's diary made after meeting with Clay early in the session, Clay vowed that he would "defy the South, the President, and the devil" to save the American System.[21]

In the House, Adams, now serving as chairman of the Committee on Manufactures, agreed out of concern for maintaining the Union to collaborate with the administration. He committed to reducing rates, but only gradually in order to continue retiring the debt and to maintain as much protection as possible. The administration proposed average cuts from 45 to 27 percent, and the House adjusted that upward and passed the bill with Adams's support. By the time it passed the Senate, the average rates had been reduced to 33 percent, but most textiles remained high at 50 percent, and rates on other import-sensitive products like iron, sugar, cotton bagging, and glass, while reduced, remained at protective levels. Clay, not especially pleased with the result, voted for the measure reluctantly, as did other protectionists.

THE FORCE BILL AND THE COMPROMISE TARIFF OF 1833

Andrew Jackson and his Democrats, including some southerners, thought these tariff reductions were sufficient to bring peace to the issue, but they were wrong as to South Carolina. The 1832 elections, in which Jackson won reelection in a landslide victory over Clay, also produced a two-thirds majority for the nullifiers in the South Carolina state elections. As prescribed in Calhoun's *Exposition*, the state legislature promptly called a constitutional convention to nullify the Tariffs of Abominations, as revised in 1832. The convention duly adopted an ordinance that forbade the collection of duties required under the tariff within the state's boundaries, effective February 1, 1833. Further, the convention declared that any act by Congress to authorize the use of force against South Carolina would be considered "inconsistent with the longer continuance of South Carolina in the Union."[22]

Jackson reacted promptly and angrily. He immediately began preparing for a war that he himself planned to lead against his birth state, vowing to hang the traitorous nullifiers. "In forty days I can have within the limits of South Carolina

FIGURE 2.2 Andrew Jackson in Lafayette Square inscribed with his anti-nullification toast: "Our Federal Union—it must be preserved"

fifty thousand men, and in forty days more another fifty thousand. . . . The wickedness, madness, and folly of the leaders and the delusion of their followers in the attempt to destroy themselves and our Union has not its parallel in the history of the world. The Union will be preserved."[23] He issued a public proclamation declaring nullification "inconsistent with the existence of the Union, contradicted expressly by the letter of the Constitution, unauthorized by its spirit, inconsistent with every principle on which it was founded, and destructive of the great object for which it was formed." The proclamation warned the nullifiers that "the laws of the United States must be executed. . . . Disunion by armed force is treason."[24] Immediately after Jackson issued his proclamation, the South Carolina legislature elected Calhoun to fill a vacancy in the US Senate, and he submitted his resignation as vice president for the remaining few months left in his term. It was just as well, since Calhoun was rumored to be high on Jackson's target list for hanging as a treasonous nullifier.

The president's strategy in resolving the nullification crisis, however, was not limited to threats and a show of force. Indeed, the week before issuing his ominous proclamation to the nullifiers, in his annual message to Congress he proposed a conciliatory offer of substantial tariff reductions to a level necessary only for basic revenue and national defense—in other words, to below protectionist levels. His treasury secretary outlined specific cuts down to the 20 percent average level of 1816, and these would gradually be reduced even further, since less revenue would be needed as the national debt was extinguished. In the ensuing weeks, opposition mounted from the protectionists, who had just made concessions in the 1832 Act only six months before, and the debate wore on, leading to little progress toward its passage in the House.

In the meantime, the president sought congressional authorization in January 1833 to take action against the South Carolina nullifiers in the so-called Force Bill, which would allow the use of the military where necessary, among other action relating to enforcing the tariff laws in that state. The tables were now turned. On this issue, Calhoun, a former Jackson supporter, and Webster, generally a Jackson critic, led the long and ponderous debates over the fate of the Union and the president's demands.

Calhoun charged that the Force Bill was a "war bill," a "bloody bill," and that Jackson was leading the nation toward military despotism. To him the question had long since gone from one of the economics of free trade to more fundamental issues of liberty and state sovereignty. He argued that the federal union was a "compact" among the states, in which powers were divided between the states and the federal government. In the present situation the irresponsible majority controlling the general government had imposed oppressive and unequal taxes upon the states and was taking resources from one section of the country and giving it to another. In such cases, did the offended states not have the right to withdraw from the compact? Referencing Jackson's proclamation that the Union must be preserved, Calhoun's rhetorical response appears ironic in light of the results of the Civil War some thirty years later. "No, no," he exclaimed, "you cannot keep the States united in their constitutional and federal bonds by force."[25]

Webster responded by emphasizing that it was the people, not the states, who had created the government of the United States. He noted that the preamble to the Constitution begins, "We the People of the United States do ordain and establish this Constitution." Thus, there is a direct relationship between the American people and the Constitution which no state can dissolve. "The people of the United States are one people," Webster said. "They are one in making war, and one in making peace; they are one in regulating commerce, and one in laying duties of imposts. The very end and purpose of the Constitution was, to make them one people in these particulars; and it has effectually accomplished its object." Furthermore, majority rule must govern. "In matters of common concern, the judgment of a majority *must* stand as the judgment of the whole." Webster called upon the patriotism of the nation to defend the Constitution against nullification as a revolutionary and unconstitutional act. "For myself, Sir . . . I shall exert every faculty I possess in aiding to prevent the Constitution from being nullified, destroyed, or impaired; and even should I see it fall, I will still, with a voice feeble . . . call on the PEOPLE to come to its rescue."[26]

Jackson, of course, was thrilled with Webster's performance, which won the senator the title "Defender of the Constitution." James Madison, one of the principal draftsmen of the Constitution, wrote Webster to express his approval. Calhoun also received some praise for his efforts, but the historical moment was not with him. As historian Robert Remeni has observed, "Like it or not, the nation was evolving into a democratic, increasingly industrial society with a strong central government able and determined when necessary, to enunciate the supreme law of the land, even if that challenged the vested rights and interests of particular states. Webster . . . rooted the legitimacy of republican government in the people, as had the Founders, and explained how the nation had actually developed, politically and constitutionally, whether or not that was the original intention of those who had established it."[27] The Senate passed the Force Bill by a vote of 32 to 1, with the nullifiers boycotting. Virginian John Tyler, a future president who was opposed to nullification but was also against sending federal troops to invade a sovereign state, voted no.

Professing fatigue, Henry Clay was also absent from the Senate along with the nullifiers at the time of the vote on the Force Bill. Although he was certainly opposed to the nullifiers' activities, some of the powers that Jackson was trying to assume to counteract them alarmed him, and he may not have wanted to vote for the bill. But he also had justification for fatigue. Clay was gravely concerned about the destruction of his American System in the president's tariff reform proposals, and in December 1832, he had begun feverishly working on a compromise proposal that would relieve the crisis, end Jackson's power grab, and preserve tariff protection for as long as possible. He began discussing the idea with businessmen and other protectionist politicians, including Webster. He got encouragement from most, except Webster who by this time was absolutely opposed to retreating from protectionist policies. He then approached Calhoun and began a collaboration intended to reconcile the nullifiers into submission. They reached a compromise to lower the tariffs marginally every two years for ten years until 1842, when they would stand at a 20 percent uniform ad valorem rate.

The debate over this legislation, known as the Compromise Tariff of 1833, which Webster referred to as Clay's "pretty little Bill," threw the National Republicans into some confusion as it pitted Clay against both Webster and Adams, with the latter opposing it in the House. Webster charged that Clay, in his "mania of pacification,"[28] was abandoning the basic principles of his American System. How else, Webster asked, could one view his "arrangement" with Calhoun? Clay's foreboding answer underscored the potential stakes of this dispute:

> Would the Senator from Massachusetts send his [Force] bill forth alone without this measure of conciliation? . . . The difference between the friends and the foes of compromise, under consideration, is, that they would, in the enforcing act, send forth alone a flaming sword. We would send out also, but along with it the olive branch, as a messenger of peace. . . . While we would vindicate the federal government, we are for peace, if possible, union and liberty. We want no war—above all, no civil war; no family strife. We want to see no sacked cities, no desolated fields, no smoking ruins, no streams of American blood shed by American arms![29]

On March 1, the Senate passed the Compromise Tariff Bill by a comfortable margin, as had the House days before, and Jackson signed it and the Force Bill the next day, just before the session ended. Based on an analysis of the House and Senate voting done by historian Maurice Baxter, there was strong support for the compromise from the Mid-Atlantic states, overwhelming support in the South, solid opposition from New England, and significant opposition from Atlantic and western states. As for the parties, Jackson's Democrats favored it two to one, and Clay's National Republicans opposed it by about the same margin. Baxter observed that of the 188 members voting on both bills in the House only 74 voted yes to both the tariff reduction and the enforcement measures. In his view some northerners who voted for the Compromise Tariff would not have done so if it had not been coupled with the Force Bill. Likewise, he noted that "there were many southern votes for the Force Bill, indicating either dislike of states-rights radicalism or acceptance of this route to tariff relief."[30]

South Carolina repealed its Ordinance of Nullification on the tariffs, but to prove a point nullified the Force Bill. This parting gesture, however, was a rather moot point at this stage since there was now nothing to force, and the crisis ended. Everyone claimed victory. Calhoun and the nullifiers claimed they had forced down the tariffs, albeit over a period of ten years. Jackson's dual-track strategy of threat and conciliation, which had drawn him into conflicting new alliances with old opponents, had worked, and the Union would remain intact for another twenty-eight years. Jackson, in his second inaugural address, given two days after signing the two bills, hailed both states' rights and the integrity of the Union as pillars of American liberty. His successful approach to ending the nullification crisis preserved both. Henry Clay, while proving himself the great political compromise tactician, took pride in having not only saved the nation from a bloody crisis but also having preserved his American System of protection for the next decade.

FREE TRADE AND THE DEMOCRATIC PARTY

It was not until new parties began to form around the forces for and against the administration of Andrew Jackson that the old Hamilton-Jefferson struggle of the moneyed classes versus the farmers and labor classes again jelled into a partisan issue. Henry Clay's euphemistic calls for an American System that promoted a "home market" were nothing more than another way of describing Hamilton's partnership between government and business based upon publicly financed internal improvements for economic development and high tariffs and subsidies protecting industry—whether infant or not. Historian Arthur Schlesinger Jr. called Clay's policies "rebaptized Federalism."[31] After his New England constituency developed a manufacturing base, Daniel Webster also took up Hamilton's role as the spokesman for the northern capitalists, bankers, and industrialists with a stake in government protection.

Although Jackson was ambivalent on tariff issues for fiscal and nationalistic reasons until the latter part of his first administration, he ultimately favored tariff reductions and never supported the Hamiltonian-Clay rationale for protective tariffs. The Jacksonian democracy embraced the "common man" and the laboring classes as its principal constituency and saw the bankers and industrialists as manipulators and profiteers seeking to use the government to steal from the labors of the workingman and farmer. According to Schlesinger, the Jacksonians were inspired by Adam Smith's arguments against the alliance of government and business, which retarded the economic growth of nations and promoted the exploitation of the people. For example, Schlesinger quotes Martin Van Buren, a Jackson disciple and his successor as president, favoring Smith's approach to ensuring to the laboring classes "a full enjoyment of the fruits of their industry":

> Left to itself, and free from the blighting influence of partial legislation, monopolies, congregated wealth, and interested combinations, the compensation of labor will always preserve this salutary relation. It is only when the natural order of society is disturbed by one or other of these causes, that the wages of labor become inadequate.[32]

Jackson's philosophy is best illustrated by his veto of the renewal of the charter of the Bank of the United States in 1832, which must have created a déjà vu moment for the then elderly Madison in his retirement. In his veto message, Jackson said in part:

> It is to be regretted that the rich and powerful too often bend the acts of government to their selfish purposes. . . . In the full enjoyment of the gifts of Heaven and the fruits of superior industry, economy, and virtue, every man is equally entitled to protection by

law; but when the laws undertake to add to these natural and just advantages artificial distinctions . . . to make the rich richer and the potent more powerful, the humble members of society—the farmers, mechanics, and laborers—who have neither the time nor the means of securing like favors to themselves, have a right to complain of the injustice of their Government. There are no necessary evils in government. Its evils exist only in its abuses. If it would confine itself to equal protection, and, as Heaven does its rains, shower its favors alike on the high and the low, the rich and the poor, it would be an unqualified blessing. In the act before me there seems to be a wide and unnecessary departure from these just principles.[33]

To the Bank's proponents, this was sheer demagoguery and a call for class warfare. Nicholas Biddle, the Bank's president, wrote to Henry Clay, the sponsor of the bank charter bill, "It is really a manifesto of anarchy, such as Marat or Robespierre might have issued to the mob of the Faubourg St. Antoine."[34] On the floor of the Senate, Daniel Webster charged, "It manifestly seeks to influence the poor against the rich. It wantonly attacks whole classes of the people, for the purpose of turning against them the prejudices and resentments of other classes. It is a State paper which finds no topic too exciting for its use, no passion too inflammable for its address and its solicitation."[35] It must be noted, however, that Webster's main constituency came from the wealthy class under attack by Jackson's veto message. In 1816 he had opposed the Bank's charter, but now that he was on retainer for the Bank his views had changed. As chairman of the Senate Finance Committee during the period when Jackson was threatening to withdraw all government deposits from the Bank, Webster wrote a private note to Biddle advising him that "I believe my retainer has not been renewed, or *refreshed*, as usual. If it be wished that my relation to the Bank should be continued, it may be well to send me the usual retainer."[36] His support for and against free trade and for and against the National Bank seem to follow a similar pattern. As Schlesinger writes, "Webster fought for it in great part because it was a dependable source of private revenue. . . . [H]e would not lead unless someone made up a purse for him."[37]

Jackson's opponents reproduced and distributed thousands of copies of his veto message in a misguided effort to damage his reelection effort. Jackson responded simply with the rhetorical question, "Shall the rights of the common man be respected or shall the rich rule the country again?"[38] As might have been predicted, his message prevailed in a landslide victory for him.

Similarly, Jackson's approach to trade, especially in his second term, began to move in a populist direction. Jackson's tariff reform policies late in his first term, which reduced the 1828 Tariff of Abominations, did little to satisfy the South Carolina radical free-trade proponents, but the protectionist interests were solidly in the opposing camp of Henry Clay's party of National Republicans. Some manufacturers even threatened to fire employees if Jackson won in 1832. Following the Nullification Crisis of 1832–33, which settled the tariff issue for ten years, Jackson's Democrats came down squarely on the side of low tariffs against the business and manufacturing interests, which marked the beginning of free trade as a central tenet of the Democratic Party for the next century and a half.

In 1834, the anti-Jackson partisans began calling themselves "Whigs," and in an effort to indict Jackson for having assumed royal powers, they dubbed him "King Andrew I." Apart from their common animosity for Jackson, however, the Whigs were an oddly heterogeneous group that included Hamiltonian manufacturers and bankers seeking the governmental partnership, as well as southern aristocrats who felt threatened by Jackson's populism and his willingness to use force against the states in the case of the South Carolina nullifiers. Southern Whigs included the sugar planters who wanted protection from Cuba, but the group also attracted for a number of years John C. Calhoun, a rabid free-trader, who joined the Whigs solely due to an intense antipathy for Jackson. The Whigs also included Anti-Masons, anti-immigrant nativists, and anti-slavery groups. The party was so diverse that when General Benjamin Harrison ran for president as a Whig in 1840, Nicholas Biddle urged Harrison's handlers to have him say or promise nothing: "Let no meeting ever extract from him a single word about what he now thinks or will do hereafter."[39] Stealing the Democrats' common-man approach, Harrison and his running mate, Virginian John Tyler, ran successfully on the campaign slogan of "Log Cabin and Hard Cider," even though both were of aristocratic heritage.

Unfortunately for the Hamiltonian wing of the Whig party, the elderly Harrison, whom Clay and Webster had hoped to control, died of pneumonia less than a month after giving a long speech during his bitter cold inauguration ceremony. Vice President Tyler, his successor, of the anti-Jackson, pro-Calhoun planter faction proved far less pliable on economic issues.

He vetoed two bills to recharter the Bank of the United States and two protective tariff bills and other measures passed by the Whig-dominated Congress. Most of his cabinet resigned as he moved more and more toward Democratic positions. Although he did finally sign the protectionist Tariff Act of 1842, which passed narrowly and brought average rates back near the levels of 1832, he was forced to do so by a depression-induced budget deficit. Having been "shamefully deceived and betrayed"[40] by Tyler, the Whigs dumped him in 1844 and nominated Clay to run for president for the third and last time on his American System platform.

The Democrats nominated a Jacksonian disciple from Tennessee, James K. Polk, who won a narrow victory against Clay in part by rallying the masses against the "money power" who sought to raise tariffs and bring back the National Bank. An issue that brought southern planters back into the Democratic fold was the annexation of Texas, which Polk openly supported, and northern Whigs did not, due to concerns that it would expand slavery. Among the mostly disconnected sectional factions now within the Democratic Party were northern and western groups who disliked slavery, small businessmen and workingmen from the North attracted to Jacksonian democracy and indifferent to slavery, and the southern planters who were pro-slavery but not particularly enamored with much of the populism of Jacksonian democracy. What united them was their desire for low tariffs.

In 1846, Polk was able to deliver for them by bringing down the tariff levels to an average level of 26 percent under the influence of his treasury secretary, Robert Walker, a strong free-trade proponent. Walker revealed Jackson's legacy on the Democratic tariff policy in his report to Congress with his sharp criticism of protective tariffs as

> a mere subtraction of so much money from the people, to increase the resources of the protected classes. Legislation for classes is against the doctrine of equal rights, repugnant to the spirit of our free institutions, and . . . may become but another form for privileged orders under the name of protection instead of privilege—indicated here not by rank or title, but by profits and dividends extracted from the many by taxes upon them for the benefit of the few.[41]

In his final State of the Union message to Congress in 1848, Polk delivered a clear statement of the Democratic manifesto on tariff policy.

It was a blistering indictment of what he termed "the miscalled 'American System,'" since he claimed it was actually modeled after the British, "who drew their wealth from the toil of the laboring millions." Whig leaders promoting the National Bank, protective tariffs, and internal improvements had, in Polk's words, "deluded" the public with popular names and simple arguments promoting "home industry" and promising higher wages to "American labor." The real effect of these elements of the American System was rather "to interpose artificial restrictions upon the natural course of the business and trade of the country, and to advance the interests of large capitalists and monopolists at the expense of the great mass of the people, who were taxed to increase their wealth." He observed that tariff revenues had increased under the lower tariffs of the Tariff Act of 1846, exceeding revenues under any of the higher protectionist periods; and manufacturing had not been harmed by reductions in the protective rates. The only effect had been to reduce the tax burden on the people and the excessive prices paid to the "favored classes." Thus, according to Polk, the only purpose that the American System served was to transfer dollars "from the pockets of the people to the favored classes . . . to build up an aristocracy of wealth, to control the masses of society, and monopolize the political power of the country."[42]

From 1828 to 1860, the Democratic Party inspired by Jefferson and Madison and reconstituted by Jackson in the political battle of the working class against the Hamilton-Clay government-business partnership lost only two presidential elections. In both instances, the victorious Whigs were able to win by avoiding economic issues and nominating popular war heroes, Benjamin Harrison in 1840 and Zachary Taylor in 1848. The Democrats' electoral success over this period drew heavily on their consistent opposition to the National Bank and protective tariffs—the key elements of Clay's American System and Hamilton's legacy. In their last successful campaign platform of 1856, the Democrats proclaimed: "The time has come for the people of the United States to declare themselves in favor of free seas and progressive free trade throughout the world."[43] Indeed, in 1857, the last Democratic administration to hold office for the next twenty-four years would reduce tariffs again to an average level of 20 percent—as close to free trade as the nation would reach in the nineteenth century and the lowest rates for most of the century to follow.

3

Civil War and Robber Barons

We swept [out] slavery & substituted Protection.[1]
—Mark Twain

Despite a lifelong effort, Henry Clay's attempt to win over the nation to his American System of trade protectionism seemed a complete failure by the time of his death in 1852. Although Clay spawned a generation of political disciples and was successful in increasing tariffs to very high levels, gradually from 1816 until 1832 and briefly again after 1842, the successors of his nemesis, Andrew Jackson, appeared to have won the philosophical debate and political war. From the mid-1840s on, tariff rates began a steady decline, met by little or no effective opposition—much as was happening simultaneously in England. In 1854, the administration of Democratic president Franklin Pierce negotiated a treaty of reciprocity with Great Britain, abolishing duties on a wide range of commercial products flowing between colonial Canada and the United States, as a first step toward free trade on the northern border. Ratification by Congress of the treaty and implementation soon after it was signed proved that protectionism was all but dead as a political force.

Likewise, support for the other pillar of Clay's American System of economic development—government-subsidized "internal improvements"—crumbled, along with hope for a revival of Alexander Hamilton's Bank of the United States. The Bank, over which Jackson and Clay had battled in the 1832 election, had not had a charter in almost two decades. Even Clay's political party, the Whigs, all but dissolved during the year of his death.

There were shocking times ahead, however, for Democrats expecting smooth sailing into a future of free trade and a government unencumbered by the interests of financiers and manufacturers. Within ten years, a seismic eruption of the slavery issue revolutionized the two-party system of Whigs and Jacksonian Democrats, which for two decades had been dominated largely by personalities and trade politics. The protectionist legacy of Hamilton and Clay would soon experience a revival with a vengeance.

SLAVERY ISSUE ECLIPSES THE POLITICS OF TRADE

Since the beginning of the republic, slavery had been a divisive, though primarily sectional, question. Views on the subject were marked by varying shades of moral, political, and economic motivations, yet periodic compromises buried the controversy over slavery just below the surface of partisan divisions. The first such compromise was written into the Constitution, with its controversial provision counting slaves as three-fifths of a person for purposes of congressional apportionment, and a clause protecting the continuance of the slave trade for twenty years. Later, the Missouri Compromise in 1820 and the Compromise of 1850, both crafted principally by Henry Clay, resolved crises that had threatened the Union by limiting slavery in the new territories gained in the Louisiana Purchase and the Mexican War, respectively, and by protecting "property" rights of slave owners against runaway slaves in free states.

These settlements came unglued in 1854 with the Kansas-Nebraska Act, which repealed the restrictions against new slave states in the northern territory and left the decision regarding slavery to the settlers based upon "popular sovereignty." Outrage broke out across the North, condemning the sponsors of the Kansas-Nebraska Act as an unholy alliance of southern Democrats desiring to expand slavery and political opportunists among northern Democrats, including most prominently Senator Stephen Douglas of Illinois. The resulting firestorm recast the constituencies of American political parties for decades.

The Whigs had already begun to disintegrate as a viable political party following the stunning defeat of Mexican War hero Winfield Scott, the Whig candidate in the 1852 presidential election. Decrying the malevolence manifested by the "slavocracy" in ending the solemn bargain that had confined the "peculiar institution" to the South, a group of anti-slavery Whigs, northern Democrats, Free-Soilers, and abolitionists met in Wisconsin and Michigan in 1854 to form a new party, calling themselves Republicans after Thomas Jefferson's original Democratic-Republicans. Adding to the mix was a third party, the Know-Nothings or American Party, which arose out of an anti-immigrant and anti-Catholic movement in the 1840s. Originally it had been a secret order whose members replied, "I know nothing," when asked about their activities.

Although the fallout from the Kansas-Nebraska Act severely weakened the Democrats, they strung together a victory in the 1856 election. The party nominated James Buchanan at the Democratic convention that year, passing over both the current incumbent president, Franklin Pierce, and Senator Stephen Douglas, due to their involvement in supporting the passage of the act. Buchanan, who had escaped the controversy through his presence in London as Pierce's minister to England, won the general election with 45 percent of the popular vote against 33 percent for Republican John Fremont and 22 percent for former president Millard Fillmore, who represented the Know-Nothings.

Over the next four years, new fires erupted over the slavery issue, further undermining the delicate coalition holding the Democratic Party together. The first of these was the landmark 1857 Supreme Court decision in the *Dred Scott* case. A slave had brought a claim for freedom based upon his having been taken into territory where slavery was barred under the Missouri Compromise. The Court, then made up of a majority of justices from slaveholding states, denied the claim, holding that Negroes were not citizens under the Constitution and therefore could not sue in a federal court—a dubious analysis considering that freed slaves had voting rights in four of the original thirteen states. Moreover, the Court added a gratuitous ruling that the Missouri Compromise of 1820 was unconstitutional because it deprived slave owners of property without due process of law under the Fifth Amendment of the Constitution. The decision sparked an outcry throughout the North that the Supreme Court had become beholden to the slavocracy, further strengthening the Republicans and splitting the Democrats.

Later that year, President Buchanan further aggravated the divisive slavery issue by siding with southern supporters in Congress who tried unsuccessfully to force a vote to admit Kansas as a state with a highly controversial pro-slavery constitution. The constitution, drafted by a rump convention of slaveholders, had not been ratified by a vote of the people in the territory. Buchanan's action brought him into sharp collision with many Democrats, including Stephen Douglas, who opposed him openly for violating the principle of popular sovereignty.

The final blow to national Democratic cohesion came with John Brown's famous 1859 raid on a federal arsenal in Harpers Ferry, Virginia, motivated by a quixotic desire to provoke a slave revolt against the South. Brown's hanging after the raid was put down elevated him to martyrdom among northern sympathizers, while his bold, if not insane, attack escalated the fears of southern conservatives against radical abolitionists. The national partition in popular opinion that had been provoked early in the decade by the publication of Harriet Beecher Stowe's *Uncle Tom's Cabin* was now nearly complete.

Meanwhile, an economic panic in the latter part of 1857 brought an abrupt end to temporary passivity in Washington regarding trade politics. Following a decade of prosperity, the New York stock market took a steep fall and the entire northeast region plunged into a sharp depression, with deflating prices and unemployment rising to crisis levels. The bursting of a speculative bubble after ten years of expansion (including the California gold rush period), feverish land speculation, and rash investment and credit decisions in the financial market likely caused the panic. Industrial interests in the North, however, blamed the 1857 Tariff Act, which had cut duties to the lowest rates since 1816. Northern manufacturers competing with European imports suddenly became decidedly hostile to the South's advocacy of low tariffs as well as its high-priced cotton and cheap slave labor. Actually, the bill had drawn very little partisan or sectional opposition when it passed. Due to an abundant treasury surplus at the time, a consensus in Congress agreed that revenues needed to be reduced, and only the representatives from Pennsylvania raised protectionist objections to the tariff reductions.[2] In any case, many northern Democrats—no doubt impacted by emotions arising out of the slavery debate—now had a new reason to abandon their old, southern-dominated party and find a new home among protectionist Republicans.[3]

In its fourth year of existence, the Republican Party approached the congressional elections of 1858 with high expectations and was not disappointed. In addition to opposing slavery in the new territories, at the crest of the economic panic, Republican candidates ran on an effective platform of protective tariffs, free homestead to encourage western settlement, and internal improvements. The new party picked up major victories in the industrial heartland of Pennsylvania, Ohio, New York, and Indiana and won plurality control of the House of Representatives for the first time. Although the Senate remained under Democratic control, the party was deeply divided. The nationally publicized Lincoln-Douglas debates, with their heavy concentration on the slavery question, highlighted the Senate elections results. Although Democrat Stephen Douglas won a slim reelection victory, the debates dampened his national appeal, brought Republican Abraham Lincoln into prominence, and underscored the issues dividing the nation.

Emotions continued at a fever pitch over the containment of slavery when the Democratic Party met to select its presidential candidate in Charleston, South Carolina, in April 1860. When the convention voted down southern proposals to preserve slavery in the new territories, most delegates from the Deep South walked out, and the party separated into northern and southern wings with each later nominating its own presidential candidate: Stephen Douglas in the North and John C. Breckinridge of Kentucky in the South. Importantly, however, while the sectional wings of the Democratic Party took different approaches to the slavery issue, they both endorsed the 1856 free-trade economic platform. That element of Jacksonian Democracy survived the great sectional schism over slavery.

In stark contrast, the Republican Party adopted the economic policies of Henry Clay's Whigs. In their May 1860 convention platform statement, the Republicans promised to adjust import duties "to encourage the development of the industrial interests of the whole country" and increase federal appropriations for a transcontinental railroad and river and harbor improvements to accommodate commerce."[4] In a renewal of Alexander Hamilton's business-government partnership, manufacturers seeking a helping hand from the government thus became a critical constituency of the Republican Party.

Adding to the confusion and ensuring that no candidate could win a popular majority, a fourth group made up of diehard Whigs, moderate southerners, former Know-Nothings, and less strident Republicans organized the Constitutional Union Party. Their goal was to preserve the Union at any cost, essentially ignoring the principal conflicts dividing the nation. This party nominated Senator John Bell of Tennessee, who had been a strong opponent of the Kansas-Nebraska Act and the pro-slavery constitution in the Kansas statehood bill. Their movement gained traction only in the border states, where the stakes for disunion were the highest.

When the tallies were finally counted, the Republican nominee, Abraham Lincoln, won a clear victory of the electoral votes—180 to 123—by carrying the northern and western states. Yet he lost the popular vote by almost a million votes to the combined totals of his three opponents. The aggregate of the popular tally for the two Democratic Party candidates exceeded the votes for Lincoln—who received slightly less than 40 percent of the total—by roughly 2,227,000 to 1,866,000, not even counting the 589,000 votes received by the Constitutional Union Party, which dominated in the upper-South states.[5] Without the benefit of modern exit polling, these numbers suggest that a majority of the electorate favored the Democratic position on trade at the time of the outbreak of the Civil War. Nevertheless, the new Republican administration heralded a new beginning for trade protection in America.

LINCOLN: A DISTRACTED PROTECTIONIST

Abraham Lincoln, consistently following his Whig roots, had been a long-standing supporter of protective tariffs but never an effective advocate for the cause. Over the years, Lincoln had made an effort to master the economics of trade policy, relying on several sources, the most prominent among them being the writings of conservative economist Henry C. Carey, who viewed free trade as a British scheme to thwart industrialization in America. Lincoln sought simple, rather than theoretical, explanations that he could relate to his political audiences. Although Lincoln was a brilliant lawyer and persuasive orator, his speeches and writings on trade policy were shallow at best. Biographer David Herbert Donald characterized his early speeches on the tariff in 1843–44 as "confused and demagogic." For example, Lincoln claimed that the protective tariff would have no effect on the common man, since it would be collected only from the rich who wished "to strut in British cloaks . . . and pantaloons." Counterintuitively, he argued that high tariffs made goods cheaper. A contemporary journalist reported that Lincoln could not explain why tariffs lowered prices and argued simply "that it was so."[6]

After he was elected to Congress and before he took his seat in December 1847, Lincoln prepared several pages of notes related to the duty reductions under the 1846 Walker Tariff Act, passed under President Polk, to use in speeches on trade. Using analogies that involved farmers, manufacturers, and even the Almighty, he attempted to show how the transportation costs required for international trade added "useless labour" that would be eliminated by protective tariffs, thus presumably attempting to explain why the protective system would be cheaper for the consumer.[7] Historian G. S. Boritt observes, "It should be clear that Lincoln was not a systematic thinker on the subject of political economy and only attained an understanding of the outlines of the economic forces at work in his day."[8]

Lincoln's economic views are perhaps best understood in the context of his position as a western Whig politician. Like Clay, he was a strong proponent of federally financed internal improvements, such as canals and railroads to transport western produce to eastern markets. There was very little manufacturing in the West to be protected before the Civil War, thus western Whigs favored high tariffs to pay for these improvements to bring economic development to their constituencies. In contrast, Jacksonian Democrats argued that federal appropriations for these purposes were simply public burdens for the benefit of limited special interests. During Lincoln's term in Congress in 1848, President James K. Polk, a Jackson disciple, vetoed two government-sponsored improvement bills. In a floor speech on the subject, Lincoln acknowledged that the benefits of internal improvements might not be distributed equally, but he offered the sweeping, vague justification that these improvements would put the entire country "on that career of prosperity, which shall correspond with its extent of territory, its natural resources, and the intelligence and enterprise of its people."[9]

By the time of his nomination to the presidency twelve years later, when the slavery question was pushing the nation to the breaking point, Lincoln was not anxious to create more political strife by forcing a new tariff bill on Congress. Many Republicans who had joined the party recently, especially those who had left the Democratic Party mainly because of the slavery issue or were from nonprotectionist regions, were not keen to see a platform dominated by protectionism. For example, Lincoln's choice to be secretary of treasury would be Salmon P. Chase, who had formerly been a free-trade Democrat and one of Lincoln's rivals for the Republican presidential nomination. During the Republican Convention in May 1860, Lincoln sought to downplay the issue. Writing to a correspondent who had asked for a public stance on the tariff question, Lincoln said:

In the days of Henry Clay I was a Henry Clay-tariff-man; and my views have undergone no material change upon that subject.

I now think that the Tariff question ought not to be agitated in the Chicago Convention; but that all should be satisfied on that point with a presidential candidate, whose antecedents give assurance that he would neither seek to force a tariff-law by Executive influence; nor yet to arrest a reasonable one, by a veto, or otherwise. . . . I really have no objection to these views being publicly known; but I do wish to thrust no letter before the public now, upon any subject.[10]

On February 15, 1861, during his train excursion to Washington before the inauguration, President-Elect Lincoln conveyed a similar reluctance to stir up the trade issue in a speech in Pittsburgh, a traditional protectionist base. After speaking on the secession crisis, he gave the standard Republican talking points for protectionist tariffs, noting their benefits to mechanics, manufacturers, and farmers. Yet with characteristic modesty, he told the audience that he was no tariff expert, saying, "I have by no means a thoroughly matured judgment upon this subject, especially as to details; some general ideas are about all." He said that he would recommend that Congress make such tariff adjustments as would be just and equal to all sections and classes of the country.[11]

REPUBLICAN CONGRESS AND THE RETURN OF HIGH TARIFFS

Congress, however, had already begun without him. Before Lincoln had even been nominated, the House of Representatives in 1860, then under Republican control, passed a bill drafted by Vermont congressman Justin S. Morrill raising tariffs back to pre-1846 protectionist levels. Seizing the moment and taking the lead on the trade issue as soon as they took the reins of power, the sponsors of the bill hoped to consolidate support for the Republican Party in Pennsylvania and other protectionist strongholds in the North prior to the upcoming election. The bill passed the House with deliberate speed, but the Senate, under the control of southern Democrats, refused to take it up.

This situation changed dramatically following Lincoln's election, when seven southern states seceded from the Union by February 1861, taking their fourteen free-trade senators with them. In fact, the Morrill Bill became a factor in secession conventions, as it was viewed as evidence of northern malevolence against the interests of the South. At a secession debate in Georgia, Senator Robert A. Toombs denounced "the infamous Morrill bill" as the product of a northern coalition of "non-abolition protectionists" and "free-trade abolitionists." "The robber and the incendiary struck hands," shouted Toombs, "and united in joint raid against the South."[12]

With most of the southern senators withdrawn, the Senate Republicans took control and passed the bill on a 25-to-14 vote, with only one Pennsylvania Democrat voting in favor. President James Buchanan signed the Morrill Tariff Act of 1861 into law on March 2, as one of his final acts as president two days before the end of his term and Lincoln's inauguration. Though Buchanan was a Democrat elected on a platform of "progressive free trade throughout the world," he was also a Pennsylvanian heading home to protectionist soil at the end of his political career.

Within six weeks, the attack on Fort Sumter would mark the commencement of the Civil War, and over the next four years the huge financial demands of prosecuting the war brought revolutionary changes to the federal fiscal system. As the war generated an enormous national debt, Congress created a national banking system, a national currency, and a vast, comprehensive scheme of internal taxation, including income and excise taxes.

In this fertile environment for major changes, tariffs were subject to constant upward pressure. Duties on some imports increased almost monthly when Congress was in session throughout the war. In the deliberation over the Tariff Act of 1862, Congressman Morrill and other sponsors argued that the rates needed to be raised again to offset the internal excise taxes being imposed on domestic producers to put them on equal footing with foreign importers. Two years later in the Tariff Act of 1864, which passed both houses of Congress in two weeks with little or no debate, Morrill was able to increase average tariffs to 47 percent, the highest percentage since the Tariff of Abominations. The Republican leadership had thus revived the legacy of Alexander Hamilton with renewed passion and enacted Henry Clay's American System with no opposition.

The eminent nineteenth-century economic historian Frank W. Taussig noted three causes of the explosive growth of tariffs during this period: (1) the urgency of military requirements, (2) the desire to balance out the new internal taxes imposed on domestic producers, and (3) the protectionist bent of those crafting and managing the financial legislation during the period.

First, the urgent call to arms after Fort Sumter and the early Union losses on the battlefield demanded new sources of revenue. Initially, many thought the Morrill Bill was a mistake and demanded its repeal when the new Confederate government, with its free-trade platform, was attracting European trade and moral support. By contrast, the Morrill Bill was having a devastating effect on northern trade and only antagonizing the European powers. With the outbreak of war and the demand for new revenue, however, the mood changed quickly, even though national protectionist sentiments remained low. Treasury Secretary Salmon Chase—a free-trade Democrat all his life until he joined the Republican Party solely because of its anti-slavery platform—went to Congress as the war began and obtained increases in the Morrill tariffs. Even the New York *Evening Post,* which had always editorialized in favor of free trade and opposed the Morrill Bill, calling it a "booby of a bill" and the "blunder of the age," came around to supporting increased tariffs: "War is an exceptional state and demands extraordinary measures. . . . [W]e are prepared to support a scale of duties at present which we should oppose if the nation were at peace."[13]

Second, the heavy new taxes on domestic manufacturing were a competitive burden against imports. The general excise tax of 5 percent on manufactured products was often repeated at each new stage of production, so that the tax collected on the finished product would generally be between 8 and 15 percent. Congress also added excise taxes to the cost of transportation, insurance, telegraph, and licenses for every branch of trade—not to mention a 5 percent income tax and 10 percent on incomes over $10,000. The equity in increasing the tariff to balance internal taxes on domestic manufacturers was as evident as the need for increased revenue to fund the war. The only question was how much was the correct amount to reach this equity and need.

Third and most important, protectionist legislators writing and managing the war tariff bills brought the Civil War tariff rates to their peaks while granting favors to business opportunists and war profiteers. According to Taussig, the new Republican leaders were willing to increase tariffs on "every possible article at the highest rate that any one had the courage to suggest."[14] The first Republican chairman of Ways and Means, John Sherman of Ohio, the brother of Major General William T. Sherman, had built his political career upon protection of American industrial interests and fierce opposition to the Democratic Party. Under his leadership, the committee instructed Justin Morrill, the New England protectionist, to construct new tariff legislation as soon as the Republicans took control of Congress. By the time the Morrill Bill finally passed the Senate in 1861, a swarm of domestic protectionist interests latched onto the measure, attaching amendment after amendment in a feeding frenzy that even shocked Morrill.[15]

Thaddeus Stevens of Pennsylvania, Sherman's successor as Ways and Means chairman, however, became chief among the protectionist leaders in Congress during the Civil War period. Stevens is best remembered as a fervent Radical Republican and often a thorn in Lincoln's side. Following Lincoln's assassination in 1865, Stevens was a strong proponent of punitive Reconstruction measures in the South and of the impeachment of President Andrew Johnson. As the most powerful member of Congress during this time, he was a ruthless autocrat, known for both his eloquence and biting, sarcastic wit. On trade protection he had no rival and gave no quarter to moderates. According to Ida Minerva Tarbell, the investigative journalist who surveyed the period in her 1911 book, *The Tariff in Our Times*:

> Duties were never too high for him, particularly on iron, for he was an iron manufacturer as well as a lawyer, and it was often said in Pennsylvania that the duties he advocated in no way represented the large iron interests of the state, but were hoisted to cover the needs of his own small and badly managed works.[16]

To be fair, Stevens's protectionism went far beyond his own self-interest as an iron manufacturer, whose business in any case was decimated in 1863. He was so hated in the South for all of his virulent anti-southern diatribes in Congress that Confederate Major General Jubal Early made a point of burning Stevens's iron works to the ground during the southern invasion of Pennsylvania before the Battle of Gettysburg. Conflicts of interest such as those of Stevens were prevalent in Congress during the nineteenth century, with few ethical standards or rules to limit their impact on legislation. The major reason tariffs exploded to new heights during this period was the inclination of those in charge to grant almost any increase requested by a domestic producer.

In addition to the domestic manufacturers seeking to protect their profits with new tariffs, there were also smugglers and corrupt importers among the war profiteers who sought higher tariffs to game the system. Smugglers had long taken advantage of the porous borders and incompetent and notoriously corrupt customs officials to import goods without paying or underpaying duties. Higher tariffs, which they encouraged Congress to pass, simply increased their prices and earnings. Besides smugglers, some legitimate importers found other ways to profit from new tariffs. They would bring in large quantities of products that were duty free or carried low duties, stockpile them in warehouses, and then lobby Congress for new or higher tariffs in order to increase the value and price of the previously imported goods in their warehouses.

The expedient demands of war may have ignited the meteoric rise in tariffs during the Civil War, but according to Taussig, the congressional sponsors were also inspired by less admirable motivations. Noting the war's "bracing and ennobling influence on our national life," Taussig lamented the "demoralizing" effect of the war on "all legislation affecting moneyed interests":

> The line between public duty and private interests was often lost sight of by legislators. Great fortunes were made by changes in legislation urged and brought about by those who were benefited by them; and the country has seen with sorrow that the honor and honesty of public men did not remain undefiled. . . . [The Tariff Act of 1864] established protective duties more extreme than had been ventured on in any previous tariff act in our country's history; it contained flagrant abuses, in the shape of duties whose chief effect was to bring money into the pockets of private individuals.[17]

POSTWAR ENTRENCHMENT OF SPECIAL-INTEREST PROTECTIONISM

After the first prewar Morrill tariff passed, all of the rate increases that followed were explained as "temporary" or provisional duties necessary to finance the war and to compensate domestic manufacturers for internal excise taxes. Thus, when the Confederates surrendered, many in Washington expected the war revenue measures to be dismantled as the war debt of $2.8 billion was paid down. The month before Robert E. Lee and U. S. Grant met at Appomattox to end the war, President Lincoln appointed David A. Wells, a New England intellectual who had supported Lincoln's financial policies, to head a national revenue commission charged with reforming the postwar revenue system. In 1866, Wells's commission recommended legislation reducing the internal taxes and reforming tariffs. Legislation for major reductions in internal taxes passed, and President Andrew Johnson signed it into law by midyear. Talk of tariff reform, however, drew immediate opposition. In fact, the outcry for even more protection drowned out the demands for mere preservation of existing protectionist levels.

Although he later converted to a free-trade approach, David Wells was a protectionist when first appointed by Lincoln, and his proposed tariff modifications hardly deserved to be called reform. He simply recommended reducing rates on raw materials—which would have aided American manufacturers—and no changes, or only slightly lower duties, on most manufactured products. The legislation Wells proposed would have actually increased rates on import-sensitive products, such as wool and woolen goods, copper, iron, steel rails, and many consumer products. It effectively maintained the 47 percent average tariff level of the 1864 Tariff Act. Yet Thaddeus Stevens, who sought even higher duties on iron, was instrumental in preventing its passage, observing, "I look upon this bill as a free trade bill from beginning to end."[18] While the defeat was a setback for those seeking even modest tariff reform, it did not stop those who had been riding the bill as a vehicle to increase protection.

The wool and woolen interests provide an illustrative scheme. During the antebellum period, woolgrowers and woolen manufacturers had been at bitter odds with one another on tariffs. While the sheep farmers had fought for high protective duties for their product, the manufacturing interests, based largely in New England, had constantly lobbied for duty-free raw wool. In fact, the manufacturers spent so much money on efforts to eliminate wool duties in the Tariff Act of 1857 that it created a scandal leading to a congressional investigation. The profitable conditions of the war economy, however, suspended the conflict between growers and manufacturers, as both flourished because of the urgent and high demand for military uniforms combined with the shutdown of southern cotton production and the lack of wartime import competition. As the war came to an end, however, the wool market began to weaken for both producers with the reemergence of foreign imports and cotton as a competitive fabric; domestic wool and woolen manufactured products lost their wartime monopoly.

In 1864, the woolens industry, led by its shrewd and sophisticated lobbyist, John L. Hayes, organized the National Association of Wool Manufacturers—one of the first effective trade associations in Washington. Hayes soon realized that his association's goal of raising protective tariffs sufficiently to shut out foreign competition could not be achieved if he sought duty-free imported raw wool for his members at the same time. The domestic woolgrowers had their own political power base centered in Ohio and reaching into other critical states like Michigan, New York, and Pennsylvania. Legislators standing up for sheep farmers would prevent Hayes from obtaining the wall of tariff protection on woolen manufactured products if he overreached and called for duty-free wool imports. In December 1865, Hayes convened a meeting of the wool manufacturers with a group of the woolgrowers to strike a collusive bargain that would satisfy both interests. The negotiators agreed to a novel legislative package that would raise tariffs on imported raw wool to protect the growers but compensate the manufacturers by increasing duties on imported woolen manufactured products in a proportionally equivalent amount.

John Hayes explained to the members of his association that the agreement would place the manufacturer "in the same position as if he had his wool free of duty; and . . . establish a truly American policy in a national legislation respecting the woolen interest as a whole."[19] Seizing the first opportunity to implement the agreement, Hayes was able to incorporate the scheme—substantially as he had written it—into the comprehensive tariff bill proposed by David Wells in 1866. Although Thaddeus Stevens blocked Wells's broad measure, John Hayes cunningly lobbied Congress to take up the wool protection package on its own strength separately and pass it as the Wool and Woolens Act of 1867.

In the period that followed the success of John Hayes's wool interests, titans of other industries took the same tack in seeking their own special attention. In 1868, the owners of the copper industry developing around Lake Superior were suffering from price competition due to imports from Chile and Cuba. They asked their powerful friends in Congress to set copper duties at prohibitively high levels. Even though the new rates would certainly destroy the shipping trade with Chile and Cuba, drive the developing American copper smelting firms that depended on imported ore out of business, and harm businesses that relied upon cheaper copper supplies, Congress passed the Copper Act of 1869 with overwhelming majorities. President Andrew Johnson vetoed the bill, but the extremely unpopular executive, who had survived impeachment by only one Senate vote the year before, was easily overridden by more than the required two-thirds vote. In his long veto message written by David Wells, who by this time had become disgusted with overreaching protectionists, President Johnson spoke like a Jacksonian channeling Adam Smith:

> It imposes an additional tax upon an already overburdened people, who should not be further impoverished that monopolies may be fostered and corporations enriched. . . . Legislation can neither be wise nor just which seeks the welfare of a single interest at the expense and to the injury of many and varied interests at least equally important and equally deserving the consideration of Congress.[20]

With the new protective duty in place, the copper companies colluded to raise domestic prices well above the international market price, while dumping their excess supplies in great quantities on the foreign markets at lower prices. In Taussig's assessment, the Copper Act increased the profits of the mine owners, "and thus for a series of years the great natural resources of the country became a cause not of abundance and cheapness, but of curtailment of supply and dearness."[21]

Of the numerous other tariffs increased to protectionist levels after the war, the most abusive examples were the treatment of steel rails and nickel. In the case of steel rails, Congress changed the tariff in 1870 from an ad valorem rate of 45 percent of the price to a specific duty based on weight, which came to $28 per ton. The effect of this change was astronomical due to new efficiencies then developing in the steel industry—specifically, the Bessemer process—which caused the price of steel to drop dramatically after 1870. The Bessemer process, patented in England in 1855, provided the first cost-effective means of mass producing steel from molten pig iron, reducing costs and multiplying the scale of production. As a result, the price of steel rails in England dropped from around $50 per ton in 1870 to $28 per ton after 1877, which made the specific duty equal to the per-ton cost of the product. Had the pre-1870 ad valorem duty of 45 percent applied, the duty would have been high, but only $12.60 per ton. Since some US steel companies acquired Bessemer patents themselves and could produce the steel rails at the same cost as the English producers, they were able to pocket the 100 percent markup based on the duty. At a time of high demand for railroad materials in the late 1870s, during a period of explosive growth of rail lines, these domestic producers made out like bandits—or, more appropriately, robber barons—until the demand finally tapered off.

One of these steel-producing robber barons—often called "robber tariff barons" in the critical media—was Andrew Carnegie, who cringed at this pejorative term and preferred to think of himself as a partner with government in nation-building. He was frequently depicted in political cartoons ascending the Capitol steps in fat cat garb seeking protection for "infant enterprises" or handing over large money bags labeled personal profits from his protected industries to well-known protectionist Republican politicians. Of course, Carnegie's fortune did not arise solely from trade protection. He was a brilliant innovator in the efficient, mass production of steel rails and the vertical integration of the manufacturing process—not to mention a shrewd and ruthless competitor in the domestic market. When he sold his steel conglomerate in 1901 to the financier John Pierpont Morgan, who formed the United States Steel Corporation, Carnegie became second only to John D. Rockefeller as the richest man in the world. But it was not until he was well into retirement that he abandoned his protectionist pleas.

The treatment that nickel received illustrates how a single person of influence was able to manipulate the system in obtaining the protection he desired. Prior to the Civil War, there was no import duty on nickel. In 1864, Congress placed an ad valorem rate of 15 percent on nickel, and then in 1870 increased it to the equivalent of 40 percent in specific duties. In a period when tariffs were generally on the rise, this might not be a remarkable event but for the fact that there was only one nickel mine in America at the time. The owner was Joseph Wharton of Philadelphia, who had acquired the mine in 1863. He was the perfect Hamiltonian prototype: a successful businessman who saw the benefits of partnering with government to ensure the profits of his business for the good of the nation. Wharton followed his successful push for a high nickel tariff with another astonishing lobbying coup. At his urging, Congress gave Wharton's nickel mine its own coin, the new five-cent piece in 1866, the "nickel." Wharton had effectively cornered the nickel market by obtaining his own tariff protection, and he was the only domestic producer. As demand skyrocketed, so did his profits until the mine's reserves were depleted and production ended in 1891.

Wharton was a skilled entrepreneur, having made a small fortune in the zinc mining business before buying his nickel mine. With the millions he made from the nickel mine, he invested heavily in many industrial enterprises, including railroads, factories, and other mining operations. He was a co-founder and the largest shareholder in what would become Bethlehem Steel Company. But, arguably, his most valuable skill was revealed in his effectiveness as a lobbyist in the halls of Congress and in the executive mansion of the presidency.

Wharton was chairman of the executive council of the Industrial League of Pennsylvania, perhaps America's most influential protectionist organization, formed in 1867 to represent all protected industries. Due to his large investments in Bethlehem Steel, he was also president of and the principal lobbyist for the American Iron and Steel Institute (AISI). Pittsburgh iron manufacturers angered by President Polk's tariff reforms first organized the AISI in 1849. In the 1860s, it became a dominant political force, often deciding the results of tariff legislation and the fate of a politician's election. Not surprisingly, Joseph Wharton was heavily involved in Republican Party politics and was close to all of the leading protectionist politicians of the period. His close political ties and lobbying skills were also valuable in obtaining contracts for Bethlehem Steel to supply armor and guns for US Navy warships in the 1880s—thus reaffirming his Hamiltonian partnership with the government, as Bethlehem Steel became an early participant in the emerging military-industrial complex. Wharton appeared often before congressional committees requesting duty increases. His success in obtaining the nickel tariff that affected only his business and none other in the country might seem all in a day's work by the standards of the period.

Wharton is perhaps best known today for the legacy of his very substantial philanthropy, particularly in higher education, rather than his association with the nickel coin or Bethlehem Steel. He and his mother, Deborah Fisher Wharton, and a group of other Quakers were the founders in 1869 of Swarthmore College, the prestigious liberal arts school outside of Philadelphia. But his most important gift for purposes of trade politics was his bequest to the University of Pennsylvania of $100,000 in 1881 to form the "Wharton School of Finance and Economy," the first collegiate business school in the world. As he described it in his plan for the school, Wharton desired that the students be taught how to run a business and deal with the cycles of economic activity, but he had a further clearly stated purpose: to advocate economic protectionism unequivocally. Wharton sought to foster in the new school disciples of the religion that he had been preaching to every politician in Washington for the previous fifteen years. His plan for the school specifically demanded that its faculty teach students

the necessity for each nation to care for its own and to maintain by all suitable means its industrial and financial independence;

no apologetic or merely defensive style of instruction must be tolerated upon this point, but the right and duty of national self-protection must be firmly asserted and demonstrated.[22]

ILLUSORY REFORM OF 1883

Wharton may have felt a growing need for new evangelists for his protectionist cause at this time, because by 1880 a growing demand for tariff reform was emerging even within the Republican Party. In the twenty-year period since the Morrill Bill had initiated the meteoric rise in rates, there had been only one significant tariff reduction—a 10 percent across-the-board cut from the historic peak in 1872—which passed at a moment when reform-minded Republicans joined free-trade Democrats in an attack on protectionism and the scandal-ridden administration of President Ulysses S. Grant. Although protectionists continued to hold sway over Congress, many of them agreed with Senator John Sherman of Ohio, who argued that there is "a great mountain of discontent against the present high rates of duty imposed on the ordinary necessaries of life. I believe in a protective system; but . . . it is better for the protected industries in this country that this slight modification of duties should be made, rather than to invite a contest which will endanger the whole system."[23] In any case, the Republican Congress repealed this reform two years later in the aftermath of the stock market panic of 1873. The serious economic depression that followed, along with Grant's unpopularity, triggered a Democratic takeover of control of the House of Representatives after the 1874 elections and also enhanced calls for tariff reform from within the Republican Party, especially from western agricultural interests and free-traders among eastern merchants.

But Republican protectionist stalwarts led by Justin Morrill remained firmly in control in the Senate, and the Senate reigned supreme on this and most other issues in the postwar thirty-year period of weak presidents and a generally disorganized House of Representatives. No longer in its "Golden Age" as a forum for classic debates dominated by great orators, the Senate was now in the beginning of the "Gilded Age," when the moneyed interests of industry and finance controlled the upper House behind closed doors. The 1872 Crédit Mobilier scandal, which exposed millions of dollars in bribes being paid to politicians by representatives of the Union

Pacific Railroad, was the first of many public embarrassments that were largely ignored by senators elected for six-year terms by state legislatures controlled by industry. Passage of the Coinage Act of 1873, which effectively put the country on the gold standard to the exclusion of silver, lengthened and deepened the depression for the benefit of the eastern financial interests. This measure reduced the money supply, strengthened the dollar, and increased the cost of repaying loans by infuriated farmers and other working-class debtors who called it the "Crime of '73." The act became a dominant political issue for decades, but the fury had no immediate impact on the well-insulated Senate. Likewise, the public views on the increasingly unpopular protectionist tariffs had no effect on the Senate.

The House Democrats had their own powerful protectionist wing, led by Samuel J. Randall of Pennsylvania. Randall was elected Speaker following the 1874 midterm elections and selected a like-minded member, the former New York City mayor Fernando Wood, to chair the Ways and Means Committee. The Democratic Party platform of 1876 demanded "that all custom-house taxation be only for revenue" and denounced the existing tariff system "as a masterpiece of injustice, inequality, and false pretence, which . . . has impoverished many industries to subsidize a few."[24] But the free-trade Democrats could not muster a majority to vote any reform measure through the House due to their division on the issue and the strength of industry lobbies opposing reform. It was not until after the presidential election of 1880 that tariff reform again came to a head.

Republican James A. Garfield was elected president promising to continue protectionist trade policies, but arch-protectionists in his party were not so sure he would keep his commitment. He was known to be only a moderate protectionist at best, however, having argued earlier in his career that

> duties should be so high that our manufacturers can fairly compete
> with the foreign product, but not so high as to enable them to drive
> out the foreign article, enjoy a monopoly of the trade, and regulate
> the price as they please. . . . I am for protection which leads to ulti-
> mate free trade.[25]

In 1871, when the call for tariff reform had been at a postwar peak, Speaker James G. Blaine (R-ME), a devoted high protectionist, reneged on a promise to appoint Garfield, with his heretical views, chairman of the Ways and Means Committee. Just before Garfield's nomination for president, Joseph

Wharton, speaking for the iron and steel industry, but calling to arms all other protected American industries, issued this warning to the nominee:

> We will support no party and no candidate who cannot be depended upon by something better than election-day promises to protect and defend home labor. It is fitting for us to call "hands off" to those who are itching to tear our tariff laws to shreds; to call upon the President in advance to refrain from meddling with commercial treaty-making and to veto . . . any measure injurious to home industry which a hostile majority in Congress may pass.[26]

The assassination of President Garfield a few months after his inauguration by a disappointed and deranged office seeker preempted a test of how his views might have affected the reform process.

In 1882, Garfield's vice president and successor, Chester A. Arthur, whose past had included a stint as a New York customs collector—a notoriously corrupt opportunity under the spoils patronage of President Grant—took up the task of dealing with tariff reform with help from lobbyists for the protected industries. Recognizing the pressure for reform brought on by blatant inequities in the current tariff system and recurring excessive revenue surpluses, Wharton's Industrial League began to see that revisions of some kind were inevitable. To retain control of the process, the League urged the establishment of a commission of experts in which domestic manufacturers would be directly represented, to recommend reforms to Congress. President Arthur adopted the idea as his own and proposed the creation of a Tariff Commission in his first message to Congress. Congress passed the bill creating the nonpartisan commission in May 1882—albeit with a heavily partisan vote, with most Republicans in favor and most Democrats opposed.[27]

President Arthur wasted no time in appointing members to the commission. In doing so, the president followed the prescription of Joseph Wharton, who outlined it in an Industrial League conference:

> Seeing that the appointments would be made by a Republican President, and that the Republican party is firmly committed to the principle of Protection to home industry, it would obviously be right that a majority of the commission should be Republicans and that a majority also should be distinctly Protectionists.[28]

Arthur's Tariff Commission included a firm majority who favored a high degree of protection and none who were predisposed to reducing protective tariffs. Each of the main protected domestic industries—iron and steel, woolen manufacturing, woolgrowers, and sugar—had their own representative on the commission. And to leave no doubt as to the intended direction of the commission, Arthur appointed as president of the commission John L. Hayes, the secretary and chief lobbyist for the Wool Manufacturers' Association and the most influential of the high protectionists in the country.

After months of hearings and meetings with a wide range of witnesses in cities across the country, however, the new Tariff Commission issued a report to Congress in December 1882, which surprisingly called for a 20–25 percent reduction in tariffs. Furthermore, the report offered strong anti-protectionist rationale for the reductions, declaring that "defensive duties," which more than counterbalance the conditions of labor and capital of foreign competitors, could not be justified except in the case of new industries. The commission felt the recommended reduction was justified in light of the development of American industry over the previous twenty years, which had allowed domestic manufacturers to compete with their foreign rivals. Along with the Tariff Commission findings, President Arthur added his recommendation for duty reductions and reforms in his December 1882 message to Congress, in which he declared: "The present tariff system is in many ways unjust. It makes unequal distributions both of its burdens and benefits. . . . [It] should be so revised as to equalize the public burden among all classes and occupations and bring it into closer harmony with the present needs of industry."[29]

The commission and the president were not the only sources of pressure on the Republican-controlled Congress to take action on tariff reform. The Democrats won a major victory in the 1882 congressional midterm elections and would take over the reins of the House in December 1883. If the Republicans did not enact their own version of tariff reform in the short remaining session, they could lose control of the process.

In both chambers of Congress, the leadership began putting together legislation to address the reform issue, giving some consideration to the Tariff Commission's recommendations. When the process bogged down in the House, however, the protectionists seized the initiative through a parliamentary move referring the measure to a conference committee of ten members, seven of whom were high protectionists. The committee included

Senators Justin Morrill, John Sherman, and Nelson Aldrich, a new member from Rhode Island, and Congressmen William Kelley of Pennsylvania, chairman of the Ways and Means Committee—known as "Pig Iron" Kelley for his ardent support of the iron tariffs—and William McKinley of Ohio, who was beginning his career as a leading protectionist. Normally, a conference committee is established to reach compromises between the positions taken in each chamber's bill, but this conference reconciled their differences in most cases by increasing the rates higher than either House had proposed. To give the appearance of reform, the conferees made numerous changes in tariff classifications and some inconsequential duty reductions but increased duties on products subject to import competition.

For example, the committee increased duties on competitive woolen manufactured goods and lowered them on noncompetitive woolens. Some duties were reduced on articles that were simply reclassified under new schedules with an equal or higher duty. In other instances, where the market prices had dropped significantly, duties were reduced somewhat but remained prohibitively high. In the case of steel rails the old protective rate of $28 per ton was equal to the purchase price when demand was high in the late 1870s. As demand and production costs had fallen, however, the committee set the new rate at $17. That rate was still too high to import the English product and allowed American producers to pocket the difference. Similar market conditions permitted some reductions in copper, nickel, and other products. Overall, there was very little consistency in the resulting bill produced by the conference committee; some rates were lowered, some were increased, but in the end the committee's bill maintained the protective system established during the Civil War.

In the opinion of economic historian Taussig, the Tariff Act of 1883, which squeaked through the Senate on a partisan vote of 32 to 31, was "a half-hearted attempt on the part of those wishing to maintain a system of high protection, to make some concession to a public demand for a more moderate tariff system."[30] Ida Tarbell attributed the results of what she called "The Mongrel Bill of 1883" to the lobbying efforts of the "organized business man":

True, they had been more or less active in every bill since the war, but never before had their right to stand day and night at the doors of Senate and House, to sit in committee, to be closeted in every leisure hour with their representatives in Congress, been conceded.[31]

FIGURE 3.1 Ida Tarbell, muckraking journalist and author of *The Tariff in Our Times* depicting the corruption in trade politics after the Civil War (Library of Congress)

It was no doubt true that the conference committee had the assistance—and in many cases the undue influence—of outside experts in the formulation of the provisions of the bill. John Hayes, wearing his hat as the Wool Manufacturers Association lobbyist and clearly one of those to whom Tarbell was referring, said of the woolen duties after passage of the Act:

> Reduction in itself was by no means desirable to us; it was a concession to public sentiment, a bending of the top and branches to the wind of public opinion to save the trunk of the protective system. In a word, the object was *protection through reduction*. We were willing to concede only to save the essentials both of the wool and woolens tariff. . . . We wanted the tariff to be made by our friends.[32]

4

The Gilded Age of Protectionism

I would not permit a single ton of steel to come
into the United States if our own labor could make
it. . . . And if you do not like it, you know what you
can do.[1]

> —Representative William McKinley
> May 18, 1888

In his 1968 presidential campaign, Governor George C. Wallace, running as a third-party candidate, often proclaimed: "There's not a dime's worth of difference between the Democrat and Republican Parties." Wallace's assessment of the parties would have been more accurate during the 1884 presidential election—especially as to the tariff issue, which had been a principal distinction between the parties from the inception of the Republican Party (GOP).

The Republicans adopted a platform in 1884 that spoke generally about protectionist principles but pledged only "to correct the inequalities of the tariff, and to reduce the surplus . . . without injuring the laborer or the great productive interests of the country."[2] The Democratic platform was for all practical purposes the same. Forsaking its bold prewar goals of "progressive free trade throughout the world" and its recent postwar pledges of "tariffs for revenue only," the party of Andrew Jackson betrayed his populism and yielded to a vague pledge "to revise the tariff in a spirit of fairness to all interests . . . without depriving American labor of the ability to compete successfully with foreign labor."[3] This tepid pronouncement reflected the strength of the protectionist elements of the Democratic Party, which had been partly responsible for the disastrous results of the 1883 reform efforts.

The Republican presidential nominee, James G. Blaine of Maine, a leading arch-protectionist, attempted to highlight the tariff issue and put the Democrats on the defensive,[4] but the election turned on other matters. One of these was a highly publicized scandal involving a favor Blaine had granted to the Union Pacific Railroad while serving as Speaker of the House. In return for the favor, Blaine had requested and received permission from the railroad to sell its bonds, for which he received a generous commission. The matter became public after some letters Blaine wrote to an executive of the company about their secret agreement and his commission found their way into the hands of journalists. Blaine closed one of his letters with the plea to "Burn this letter," and was famously reminded of this plea by placards repeating the phrase in Democratic rallies during the campaign.

The issue of financial corruption led to the defection of a number of prominent Republicans who campaigned openly for the Democratic candidate, Grover Cleveland. Detractors derisively named the defectors "Mugwumps," a term derived from a Native American word implying sanctimonious. Another factor in the election was the Irish Catholic vote, which was stirred against Blaine by one of his supporters—a Protestant minister, who charged that the Democrats were run by "Rum, Romanism, and Rebellion." The implication that Republicans were anti-Catholic Prohibitionists still waving the "bloody shirt" of the Civil War was not well received in the Irish immigrant community. Historians debate the impact that the Mugwumps had on the outcome of the election, but Blaine lost to Cleveland by fewer than 30,000 popular votes nationwide and lost New York by less than 1,200. A difference of 600 Mugwumps and Irish Catholics would have given Blaine the New York electoral votes and the presidency.

GROVER CLEVELAND TAKES ON TARIFF REFORM

There is little evidence that Grover Cleveland had given much attention to the issue of trade policy before his election to the presidency, an event that ended twenty-four years in the wilderness for Democrats since James Buchanan had left the executive mansion in 1860. Before he was nominated to run for president, Cleveland's political career was hardly three years old; he had been mayor of Buffalo in 1882 and governor of New York during the years 1883–84. In his short tenure he had acquired a reputation for integrity and fighting graft, which contrasted nicely with Blaine's reputation for corruption. In the particularly nasty 1884 campaign, however, the Republicans revealed that Cleveland, a bachelor, had fathered an illegitimate child ten years earlier. Paternity of the child was actually questionable, but Cleveland candidly and without hesitation accepted responsibility. With issues like this personal attack—which, while embarrassing, had the unintended consequence of enhancing Cleveland's reputation for honesty—and Blaine's "Burn this letter" incident dominating the campaign, tariff policies took a backseat.

Although he was cautious and gradual in his approach, the new president soon picked up on the tariff issue, taking the side of the moderate reformers. In his first annual message to Congress in December 1885, he reflected his fiscally conservative bias when he justified proposals for reductions in customs duties with the simple observation that "our revenues are in excess of the actual needs of an economical administration of the Government." In an effort to avoid a philosophical and political quagmire, Cleveland studiously added, "The question of free trade is not involved, nor is there now any occasion for the general discussion of the wisdom or expediency of a protective system." Throwing a bone to the protectionists, he further cautioned that the reductions should be done "in such manner as to protect the interests of American labor. . . . Its stability and proper remuneration furnish the most justifiable pretext for a protective policy." His only directive regarding the selection of tariffs to reduce was to focus on duties "upon the necessaries of life" so as to "lessen the cost of living in every family of the land and release to the people in every humble home a larger measure of the rewards of frugal industry."[5]

Modest as it was, Cleveland's proposal did not win approval in Congress. Although Democrats controlled the House with a comfortable majority— protectionist Republicans still maintained a slim rule over the Senate—a sizable faction of Democratic votes could be expected to line up against any tariff reduction. Hence, when the Ways and Means Committee produced a bill containing moderate tariff reductions supported by the president, the Republicans with the aid of thirty-five Democratic dissenters were able to defeat a motion to bring it to the House floor for a vote.

In the months that followed, Cleveland became more determined to address the growing surplus in the government treasury and more infuriated with the inequity of protectionist tariff policies. In his second annual address to Congress in December 1886, he renewed his tariff reduction proposal using language that contrasted sharply with that in his soft-pedaling proposal the year before. In a section much longer than in his previous address, he wrote passionately about the plight of the American farmers, who were "forced to pay excessive and needless taxation, while their products struggle in foreign markets." Assuming an Adam Smith perspective and a Jacksonian posture, he pointed out the "abnormal and exceptional business profits, which . . . increases without corresponding benefit to the people at large the vast accumulation of a few among our citizens, whose fortune, rivaling the wealth of the most favored in antidemocratic nations, are not the natural growth of a steady, plain, and industrious republic."[6] Despite its more passionate approach, the president's message again failed to move Congress, which adjourned in March the following year without taking a vote on a tariff bill.

Adding to the president's frustrations, Republican protectionist forces, led by the secretary of the American Tin Plate Association, had trooped into the Illinois district of Cleveland's tariff reform workhorse, Ways and Means chairman William R. Morrison, and marshaled his defeat. A number of other tariff reform candidates lost in the 1886 midterm elections, reducing the Democratic majority in the House to a narrow margin.

Despite bleak odds and his poor track record, Cleveland resolved over the summer and fall of 1887 to force the tariff reform issue in a bold and unprecedented fashion that would define his presidency. Taking few into his confidence, the president decided to devote his entire annual message to Congress in 1887 to the tariff issue. Following the tradition of his predecessors, his previous annual messages had been long, ponderous briefs, covering a multitude of "State of the Union" issues on domestic and foreign affairs with a variety of legislative recommendations scattered throughout. This year the input his cabinet secretaries provided on the sundry matters of concern within their departments was a wasted effort. Cleveland wanted no distractions from other public issues. He intended to present the tariff issue in a manner that would shock the conscience of the public, if not Congress. With only a few edits from close advisers, the president was solely responsible for the message. In making a methodical and straightforward case against protective tariffs, he wrote the address in the fashion of a lawyer's appeal, though he spiced it with a fair share of emotive, political rhetoric.

Cleveland began by laying out the central problem of the government's growing surplus, which he said was turning the public treasury into "a hoarding place for money needlessly withdrawn from trade and the people's use, thus crippling our national energies . . . and inviting schemes of public plunder." He charged that collecting more revenue from citizens than was necessary to maintain the government was a "perversion" tantamount to "indefensible extortion and a culpable betrayal of American fairness and justice." Reviewing the current fiscal picture in some detail, he warned that the surplus would almost triple in the next year with no productive use for the surplus funds. All of the government's bonded indebtedness that could be paid off without premium or penalty had already been retired. Cleveland was opposed to "unnecessary and extravagant appropriations"; he also objected to depositing US Treasury money in private banks because it established "too close a relationship between the operations of the Government Treasury and the business of the country . . . thus fostering an unnatural reliance in private business upon public funds." Predicting disaster if Congress continued its inaction, the president said "the gravity of our financial situation" demanded a remedy and turned his attention to the cause of the problem.

The system of taxation that had caused this "needless surplus" consisted of import duties and internal excise taxes levied on tobacco and alcoholic beverages. Since the latter were not in Cleveland's view, "strictly speaking, necessaries," consumers of alcohol and tobacco had no just complaint as to this tax. On the other hand, the tariff laws, which he called "the vicious, inequitable, and illogical source of unnecessary taxation," should be revised and amended "at once." These laws, he contended, raised the price not only of all imported goods but all domestic goods that were protected by tariffs as well, because domestic producers increased their prices to correspond with the protective duty. Cleveland said he was not proposing to eliminate protection of American labor or manufacturing interests but only the protection of "immense profits instead of moderately profitable returns." In the midst of the United States' centennial celebration, he scorned those who justified this unreasonable tariff scheme under Alexander Hamilton's infant industry argument, condemning domestic manufacturers "still needing the highest and greatest degree of favor and fostering care that can be wrung from Federal legislation" after 100 years.

As to the protectionist argument that high tariffs shielded the American workingman from the conditions of "pauper labor" of Europe, Cleveland observed that of the approximately 17.4 million workers engaged in all American industries only 2.6 million were employed in manufacturing industries that benefited from high tariffs. He was careful not to suggest that the protected workers—who were in the minority—should forgo the benefit that high tariffs might have on their wages in order to lower prices for the majority of wage earners. But, with a degree of understatement, Cleveland noted that the protected workers "will not overlook that they are consumers with the rest."

He then turned to the effect of the tariff on the farmers, "who manufacture nothing, but who pay the increased price which the tariff imposes upon every agricultural implement, upon all he wears, and upon all he uses and owns." Addressing the wool tariff issue, Cleveland said that the farmer who had no sheep was forced "to pay a tribute to his fellow-farmer as well as to the manufacturer and merchant." He said the benefit even to sheep farmers was "illusory," because most sheep were raised by farmers in small flocks of twenty-five to fifty sheep, which at then current prices would allow a tariff profit of only $18 to $36, depending upon the number in their flock. When the wool was manufactured into cloth, he observed, a further sum was added to the price to benefit the tariff-protected woolen product manufacturer. By the time the sheep farmer purchased his own woolen goods for his family for the winter, he had lost his tariff profit through the cost of his new merchandise. Considering the small number of sheep farmers in proportion to the rest of the country's population and the illusory value of the wool tariff even to them, the president concluded that "it constitutes a tax which with relentless grasp is fastened upon the clothing of every man, woman, and child in the land" and should be removed or reduced.

Taking up a theme addressed by Adam Smith a century earlier, Cleveland attacked monopolies, which had come of age in America's Gilded Age in the form of trusts. He noted that among protected domestic industries,

> competition is too often strangled by combinations quite prevalent at this time, and frequently called trusts, which have for their object the regulation of the supply and price of commodities made and sold by members of the combination. The people can hardly hope for any consideration in the operation of these selfish schemes.

Indeed, it was the link between high prices brought on by protective tariffs and the formation of cartels to prevent price wars that prompted the president of the American Sugar Refining Company and leader of the US sugar trust, Henry O. Havemeyer, twelve years later to make the widely repeated remark that the "mother of all trusts is the customs tariff bill."[7]

In the conclusion of his address, Cleveland urged Congress to approach the difficult task of revising the tariff laws "in a spirit higher than partisanship," appealing to the members' "regard for patriotic duty." And he cautioned them not to base their decisions on theories of protection and free trade:

> It is a condition which confronts us, not a theory. . . . The question of free trade is absolutely irrelevant; and the persistent claim made in certain quarters, that all the efforts to relieve the people from unjust and unnecessary taxation are schemes of so-called free traders, is mischievous and far removed from any consideration for the public good.

The tariff revisions the president proposed could be made "without danger to the opportunity for remunerative labor which our workingmen need," and with benefits to all "people by cheapening their means of subsistence and increasing the measure of their comforts."[8]

THE GREAT TARIFF DEBATE OF 1888

The reaction to Cleveland's address was immediate and explosive. According to historian Joanne Reitano, "Not since Lincoln issued the Emancipation Proclamation in 1863 had a presidential document been received with such excitement and acclaim."[9] Although the message was not a new one and, actually, was rather conservative in terms of the reforms it proposed, the surprising boldness with which it was presented catapulted trade politics into prominence not experienced since before the Civil War. Almost instantly, the president's speech broke the political parties out of their stalemate on the tariff issue and firmly recast their respective sentiments back to their traditional positions. Most protectionist-leaning Democrats began retreating into the reform camp. At the same time nearly all Republicans saw Cleveland's attack as an opportunity to return to power and rallied around the protectionist flag, regardless of misgivings some may have had about abuses in the tariff system.

In essence, the president's polemic against the "indefensible extortion" of the "inequitable" tariff system, which he claimed favored rich manufacturers, monopolies, and trusts and increased the cost of living for the laboring classes, represented a return to the political themes of Andrew Jackson. These themes had worked for decades in the antebellum period and now would help cleanse Democrats of the "bloody shirt" stains of the Civil War that had limited their political growth since the war. It was also an asset for the party to be identified with Cleveland and his reputation as a corruption-fighting, straight shooter now out to reform an abusive tariff system. Yet the Republicans, after the initial shock of the president's address, believed that he had handed them a winning issue—*free trade*—that would serve as a scary call to arms, in the way that references to communism or socialism did in a later era. They had lost the last presidential election on the perceived corruption of their candidate. They hoped to win the next one with President Cleveland's threat to the values of the American system of protection.

In the spring of 1888, Congressman Roger Mills, a Texas Democrat and the new chairman of the Ways and Means Committee, introduced, with Cleveland's blessing, a tariff reform bill. Although it proposed tariff cuts averaging only 7 percent, the Mills bill sparked a debate that lasted for over a month, contained 151 speeches, and became known as "the Great Tariff Debate of 1888." Before the debate had even begun, the ranking Republican member on the committee, William McKinley—with hyperbolic overkill that will sound familiar to observers of modern political debates—predicted that the Mills bill would wreck the American economy. Similarly, the American Iron and Steel Association renamed it a "Bill to Destroy American Industries." Even its proponents seemed to give more significance to the legislation than its actual reform proposals deserved. The *New York Times* described the bill as "by far the most important fiscal measure brought before Congress since the close of the war."[10] It was the manner in which Cleveland had framed the issue and brought it to a head in a year when a Democratic president was standing for reelection for the first time in over thirty years that enhanced the impact of the debate and overshadowed the modest substance of the bill.

Mills commenced the debate on the Democratic side by appealing to Jacksonian populism rather than addressing the details of his specific tariff proposals. He first reminded the House that high tariffs had been imposed as a war measure, quoting their original author Justin Morrill's assertion that they were intended to be "a temporary measure." But unlike other war taxes, including income taxes, which had been removed from "the shoulders of the wealthy," the tariff burden had increased for consumers in the twenty years since the war ended. "Congress," he said, "lent a willing ear to the demands of wealthy corporations and individuals and took all the burden from them, but the war taxes on clothing, like the poor, we have always with us." He attributed the Republican tax policy priorities to "favoritism to the wealthy" and based on "special privileges to rich and powerful classes."[11] He went to great lengths to prove with statistics that high tariffs did not produce high wages for labor and that wages vary based on the principle of supply and demand. Prompting laughter on the House floor, Mills offered a colorful illustration of his point that higher wages for workers did not arise from extra profits gained by the manufacturer as a result of protection:

> Mr. Jay Gould, with his immense income from his railroad property, is able to pay his bootblack $500 a day, but does he do it? Oh, no; he pays the market price of the street. He gets his boots blacked and pays his nickel like a little man.[12]

Mills argued that any wage increases since the 1850s had occurred as a result of enhancements in industrialization which produced higher productivity and lower labor costs overall. He concluded, "The tariff conferred no benefit on the laborer; none whatever. . . . This 'great American system' that is intended to secure high wages for our laborers is so perverted that all its beneficence intended for the poor workman stops in the pocket of his employer."[13] With the rise of monopolies and "trusts" controlling production and increasing prices, the laborer's life is even darker. He charged that the protectionist tariff system was deeply dividing the country into "two classes—one numerous, but poor; one small, but powerful and rich."[14] His bill was intended to address the growing disparity in economic prosperity and to "send comfort and happiness into the homes and bosoms of the poor laboring people of this country."[15] Although the modest provisions of his legislation might not have lived up to his rhetoric, he was effective in putting the Republicans on the defensive at least initially.

The Republican response, led by William "Pig Iron" Kelley of Pennsylvania, was emotionally charged and largely ignored Mills's argument and the substance of the bill. Kelley proclaimed that protective tariffs had lifted the country from "national bankruptcy" caused by the tariff reductions of 1846 and 1857 and "had exalted us to the lofty prominence among nations."[16] Although the Mills bill would have only reduced the average tariff rate on dutiable goods from 47 percent back to 40 percent, Kelley said the obvious intent of the legislation was to overthrow the protective tariff system "and scatter to the winds the magnificent results achieved in less than a quarter century under its fostering influence." He forecast that the measure would, if enacted, "instantly paralyze the enterprise and energy of the people."

Kelley resorted to an old tactic to enhance the moral appeal of protectionism and to counter Mills's attacks on its special privileges for the wealthy. He retrieved the "bloody shirt" of Civil War sectional animosities by noting that all but two of the congressmen who had drafted this "partisan measure" were "representatives of what was slave territory." Kelley accused the Democratic Party leaders of being "oblivious to the overwhelming social and economic changes wrought by the abolition of slavery." He said that "free trade was essential to the perpetuity of slavery," and that "it was in the interest of free trade that the country was involved for more than four years in a fratricidal war." Thus, having not only linked free trade to slavery, Kelley made it the cause of the Civil War. He condemned the Mills bill as an "anachronism," belonging "to the saddest epoch in our national history, the period between 1832 and 1861."[17]

Finally, Kelley devoted a substantial portion of his speech in its concluding section to attacking the "whiskey trust," which he argued was the source of many of the nation's social problems. Declaring that the politics of the country were dominated by this trust as they had been by a "slave oligarchy" before the war, he observed, "King Alcohol is proving that he is as hostile to national development as King Cotton ever was." As a means of reducing the treasury surplus, Kelley proposed the elimination of alcohol excise taxes, which he argued help to create and sustain the whiskey trust. He accused Democratic politicians of being in the pockets of Kentucky banking interests for preserving these taxes, as they promoted the president's "free trade message" and the bill prepared by "the Southern gentlemen who have dominated the counsels of the Committee on Ways and Means."[18] Thus, Kelley's effort offered a buffet of diversions to draw attention away from the reformers' arguments about inequities in the tariff system with an appeal to economic fears, Prohibitionist politics, and lingering sectional divisiveness.

Throughout the debate, the Democrats continued with inspiration from Adam Smith to condemn economic inequality in a system that produced "colossal fortunes" for the protected manufacturers and persistent poverty for the workers. Some Republicans responded indirectly to this indictment by espousing the Hamiltonian position that it was the duty of the government to protect and defend American business from foreign competition. They argued that laborers benefited broadly from protection by the jobs that were preserved. As to the inequitable sharing of the protectionist profits, Andrew Carnegie spoke for the manufacturers when he wrote that "the millionaire will be but a trustee for the poor, entrusted for a season with a great part of the increased wealth of the community, but administering it for the community far better than it could or would have done for itself."[19] Carnegie's answer was not well received in a period of increasing labor unrest and violent strikes, including strikes against Carnegie Steel. Working conditions in factories were abysmal and included fourteen-hour workdays, six days a week for a dollar a day. While both sides presented charts and statistics to support their respective positions on wages, the Democratic arguments favoring more economic opportunity to prosperity gained a stronger following among the working class. The persistent labor strife at a time when protectionist tariffs were at their historical peak became a political liability for the protectionists.

Another apparent problem for the protectionist side was that the classical economists—most prominently Adam Smith and John Stuart Mill, who supported freer trade as a means of benefiting the workingman—enjoyed much favor in American academia at the time. But the Republicans turned this to their advantage with a heavy dose of anti-intellectual and anti-British rhetoric. Representative William McKinley, for example, observed that America prefers a "political economy founded upon the everyday experience of the puddler or the potter [rather] than the learning of the professor."[20] Former House Speaker Thomas B. Reed, a protectionist Republican from Maine, took a similar stance condemning "the Herr Professor of political economy" for taking too theoretical an approach regarding labor and ignoring the "soul of man," which high tariffs presumably protected.[21]

The Republicans persistently charged that the Democrats were enamored of "free trade," accusing them of following a British craze, although President Cleveland had specifically denied its relevance to his proposed reforms. While engendering fears of a British invasion "whether it be [with] armed forces . . . [or] manufactured products," the protectionist speakers called the tariff reformers "Anglomaniacs" and "American pets of British free trade aristocracy."[22] The political cartoonists in the protectionist-leaning magazine *Judge* frequently portrayed tariff reform Democrats in some demeaning relationship with an oversized John Bull, taking "free trade" advantages detrimental to American prosperity.

The final vote on the Mills bill came in mid-summer and passed with a comfortable margin, but along party lines. Unlike the opposition to previous tariff reform legislation, this bill drew only four "nay" votes from Democrats, down from 41 in 1884. But the measure received a cold reception when it moved to the Senate.

In contrast to the House of Representatives, which the Democrats controlled during eight of ten Congresses in the two decades between 1874 and 1894, the Republicans maintained majority control of the Senate for seven Congresses during the same period. A principal reason for this dominance was the manner in which senators were elected prior to the adoption of the Seventeenth Amendment to the Constitution in 1913, that is, by state legislatures rather than direct popular elections. Throughout the Gilded Age, beginning in the 1870s, large business interests—bankers, railroad magnates, and manufacturers—effectively ruled many state legislatures directly or through the state "boss" system and handpicked the senators to be sent to Washington. In many cases, wealthy tycoons simply bought their own seats, which transformed the upper house of Congress into a "Millionaire's Club." The particular business interest represented by an individual senator was often so blatant that he became better known by the interest than the state that he represented, as in the senator from Standard Oil, rather than Ohio. This dominance was portrayed in a political cartoon in the weekly magazine *Puck*, captioned "Bosses of the Senate." The cartoon, by Joseph Keppler, portrayed a row of overweight "bosses" wearing top hats and labeled "Copper Trust," "Sugar Trust," "Tin Trust," and "Standard Oil Trust," all hovering over the Senate in front of a sign that read: "This Is A Senate of the Monopolists, By the Monopolists, and For the Monopolists." Keppler depicted the "People's Entrance" as locked and "Closed."[23] Because so many senators answered to business interests protected by tariffs, "the mother of all trusts," it is not surprising that the Mills tariff reform legislation was dead on arrival in the Senate.

In 1888, Senator Nelson W. Aldrich, Republican from Rhode Island, had become the leading influence in the Senate on the tariff issue. Aldrich, whose daughter later married the only son of John D. Rockefeller, was the prototypical senator of the Gilded Age, a wealthy investor who believed that the national interest coincided with the interests of business and, like

Alexander Hamilton, that government should partner with business to achieve national prosperity. A shrewd and skilled legislator, he was an invaluable ally to protected industries, especially the American Sugar Refinery Company. Although Rhode Island had no sugar refineries, Senator Aldrich became the Sugar Trust's "man in Washington."[24] His reaction to the Mills bill was to reject it altogether and start over with a new Senate bill, which in some cases increased existing rates or kept them at prohibitive levels based on the argument that reducing imports would decrease the surplus in government revenue. One exception was Aldrich's proposal to reduce rates on raw sugar by 50 percent in order to lower costs for domestic sugar refiners. After adjourning one of the longest sessions in congressional history, the Senate passed the Aldrich bill by a partisan vote of 32 to 30 in January 1889. Yet when the revised bill arrived back in the House of Representatives, the Ways and Means Committee refused to consider it. The House leadership objected that the new Senate version was so radically different from the Mills bill that it was a new measure, which violated the constitutional requirement that all revenue measures must originate in the House.

THE ELECTION OF 1888

The two major parties held their respective political conventions for presidential nominations at the height of the "Great Tariff Debate" in the House. The Democrats renominated Cleveland by acclamation and adopted a platform dominated by denunciations of "unjust and unequal tax laws," and endorsing the president's last message to Congress and "the efforts of Democratic Representatives in Congress to secure a reduction of excessive taxation."[25] For their part, the Republicans nominated Civil War general Benjamin Harrison as a compromise candidate and declared in their platform:

> We are uncompromisingly in favor of the American system of protection; we protest against its destruction as proposed by the President and his party. They serve the interests of Europe; we will support the interests of America. . . . We denounce the Mills bill . . . and we heartily indorse the consistent and patriotic action of the Republican Representatives in Congress in opposing its passage.[26]

Tariffs, for the first time, became the principal issue in a presidential election campaign. Harrison, the grandson of President William Henry Harrison who had run under the slogan "Tippecanoe and Tyler too," picked up a modified slogan, "Tippecanoe and tariff too." Big business interests ignited the most sophisticated fundraising organization in history for the Republicans. Pennsylvania senator Matthew Quay—a cunning political operative known for trading political favors for company stock—was Harrison's campaign chairman. John Wanamaker, a retail department store magnate from Philadelphia, led the campaign finance committee, drawing from the enormous wealth of "robber tariff barons" seeking to protect their domain. Many donors were promised favors from a new administration and all were anxious to bring a business-friendly Republican back to the executive mansion. Investigative journalist Ida Tarbell called it a "campaign for protection backed by the protected."[27] James P. Foster, president of the Republican League, famously ordered Republicans who were benefiting from the "bulwark of prosperity" provided by protection to ante up. He called for the protected manufacturers, especially Pennsylvania manufacturers, to be "put over the fire and all the fat fried out of them."[28] Indeed, the American Iron and Steel Association, led by James M. Swank, supplied Harrison with "a bottomless bucket of funds."[29]

The Republicans raised four times the amount of money that Democrats generated. According to the *New York Herald*, "Pennsylvania bled at every pore in the interests of protection."[30] In an election the *Baltimore Sun* called the most corrupt in history, massive vote-buying schemes were deployed in critical states like New York, Pennsylvania, and Indiana. Matthew Quay and his operatives imported thousands of Republican voters across state lines to tilt the balance in Harrison's favor and published reams of pro-protection propaganda threatening plant closures and layoffs if Cleveland was reelected.

Democrats engaged in voter fraud schemes as well but did not have the financial capacity to reach the Republican scale of operation. In fact, the Democratic campaign was altogether anemic. President Cleveland refused to campaign or even vote for himself, considering such activity undignified for a sitting president. Despite having a strong tariff reform platform, the Democrats hedged their bets by nominating a protectionist vice presidential candidate, Allen G. Thurman of Ohio, and softened their attack on tariff abuses. In the rhetoric war, the Republicans won a significant point by tricking the British minister to the United States into writing a letter declaring that Cleveland would be the best choice on issues affecting Britain. Referring to some recent anti-British remarks made by the president, the minister indicated that Cleveland had been insincere and had rendered the remarks only for political purposes. Although the diplomat intended the letter to be confidential, Harrison's Republican managers released it to the press in the last week of the campaign as evidence of Cleveland's devotion to British free trade and anti-Irish policies. Meanwhile, a major political rift arose in New York, which split Cleveland's support and cost him that state's critical electoral votes. Thanks to the tallies in the solidly Democratic South, Cleveland won the popular vote by nearly 100,000, exceeding the margin in his previous election victory, but Harrison won the decisive electoral vote margin.

THE MCKINLEY TARIFF AND ITS FALLOUT

Despite the narrow victory and significant nontariff influences on the outcome, leading Republicans, with new majorities in both houses of Congress, heralded the election as a mandate for higher protection. William McKinley of Ohio, the new chairman of the House Ways and Means Committee, reported out a tariff bill in the new session based largely on Senator Aldrich's answer to the Mills tariff reform bill, explaining:

> I have interpreted the victory to mean . . . that a revision of the tariff was not only demanded by the votes of the people but that such revision should be . . . in full recognition of the principle and purposes of protection. The people have spoken.[31]

Hubris overwhelmed the Grand Old Party after four years out of power. The new Republican Speaker of the House, Thomas Brackett Reed of Maine, reflected this attitude, observing: "The danger in a free country is not that power will be exercised too freely, but that it will be exercised too sparingly."[32] The most prominent offspring of this attitude and the assumption of an electoral mandate was the Tariff Act of 1890. This act became known as the McKinley Tariff, even though it was based on the Senate substitute for the Mills bill and Senator Nelson Aldrich orchestrated its final amendments.

The McKinley Tariff raised the overall average duties to nearly 50 percent. Lobbyists for the key protected interests—sugar, wool, textiles, and iron and steel—were effectively allowed to draft their own schedules. The Sugar Trust, through Aldrich's oversight, made sure that the tariff on raw sugar was eliminated to the advantage of domestic refiners who continued to enjoy protective rates on refined sugar. In exchange, domestic producers of the raw product were given a generous subsidy to ensure profitability when competing with imports, even though many considered the subsidies unconstitutional—much as Thomas Jefferson did when opposing Alexander Hamilton's proposed bounties. Despite huge productivity innovations in the American iron and steel industries over the previous twenty years, the rates on their products were kept at prohibitive levels.

Andrew Carnegie—who was pilloried in political cartoons of the anti-protectionist *Puck* magazine, depicting him delivering sacks of money to the Harrison campaign in an effort to buy more protection—personally lobbied the president and congressional leaders to protect his business and wrote several essays defending the McKinley Tariff. The Tin Plate Association obtained a specific duty on tin plates, which effectively increased the price of imports of this product by 70 percent, even though there was practically no American tin plate production at the time. Ida Tarbell explained the legislative process leading to the McKinley Tariff as being based on the "openly expressed principle in political circles that your protection shall be in proportion to your campaign contribution."[33]

The 1890 tariff act had an immediate effect on imports and on politics. Pig iron imports fell off 50 percent within a year of the bill's enactment, and imports of iron and steel products fell by 50 percent over the next five years. The new tin plate industry blossomed under the shelter of its new protection. However, the high-handed manner with which the new Republican majority imposed its rule triggered an unprecedented blowback from the public. The McKinley Tariff was widely seen as an unnecessary new tax on the public for the benefit of the rich. And for the first time in history, Congress appropriated over a billion dollars in public spending in support of business interests. Democrats went on the attack, charging that the "Billion Dollar Congress" led by Republicans was raising taxes and wasting public funds as it raised the cost of living for working-class Americans. One Democratic speaker exclaimed: "The McKinley bill is with us always, at the table, at the bedside, in the kitchen, in the barn, in the churches and to the cemetery."[34] The popular Democratic mayor of New York City, Abram

S. Hewitt, who was himself an ironmaster, refuted the Republicans' argument that protection benefited workers. Based upon a statistical analysis of the steel industry, he concluded that the tariff on steel rails

> is not to benefit the working classes, who are not paid at any higher rate than they would be paid in any other branch of business, but to take from the community at large at least fifteen times, if not twenty times, as much profit as the general average business of the country will warrant. It is thus that the rich grow richer and the poor poorer.[35]

The midterm elections of 1890 reflected the depth of the disastrous fallout from the McKinley Tariff. The Republicans lost seventy-eight seats in the House—including William McKinley's seat due in part to gerrymandering—giving Democrats a 235 to 88 majority. Matters grew even more dismal for the GOP over the next two years as labor strikes broke out around the country. The worst of these occurred in June 1892 at the Carnegie Steel Company's Homestead Steel Plant near Pittsburgh following a management decision to lower wages. The Amalgamated Association of Iron and Steel Workers called the strike, which led to a bloody battle between the union members and strike breakers supported by 300 Pinkerton detectives and resulted in thirteen deaths and more than 100 wounded.

While no direct connection existed between this tragedy and the imposition of high tariffs, the resentment toward Andrew Carnegie—whose wealth was facilitated by protectionist trade policies, as he lowered wages for steel workers—carried over to the Republicans deemed responsible for his fortune. Democrats were not hesitant to place blame on the high tariffs of the McKinley Act as the underlying cause of the Homestead Steel Plant casualties. As Grover Cleveland received his party's nomination again for the 1892 presidential election, he referenced Homestead sarcastically as "the tender mercy the workingman receives from those made selfish and sordid by unjust governmental favoritism."[36] In a clear rebuke to the overreaching of business interests in control of government, the voters returned Cleveland to the presidency in a solid defeat of President Harrison. Cleveland received 277 electoral votes to 145 and a popular vote margin of 400,000. Also winning majorities in both houses of Congress, the Democrats were now in full control of government policy for the first time in thirty-four years.

OUR ROBBER BARONS.

FIGURE 4.1 *Puck*'s late nineteenth-century satirical depiction of collusion among Congress and the corporate monopolies to rob taxpayers through protectionist tariffs: "Our Robber Barons" (in author's collection)

REFORM FAILS AGAIN

The political landscape in 1893 was far more fertile for tariff reform and, in particular, for reversing the direction of the McKinley Tariff than it had been four years earlier when Cleveland's last initiative aborted. The connection between protectionist tariffs—"the Mother of all Trusts"—and abusive monopolies driving up consumer prices now trumped the Anglophobic rhetoric tying pauper wages to British-style free-trade policy. But several significant distractions and obstacles—some new and some familiar—frustrated the process. The "Free Silver" issue and the Panic of 1893 both proved to be major diversions impeding action on tariffs, and the conservative Senate dominated by business interests, even with a Democratic majority, was far from convinced of the need for reform.

The Coinage Act of 1873, which had demonetized silver, sparked the Free Silver movement, an effort to bring back silver coinage and expand the monetary base. This cause united a coalition of farmers hoping to pay back their debts with inflated dollars, silver miners desiring more demand for their work product, and a growing movement of Populists from the West and the South. Eastern financial tycoons, who would be hurt by an inflationary, expanded money supply, opposed the "silverites." The movement split both political parties. The Republicans generally favored the interests of the eastern financial establishment, but a strong contingent of western Republicans favored free silver. Cleveland, as a fiscal conservative and "sound money" man, was firmly against a return to silver, while a substantial element of the Democratic Party favored the Populist free coinage cause. The Republicans had attempted to assuage their silverites with passage of the Sherman Silver Purchase Act of 1890, which required the federal government to buy millions of ounces of silver with special treasury notes redeemable in gold or silver. Following his inauguration in 1893, Cleveland shifted the focus of his attention from tariff reform to the repeal of the Sherman Silver Purchase Act, which had resulted in a depletion of the nation's gold reserves.

Shortly before Cleveland took office, the United States fell into a deep economic depression with the Panic of 1893. Democrats blamed the McKinley Tariff and the Sherman Silver Purchase Act for the crisis, and Republicans attributed the cause to the fear of Cleveland's plan to lower tariffs. The panic was an international phenomenon, more likely the result of the bursting of an economic bubble; deflation followed an enormous expansionary period of growth and overbuilding, particularly in the railroad industry. Whatever the cause, a significant new Treasury deficit arose from the profligate spending by the "Billion Dollar Congress" and the loss in revenues resulting from the McKinley Tariff's prohibitive rates. This deficit, combined with the effects of the Panic, inspired considerable trepidation among tariff reformers and dampened the mood for another fight.

Nevertheless, after giving primary attention to the silver question by calling a special session of Congress to repeal the Sherman Act, Cleveland turned again to tariff reform in the regular session beginning in December. The new Ways and Means chairman, William L. Wilson of West Virginia, began by writing a new bill eliminating duties on many raw materials— including wool, iron ore, and coal—and reduced the rates on farm machinery and supplies in order to lower the cost of domestic production. He did not propose major reductions on manufactured products. While Wilson lowered the rates on refined sugar, steel rails, and what he called the "bogus industry" of tin plates, he kept them at prohibitive levels. Overall, the Wilson bill reduced the McKinley rates by 15 percent. President Cleveland praised the bill as it emerged from the committee, but many Democrats panned it for not going far enough toward the goal of "tariff for revenue only." One critic charged, "It is merely better than the McKinley Bill in degree, not in kind," and would be ineffective "in the age of Carnegies and Goulds." In the committee report on the bill, Wilson countered that "the legislator must always remember that in the beginning temperate reform is safest."[37]

The House passed the bill easily and quickly, but the Senate again gave reform a hostile reception. The Democrats held a 44 to 38 majority in the upper house with an additional four senators from the new Populist Party who voted with the Democrats on tariff issues. However, Senator Arthur P. Gorman (D-MD) led a group of Democrats who represented protected interests affected by reductions in the Wilson Bill and who could defeat the bill if they were not satisfied. This faction put Gorman in charge of revising the bill, leading to the addition of 634 amendments. With Gorman's group breaking the Democrats' unity, Republicans joined the fight to weaken the House reforms. Senator Quay filibustered the bill for twelve days— threatening to "talk it to death"—and secured increased tariffs for hundreds of products, with particular emphasis on iron, steel, and cotton products. The Sugar Trust also came into the game, pouring six-figure sums into the coffers of both political parties during consideration of the bill. An investigation proved that senators were also speculating on sugar stocks during the process. In the end, the Senate approved amendments raising the tariffs on raw sugar from 0 to 40 percent and retained the effective protective tariffs on refined sugar.

After passage of the bill in the Senate, an outraged President Cleveland wrote a letter of protest to be read into the record by Wilson, urging rejection of the Senate amendments. Cleveland charged that the Senate version represented an abandonment of Democratic pledges of tariff reform and meant "party perfidy and party dishonor." Pointing to the "inconsistent absurdity" of removing tariffs on the wool of the farmer, while maintaining protective tariffs on "the iron-ore and coal of corporations and capitalists," he asked, "How can we face the people after indulging in such outrageous discriminations and violations of principles?"[38]

The president's letter only enraged the Senate sponsors of the amended bill, leading to their refusal to compromise and come to terms with the House in conference over the measure. Ultimately, the House had no choice but to accept the Senate amendments and passed the bill. Assuming that a veto would likely be overridden, and recognizing that the Wilson-Gorman Tariff Act—as bad as it was—was an improvement over the McKinley Tariff, President Cleveland let the bill become law without his signature under the pocket veto provision of the Constitution. For all his bold and well-intended initiatives, in the final analysis, Cleveland lacked the political skill and the critical drive necessary to lead the effort to enact effective tariff reforms. After presenting his case in the traditional written message to Congress, he had left to others the labor of finishing the job. In an era when the protected interests controlled a majority of votes in the Senate, more was needed from the president to win transformational reform.

THE INCOME TAX

The inconsistent tariff revisions, however, were not the only attempts at fiscal reform in the Wilson-Gorman Act. The bill also included for the first time since the end of the Civil War an income tax, which proponents argued was the "handmaid of tariff reform" necessary to compensate for the regressive tariff tax on consumption that fell largely on the poor and working class. Cleveland had agreed to include a small tax on corporate income in his address to Congress, but he and Wilson feared the political fallout that adding an income tax to the equation might bring. Led by Congressman William Jennings Bryan (D-NE) and Benton McMillin (D-TN), sponsors of the income tax argued that it was needed to supplement tariff revenue and shift some of the burden to the wealthy. Bryan sought a comprehensive graduated tax on all incomes above $2,500, but Wilson reluctantly accepted a committee amendment, which was included in the final bill, placing a flat 2 percent tax on all individual and corporate incomes over $4,000. The Treasury Department estimated that only about 85,000 of the 65 million Americans at that time had taxable incomes of this size. Most of these high earners lived in the northeastern states. Opponents called the measure socialistic and an attack on thrift and the creators of wealth. No Republican voted for the bill in either chamber, and the few Democrats who voted against it came mainly from the Northeast.[39]

Less than three months after the date the Wilson-Gorman Act went into effect on January 1, 1895, the United States Supreme Court heard the case of *Pollock v. Farmers' Loan and Trust*[40] and struck down the income tax provision as unconstitutional in a highly controversial, sharply divided 5 to 4 opinion. It was a surprising decision, reversing nearly a century of judicial precedent, and came only fourteen years after the Supreme Court had upheld the Civil War income tax.[41] The court held that the congressional power of "direct" taxation under the Constitution must be apportioned among the states according to population in the same manner as congressional representation. Chief Justice Melville Fuller, speaking for the *Pollock* Court, observed that the drafters of the Constitution believed that "in adjusting a system of representation between the states, regard should be had to their relative wealth, since those who were to be most heavily taxed ought to have a proportionate influence in the government."[42] However, in 1796, a unanimous Supreme Court—which included three members of the 1787 Constitutional Convention—had held in an opinion, included among the body of cases prominently reversed by *Pollock*, that "direct taxes" did not include taxes such as income taxes and need not be apportioned among the states.[43]

The debate reflected in the opinions of the justices mirrored the emotional congressional debate. Mr. Justice Stephen Field in his concurring opinion opined simply that the income tax

> discriminates between those who receive an income of $4,000 and those who do not. It thus vitiates, in my judgment, by this arbitrary discrimination, the whole legislation .... [I]t is class legislation, and leads inevitably to oppression and abuses, and to general unrest and disturbance in society.... The present assault on capital is but . . . the stepping-stone to . . . a war of the poor against the rich.[44]

Mr. Justice Edward Douglass White's dissenting opinion declared that the majority, in abandoning the settled conclusions of its predecessors, was denying Congress "a power conceded to it by universal consensus for 100 years." Great constitutional questions were being determined by this Court, he wrote, "according to the mere opinion of those who temporarily fill its bench, and our constitution will . . . be bereft of value, and become a most dangerous instrument to the rights and liberties of the people."[45] Mr. Justice Henry Brown, another dissenter, called the majority opinion "a surrender of the taxing power to the moneyed class" and expressed the hope that it was not "the first step toward the submergence of the liberties of the people in a sordid despotism of wealth."[46]

The most impassioned dissent came from Mr. Justice John Marshall Harlan, later known as "the Great Dissenter." Like the other dissenters, he premised his conclusion with erudite legal reasoning and precedent. But he peppered his opinion with references to the discrimination the decision placed on "the greater part of the people" burdened disproportionately by current taxes in favor of "the dominion of aggregated wealth." The manner in which Harlan delivered his opinion from the bench became the topic of great controversy in the conservative press. The *New York Sun* wrote that "he pounded the desk and shook his finger under the noses of the Chief Justice and Mr. Justice Field, turned . . . angrily upon his colleagues of the majority, and expressed his dissent . . . in a tone and language more appropriate to a stump speech at a Populist barbecue than to an opinion on a question of law before the Supreme Court." A San Francisco paper accused Harlan of giving a "Democratic stump-speech," ignoring the fact that Harlan was a Republican, having run twice as a GOP candidate for governor of Kentucky. Harlan had played a key role in the 1876 Republican National Convention nominating Rutherford B. Hayes, who as president named him to the Supreme Court the following year. Among other newspapers criticizing Harlan's dissent, the *New York Times* quoted an anonymous Ohio attorney who said, "It is well known that Justice Harlan has presidential ambitions" and claimed that he was hoping to "strike a responsive chord in the country." With all the controversy his opinion had stirred, Harlan wrote a long letter to his sons urging them not to be "at all alarmed by the reports sent out by lying newspaper correspondents," and explained his concern about the case:

> This recent decision will become as hateful with the American people as the Dred Scott case was when it was decided. That was the attempt of the owners of slave property to dominate the freemen of America and compel them against their wishes to sustain the institution of slavery. The recent decision will have the effect, if the country recognizes it permanently as good law, to make the freemen of America the slaves of accumulated wealth.[47]

The Supreme Court majority was already being dubbed the tool of vested corporate interests, having just handed down decisions sanctioning injunctions against labor strikes (*In re Debs*)[48] and dismantling the Sherman Anti-Trust Act (*United States v. E. C. Knight Co.*).[49] This was also the Court that handed down the decision in *Plessy v. Ferguson*[50] in 1896 that sanctioned the Jim Crow racial segregation system for the next half century. But it was the *Pollock* decision that became the most widely condemned decision since *Dred Scott*. While many eastern newspapers endorsed the decision, papers throughout the country took up the cause of the Court's dissenting opinions, as did Bryan and most Democrats and Populists. The *Augusta Chronicle** in Georgia charged that *Pollock* "robs the masses . . . for the few who own the wealth of the country." The *St. Louis Post-Dispatch* wrote that the opinion confirmed that "corporations and plutocrats" were "securely intrenched in the Supreme Court," and the *New York World* called it "a triumph of selfishness over patriotism."[51] Although by the end of 1895, congressional Democrats introduced a constitutional amendment to overturn the decision, the effort would have to wait another eighteen years before prevailing in 1913 with the ratification of the Sixteenth Amendment.

MCKINLEY AND THE DINGLEY TARIFF

President Cleveland's failure on tariff reform in the Wilson-Gorman Act was not his only problem. When he called in federal troops in July 1894 to put down the Pullman strike in Chicago—the first national strike in US history—Cleveland drew the unmitigated wrath and condemnation of organized labor on his administration. Likewise, his attack on silver cost him the increasingly significant Populist vote. These actions, coupled with the devastating impact of the economic depression following the Panic of 1893, led to record Democratic losses in the 1894 midterm elections and the removal of Cleveland from the Democratic ticket in the 1896 election. Cleveland's political demise marked the beginning of a sixteen-year Republican reign over both ends of Pennsylvania Avenue.

The precipitous decline of Cleveland's viability in the Democratic Party during his second term corresponded with the ascendancy of William

---

* Ironically, this newspaper's editorial page today is one of the most conservative in the United States. In the interest of full disclosure, it is noted that after I voted for the 1993 "Clinton Budget," which included an income tax increase, the *Augusta Chronicle* printed an editorial apologizing for having previously endorsed my candidacy for Congress.

Jennings Bryan. Elected to Congress as a Democrat from Nebraska in 1890 in the wake of the fallout from the McKinley Tariff, Bryan made his first floor speech in support of tariff reductions—a three-hour stem-winder that established his mark as a powerful orator. The speech also made him a leading voice against protectionism, which he described as "conceived in greed and fashioned in iniquity."[52] After only two terms in the House and a failed Senate bid, Bryan shockingly emerged as the 1896 presidential nominee for both the Democratic and Populist Parties at the age of thirty-six. In addition to his oratorical skills, what distinguished Bryan from Cleveland was his stand against the gold standard and for the free coinage of silver. The rise in popularity of silver in the Democratic Party represented a move from Cleveland's fiscal conservatism to Bryan's economic radicalism. Bryan, who became known as the Great Commoner, carried the day for "free silver" within his party and sealed the first of three Democratic presidential nominations with his famous "Cross of Gold" speech at the 1896 national convention:

> What we need is an Andrew Jackson to stand, as Jackson stood, against the encroachments of organized wealth . . . . [M]y friends, the question we are to decide is: upon which side will the Democratic party fight; upon the side of "the idle holders of idle capital" or upon the side of "the struggling masses"? . . . [W]e will answer [the Republican] demand for a gold standard by saying to them: You shall not press down upon the brow of labor this crown of thorns! You shall not crucify mankind upon a cross of gold![53]

While support for silver was strong among many Republicans from the mountain and western regions, the GOP focused on the tariff issue. They blamed the Panic of 1893 and the depression that followed on tariff reform, even though Cleveland's reform effort, dysfunctional as it was, did not take place until 1894. The Republican national convention chose as its nominee Ohio governor William McKinley—returning to the national scene as the namesake of the controversial McKinley Tariff—to run on a protectionist platform.

Mark Hanna, a rough-edged industrialist and firm disciple of Alexander Hamilton's prescription of mixing business interests with government policy, managed McKinley's campaign. Hanna believed that all issues decided in a democracy were "questions of money" and later assumed the quintessential role of the wealthy businessman turned Gilded Age senator. Political cartoons in William Randolph Hearst's New York *Journal* portrayed Hanna covered with dollar signs as the commercial power controlling McKinley. Hearst later used similar cartoons attacking President McKinley's reluctance to go to war with Spain in Cuba because of opposition from business interests represented by Mark Hanna.[54] Deploying modern techniques for smothering the electorate with scary warnings about a potential Bryan presidency, Hanna was able to raise unprecedented amounts of campaign funds—dwarfing by twelve to one the amount raised by the Bryan campaign. The money came largely from manufacturing and financial interests opposed to lowering tariffs and ending the gold standard. In *Age of Betrayal*, a book devoted to the corrupting influence of money in politics in the post–Civil War era, author Jack Beatty concludes, "In 1896 corporations bought a controlling stake in the GOP."[55] Hanna's tactics employed to create a permanent Republican majority served as a model for modern campaigns and attracted the admiration of GOP political strategist Karl Rove, mastermind of a similar design a century later.

Finessing the silver issue by promising to take it up in an international agreement, McKinley promised a return to national prosperity through increased tariffs. The Republican candidate won with nearly 51 percent of the popular vote, by taking all of the industrial states of the North and East. Bryan, who blamed Grover Cleveland's legacy for his defeat, won all of the southern and most western states. It is entirely possible that Cleveland's "Gold Democrats" made the difference by voting for McKinley.

True to his promise, McKinley called Congress into extra session immediately after his inauguration solely to take up a bill to raise tariffs again. Nelson Dingley, a protectionist Republican from Maine, had in fact been working on such a bill for two years. Dingley had been named chairman of Ways and Means following the GOP takeover of the House in the 1894 election, in which his predecessor in the chair of Ways and Means, William L. Wilson, went down in defeat along with 112 other Democratic House members. The protected interests—particularly iron, steel, and wool—which had answered Mark Hanna's demand for contributions to the McKinley campaign, were now calling for their dividend. Dingley responded with a bill that restored many of the duties that had been reduced or eliminated in the 1894 Wilson-Gorman tariff bill and passed it out of the House two weeks after the session began.

The Senate took more time with the measure and, in keeping with its tradition, lowered some rates while awarding higher protection to industries simply for the asking. The secretary of the National Association of Wool Manufacturers even maintained a desk in the office of Finance Committee chairman Nelson Aldrich, as if he were the senator's clerk instead of being on the payroll of the wool interests. His efforts raised the rates on raw wool back to the level of the McKinley Tariff of 1890, and manufactured woolens received a record 55 percent tariff. The final bill of the House and Senate conference committee report raised the duties on many other products higher than the rates passed in either house because of new demands to equal the treatment favored to wool. The resulting Tariff Act of 1897, called the Dingley Tariff, pushed the protectionist envelope in many categories to new heights with average tariffs at 50 percent.

The Dingley Tariff, however, also opened the door to the possibility of negotiated tariff reform. The act provided the president authority to negotiate bilateral trade treaties with any other country in order to lower tariffs on the basis of reciprocity, subject to Senate ratification. After several decades of maintaining the most protected market in the world, the United States was finding more and more foreign markets closed to its own exports in retaliation at a time when the phenomenal growth of American industry had reached the saturation point in the domestic market. President McKinley, who had included reciprocity provisions in his 1890 act only to see them removed in the 1894 act, saw reciprocity negotiations as a complement to protection in expanding opportunities for domestic industry. He immediately appointed a special plenipotentiary to conduct bilateral trade negotiations and by the turn of the century had signed treaties with France, Germany, Italy, Argentina, and Portugal. The Republican leadership in the Senate, however, refused to take them up.

In the summer of 1901, following his overwhelming reelection victory the preceding year, McKinley began an effort to persuade the Senate to ratify the treaties. In what became his last speech—one he described as "the most important of my life"[56]—at the Pan-American Exhibition in Buffalo, New York, McKinley explained the simple rationale for reciprocity agreements:

> We must not repose in fancied security that we can forever sell everything and buy little or nothing. . . . The period of exclusiveness is past. The expansion of our trade and commerce is the pressing

problem. Commercial wars are unprofitable. A policy of goodwill and friendly trade relations will prevent reprisals. Reciprocity
treaties are in harmony with the spirit of the times; measures of
retaliation are not. If, perchance, some of our tariffs are no longer
needed for revenue, or to encourage and protect our industries at
home, why should they not be employed to expand and promote
our markets abroad?[57]

The next day, an anarchist shot and mortally wounded President
McKinley. In his first statement upon succeeding from his position as vice
president to the presidency, Theodore Roosevelt pledged "to continue absolutely unbroken the policy of President McKinley for the peace and prosperity and the honor of our beloved country."[58] But he quickly abandoned
this pledge, telling journalists on his first day in the White House, "I am
President and shall act in every word and deed precisely as if I and not
McKinley had been the candidate for whom the electors cast the vote for
President."[59]

5

Trade Reform in the Progressive Era

The question of monopoly and special privilege
undoubtedly centers in the tariff. That is the nest
where the brood is hatched.[1]
—Governor Woodrow Wilson, 1912

The promotion of prosperity for the American workingman was a prominent theme in speeches favoring protective tariffs throughout the Gilded Age. Proponents of protection argued that even marginally lower rates—often exaggerated as "free trade"—would stunt job growth and inevitably lead to the "pauper wages" paid in British industries. Yet, after nearly five decades of protectionist trade policy promoted in the name of labor, most wage earners in protected industries saw little or no benefit from high tariffs for favored industries while workers in nonprotected industries saw only higher prices. Income inequality and labor strife reached historic levels in the final decades of the nineteenth century. At the turn of the century, nearly 2 million children were working together with desperate women twelve hours daily, seven days a week in windowless sweatshops. Industrial and mine workers lived like serfs in company towns and city slums. And farmers struggled to survive in markets controlled by banks, railroads, and high tariffs.

Upton Sinclair, as a twenty-seven-year-old writer of fictional realism closely aligned with the investigative journalists of the emerging progressive era, gave a vivid and sensational description of the "wage slavery" common in industries at the turn of the century. His portrayal of the wretched, unsanitary working conditions in the Chicago meatpacking industry of the beef trust in his best-selling novel, *The Jungle*, accelerated nationwide attention to the stark divide between capital and labor during this era. "All day long," Sinclair writes of a fictional assembly worker paid on the basis of piece work production, "this man would toil thus, his whole being centered upon the purpose of making twenty-three instead of twenty-two and a half cents an hour: . . . and jubilant captains of industry would boast of it in their banquet halls, telling how our workers are nearly twice as efficient as those of any other country."[2]

The book, first serialized in 1905 in the socialist weekly newspaper *Appeal to Reason*, received immediate praise from President Theodore Roosevelt (TR). The president invited Sinclair to lunch at the White House and followed with his own investigation of the slaughterhouse and meat packaging industry, which led to passage of one of the first American consumer protection laws, the Pure Food and Drug Act in 1906. Sinclair's work drew worldwide attention as well, attracting a highly favorable review from a new member of the British Parliament, Winston Churchill, who was horrified by the "filthy, tragic, detestable details" presented in the book, for which society was indebted to its author if "only one-tenth part be true."[3]

The abusive effect of tariff protectionism upon workers and consumers is also condemned in the broad sweep of indictments that *The Jungle* brings against industry. In one scene Sinclair draws attention, with some irony, to a fictional GOP senator's campaign speech extolling the benefits of high tariffs to wage earners:

> The eloquent senator was explaining the system of Protection; an ingenious device whereby the working-man permitted the manufacturer to charge him higher prices, in order that he might receive higher wages; thus taking his money out of his pocket with one hand, and putting a part of it back with the other. To the senator this unique arrangement had somehow become identified with the higher verities of the universe.[4]

Investigative journalism, which proved to be a driving influence in the progressive movement, also weighed in for tariff reform. The most acclaimed group of journalists practicing in this genre—Ida Minerva Tarbell, Ray Stannard Baker, Lincoln Steffens, and William Allen White—staffed *McClure's Magazine*, an illustrated literary and political monthly first published in 1893. *McClure's* creator, Samuel S. McClure, was a temperamental genius bubbling over with ideas for political investigation and with a remarkable eye for literary talent. He introduced his American readers to Rudyard Kipling, Arthur Conan Doyle, J. M. Barrie, and Robert Louis Stevenson, and brought Willa Cather and Stephen Crane on staff. It was the thorough and blistering political pieces, however, that brought *McClure's* to national prominence as the progressive standard-bearer. Ray Baker's comprehensive analysis of J. P. Morgan's predatory and anti-competitive consolidation of multiple steel manufacturers into the U.S. Steel Corporation and Ida Tarbell's serialized account of the abusive business practices of John D. Rockefeller in creating the Standard Oil monopoly brought fame to the writers and spurred public condemnation of the trusts. Receiving wide acclaim for her Standard Oil series later published as a two-volume book, Tarbell, according to Sam McClure, became "the most famous woman in America."[5]

Following a dispute with the mercurial Sam McClure, Ida Tarbell and the other stars on *McClure's* staff left the magazine in 1906 and formed a rival, *The American Magazine*. A central theme in the work of these journalists addressed the poor working conditions for American labor and the vast inequality of income and wealth dividing labor and capital at the turn of the century. Tarbell considered "the question of special privilege, and the unequal distribution of wealth which special privilege entails" to be "the greatest issue before the American people." She held that the protective tariff, which "fosters special privilege," was "responsible for many of those social inequalities which are the curse of the body politic," and contributed to the centralization of American "wealth in the hands of a few individuals."[6] As her first exposé in the new journal, Tarbell wrote a six-part series, published in 1906–07, depicting the overbearing special interests and corrupt politics of tariff-making in the half century since the Civil War.

TR AND TAFT

President Roosevelt developed close relationships with the team at *McClure's* and drew support from them in his own attacks on the trusts, even though this relationship was strained a bit when the president attacked investigative reporters in a 1906 speech in which he dubbed them "muckrakers."

FIGURE 5.1 Presidents Theodore Roosevelt and William Howard Taft c.1909 (Library of Congress)

TR explained to Ray Baker that he was referring to the scandal writers at the Hearst newspapers, but he had painted the muckraker title with a broad brush and investigative reporters everywhere adopted the smear as a badge of honor. Another difference the president had with the group was that he remained unmoved by the growing anti-protectionist faction of the progressive movement.

On the tariff issue, Roosevelt had a history of benign ambivalence. While a student at Harvard, he had favored a free-trade philosophy, but upon entering Republican politics he easily shed his liberal trade policies for the safer political position as a protectionist. "Thank God I am not a free trader," he wrote in 1895, and protectionists often quote him as one of their own.[7] The truth is that the subject never excited him one way or the other—especially not to the degree that he was enthused by war, territorial expansionism, and later by conservation, anti-trust, and business regulation. In an early draft of his first message to Congress he included a passage promoting McKinley's reciprocity treaties. Only a month after McKinley's death, however, Roosevelt began his reeducation on trade politics in a meeting with Joseph Wharton, the protectionist steel maker and lobbyist from Pennsylvania. When Wharton opposed the draft reciprocity language that Roosevelt shared with him in the meeting, the new president decided to confer on the matter with Senator Aldrich, who now effectively ran the Senate for the Republicans. Following an afternoon with Aldrich, who advised him that there should be "no tinkering with the tariff," Roosevelt backed off the McKinley reciprocity policy.[8]

One could hardly accuse the intrepid leader of the Rough Riders' charge up San Juan Hill of timidity, but the young president's progressive ideals were in this case tempered by political realism. Roosevelt may have been a "damned cowboy," as Mark Hanna referred to him, and he did end the post–Civil War period of weak presidents, but he could not afford a near certain loss in a major legislative battle this early in his presidency. Even if he could have gotten McKinley's reciprocity treaties ratified with a two-thirds vote in the protectionist-dominated Senate—which was highly unlikely—the chance that the Republican House leadership would pass legislation implementing the treaties' lower tariffs was at best minimal. Uncompromising devotion to protection had been a core Republican principle for over four decades. Senator Hanna, then chairman of the Republican National Committee and a prominent rival for the 1904 presidential nomination, warned TR, "As long as I remain in the Senate and can raise a hand to stop you, you will never touch a schedule of the tariff act."[9] Unlike Grover Cleveland, Roosevelt was not willing to wager all of his political capital against such odds. Besides, he considered tariffs a rather boring issue "of expediency and not of morality."[10] He was preparing an attack against corporate trusts—which *was* an issue of morality for him—and did not want a defeat over tariffs to diminish his credibility.

Roosevelt even submitted his speeches on tariffs and monetary matters to Aldrich for approval to be sure that what he said was "along lines upon which all of us can agree." Any tariff modifications, he said, should be made "primarily from the standpoint of business interests."[11] Except for his unsuccessful effort to lower tariffs for Cuba and the Philippines, motivated by a moral obligation he felt following the Spanish-American War, Roosevelt avoided the tariff issue for the remainder of his first term.

While the protective tariff remained a key part of the GOP campaign in the presidential election of 1904, the movement for tariff reform was gaining momentum within the party. The National Association of Manufacturers began calling for negotiation and passage of reciprocity treaties in 1900 to provide a market for "excess production." International reaction to the Dingley Tariff had sparked a trade war against American exports in many parts of the world, and American agricultural exports were effectively shut down. Republicans in the western agricultural states reacted passionately. The view of Mark Twain—who had defected with the Mugwumps in supporting Cleveland over the scandal-ridden James Blaine in the 1884 election—was typical of many western and progressive Republicans who felt that high tariffs discriminated against the West and fostered monopolies:

> By a system of extraordinary tariffs [the Republican Party] has cre-ated a number of giant corporations in the interest of a few rich men & by most ingenious & persuasive reasoning it has convinced the multitudinous and grateful unrich that the tariffs were insti-tuted in their interest.[12]

Iowa governor Albert B. Cummins, a progressive Republican, pro-posed the "Iowa Idea" to eliminate all tariff protection on products of industries that were part of a trust. Though many believed that the tariff was the "mother of all trusts," Roosevelt separated the tariff issue from his progressive agenda against the monopolists he called masters of "predatory wealth . . . accumulated on a giant scale by all forms of iniquity."[13] He blamed these "malefactors of great wealth"[14] for the Panic of 1907. Nevertheless, reformers like Mark Twain, who never returned to the Republican Party, could not accept Roosevelt as a true opponent of monopolies so long as he continued to support protectionist tariffs.

Roosevelt talked about proposals to revise the tariffs from time to time in his second term but was never willing to enter a futile and politically damaging fight over the issue with the conservative Republican leadership in Congress. This leadership now included not only Nelson Aldrich—*the* power in the Senate at this time—but also the new dictatorial Speaker of the House, Joseph G. Cannon (R-IL), a diehard protectionist of the GOP's "Old Guard," with whom the progressive president was often at odds. Roosevelt considered his struggle for anti-trust and corporate regulation a matter of principle for which he was willing to fight. "On the tariff," he said, "I shall not break with my party."[15] "By all signs," Ida Tarbell observed, "Theodore

Roosevelt should have been the Richard Cobden of our tariff reform, but he did not see it as a dragon worthy of his steel."[16]

One of Roosevelt's close confidants, however, did favor tariff revision—his secretary of war and handpicked successor in the White House, William Howard Taft. Like Roosevelt, Taft had been taught to appreciate the virtues of free trade during his Ivy League education. His teacher had been the famous free-market economist and sociologist William Graham Sumner at Yale. Even after he entered the political arena, Taft consistently opposed high tariffs. As governor-general of the Philippines, he argued for free trade between the United States and its new territorial bounty from the war with Spain. When he entered the presidency in 1909, Taft, as TR's protégé, openly committed to carrying out his predecessor's unfinished progressive agenda and vowed to go further by revising tariffs. Soon, however, the new president would gravely disappoint Roosevelt, as it soon became clear that he was ill-prepared to be an effective advocate of the TR progressive agenda and his own promise of tariff reform. Like Grover Cleveland before him, Taft was well intentioned on reform but lacked the political skill, personality, and stamina to carry it out.

In the beginning, Taft did make an effort to fulfill his promise on tariffs, and the time was ripe for revision. Protectionism appeared to have reached its peak even within the Republican Party. A contingent of "insurgent" Republican senators—prominently led by Robert La Follette of Wisconsin—was ready to carry the progressive movement fostered by Theodore Roosevelt to the next level. Gaining more and more influence within the party, they demanded sweeping reform, including lower tariffs. Even the old "robber tariff baron," Andrew Carnegie, now retired to a life of leisure and philanthropy after selling his steel business to the financial conglomerate led by J. P. Morgan, called for dismantling protection for most imports in an essay he titled "My Experience with, and Views upon, the Tariff." Subpoenaed by Congress to defend his essay, Carnegie testified: "The time for free trade has come so far as steel is concerned." To the outrage of his successors at the U.S. Steel Corporation, who were still very much insisting on protection and saw Carnegie's comment as a hypocritical betrayal, he maintained that the steel companies would be better off without the tariff than continuing under "the present coddling system."[17]

In the spring of 1909 as Congress began taking up Taft's trade proposal, Ida Tarbell added more articles to her anti-tariff series, which would later be published in her book *The Tariff in Our Times*. In one article entitled

FIGURE 5.2 *Puck*'s portrayal of ex-robber baron Andrew Carnegie as "Brutus" turning against protection for the steel industry after he sold his interest: "Et tu, Andy!" (Library of Congress)

"Where Every Penny Counts," she observed that "a recurring note" in the congressional tariff hearings "was contempt for the suggestion that this or that duty made an article cost a cent or two more at retail." Reviewing in detail the average wages of workers in a number of protected industries, including steel, textile, and shoe manufacturing, she found that millions of American families earned less than $500 a year. "To these families," Tarbell wrote,

> an increase of a cent in the price of a quart of milk is something like a catastrophe . . . . [E]very penny added to the cost of food, of coal, of common articles of clothing, means simply less food, less warmth, less covering, when at the best they never can have

enough of any one of these necessaries. These budgets are a powerful demonstration that the rapid rise in the cost of living under the
Dingley Bill was to a vast number of people of this country nothing
less than a tragedy.

Average commodity prices rose over 35 percent in the ten years following the Dingley Tariff Act of 1897, as national wealth grew at "sensational"
levels but wages for manufacturing workers grew at less than 2 percent
per year.[18] Tarbell had genuine affection for President Taft, considering
him "one of the most kindly, modest, humorous, philosophical of human
beings."[19] Both she and her colleague Ray Baker believed that he was sincere about tariff revision, and her series of articles added momentum to his
effort. Unlike TR in his anti-trust efforts, Taft never took advantage of the
journalists' offer of support to the tariff reform effort.

Regardless of the growing strength of the reform movement among progressives, the eastern establishment and Old Guard Republican conservatives still held the balance of power in Congress. From the outset, Speaker
Joe Cannon—whom the proper and judicious Taft considered a rube and
reactionary tyrant—was his principal obstacle. With the power to appoint all
committee members and chairmen, control all legislation, and require members to obtain his advance permission to speak on the House floor, Cannon
was the most powerful speaker in US history. He had opposed Taft's plank
in the Republican Party platform pledging tariff revision. Knowing that Taft
intended to call Congress into an extra session for tariff reform as soon as
he was sworn in, the speaker threw down the gauntlet after Taft's election
with a protectionist speech opposing any significant reductions and implying that the platform position on tariff reform should not be taken seriously.
Taft was furious, observing that the speech "was of a character that ought to
disgust everybody who believes in honesty in politics and dealing with people squarely."[20] The president responded by deciding to assist the progressive Republican "insurgents" in Congress in defeating Cannon's reelection
as speaker or at least in modifying the rules so as to strip Cannon's dictatorial power in the House. Taft soon abandoned his effort to defeat Cannon's
reelection after being warned by close allies, including TR, that it was a quixotic and highly risky move, certain to fail. Nevertheless, he maintained hope
that the rules could be changed to neutralize Cannon.

After thirty progressive Republicans refused to join the party caucus in
pledging to vote for the existing rules, Cannon—joined by Senator Aldrich,

and Ways and Means chairman Sereno E. Payne of New York—paid a visit to the White House. They advised Taft that if the rules went down in defeat, tariff reform was doomed to suffer a similar demise. On the other hand, they promised that if the president would support the existing rules, the three legislative leaders would agree to follow his lead on tariff reform. Taft accepted the deal, losing forever his credibility with the progressive insurgents with whom he had been aligned to dethrone Cannon.

Following a weak presidential message opening the special session, which the clerk read in two minutes to the great disappointment of progressives, Chairman Payne introduced a bill containing tariff reductions that were not as deep as the president had desired, yet substantial enough for him to accept. Payne's proposal contained significant reductions for raw materials and for farm and manufacturing tools. At Taft's request—and over Cannon's objection—the bill also eliminated tariffs on iron, coal, and hides. Within a month, the House passed the bill on a party-line vote and sent it to the Senate, where Senator Aldrich took control. As the *New York Press* observed, "The house makes the tariff, Senator Aldrich, pretty much single-handed, remakes it."[21]

Aldrich revised the bill in the Finance Committee, allowing over 800 amendments, which he claimed provided more rate cuts than the Payne bill. Although many of the amendments were technical and difficult to decipher, it soon became clear that, in fact, the Aldrich bill moved rates higher and that new protections were concealed in the details of obscure new classifications hidden in vastly expanded tariff schedules intelligible only to experts. "As a rule, it is safe to say that a Congressman understands rarely the real meaning of the rates he votes for," Tarbell observed. "What he understands is that the Committee has made the bill for what it considers sound party reasons, . . . and he accepts it without too much scrutiny."[22] The progressives in this case, however, studied Aldrich's work carefully and exposed the fact that the new Senate bill actually increased average rates above those in the Dingley Tariff of 1897. Cheered on by Democrats who were otherwise hamstrung in the minority, Senator La Follette led the progressive midwestern Republicans in attacking Aldrich and his conservative allies on the Finance Committee—prominently including Henry Cabot Lodge of Massachusetts and Reed Smoot of Utah.

At first, President Taft was shocked by the Aldrich bill and encouraged the insurgents to keep up the fight for lower rates. He advised La Follette that he would veto the bill if it were not improved. But after several conferences with Aldrich and Cannon, the president again abandoned the reformers and gave his support to the Aldrich camp. Taft's shifting position revealed not only a new respect and personal affinity for Aldrich but also an increasing disdain for the "so-called progressives," as he began to refer to them. He simply did not have the inclination to attack the leaders of his party in Congress, even as he knew that such an attack would have been popular with the public. As the tariff debate continued and his friendship with Aldrich grew stronger, Taft came to view the progressives as "self-centered, self-absorbed" and their attacks on Aldrich and Cannon as demagogic. He said they were not Republicans, but only "assistant Democrats."[23]

Progressives working in coalition with Democrats also introduced another element in the Senate bill, namely, income tax, further complicating matters for Taft. Congressman Cordell Hull of Tennessee—only in his second term and following in the footsteps of a predecessor and mentor, Benton McMillin, co-author of the 1894 income tax—proposed the adoption of an income tax in the House bill. After Speaker Cannon blocked consideration of his amendment, Hull encouraged a Senate sponsor to take up his proposal. Similar to the approach taken in the 1894 Wilson-Gorman Act, insurgent Republicans and Democrats agreed to propose taxing 2 percent of individual and corporate incomes exceeding $5,000. Even though Taft had previously advocated an income tax, he joined Aldrich in opposing the coalition's amendment, which had garnered a majority in the Senate of supporters to challenge the Supreme Court's *Pollock* decision. Aldrich disliked the measure not only for its effect on the wealthy but also due to his fear that it would generate so much revenue that the case for continuing protective tariffs would be further weakened. With support from Taft, Aldrich offered a compromise: a proposed constitutional amendment, overruling *Pollock* and granting Congress broad taxing powers "on incomes, from whatever source derived, without apportionment among the several States."

Aldrich's plan was disingenuous; he knew how difficult it would be to obtain ratification of the amendment by the required three-fourths of the states and believed ratification failure would kill forever the chances of reviving an income tax as an alternative to tariff revenues. Although many of the coalition supporters of the income tax provision saw Aldrich's shrewd maneuver as insincere, he won over enough insurgents to support it and boxed in the remaining opposition. After an overwhelming vote approving the constitutional amendment, Aldrich was able to push his tariff bill through by threatening to reduce tariffs on goods produced in the states of senators voting against the bill. On the income tax amendment, Aldrich proved to have outsmarted himself. His state of Rhode Island—where his political influence reigned supreme—voted it down in 1910. By 1913, however, following a wave of Democratic and Progressive legislative victories across the country, forty-two states had ratified the amendment, giving it six states more than were required for adoption.[24]

On tariffs, President Taft believed that he could obtain improvements on the Senate bill in the conference committee appointed to resolve the House and Senate differences. Aldrich had convinced him that the excesses in the Senate bill were forced on Aldrich to get the measure through his chamber and could be sacrificed in conference. Both Cannon and Aldrich had assured Taft that he would be allowed to have great influence on the final bill in conference, although the two leaders had made sure that only high protectionists were appointed to the committee. After a protracted struggle, Taft was able to get the conference committee to include solid reductions on a number of products, including some raw materials—coal, iron ore, and hides—and a few manufactured products such as boots and shoes. The final bill also included the creation of a tariff commission to recommend rates based on "scientific" schedules and an income tax on corporations doing interstate business. It gave the president the authority to raise tariffs by 25 percent of value on products from countries "unduly" discriminating against the United States. While the Payne-Aldrich Tariff Bill that emerged from conference leaned heavily toward the Aldrich version, maintaining in some form most of more than 800 Senate amendments, Taft declared victory, hailing it as "a substantial achievement in the direction of lower tariffs and downward revision" and "the best tariff bill that the Republican Party has ever passed."[25]

Outside the eastern Republican establishment, however, there were few, if any, endorsements of the analysis and accolade that Taft bestowed upon the Payne-Aldrich Tariff. The midwestern progressives in his party, who had voted against the measure, charged that Taft had been duped. They attacked Aldrich and Cannon as shills for big business monopolies and financial tycoons who had betrayed the Republican platform pledge to lower tariffs. La Follette called the act "the consummation of privilege more reprehensible than had ever found a place in the statutes of the country."[26] Many progressive newspapers agreed, demanding the removal of the "trust serving" legislative dictators. Governor John A. Johnson, Democrat of Minnesota, drew applause from a Seattle audience, which included many Republican journalists, when he urged progressives in the West to join Democrats in the South in a political rebellion against the Old Guard

Republicans. Following passage of Payne-Aldrich, Ida Tarbell wrote that Senator Aldrich had managed the process by "carrying on a traffic in duties" and concluded that the powerful senator had been motivated by the principle "that the tariff, properly worked, was the surest road to power and to wealth that this country offered to a politician."[27] With this bill, however, the road ahead appeared less certain. Payne-Aldrich brought no measurable "downward revision," as Taft had claimed it would, and effectively placed protectionist politicians on the defensive with a tariff-weary public. Tarbell, who had had high hopes for Taft's reform effort in the beginning, lost faith in him completely following the signing ceremony, which she considered a "defeat of the popular will." To her friend and colleague William Allen White, she wrote, "Taft is done for, I fully believe."[28]

By 1910, protectionist Republicans—who had claimed credit for the economic boom following the Dingley Tariff of 1897—were awarded the blame for the economic depression that began with the Panic of 1907 and continued after passage of the Payne-Aldrich Tariff of 1909. Both Democrats and progressive Republican insurgents attributed the soaring cost of living afflicting the working class to protectionism and its byproduct, the despised monopolies that had a stranglehold on the American economy.

While there were causes other than high tariffs contributing to the economic stress of average Americans, the perception of blame cast upon the protectionist leaders of the Republican Party dominated the political atmosphere. The Democrats triumphed on this issue in the congressional midterm elections in 1910—picking up fifty-six seats and control of the House for the first time in sixteen years. Republicans also lost ten seats in the Senate, but retained control and became the perfect foil for Democrats and GOP progressives attempting to pass trade reform in the House knowing that the conservative "standpatters" in the upper house would oppose it. The stage was thus set for tariffs to become the primary issue of the 1912 presidential election.

NEW NATIONALISM AND THE DIVIDED REPUBLICAN PARTY

If the ongoing economic crisis were not enough to threaten the GOP's sixteen-year reign over the White House, a sharp division rising within the party was also emerging to cripple its hopes of retaining power. Having seen President Taft align himself with eastern conservatives early in his administration, western progressives in the party realized that they needed a candidate more sympathetic to their views for the next election. Senator Robert La Follette began organizing a challenge, but he was viewed as too extreme by many and had difficulty drawing a following outside his home base in Wisconsin. Eventually, it was Theodore Roosevelt—Taft's friend and political benefactor—who became the principal progressive threat to Taft and ultimately to the Republican Party.

After attending Taft's inauguration in March 1909, Roosevelt departed on a yearlong safari in Africa and grand tour of European capitals. While he was abroad, Roosevelt learned that his old friend was failing on his promise to carry on the TR progressive agenda. Taft had even fired Roosevelt's close friend, Chief Forester Gifford Pinchot, who had been in charge of implementing the former president's aggressive conservation measures. Although he was not ready to begin a campaign against Taft when he returned in 1910, Roosevelt was no doubt flattered by the appeals he received from progressives who had begun establishing "Back from Elba" clubs to draft his nomination.[29]

While on a western speaking tour—as he put it, "to announce myself on the vital issues of the day"—Roosevelt presented a radically progressive platform for his potential campaign in late August in Osawatomie, Kansas. The occasion of the speech, before a crowd of 30,000 adoring enthusiasts, was the dedication of the John Brown Memorial Park near the location where the fanatical abolitionist had led a skirmish against pro-slavery men in the "Battle of Osawatomie." But the former president, hardly mentioning Brown, chose an entirely different theme for his speech that became known as the "New Nationalism Address." Endorsing Abraham Lincoln's declaration that "Labor is the superior of capital, and deserves much the higher consideration," Roosevelt called for "equality of opportunity" in the conflict between "the men who possess more than they have earned and the men who have earned more than they possess." He urged freeing the government of the "sinister influence" of the "great special business interests [which] too often control and corrupt the men and methods of government for their own profit."

Roosevelt's New Nationalism went far beyond his previous slogan promoting a "Square Deal" for all, with the federal government merely acting as an objective umpire. He now proposed a powerful federal government that would boldly intervene and regulate the economy to guarantee social justice for laborers in conflict with capitalists. This executive power would be "the steward of the public welfare," with the judiciary to be focused on "human welfare rather than . . . property" and the legislature to "represent all the people rather than any one class." Observing that corporate political expenditures were "one of the principal sources of corruption in our political affairs," he called for federal laws prohibiting the use of "corporate funds directly or indirectly for political purposes." In a prescient portrait of the modern, post–New Deal welfare state, he proposed strict control over business activities, regulation of child labor and women in the workplace, minimum wage laws, comprehensive workman's compensation acts, enforcement of sanitary and safe working conditions, and expanded public education opportunities for workers. He also urged enactment of a graduated income tax and a graduated inheritance tax "on big fortunes."[30]

Historian George E. Mowry called the New Nationalism Address "the most radical speech ever given by an ex-President" and, from the perspective of 1910, "nothing short of revolutionary."[31] Contemporary reaction was mixed. The conservative press in the East unloaded on Roosevelt, calling him "self-seeking, hypocritical" and "frankly socialistic" and warning "every honest and patriotic citizen to prepare himself against this new Napoleon" who was out "to overthrow and destroy in the name of public opinion . . . and personal advancement."[32] On the other hand, the progressive insurgents loved the speech, taking it as an indictment of Taft. Indeed, Gifford Pinchot, Roosevelt's close associate who had been fired by Taft, had drafted the speech and was among the entourage of progressives traveling with TR in Kansas. The former president remained on the fence, nonetheless, refusing to endorse Taft while resisting entering the race himself.

Meanwhile, Taft, with a boost from Old Guard Republicans offended by Roosevelt's speech, commenced his campaign for renomination. Responding to the avalanche of criticism he had received for the Payne-Aldrich Tariff, the president began several initiatives to address his weakness among progressives. During the summer of 1910, he moved for trade liberalization by initiating negotiations for a reciprocity agreement with Canada that would have eliminated tariffs on agricultural products and dramatically reduced industrial tariffs in both countries as a means of slowing the soaring cost of living. When announced early the next year, the agreement drew strong opposition from Republican standpatters and praise from some, but not all, progressives. Since many of the insurgent

Republicans represented western farmers who feared a surge of agricultural imports from the North, Taft had to rely heavily on Democrats for passage of implementing legislation. Embarrassingly, however, the initiative fell flat when the Canadian Parliament failed to approve their side of the bargain.

In another move intended to boost Taft's progressive credentials, the Justice Department filed an anti-trust case against the U.S. Steel Corporation, J. Pierpont Morgan, John D. Rockefeller, Andrew Carnegie, and others for illegal monopoly activities, stifling competition in restraint of trade. This action backfired politically, however, as a widely publicized allegation included in the legal petition asserted that former president Roosevelt had been duped into allowing U.S. Steel to acquire a competing firm during the Panic of 1907. The insult inferred by this accusation infuriated TR, who publicly defended his approval of the acquisition and charged the president with hypocrisy, as Taft had also approved the deal while serving as a member of TR's cabinet. This incident proved to be the coup de grâce for the friendship between the temperamental Roosevelt and Taft. Within three months Roosevelt entered the race for president, announcing his candidacy for the nomination in February 1912.

Roosevelt famously declared that he was "fit as a bull moose," when asked by a reporter whether he was up for the challenges ahead, and soon began charging aggressively like an enraged moose, as he launched bitter personal attacks against his old friend, the incumbent president. Taft, however, had a firm hold on the conservative leadership in most state parties that controlled delegate selection for the GOP's nominating convention. Undaunted, Roosevelt called for presidential preference primaries to allow selection of the delegates by rank-and-file voters among whom he had broad support. Of the thirteen states that held primaries, Roosevelt won nine of them, including Taft's home state of Ohio, with Taft and La Follette splitting the remaining four. While Roosevelt also picked up a large number of delegates from state conventions, Taft and the Old Guard maintained a firm grip on the national convention's proceedings in Chicago and overruled every challenge posed by Roosevelt supporters to unseat seventy-two Taft delegates whom they claimed had been fraudulently chosen. Taft won the nomination on the first ballot. Outraged by the manner in which he had been steamrolled at the convention, Roosevelt soon accepted the call of his supporters to run on the ticket of a newly formed third party, the Progressive, or as the newspapers dubbed it, the "Bull Moose" Party.

WILSON, DEVOTED FREE-TRADER, EMERGES

With the Republicans now formally split down the middle and GOP economic policies in widespread disfavor, the Democrats had high hopes for recapturing the White House. But they were without a leading candidate. William Jennings Bryan—the Great Commoner who had been the party's nominee in three of the previous four elections—was finally fading as an effective standard-bearer and the door was open for new leadership. Two prospects with deep political roots emerged from the House of Representatives: Speaker Champ Clark of Missouri, a progressive from the Bryan wing of the party, and the more conservative Oscar W. Underwood of Alabama, chairman of the Ways and Means Committee and political leader of the tariff reform movement. It was a third unlikely candidate, however, who survived the nomination process: the cerebral scholar, Woodrow Wilson.

With less than two years in elective politics as the governor of New Jersey, Wilson, having spent the previous twenty years in academia, was largely unknown nationally. He certainly had an impressive academic pedigree garnered at Davidson College, Princeton, and the University of Virginia Law School. After a brief, unpleasant attempt at practicing law in Atlanta, Wilson finished his education with a PhD in political science from Johns Hopkins University. An accomplished orator, Wilson had an abiding interest in entering politics but ultimately found his calling as a highly popular professor of jurisprudence and political economy at Princeton. In 1902, the Princeton trustees elevated Wilson to president of the university. In that capacity he initiated a reform program, which effectively raised Princeton to the top echelon of American academic institutions. However, some of his reforms—such as his unsuccessful effort to ban Princeton's social "eating clubs"—created turmoil among wealthy alumni and great stress to his health. Fortunately, the publication of his five-volume work, *History of the American People*, which was first serialized in *Harper's Weekly* and became a bestseller, put him on the speaking circuit and created an escape from his academic burdens. Wilson soon attracted attention as a frequent speaker on national political issues before a wide variety of audiences.

During his academic years, Wilson was a political disciple of enlightened conservatives, especially the English statesman Edmund Burke, favoring the promotion of social harmony through evolutionary, not revolutionary, reform. Wilson strongly opposed the emerging socialist movement and the violent labor strikes prevalent in his formative years. He was a Democrat in the philosophical mold of Grover Cleveland, with no taste for Bryan populism. As a "Gold Democrat" he was appalled by Bryan's "Cross of Gold" speech at the Democratic convention. He voted for the "National Democratic" splinter ticket against Bryan in the 1896 election. As late as 1908, Wilson described Bryan as "the most charming and lovable of men personally, but foolish and dangerous in his theoretical beliefs."[33]

Born in Virginia and raised mainly in Augusta, Georgia, and Columbia, South Carolina, Wilson was a southerner at heart and was guided by the deep moral and religious influence of his father, a Presbyterian minister. Even as he moved to the progressive left on most issues in the lead-up to his run for president, he always adhered to the white southern evangelical view that racial segregation was ordained by God. The length to which he enforced Jim Crow segregation in the executive branch when he became president was often cruel and inexcusable. After watching the first motion picture to be shown in the White House, D. W. Griffith's controversial 1915 silent film, *The Birth of a Nation*, which depicted African Americans despicably and the Ku Klux Klan favorably, he is often reported to have remarked, "It is all so terribly true."[34] Whether or not he actually made this comment, his segregationist views and policies on race never advanced beyond his regional heritage and would be a permanent stain on his record of progressive achievements as president.

Wilson's political philosophy combined a Calvinist view of moral law with British economic liberalism. His keen interest in trade policy was evident from the beginning of his education. As a Princeton undergraduate, he won a debate favoring the proposition that protective tariffs were not necessary for the protection of domestic industries. When applying to Johns Hopkins, he expressed interest in examining "the phases of the free trade controversy and . . . the general topics of political economy."[35] His views on the political economy were no doubt influenced by his southern heritage but were intellectually based on Adam Smith's *Wealth of Nations* and Burke's *Thoughts and Details on Scarcity*. He was particularly enamored of their insistence on the separation of government and business to allow the laws of nature and God to prevail in broadening economic opportunity and prosperity. The Hamiltonian concept of marrying government with the interests of the wealthy was anathema to Wilson's moral and intellectual principles. He was a devoted follower of the Manchester School of free-trade economics and social reforms, as espoused by the Liberal

British politicians Richard Cobden and John Bright. Along with images of his father and Burke, Wilson kept portraits in his Princeton study of ardent free-traders: Walter Bagehot, British essayist and early editor of the *Economist* magazine; and William Gladstone, British prime minister and leader of the Liberal Party.

Wilson's passion for free trade manifested itself in his very first public political statement, nearly three decades prior to his entry into elective politics. As a diversion from his preparation for his bar examination in Atlanta, Wilson testified in September 1882 before the US Tariff Commission, which was making its way around the country taking evidence for the purpose of possible tariff revisions. The young lawyer gave them an earful, calling for the repeal of all protective tariffs because "manufacturers are made better manufacturers whenever they are thrown upon their own resources and left to the natural competition of trade than when they are told, 'You shall be held in the lap of the government, and you need not stand upon your feet.'"[36] Wilson expressed privately at the time that tariffs were the most burdensome of all taxes, "for their weight falls most directly and most heavily on the poor and is least felt by the rich."[37] After his testimony, Wilson formed an Atlanta branch of the Free Trade Club of New York.

The lead-up to Wilson's first candidacy for public office in 1910 was an era peppered with explosive exposés of abusive monopoly practices written by muckraking journalists such as Ida Tarbell, Ray Baker, and Lincoln Steffens. Wilson soon became convinced that equal economic opportunity could not be achieved through natural law and free-market competition alone, and he began shifting his views decidedly leftward—from enlightened conservatism to passionate progressivism. Following the Panic of 1907, he declared that the lingering economic difficulties had in large part been brought on by the "privileged interests" and endorsed governmental restraint upon "those who enjoyed the very privilege which [the government] itself had granted."[38] For Wilson, offering praise for governmental intervention and restrictions on business was a significant move. Previously a devotee of laissez-faire economics, he had harshly criticized Theodore Roosevelt's "regulative passion." Similarly, his position on tariffs took a more combative political tack. After Congress passed the Payne-Aldrich Tariff in 1909, Wilson blasted the Republicans for collusion with protected monopolies— trading tariff favors for campaign contributions. He condemned the "pure favoritism and . . . dangerous and demoralizing special privilege" granted by the tariff legislation written under "the great and sinister hold [of] the chairman of the Finance Committee of the Senate," Nelson Aldrich.[39] And despite his long-held disapproval of aggressive union activities, Wilson hailed organized labor's fight with the trusts over increased wages.

In May 1909, Wilson's friend and early political champion George Harvey, the editor of *Harper's Weekly*, wrote in his newspaper: "We now expect to see Woodrow Wilson elected Governor of the State of New Jersey in 1910 and nominated for President in 1912 upon a platform demanding tariff revision downward."[40] Although the odds on Harvey's prediction were long when he wrote it—and he famously broke with Wilson before the presidential nomination—his commentary proved prescient. With the aid of the political machine of Democratic boss James Smith Jr., the president of Princeton University was elected governor of New Jersey in the national Democratic sweep of the 1910 elections. As a US senator in the 1890s, Smith had been called "Sugar Jim" for supporting tariffs favoring the sugar trust while investing in sugar stocks.[41]

During his first year in office, Wilson established his progressive bona fides by turning his back on the corrupt Smith machine, refusing to endorse Smith's return to the Senate and enacting an impressive record of liberal reforms. With strong bipartisan, progressive support, the Democratic-controlled legislature passed, among other reforms, Wilson's proposals for a corrupt practices act, election reform, workmen's compensation, and a public services commission to set utility rates. The Republicans regained control of the New Jersey legislature in 1911 and largely ignored the governor's 1912 proposals. But by then Wilson was preoccupied with running for president.

The first step Wilson took before formally entering the race was to confirm and nationalize his credentials on the most important issue of the day: tariff reform. While he had been consistently on the free-trade side of the argument for thirty years, Wilson lacked the political credibility on the issue enjoyed by his main Democratic opponents. Both Clark and Underwood had been at the forefront of the congressional tariff reform debate. To begin to address this problem, Wilson arranged an interview on the subject in late December 1911 with Joseph Pulitzer's Democratic-leaning *New York World*. He declared to the reporter that the tariff issue would be the "greatest" issue of the presidential campaign and added: "The tariff question is at the heart of every other economic question we have to deal with, and until we have dealt with that properly we can deal with nothing in a way that will be satisfactory and lasting."[42]

Wilson followed this interview with a stem-winding anti-tariff speech early the next month, setting the tone for the nomination campaign. He vowed to keep government and big business at arm's length on tariffs and blasted Republicans for being "controlled by business men," and for allowing them to write their own protective rates. "As a politician I'll agree not to trouble this country's business if this country's business men will agree not to trouble politics." On the protectionist claim that high tariffs are good for American workingmen, he responded, "I'd like to hear of any case in which any American businessman ever divided his tariff-obtained profits with his workmen." The theory that "if we make the captains of industry rich they would make the country rich," he exclaimed, "is like conferring charity on millionaires." Turning to face one side of the room and then the other, with his hand clenched and raised dramatically in the air, he shouted, "Oh, the infinite selfishness of these business men."[43]

At the same time, Wilson began moving even further into the progressive camp by offering an olive branch to the Great Commoner. Early in 1912, in an effort to divide the Democratic Party, the *New York Sun*—a conservative Republican and sharply anti-Wilson paper—published a five-year-old private letter from Wilson to a Princeton trustee critical of Bryan. "Would that we could do something at once dignified and effective," Wilson wrote, "to knock Mr. Bryan once and for all into a cocked hat." The evening after the letter was published, in Bryan's presence at a Jackson Day Dinner in Washington, Wilson acknowledged that he had occasionally differed with Bryan but offered penance by praising "the steadfast vision" and "the character and the devotion and the preachings of William Jennings Bryan."[44] The remark pleased Bryan and markedly enhanced the New Jersey governor's chances at the Democratic convention five months later in Baltimore.

Speaker Clark arrived at the convention with a nearly two-to-one lead in pledged delegates over Wilson, but far short of the two-thirds margin necessary for nomination. Having been a loyal lieutenant in Bryan's populist wing of the party, Clark was the presumed heir to the legacy of the perennial nominee. Going into the convention, Bryan had been officially neutral in the struggle between Clark and Wilson, the two leading progressives. But when Bryan heard that Clark had cut a deal to receive the endorsement of New York's Tammany Hall, including its notorious Wall Street plutocrats, Bryan proposed a resolution demanding that the convention oppose any nominee "under obligation to J. Pierpont Morgan . . . or any other member of the privilege-hunting and favor-seeking class."[45] In support of his resolution, Bryan charged, "An effort is being made right now to sell the Democratic party into bondage to the predatory interests of this nation . . . [and] to make the nominee the bond-slave of the men who exploit the people of this country."[46] The anti–Wall Street resolution passed by a wide margin with the support of Wilson's delegates. When the Tammany-led New York delegates eventually did switch their votes to the speaker, Bryan completely abandoned Clark. Although Bryan did not actually endorse the New Jersey governor, his followers and others moved to Wilson as the balloting progressed. Wilson finally won the nomination on the forty-sixth ballot and later appointed Bryan secretary of state, despite his limited foreign policy credentials, following the general election.

Returning to the Jacksonian Democratic demand that tariffs be collected "for revenue only," the convention also adopted the strongest tariff reform language since the Civil War. Charging that "excessive prices result in large measure from the high tariff laws enacted and maintained by the Republican party and from trusts and commercial conspiracies fostered and encouraged by such laws," the platform provided in its primary declaration:

> The high Republican tariff is the principal cause of the unequal distribution of wealth; it is a system which makes the rich richer and the poor poorer; under its operations the American farmer and laboring man are the chief sufferers; it raises the cost of the necessaries of life to them, but does not protect their product or wages.[47]

THE GENERAL ELECTION OF 1912

On the surface, the 1912 election was a three-way race among the incumbent president Taft, former president Roosevelt, and Governor Wilson. Taft adopted the mantle of the Old Guard conservatives of his part while TR largely represented the GOP progressives, though some prominent insurgents stuck with Taft, refusing to abandon their party; others, such as La Follette, infuriated with both Taft and TR, supported Wilson, the progressive Democrat. The tide had turned on the conservative Republicans, however, and Taft soon became practically irrelevant to the main event between the competing progressives in the new century's liberal political climate. As a sign of the mood of the country, even Eugene V. Debs, the labor leader imprisoned for his involvement in the violent 1894 Pullman strike,

FIGURE 5.3 Woodrow Wilson and William Jennings Bryan as a team in 1912 (Library of Congress)

was attracting a substantial following as the Socialist candidate. Clinging to the traditional approach for sitting presidents, Taft hardly campaigned; his challengers set a new standard for modern elections with whistle-stop speaking tours across the country, selling their respective, yet similar, progressive platforms to a receptive public. With most conservatives and the titans of big business having contempt for both Roosevelt and Wilson and the far left leaning toward Debs, the progressive candidates were fighting over the middle class and small business constituencies.

With guidance from Louis D. Brandeis—the progressive intellectual whom he would later appoint to the Supreme Court—Wilson responded to Roosevelt's "New Nationalism" with his own progressive program, which he called "New Freedom." While the social and economic goals of the two programs may have been parallel, the means of achieving them were not. Wilson criticized the preceding Republican administrations for taking the approach of Alexander Hamilton, in which "the only people qualified to conduct [government] were the men who had the biggest financial stake in the commercial and industrial enterprises of the country."[48] According to Wilson, Roosevelt's New Nationalism continued this failed approach by forming a partnership between the government and the trusts, which made the US government the "foster-child of the special interests."[49] Wilson pointed out that trusts had prospered more during Roosevelt's presidency than ever before. Rather than simply regulating the monopolies as Roosevelt proposed, Wilson planned to dismantle them altogether and adopt regulations to restore competition to the free enterprise system. Wilson's New Freedom called for an Adam Smith approach, in which the government would be freed from the interference of plutocrats and monopolies. He called for a "crusade" against the ruling monopolies "that have set us in a straight jacket to do as they please." "If America is not to have free enterprise," Wilson declared, "then she can have freedom of no sort whatever."[50]

In the same vein, Wilson's New Freedom persistently attacked protective tariffs as an impediment to free competitive enterprise, in sharp contrast to Roosevelt's approach. In his New Nationalism speech, Roosevelt had accepted as probably true the widely held opinion that special interests had been too influential in crafting tariff legislation and acknowledged that Republican tariff policy "put a premium on selfishness." Yet Roosevelt's ideas on tariff reform were quite conservative compared to his other more radical reform proposals. He continued to proclaim his belief in tariff protection, couching his goal in progressive terms: "to make it certain that protection is given to the man we are most anxious to protect—the laboring man."[51] With little deviation from then prevailing Republican positions, Roosevelt proposed only that an expert tariff commission—removed from political pressure or "improper business influence"—make revisions based on the difference between foreign and domestic labor costs. Wilson scoffed at this proposal, calling "cost of production" a "will-o'-the-wisp" and laughable as a basis for tariff legislation.[52] He opposed the expert tariff commission as nothing more than a delaying tactic and unnecessary for carrying out reforms designed simply to eliminate protectionist tariffs imposed for private profit. Under the New Freedom, Wilson declared, tariff reformers would enact fiscal laws, "not like those who dole out favors, but like those who serve a nation."[53]

The striking differences in the personalities and presentations of Roosevelt and Wilson often overshadowed their differences on economic issues. Roosevelt was jingoistic, impulsive, temperamental, and bombastic. Wilson was idealistic, cautious, serene, and aloof. Nearly a century later, the mannerisms of John McCain, a TR admirer, and Barack Obama in the 2008 presidential campaign mirrored their contrasting political personalities.

Despite the sharp personal and economic policy distinctions among the three candidates, the election results came in predictably along partisan lines. The hardcore conservative Republicans went to Taft with 23 percent of the vote. Most of the GOP progressives and TR loyalists stayed with Roosevelt, giving him 27 percent. Debs, representing the Socialists, took a surprising 6 percent. And Wilson won with a plurality of 42 percent of the popular vote and a landslide in electoral votes, by capturing both conservative and progressive Democrats and a substantial number of Mugwump Republicans disillusioned with Roosevelt.

Beyond the remarkable upheaval in the Republican Party, Wilson also received a boost from the first president of the American Federation of Labor (AFL), Samuel Gompers, who brought much of the organized labor vote to the Democratic ticket. This was a dramatic move for Gompers, as the New Jersey governor had been no ally to unions in the past and the AFL had generally been neutral on partisan politics and tariff issues.

Since its founding in 1886 under Gompers's leadership, the AFL had officially maintained a position of neutrality on protectionist trade policy due to the conflicting views of its participating unions and the possibility that the issue could become a wedge blocking unity among the AFL member unions. Some unions representing workers in import-sensitive industries favored protection, but many did not due to its effect on the cost of living and a general animosity toward the protected robber barons. In 1881, at the first convention of the AFL's predecessor, the Federation of Organized Trades and Labor Unions, a bitter dispute arose over a resolution favoring protection, which the protectionists won by a close margin. The following year, the organization voted again and withdrew its high-tariff endorsement in favor of neutrality. One of the Federation's early leaders, Frank K. Foster, read a paper in support of neutrality entitled "Protectionism *vs.* Wages," stating:

> Protection does not protect labor; the rate of wages depends upon other causes than the tariff; and labor, as the prime creator of wealth, is obliged to pay . . . enormous and unjust taxes that capital may benefit therefrom. . . . I appeal to you all to erase from the platform of the organized workers . . . this monopoly-nurturing, freedom-restricting section.[54]

John Jarrett, president of the Amalgamated Association of Iron and Steel Workers, who had led the fight for the protectionist side, withdrew his

FIGURE 5.4 AFL president Samuel Gompers at Democratic National Convention 1912
(Library of Congress)

union from the Federation for several years because of this issue. Over the
years, other unions also supported protection, but Gompers, as leader of
the AFL, maintained the neutrality policy until his death in 1924. Gompers
argued that American workers should depend on the labor movement
for their economic improvements, not government fiscal policy. Clearly,
Gompers personally opposed protectionism, seeing little benefit in it for
workers. His views seemed similar to those of another contemporary organization, the Knights of Labor, which maintained neutrality to avoid dissension among its members in the beginning but later condemned protective
tariffs as a tool of the industrial trusts that offered nothing for workers.[55]

THE UNDERWOOD TARIFF OF 1913

In his first inaugural address, President Woodrow Wilson outlined the
principal tasks his administration would pursue in implementing the New
Freedom: tariff reductions, banking and currency reforms to expand credit
for small business, and strengthening the Sherman Antitrust Act. He promised to address "the human cost . . . of our industrial achievements. . . . The
great Government we loved has too often been made use of for private and

selfish purposes, and those who used it had forgotten the people." His first priority was to lower the tariff, which, he noted, "cuts us off from our proper part in the commerce of the world, violates the just principles of taxation, and makes the Government a facile instrument in the hands of private interests."[56]

Wasting no time, the new president called Congress into session the month following his inauguration for the special purpose of passing tariff reform. Unlike Grover Cleveland, who transmitted his bold tariff reform speech to be read to Congress by the secretary of the Senate and offered little or no active involvement in enacting the reforms he had proposed, Wilson personally presented his case and engaged the full power of the presidency to see the process through.

An unabashed admirer of the British parliamentary system, Wilson had long favored a stronger relationship between the executive and legislative branches and took on the role of prime minister in pushing his legislative agenda. Opening the special session with a speech to both Houses, he became the first president to personally address Congress since Thomas Jefferson abandoned the practice in his first term. Relying on his own oratorical skills rather than a perfunctory reading by the clerk, Wilson sought

FIGURE 5.5 President Wilson was the first president to address Congress since John Adams when he called a special session for tariff reform in 1913 (Library of Congress)

to convey the importance of tariff reform in a more persuasive manner. Some in the congressional leadership were not pleased by what they saw as an invasion of their turf—Champ Clark, after all, had remained as speaker after losing the bitter nomination battle with Wilson. Fewer objections came from Republicans than from the president's own party, who preferred the "simple and democratic custom of Jefferson" to "a worn-out Republican custom," alluding to the practices of Federalists George Washington and John Adams. One southern senator likened Wilson's address to a "speech from the throne" and called it a "cheap and tawdry imitation of English royalty."[57] But the move proved highly effective and established an indispensable practice used by all of Wilson's successors. The practice of presidents in personally delivering annual State of the Union addresses to a joint session of Congress is one legacy of Wilson's innovation of personal engagement with Congress that began with this push for reduced tariffs.

Following his New Freedom theme, Wilson called for abolishing "the semblance of privilege or . . . artificial advantage" of protective tariffs and for putting American producers under "a constant necessity to be efficient, economical, and enterprising." The object of tariff duties, he said, should "be effective competition, the whetting of American wits by contest with the wits of the rest of the world."[58] After coming down from the rostrum, the president continued to press his case in informal discussions with members of Congress throughout the spring as Majority Leader and Chairman Oscar Underwood began drafting the bill in the Ways and Means Committee. In less than a month the measure rolled through the heavily Democratic House, reducing average tariffs from around 40 percent to 29 percent and putting a number of previously protected products on the duty-free list— including politically sensitive products, such as wool and sugar, the tariff for which was reduced to 1 percent and scheduled to become free of duty in 1916. Only five Democrats voted against the bill, four of whom were from sugar-producing Louisiana.

With tariffs at this time making up three-fourths of all federal government revenue, the bill also included a new revenue measure to compensate for the reduction in tariff income: an income tax authorized under the Sixteenth Amendment, which had been ratified largely as a response to the inequities of the regressive tariff system only two months prior. Congressman Cordell Hull, who drafted the income tax provisions in the House and managed their passage on the floor, hailed the new progressive tax as "the one great equalizer of the tax burden" in the long fight to lift the "vast burdens in consumption taxes from the backs of the poor and the masses generally and therefore a tremendous agency for the improvement of social conditions."[59] The new tax created a progressive structure with exemptions for low wage earners and with the top earners paying up to 7 percent. The tax affected less than 1 percent of the population, but easily produced more than sufficient revenue to offset the revenue from the tariff reductions.

As expected, the reform process brought on an onslaught of heavy pressure from lobbyists for the protected interests in the Senate, where the Democrats had only a six-vote majority, including several protectionist Democrats from wool and sugar-producing states. According to historian H. W. Brands, the "protection gang defended every ingot of steel, bolt of cloth, pair of shoes, sack of sugar, and bale of cotton as though the survival of the republic hung in the balance."[60] Wilson responded by calling them out for public condemnation from his new bully pulpit. "Washington has seldom seen so numerous, so industrious, or so insidious a lobby," he declared. "There is every evidence that money without limit is being spent to sustain this lobby, and to create an appearance of a pressure of public opinion antagonistic to some of the chief items of the tariff bill." He chastised the protectionists as "astute men" seeking "to overcome the interests of the public for their private profit," while the "people at large" without lobbyists are "voiceless in these matters."[61]

Wilson's offensive against the trade lobbyists was an unqualified success. The Senate formed a special committee to investigate the lobby and required senators to disclose any personal financial interest that might be affected by tariff revisions. The committee found that millions of dollars had been disbursed to keep the sugar tariff in place. Wilson's relentless attack put the brazen Senate protectionists in a box, foreclosing their tradition of successfully defending and maintaining the closed market system. In an unprecedented break with its past, the Senate voted to add more products to the free list, reduced the average tariff to 26 percent, and increased the rates of the highly controversial new income tax. Only two Democratic senators, both from Louisiana, voted against it, and two progressive Republicans, including La Follette, voted in favor. The result was shocking even to Wilson's supporters. "Think of it—a tariff reduction downwards after all," observed Agriculture Secretary David F. Houston, "Lower in the Senate than in the House! . . . A progressive income tax! I did not much think we should live to see these things."[62] One opponent, Senator Albert B. Cummins, a progressive Republican from Iowa who would often support Wilson initiatives, complained that the congressional surrender to the new president's "single will" showed that he had "more influence in the Congress of the United States than any man ever before had."[63]

Even so, the Tariff Act of 1913, known as the Underwood Tariff, was far short of the Democratic Party's traditional free-trade standard of "tariff for revenue only." Advocates of the bill called it a "competitive tariff," which the renowned economic historian of the period Frank W. Taussig defined as meaning "merely that protection should not be unnecessarily high, yet high enough to ensure the maintenance of domestic production."[64]

While it did not bring an end to protectionism, the Underwood Tariff was a major victory for Wilson against entrenched interests in both political parties. He had shrewdly manipulated Congress to produce the first substantial tariff reduction in more than fifty years. By reducing rates on dutiable products by one-third and expanding the free list to include more consumer "necessities" such as food, leather, and wool, he hoped to have established a precedent that would lead incrementally to free trade. Signing the bill on the evening of October 3, 1913, Wilson established a new tradition by using two gold pens, which he presented to Underwood and Senate Finance Committee chairman Furnifold M. Simmons of North Carolina, in an elaborate ceremony witnessed by at least fifty members of Congress and cabinet officials, including Assistant Secretary of the Navy Franklin D. Roosevelt and Congressman Cordell Hull, crowded around the president's desk in the Oval Office. Quoting from Shakespeare's *Henry V*, Wilson said, "If it be a sin to covet honor, then am I the most offending soul alive," explaining, "I have had the accomplishment of something like this at heart ever since I was a boy."

In an informal nine-minute speech, he gave credit and expressed "profound gratitude" to those in the room who had contributed to the great service to "the rank and file of the people of this country" in setting American business "free from those conditions which have made monopoly not only possible, but, in a sense, easy and natural." As if he were on a divine mission, Wilson concluded that he felt as though he were halfway along a journey at the end of which he would sleep "with a quiet conscience, knowing that we have served our fellow men, and have thereby tried to serve God."[65]

NEW FREEDOM, THE FEDERAL RESERVE,
AND TRADE EXPANSION

Tariff reform, coupled with the first permanent income tax, was only the first step in the implementation of the New Freedom reforms. Within eighteen months after his inauguration, during the longest legislative session in American history up to that time, Wilson also pushed through the enactment of the Federal Reserve System, the Clayton Antitrust Act, and the Federal Trade Commission. In view of these reforms and the labor and financial reforms passed later in his first term, Wilson biographer John Milton Cooper Jr. ranks him among the top three great legislative presidents along with Franklin Delano Roosevelt and Lyndon Baines Johnson.[66] Ending a period dominated by robber barons, monopolies, and their advocates in Congress, Wilson's legislative agenda marked the beginning of a fundamentally new epoch in the US economy, and the foundation of a new era in the global economy in which the United States would play a predominant role.

When Woodrow Wilson entered the White House, the United States was alone among the major world economies without a central bank. As with the free-trade movement, British liberals in the mid-nineteenth century led in transforming the Bank of England into a central bank and lender of last resort to stabilize the banking system and minimize the uncertainty of fluctuating currencies in international business. The Bank of England was originally a private institution chartered in 1694 to finance the Royal Navy and became instrumental in catapulting the British financial system to a leading role in the world market, especially after Prime Minister Robert Peel gave it a monopoly on issuing bank notes in 1844. In the United States, Alexander Hamilton convinced Congress to charter the First Bank of the United States in 1791 when there were only four other banks in the country. Allowed to lapse in 1811 during James Madison's presidency and renewed five years later, the Bank finally met its demise in 1832 when, with much populist fanfare, President Andrew Jackson vetoed the renewal of its charter. For the next eighty years, the American economic system survived with a weak, fragmented system of private banks periodically vulnerable to financial panics.

During the 1907 financial crisis, the era's leading financier, J. Pierpont Morgan, came to the country's rescue as he had in the previous decade by bailing out the federal government to prevent it from defaulting on European loans. In an inverted twist on the federal government bailout of

Wall Street a century later during the financial crisis of 2008, Morgan led a private effort in 1907 to raise enough money to save the nation's banking system from collapsing, but the crisis exposed the critical need for a better solution.

In 1908, the Republican-controlled Congress established the National Monetary Commission to study the banking system and make reform recommendations and appointed Senator Nelson Aldrich its chairman. Endorsing the call for reform, Aldrich observed, "We may not always have a Pierpont Morgan with us to meet the country's crisis."[67] Strongly influenced by a group of elite New York bankers who secretly convened with Aldrich at the exclusive tycoon retreat on Jekyll Island off the coast of Georgia, the commission proposed forming a central bank but leaving control of the financial system in the hands of the Wall Street banks. When Wilson assumed the presidency in 1913, however, Aldrich was not the new administration's ideal candidate as a credible advocate for banking reform. For more than a decade the wealthy protectionist had carried the water in the Senate for the special interests Wilson found most offensive. Democrats and progressive Republicans lined up against the Aldrich plan. Nonetheless, Wilson—whose party had opposed the establishment of a central bank since the founding of the party by Jefferson and Madison and certainly since its reconstruction under Andrew Jackson—found progressive reasons to abandon the Jefferson-Jackson opposition.

As governor in 1911, Wilson declared, "The great monopoly in this country is the money monopoly." A small group of "capitalists" controlled credit, he remarked, and a combination of New York banks "now practically exercises all the powers of a central bank . . . without any of the public responsibility which a central bank organized by Federal statute would necessarily have imposed upon it":

> The control of the system of banking . . . must be public, not private, must be vested in the Government itself, so that the banks may be the instruments, not the masters, of business and of individual enterprise and initiative.[68]

Wilson's views were fully documented and confirmed by Congressman Arsène P. Pujo, a Louisiana Democrat who chaired a 1912 House investigation into the powerful Wall Street "money trust" that dominated the nation's credit facilities. Louis Brandeis, a key Wilson adviser, popularized the work of the Pujo investigation in his book *Other People's Money,*[69] describing how an oligarchy of investment bankers stifled competition by funneling financial resources to companies in which they held interests.

In addition to providing more stability and fair competition to the financial system through the Federal Reserve Act, Wilson hoped to create a strong financial system independent of Europe in order to facilitate US export expansion. As in the case of tariff reform—where the principal purpose was to relieve the burden from the working class of an inequitable tax system favoring special monopoly interests—an important secondary purpose of tariff reform and the Federal Reserve Act was to open new markets for American exports. "We need foreign markets," he said in his speech accepting the Democratic nomination in 1912. "The tariff was once a bulwark; now it is a dam. For trade is reciprocal; we can not sell unless we buy."[70] To promote the opening of new markets for American products, Wilson championed lifting the legal restrictions that precluded national banks from engaging in foreign banking and forced American exporters to finance their trade transactions through foreign banks. Wilson corrected this disadvantage in the Federal Reserve Act by allowing national banks to accept drafts drawn on foreign trade and to establish foreign branches. He considered the Federal Reserve Act to be one of the great initiatives of his presidency in promoting international trade.

Wilson's initiative to open foreign markets also included a significant exception to his general abhorrence of trusts and monopolies. In most cases the president equated laissez-faire competition with business efficiency and believed it to be fundamental to a strong domestic economy. He felt that high tariffs, price fixing, and other unfair trade practices skewing the market in favor of the trusts undermined the natural efficiencies derived from fair competition. Despite some of his rhetoric, Wilson was not an enemy of big business as long as its success was based on competition and not monopolistic business tactics. On this point, Wilson saw a distinction between domestic competition and US export promotion. In its efforts to encourage business to go abroad, however, the Wilson administration supported exemptions from anti-trust laws codified in the Webb-Pomerene Act of 1918. These included "export combinations," that is, multi-company collusive arrangements that were essentially monopolies for export purposes. This policy acknowledged that foreign competition included combinations permitted under European trade expansion programs. William C. Redfield—Wilson's secretary of commerce and the first person to serve in that position after it became a separate department in 1913—believed that larger, integrated businesses were better able to compete in foreign markets than small firms. Redfield also made an exception to the standard Jacksonian Democratic opposition to business-government partnerships by adding commercial attachés to American embassies in key foreign markets in order to assist in locating buyers for US products.

TRADE AND THE CONSEQUENCES OF WAR

The eruption of war in Europe in August 1914 transformed the trade environment for US manufacturers and for the architects of trade policy. The war wreaked havoc on commercial markets all across the European continent and provided new opportunities for American exporters to supply the belligerents with goods no longer available from enemy sources. It also opened new foreign markets traditionally supplied by war-strained European exporters. By early 1915, the trade focus in both the public and private sectors centered on Latin America, whose import markets had long been dominated by Europeans. But the withdrawal of European vessels as a result of the war also engendered a crying need for new shipping capacity. A need for alternative financial facilities for foreign transactions was also revealed as London financial institutions, which had previously controlled the international credit market, became preoccupied with the demands of the war. To address these problems, Secretary of the Treasury William G. McAdoo in May convened the Pan-American Financial Conference; all members of the president's cabinet, the Federal Reserve Board, and prominent business leaders and financiers attended. By the end of 1916, US banks had established foreign trade facilities and a foreign exchange market in American dollars, which began to supplant British sterling as the dominant world currency, and Congress had begun to create a government-owned and -operated merchant marine service.

Transatlantic commerce, however, proved more and more difficult for merchants and travelers from the United States after war had broken out and the belligerents had imposed blockades. Wilson protested to both the British and Germans about abuses of the rights of neutrals and the freedom of the seas resulting from the enforcement of their respective blockades. The sinking of the British ship *Lusitania* by a German submarine in May 1915, which caused the deaths of almost 1,200 passengers, including 128

Americans, was a turning point for Wilson. The president issued a strong protest and warning to Germany—so strong, in fact, that it prompted his secretary of state, William Jennings Bryan, to resign in protest, claiming that Wilson's message undermined the neutrality of the United States. Over the next two years, the president offered to mediate a peaceful settlement of the war, while narrowly winning reelection in 1916 with the campaign slogan, "He kept us out of war." But when the Germans defied his ultimatum and began attacking American ships in 1917, Wilson asked Congress for a declaration of war, famously declaring: "The world must be made safe for democracy."[71]

The war brought on a provisional retreat by Wilson from his campaign to lower tariffs. Under pressure to finance the military requirements of war, Wilson and Congress agreed to amend the Underwood Tariff to retain the revenue-rich protective tariff on sugar, which had been scheduled to phase out in 1916, and to raise duties on chemicals with the goal of protecting American manufacturers against German competitors.

Wilson also reversed his position on the creation of a tariff commission. When President Taft had proposed it, Wilson and most Democrats had been hostile to the idea as simply another bureaucratic obstacle to ending the protectionist tariff system. Now, as president, Wilson saw political expediency in moving to a "scientific" approach to trade policy, especially after having already taken the first significant step toward dismantling protectionism with the Underwood Act. The Tariff Commission, which was to be strictly bipartisan in membership, would study and compare the production costs and tariffs on goods produced in the United States and other nations in order to aid in the negotiations with the European powers during the war. To ensure that the commission did not become a protectionist tool, Wilson appointed the liberal Harvard economist Frank W. Taussig to be its first chairman. He also offered a commission appointment to the anti-protectionist muckraker Ida Tarbell, who, however, declined.

That Wilson's devotion to free trade was not diminished by the advent of war was evident in his efforts to bring about permanent peace at the end of the war. In his famous Fourteen Points spelling out his peace terms proposal, he called for "absolute freedom of navigation upon the seas" and the "removal, so far as possible, of all economic barriers and the establishment of an equality of trade conditions among all the nations consenting to the peace."[72]

The president's free-trade philosophy was also manifested in the transformation of the revenue base that funded the war. While Wilson, prompted by the war, made concessions on sugar and chemical tariff protection, he financed the preparation for war largely through major increases in other revenue sources. The Revenue Act of 1916 doubled the "normal" income tax on personal income from 1 to 2 percent and added graduated "surtaxes" progressively from 2 percent up to a combined normal and surtax rate of 15 percent on incomes exceeding $2 million (equivalent to more than $40 million in current dollars). The act also doubled the 1913 tax on corporate incomes and imposed the first estate tax since the Civil War, along with a wartime "excess profits" tax on munitions manufacturers.[73] Congress under Wilson's leadership increased taxes again in 1917 with the highest combined rates, including surtaxes, going to 67 percent. The Revenue Act of 1918 increased the maximum combined income tax rate to 77 percent and the excess war profits tax to a maximum of 65 percent to combat war profiteering.[74] Revenue of $8 billion derived from this act funded one-third of the costs needed to prosecute the war, with the remainder largely funded by government indebtedness through the Victory Liberty Bond Act. In 1913, import duties funded nearly half of all federal revenues with less than 5 percent coming from income taxes. By 1918, nearly 70 percent of all federal revenue came from income taxes and less than 5 percent came from tariffs.[75]

This shift in the source of federal revenue from wage-earning consumers to wealthy producers brought charges from Republican opponents that the new tax structure represented a socialistic attempt to redistribute the country's wealth. With income inequality at a new peak, only the top 5 percent of Americans were subject to the income taxes under the new law, even though it taxed income levels beginning at $1,000, or $2,000 for married couples, above basic exemptions and allowable deductions. Undeniably, the law did have a social agenda in addition to revenue enhancement. One new provision added a 10 percent tax on the net profits of employers of children under the age of sixteen working in mines or fourteen in other places of employment. This tax was intended as a substitute for the recently passed prohibition of child labor, which the Supreme Court had ruled unconstitutional. Purchasers of yachts, automobiles, furs, expensive clothing, and other "luxuries" also saw a new excise tax burden, as did purchasers of the products of sin, including tobacco, alcohol, and opium. Revenue from alcohol taxes, however, was expected to go down by $500 million with the ratification of Prohibition. Obviously, the effort to legislate "fair, equitably distributed taxation" involved political value judgments, but Wilson focused on the patriotic need to support the American troops fighting in

Europe in the most productive manner possible. As to partisan debate over these value judgments, Wilson simply declared: "Until the enemy shall be beaten and brought to a reckoning with mankind . . . Politics is adjourned."[76]

Although Wilson did not enjoy the benefit of strong progressive majorities in his second term, he received a reprieve from protectionist pressures during most of the war years. During the first session beginning in 1917, the Democratic majorities were cut to a slight margin, but the two parties arranged a truce on tariffs to focus on the prosecution of the war. In any case, tariffs were not a major issue during this period, because the economy was thriving and the war had eliminated European imports to a degree that protection was practically meaningless. For the same reason, revenue from import duties was not a significant factor in American budgetary requirements.

The political and economic environment began to change dramatically in the months after the war ended. As a result of war conditions, industries had developed and prospered free from foreign competition, a state of affairs that would diminish after 1918. At the same time, the demand for American agricultural products dropped dramatically, creating panic and disaster in the farm economy. Even in the agricultural West, a desperate search for a solution caused protectionist pressures to emerge where they had previously never existed. As the economy began to enter the postwar decline, the Democrats began losing their grip on the levers of power in Congress, and Wilson's tariff reforms soon came under attack.

WILSON'S FINAL YEARS

In contrast to the many triumphs Wilson enjoyed during the first six years of his presidency, including his transformational economic reforms and military victory in Europe, his last two years in office must be counted as a failure. The essence of this failure was the progressive president's declining dominance over the legislative branch, the Senate in particular. As historian Robert Caro writes, "The tariff reduction bill was the signpost of the beginning of Wilson's relationship with the Senate; the signpost at the end was the Treaty of Versailles."[77] In the same month that the Armistice ending World War I was signed, the American voters returned control of both houses of Congress to the Republicans in the 1918 midterm elections. In 1919, against the counsel of his advisers Wilson took a risk that was unprecedented as a head of state, leading the US delegation in the six-month negotiations of the Versailles Peace Conference. The conference produced much frustration for the president and a flawed treaty but secured his goal of creating the League of Nations. Unfortunately, Wilson's hopes for Senate ratification of the treaty and US membership in the League were later dashed by Henry Cabot Lodge, the Republican leader in the Senate following Aldrich's retirement, serving as the unofficial majority leader and chairman of the Foreign Relations Committee.

Lodge shared not only the nationalistic, unilateralist ideology of his late friend and ally, Theodore Roosevelt—who had died suddenly while Wilson was in Europe—but also TR's deep personal and partisan enmity of Woodrow Wilson. Lodge wrote a friend that he "never expected to hate anyone in politics with the hatred [he felt] toward Wilson." The feeling was mutual; on at least one occasion Wilson refused to sit on the same platform with Lodge. A well-published historian with a PhD from Harvard, Lodge had been known as "the Scholar in Politics" before Wilson became president and took over that unofficial title. Wilson classed Lodge among other Senate Republicans whom he considered "pygmy-minded—narrow ... selfish ... poor little minds that never get anywhere but run around in a circle and think they are going somewhere."[78]

Adamantly refusing to compromise with Lodge, Wilson took his bully pulpit on the road to sell the importance of the League to the American people. But after an excruciating schedule of speeches across the country, stress and hardening arteries combined to end his campaign with a debilitating stroke in September 1919, leaving him physically incapacitated for the remainder of his presidency.

By the spring of 1920, the Republicans' aspirations for retaking the White House were becoming a near certainty as the American economy entered a period of depression. The expanded prosperity during the war years had created wealth for many sectors of the economy but brought serious inflation along with it. The cost of living increased by over 100 percent between 1914 and 1920. When the overextended world economy suddenly collapsed, deflation set in with a vengeance, with agriculture prices dropping precipitously by nearly 60 percent and labor earnings declining as much as 20 percent over the next year. Republicans and the conservative press blamed Wilson for being more interested in recovery in war-torn

Europe than his own country's economy, but the president was too ill to respond.

Despite his illness, Wilson made a feeble attempt to gain a third presidential nomination. At the Democratic Convention in June, however, the nomination went to dark-horse candidate James M. Cox, the former governor of Ohio, on the ticket with a young Wilson protégé, Franklin D. Roosevelt, a distant cousin and nephew by marriage of Theodore.

The Republicans nominated Warren G. Harding from Ohio, who was completing his first term in the Senate, along with Governor Calvin Coolidge of Massachusetts as his running mate. Harding—a Taft "standpatter" of the first order—was a compromise candidate favored by the conservatives to reverse Wilson's reforms and block any reform attempts from Republican progressives. Chosen to give the nomination speech for Taft at the Republican Convention in 1912, Harding had drawn heckles from Theodore Roosevelt's supporters when he declared, "President Taft is the greatest progressive of the age."[79] A newspaper publisher prior to entering the Senate, Harding editorialized for tariff protection, predicting depression would follow Wilson's tariff reforms. During the campaign, he promised an end to the dramatics of the Wilsonian revolutionary period and to bring back "normalcy" to heal the country's problems. Except among conservatives who liked his strong stand against labor unions, Coolidge was hardly known outside of his home state. They were not a dynamic campaign team, but this was not a competitive year for the Democratic Party and they were a safe bet for the conservative cause.

The Harding-Coolidge ticket won in a landslide, with 404 electoral votes to 127 for Cox-Roosevelt. Democrats were in the wilderness again, and the reversal of Woodrow Wilson's divine mission to bring free trade to America had already begun. Though tariffs played only a small role in the 1920 election, the GOP victors took up their traditional stance and began tariff hearings in the Ways and Means Committee early in 1921 in anticipation of the incoming regime. In the final days of the Wilson administration, Congress passed an Emergency Agricultural Tariff Act, imposing protective duties on farm products, only to have it vetoed by President Wilson on his last day in office.

While invoking the anti-protectionist themes of his first public statement in 1882 that the bill promoted "selfish interests which will foster monopoly," Wilson's veto message offered prescient warnings about the trade legislation that would be enacted in the decade that followed his administration. He wrote that this "emergency" bill would not offer the relief promised by its authors. What the farmer really needed, he argued, was a better system of domestic marketing and credit and "especially larger foreign markets for his surplus products." This legislation would be counterproductive to that goal, Wilson maintained. The United States had become "a great creditor Nation," holding enormous public and commercial indebtedness of European nations. "If we wish to have Europe settle her debts," he said, "we must be prepared to buy from her, and if we wish to assist Europe and ourselves by the export either of food, of raw materials, or finished products, we must be prepared to welcome commodities which we need and which Europe will be prepared, with no little pain, to send us." As if making a final admonition to his successors, he declared, "Clearly, this is no time for the erection here of high-trade barriers."[80]

6

The Roaring Twenties and the Path to Smoot-Hawley

Prosperity will inevitably follow the readjusted tariff of 1929. . . .

The people elected a Republican President and Congress in order that a readjustment of the tariff might be in the hands of the friends of protection.[1]
— Senator Reed Smoot (R-UT)
September 12, 1929

On May 17, 1923, President Warren G. Harding and his treasury secretary—the multimillionaire Pittsburgh banker and industrialist Andrew Mellon—unveiled a bronze statue of Alexander Hamilton on the south terrace of the Department of the Treasury. Harding had long been a student of Hamilton's life and achievements and often praised him in his speeches before entering the White House. In this tribute, given with much fanfare before an audience of 5,000 Washingtonians, the president hailed Hamilton's "matchless contribution" as the first treasury secretary in leading "the young republic from the depths of seeming hopelessness to the very heights of confidence." Without naming them, Harding chastised those, like Jefferson and Madison, who had called Hamilton "a monarchist and the foe of liberty . . . the enemy of democracy." Observing that Hamilton never sought to "echo ephemeral popular opinion," Harding praised him for his efforts to build a nation "strong enough to guarantee the security of liberty."[2] The memorial to Hamilton inscribed on the base of the statue reinforced Harding's point:

HE SMOTE THE ROCK
OF THE NATIONS RESOURCES,
AND ABUNDANT STREAMS
OF REVENUE GUSHED FORTH.
HE TOUCHED THE DEAD CORPSE
OF THE PUBLIC CREDIT,
AND IT SPRUNG UPON ITS FEET.

Hamilton had become a Republican icon following the Civil War, and his philosophy of ensconcing the moneyed class into the public policymaking process became the guiding light of the Gilded Age. The unveiling ceremony by Harding and Mellon—under the approving gaze of conservative Republican platform guests led by Senator Henry Cabot Lodge, a Hamilton scholar and the editor of his multivolume works—broadcast the symbolic message that the Hamiltonian approach to stability founded upon protectionist trade policies in a business-government partnership had returned in full force. It would not be until 1947 that a Democratic administration erected the statue of free-trader Albert Gallatin, Jefferson's treasury secretary, at the north entrance to the Treasury Building.

To be fair, President Wilson had also been an admirer of Hamilton and had actually proposed the statue in 1917. Wilson had even revived the Hamiltonian concept of the National Bank, long buried by Andrew Jackson, with the enactment of the Federal Reserve System, albeit without the partnership with Wall Street bankers favored by Hamilton and his philosophical descendants. But the era of Wilson's progressive reforms seemed in the distant past as Harding, in his first two years, began to fulfill his slogan of "less government in business and more business in government."

Immediately after his election, Harding had promised to "repeal and wipe out the mass of executive orders and laws which, failing to serve effectively to prevent profiteering and unfair practices, serve only to leave American business drifting and afraid." Committing to readjusting tariffs, he promised to "give Government co-operation to business" and to protect American business at home and abroad by "a restoration of our self-respecting measure of American protection to her citizens wherever they may go upon righteous errands."[3]

FORDNEY-MCCUMBER TARIFF ACT OF 1922

Wilson's tariff reforms in the Underwood Tariff Act of 1913 had remained largely intact for nine years, giving the measure a longer life than all but one tariff act enacted in the previous forty years. Democrats had controlled Congress with overwhelming majorities during Wilson's first term and, along with the progressive Republican insurgents, kept in place this significant departure from the entrenched protectionist system. Wilson's progressive move to more liberal trade stalled during his last two years in office, however, and President Harding began abruptly reversing course the moment he took the oath of office.

The day after President Wilson vetoed the Emergency Agricultural Tariff Act on his last day in office with a warning of the dangers of high trade barriers, President Harding used his own inaugural address to deride "the theory of banished barriers of trade" as a "luring fallacy," observing that the preservation of American standards with higher production costs would require higher tariffs on imports.[4] Within six weeks the new president called a special session of Congress to address tax reform and emergency tariffs. With strong support from a number of senators and representatives largely from the Middle West and the South coalescing as the Agricultural or Farm Bloc, Congress passed a new Emergency Tariff Act, which Harding signed on May 27, 1921. This act imposed an embargo on German chemicals and dyestuffs, prohibited dumping (sale at less than "fair value") of foreign goods in the US market, and imposed prohibitive tariff rates on about thirty agricultural products, including wheat, corn, meat, wool, and sugar. The emergency duties were supposed to remain in effect for only six months but were extended until the next permanent tariff increase. Wilson's prediction that the measure would not provide a solution to the farmer's problems proved correct. According to economic historian and Wilson's Tariff Commission chairman, Frank Taussig:

> As a means of meeting the emergency of the time it was hardly more than an amiable gesture. The prices of the several products continued to decline; hardly better proof could be found of the failure of tariff duties to serve as a remedy of immediate efficacy.[5]

The hearings in the Ways and Means Committee for a permanent repeal of the Underwood Tariff Act began before the emergency tariff bill was passed. Chairman Joseph W. Fordney (R-MI) introduced the bill in the House, declaring, "I am a protectionist and I am a Republican, without any apologies for my protection or Republican views. [Applause] But, my friends, it has been my earnest purpose . . . that no prohibitive rates shall be written into the law. It is my purpose also to see that the rates are sufficiently high to offset the difference between cost of production in this country and the cost abroad."[6] Under a strict rule that limited debate and floor amendments, the bill passed in the House on a party-line vote in a matter of days. As was its tradition, however, the Senate took its time in exercising its prerogative in rewriting the measure.

Senate Finance Committee chairman Porter J. McCumber (R-ND) presented the bill in the Senate chamber nine months later. With over 2,000 amendments to the House bill—in most cases increasing the already high tariffs—McCumber observed, "We do not believe we have made any rate so high as to prevent reasonable foreign competition."[7] Regardless of this assurance, the final measure increased average tariffs 64 percent higher than the average rates under the 1913 Act, reaching an average level of 38.4 percent—an outcome higher than the protective measures of 1890, 1897, and 1909.[8] Although some interest groups had spoken against raising tariffs—for example, the increasingly influential American automobile manufacturers, who dominated the market but worried about foreign tariff retaliation—the pressure for higher protection had been overwhelming. Western agricultural interests represented by the Farm Bloc demanded protective tariffs for farm products to the same extent that protection was given the products of any other industry. A poll of the membership of the United States Chamber of Commerce on the question of whether to raise the tariff rates immediately resulted in a tally of 1,140 for and 723 against.[9] When the vote on the bill came, the Senate, like the House, voted along party lines with no Democrats voting in favor and only two progressive Republicans, including La Follette, opposed.

In the wake of its passage, Representative Fordney defended the measure against Democratic charges that it would increase the cost of living to American consumers with an appeal to nationalism:

> Already American prices are extraordinarily high. . . . This act
> reaches out to gather in more of the foreigners' outrageous profits
> in reduction of the taxes of our people . . . and to divert some of the
> billions of our money from foreign channels in aid of American

manufacturers and producers and labor, rather than the upbuild-
ing of the foreign factory and aiding the foreign producer and
feeding foreign labor. . . . The proponents of this act believe in
American institutions, in American industry, in American labor,
in American men and women, and by this law present to the country a purely American act.[10]

FLEXIBLE TARIFF AUTHORITY

The return to the high protective tariffs of the Fordney-McCumber Act
may have simply represented the "return to normalcy" that Harding had
promised, but the act also included an unprecedented delegation of congressional authority to the president to raise or lower rates under limited
circumstances. During the course of deliberations on the bill, some members of the business community expressed concerns about the negative
effects of a resumption of extreme protection on export trade and warned
of potential political backlash as had occurred following passage of the
excessive McKinley and Payne-Aldrich Acts. Harding, suddenly less comfortable with his strict protectionist approach, began looking for a solution
more palatable to the exporting community. He found it in advice from
Tariff Commissioner William S. Culbertson, a moderate protectionist and
progressive Republican. In lengthy memoranda, Culbertson convinced
Harding that adding a flexible tariff mechanism to the law would be economically and politically beneficial. With the aid of the Tariff Commission,
which could independently and "scientifically" compute the difference
between foreign and domestic production costs and thus give expert advice
on the appropriate duty, the president could adjust the duty in a judicious
manner, thus correcting congressional political guesswork.

In his first State of the Union message, delivered before the Senate
Finance Committee began work on its version of the bill, Harding asked for
authority to make scientific adjustments to duties with the goal of making
tariffs "equitable, and not necessarily [burdening] our imports and [hin-
dering] our trade abroad."[11] Despite strong opposition from congressional
Democrats who argued that it was unconstitutional—one called it an act of
despotism—the flexible tariff authority was included as Section 315 in the
final version that passed. The act stated explicitly for the first time by statute
that the intended policy underlying the protective tariff was to equalize the

differences in the costs of production in the United States and competing foreign countries. Although this policy, as discussed below, was based on unsound economics, it at least put a fig leaf over the purely anti-competitive, special-interest favoritism for which protective tariffs had been tradition- ally criticized. Under Section 315, the president was authorized to raise or lower duties in the act by an amount not exceeding 50 percent for purposes of equalizing the production costs. Before exercising this authority, how- ever, an investigation of cost of production by the Tariff Commission was required and the president's action was to be based on the recommendation of the commission.

At a signing ceremony at the White House on September 21, 1922, wit- nessed by Fordney, McCumber, and members of the House Ways and Means and Senate Finance Committees, President Harding was obviously relieved and hopeful after the sixteen-month legislative process. "This law has been long in the making," he said. "I don't know how many are in accord with me, but if we succeed in making effective the elastic provisions of the measure it will make the greatest contribution to tariff making in the nation's history."[12]

On its face, the flexible tariff authority appeared to have offered a prom- ising method to correct and moderate political excesses, and it broke new ground in the delegation of congressional trade policy authority. But the innovation suffered from three fatal weaknesses: a fundamentally flawed formula, a conflicted Tariff Commission, and, ultimately, a president not committed to it.

The ostensible policy basis for the Fordney-McCumber protective tar- iffs and guiding formula for the flexible tariff—the equalization of differ- ences in the costs of production between the United States and competing foreign countries—had in recent years become the mantra for Republicans as a justification for protective tariffs. Frank Taussig described the policy as having become "a sort of fetish among the protectionists" and found it "fatally unsound as a matter of tenable or consistent theory."[13] Taussig had served as the first chairman of the Tariff Commission but resigned in 1919 as the Republicans regained control of Congress and began to formulate plans to raise tariffs again. He had taught classical economics at Harvard since 1882 and subscribed to David Ricardo's doctrine of comparative advantage as the fundamental basis for trade. The concept of comparative advantage, a foundational theory of trade economics, would be entirely nullified by a tariff equalizing the differences between domestic and foreign costs of pro- duction. Equally important, Taussig believed it was practically impossible in the 1920s to obtain accurate company accounting and production records pertaining to foreign products sufficient to dependably ascertain and maintain assessments of the cost of production in foreign countries.

For those who may have hoped that the flexible tariff provision would provide some relief from the high tariffs of the Fordney-McCumber Act, Harding's appointments to the Tariff Commission soon brought disappointment. When Harding entered the White House, the commission had in place four Wilson incumbents—Culbertson, the only Republican, alongside two Democrats and a Progressive. To appease the high protectionists, Harding filled the two open Republican seats with prominent protectionist lobbyists for manufacturing interests. At the urging of Senator Lodge, Harding soon after named one of these appointees chairman, namely, Thomas O. Marvin, secretary of the protectionist Home Market Club of Boston. When one of the Democratic commissioners resigned, the president replaced him with a protectionist Democrat. The conflicts that subsequently arose among the commissioners involved not only basic trade policy issues but fundamental procedural questions concerning the role of the commission in deciding which rate cases to investigate. Marvin argued that the commission could not initiate a case without approval from the president, while Culbertson sought independence for the commission and the discretion to review all tariff rates.

With support from the Progressive and free-trade Democratic commissioners, early in 1923 Culbertson proposed a list of cost investigations for a broad review of nearly all tariff rates to which Marvin objected. Culbertson appealed to the president and his cabinet for support, warning of political backlash against the Fordney-McCumber Act and the potential failure of the Section 315 flexible tariff provision. Secretary of Commerce Herbert Hoover weighed in supporting Culbertson's effort, as did several western congressmen. In April, the president agreed that the commission could initiate an investigation based on petitions from interested parties, or in the absence of a petition, when the commission had evidence indicating that duties did not equalize competitive conditions after first conferring with the president.

Despite this agreement, the commission remained conflicted and could not reach agreement on the investigations to pursue. Culbertson continued to target broad-scope revision while Marvin sought to limit investigations to minimal single targets with limited application. Harding, who had created the turmoil by adopting Culbertson's proposal for the flexible tariff and then appointing commissioners who would ensure its failure, refused to intervene to resolve the impasse. As the commissioners continued to squabble over the procedural agenda, Harding left on a speaking tour in the western states. The commission finally agreed to take up twenty-nine investigations, but it is impossible to know how Harding would have acted upon the recommendations of the Tariff Commission concerning its investigations under Harding's flexible tariff authority. He died of a heart attack in San Francisco on August 2, 1923, leaving the troublesome issue to his successor, Calvin Coolidge.

Commissioner Culbertson made an effort to convince the new president of the political and economic value of the flexible tariff provision, but with no success. In his first address to Congress in December 1923, Coolidge praised the high tariffs of the Fordney-McCumber Act for securing "abundant revenue and . . . an abounding prosperity."[14] He saw no reason to make adjustments that could only disturb what he believed was tariff-driven prosperity. He admitted to Culbertson that "we will have to seem to be doing something," but commented to humorist Will Rogers that he avoided using his authority for duty adjustments to keep from alienating either manufacturers or consumers. He simply ignored Tariff Commission recommendations or delayed acting on them indefinitely by asking for more information. Over time, Coolidge was able to replace the Wilson appointees and pack the commission with a protectionist majority—Culbertson accepted an appointment as minister to Romania—and made only thirty-eight Section 315 rate changes in seven years. Of these adjustments, thirty-three were increases and only five were reductions for such nonsensitive commodities as live bob-white quail and paint brush handles. The president expressly refused to follow the commission's controversial recommendation to reduce the duty on raw sugar and simply ignored many others. In a comment after he left office, Coolidge declared that in his judgment the whole idea of trying to derive a "scientific tariff" by comparing costs of production was only a "delusion."[15]

COOLIDGE PROSPERITY

During the Coolidge administration, John Maynard Keynes published a pamphlet based on one of his lectures entitled *The End of Laissez-Faire* (1926). In the lecture, Keynes gave a history of the principle of laissez-faire and how it became a tenet of classical economics. Noting that the phrase is nowhere mentioned in the works of Adam Smith, David Ricardo, or Thomas Malthus, Keynes observed that the term gained great popularity in the nineteenth century by being contrasted with two scientifically deficient opposing doctrines—protectionism and Marxist socialism. He said Adam Smith's advocacy of free trade and natural liberty led him to oppose mercantilism and eighteenth-century trade restrictions, but he was not a dogmatic opponent of government involvement in regulating commerce. Keynes at this time was still a devout believer in the virtues of free trade but found fallacy with the assumption basic to the principle of laissez-faire, as it pertained to unregulated capitalism, that people are driven by their own self-interest to act in the public interest. "It is *not* a correct deduction from the Principles of Economics," wrote Keynes, "that enlightened self-interest always operates in the public interest." In an early statement of his views favoring capitalism mixed with government intervention, Keynes concluded, "I think that Capitalism, wisely managed, can probably be made more efficient for attaining economic ends than any alternative system yet in sight."[16]

If President Coolidge ever had occasion to read the Keynes pamphlet, he was certainly not influenced by it. His devotion to a hands-off, laissez-faire approach to governing business knew only one limitation, namely, protective tariffs, which he refused to reduce in each of his annual messages to Congress. Famously proclaiming that "the chief business of the American people is business,"[17] Coolidge followed Harding in appointing pro–big-business advocates to the new federal regulatory agencies, including the Interstate Commerce Commission, the Federal Reserve Board, and the Federal Trade Commission (FTC). Although the Coolidge appointments did not result in the scandal-ridden nightmare that plagued Harding's legacy—the worst of which was the infamous Teapot Dome scandal—they did manage to infuriate progressives of both parties. Senator George W. Norris, a progressive Republican from Nebraska, charged that Coolidge was in effect nullifying federal law through the appointment process. Norris called for abolishing both the Tariff Commission and the FTC because these agencies had "fallen into the hands of reactionaries and no longer served the purposes for which they were created."[18] As Coolidge biographer Robert H. Ferrell observes, "Regulation in the Coolidge era was thin to the point of invisibility."[19]

A key goal of the Coolidge pro-business agenda was reducing the high tax rates and national debt still lingering from the Wilson administration and World War I. He worked in close partnership with Secretary Mellon, whose 1924 book, *Taxation: The People's Business,* reads in parts like a "supply-side" tract. According to Mellon:

> The history of taxation shows that taxes which are inherently excessive are not paid. The high rates inevitably put pressure upon the taxpayer to withdraw his capital from productive business. . . . It seems difficult for some to understand that high rates of taxation do not necessarily mean large revenue to the Government, and that more revenue may often be obtained by lower rates.[20]

Coolidge's persistence and success on tax reduction and deregulation of business have endeared him to modern Republican partisans. When Ronald Reagan became president in 1981, he placed a portrait of Coolidge in the Cabinet Room of the West Wing, replacing one of President Harry S. Truman.

The treasury secretary began his tax reform effort with Harding by pushing through the Revenue Act of 1921, which brought the top marginal rates down from 73 to 50 percent. In 1924 Mellon and Coolidge were able to persuade Congress to lower individual rates again, but with an increase in estate and gift taxes. Finally, under intense administration pressure, Congress passed the Revenue Act of 1926, which reduced top marginal rates to 24 percent, cut estate taxes in half to 20 percent, and abolished the gift tax. The tax cuts would reduce federal revenue by 10 percent, forcing a return to the pre–Wilson era reliance on high tariffs. Coolidge was delighted.

While the 1926 tax cuts passed with a strong bipartisan vote, progressive critics like Congressman Fiorello H. LaGuardia (R-NY) charged that the measure was designed to benefit only the wealthiest taxpayers. Senator James J. Couzens, a progressive Republican from Michigan, who was himself a wealthy former Ford executive, accused the Treasury Department of giving refunds and credits amounting to billions of dollars to favored businesses, including some controlled by Mellon. But despite the truth of these charges, the relatively widespread prosperity of the period—dubbed the "Coolidge prosperity"—insulated the president from political damage.

After overcoming the brief postwar depression of 1920–21, the American economy, driven by a confluence of forces, began to revive and benefit from the advantages of its wartime experience. The American industrial sector of the late nineteenth century received a boost from World War I, and by 1926–29, US manufacturing output had risen to 42.2 percent of world production, exceeding the total production of all eight competitive industrial economies (Germany, Britain, France, Italy, Canada, Belgium, Japan, and the Soviet Union).[21] Greater use of electricity, higher mechanization, assembly lines, and other manufacturing innovations enhanced efficiency of production such that these economies could capitalize on pent-up wartime demand. Led by Henry Ford's Model T, American automobile manufacturing, along with its supply industries, dominated the world market and had a dramatic impact on the US economy. The Federal Reserve Board consistently kept interest rates low, stimulating economic growth as construction boomed and the stock market soared on speculative brokers' margin lending. No doubt the Harding-Coolidge hands-off approach to business regulation also spurred a high degree of business confidence and exuberance.

A critical weak spot in the economy throughout the 1920s remained, however, in agriculture. Farmers had gone into debt to expand production in meeting the war demand but were left with only the debt when demand evaporated and prices fell at the end of the war. The high tariffs that Congress had passed for agricultural products in 1922 failed to help shore up prices, and Harding had refused to support direct aid to the farmers. Many foreign governments had imposed retaliatory tariffs and import quotas on American farm products and gave subsidies to their own domestic farm producers. In 1924, Senator Charles L. McNary (R-OR) and Congressman Gilbert N. Haugen (R-IA) first introduced a new solution supported by a broad range of agricultural interests to guarantee a fair domestic price for farm produce. Under the McNary-Haugen bill, a government-sponsored corporation would buy farm surpluses at a price based on the tariff level set at prewar market prices and then "dump" them abroad at world prices. The ensuing losses would be charged to farmers in the form of an "equalization fee." Despite strong support from the Farm Bloc, the bill attracted preemptive opposition from Coolidge and highlighted the strength of manufacturing interests over agriculture in Washington.

Coolidge, Mellon, Hoover, and other critics complained that the scheme amounted to price fixing and a "vicious" form of taxation, which increased the cost of living to consumers and paid an unearned bonus to producers. While these were valid objections, the same objections applied equally to protective tariffs for industrial products. McNary-Haugen's two-price system for domestic versus export sales was unsound economically but mirrored the practice of protected industries, such as steel, which often had sold high in the protected domestic market while surplus product was dumped abroad. The two-price issue was an even more serious problem for some agriculture products, like cotton, which depended heavily on the export market. But when the price of cotton dropped precipitously after 1925, southern congressmen joined in support of the bill. Despite strong opposition from Coolidge and the business community, the McNary-Haugen Act finally passed in February 1927 and Coolidge vetoed it. Congress modified it in an effort to address some of the president's objections and passed it again in May 1928 with larger majorities, only to have Coolidge promptly veto it again.

If the president's veto was not well received in Congress, it did not matter. On the fourth anniversary of Harding's death on August 2, 1927, Coolidge had made a surprise announcement: "I do not choose to run for president in nineteen twenty-eight." Calvin Coolidge believed that he was leaving at the top of his game. Apart from the agricultural problems that had plagued the country for a decade and would be passed along to his successor, the Coolidge prosperity appeared solid as his laissez-faire legacy. In his final annual message to Congress he was complacent: "The country can regard the present with satisfaction and anticipate the future with optimism."[22]

HERBERT HOOVER: THE "WONDER BOY"

In the wake of President Coolidge's cryptic withdrawal from consideration for renomination, the clear favorite to lead the 1928 Republican ticket was Secretary of Commerce Herbert Hoover. Contrary to his historical legacy as the dour and callous bungler whose administration is popularly blamed for the Great Depression, for most of the 1920s Hoover was considered a dazzling superstar among public figures.

From a meager start as an Iowa orphan, Hoover worked his way through the first graduating class of Stanford University to become a self-made millionaire in the mining industry in Australia, China, and other parts of the world. When war broke out in 1914, he was living in London and helped organize the return of 120,000 Americans in Europe to the United States. With exceptional management skill and fourteen-hour workdays, Hoover voluntarily chaired the food relief effort for millions of starving victims of the German invasion of Belgium. When America entered the war in 1917,

President Wilson appointed him to head the US Food Administration to introduce efficiencies in the conservation of food resources for the Allied cause. After the war, he organized relief efforts in Europe and for the famine victims in Soviet Russia despite opposition from Republican leaders like Senator Henry Cabot Lodge. In 1914, Hoover was known in his profession as the "Great Engineer," but by 1920, he had gained international fame as the "Great Humanitarian."

As ambitious young members of the Wilson administration, Hoover and Assistant Secretary of the Navy Franklin Roosevelt became friends during the war. Among other Democrats, Roosevelt considered Hoover a good prospect to succeed Wilson on the Democratic ticket with Roosevelt in 1920. Hoover had been a progressive Republican—supporting Theodore Roosevelt's Bull Moose Party over Taft in 1912—and now had served in the progressive Wilson administration and even supported the Versailles Treaty with minor reservations. Franklin Roosevelt urged Hoover to declare himself a Jeffersonian Democrat and be welcomed into the party. Colonel Edward House, recently a senior aide to Wilson, considered a Hoover-Roosevelt ticket the Democrats' best chance to hold the White House.[23] After dining with the Roosevelts earlier in the month and remaining coy about his decision, Hoover announced at the end of March 1920 that he was a progressive Republican. He made a brief attempt at the Republican nomination by running and losing in the California primary and then endorsing Harding. After the election, Harding rewarded him with what was then a minor cabinet position at the Department of Commerce.

Commerce under Hoover was anything but a *minor* cabinet position when he finished with it. He was a star in both the Harding and Coolidge cabinets, where he aggressively reorganized and expanded the role of the still new department, offering new services to business and industry both at home and abroad. He developed the new radio broadcasting industry, organized air travel, and promoted corporate America. In 1927, he oversaw the relief effort following the flooding of the Mississippi River, which left 1.5 million people homeless. He also created an innovative and effective public relations staff that broadcast his accomplishments widely. While he received much well-deserved credit, some resented his efforts at empire building as he crossed into the turf of other departments. His rivals referred to him as the "Secretary of Commerce and the Undersecretary of Everything Else." Among those least impressed by Secretary Hoover was President Coolidge himself, perhaps having grown weary of being upstaged by his subordinate, to whom he referred derisively as "wonder boy." When asked if he would back Hoover's nomination to succeed him, Coolidge replied, "That man has offered me unsolicited advice for six years, all of it bad!"[24]

Notwithstanding the misgivings of his predecessor, Hoover was unstoppable. He even drew supporting accolades from Wilsonian progressives like Ida Tarbell and Supreme Court Justice Louis Brandeis, who cheered, "I am 100 percent for him."[25] The Democrats nominated Governor Alfred E. Smith of New York, who in most respects represented the antithesis of Hoover. Like Hoover, Smith had grown up poor but he came from the urban tenement districts of the Lower East Side of New York and earned his way to the top of his field through the machine politics of Tammany Hall. Hoover was a Quaker who thought Prohibition a great and noble economic experiment while Smith was Irish Catholic at a time when much of the country had an anti-Catholic and anti-immigrant prejudice and he made ending Prohibition a top issue in the campaign.

Only on economic issues did the two candidates share views. Although Smith had enacted a number of progressive reforms as governor, in 1928 his pro-business approach was barely distinguishable from that of Hoover. Even on tariffs, Smith abandoned the traditional Democratic position of "tariffs for revenue only" in favor of minimum protective duties. The Democratic platform in 1928 basically punted on the issue, proclaiming "a Democratic tariff based on justice to all."[26] Smith attempted to distance himself from Hoover on the agriculture issue by weighing in against industry in support of the McNary-Haugen program vetoed by Coolidge. But the sections of the country where this position would have helped most—the South and West—were those most affected by an anti-Catholic bias that weighed against him.

Hoover was nominated on the first ballot at the Republican National Convention on a platform that credited the Coolidge administration with lifting the country "from the depths of a great depression" and reaffirmed the "belief in the protective tariff as a fundamental and essential principle of the economic life of this nation."[27] In his acceptance speech given at Stanford, Hoover promised that the prosperity the country was then enjoying under the Republican Party was only going to get better:

> We in America today are nearer to the final triumph over poverty than ever before in the history of any land. The poorhouse is vanishing from among us. We have not yet reached the goal, but given

a chance to go forward with the policies of the last eight years, we shall soon with the help of God be in sight of the day when poverty will be banished from this nation.[28]

Hoover won in a landslide, even taking Smith's home state of New York, where Franklin Roosevelt won a close election as Democratic governor. On his coattails, Hoover brought in overwhelming Republican majorities to both houses of Congress.

THE SMOOT-HAWLEY TARIFF ACT OF 1930

Drawing praise from all corners, the "Great Engineer" began taking bold actions immediately after the inauguration that distinguished him from his two immediate predecessors. After ordering the removal of oil lands from access to further leasing and also requiring the publication of large income tax refunds—actions that would have prevented scandals under Harding and Coolidge—the liberal *New Republic* complimented him for acting "with a promptness and decision which have not been seen in the White House since Mr. Wilson's early days."[29] Indeed, Hoover wrote in his memoirs that he had hoped to revive the era of progressive reforms under Wilson, which had been stalled by the war and buried by Harding and Coolidge.[30] However, the strong convictions on the limited role of government Hoover described in his 1922 book, *American Individualism*, circumscribed his reform programs. His vision of the "rugged" American individual was based on a strong spirit of voluntary service as he had experienced it in his Belgian relief work during the war and was anathema to government bureaucracy or government subsidies. Support for protective tariffs was a notable exception to Hoover's vision of rugged individualism.

To tackle the country's most difficult problem—agriculture—Hoover called Congress into special session six weeks after his inauguration "to redeem two pledges in the last election—farm relief and limited changes in the tariff."[31] In one respect the president's effort in the special session began with great success. Within two months he was able to pass the Agricultural Marketing Act sponsored by his administration with the intent to stabilize farm commodity prices by creating a Federal Farm Board with a revolving loan fund of $500 million. This measure did not please the most activist farm groups such as the National Grange, which advocated the McNary-Haugen

FIGURE 6.1 Representative Willis Hawley (left) and Senator Reed Smoot in 1929, authors of the Smoot-Hawley Tariff Act of 1930 (Library of Congress)

styled export subsidies. The Farm Board could make loans to cooperative associations and certain stabilization corporations to buy agriculture commodities for the purpose of controlling surpluses. It was not authorized to fix prices, but in effect it had the discretion to do so. The Farm Board, however, never worked as intended to prevent price declines, especially after the stock market crash in October 1929.

The president's goals for tariff revision in the special session were restricted to curing specific problems. First, he was committed to raising duties on agricultural imports to help farmers. Second, he wanted to strengthen the Tariff Commission and the "flexible tariff" in order to limit the effect of congressional "logrolling" and excessive and arbitrary protection. Third, he saw "the necessity for some limited changes" in tariffs for industries other than agriculture created by economic shifts taking place since the 1922 Act. According to Hoover, "the test of necessity for revision is in the main whether there has been a substantial slackening of activity in an industry during the past few years, and a consequent decrease of employment due to insurmountable competition in the products of that industry."[32] As reasonable as it may have seemed, Hoover's call for these "limited changes" unleashed a legislative "free-for-all" that resulted in one of the most controversial and arguably damaging pieces of legislation in congressional history: the Smoot-Hawley Tariff Act of 1930.[33]

One of the remarkable ironies associated with the development of the infamous Smoot-Hawley tariff is the absence of the type of conditions that normally prompted major tariff measures. As Frank Taussig observes in the final chapter of his treatise *The Tariff History of the United States*, every previous tariff revision since the Civil War had been preceded by a financial crisis or political party upheaval fought over tariffs. Not only had there not been a political party turnover in the 1928 election, but tariffs had not even been an issue between the major candidates. Apart from the depressed prices farmers had been enduring since the end of the war, the country was at the peak of the Coolidge-era prosperity when Congress took up tariff adjustment in the special session. Based on the test laid out by the president, only moderate revisions might have been expected. Yet in the two months prior to Hoover's inauguration, the House Ways and Means Committee had already heard from nearly 1,100 witnesses in forty-five days of hearings and accumulated 11,000 pages of tedious testimony and briefs.[34] Most of the testimony came from special-interest producers seeking to increase or preserve protection, as most of the large manufacturers at this time, such as the automotive industry, were seeking favorable export markets and opposed higher tariffs.

In the political system that had matured over the previous seven decades, however, the tradition of logrolling trumped most policy debate in the tariff making process. In his classic study of the Smoot-Hawley process, E. E. Schattschneider called the logrolling process "reciprocal noninterference," meaning that support for a tariff increase on one product was traded in exchange for support for an increase on another.[35] By the time the president called for a special session, the Republican chairmen of the Ways and Means subcommittees were already meeting in closed session exclusively with their majority colleagues writing the bill. It was in these secret meetings that the logrolling began. There were fifteen Republicans on the committee, each of whom served as chairman of a subcommittee of three covering a certain tariff schedule that involved products of interest to the chair's constituency. A member from New England, for instance, would chair the textile subcommittee, and the other two members would defer to him on that schedule. Likewise, the two members on the subcommittee chaired by the member from Pennsylvania in charge of the iron and steel schedule would defer to his direction on that tariff. The hearings were held in public before the full committee, but the deals were made in private where there would be no objections from among the friends of protection.[36]

On May 9, 1929, Congressman Willis C. Hawley (R-OR), chairman of the Ways and Means Committee, presented the product of the committee's work on the House floor. After observing that the country had given "emphatic [endorsement] to this program by electing the candidate of the party that has always been the protectionist party to the Presidency by a great vote," the Republican members of the committee had "cross-examined with great diligence" the subcommittees that had prepared the revised tariff schedules. He noted that the revisions were not limited to agriculture, as proposed by a few, because that "would not have satisfied the Congress or the country, for the reason that we believe the equal protection of the law should be extended to everybody and every industry."[37] Hawley and the committee report on the bill downplayed the extent of tariff modifications in the proposal. The report proclaimed that "although a percentage of duties have been readjusted, the average rate on dutiable imports will not be materially changed." It claimed the proposal should not even be "properly designated as a revision but as a readjustment."[38] Hawley was vague in his description of the changes, but estimated the modifications to be only about "15 or 20 per cent" of the items on the tariff schedule. However, in an analysis provided in Douglas A. Irwin's account, *Peddling Protection: Smoot-Hawley and the Great Depression*, Hawley's proposal modified close to 35 percent of the rates in the 1922 Act, over 90 percent of which were increases.[39]

The purpose of the duty revisions provided in the bill were, according to the committee report, intended to adjust the differences in competitive conditions at home and abroad—particularly foreign labor, which the committee reported "receives less than 40 per cent of American wages." Addressing this labor disparity "is a most important factor in tariff making." The report added: "Foreign competitors have an uncanny aptitude for discovering what goods, wares, and commodities are [insufficiently] protected, and attacking them."

One of the stated principal purposes of the bill was "to protect American labor," and the report concluded with the observation that the Republican members had given special attention to the importance of the tariff adjustments "to our wage-earning population."[40] However, organized labor took no position on the measure. In 1929, the president of the American Federation of Labor (AFL), William Green, confirmed that his organization had "never committed itself to the support of a protective tariff or free trade. We have avoided most scrupulously and carefully that controversial field." Samuel Gompers, founder of the AFL, established this position on tariffs in 1906. While some unions supported protectionism and others favored free trade, Gompers—quite unlike many of his modern-day successors—believed that the livelihood of American workers was best advanced by the labor movement and not government tariff policies.[41]

Congressman Cordell Hull (D-TN), a southern Democrat and true believer in the Manchester School of free-trade economics, led the opposition. Democratic Minority Leader John N. Garner from Texas—later FDR's first vice president—was the ranking Democrat on Ways and Means, but he favored high tariffs, especially for agriculture. For that reason Hull took the lead for the minority during the hearings. Schattschneider's study praised Hull for asking the committee's best questions during the testimony.[42] Hull gave a scathing and highly partisan review of the bill in a minority report published two days after Hawley unveiled it. He noted that time did not permit a detailed analysis of the proposed rate changes but pointed out that agriculture received "benefits wholly minor and disproportionate to those assured to manufacturing industries"—a circumstance also criticized by midwestern, progressive Republicans. Practically all of the prohibitive rates of the Fordney-McCumber rates had been "left untouched and intact," Hull observed. The Republicans had flouted and shunted aside "all formulas and fact-finding agencies" with tariff rates "generally dictated by beneficiaries," effectively continuing "the old and worst type of logrolling and political pressure of conflicting interests." The congressman minced no words in describing the GOP's "corrupt partnership" with protected industries evidenced by the "Republican practice of accepting large campaign funds from tariff beneficiaries and later permitting them to come to Washington and write their own rates on the plea that the tariff must be revised by its 'friends.'"

Calling the notion of equalizing tariff benefits between agriculture and industry "absurd," Hull asserted, "the tariff is the most inequitable of all taxes." After the experience of the farm tariffs in 1921 and 1922, any attempt to make these tariff benefits proportionate was "now beyond the pale of controversy." In any case, the higher agriculture tariffs, he argued, had not benefited farmers. "Agriculture today is $20,000,000,000 worse off than in 1920. . . . Can the same farmers be thus fooled a third time in succession?"

Hull gave no credence to the argument that high tariffs were responsible for high wages and high living standards in the United States, which he said had become a permanent part of the American industrial system before the Fordney-McCumber Tariff. Real wages, he noted, had not increased much over 2.5 percent since 1923, during the Coolidge prosperity, and working hours were greatly reduced prior to 1921. He attributed higher wages and economic growth to industries not sheltered by tariff protection and by "unlimited raw materials and foodstuffs, mass production, and increased productivity of labor, automobile expansion, our vast gold and credit structure, the expenditure of billions annually in building, highway, and railway construction and improvement, and installment sales of two and three-fourths billion dollars per annum." The major effect of high tariffs during this period, Hull observed, had been "to transfer wealth from one class to another without affecting the Nation's total."

Hull decried the growing surpluses in US productive capacity, which were estimated at "25 per cent in excess of our ability to consume," and lamented that American products were being denied full access to foreign markets due to the impact of "our system of superprotection." In a prescient observation five months before the great Wall Street Crash of 1929, Hull wrote that these surpluses had produced "much idle labor and vast aggregations of idle capital, billions of which have gone into stock brokers' loans, for gambling purposes, thereby seriously affecting the stability of both our money and trade structure." Hull ranked the Republicans' tariff barriers, along with those of Spain and Russia, as the highest in the world, "inordinate, air-tight, superprotection intended to exclude every item of imports remotely competitive." The effect would be to invite retaliation, "which largely cuts us off from all markets for our surpluses," he concluded. "They dare not defend it upon grounds of revenue or equity or morals."[43]

President Hoover was also not happy with the committee's bill and called the Republican members in to meet with him at the White House. Insisting that the rates on industrial tariffs be reduced, that agricultural rates be increased, and that the flexible tariff authority be enhanced, he received some support from Chairman Hawley. Meeting resistance from the arch-protectionists led by Speaker Nicholas Longworth (R-OH), Hoover called the leadership in a week before the vote and again went over his objections, but to no avail. On May 28, the House approved the bill with its customary limited rule on amendments on a largely party line vote of 264 to 147. Thirteen percent of the Democrats—mainly from sugar-producing districts in Florida and Louisiana—voted for it, and 5 percent of the Republicans—mainly progressives—voted against it.[44] Midwestern Republicans and protectionist Democrats such as Congressman Garner opposed it because of the continued disparity benefiting industry over agriculture and the failure to pass export subsidies for farm products.

As usual, the process in the Senate proved much more complicated; in fact, it turned into a ten-month melee during which the controversial legislation nearly died. The leader of the effort was Finance Committee chairman Reed O. Smoot of Utah, described by Taussig as "an out-and-out protectionist of the most intolerant stamp" in whose committee "the familiar process of mutual concessions" prevailed, and all "pretense of limited revision disappeared."[45] One of twelve apostles in the Mormon Church,[46] Smoot in nearly three decades in the Senate had become known as the "Apostle of Protection" and an ardent advocate for the parochial interests of his district—beet sugar, lead, and wool. In 1925, the *American Economist*, a journal published by the American Protective Tariff League, gushed: "Senator Smoot is the greatest Tariff expert who has ever held a seat in the United States Senate."[47] This accolade, which lifted Smoot above such Senate protectionist legends as Henry Clay, Justin Morrill, and Nelson Aldrich, might be dismissed as hyperbole from an obsequious trade association but for Smoot's tireless, winning efforts to steer his infamous namesake legislation through to final passage. He was even successful in having the act most commonly referred to as Smoot-Hawley rather than the common practice of leading with the House author first, as in Hawley-Smoot.

Smoot's troubles began just as his committee began hearings on the bill. Midwestern Republicans, led by insurgent Senator William E. Borah (R-ID), proposed a resolution restricting the Finance Committee to the revision of only agricultural tariffs, barring changes to the industrial tariffs. On June 17, in an ominous signal of the difficulties ahead, a strong coalition of twenty-five Democrats and thirteen insurgent Republicans supporting the resolution failed to pass the restriction by only one vote—39 to 38.[48]

Following five weeks of hearings, which included nearly the same amount of testimony as was presented in the House, and another month of secret markup sessions, Senator Smoot presented the committee bill to the Senate on September 12. To please the president, he included the flexible tariff provision in his bill and made an effort to satisfy the mid-westerners by adding to the agricultural tariffs and decreasing some of the industrial rates in the House bill. Nonetheless, the insurgent Republican and Democratic coalition forces immediately attacked it. On October 2, the Senate voted to delete the flexible tariff authority from the bill by a vote of 47 to 42 (13 Republicans and 34 Democrats in favor), and on October 19 it voted to add export subsidies for agricultural products by a vote of 42 to 34 (14 Republicans and 28 Democrats in favor).[49] Both of these votes were a slap against Hoover and the protectionist Republican leadership. The coalition then moved against industrial tariffs, reducing rates on a high protectionist favorite in Pennsylvania, pig iron, and a host of other industrial products commonly used by farmers. Senator David Reed (R-PA) charged that in lowering industrial tariffs, the insurgents representing the "corn belt so called" were trying to pull down the industrial East to the same level of "common misery" as the agricultural West. He pronounced the bill effectively dead.[50] When the Senate adjourned in November, Smoot admitted that his committee had lost control of the bill. Refusing to intervene, Hoover remained essentially silent.

Soon after the Senate reconvened in early 1930, however, the anti-tariff coalition began losing votes to the protectionist Old Guard, as the logrolling tradition began to revive. Along with Smoot, one of the leaders of the effort to reverse the coalition's early success was newly appointed senator Joseph R. Grundy (R-PA), who had only recently been vice president of the American Protective Tariff League, president of the Pennsylvania Manufacturers' Association, and a key tariff lobbyist and Republican fundraiser. Grundy's bold tactics in openly demanding tariff rewards for industries giving campaign contributions and his success in overturning coalition successes with logrolling excesses led some Democrats to begin calling the bill the "Grundy Tariff." President Hoover and Senator Smoot frequently pointed out the fact that many Democrats voted for Grundy amendments increasing tariffs favoring their constituent interests and then voted against final passage of the bill.

The extensive debate on the bill was not exclusively about tariffs. Senator Smoot spent two days in March debating an amendment that would have eliminated the authority of the US Customs Service to prevent the importation of any "book, which taken as a whole offends the moral sense of the average person." As an example of the "disgusting . . . beastly, beastly" foreign works being imported, Smoot presented on the Senate floor *Lady Chatterley's Lover*, by English novelist D. H. Lawrence. The author of the amendment asked Smoot how he knew the book was so evil after Smoot admitted he had read only a page. Smoot responded that one page was "enough to indicate that it is written by a man with a diseased mind and a soul so black that he would even obscure the darkness of hell." A junior Democratic senator from Alabama, Hugo L. Black—who would later gain eminence on the US Supreme Court for his First Amendment opinions—objected to giving the Customs inspectors the unfettered discretion to determine at the border what materials are obscene. The issue was finally settled by a compromise offered by Black, and reluctantly accepted by Smoot, to permit the importer to request judicial review of the Customs decision.[51]

When the bill came for a final vote in the Senate, there was, according to Taussig, "no rhyme or reason in it."[52] Senator Grundy had worked with the insurgent Republicans to increase rates on agricultural products in exchange for keeping rates high on industrial products. But this arrangement proved highly inconsistent, as it was kept in some instances and deviated from in others, with chaos resulting. The most devout progressives—for example, Senator Robert M. La Follette Jr., who had taken up his late father's torch— were unbending, calling the rates unfair to farmers, just another gift to special industrial interests, and "the worst tariff bill" in the nation's history. But most of the insurgents were pacified by the continued inclusion of export subsidies for farm products and the exclusion of the flexible tariff provision desired by the president. The Senate bill passed easily on a partisan vote of 53 to 31. Only five Republicans voted against it and seven Democrats voted for it.

The House and Senate conference committee met in April to begin resolving the differences between the two chambers and found that tariff rates were not a problem. In most cases where there were differences in the rates, the conference committee simply adopted the higher level. The problem came with the Senate's insistence on including agricultural export subsidies and eliminating the flexible tariff—positions not only opposed by the House leadership but certain to draw a presidential veto if they were part of the final compromise. When the conference deadlocked over these provisions in mid-May, Smoot introduced resolutions in the Senate seeking to release the conferees from their position on these issues. Both votes barely passed. On the export subsidy provision, the Senate voted 43 to 41 to release its conferees to drop the provision. The vice president broke a 42-to-42 tie to allow the conferees to negotiate the flexible tariff provision.[53] On May 24, President Hoover, who had not been involved in the details of the bill during most of the process, wrote out the terms of the flexible tariff provision that he desired and sent word that he would veto the bill unless his formula was adopted. The result, he claimed, "was a complete victory for the flexible tariff in the conference report."[54]

The final vote in the Senate on the conference bill was 44 to 42, with five Democrats voting in favor while eleven Republicans voted no. Several of the insurgent Republicans who had previously voted for the bill switched to negative on the conference version because of the agricultural subsidy issue. Senator Borah, for instance, announced that the bill was now worthless to agriculture. On the other hand, the Republican majority leader predicted the bill would regain the prosperity lost in the October stock market crash within thirty days of enactment and assailed opponents like Henry Ford and General Motors president Alfred P. Sloan as "international financiers and industrialists" motivated by the desire for cheap labor.[55] As an indication of the strength of partisanship over constituent economic interests, it is interesting to note that all of the Michigan delegation except one absent member voted in favor of the bill despite the opposition of Ford and General Motors.[56]

In the House, where the vote for final passage was tightly controlled and the debate predictable, the balance was much stronger in a highly partisan tally of 222 to 153.[57] Democratic leader Garner said the bill violated every notion of common sense and justice, charging that the Republican majority had inflicted upon farmers the burden of inequitable industrial tariffs that would reduce or eliminate foreign markets. But according to Chairman Hawley, the bill would bring

> a renewed era of prosperity . . . in which all of the people of the United States in every occupation, every industry, and every employment will share . . . , which will increase our wealth, our employment, our comfort, the means of supplying our necessities, that will promote our trade abroad, and keep the name of the United States still before the world as the premier nation of solid finance, fairness, and justice to all the people, and one which for all time intends to provide for its own.[58]

Six weeks before the Smoot-Hawley Tariff Act reached President Hoover's desk for signature, 1,028 economists and businessmen from forty-six states and 179 colleges and universities joined in a public statement to the president and Senator Smoot and Representative Hawley in opposition to the bill and urging the president to veto it should it pass.[59] The signers, who included nearly every reputable economist in the United States at the time, argued that the bill would raise the cost of living, increase unemployment, hurt rather than help the vast majority of farmers, inject bitterness into international relations, and harm American export trade. If their opinions were not enough, the president received advice and counsel from countless others urging him to veto the bill, including Secretary of State Henry Stimson, who warned that it would disrupt the international financial community. Hoover's influential economic adviser Thomas Lamont, acting head of J. P. Morgan and Company, claimed, "I almost went down on my knees to beg Herbert Hoover to veto the asinine Hawley-Smoot Tariff."[60]

Smoot, Hawley, and the protectionist leaders of Congress dismissed the economists' objections as impractical and unpatriotic, detached from the problems of ordinary Americans who had to do real work for a living. As for Hoover, even if he had been willing to listen to the academics and the other influential opponents of the bill, he had painted himself into a corner in which a veto was not a likely option. Although both the Senate and the House had gone well beyond his requested "limited revisions," the president had been silent during the entire legislative process except for his veto threat over the flexible tariff provision and his objections to export subsidies. He displayed no leadership in attempting to limit Congress on the tariff provisions and had declared "a complete victory for the flexible tariff in the conference report."[61] When presented with a bill containing the essential provision he had demanded, Hoover was not in a position to veto it.

The president signed the bill with six gold pens on June 17, 1930, remarking that he believed the flexible provisions could "within reasonable time remedy inequalities" and, hopefully, would take "the tariff away from politics, lobbying, and logrolling." Like Smoot and Hawley, Hoover remained forever defensive about the bill, describing it in his 1952 memoirs as statistically comparable to other historical tariff acts, although the statistics he selected for comparison were misleading. Hoover concludes his chapter on Smoot-Hawley by saying that "raising the tariff from its sleep was a political liability despite the virtues of its reform."[62]

President Hoover may have been dreaming about the "virtues" of its reform, but his assessment of Smoot-Hawley as a political liability was correct, only grossly understated. Although he had come to the White House with widespread high expectations as the Great Engineer, the reviews of his performance on tariff reform were universally blistering. Walter Lippmann, who had praised Hoover in 1928 as "a reformer who is probably more vividly conscious of the defects of American capitalism than any man in public life today," wrote after Hoover signed the tariff bill that he had "surrendered everything for nothing. He gave up the leadership of his party. He let his personal authority be flouted. He accepted a wretched and mischievous product of stupidity and greed."[63] Historian Allan Nevins called Hoover's handling of the whole process "astonishing clumsiness," and a favorable biographer, Harris Warren, called it a "political disaster," writing that "probably nothing was so damaging to Hoover's reputation during his first two years in the presidency as his handling of the tariff." Biographer William E. Leuchtenburg writes that well before the Wall Street crash Hoover's failures on the tariff bill "exposed [him] as politically inept and incapable of mobilizing his own party."[64] Taussig observed, "The judgment of sober men of all parties, and even of the staunch protectionists, was that there had been a sad exhibition of political ineptitude."[65]

THE SMOOT-HAWLEY LEGACY

Smoot-Hawley—or the Tariff Act of 1930, as it is formally known—is the most infamous piece of legislation in American economic history due largely to its association with the Crash of 1929 and the Great Depression that followed. Because most of the duties were "specific" (assessed per pound) and not ad valorem (assessed by value), as prices fell precipitously with the Depression, the average percentage increased from rates of 45.4 percent on dutiable goods in 1930 to nearly 60 percent in 1932—a rate second only to the Tariff of Abominations of 1828.[66] These extraordinarily high rates at a time of world economic crisis brought on an immediate international reaction. In a seminal 1934 study on foreign retaliation to the act, Joseph Jones wrote, "The world depression and the Hawley-Smoot tariff are inextricably bound up one with the other, the latter being not only the first manifestation but a principal cause of the deepening and

aggravating of the former."[67] Jones cited the numerous retaliatory measures taken by European countries, including Spain, Italy, Switzerland,
and France, against US exports, including boycotts, quota systems, and
retaliatory tariffs. Britain and Canada, where American exporters found
their best foreign markets before 1930, squeezed out American products
with a bilateral trade agreement. Many retaliatory measures were aimed
at the dominant American automobile manufacturers but also included
food exports, hurting the ailing farmers and contributing to the ubiquitous
bank failures across the country.[68] Between 1929 and 1933, US foreign trade
fell through the floor, with exports plunging from $5.16 billion to $1.65
billion in 1933 and imports dropping from $4.4 billion to $1.45 billion.[69]
Most of this decline resulted from the deflating prices and falling demand
spurred by the world depression, but Smoot-Hawley garnered its share of
the political blame.

In the summer of 1932, the United Kingdom convened an Imperial
Economic Conference in Ottawa, Canada, which inaugurated a comprehensive system of mutual trade preferences between the United Kingdom
and the British Colonies and autonomous Commonwealth Dominions. The
Ottawa Agreements effectively restricted trade within the Empire to favor
its component parts and at the same time all but shut out American exports
from a quarter of the globe. These imperial preferences would prove to be a
major thorn in the Anglo-American relationship for decades.

Most economic historians debating the impact of Smoot-Hawley on
the stock market crash and the Great Depression have concluded that other
economic forces—predominantly the restrictive monetary policy of the
Federal Reserve—played a more damaging role in the economic disaster
of the 1930s.[70] Nevertheless, the legacy of Smoot-Hawley has continued to
loom heavily over trade policy debates in the decades following its passage. As a young lawyer on the Ways and Means Committee staff during
the markup of the bill later enacted as the Trade Act of 1974, I remember
vividly Congressman Sam M. Gibbons (D-FL) pointing up to the portrait of
Chairman Willis Hawley hanging in the committee room in the Longworth
House Office Building and warning against what he deemed were protectionist provisions in the bill and a resurrection of the policies that took the
country into the Great Depression.

In the famous 1993 CNN debate between Vice President Al Gore and
the then former independent presidential candidate, Ross Perot, over the
North American Free Trade Agreement, favored by Gore and opposed by

Perot, Gore presented a framed picture of Mr. Smoot and Mr. Hawley to Perot and said:

> They look like pretty good fellas. They sounded reasonable at the time; a lot of people believed them. The Congress passed the Smoot-Hawley Protection Bill. He [Perot] wants to raise tariffs on Mexico. They raised tariffs, and it was one of the principal causes, many economists say the principal cause, of the Great Depression in this country and around the world. Now I framed this so you can put it on your wall if you want to.[71]

Whatever effect Smoot-Hawley may have ultimately had on the catastrophic economic decade that emerged in 1930, the combination of the downturn with the negative reaction to the new tariffs had an immediate, explosive political impact. The Tariff Act of 1930 proved to be the beginning of the end of the Hoover administration. The 1930 midterm elections were a disaster for the Republicans even before the full effects of the Depression had set in. The GOP lost fifty-one seats and control of the House of Representatives. Though Republicans retained control of the Senate by one vote, insurgent Republicans working closely with Democrats—who had made Smoot-Hawley and agriculture the major issues in the election— gave progressives control on trade issues. Cordell Hull, the leading trade reformer in the House, won a Senate seat and began circulating a plan to roll back Smoot-Hawley before the new Congress was even sworn in.

Hull denounced the "narrow and selfish spirit of economic nationalism [of the Harding, Coolidge, and Hoover years] as the greatest danger to world peace today . . . [and which] more seriously threatens the world with bankruptcy than war itself." He advocated a three-point program to restore the American export market and "help pull the country from depression." He urged that the president call a permanent world economic congress to promote trade liberalization, that Congress grant the president authority to negotiate reciprocal trade agreements with other countries based on mutual tariff concessions, and that Congress proceed toward gradual readjustment downward of excessive tariffs.[72] Responding to Senator Hull's call, a coalition of Democrats and insurgent Republicans controlling Congress passed the Collier Tariff Bill in early 1932, which, among other things, called for an international conference on trade and requested that the president negotiate reciprocal trade agreements with foreign governments under a policy of mutual trade concessions. But President Hoover had the last word. The embattled president, suffering through a brutal campaign year, vetoed the bill on May 11, 1932.

Hoover may have perceived the bill as simply an effort by the Democrats to undermine his reelection effort, but his final message on trade was true to his protectionist principles. He wrote that the idea of an international conference on trade was unacceptable and would be a "radical change in historic policies." From the time of Washington's administration, he said, "one of our firm national policies has been that tariffs are solely a domestic question in protection of our own people." As to the notion of tariff reductions, he declared, "There has never been a time in the history of the United States when tariff protection was more essential to the welfare of the American people than at present."[73] After two years' experience with the disastrous effects—both political and economic—of the Tariff Act of 1930, Herbert Hoover was determined in his path and unrepentant.

Reed Smoot and Willis Hawley also made their last official statements on trade that year. Both went down in defeat in the election of 1932.

PART TWO

Transformation

The Creation of the Liberal Economic Order

7

FDR and Cordell Hull

If I were President of the United States, I should . . .
propose to all commercial nations at the close of
the present European war an international trade
conference . . . for the purpose of establishing a
permanent international trade congress . . . to
formulate agreements . . . designed to eliminate and
avoid the injurious results and dangerous possibilities
of economic warfare, and to promote fair and friendly
trade relations among all the nations of the world.[1]
                           —Representative Cordell Hull
                                         July 8, 1916

Franklin Roosevelt met Cordell Hull for the first time at the 1912 Democratic Convention in Baltimore, where both were supporting the then unlikely presidential candidacy of Woodrow Wilson. Roosevelt, a thirty-year-old progressive Democrat completing his first term in the New York State Senate, was enjoying his initial exposure to national politics. He had been passed over by the Tammany-controlled power structure to attend as a convention delegate but was able to wrangle floor credentials as chair of a rump group of New York Wilson supporters. Roosevelt spent most of his time glad-handing with delegates in the hotel and convention lobbies, promoting Wilson, and making new friends. Among those new friends would be two southern-ers: Hull and a North Carolina newspaper editor, Josephus Daniels, who would soon become Wilson's secretary of the navy and Roosevelt's boss.[2]

CONTRASTING COMMONALITIES

Cordell Hull at forty was a three-term liberal congressman from rural Tennessee enamored of Wilson's idealism and views on free trade. Although he had never met Wilson and had a close working relationship with the leading Democratic candidates, House Speaker Champ Clark and fellow southerner, Ways and Means chairman Oscar Underwood, Hull had studied Wilson's speeches and brief political record. He recalled later, "There was no doubt that Wilson's principles were mine." With Wilson's ultimate victory in November, Hull noted the "great rejoicing among the progressive forces at the defeat of the powerful reactionary phalanx that had ruled the nation as with a rod of iron for sixteen years."[3]

During the Wilson years, Roosevelt moved to Washington after being appointed assistant secretary of the navy—a position he coveted because of his love of the sea and because his fifth cousin Theodore had held it on his path to the White House. Congressman Hull and the aggressive young sub-cabinet official would often come in contact, though their official positions did not require it and they certainly did not run in the same social circles. Hull was not married until 1918 and rarely participated in Washington society, but if he had, he would not have had much in common with Roosevelt beyond Democratic politics and Wilsonian idealism.

Hull rose from the hardscrabble life in the foothills of Appalachia, where he was literally born in a log cabin. He and his four brothers were taught their ABCs and the Bible by their mother between her chores on the spinning wheel and in the farmyard. By contrast, Franklin Roosevelt was born into the American aristocracy of the Gilded Age and grew up among the landed gentry of the New York Hudson River Valley in a comfortable seventeen-room mansion on the wooded estate of Hyde Park with private tutors and a full-time hovering mother. Franklin's father, James, was fifty-three when Franklin was born and in ill health during much of the period before he died, when Franklin was a freshman in college. Biographer Jean Edward Smith writes, "The most important figure in Roosevelt's life was his mother, Sara."[4] Roosevelt was known as a "Mama's boy" most of his life.

Hull's character was most influenced by his father, William, a yeoman farmer and later a successful logger and general store owner, driven by relentless determination and a fierce temperament. With apparent pride, Cordell illustrates his father's determination and temperament with an anecdote in his memoirs. Near the end of the Civil War, William was attacked by "Yankee guerrillas" who killed a man who was with him and shot William through the right eye with the bullet passing out of the back of his head. He was left for dead, but recovered partly, losing sight in his right eye. At the end of the war, William tracked down one of the men responsible for the attack two states away in Kentucky and, according to Cordell, "went straight to him without ceremony and shot him dead."[5]

Both the famous Roosevelt temperament—intuitive, almost effeminate geniality—and Hull's contrasting stiff, reserved, but often feisty personality might be attributed to influences derived at home.

There were similar stark differences in their educational pedigrees. Roosevelt naturally followed a privileged path—beginning at the prestigious Groton School in Massachusetts, then going on to Harvard College, and finishing at Columbia University Law School. While his scholastic record was undistinguished, he was elected editor of the *Harvard Crimson* and maintained a full social calendar. He often hosted parties at the home his mother rented in Boston to be close to him after his father died. During his first year of law school, Franklin married his fifth cousin once removed, Anna Eleanor Roosevelt, the daughter of President Theodore Roosevelt's brother Elliott, who had died eleven years earlier. TR gave Eleanor away in a highly celebrated New York ceremony in March 1905. Before finishing his law degree, Franklin passed the New York bar in 1907 and joined one of the most prestigious Wall Street law firms, Carter, Ledyard and Milburn, as an unsalaried apprentice. The firm represented J. P. Morgan during the Wall Street Panic of 1907 and later handled anti-trust cases for John D. Rockefeller's Standard Oil Company and the American Tobacco Company.

The opportunities for education were few in the territory where Cordell Hull's father's farm was located. But in 1886, when he was fifteen and his father's logging business was prosperous enough, Cordell was sent twelve miles away to Celina, Tennessee, to the Montvale Institute for five months of intense study of algebra, geometry, trigonometry, advanced English, rhetoric, Latin, Greek, and German. He already had developed a strong interest in history and literature and was steeped in Gibbon's "Rome" and Shakespeare. Like most Tennesseans he idolized Andrew Jackson and learned about the Civil War from veterans' stories told in country stores. His principal teacher and strongest inspiration at Montvale was Professor Joe S. McMillin, whose brother was local congressman Benton McMillin. Benton served on the Ways and Means Committee and was an avid opponent of high tariffs and the co-author with then congressman William Jennings Bryan of the income tax provision held unconstitutional in the controversial 1895 US Supreme Court decision.[6] Another brother was John McMillin, a brilliant Celina lawyer. In Celina, Hull attended court whenever he had a chance and read his first daily newspaper. He developed an intense interest in public affairs and decided he wanted to become a lawyer. After his term at Montvale, Hull attended "normal" schools for teachers in Bowling Green, Kentucky, and Lebanon, Ohio, and read law in John McMillin's office while working on his father's farm in the summers. Before he was seventeen, in the summer of 1888, he made his first political speech supporting tariff reform and Grover Cleveland's reelection. In 1891, he attended Cumberland Law School in Lebanon, Tennessee, and graduated after ten months, passed the bar at age nineteen, and immediately began practicing law.

A month after turning twenty-one, Hull was elected to the state legislature. During the next year, he made his first trip to Washington, where Congressman McMillin took him to meet with President Cleveland in the president's Oval Room office in the upstairs of the White House. Cleveland had just been inaugurated to his second nonconsecutive term promising tariff reforms—an issue that had defeated him in his bid for reelection four years earlier. The president graciously received the young Tennessee legislator, and Hull, a great admirer of his tariff policies, praised the president's achievements as among the best of those who had served in that office. Despite his admiration for the president on trade policy, Hull followed McMillin and most Tennesseans in splitting with Cleveland on the silver issue in 1896.

Coincidentally, Franklin Roosevelt had also visited President Cleveland at the White House. James Roosevelt, a staunch Democrat and old friend of Cleveland's from New York politics, took five-year-old Franklin to meet the president during his first term in 1887 in the midst of a particularly trying period for Cleveland. As FDR enjoyed telling the story later, "My little man, I am making a strange wish for you," Cleveland said to him, while patting Franklin's head, as he and his father were departing the executive mansion: "It is that you may never be president of the United States."[7]

Thirteen years after making that first trip to Washington, Cordell Hull was elected to fill the congressional seat of his old friend and mentor Benton McMillin, who had retired several years earlier. From the beginning of his career, Hull earned a reputation for persistence, diligence, and focus. He was by his own admission a poor public speaker; he spoke in a high-pitched, raspy voice with a lisp, pronouncing his favorite phrase, for example, "fwee twade." But he worked hard at mastering what he considered the two most important government issues, though they were the dullest to most members—taxation and public expenditures—and made sure that he knew more about those matters than anyone else in Congress. He chose those issues because, like Wilson, he was a true believer in Gladstone liberalism and had become convinced that the wealthy were dumping their burdens on the working classes. Only twelve days after entering Congress, he introduced a comprehensive income tax bill. And although the dictatorial Speaker Joe Cannon refused to give him a significant committee assignment during his first two terms, Hull persistently made sure his voice was heard on all tax and tariff issues during that period.

In his maiden speech, Hull came out forcefully for a national income tax and vigorously attacked "the king of evils," protective tariffs, which, he claimed, were the forebears of monopolies and trusts. "The flag of monopoly has always floated above the ramparts of protection," Hull said, as he attacked President Theodore Roosevelt for having loudly inveighed against the evils of trusts, yet championed the protective tariffs that fostered trusts. "The American people," Hull observed, "are merely experiencing an optical illusion due to the pyrotechnic display of the President." Hull, who called the GOP "the toady, the lackey, the flunky of the trusts," gave his speech during a highly partisan period when the Republican Old Guard, whom Hull dubbed "the criminal plutocracy," dominated Congress and several years before TR had adopted his full-throated Bull Moose progressive program. He accused the president of "paternalism" that failed to suppress lawless business combinations, to properly curb corporate wealth, and to secure to labor its just rights. "The President," he said, "is paternally and eternally advocating doctrines so extremely Federalistic and paternalistic . . . as would have put to shame Alexander Hamilton himself."[8]

When the Democrats took control of the House of Representatives following the 1910 elections, the leadership selected Hull to be among those to reorganize the committee system. Earlier, in March 1910, a coalition of progressive Republicans and Democrats had stripped Speaker Cannon of his autocratic powers, including the power to make all committee assignments for both Democrats and Republicans. The new Democratic leaders were not inclined to return this power to a Democratic Speaker. The reformers decided to give the power of committee appointments to the Democrats on the Ways and Means Committee, who would be appointed by party caucus. Ways and Means thus became the steering committee of the House and nominated the membership of all other committees of the House, subject to the approval of the full party caucus. This rule continued in place until the post-Watergate reforms in the mid-1970s. Hull was immediately selected as a member of the Ways and Means Committee; others were not so fortunate in the selection process, which required a qualification interview with the party leadership and a teamwork pledge. Edward Pou of North Carolina, for example, was removed from Ways and Means because he had once voted for a tariff on lumber.

Hull was especially proud of the progressive record of reforms that the Sixty-Second Congress passed during 1911–12. Among the House-passed bills that he lists in his memoirs are the establishment of an eight-hour workday, the creation of the Department of Labor, tariff reductions, the provision of an excise tax on individuals, a resolution calling on the president to abrogate the Treaty of 1832 with Russia because of Russian persecution of Jews, the creation of a legislature for Alaska, the founding of agricultural extension departments, campaign finance reforms for congressional elections, and the proposal of an amendment to the Constitution to elect US senators by direct popular vote.[9]

Following the inauguration of President Wilson in 1913, Hull worked closely on Ways and Means with Chairman Underwood in framing the tariff reforms in the Underwood Tariff Act and wrote and managed on the House floor passage of the income tax to replace the revenue lost in tariff reductions. His role in this legislation not only made him the father of the modern income tax; it also raised his status as a national political figure and a key ally for Wilson's progressive agenda. Named to the executive committee of the Democratic National Committee (DNC), he moved to New York City for several months to help organize Wilson's reelection in 1916. But his main contributions remained in the House, where he built on his reputation as the leading expert on fiscal issues in Congress. Among other legislative accomplishments, he wrote and managed estate tax and excess profit tax bills that would provide the basis for financing the American efforts in the First World War.

The philosophy guiding Hull's support for lowering trade barriers evolved as war became more imminent for the United States in 1916. Whereas he had previously emphasized the goal of equalizing the tax burdens between the working and wealthy classes, he now began prominently to include the objective of promoting peace. He came to believe—and carried this belief through his service as secretary of state during the Second World

War—that free trade was associated with peace and that trade barriers and unfair economic competition bred war. He thus proposed a resolution calling for a "permanent international congress," along the lines of today's World Trade Organization in Geneva, to consider all international trade practices that create commercial disputes and bitter economic wars and to reach agreements to promote fair trade relations among the world's nations. Although this idea was far ahead of its time and Wilson's State Department rebuffed him on it, he claims in his memoirs that it became the forerunner of Point Three of Wilson's Fourteen Points in the Versailles peace talks calling for elimination of international trade barriers.[10] True or not, Hull's record of service clearly impressed the president, as Wilson listed Hull among the three Democrats most qualified for the vice presidency in 1920.

On a different track, Franklin Roosevelt also raised his national political profile during the two Wilson terms. He reveled in his work at the Navy Department, where he learned the intricacies of bureaucratic manipulation and used his unparalleled social skills to expand his base to every corner of Washington's power structure. His role as assistant secretary may have been limited, but he boasted that he was able to get his "fingers into just about everything and there's no law against it."[11] Roosevelt maintained a good relationship with his boss, Secretary Josephus Daniels, even though some of his actions bordered on insubordination. In testimony before the House Committee on Naval Affairs he observed the need for more ships and enlistments for naval readiness in case of war, which directly contradicted the position taken by his superiors. Daniels and Secretary of State William Jennings Bryan believed that such increases might draw the United States into the European war. Roosevelt recognized that his position might get him into trouble, and told Eleanor so, but also that he was prepared to stand by it. "The country needs the truth about the Army and the Navy," he said, "instead of the soft mush about everlasting peace which so many statesmen are handing out to a gullible public."[12] An unabashed self-promoter, Roosevelt even hired his own publicist to support his positions. Through it all, he gained a formidable reputation for his naval expertise among the hawks on Capitol Hill and the military brass. Eventually, President Wilson, increasingly concerned about German war plans, came to agree with him and in December 1915 authorized the largest peacetime naval expansion in history. Because his responsibilities included handling labor issues at the Naval Yard, Roosevelt also established a reputation as a problem solver on labor issues and fostered valuable relationships with union leaders.

In 1914, following ratification of the Seventeenth Amendment to the Constitution, which provided that Senate elections would be determined by popular vote, and while retaining his position at the Navy Department, Roosevelt made a quixotic run for the US Senate in New York. He lost the primary in a landslide to a Tammany-supported candidate, James W. Gerard, who was serving as Wilson's ambassador to Germany and did not leave his foreign post for the duration of the campaign. With no visible candidate present to run against, the progressive Roosevelt had railed against the corrupt politics of Tammany "bossism" and refused to support Gerard, who ended up losing to a Republican in the general election. Although he never forgave Gerard for giving him his first taste of political defeat, Roosevelt soon acknowledged the error of his ways and came to terms with the power of Tammany in order to salvage his political career in New York. At the urging of his key political adviser, Louis Howe, Roosevelt made peace with Tammany boss Charles Francis Murphy and endorsed Tammany candidates for the remainder of the decade.

THE TWENTIES

At the 1920 Democratic convention, Roosevelt gave a rousing, widely praised seconding speech to Murphy's favorite-son candidate, New York governor Alfred E. Smith, and gained Murphy's rather reluctant endorsement as the nominee for vice president on the ticket with the ultimate presidential nominee, Governor James Cox of Ohio. Roosevelt was only thirty-eight years old, but he was handsome, athletic, progressive, and in possession of a well-respected wartime record and famous name. He was also from New York, which held forty-five electoral votes, more than any other state in the nation. FDR's nomination, which was granted by acclamation, received applause from a broad range of political perspectives. Walter Lippmann, the influential liberal columnist from the *New Republic* and later a caustic FDR critic, called it "the best news in many a long day." Herbert Hoover, a Wilson administration colleague with whom Roosevelt had been tagged as a possible 1920 Democratic ticket before Hoover declared allegiance to the GOP, wrote to Roosevelt that he considered the nomination "a contribution to the good of the country" and noted that "it will bring the merit of a great public servant to the front."[13] The election brought a national spotlight upon the young, ambitious Roosevelt as he barnstormed across the country, extolling the virtues of the League of Nations and Wilsonian internation-alist idealism.

But 1920 was not a good year for Democrats, and both FDR and Cordell Hull suffered from anti-Wilson sentiment and harsh postwar economic conditions. The promise of a "return to normalcy" by the amiable Warren G. Harding, with whom Roosevelt had often golfed at the Chevy Chase Country Club, proved to be the prescription desired by the American elec-torate. The Cox-Roosevelt ticket lost in a landslide to Harding-Coolidge, whose coattails brought in Republican supermajorities in both chambers of Congress. Among the Democratic seats lost in the House was that of Cordell Hull. He lost by fewer than 300 votes in a Tennessee district that had always been closely divided by party. For Roosevelt, however, the loss of his election was dramatically eclipsed by the misfortune he suffered the following year when he suddenly contracted poliomyelitis. The crippling affliction appeared likely to terminate his meteoric rise to national promi-nence as well as the great promise for his political future.

In Hull's case, political exile was short-lived. Soon after his failed bid for reelection to Congress, he was chosen to be national chairman of the Democratic National Committee, which was deeply in debt following the debacle of the 1920 election. He spent most of the next two years traveling around the country, raising money for the party, building state organiza-tions, and giving speeches condemning Republican high-tariff economic policies embodied in the Fordney-McCumber bill then under consider-ation. He also fostered strong political relationships around the nation, including his relationship with FDR and chief adviser and confidant, Louis Howe. While remaining DNC chair through the 1924 Democratic conven-tion, Hull returned to Tennessee and regained his House seat in 1922 by a 7,000-vote margin. He attributed his victory in part to the women's vote authorized by the recently ratified Nineteenth Amendment initiated during the Wilson administration.

Despite the severe limitations imposed by polio, Roosevelt soon got back into the political game. He endured and masked his painful handicap with characteristic optimism and a cheerful stiff-upper-lip disposition. Roosevelt gradually reestablished his New York political base from his wheelchair with a letter-writing campaign to partisans around the state and with able assistance from his dedicated aide and adviser Louis Howe and his wife, Eleanor. Howe, an unkempt, chain-smoking former journal-ist who latched on to FDR during his state senate tenure, was physically

FIGURE 7.1　Representative Cordell Hull as chairman of the Democratic National Committee in 1924 (Library of Congress)

the opposite of Roosevelt. According to Eleanor, Howe was "a gnome-like looking little man,"[14] and by Howe's own description, his face was "one of the four ugliest" in New York.[15] But Howe's shrewd, unvarnished political insight—not to mention his complete devotion to Roosevelt's journey to the White House—appealed to the ambitious young politician. Both Howe and Eleanor substituted for him at public events as he came to terms with the early stages of his paralysis. Eleanor did so despite her distaste for politics, discomfort with public appearances, and the permanent injury caused by her shocking discovery in 1918 of secret love letters between FDR and her former social secretary, the attractive Lucy Mercer. As a tribute to the success of these efforts, Tammany Hall approached him in 1922 about running as their candidate for governor. Roosevelt ultimately demurred for health reasons, but played a public role in both promoting the nomination of Al Smith, who had been defeated for reelection in 1920, and stopping that of the controversial newspaper magnate William Randolph Hearst.

By 1924, however, Roosevelt was ready to enter the national stage again and did so by chairing Al Smith's campaign for president and giving a dramatic nominating speech for Smith at the Democratic convention in Madison Square Garden. With the aid of his sixteen-year-old son James, heavy leg braces, and crutches, he made it to the platform while sweating profusely, and walked the last steps alone to the podium, which he grasped firmly, imposing his weight on the stand. The audience of 8,000 in the Garden burst into tumultuous applause while watching this painful feat. In his booming tenor voice, which was electronically amplified and broadcast across the nation on radio for the first time at a political convention, FDR presented a litany of Governor Smith's progressive accomplishments for the common people, including outlawing child labor and night work for women as well as sponsoring a workmen's compensation law, state pensions for widowed mothers, labor boards to mediate disputes between employer and employee, and "the best factory laws ever passed in any state." Roosevelt concluded his half-hour speech with a phrase borrowed from a Wordsworth poem by Smith's speechwriter but forever associated with FDR rather than Smith: "He is the 'Happy Warrior' of the political battlefield."[16] As he finished, the crowd again broke out in cheers and Roosevelt had become "the most popular man at the convention," according to the *New York Times*.[17]

People close to FDR both before and after he contracted polio noticed a change in him in the period following the development of his paralysis. They observed that he became more genuinely concerned and truly sympathetic toward the plight of the infirm and the underprivileged classes. Many who knew him during his early days in politics—including Francis Perkins, whom he later appointed secretary of labor and the first female cabinet official in US history, thought of him as an arrogant dilettante with "deafness to the hopes, fears, and aspirations which are the common lot." Perkins wrote, "I believe that at that time, Franklin Roosevelt had little, if any, concern about specific social reforms. . . . The marvel is that these handicaps were washed out of him by life, experience, punishment, and his capacity to grow."[18] Eleanor, Howe, and others came to believe that his paralysis made him more sensitive to the struggles many faced that he had never before personally experienced.[19] At Warm Springs, Georgia, where he retreated for mineral spring treatment of his polio, he witnessed up close and every day the effects of extreme rural poverty and Jim Crow racism. Perhaps it was during this period that he became ensconced in the attitude that would inspire some to denounce him as a "traitor to his class."

In 1925, he published a letter written to the leadership of the Democratic Party urging the party to be "unqualifiedly the party representative of progress and liberal thought":

> In other words, the clear line of demarcation which differentiated the political thought of Jefferson on the one side and of Hamilton on the other must be restored. The Democracy must make it clear that it seeks primarily the good of the average citizen . . . as opposed to the Republican Party, which seeks a mere moneyed prosperity of the nation through the control of government by a self-appointed aristocracy of wealth and of social and economic power.[20]

In December of the same year, FDR wrote a review of the book *Jefferson and Hamilton*, by Claude Bowers, for the *New York Evening World*. In the piece, Roosevelt depicted the development of the first political parties with Jefferson attempting to mobilize the masses against Hamilton's "autocracy of the few." While the "organized compact forces of wealth, of birth, of commerce" backed Hamilton's party, Jefferson could only count on "the scattered raw material of the working masses, difficult to reach, more difficult to organize." Obviously referring to the Republicans' control of government in the twenties, FDR wrote, "Hamiltons we have today. Is a Jefferson on the horizon?"[21] Though nurtured among the forces of wealth, birth, and commerce in the Hudson River Valley, Roosevelt was now clearly aligning with the tradition carried forward from Adam Smith by Jefferson, Jackson, Cleveland, and Wilson on the side of the working-class struggle against the protectionist special interests of the moneyed class.

Cordell Hull, emanating from an entirely different foundation, found much in common with Roosevelt's political sentiments. Hull's attacks against trade protectionism always included the populist arguments of Jefferson and Jackson, pitting the struggle of workers and small farmers against the eastern industrial and financial interests. And Roosevelt had consistently taken the Democratic position on tariff reform incessantly espoused by Hull. As each of them gained more prominence on the national political scene in the mid-1920s, they became natural allies, conferring often when Roosevelt came through Washington on his trips to Warm Springs. Hull was in constant communication with Louis Howe, who was perpetually navigating FDR's path to the White House.

Although both Hull and Roosevelt supported Governor Al Smith's campaign for president in 1928—Roosevelt again gave an eloquent nominating speech for Smith at the convention—they did not agree with the direction taken by Smith and his campaign manager, John J. Raskob, to attract the support of conservative businessmen. Raskob was himself a multimillionaire, a former General Motors executive who had left the Republican Party to chair the Democratic National Committee for Smith. Like Smith, Raskob was an Irish Catholic and a "wet," favoring repeal of Prohibition—both of which represented Smith's major weaknesses in uniting the party behind his candidacy. He was also a trade protectionist and led Smith to take a similar stance. In what Hull called "a typical high-tariff speech" during the campaign at Louisville, Kentucky, Smith said that due to the "economic ruin of the rest of the world" the Democratic Party should "stand in favor of such tariff schedules as will to the very limit protect legitimate business enterprise as well as American labor from ruinous competition of foreign-made goods." At his insistence, the Democratic Party platform adopted the long-held Republican position of promoting tariffs that "would equalize the difference between costs of production abroad and at home." In Hull's view, this policy would effectively impose an embargo on imports due to the added costs of transportation, insurance, and currency exchange and consequently represented "the unconditional surrender of the Democratic Party to the forces of high-tariff greed and privilege."[22]

THE 1932 PRESIDENTIAL NOMINATION

Following the landslide victory for Herbert Hoover over Smith in the 1928 election, Cordell Hull quietly began a move to replace Smith and his allies, most prominently Raskob, from control of the Democratic Party. Roosevelt, who had reluctantly accepted a draft by Smith for the Democratic nomination for governor of New York, managed to succeed Smith by narrowly claiming one of the few Democratic victories in 1928. In 1930, Hull also moved up politically as a result of his election to the US Senate. He had grown weary of his service in the House, especially after having vainly butted heads with the Republican leadership over the Smoot-Hawley Act, and was considering retiring in frustration when the Senate seat opened up unexpectedly with the death of the incumbent. In the same year, Roosevelt won reelection as governor with the highest margin in the state's history. As Smith had moved to a more conservative stance, FDR established himself as the most progressive voice in the party by launching a number of pro-labor initiatives to address the budding Depression, including workmen's compensation, unemployment relief, and expansive public works projects.

Early in 1931, Smith and Raskob attempted to move the DNC to adopt platform policies for the next election, including most prominently tariff protection and repeal of Prohibition. Smith argued that tariffs should be taken out of politics by minimizing the partisan distinction on the issue. Hull was outraged and gave a speech condemning the idea of merging the economic policies of the two parties "under the false but attractive plea to 'take the tariff out of politics.'"[23] Roosevelt, who had been in Smith's camp for years, called Hull and offered his support to arrest Smith's and Raskob's attempt to impose their views on the Democratic platform. In a letter to another friend just before the meeting, Roosevelt explained that the party must not yield to Raskob and "make our party a party of high tariffs and a friend to those vested interests which have so completely dominated the Republican organization for so many years. If we win, we must win because we are progressive."[24]

At the March 5, 1931, DNC meeting where Raskob planned to have his proposals adopted, Roosevelt sent his campaign manager and chairman of the New York Democratic Party, James A. Farley, to sit next to Hull to make manifest his support. Both Hull and Roosevelt had worked the phones prior to the meeting to gain more than enough support to defeat Raskob. Hull and Raskob made competing speeches on the tariff and Prohibition issues, but Raskob dropped the effort to have the committee adopt preemptive positions for the party platform. According to Hull, Roosevelt's maneuver regarding this meeting established his independence from the Smith organ-ization and was a turning point in attracting southern and western leaders to his presidential candidacy to defeat another Smith nomination in 1932. It also confirmed to Hull that Roosevelt shared his anti-tariff and "damp" (neither "wet" nor "dry," let the states decide) views on Prohibition, even though the basis for Roosevelt's views may have been more political prag-matism than deep substantive conviction. As historian Arthur Schlesinger Jr. observes in connection with the Prohibition issue, FDR "wanted nothing to distract the old Bryan group [who were 'dry'] from a fight against busi-ness rule. . . . For by the spring of 1931 Roosevelt was drawing clearly ahead as the candidate for 1932, and Roosevelt's candidacy was aggressively identified with the liberal wing of the Democratic party."[25]

Over the next year, leading up to the Democratic National Convention in Chicago, Roosevelt filled the nation's radio airwaves with speeches denouncing Hoover and the Republican Party and formally announced his candidacy on January 23, 1932. Hull, now fully committed to Roosevelt's nomination, praised all of the speeches but one. FDR greatly disappointed Hull and other Wilsonian internationalists, including Eleanor, in a speech aimed to satisfy the powerful and nationalistic publisher William Randolph Hearst. In it the candidate announced that he no longer supported American participation in the League of Nations. Making no apology for having supported it as the "single paramount issue" while running for vice president in 1920, Roosevelt said the League had "not developed through these years along the course contemplated by its founder." The League was designed by Wilson to promote world peace, he said, but had become a vehicle for dealing only with European political differences, a role the United States should avoid. Parts of the speech must have pleased Hull, because in it Roosevelt also blasted the Smoot-Hawley Act and called for an international trade conference to break down high tariff walls that had "paralyzed world trade and thrown millions here and abroad out of useful work."[26] Thus, the speech reflected an FDR move away from political internationalism while carefully steering clear of economic nationalism.

Hull especially liked FDR's "forgotten man" radio speech on April 7, parts of which Roosevelt repeated often in the months prior to the convention. In contrast to Hoover's policies, the speech argued that prosperity should come "from the bottom up and not the top down." He said the working class, "the infantry of our economic army," had been ignored by Hoover. Roosevelt urged putting "faith once more in the forgotten man at the bottom of the economic pyramid." Government should "provide at least as much assistance to the little fellow [to avoid foreclosure] as it is now giving to the large banks and corporations." He called for restoring purchasing power to the farmers and reducing the "foolish tariff" through reciprocal trade agreements so that Americans could sell their products to those nations desiring to sell to Americans. What was needed was "a tariff policy based upon economic common sense rather than upon politics, hot-air, and pull."[27]

Hull had only recently used the "forgotten man" reference in an anti-tariff speech in the Senate and assumed that FDR had gotten the idea from him. But, ironically, Raymond Moley, a new speechwriter for Roosevelt and leader of the "Brains Trust" which soon would be battling with Hull for Roosevelt's attention on tariff issues, claimed that he, Moley, had "scraped" the phrase from his own memory.[28]

In his last pre-convention speech given at the commencement ceremonies of Oglethorpe University in Atlanta, Roosevelt expanded on the theme that inequality between the producers and consumers in the American economy had grown in the 1920s, with excess corporate profits far outpacing growth in workers' wages and diminishing farm incomes. In what would become the model for the New Deal approach to government intervention addressing this disparity and ensuring that "all who are willing and able to work receive . . . at least the necessities of life," he urged "bold, persistent experimentation." In contrast to Hoover's inaction, which relied upon cures provided by the voluntary efforts of private enterprise, Roosevelt stressed that the economic woes affecting the nation called for action. "It is common sense to take a method and try it: If it fails, admit it frankly and try another. But above all, try something."[29]

Prominently among those who did not like the Roosevelt message decrying income inequality was his former ally, Al Smith. Not ready to abandon his own presidential quest, Smith had made public two weeks after FDR announced his candidacy that he was available to "make the fight" if the convention should decide, "after careful consideration," that it wanted him to lead the ticket.[30] In the wake of FDR's invocation of the "forgotten man," Smith proclaimed in mid-April that he would "take off his coat and fight to the end against any candidate who persists in any demagogic appeal to the masses of the working people of this country to destroy themselves by setting class against class and rich against poor."[31] Roosevelt brushed off Smith's criticism and continued moving his campaign away from the more conservative stance that had failed Smith in 1928. As Ray Moley wrote in a memorandum to FDR one month before the convention, "There is no room in this country for two reactionary parties." According to Moley, Al Smith believed favoring the wealthy interests would create prosperity that would "leak through"—as in "trickle down"—to the laboring classes, whereas Roosevelt's Democrats would be the "party of liberal ideas, of planned action" for them.[32]

In the weeks prior to Chicago, Cordell Hull was in frequent contact with Roosevelt and Louis Howe on planning for the convention. Hull and other intimate supporters would visit FDR at Hyde Park on Sundays, and Howe would make Hull's Senate office his headquarters on his frequent trips to Washington. Roosevelt asked Hull to chair the Committee on Platform and Resolutions at the convention, but Hull demurred, saying that he thought he could be of more value defending Roosevelt's positions on the convention floor. Besides, he and Woodrow Wilson's attorney general, A. Mitchell Palmer, had already drafted the platform, which included a harsh condemnation of Hoover's tariff policies.

Hull was correct in predicting that there would be difficult fights over certain parts of the platform, especially on Prohibition and tariffs. Hull and Roosevelt favored allowing the states to decide Prohibition. While Hull made a valiant effort defending that position, FDR, however, refused to risk the fight and, through his campaign manager, Jim Farley, advised his delegates to vote as they wished on it. The "wets" won and adopted a plank urging outright repeal of the Eighteenth Amendment. Otherwise, Hull's draft largely prevailed. It blamed the Depression on "the disastrous policies" pursued by the Republican government since the World War and, among other things, called for an income tax based on ability to pay, unemployment relief, extensive public works, aid to agriculture, mortgage assistance, regulation of the securities industry, protection of bank deposits, and campaign finance reform. Hull was the clear victor on tariff reform, with the adoption of his language calling for "a competitive tariff for revenue . . . reciprocal tariff agreements with other nations, and an international economic conference designed to restore international trade." The platform specifically singled out the Smoot-Hawley Tariff Act for condemnation, saying it had "resulted in retaliatory action by more than forty countries, created international hostilities, destroyed international trade, driven out factories into foreign countries, robbed the American farmer of his foreign markets, and increased the cost of production."[33]

After adopting the platform, the convention began to take up nomination and balloting for the Democratic ticket at 3:00 in the afternoon on June 30. The speeches and four roll-call votes by the delegates went almost nonstop through the following evening when Roosevelt received the required two-thirds majority on the final ballot and was proclaimed the nominee at 10:32 P.M. Both of FDR's principal opponents—Al Smith and Speaker of the House John Nance Garner—were protectionists, which made Hull all the more relieved as the organist played the new Roosevelt campaign theme song, "Happy Days Are Here Again." While Smith never conceded, Garner abandoned the fight after the third ballot, when Roosevelt committed to support his nomination for vice president—an office Garner once declared not worth "a pitcher of warm piss."[34] Roosevelt, who had been following the convention proceedings from the New York governor's mansion in Albany, announced through the convention chair that he would fly to Chicago the next morning to personally accept the nomination. It was a dramatic move, not only because of the dangers associated with flying in 1932, but, more important, because it broke the long tradition of giving acceptance speeches in the nominee's hometown weeks after the convention concluded.

Arriving hours late due to severe headwinds and two stops for refueling, Roosevelt appeared on the stage again with the aid of his son, James, before the wildly enthusiastic thousands standing in the hall to greet him and millions listening on the radio. In the speech, which he had cobbled together with input from Louis Howe, Ray Moley, and his chief counsel Samuel I. Rosenman on the plane and during the car ride to the convention, FDR admitted that his decision to be there might be "unprecedented and unusual, but these are unprecedented and unusual times." And it was time for the Democratic Party "to break foolish traditions." The theory that government favoritism to the wealthy based on the hope "that some of their prosperity will leak through, sift through, to labor, to the farmer, to the small business man . . . belongs to the party of Toryism." The choice offered to the people was that reactionary doctrine or "a party of liberal thought, of planned action, of enlightened international outlook, and of the greatest good to the greatest number of our citizens." He committed the party to governmental action to deal aggressively with the causes and byproducts of the Depression, including securities regulation, public works, shorter workweeks, reforestation, agricultural production planning, and tariff reduction. Then the candidate finished with a promise that included the phrase picked up by the press as the slogan of his administration's progressive economic programs:

> I pledge you, I pledge myself, to a new deal for the American people. Let us all here assembled constitute ourselves prophets of a new order of competence and courage. This is more than a political campaign; it is a call to arms. Give me your help, not to win votes alone, but to win in this crusade to restore America to its own people.[35]

The following day a political cartoon depicted a farmer gazing up at an airplane marked "New Deal."

8

The Brain Trust

World trade is, after all, only a small percentage of the
entire trade of the United States. This means that our
domestic policy is of paramount importance.[1]
    —Assistant Secretary of State Raymond Moley
                                        May 20, 1933

While the Democratic Convention audience roared with approval and left
Chicago with hope and optimism that happy days might truly be here again
with a "new deal for the American people," some observers were less impressed
with FDR and his promises. Many of the political cognoscenti considered him
wishy-washy and unprincipled. The two most renowned pundits of the period,
Walter Lippmann and H. L. Mencken, were both decidedly underwhelmed.
Lippmann, who thought Roosevelt was an intellectual lightweight and dismissed him as an "amiable boy scout," wrote, "Franklin D. Roosevelt is no cru-
sader. He is no tribune of the people. He is no enemy of entrenched privilege.
He is a pleasant man who, without any important qualifications for the office,
would very much like to be President."[2] Similarly, Mencken piled on with biting
appraisals, observing that Roosevelt was "the most charming of men, but like
many another charming man he leaves on the beholder the impression that he
is also somewhat shallow and futile." Of course, Roosevelt was in good company as the subject of Mencken's ridicule. The "sage of Baltimore," as Mencken
was known, called the first President Roosevelt a "national Barbarossa" and
President Wilson "the self-bamboozled Presbyterian, the right-thinker, the
great moral statesman, the perfect model of the Christian cad."[3]

Later, Supreme Court Justice Oliver Wendell Holmes Jr. was often quoted as having tagged FDR with a "second-class intellect but a first-class temperament." While the Holmes quote is disputed by some as directed at TR rather than FDR, or simply apocryphal, it may come closest to depicting FDR's political assets. He was not an intellectual, but the combination of his determined, indefatigably optimistic outlook and masterful intuition in reading, manipulating, and benefiting from those around him produced a "temperament" that was indeed first class. This temperament, complemented by his acute sense of timing and policy instincts, often proved to be a formula for political genius.

THE PRIVY COUNCIL TO THE NEW DEAL

In March 1932, at the suggestion of his legal counsel in the governor's office, Sam Rosenman, Roosevelt assembled a group of academic experts to advise him on national issues for the campaign. Led by Ray Moley, Rexford G. Tugwell, and Adolf A. Berle Jr., all of Columbia University, the group was dubbed the "Brains Trust" by *New York Times* reporter James M. Kieran and later usually referred to collectively as the "Brain Trust." Their collaboration laid the conceptual groundwork for the economic plan for the New Deal. Moley was a political scientist with a substantive focus on criminal justice and had a special speechwriter's talent for turning memorable phrases; Tugwell was an innovative and radical agricultural economist; and Berle, who had voted for Hoover in 1928, was a brilliant corporate law professor who offered expertise mainly on banking and finance reform.

This "privy council," as Roosevelt initially referred to the collective, approached its task with what Moley called the "Look Homeward, Angel" interpretation of the Depression, meaning they believed "that the causes of [the economic] ills were domestic, internal, and that the remedies would have to be internal too."[4] This view rejected President Hoover's thesis that the Depression was caused by an international crisis and largely ignored or subordinated Hull's constant plea to expand foreign trade as a solution to the surplus production problem. Tugwell argued that the failure of American business to distribute the benefits of increased productivity through higher wages or lower prices had resulted in diminished purchasing power by consumers, leading to under-consumption and inevitably to the Depression. The solution had to focus on increasing domestic purchasing power, and trade promotion policy would not be a primary goal for the Brain Trust. Generally viewed as economic nationalists, they were not enamored by free-trade philosophy and feared that a focus on tariff reform might be at cross purposes with their own New Deal recovery plans.

Nevertheless, before the Chicago convention, the trade issue played a significant role in speeches because of the low tariff tradition of the Democratic Party and because Smoot-Hawley was such an attractive political target. Roosevelt especially needed a strong vote from the pro-trade southern and western delegates to distinguish himself from his main competitors for the nomination, Al Smith and Speaker Garner, in order to get the necessary two-thirds majority. As Tugwell observed, there would be difficulty on the trade issue with "Cordell Hull's uncompromising laissez faire; no old-line Democrat could go back on so traditional a doctrine, even if hardly anyone wanted to see it implemented."[5] After the nomination, Roosevelt put Moley in charge of all of his speeches, and all policy recommendations from others would have to be filtered through him. This gave Moley and the Brain Trust supremacy on clearing policy ideas presented to FDR over Louis Howe and Jim Farley, who were closest to Hull. The Brain Trust largely avoided Hull, whom Tugwell dismissed as a "Tennessee mountain politician, a bumbling free-trade advocate."[6]

In his first significant speech after becoming the Democratic candidate, Roosevelt supported the platform regarding tariffs as he urged the lowering of trade barriers "as quickly and definitely as possible" through negotiation "to set international trade flowing again."[7] But soon he began to vacillate on the issue as he was torn between the competing influences of the Brain Trust and other advisers. In August, Moley was preparing a new tariff speech and sought input from Hull, who was at home in Tennessee, through Charles W. Taussig, president of the American Molasses Company and a relative of the famed economist Frank Taussig. Taussig returned from Tennessee with a tariff speech that he and Hull had drafted which "stunned" the Moley team. Moley wrote that "there were groans of anguish" as the Hull-Taussig draft was read to the group. It recommended that FDR come out for unilaterally cutting all tariffs by 10 percent across the board. They began work immediately on an alternative draft that called for bilateral negotiations, using "old-fashioned Yankee horse-trades," to find markets for domestic surplus production in exchange for lower tariffs on foreign imports "which would least disturb the domestic system." Moley presented both drafts to FDR, who after reading them left Moley "speechless" with the "impossible assignment" to "weave the two together."[8]

With further revisions added by two protectionist-leaning Democratic senators, Thomas J. Walsh of Montana and Key D. Pittman of Nevada, Moley presented a new draft accepted by Roosevelt. The governor called it "a compromise between the free traders and the protectionists,"[9] but, apart from characterizing some of the Smoot-Hawley rates as "outrageously excessive," it proved to be a profound disappointment to Hull and other free-traders. In essence the speech represented a retreat to the Smith-Raskob stance, minimizing the differences between the Republican and Democratic positions. Roosevelt said that "despite the effort, repeated in every campaign, to stigmatize the Democratic Party as a free trade party," duties were always levied in tariff acts "with a view to giving the American producer an advantage over his foreign competitor." He promised tariff revisions that "would injure no legitimate interest."[10] A liberal columnist for the *Nation* accused Roosevelt of abandoning the Democratic anti-protectionist tradition and eliminating any difference between Roosevelt and Hoover on the tariff. The writer observed, "Presidential elections [have] usually been bought by the tariff magnates," and in this case neither candidate wished "to offend the protected big boys who hold the money bags."[11]

In the final weeks of the campaign, FDR continued to hedge as President Hoover challenged him to list the tariffs he would reduce from the Smoot-Hawley levels. The week before the election, Hoover declared that if Roosevelt were elected president and the Democratic tariff policy adopted, "The grass will grow in the streets of a hundred cities, a thousand towns; the weeds will overrun the fields of millions of farms if that protection be taken away."[12] Ignoring the challenge, Roosevelt shored up his position with farmers, saying that "it is absurd to talk of lowering tariff duties on farm products. . . . I know of no effective excessively high tariff duties on farm products. I do not intend that such duties shall be lowered." He promised "continued protection for American agriculture as well as American industry" and advocated "measures to give the farmer an added benefit, to make the tariff effective on his products."[13] While continuing to blur his differences with Republican tariff policies in some respects, Roosevelt did not hesitate to continue his attack on Smoot-Hawley tariff levels and call for reciprocal trade negotiations with other countries. Only days before the election, FDR rationalized his ambivalent approach in an interview with the *New York Times Magazine*. He said that trade-prohibiting tariffs were "strangling civilization" and were "symptoms of economic insanity." The governor predicted that if "the present tariff war continues, the world will go back a thousand years." Yet until "the crazy system could be revised as a whole," he concluded, "farm products had to have emergency protection."[14]

THE PRESIDENT-ELECT AND THE SECRETARY
OF STATE DESIGNEE

The magnetic, though often evasive, candidate Roosevelt presented nothing but frustration to the glum incumbent. The president called his challenger "a chameleon on Scotch plaid"[15] and warned that his old colleague from the Wilson days would overturn the American economic and social system for the next hundred years. The problem for Hoover was that along with the Great Depression and the end to Coolidge prosperity came the hope for just such a revolutionary change. Hoover claimed that employment was rebounding as the economy recovered on its own and vetoed a federal relief and public works bill. The soup lines and squalid encampments of homeless people out of work on the edge of major cities, commonly called "Hoovervilles," only reinforced the belief that the president was doing nothing to address the country's economic woes while Roosevelt was promising "bold experimentation," though vaguely defined, to overcome the plight of the unemployed millions of "forgotten men." On Election Day, the FDR landslide was inevitable. Hoover lost all but six states, and the margin for Roosevelt exceeded 7 million popular votes in an electoral vote victory of 472 for FDR to Hoover's 59. The election also swept a two-to-one Democratic majority into the House and a plus-fifteen majority into the Senate. "All informed observers agree," wrote the *New Republic*, "that the country did not vote for Roosevelt; it voted against Hoover." The liberal journal offered little promise for partisan loyalty to the new president-elect in leading the nation out of its great and perplexing difficulties, observing: "The Democratic party is one of the most ill assorted coalitions in the history of constitutional government."[16]

In the long four-month interval between the election and the inauguration on March 4, 1933, Roosevelt began organizing his administration in the midst of the increasingly intense economic crisis. In a late November meeting at Warm Springs, he advised Moley that he had decided to give the title of secretary to the president to Louis Howe—to whom, along with Jim

Farley, FDR gave credit for his victory. To keep Howe happy, Roosevelt said he would do away with the three administrative assistants to the president, positions maintained in the Hoover administration. The president-elect continued that he had been "digging through the Congressional Directory" and found "that the office of Assistant Secretary of State is the only one of importance that seems completely free of statutory duties." If Moley would take this title, Roosevelt said, he could continue working as he had been during the campaign, giving confidential assistance, and answering only to the president. The State Department was then housed with the Navy and War Departments next door to the White House, and Moley would have close proximity to the president, and vice versa, to assist in formulating and carrying out New Deal policies. According to Moley, Roosevelt said, "You've got to have a job with enough prestige to make it possible for you to deal with people of importance for me."[17]

In the meantime a foreign crisis erupted when France and Great Britain advised Hoover just after the election that they desired renegotiation of their World War I debts to the United States and wanted to postpone the installment due on December 15. To avoid further deterioration and possible collapse of the European economy, Hoover had granted a one-year moratorium on debt repayment in 1931 that had now expired. The lame-duck president requested a meeting with the president-elect for collaboration on a plan to deal with the dilemma. Roosevelt agreed, bringing Moley along with him, to meet with Hoover and his treasury secretary, Ogden Mills, but he was resolved not to be drawn into Hoover's plans. FDR believed that any substantive collaboration would preempt or at least limit the actions he might be able to take after his inauguration. His reluctance to participate in a collaborative action to avert further economic damage from the Great Depression contrasts sharply with the willingness of president-elect Barack Obama to work with the outgoing George W. Bush administration in formulating solutions to the parallel 2008 crisis involving the Great Recession. One major reason for the reluctance of Roosevelt and Moley was the opposition of the Brain Trust to traditional "internationalism." Despite his unwavering commitment to trade protectionism, Hoover was more of an internationalist than FDR at this stage. Roosevelt and the Brain Trust believed that the heart of the recovery program must be domestic. Intervening in complicated negotiations with foreign nations, they feared, could only jeopardize it.

After giving his successor an hour-long lecture on the intricacies of international finance, Hoover proposed that they jointly appoint a debt commission to deal with the foreign debt issue. The next day Roosevelt issued a public statement rejecting the commission and left the issue in the hands of Hoover and the lame-duck Congress. In mid-December, Hoover reached out again to Roosevelt with an appeal that they jointly select a delegation to represent the United States at the highly anticipated World Economic Conference being planned for the following June. Again FDR demurred, as he also refused on March 3—the eve of his inauguration—when Hoover asked him to join in a proclamation to close the banks being threatened by bank runs across the nation. Roosevelt and his Brain Trust wanted no part in a coalition with the tainted Hoover administration that might limit the freedom of action in FDR's own plans to deal with the growing crisis.

During this transition period—indeed, during the entire post-nomination period of the campaign—Cordell Hull was not often in contact with Roosevelt. Feeling a bit estranged from FDR's inner circle of advisers during this period, Hull was preparing to continue his work in the Senate with proposals in December to reduce all permanent tariff rates by 10 percent, declaring a "truce" on any new increases, and further reducing trade barriers through reciprocal agreements based on unconditional most-favored-nations treatment. On the war debt issue, Hull declared that the European borrowers "should indicate their attitude toward the broader and more fundamental program of reducing trade barriers" before asking for debt reduction.[18] FDR, however, did not consult Hull on the diplomatic issues involving the European debt question.

In mid-January, Hull was surprised to receive a request from Roosevelt to meet with him on his way to Warm Springs in Washington's Mayflower Hotel. At the meeting, with very little prior notice as to its purpose, Roosevelt offered to appoint the senator secretary of state. Hull later wrote that he was "almost thunderstruck" by the offer, having had no hint that he was even being considered. He thanked him, but asked for some time to consider it. "The post of Secretary of State," he told the president-elect, "has not been any part of my personal planning for the future."[19] To Roosevelt and Louis Howe, the senator's main supporter among FDR advisers, Hull was the first choice to head the State Department. They both had great respect for Hull's idealism and high-minded dignity, and they were grateful to him for the influence he wielded in bringing the support of southern Democrats to FDR's nomination in Chicago. "Cordell Hull is the only member of the Cabinet," Roosevelt would say, "who brings me any political strength that

I don't have in my own right."[20] But to others, especially Ray Moley, the appointment made absolutely no sense. Moley saw a fundamental conflict between Roosevelt's New Deal plans and what he called "Hull's Adam Smith economics."[21]

In the interim following the offer to Hull, Moley found support for his views on Hull from five unnamed Democratic senators. They told Moley that they were fond of Hull and thought that he would fit well in the Treasury Department, but they had serious concerns about his suitability at State. The senators argued that Hull knew little about foreign policy generally and was so absorbed with reducing tariffs that it was unlikely that he could ever broaden his perspective. "Why, it's an open secret that he's got only one string to his bow," one said. "And every time he makes his speech on tariffs, he clears the floor of the Senate." But when Moley called FDR in Warm Springs to relay these comments, the president-elect simply responded: "Well, you tell the senators I'll be glad to have some fine idealism in the State Department."[22]

Seeing that the president-elect had made up his mind on the Hull appointment (as Moley put it, Roosevelt's "Dutch was up" on the decision), Moley followed up his call with a trip to Warm Springs to meet with FDR in person to express misgivings about his own appointment as Hull's assistant secretary of state. Moley, who thought of himself as "a symbol of the new order," believed that to be housed "with the living embodiment of what the New Deal was not would be tempting providence." Besides, he said, Hull would naturally resent being Moley's "boss-in-name-only." He would not be "overjoyed at having an Assistant who saw the President more often than he, who knew the President's mind better, and who was asked to handle matters of which the Secretary knew nothing." But FDR would not budge. "Hull knows all about it," Roosevelt responded. "There will be no misunderstanding with him if he takes the job. You're going to work with *me*." Moley finally acquiesced after FDR dictated a brief statement that Moley's duties would include the handling of "the foreign debts, the world economic conference, supervision of the economic adviser's office and such additional duties as the President may direct in the general field of foreign and domestic government."[23]

Senator Hull kept the president-elect waiting for a month before finally accepting his appointment. His primary concern came from the neglect he experienced from Roosevelt and his advisers following the convention and press leaks that seemed driven by a desire to scuttle or diminish the status of his appointment. Word of Moley's appointment also discouraged him. A prominent colleague of Moley on the Columbia political science faculty contacted one of Hull's closest Tennessee political confidants, George Fort Milton, editor of the *Chattanooga News*, and urged Hull, through Milton, to keep Moley out of the State Department. He warned that Moley knew nothing of international affairs and, stemming from his "tremendous inferiority complex," Moley was given to "violent rages" when people disagreed with him.[24]

Hull was also concerned about the costs of entertaining required by the job, until Roosevelt agreed to appoint William Phillips, a wealthy and experienced former Wilson diplomat, to the post of undersecretary of state to take charge of the social functions at State. Senior Roosevelt advisers, including Jim Farley and even Moley, met with Hull in an effort to ease his concerns. After meeting again with the president-elect in Warm Springs and finally on the train from Richmond to Washington in mid-February, Hull agreed to accept the post after FDR assured him that he would be a full partner in formulating and conducting the president's foreign policy.

THE FIRST HUNDRED DAYS

Frances Perkins, FDR's incoming labor secretary, likened his inauguration to a revival meeting. She had followed his development from the pretentious and arrogant state senator who appeared to be "looking down his nose at most people" through his pince-nez, to the empathetic social reformer he embodied as the governor for whom she worked two decades later. Roosevelt was a religious believer "who had no doubts," Perkins wrote in her remembrance of him. "He just believed with a certainty and simplicity that gave him no pangs or struggles."[25] In the most quoted phrase from his famous first inaugural address, FDR offered faith, hope, and courage in reassuring the American people that "this great nation will endure as it has endured, will revive and will prosper," he declared, asserting his "firm belief that the only thing we have to fear is fear itself." Evoking the image of Jesus cleansing the temple in Jerusalem and rendering a new covenant with humanity, Roosevelt railed against Wall Street's "unscrupulous money changers," who knew "only the rules of a generation of self-seekers," and "the rulers of the exchange of mankind's goods," who had failed to employ and fairly distribute the abundant resources available to the American economy. Through

FIGURE 8.1 President Hoover and FDR on the way to the US Capitol for Roosevelt's inauguration March 4, 1933 (Library of Congress)

"stubbornness" and "incompetence" they had failed and abdicated. "The money changers have fled from their high seats in the temple of our civilization. We may now restore that temple to the ancient truths."

The greatest primary task, said the new president, was "to put people to work." And to accomplish this task, he observed, "This Nation asks for action, and action now." Reflecting the views of the Brain Trust, he called for projects to stimulate and reorganize the use of the country's natural resources; for efforts to raise the values of agricultural products while increasing the nation's purchasing power; for unifying relief activities, which he said were then "often scattered, uneconomical, and unequal"; and for national planning and supervision of transportation, communications, and other public utilities. To safeguard "against a return of the evils of the old order," he said it would be necessary to require strict supervision of banking and investments to put "an end to speculation with other people's money"; and to make "provision for an adequate but sound currency." He would recommend measures for Congress to implement his plans; but if

Congress failed to respond, he promised to ask for "broad Executive power to wage a war against the emergency, as great as the power that would be given to me if we were in fact invaded by a foreign foe."

On foreign policy, Roosevelt had little to say other than that he would follow "the policy of the good neighbor," which he defined as "the neighbor who respects his obligations and respects the sanctity of his agreements in and with a world of neighbors." The "good neighbor" policy was not a new concept. President Hoover had invoked the phrase in Latin America to smooth over diplomatic problems caused by the Coolidge administration's armed interventions in Haiti and Nicaragua. Original or not, the policy pleased Cordell Hull, and he made effective use of it in later years. A more troublesome paragraph for Hull in the president's speech, however, addressed the administration's priorities affecting foreign trade:

Our international trade relations, though vastly important, are in point of time and necessity secondary to the establishment of a sound national economy. I favor as a practical policy the putting of first things first. I shall spare no effort to restore world trade by international economic readjustment, but the emergency at home cannot wait on that accomplishment.

The new president closed his short, powerful revival message, which dedicated the nation to "direct, vigorous action" to lift the economy and spirit of "a stricken Nation in the midst of a stricken world," by asking for God's blessing: "May He guide me in the days to come."[26] The new secretary of state must have hoped that this divine guidance would ultimately prevail above the influence of Ray Moley and the Brain Trust in the conduct of trade policy.

The next day, Roosevelt issued a proclamation calling Congress into extraordinary session to begin fulfilling his promise to act. Within 100 days after the special session began, Congress enacted fifteen major new bills under the president's leadership, which represented the most comprehensive package of economic reforms in history. Starting with the Emergency Banking Act—which the House passed by unanimous voice vote before it had been printed and the Senate overwhelmingly approved and the president signed, all within eight hours after FDR sent it to the Hill—Congress gave the president extensive authority over the nation's financial system and ended the banking panic less than two weeks after the inauguration.

He sent proposals for unemployment relief calling for a Civilian Conservation Corps to put unemployed young men to work on forestry, conservation, flood control, and park projects. Similarly, he called for the creation of the Federal Emergency Relief Administration to administer and enhance federal unemployment assistance. The new Public Works Administration and the Tennessee Valley Authority offered new sources of development and public employment, while the Agriculture Adjustment Act and the Farm Credit Administration were put in place to help the long-depressed farm economy. As ratification of the Twenty-First Amendment repealing Prohibition made its way through the states, Congress passed the Beer-Wine Revenue Act, legalizing and taxing the sale of 3.2 percent beer and light wine. As a counterbalance to the new spending programs, the president requested authority to cut around $500 million from the $3.6 billion federal budget, by cutting veterans' benefits and eliminating some government agencies and reducing the pay of all federal employees—civilian and military.

The "Hundred Days" also included the establishment of the Federal Deposit Insurance Corporation (FDIC) to guarantee bank deposits, a proposal that FDR had initially opposed, and the Home Owners Loan Corporation to refinance mortgages and avoid foreclosures, as well as the enactment of the Glass-Steagall Banking Act, walling off commercial from investment banking activities. And Congress passed the Federal Securities Act requiring investment promoters to fully disclose financial information about new stock issues and giving authority to the Federal Trade Commission (later transferred to the Securities and Exchange Commission created in 1934) to regulate stock transactions.

This period of frenetic legislative action strongly reflected the promise of FDR's speech at Oglethorpe University the previous year when he had called for "bold, persistent experimentation"—that is, try a method and if it fails, admit it and try another—but insisted, "above all, try something." As one senator described it in his diary, Roosevelt sent so many proposals to Congress during the special session "that one grew dizzy. Before we could analyze one message from the White House, swiftly upon that message would come another and yet another."[27] Humorist Will Rogers quipped that "Congress doesn't pass legislation any more; they just wave at the bills as they go by."[28]

The new president offered a stark contrast from his predecessor, who had insisted that the economy was improving on its own and that under his concept of "rugged individualism" relief should come largely from the states and private charity. Although Hoover finally signed a bill allocating $300 million to the Reconstruction Finance Corporation to be distributed to the states for loans to relieve unemployment, he consistently spoke against and vetoed relief measures. The press and the public generally depicted him as resisting action to counter the Depression. Even the *Wall Street Journal* wrote in mid-March that Roosevelt's actions "marked an end to three years of a nation's drifting from bad to worse, an end to helpless acceptance of a malign fate. . . . [W]e must look to the fact that the new Administration in Washington has superbly risen to the occasion."[29]

Throughout the Hundred Days, Ray Moley consistently served as FDR's policy adviser in developing and implementing the New Deal legislative strategy. He was now far advanced from the behind-the-scenes role he had played in leading the Brain Trust during the campaign. In May, *Time* magazine did a cover story on Moley, calling him the president's "closest, most intimate adviser" and observing: "He is not a great man but he is a powerful one. . . . Through his ear is the shortest and swiftest route to the heart of the White House."[30] But Moley claimed not to have been involved in the process of drafting the last and most controversial of the spring New Deal legislation—the National Industrial Recovery Act (NIRA)—which he called "a thorough hodge-podge of provisions designed to give the country temporary economic stimulation and provisions designed to lay the groundwork for permanent business-government partnership and planning."[31] The NIRA represented a break from the Democratic tradition of opposing the Hamiltonian business-government partnership and Henry Clay's promotion of public aid to foster private development.

Roosevelt had viewed his inaugural parade from a reviewing stand constructed in front of the White House as a replica of the portico of Andrew Jackson's Hermitage plantation near Nashville, but two months later he seemed to be adopting policies of the political foes of Old Hickory. Woodrow Wilson, the previous Democratic president, had insisted on separating government from business and letting businesses compete among themselves while government only intervened to regulate against monopolistic and other abusive practices. As Moley reviewed the text of FDR's second fireside chat, in which Roosevelt planned to defend the new partnership with business, he remarked to the president, "You realize, then, that you're taking an enormous step away from the philosophy of egalitarianism and laissez-faire?" After a few moments of silence, the president responded gravely, "If that philosophy hadn't proved to be bankrupt, Herbert Hoover would be sitting here right now."[32]

The main purpose of the act was to counteract the national emergency reflected in the huge unemployment numbers and, as Roosevelt described it, to bring order out of chaos in the industrial economy. It was to accomplish this purpose first by loosening the anti-trust laws to permit trade associations to write "codes of fair competition" aimed at preventing "disastrous overproduction" and "cut-throat prices" and rigorously enforced by government licensing provisions. To counter a bill sponsored by Senator Hugo Black limiting the workweek for employees engaged in interstate commerce to thirty hours—a measure FDR opposed, but which easily passed the Senate with strong labor support—the NIRA codes would include minimum wage, maximum hour, and child labor protections. The NIRA also guaranteed collective bargaining and the right to organize labor unions. Second, the bill authorized $3.3 billion for public works projects to be administered by the Public Works Administration, which Roosevelt was convinced would "put the largest possible number of people to work." Both business and organized labor endorsed the bill with enthusiasm. The president of the US Chamber of Commerce, while seeking to eliminate the collective bargaining guarantee, deemed it "one of the most important measures ever presented at any time to any Congress." The president of the American Federation of Labor gave it a similar accolade and predicted that it would generate 6 million jobs.[33]

Roosevelt called the codes "modern guilds" in which employers in each trade could bind themselves and agree to act together. This comparison to one of the egregious elements of the mercantilist system was an apt reminder that the NIRA was a backward step in the long battle against trusts and monopolies. The president's advisers, including Moley and Tugwell, rejected "the nostalgic philosophy of 'trust-busters'" and "the traditional Wilson-Brandeis philosophy that if America could once more become a nation of small proprietors, of corner grocers and smithies under spreading chestnut trees, we should have solved the problems of American life."[34] Progressives from both parties in the Senate objected to its anti-trust exemptions, warning against price fixing and the opportunity the measure provided for big business to run small ones into bankruptcy. Hugo Black voted against it in the end, arguing that it would be "a very advanced step toward the ultimate concentration of wealth."[35] According to historian H. W. Brands, Roosevelt's promotion of industrial planning to business leaders "constituted, at bottom, a cartelization of America's major industries, with the federal government acting as a non-profit partner. Big government would join with big business and perhaps big labor to prop up prices, apportion markets, and prevent small operators from undercutting the deal."[36] With strong support from business and labor, however, the administration pushed the bill through Congress with a wide margin in the House and a closer Senate vote, which included fifteen Democrats in the tally against it.

The NIRA proved over the next two years to be one of the New Deal "experiments" that failed. Critics charged that the 750 codes created under the act favored big business and stunted economic growth. Large producers worked the system to increase prices and decrease production output. The program was rapidly growing more and more unpopular when, in 1935, the Supreme Court held the delegation of code-writing authority to the president to be unconstitutional in a unanimous decision that included liberal Justices Louis Brandeis and Benjamin Cardozo.[37] By this time, FDR realized that the codes and their anti-trust exemptions had been a mistake—he described the code process as a "mess" and a "headache"[38] to Frances Perkins—and was actually relieved by the Court's decision. However, he continued the public works projects at an advanced pace. Largely without support from Roosevelt, the workers' rights provisions were ultimately revived in Senator Robert F. Wagner's (D-NY) "Magna Carta for Labor," the National Labor Relations Act of 1935, and Senator Hugo Black's Fair Labor Standards Act of 1938.

THE LONDON ECONOMIC CONFERENCE

During the first three months following his swearing-in as secretary of state, Cordell Hull occupied himself entirely with matters of foreign affairs and settling into his new role in government. Unlike FDR, who had learned how to manipulate and maneuver his way through the federal bureaucracy during his eight years in the Navy Department, Hull, coming off twenty-five years in the legislative trenches, was not prepared for the combative interpersonal political struggles over access to the president's attention. Reserved, courtly, and with a Confucian respect for hierarchy, he lacked the personality traits needed to impose his views on domestic issues even when they affected foreign policy and infringed upon his trade policy priorities.

He was invited only once to a White House meeting to discuss a domestic economic issue in these months. After listening quietly to a discussion about regulating commodity prices through the modification of the gold standard, Hull finally questioned the efficacy of the theory and was not invited back again. He claimed to be happy that he was not to be invited into White House meetings with what he called the "extreme liberal or semiradical" group, personified by Moley and Tugwell, closely advising the president.

Hull was a southern liberal with a strong pro-labor legislative record reflecting a mixture of Jacksonian populism and Wilsonian internationalism. Like Wilson, he had also studied and admired the Gladstone school of liberalism. Hull told Roosevelt that he "was 1000 per cent with him in all needed reforms and social welfare legislation," just as he had supported the reforms inaugurated when the Democrats had taken control of the House in 1910. His break with the New Dealers' approach to reform was over what he called "paternalism in government." He had seen "the predatory group of financiers and big-business . . . run away with Federal rule" in the decades before the Wilson presidency and did not want to see the opposite extreme "plant themselves" in the place of the capitalists as their paternalistic successors. Part of his objection was based on his southern philosophy of limited government inherited from Jefferson, but it also derived from his fiscal conservatism and views on sound money. He was willing to relax his opposition to paternalism to some degree due to the extraordinary economic crisis existing in 1933, but he believed that the president was in some instances "adopting cures too sweeping for the disease—cures that might bring on other ailments."[39]

According to Ray Moley, when the president told his financial advisers and senior cabinet members in April—the day before he announced it publicly—that he was taking the country off the gold standard, "Secretary Hull said nothing at all, but looked as though he had been stabbed in the back."[40] Only two weeks earlier, Hull had sent a State Department memorandum to the president asserting, "The maintenance of an international gold standard in some form is an essential to world recovery."[41] Wholesale commodity prices had dropped 40 percent below pre-Depression levels, and faced with domestic and foreign pressures to inflate prices, Roosevelt had originally planned to address the problem through his recovery programs, but he came to realize that he needed a more immediate solution. Many in Congress, supported by the Brain Trust in the administration, were pressing for inflationary measures to relieve the long depressed farm belt. By forbidding US gold exports and removing gold backing of the dollar abroad, FDR expected gold prices to fall, other commodity prices to increase, and the dollar to be devalued. A cheaper dollar brought greater demand for American agricultural exports, and with increased demand came higher domestic prices for the suffering farmer. An article by Walter Lippmann that appeared the morning FDR announced his decision to Hull may have influenced the president. Lippmann argued that it was impossible to keep prices up at home while defending the gold content of the dollar abroad.[42]

Although the Brain Trust advisers hoped to isolate the domestic recovery programs from foreign influences, the actions of other nations in the aftermath of Smoot-Hawley and the onset of worldwide depression contributed to the collapse of American price levels. Some thirty nations had gone off the gold standard by the time Roosevelt took action, and they were manipulating their currencies to enhance exports and limit imports. Britain had abandoned the gold standard in September 1931. John Maynard Keynes had promoted the move since the early 1920s, calling the gold standard "a barbarous relic" and an "outworn dogma" to which the stability of prices, business, and employment was being sacrificed.[43] In 1932 the British Parliament also renounced its traditional views on free trade by adopting protective tariffs on all imports and creating the imperial preference system, which imposed a wall around the territories of the British Empire. This preference system curtailed the competitive position of American producers in relation to Canada and all other Commonwealth nations. While France remained on the gold standard, it initiated, along with many other US trading partners, import quota systems and other nontariff trade restrictions that severely limited American export opportunities in a mercantilist renaissance.

Hull was disappointed with the president's decision, as were the other "sound money" advisers. Budget Director Lewis Douglas said the move marked "the end of Western civilization."[44] Hull sent out cables to the Foreign Offices in London, Berlin, Paris, and Rome, with a strained explanation that the action "was required by circumstances . . . to work out an improvement in prices" and was not intended "to seek any special American advantage."[45]

In order to preserve influence for his main goal of trade reform, Hull resisted an appeal to reverse the decision. His trade goals, however, had already been undercut by New Deal legislation adopted in the Hundred

Days. The Agricultural Adjustment Act authorized the president to impose compensating duties and quotas on imports to offset the act's price-enhancing measures. Likewise, the NIRA authorized the president to limit or prohibit imports that might infringe on the operation of the new industrial codes. These measures designed to insulate the domestic price recovery program from foreign imports troubled Secretary Hull, but the president's continued public support for legislation authorizing reciprocal trade agreements provided him solace. Hull began drafting the legislation and was convinced that the president would introduce it shortly.

Ray Moley came to a different conclusion. He believed that Hull's endless talk about tariff reduction was meaningless in light of the New Deal tariff measures that were being adopted, not to mention the new British protectionist approach to trade. True, Roosevelt had authorized Hull to begin drafting the reciprocal trade agreements bill but told him to seek an interagency agreement on the proposal approved by the secretaries of agriculture, commerce, and labor. In Moley's opinion, achieving this approval would be as easy as getting "the College of Cardinals to endorse the Communist Manifesto." Moley concluded that FDR's "strategy was to let Hull's low-tariff talk screen the movement of the rest of the administration in the other direction." But since Roosevelt kept his own counsel on strategy—which seemed often determined momentarily by instinct—Moley could not be sure. "It occurred to me," he later wrote, "that it might, after all, be *my* leg that F.D.R. was pulling, and not Hull's. (It proved, eventually, to be the legs of us both.)"[46] Actually, it was not clear what the president's true feelings were on the subject at this time because, as Rex Tugwell observed, he "was not then defending any policy, he was trying to arrive at one."[47]

For Hull, the World Economic Conference in London offered the opportunity to begin putting into effect the views he had entertained on trade reform for thirty years. In late April and early May, he gave widely reported speeches to the American Society of International Law and the American Chamber of Commerce promoting "fair, friendly and normal trade relations" as the means to solving the world's economic woes and avoiding military conflict. The idea for the conference had originated during the Hoover administration under the auspices of the League of Nations. In preparation for the talks, Roosevelt invited the leaders of eleven nations—including the new fascist leader of Germany, Adolf Hitler, who declined but sent a representative—to come to Washington in April to consult on the issues to be covered. British prime minister Ramsey MacDonald, the

Labor Party leader then heading a national coalition government with the Conservatives, was able to get the president to agree to hold the conference in London commencing on June 12. Roosevelt had wanted the conference in Washington at a later date because Congress would still be in session and in the process of enacting his domestic program, but MacDonald insisted that any later date would conflict with the grouse season and therefore threaten full participation from the British delegation. This concession by Roosevelt to MacDonald on venue and schedule appeared minor at the time in comparison to the president's refusal to allow discussion of negotiations on the European war debts to the United States and restriction of the talks to currency stabilization and reduction of trade barriers. But by limiting Roosevelt's direct participation in the conference held in London and scheduling it to begin before clear administration goals were defined, the concession would prove to be a fatal mistake.

While the preliminary talks resulted in very little of substance that would advance the London agenda, the British and French agreed to support a temporary truce on new tariffs and other trade restrictions for the duration of the conference. This truce might not seem significant for a conference that was expected to last only two or three months, but it was a bitter pill for the Europeans, who were infuriated by the American abandonment of the gold standard and frustrated by its comprehensive protectionist system. The British, whose recently adopted protectionism was hardly in place, worried that even a temporary acceptance of the status quo left them vulnerable to competition from the more advanced protectionist states. Still clinging to the gold standard, the French were especially tormented by the wildly fluctuating—mainly downward—value of the dollar. The joint declarations released following each of the talks were filled mainly with platitudes and included hardly any agreements on how the countries would fulfill their promise of "a fresh impetus to the solution of the problems that weigh so heavily upon the . . . men and women of the world." In describing the upcoming conference in his second fireside chat on May 7, the president said that its intent was to seek a reduction in trade barriers and a stabilization of currencies "to restart the flow of exchange of crops and goods between Nations."[48]

Later that month FDR began to realize that he might have gone too far in instilling hope that the conference would bring great solutions to the world's problems. The dollar was sliding to new lows while domestic commodity prices and the stock market were on the rise. The president told

Moley privately that he was in no rush to stabilize currencies while new purchasing power and his bargaining position were being enhanced. "This stimulating movement must not be stopped," he maintained, according to Moley. "This was recovery—not a dangerous speculative spree!" As the dollar continued to drop, both the French and British demanded a provisional stabilization of the dollar before the conference could commence, but they were effectively ignored. Roosevelt's position on tariff negotiations also seemed now to be in retreat. Where he had previously stated publicly that he would have Hull's trade legislation introduced in the current session, in late May he would only say that it was "probable" that he would send it forward.

Without consulting Hull, but after obtaining Roosevelt's approval, Moley took it upon himself to tamp down optimism for the conference goals. In a syndicated article, the substance of which he repeated in a radio speech delivered on May 20, Moley wrote:

> The problems most difficult of solution will be related to trade, the barriers against trade and the readjustment of these barriers. Tariffs and other restrictive devices are deeply rooted in the policies of the various countries and are closely integrated parts of their economic life. All of the nations, including our own, have been moving toward self-support for a long time. Industrial and agricultural life has developed in that direction with remarkable rapidity of late. . . . Thus a combination of forces is arrayed against extensive attacks upon trade barriers. Moderate results must be anticipated. The groundwork can be laid for many bilateral agreements and a more enlightened point of view. But we shall not have a vast new commerce on the seven seas, even after a successful Economic Conference.[49]

After reading a draft of the article, Roosevelt approved it and, to Moley's astonishment, commented that it "would be a grand speech for Cordell to make at the opening of the Conference." Moley had "never known him to employ irony," but then realized that the president was not being ironic but rather was "in dead earnest." Roosevelt, Moley perceived, "had returned to an intellectual region into which I could not follow."[50] Reaction from the liberal, free-trade press to Moley's speech immediately recognized and expressed regret over the "clash" it reflected between Hull and his assistant secretary. Hull was furious. He saw it as undermining the American position in London and his standing as head of the delegation. "Moley deserved a severe call-down from the President," Hull wrote, "but unfortunately Mr. Roosevelt sometimes gave his intimates undue liberties over his other friends."[51] Yet the secretary kept his anger largely to himself, tenaciously holding to the hope that the conference would fulfill his goals on tariff reduction and make up for any slights he had suffered in reaching them.

Another impediment hampering Hull's aspirations for London, however, was the eclectic delegation that FDR chose for Hull to chair without consulting him. To avoid the mistake Wilson had made at Versailles in not including congressional representation, the president selected two senators and one congressman. But of the six total members, Hull could not be sure of support for his low-tariff goals. Both senators, including Chairman Key Pittman of the Foreign Relations Committee, were trade protectionists. Pittman, from Nevada, was also an ardent silverite, whose incessant pro-silver arguments put the other delegates to sleep; and because of his prominent position in the Senate and his serious drinking problem, he would prove a destructive force to Hull's efforts in leading the delegation. Former Ohio governor James Cox, with whom Roosevelt had run on the 1920 presidential ticket, would be Hull's vice chair. Cox supported Hull's pro-trade views, as did two others on the delegation, the congressman and a Texas businessman recommended by Vice President Garner. None of the delegates had ever attended an international conference, and none, except Hull, had any expertise in the international economic issues that were to be discussed.

The only salvation to Hull was that his most troublesome adversary, Ray Moley, was to stay in Washington to assist the president while Congress remained in session completing the One Hundred Days legislative program. But while Hull had a slight majority among the delegates supporting his views, he had to be concerned about Moley continuing to undermine him with Roosevelt in Washington.

In a final meeting with the delegation the day before they were to leave for London, Roosevelt instructed them not to discuss war debts—the topic of highest priority to the Europeans. Instead, they were to confine their discussions to issues related to the coordination of monetary and fiscal policies to stimulate growth and improve prices, currency stabilization, and an agreement for the gradual abolition of artificial barriers to trade, including import quotas and export subsidies. Hull was disappointed with the limitations imposed by the president; he had wanted to use the war debt issue to gain trade concessions from the debtor nations. Nevertheless, he was content with the mandate he believed he had to begin implementing his trade reform dream. He had every expectation that the bill authorizing his negotiation of trade agreements would be introduced and possibly enacted by the time the conference began.

Hull set sail for London on May 31 with a draft of the reciprocal trade agreements bill in his pocket. He was eager to show the bill to his counterparts in London as evidence of American determination to dismantle its high-tariff regime. He predicted on leaving that there would be an agreement on the fundamental issues of currency stabilization and trade barriers "in a few weeks."[52] The old Brain Trust leaders, Moley and Rex Tugwell, however, had a different view. "The argonauts leave this morning," Tugwell recorded in his diary. "Moley pronounces the word sardonically and I think we feel alike that the results of the Conference are sure to be pretty slim—in the vague, hazy sense that Hull means. His rambling, lisping speeches on the evils of protection, and his extolling of the old *laissez-faire* internationalism have become harder and harder to bear."[53]

Before arriving in London, Hull began receiving disturbing cables from his staff at the State Department indicating that the president had not sent the trade bill to Congress yet and seemed anxious for adjournment as early as possible. Hull, who was basing success in London almost entirely upon the bill, became distraught and wired the president, hoping to dispel the rumors. He wrote that he trusted the reports to be unfounded because to defer passage until 1934 would be "a major error" and would "most seriously [handicap] the mission of our delegation," reducing it "to a passive role at the Conference rather than the active role contemplated." FDR replied that while he understood Hull's anxiety, the "situation in these closing days of the session is so full of dynamite that immediate adjournment is necessary" to avoid passage of other legislation damaging to his programs. "Therefore, tariff legislation seems not only highly inadvisable, but impossible of achievement," Roosevelt wrote. The president told Hull that he had full authority to negotiate general reciprocal commercial treaties based on mutual tariff concessions, which would be submitted to Congress for approval in the next session.[54] But Hull knew that obtaining the required two-thirds majority of the Senate to approve such commercial treaties was "a dismal and hopeless prospect." The Senate had never approved a trade treaty negotiated by the executive branch that materially reduced tariffs. "Such a tariff reduction," Hull observed, "was always beaten outright or filibustered to death after protected interests brought pressure on their Congressmen."[55] No country, Hull believed, would negotiate tariff concessions subject to Senate supermajority approval.

Hull, who, correctly or not, saw Moley's fingerprints all over FDR's decision, was devastated. While protectionist interests were lining up to defeat or delay the bill's passage for as long as possible, Hull believed that it would pass without difficulty. Moley, on the other hand, observed that "congressional leaders told [FDR] point-blank that no matter what he and Secretary Hull had agreed upon Congress would refuse to give the administration authority to reduce tariffs."[56] Hull confided to his friend the US ambassador to Britain, Robert W. Bingham, that he would not have come to London had he thought that he would not have congressional authority to negotiate trade agreements. Hull began to regret aloud that he had given up his Senate seat to join the cabinet and confided to James Cox that he was preparing to resign. Recognizing the devastating impact the resignation would have on the new administration, Cox and Hull's special assistant William C. Bullitt cabled Roosevelt urging him to reassure Hull immediately of his personal loyalty to him and his continued support for trade reform. The day before the conference opened, Hull received a second message from the president, prompted by Cox and Bullitt, urging him not to "worry about situation here in regard to tariff reductions and removal of trade obstacles. . . . I am squarely behind you and nothing said or done here will hamper your efforts. There is no alteration of your policy or mine."[57] Bullitt sent a confidential message to the president, thanking him for easing the situation with Hull, whom he described as having been "broken up" and in a condition of "complete collapse" with his immediate resignation ready to be telegraphed to Roosevelt.[58] Hull withheld his resignation, but he was not consoled. "I left for London with the highest of hopes," he wrote, "but arrived with empty hands."[59]

The secretary suffered frustration on several fronts. Not only did he lack statutory authority to negotiate for tariff agreements, but the president had even broken the tariff truce by increasing cotton tariffs under the new Agriculture Adjustment Act. Second, France and the other gold-standard countries blocked trade reform discussions until currency stabilization was resolved. Hull considered this issue beyond State's portfolio and deferred on currency issues to the Treasury Department, which had sent its own delegates. Third, the British and other Europeans continued to seek negotiations on debt settlement, but the president had prohibited the American delegates from even discussing that topic. Finally, Hull's own delegation was strongly divided personally and on the critical issues. He and Pittman, the pro-silver protectionist, got into an open dispute before arriving in London, and Pittman's drunken binges were a nightly embarrassment and often out of control. The chairman of the Senate Foreign Relations Committee not only shot out London streetlights with a six-shooter but chased a senior adviser to the American delegation around the halls of the delegation's headquarters at Claridge's Hotel with a bowie knife. The conference seemed to Hull "to be moving and operating most of the time in a dense fog."[60]

Yet Hull did not miss an opportunity to expound upon the virtues of free trade in bringing peace and prosperity to the world. Even though his first speech to the delegates of sixty-six nations attending the conference was heavily pared and toned down by the White House before he delivered it, his message seemed to have been directed as much to his New Deal colleagues in Washington as to the foreign delegates. Declaring that the "cherished idea . . . that each nation singly can, by bootstrap methods, lift itself out of the troubles that surround it has proven fruitless," he urged the conference to "proclaim that economic nationalism . . . is a discredited policy." While praising President Roosevelt for adopting within three months "an effective domestic program to promote business improvement in the fullest possible measure," he pointed out the "equal necessity for an equally important international program of remedies."[61] The secretary's speech was not especially well received on either side of the Atlantic. Despite the speaker's personal devotion to the cause, the Europeans did not place much value on a sermon on free trade delivered by the representative of the most protected developed nation in the world. In Washington, Tugwell dismissed it as "Hull bumbling about free trade."[62] Moley said the tenor of the speech "was the tip-off that worse was still to come." In continuing to vehemently attack "bootstrap methods" of recovery, it was apparent to Moley that, despite the White House edits, Hull had "decided to have his say in London."[63]

At the insistence of the British and French, tripartite negotiations on currency stabilization began as soon as the Treasury delegation arrived and preempted any discussion of tariffs. In mid-June word leaked that US Treasury negotiators had assented to a temporary agreement to stabilize the dollar with the franc and pegging it to the pound at around $4.00, with a 3 percent fluctuation range. The exchange rate on June 12 had the dollar falling to $4.18 against sterling. News of the agreement increased the dollar's value to $4.02 on June 16 and spawned an immediate fall in US stock and commodity prices. Viewing the agreement as a European attack on his domestic recovery programs that limited his use of monetary flexibility as a policy tool, FDR rejected it out of hand before seeing it. He then left for a two-week vacation after Congress adjourned on June 16 to sail the New England coast to his family island home at Campobello in Canadian waters off the coast of Maine.

In the wake of Roosevelt's rejection of the temporary stabilization agreement, Hull entered the fray again by proposing to the conference a 10 percent across-the-board tariff reduction. The proposal was similar to one he had proposed without success to Roosevelt during the 1932 campaign and again after the inauguration. But the motion gained no traction in large part because both senators in his delegation campaigned against it to the press, and it was soon withdrawn. The US delegation and the conference now seemed hopelessly disoriented.

At Moley's suggestion, Roosevelt decided to send him to the conference in London to convey the message that his primary international goal was to raise world price levels. If the dollar could be stabilized without halting the advance of American prices, which had occurred since going off the gold standard, Roosevelt said he would consider an agreement to do so. As word of Moley's trip spread, the press on both sides of the Atlantic reported rumors that the assistant secretary was coming to take over the delegation and save the conference. The rumors were enhanced by Moley's dramatic journey—covered by the media at every stage—by a US Navy plane and destroyer to the president's schooner for final instructions before sailing to England. Arthur Krock, Hull's confidant at the *New York Times*, criticized the administration for "changing its mind in public, humiliating its envoys in London, and then sending off Dr. Moley to England to sink or salvage what?"[64]

Hull, of course, *was* humiliated and dismayed by the signal Moley's trip conveyed, whether the worst rumors were true or not. "Moley's reception in London," Hull later wrote, "was surpassed only by those given to kings. . . . During the few days that followed, prime ministers and other top officials of governments flocked after Moley as if he were the Pied Piper." The secretary's outward response was characteristically subdued, while his blood was boiling internally. Hull remained "in the background as if [he was] the most insignificant individual hanging about the conference." He decided to give Moley "all the rope he might want and see how long he would last in that London situation."[65]

For his part, Moley made a superficial effort to keep Hull informed, but for "the purposes of this mission," Moley asserted, "Secretary Hull was in no sense my superior officer."[66] To make clear he was not part of Hull's delegation, but rather the president's "liaison" to the conference, he stayed at the American Embassy rather than at Claridge's with the other American delegates.

Moley began almost immediately meeting on the currency question with key foreign delegates who were in a state of high anxiety as the dollar continued to plummet after Roosevelt rejected the Treasury officials' stabilization proposal. FDR had advised Moley on the schooner that he might be willing to agree to a stabilization range between $4.05 and $4.25 per pound, but by the time Moley got to London, the dollar had already fallen to $4.43 per pound. On the second day after Moley arrived, Neville Chamberlain, then chancellor of the exchequer, came to the embassy to meet with Moley and to present a declaration that Chamberlain felt sure would not impose any limitation on Roosevelt's steps to raise prices through monetary action. It only committed the president to ask the Federal Reserve to cooperate in limiting fluctuations caused by speculation. The chancellor also expressed confidence that this declaration would end the panic on the Continent among the gold countries. Later that day Moley met at 10 Downing Street with a very emotional Prime Minister MacDonald, who pleaded with him to urge the declaration upon Roosevelt in order to save the conference from being wrecked and to end the panic then gripping Europe. Considering the declaration innocuous and certainly not a stabilization agreement limiting American monetary policy, Moley agreed to do so, and knowing "F.D.R.'s state of mind," had no doubt that he would approve it.[67] But the president was then at Campobello without phone service, so Moley conveyed the message through cable messages and calls with senior Treasury officials in New York, who promised to endorse it.

Over the next two days Moley had several bitter exchanges with Hull. The conversations are described very differently in their separate memoirs, with Moley's description coming off as defensive, but respectful, and Hull's being understated, but manifesting undisguised anger and bitterness. Moley first requested Hull to sign the agreement at 10 Downing Street once the president had approved it, as Moley fully expected Roosevelt would. Hull adamantly refused, stating that he had nothing to do with the stabilization talks.

A cable finally arrived the next day from Roosevelt rejecting the declaration. With the dollar continuing to drop in favor of his recovery plans, the president saw the declaration as a preliminary step toward a stabilization agreement limiting the freedom of the United States to raise domestic prices, and additionally, he said he did not know how governments could prevent speculation. Knowing that the president was presently isolated from his principal economic advisers, Moley blamed the rejection on his White House rival, Louis Howe, who, Moley observed, "didn't know beans about monetary questions."[68] Moley again approached Hull for help. But the secretary's anger with Moley was no longer in any way subdued. According to a description of the conversation later related by Hull to a friend in Tennessee, he responded:

> I never sent over the stabilization plan. I know nothing about it, and I'll have nothing to do with it now. You have been a traitor to me from the very minute you went into the Department. You have been pretending to my face to be for me and you have been conspiring against me behind my back. You have been making radio speeches against my policies. You Goddamn, little son of a bitch, you and all your stabilization can go straight to hell.[69]

Both Hull and Moley, separately, began to prepare a statement to present to the foreign delegates explaining the president's decision in a manner that might save the conference from disintegrating. It was no easy task; neither of them agreed with the policy action they were obligated to endorse. Regardless, it would prove to be a wasted effort. Roosevelt preempted his representatives in London from offering any diplomatic explanation by releasing his own message from the battleship *Indianapolis* on his way back to Washington—a message that would instantly become known as "The Bombshell." It read in part:

> The world will not long be lulled by the specious fallacy of achieving a temporary and probably an artificial stability in foreign exchange on the part of a few large countries only.... [O]ld fetishes of so-called international bankers are being replaced by efforts to plan national currencies with the objective of giving to those currencies a continuing purchasing power which does not greatly

vary in terms of the commodities and need of modern civilization. . . . That objective means more to the good of other Nations
than a fixed ratio for a month or two in terms of the pound or
franc. . . . Restoration of world trade is an important factor both in
the means and in the result. Here also temporary exchange fixing
is not the true answer. We must rather mitigate existing embargoes
to make easier the exchange of products which one Nation has and
the other Nation has not.[70]

The message not only repudiated Moley, but its belligerent tone, together
with its uncompromising substance, caused deep resentment among the
senior delegates from other nations. The delegates began calling for adjournment of the conference and hanging the blame around the neck of FDR.
The European press furiously blasted Roosevelt's "preaching." Only John
Maynard Keynes praised the message in an article declaring the American
president "magnificently right," to which Moley commented, "Magnificently
left, Keynes means."[71] In an effort to redeem the American position and save
the conference, Moley solicited the aid of Keynes and Walter Lippman, who
was in London covering the conference for the *New York Herald Tribune*,
to write a less offensive restatement of the president's position in terms
that would at least unite the non–gold bloc countries and help to salvage
the conference. After working until dawn on the statement, which aggressively but diplomatically defended the rationale of the New Deal monetary
policies prompting Roosevelt's action, Moley sent it to the president.[72] Upon
receiving the president's approval, Moley gave it to Hull to deliver to the
conference. Despite continued criticism of the US position reflected in the
president's message, Hull effectively defended FDR's decision and gained
critical support to continue the conference from Neville Chamberlain and
other delegates outside the gold bloc led by the French.

Before leaving to return to America, Moley sent a cable addressed "to the
President alone and exclusively, with no distribution in the Department," in
which he rendered a brief assessment of the state of play at the conference,
including an excoriating appraisal of the American delegation. In an indirect attack on its chairman, he advised that Senator Pittman was the "only
member of delegation able intellectually and aggressively to present your
ideas to conference." He recommended a recess in the conference for up
to ten weeks and that the entire delegation, including Hull as chairman, be
"reconstituted." In an obsequious gesture to regain favor with the president,

Moley concluded the cable by saying, "I consider your message splendid. It was the only way to bring people to their senses, and do not be disturbed by complaints about severity of language. It was true, frank and fair."[73] Moley's faith in the confidentiality of the State Department channels through which he transmitted the message was misplaced, however, and Hull's friend, Ambassador Bingham, quickly placed it in the secretary's hands.

In the words of historian Michael A. Butler, "An angry Hull subsequently embarked on a textbook example of the destruction of a political enemy." With a determination reflecting that of his father in tracking down his Yankee attackers after the Civil War, Hull immediately initiated a strategy to undermine Moley in both London and Washington. He promptly shared the message containing Moley's attack on the American delegation with the rest of its targets. He described Moley to one of them as a "piss-ant" who had "curled up at my feet and let me stroke his head like a hunting dog and then he goes and bites me in the ass!"[74] With Bingham's help he formed a lobby at the American Embassy to repeat the case against Moley to every prominent American who came to London. Hull and Bingham were also the likely source of leaks to the press about excessive, unapproved expenses incurred by Moley while in London. But the secretary directed his main campaign against Moley to the White House. Through his ally Louis Howe he complained about the difficulties he labored under in London, including "the concerted and deliberate plans of certain influences to undermine and destroy me." Mentioning the sacrifices he had made in giving up "an indefinite tenure in the Senate," Hull hinted that he might resign if the conditions infringing on his ability to do his job were not improved.[75] Following up with a cable to the president, he outlined a list of specific grievances against "Professor Moley." The drama portrayed in the press, Hull wrote, that Moley came "to speak and act for you and to take charge of American interests in London . . . with headlines morning and afternoon here about how Moley was coming to dispense salvation to every part of the world" made it impossible for the American delegation to function. Hull concluded that the attitude and conduct of his subordinate in attempting "secretly to undermine and destroy" him "while openly professing both friendship and loyalty" had been "utterly dumbfounding" to him.[76] The combined messages in essence conveyed an ultimatum, making clear that Moley must be removed from State if Hull was to remain its secretary.

In the meantime Hull was being praised in the press and by State Department allies for his diplomatic success in reviving the conference from near death following the "Bombshell" fallout. While the conference continued for only three weeks before adjourning for an indefinite recess and never reconvening, Hull received credit for protecting the president and the United States from a full blast of blame for wrecking the whole event. In the waning days before the recess, Hull made a final effort to bring trade back to the table by offering a resolution calling for lowering world tariff levels. Before it was approved by the White House, however, the resolution had been watered down with reservations, including exceptions for the new tariff safeguard authority in the NIRA and the Agriculture Adjustment Act. While not as strong as he would have liked, the measure at least put the United States on record for trade reform in an international forum and laid the groundwork for future bilateral trade negotiations.

As Hull and the delegation sailed back across the Atlantic, Ambassador Bingham continued to wage the battle against Moley, communicating with Howe and directly with the president. FDR now knew that he had to make a choice, and it was a choice that weighed heavily in favor of his old friend from Tennessee. Moley had a number of supporters among the New Deal advocates, but Hull was insulated well politically by a Democratic phalanx that included both southerners and Wilsonian internationalists. Moley offered talents that had served the president well in the campaign and the Hundred Days following his inauguration, but Roosevelt could not afford to lose the political value Hull embodied. As a strong indication of what his decision would be, the president invited Secretary and Mrs. Hull to visit him at Hyde Park upon their arrival in New York with further assurances of his "affectionate regard for . . . and confidence in" Hull. "You have admirably faced great difficulties," Roosevelt wrote Hull, "and through your own courage and sincerity saved the principle of continued international discussion of perplexing world problems from a collapse which would have made further deliberations impossible."[77] Following his visit with the president at his home in the Hudson River Valley, during which Roosevelt confided to Hull that Moley's actions and the fanfare surrounding him in London had "surprised him greatly," Hull sent a report of the meeting to Bingham. "Personnel matters about which you and I talked," he wrote to the ambassador, "are clearing up in a most satisfactory manner."[78]

Within weeks of Moley's return from London, the president transferred him temporarily to work on a criminal justice project in the Justice Department.[79] A few weeks later, Assistant Secretary Moley, the man whose face only three months prior had appeared on the cover of *Time* as the president's "closest, most intimate adviser," submitted his resignation to FDR. For several years after his resignation, Moley continued to maintain relations with the president and occasionally assisted with advice and speechwriting. But as time passed, the founder of the Brain Trust, who as a young man had admired the leftist populism of William Jennings Bryan, began tacking to the right of New Deal liberalism.

By 1939, with the publication of his memoirs, *After Seven Years*, reflecting on his time with Roosevelt, Moley finally cut ties with his former boss. The *New York Times* called the book a "long and hostile analysis not only of [the president's] policies but of his motives and intelligence."[80] Observing that Moley's "loyalty turned to hatred and his progressivism turned to reaction," even his friend and fellow Brain Trust member, Rex Tugwell, could not answer when asked, "What happened to Ray Moley?" "*After Seven Years* is, in fact, one of the cruelest books I know of," Tugwell wrote, calling Moley's move to the opposition "the ultimate political apostasy."[81] Roosevelt himself called it a "kiss-ass-and-tell" book.[82] Warning of a drift toward socialism in the United States, Moley continued moving further and further to the political right until becoming a Barry Goldwater Republican in the 1960s.

On April 22, 1970, President Richard M. Nixon, declaring that Moley had been his "very close personal friend and very valued counselor," awarded FDR's one-time top aide the Presidential Medal of Freedom.[83]

As for Cordell Hull, the conclusion of the London conference brought mixed emotions. His leadership and persistence in the final weeks following Moley's repudiation and departure had enhanced his public image and his stature within the administration and had even laid a foundation for implementing his goals in future trade negotiations. But the president's aloofness and decision-making process during the first weeks of the conference were disturbing and left him with an uncertain view of the path ahead. Hull continued to believe that Roosevelt fundamentally supported trade liberalism, but with the White House continuing to hedge its bets politically, the issue remained in flux. The one bright spot in the picture for Hull was the absence of Moley as a filter through which proposals to the president were strained or blocked. As one journalist put it, "Hull's gaunt figure and downcast eyes are enough to move one to tears, until one remembers the stiletto protruding from Moley's back."[84]

9

The Dawn of the Multilateral Trading System

Having once started on the road away from the
medieval mercantilism . . . progress should now be
more rapid and the movement gain momentum.[1]
   —Secretary of State Cordell Hull, upon signing
   the first trade agreement under the Reciprocal
   Trade Agreements Act, February 2, 1935

Cordell Hull may have enjoyed a personal victory in London in disposing of his principal adversary, Ray Moley; and he certainly enhanced his
political credibility by saving the president from blame for the diplomatic
collapse of the conference, but he was far from ready to charge ahead with
his trade reform agenda upon his return to America. While Roosevelt
continued to offer him words of encouragement on trade, the secretary
could not be confident as to when, or *if*, the critical support from the
White House would materialize. The president continued to emphasize
that domestic economic recovery was his paramount goal, and interagency competition over control of trade policy remained fierce. Hull's
cautious reluctance to push his trade agenda was a reflection of his characteristically plodding nature, deference to presidential authority, and
the demands of the State Department's full plate of diverse foreign policy
concerns—including disarmament in Europe, Japanese aggression in
China, diplomatic recognition of the Soviet Union, and political unrest
in Latin America.

MONTEVIDEO

In December 1933, the United States was scheduled to participate in the seventh Pan-American Conference in Montevideo, Uruguay. In the months leading up to the conference, however, the governments of Argentina, Brazil, Colombia, and Chile recommended postponing it in view of political turmoil in Latin America. Bolivia and Paraguay were at war with each other, and Peru and Colombia were on the verge of conflict over a border dispute. Cuba's government had been overthrown in September and the ensuing riots threatened lives and property, prompting the possibility of US intervention under the controversial Platt Amendment to the Cuban-American Treaty of 1903. Even the host government of Uruguay was under threat of revolution, but it opposed postponing the meeting.

Hull was himself deeply concerned about the impediments to success at Montevideo. Some of his friends urged him not to go, telling him that he could not afford another diplomatic failure after what had occurred in London. Many of the Latin American countries, his advisers argued, were likely to gang up and block any US economic proposal as simply another hegemonic tactic of intervention in their respective regimes. The last Pan-American conference held in Havana in 1928 had been dominated by attacks against "Yankee imperialism" after Charles Evans Hughes, a former secretary of state and chairman of the US delegation, defended America's right to intervene. The Montevideo conference had already been postponed a year beyond the customary four-year schedule. Hull observed that a "powder magazine was built at Havana which could easily explode into numerous discordant factions among the twenty-one American nations."[2] After conferring with FDR, however, he agreed to lead the US delegation, even though the president had very limited hopes as to what might be accomplished.

A few days before Hull left for Uruguay, Louis Howe approached him on behalf of Roosevelt and said, "We don't think you need to undertake much down at Montevideo. Just talk to them about the Pan-American highway from the United States down through Central and South America."[3] Although Roosevelt had proposed the highway as the goal of the conference, Hull saw no wisdom in sending a delegation to the conference "empowered only to build a road."[4] Over the next twelve days as he sailed for Montevideo, the secretary pleaded with the president through State

Department cables for approval to propose a comprehensive resolution for a tariff truce and negotiations to eliminate trade restrictions in the Americas. At first Roosevelt refused, citing the failure of such proposals in London and the risk of jeopardizing the administration's domestic recovery efforts. He instructed Hull to pursue lifting trade barriers through bilateral negotiations, not multilateral commitments in this period of unpredictable domestic economic conditions. Hull later observed that the president's message manifested "that the old struggle between the nationalistic philosophy of the New Deal group about the President and my international philosophy of economics was still acute."[5] Hull saw no chance that bilateral trade agreements would be ratified by the Senate and in his response urged the pursuit of a broader proposal to keep the policy of reducing trade restrictions alive for the future. Worn down by Hull's persistence, the president finally authorized a cable approving a tariff-reduction proposal as long as it allowed exceptions for the emergency tariff provisions in his National Industrial Recovery Act and Agriculture Adjustment Act. Hull was delighted with this authority, which he had not had in London, and spent days penning the resolution, which he intended ultimately to have worldwide application.

Huge billboards reading "Down with Hull" greeted the delegation as it sailed into Montevideo four days before the conference was to begin. Local newspapers warned of the selfish intentions of the "big bully" from the North. Hull knew well that he had much work to do to win over the confidence and cooperation of the other nations of the hemisphere. "The whole atmosphere and surroundings," he would remember, "were like a blue snow in January."[6]

Against the advice of his delegation, he began immediately to personally call on each of the delegations of the other twenty countries in attendance. Leading the delegation of the largest nation participating in the conference, Hull's informal visits to the delegates in their hotels broke with the great power tradition of granting an audience to, rather than modestly requesting an audience with, the delegations of smaller nations. He was determined to overcome the prevalent suspicions of American intentions regarding hemispheric dominance and thereby calm the atmosphere for negotiating his primary goal.

A principal target of the secretary's personal diplomacy was Carlos Saavedra Lamas, the astute and stubbornly strong-willed Argentine foreign minister. Saavedra Lamas, who saw the United States as a rival to Argentina's

leadership in Latin America, had played a key part in blocking US diplomatic goals at the 1928 Havana conference. Hull knew from discussions
with the Argentine ambassador in Washington that the foreign minister's
main interest at the conference was to gain approval of a regional Antiwar
Pact he had drafted, which condemned acts of aggression among the signatory nations and committed them to the peaceful resolution of disputes in
accordance with international law. Prior to Montevideo, the United States
had withheld its approval of the Antiwar Pact in favor of its own brainchild,
the 1928 Kellogg-Briand Pact, which renounced war as an instrument of
national policy and which Argentina had refused to sign.

Initially, the Argentinians were reluctant even to participate in the
conference and planned to obstruct from Buenos Aires every proposal the
United States might table. On the day before the conference began, however, the Argentine delegation, led by Saavedra Lamas, checked into a resort
fourteen miles from the conference venue. Immediately upon hearing of
their arrival, Hull had his secretary telephone ahead to advise the foreign
minister that he was on his way to call upon him. Saavedra Lamas received
his American visitor diplomatically, but remained aloof and skeptical as to
Hull's intent. Hull assured him that the goals of the US delegation were to
promote regional peace and economic welfare consistent with Roosevelt's
Good Neighbor doctrine, which recognized the territorial and political sovereignty of all nations in the hemisphere. Praising the Argentinian's reputation as "an outstanding Latin American statesman and advocate of peace,"
Hull professed to have come to seek his counsel. Saavedra Lamas, dressed in
dapper attire with a high, stiff collar and smoking incessantly, listened cour-
teously and perked up when he heard Hull remark that the United States
was now prepared to sign his Antiwar Pact.

Hull advised the Argentinian that he had drafted two resolutions—
one on economics containing his trade proposals and the other approving five peace agreements, including both the Kellogg and the Saavedra
Lamas Pacts. He proposed that the foreign minister introduce the peace
resolution, due to his world-renowned reputation as an advocate of peace,
and promised the utmost support of the United States. As he waited for a
reply, Hull suggested that if Saavedra Lamas did not think it appropriate
to introduce this resolution, it would be necessary to select another sponsor, such as the head of the Brazilian delegation—a rival diplomat within
Latin America. After asking for time to consider the idea, within twenty-
four hours Saavdra Lamas came to visit Hull at his hotel and agreed to offer

the peace resolution and support Hull's economic resolution, even though he said that his government did not favor portions of it. "We shall be the two wings of the dove of peace," he told Hull, "you the economic and I the political."[7]

With the support of the Argentinians and most of the other delegations personally wooed by Hull, the conference became in Roosevelt's words, "a splendid success."[8] Eschewing leadership of any conference committees, the secretary worked behind the scenes to achieve his goals until rising to speak for his economic proposal. At that point Hull passionately urged the elimination of trade barriers through bilateral agreements in the Americas, which would lead ultimately to freer trade around the world and also endorsed a conference convention, aimed at the United States, prohibiting foreign intervention in the domestic affairs of other states. Fulfilling his promise to Saavedra Lamas, Hull spoke equally passionately in favor of the peace proposal, asserting that under the "enlightened liberalism" of the New Deal "the so-called right of conquest must forever be banished from this hemisphere."[9] Both resolutions passed easily and won Hull praise from Latin American leaders and the American media. The *New York Times* reporter covering the conference noted that the most important reason for its success was "the personality of Secretary of State Cordell Hull" with the humility "and obvious sincerity" of his diplomacy.[10] Yet the White House issued the approval of Hull's "splendid success" that mattered most.

RECIPROCAL TRADE AGREEMENTS ACT

Based significantly on the success in Montevideo and Hull's well-received trade speech at the conference, FDR agreed to initiate action to obtain legislative authority for the secretary's trade negotiation program. By the end of February 1934, an interagency committee agreed on a draft bill that the president sent to Congress on March 2. FDR's message that accompanied the bill cited the "startling" 70 percent decline in world trade volume and 52 percent drop in US export volume since 1929: "This has meant idle hands, still machines, ships tied to their docks, despairing farm households, and hungry industrial families." The president declared, "A full and permanent domestic recovery depends in part upon a revived and strengthened international trade," and added that "American exports cannot be permanently increased without a corresponding increase in imports." Promising not to disturb any "sound and important American interest," he maintained that this legislation was "an essential step in the program of national economic recovery . . . as part of an emergency program necessitated by the economic crisis through which we are passing."[11] With Democrats commanding supermajorities in both chambers of Congress, the Reciprocal Trade Agreements Act (RTAA) passed the House in less than three weeks by a highly partisan vote of 274 to 111. Two and a half months later, the Senate, following a more protracted and politically polarizing debate, passed it by a vote of 57 to 33 with five Democrats voting no and an equal number of progressive Republicans voting in favor. The *New York Times* called it "a Democratic victory from start to finish."[12]

The ranking Republican on Ways and Means, Congressman Allen T. Treadway (R-MA), who led the opposition in the House, denounced the bill as an abdication by Congress of its authority over international trade. He cited the congressional speeches of Cordell Hull and other prominent Democrats who had made similar denunciations of the far more limited "flexible tariff" authority granted to presidents under Republican trade bills. Less than two years earlier, Treadway observed, Hull had urged repeal of the flexible tariff, calling it the largest surrender of fiscal authority "since the British House of Commons wrenched the taxing power from an autocratic King." Treadway declared that "this bill gives the President the power of life and death over every domestic industry, whether manufacturing or agricultural, and over every section of the country, . . . [and] will only enable him to go on a wild goose chase for foreign markets that no longer exist, all at the expense of domestic trade and industry. The world has comparatively little that we want or need."[13]

In the Senate, William E. Borah (R-ID), Hiram W. Johnson (R-CA), and Arthur H. Vandenberg (R-MI) led the fight for the opposition. Borah, a progressive western populist who had supported tariff reform in the past and voted for some parts of the New Deal, used his famous oratorical skills to lambast the bill from an isolationist perspective, as he had in opposing the League of Nations. Further, he felt that it was inconceivable for a western senator to surrender the power to protect farm constituencies in order to benefit eastern industrial exporters. Despite receiving reports that California sentiment widely favored the bill, Johnson responded that he would not place authority over farm tariffs "in the hands of two ardent internationalists and enthusiastic free traders like [Agriculture Secretary] Wallace and Hull." He believed that Hull had "more delusions concerning the world than a dog has fleas."[14] Vandenberg called the bill "Fascist in its philosophy, Fascist in its objective," "economic dictatorship come to America," and "palpably unconstitutional."[15] But while delegations of congressional authority often raise constitutional issues, the Supreme Court had already sanctioned the delegation of trade negotiating authority, including the flexible tariff authority.[16] In *United States v. Curtiss-Wright Export Corporation*,[17] the Court explained that congressional delegations of authority to be implemented by the president through international negotiations must be granted with "a degree of discretion and freedom from statutory restriction which would not be admissible were domestic affairs alone involved."[18]

Hull made a point of selling the bill to Congress and to the public, not as a move toward free-trade idealism but rather as a means to open new markets for American exports and to create jobs for American workers. The Ways and Means Committee majority report on the bill adopted Hull's argument, emphasizing the importance of the measure to the plight of "millions of farmers and working men who would normally be engaged in agriculture and industry to produce goods for our foreign trade."[19]

Hull intentionally drafted the bill to be short and uncomplicated—originally only three pages. Very simply, it authorized the president to negotiate reciprocal agreements raising or lowering tariffs by up to 50 percent of their Smoot-Hawley rate levels on a product-by-product basis—that is, no across-the-board, horizontal cuts were permitted. The president's bill had proposed that the authority be made permanent, subject only to repeal by future legislation, but the House amended the bill to limit the delegation of authority to three years. Since the act required no congressional ratification or implementing legislation for the tariff modifications adopted in the agreements negotiated under this authority, this time limitation provided the only leverage Congress had in overseeing the program. Unlike the more limited presidential "flexible tariff" authority to raise and lower tariffs granted in the 1922 and 1930 Tariff Acts, the president was not required to consider the factor of equalizing the "cost of production" in the decision to modify rates. Hence, in negotiating the reciprocal trade agreements under the act, the critical concern was enticing lower tariffs for American exports in foreign markets. Like much of the New Deal legislation, the RTAA laid down only broad policy outlines and left many of the details in application within the president's discretion.

Hull actually would have preferred legislation giving executive authority to enter into multilateral agreements with sweeping tariff reductions, or even unilateral cuts in the Smoot-Hawley rates, but he realized that this was politically impracticable. Based upon historical experience with the disastrous consequences of opening up the tariff schedules for legislative reform, he feared that a more comprehensive bill would likely lead to failure and a return to legislative logrolling.

As he watched the president sign the bill in the White House on the evening of June 12, Hull felt a message of happiness enter his heart with each stroke of the pen. "My fight of many long years for the reciprocal trade policy and the lowering of trade barriers," he believed, "was won."[20] But the victory was short-lived.

GEORGE PEEK: A NEW RAY MOLEY?

The RTAA required the president when negotiating trade agreements to seek advice from the Tariff Commission, as well as the Departments of State, Treasury, Agriculture, and Commerce. For this purpose, FDR established the Committee on Trade Agreements made up of representatives from the designated agencies to be chaired by the State Department, thus placing the program under Secretary Hull's supervision. A problem developed, however, when the president appointed George N. Peek, in December 1933, to be his own special assistant on foreign trade. "If Mr. Roosevelt had hit me between the eyes with a sledge hammer," Hull would recall, "he could not have stunned me more than by this appointment."[21] Hull saw the greatest threat to his trade agreements program now coming not from the politically impotent Republicans, nor from protected industrial and agricultural interests, but again, as with his conflict with Ray Moley, from within the Roosevelt administration itself. Hull's fears were justified. Much of the trade policy debate throughout 1934 and 1935 was dominated by his internecine struggle with Peek, which posed Hull's internationalist approach against Peek's nationalistic perspective.

Peek was a former farm implement manufacturer, who had been vice president of John Deere and Company and president of the Moline Plow Company. He had been a principal proponent of the McNary-Haugen Act, which supported a two-price system for agriculture—a higher than market price domestically and a below-market price for exports; it was vetoed twice by President Coolidge in the 1920s. A firm believer in maintaining a favorable balance of trade through export subsidies and dumping surplus agriculture products in foreign markets, Peek had been trying to implement his trade beliefs as head of the Agriculture Adjustment Administration (AAA) before becoming FDR's foreign trade assistant in the White House. At the AAA, he came into direct conflict with Secretary of Agriculture Henry A. Wallace and Undersecretary Rex Tugwell. Wallace, a progressive Republican and son of the agriculture secretary under Harding and Coolidge, had become one of Hull's allies on trade. His influential pamphlet, *America Must Choose*, supporting the RTAA, had even attracted the endorsement of Henry L. Stimson, Hoover's secretary of state.[22] Tugwell, one of the original members of the Brain Trust, was no friend to Hull's laissez-faire trade policies, which he considered anachronistic, but because he was attempting to raise farm prices and reduce surplus agriculture through domestic production controls, he strongly opposed Peek's dumping proposals. He advised Wallace that dumping "has been condemned in every international conference" and would only provoke retaliation. The president realized that he would need to remove Peek from the AAA, but for political reasons he did not want to fire him. When Tugwell suggested that Peek could do something involved in developing foreign markets, Roosevelt responded, "Lordy, Lordy, how Cordell Hull will love that."[23]

Roosevelt often chose subordinates with conflicting views so that he could play one against the other and be free to make his own decisions. The president's selection of Peek, first perhaps to counterbalance Wallace and then to spar with Hull, suited this decision-making process.

George Peek saw in his new job an opportunity to take over trade policy coordination and to neutralize Hull's liberal trade goals. While Hull was still in South America, Peek submitted a plan to the president for reorganization of the administration's trade policy apparatus which put himself at the helm. Opposition to Peek's plan came naturally from State, with Wallace and Commerce Secretary Daniel C. Roper also weighing in on Hull's side. Roosevelt ultimately confirmed that Hull and the State Department would be in charge of RTAA trade negotiations, but not before he further entrenched Peek as head of the newly created Office of the Special Adviser on Foreign Trade. Further, the president endowed Peek's office with a huge budget for statistical analysis and appointed him president of the newly established Export-Import Bank of Washington (Exim Bank). The Exim Bank was created initially to finance export sales to the Soviet Union and

Cuba, but Peek immediately began to use it to pursue his own trade program, which ran diametrically counter to Hull's efforts.

For Hull, a critical aspect of the trade program was the requirement he had imposed that agreements under the RTAA be negotiated under the *unconditional* "most-favored-nation" (MFN) principle—that is, on a non-discriminatory basis with all trading partners that did not discriminate against the United States. This requirement allowed Hull to multilateralize the tariff reductions obtained in bilateral agreements. Simply stated, it worked as follows: If in bilateral negotiations with country X, the United States agreed to reduce tariffs on a particular product, it committed also to grant this tariff reduction on the same product from all other countries that maintained non-discriminatory tariffs on imports from the United States. Likewise, if country X later reduced the tariff on a product for a third country below the rate established in the agreement with the United States, country X committed to grant the same reduction on that product when imported from the United States. Thus, among the group of nations that practiced non-discriminatory trade policies, trade restrictions reduced in bilateral agreements benefited all trade.

MFN clauses had been included in bilateral trade agreements for centuries. The principle was employed in the first United States treaty, a 1788 agreement with France, and in the controversial Jay Treaty with Great Britain in 1794. George Washington endorsed the concept in his famous Farewell Address, in which he declared "our commercial policy should hold an equal and impartial hand; neither seeking nor granting exclusive favors or preferences."[24] But since the eighteenth century most of these clauses were employed in a *conditional* form. Under this practice concessions granted by the United States in bilateral trade agreements were extended to third countries only on the condition that the third country "pay" for them by granting concessions of equivalent value to the United States. Although the conditional approach sounds reasonable in theory, the practical effect of requiring specific payments for non-discriminatory trade concessions produced perpetual market distortions as countries haggled over an acceptable "price" for each concession in negotiations that had to be repeated every time a country granted a new concession undercutting rates included in previous agreements. Even when an agreement resolved the distortion in rates, exporters lost market share during the period of discrimination and the process was never-ending. The conditional approach also made broad tariff reductions difficult, if not impossible, to implement.

During the Harding administration, Secretary of State Charles Evans Hughes finally abandoned the use of conditional MFN policy in favor of the unconditional approach. The United States signed the first unconditional MFN agreement after this decision with Germany in December 1923 and converted a number of existing preferential agreements to non-discriminatory arrangements. But as exorbitant rates—guarded by ardent Senate protectionists—prevailed in the decade that followed, there was little interest in or hope for ratification of trade agreements of any kind. Many agreements with major trading partners, such as Great Britain, continued in the conditional format, and some agreements had no MFN provision at all, as was the case with Canada.

In stark contrast to Hull's almost religious fervor for an international trading system with reduced barriers and no preferences or discrimination, George Peek saw the reciprocal trade program as an opportunity to sell surplus American products through one-on-one horse trading for national advantage without regard to broader multilateral implications. He urged the president to "return to the traditional realistic policy of conditional most-favored-nation treatment," charging that Hull's unconditional MFN policy amounted to "unconditional economic disarmament."[25] The RTAA provided that duties arrived at under the contemplated agreements and proclaimed under the act would apply to imports from "all foreign countries" except countries that discriminated against American commerce and Cuba, which had an established US tariff preference program. This provision appears to have supported Hull's view, but the language was vague enough for alternative interpretations, especially in view of the act's express purpose of "expanding foreign markets for the products of the United States."[26]

Peek believed that exchange controls were more damaging to trade than tariffs and that the reciprocal agreements should focus on barter arrangements on specially selected products decided on a country-by-country basis without reducing American restrictions to all foreign imports. He was outspoken in his criticism of the State Department policy, telling one audience that the United States could not dispose of its surplus farm products "because we have in this country a school of international altruists which still believes in free trade as a means of raising the standards of living in all the world, notwithstanding the fact that such a practice can result only in diluting our strength with the world's weakness."[27]

Hull complained that Peek would "take basketfuls of statistics" on bilateral trade balances to the White House to support his views and "came perilously near supplanting my whole set of international economic policies and my program to extend their application over the world."[28] By the fall of 1934, Hull began to fear that Roosevelt, preoccupied with his domestic recovery reforms, had lost interest, if not faith, in the foreign trade policies the president campaigned on before his election and was vulnerable to the persistent appeals for economic nationalism from Peek. In late November, an informal note to him from FDR confirmed his fears:

> Like most problems with which you and I have been connected during many years, there are two sides to the argument. In pure theory you and I think alike, but every once in a while we have to modify a principle to meet a hard and disagreeable fact! . . . I am inclined to think that if you and George Peek, who represents the very hard-headed practical angle of trade, could spend a couple of hours some evening talking over this problem of the most-favored-nation clause, it would be very helpful in many ways.[29]

Hull did have a talk with Peek, as the president requested, but it went nowhere and afterward the secretary sent three memoranda reinforcing his position to FDR recuperating in Warm Springs, Georgia. He wrote that all of the administration's principals involved in trade policy decisions, as well as the press generally, supported his views, "with the sole exception of our good friend Peek." Yet the president continued to favor Peek's approach, telling a press conference that in the present international reality, with most nations having withdrawn into a policy of economic nationalism and self-sufficiency, his best hope for the trade program was "to get some special agreements with different countries . . . on a barter basis."[30] While on his way back from a Tennessee speaking engagement in mid-December, Hull received an urgent message from his undersecretary, William Phillips, that the president had approved a barter agreement just negotiated by Peek with Germany. Fortunately, Phillips had obtained a promise from the White House that final word on approval would await Hull's return.

Essentially, the agreement provided for the sale of 800,000 bales of cotton through the Exim Bank under a complicated formula that allowed the Germans to pay one-fourth of the price to the bank in dollars and the remainder in Deutschmarks. The bank would then sell the German currency at a discount to American importers exclusively for the purchase of wine, fertilizer, and other goods from Germany. Under the fiercely

nationalistic economic policies implemented by Adolf Hitler and his minister of economics and Reichsbank president, Dr. Hjalmar H. G. Schacht,
to finance German recovery and rearmament, Germany was entering into
bilateral barter arrangements. It recently announced that it would terminate its unconditional MFN commitment with the United States. The new
deal effectively subsidized German exports to the United States, thus discriminating against competing exports from other foreign sources. Hull
was shocked and outraged. He knew that Peek had been negotiating with
the Germans but was preoccupied with his own negotiations with Brazil,
which he hoped would lead to the first agreement under the RTAA.[31] If the
German deal went through, it would stop the Brazilian negotiations in their
tracks and potentially destroy Hull's entire trade program.

The actual bilateral trade implications of the potential agreement
with Brazil were not significant. Most of the products Brazil exported to
the United States were already on the duty-free list, and Brazil's foreign
exchange controls on its devalued currency presented more of a problem
for American exporters than did Brazilian import tariffs. To Hull, however, the issue was much bigger than bilateral trade benefits. This kind of an
agreement—one committed to unconditional MFN treatment with the
largest economy in Latin America—would lay the cornerstone for his policy in the Americas. It would also make an important statement promoting his goal of ending trade restrictions in a new world economic order.
Peek, on the other hand, favored a bilateral foreign exchange arrangement
with Brazil rather than a broad MFN trade agreement and issued a report
advocating his approach to the president. In a 7-to-1 vote of the interagency
committee approving Hull's draft proposal for the Brazilian trade agreement, Peek was the lone dissenter. Despite his apparent drift toward Peek's
point of view, the president approved the draft from Warm Springs.

When the Brazilian negotiators got word of the deal that Peek was making with the Germans, they submitted a protest to the State Department
with a reminder that Brazil was also a major cotton exporter and that they
had been stalling a German delegation seeking the same preferential barter
with Brazil. If the United States went through with the German agreement,
the Brazilians said that they would have to accept their own German offer
and defer negotiations with the United States indefinitely. Other countries
followed with reprisal threats in reaction to the possibility of American
preferential treatment for German imports that were competitive with their
own. Chile, for instance, threatened to dump its fertilizer on the American

market if it had to in order to compete with the German product shipped under preferential conditions.

Hull met with the president and presented the case that the German agreement posed a devastating threat to the Brazilian negotiations and to all other possible agreements under the act. He believed that the agreement contravened the RTAA's provision requiring equality of commercial treatment and that the act did not contemplate discriminatory barter transactions. The secretary argued that a deal giving discriminatory market access to German imports was not even necessary to sell American cotton to Germany—a country desperate for cotton. He thought the Germans, who were openly in default on $2 billion in debt to the United States, were acting in bad faith in seeking a trade agreement with a creditor they had previously snubbed. The agreement was, Hull said, "a very good trade bargain for Germany, but with little gain and large risks for the United States. . . . The proposed plan is almost certain to engender extreme resentment among that large section of the American public which is violently opposed to the Hitler regime."[32] Under the weight of Hull's argument, affirmed by the support of all the relevant cabinet secretaries, Roosevelt relented and withdrew his approval of Peek's agreement.

Peek did not accept defeat gracefully. He attempted to raise the barter proposal again with FDR a few months later, but the president refused to reconsider the matter, replying that it conflicted "with the foreign commercial policy of the United States, and the particular form of the proposal was open to very serious economic objections."[33] By July, Peek offered to resign, but Roosevelt urged him to stay on as president of Exim Bank even after abolishing the Office of Foreign Trade Adviser, with the comment that "we are not so far apart in our views" and implying that these views might prevail in the long run. The Hull-Peek dispute received wide coverage in the media with the *New York Times*, where an editorial asserted that the "controversy has become so sharp and inexcusable that it is rapidly taking on the air of a first class government scandal."[34] The *Times* opinion joined an earlier critical editorial in the *Washington Post*, entitled "Mr. Hull and Mr. Peek," in which the *Post* sided against Peek's "essentially unworkable plan of action," versus the "strong ground" upon which Hull stood. While Hull's hopes "may seem quixotic," the *Post* observed, "it is only along the lines indicated by him that any considerable [trade] expansion can be expected in the future."[35] Most economic scholars also favored Hull's policy, derisively referring to the views of his opponent as "Peekonomics." But Peek had his own political and academic supporters, mainly from the isolation-ist and protectionist camps. The influential historian and later a prominent isolationist critic of FDR, Charles A. Beard, called Peek "the realist among the administration men engaged on the foreign trade side," observing that "Peek's mind does not seem to be encumbered by a thousand exploded eco-nomic dogmas that no longer fit the world of reality."[36]

Peek decided to stay on as Exim Bank president for the time being, but he continued publicly and ruthlessly to disparage the State Department's trade policies. At an Armistice Day speech he finally stepped over the line. He declared that the choice for the United States on trade policy and a broad range of other issues was between Americanism and international-ism. "When we Americans choose—let us choose America," he concluded, implying that the administration was moving in an un-American direction with laissez-faire policies that opened US markets to foreign advantage. The pro-Republican *Washington Herald* reported on Peek's speech highlight-ing the slanted details of the choice, with a supporting editorial headlined, "Sane Nationalism or Fatuous Internationalism—Which Shall It Be?"[37] Roosevelt reacted with a letter to Peek, denouncing his misrepresentations of administration policy and calling the speech "rather silly," and claiming it sounded "like a Hearst paper." The president denounced one point in Peek's speech as "a deliberate lie."[38] This time when Peek offered his resignation, the president promptly accepted.

Peek continued his fight against Hull's trade policy and ultimately, like Moley, did his best to defeat Roosevelt. He co-authored a book with extreme isolationist William Crowther entitled *Why Quit Our Own*, which was distributed broadly by protectionist interests. But with Peek's departure, Hull had finally triumphed within the Roosevelt administration. As Arthur Schlesinger Jr. writes in *The Age of Roosevelt*, "Once again a hard-boiled political infighter had fallen victim to the long knife of Cordell Hull."[39]

Hull's victory over Peek marked a turning point for his trade program, embedded internationalism into the economic fabric of the New Deal, and signaled the beginning of a revolution in the governance of world trade. With his trade philosophy now predominant and unchallenged within the administration, Hull signed the Brazilian agreement on February 2, 1935, and secured unconditional MFN agreements with seven more countries by the end of the year.

But success for his ultimate goals remained far from certain on the road ahead. The Brazil deal drew virulent reaction from American manufacturers of products competing with imports receiving tariff concessions under the agreement. Prompted by Peek, domestic producers worried about the MFN benefits to third-country imports and brought their concerns to Congress where intense bipartisan criticism erupted. In response, Hull and Roosevelt, who was still not at all comfortable with the unconditional MFN principle, decided to moderate concessions offered in negotiations with Belgium as Hull took the program to Europe. Thinking that a moderate agreement would be better than risking political backlash from a deal that went too far, Hull withdrew a 30 percent cut in iron and steel tariffs from his draft proposal. In a turnabout, however, Roosevelt had Hull keep these sensitive cuts in the agreement in order to lower costs for domestic construction in reviving the American economy.

Following the Belgian agreement, countries began lining up to become a part of the American MFN regime to get out from under the

FIGURE 9.1 Secretary of State Hull signs the first trade agreement under the RTAA with Brazil in the Oval Office in the presence of President Roosevelt with the Brazilian minister of finance Arthur Souza Costa and Brazilian ambassador Oswaldo Aranha (Library of Congress)

Smoot-Hawley rates imposed on imports from countries without a non-discriminatory commitment to the United States. By the end of 1936, Hull had reached agreements with fourteen countries, and US exports began to rise rapidly in those markets, especially in comparison to trade with other countries.

THE 1936 ELECTION

A principal target for the State Department's trade program was the United Kingdom and its empire. Throughout his career, which began at a time when Anglophobia in American politics had been rampant for well over a century, Hull had often sung the glories of the British free-trade regime with worshipful praise for its proponents in the Liberal Party, such as Richard Cobden, William Gladstone, and Lloyd George. Following the British abandonment of the gold standard in 1931, their adoption of protectionist tariff increases, and the creation of a wall of trade barriers around the Commonwealth at the Ottawa Imperial Conference in 1932, however, Hull's perspective changed. In response to Smoot-Hawley, the Ottawa agreements enhanced imperial trade preferences and established a "Sterling Bloc" that was nearly impenetrable to US exports. Even outside the Commonwealth, Britain was busily signing preferential bilateral trade agreements effectively limiting American access. The US-British "special relationship" formed during the Second World War could not be foreseen at this time, when the United Kingdom stood as a fierce commercial adversary and a threat to American trade policy. Since the Ottawa preference commitments extended until October 1937, after the president's authority was to expire, and 1936 was an election year when sensitive negotiations would be postponed, Hull and the president decided to wait until after the election to attempt negotiations with London.

But Canada offered a different opportunity. Late in 1934, the Canadian government sent an official request for trade negotiations to the State Department. As a primary proponent and beneficiary of the imperial preference program, Canada's request was significant. Both the Liberal and Conservative Parties in Canada had supported retaliatory trade measures against the United States following Smoot-Hawley, but the size and proximity of the American market attracted a shift in policy after Hull's new trade policy began to take shape. Canada, too, was facing elections, and a

North American trade deal was now popular in both parties. The Liberals, representing the traditional free-trade party, had the edge, however, and won the election.

In light of the critical fallout from the Brazilian agreement, Hull stalled the talks with the Canadians and let the negotiations drag on through most of 1935. Finally, the newly elected Liberal prime minister Mackenzie King came to Washington himself, announcing that he was committed to Hull's trade program and planned to stay until an agreement was signed. Although Canada maintained for the time being its imperial preferences, it agreed to unconditional MFN treatment for trade outside the Dominion territories. Both Roosevelt and Hull thought the deal generally favored the American side, and the agreement initially received favorable public reaction. While a substantial increase in annual bilateral trade followed this first formal agreement between the two neighbors since the 1860s, it also supplied campaign fodder for the Republicans in opposing Roosevelt's bid for reelection.

While the early agreements obtained substantial concessions for American exports and allowed only minimal new market opportunities for imports, they did little to alleviate domestic agricultural discontent. This was an especially tough time for American farmers, who were beginning to suffer the devastating Dust Bowl drought that eventually persisted through the 1930s. Hull had kept agricultural tariffs in the Canadian agreement at the high level imposed in the 1922 Fordney-McCumber Act and advised the president that Republicans would be hard put "to conjure up a political issue" based upon that agreement.[40] He could not imagine the GOP now calling for a return to the widely discredited Smoot-Hawley levels. Yet Senate Minority Leader Charles L. McNary (R-OR) revived the standard refrain from western agricultural interests that the agreement sacrificed farm producers for the benefit of eastern industrialists. This type of criticism prompted some officials in the Agriculture Department to grumble that the new trade policy was not working fast enough and needed a boost in the form of export subsidies. Secretary Wallace firmly rejected this suggestion, but Hull responded to the attacks by cautiously deciding to put future agreements on hold for most of the 1936 election year.

Predictably, this moratorium did not stop the criticism. Protectionist interests like the iron and steel industry, which loudly objected to concessions in the Belgian agreement, forecast doom for the high-paying jobs throughout the national industrial regions. A surge in "Made-in-America" organizations arose across the country, revealing a nationalistic fervor prevalent among small businessmen and farm producers. Critics homed in on Hull's unconditional MFN treatment, calling it a giveaway program, and on the confidentiality of the negotiations, which they deemed undemocratic and deaf to the voices of economic interests affected by them. Former president Hoover picked up on these points, blasting Roosevelt for opening American markets to foreign farmers "in secret determinations of tariffs in back rooms without public hearings through so-called reciprocal tariff negotiations" and depriving Americans "of their livelihood by secret covenants secretly arrived at."[41] As candidates for the Republican presidential nomination, both Senators Borah and Vandenberg attacked the Canadian agreement and the reciprocal trade program, attempting to make FDR's trade policy a major issue in the campaign. Borah proclaimed, "It is our duty to preserve the American standard of living, to preserve the American scheme of life and to preserve civilization, and to do that we must protect our people from importations from the cheap labor countries."[42] Vandenberg, who had often consulted with George Peek and favored his trade policies, urged the adoption of an export subsidy program and "a realistic selective trade policy" to dispose of the nation's agricultural surplus. He asked, how can a private business remain "healthy if it depends upon tariff protection, as many do, when it doesn't know what moment a free trade State Department will bargain away all of its essential protection in response to some swivel chair theory of international commerce?"[43]

Nonetheless, a number of influential Republicans were now supporting Hull's trade policy. The two senior officials in Hoover's cabinet, Henry Stimson and former treasury secretary Ogden Mills, were both publicly on record in favor of it. Although support from the business community was mixed, a number of prominent leaders were outspoken in their endorsements, including Hoover's former financial adviser, Thomas Lamont of J. P. Morgan & Co. Thomas J. Watson, president of the International Business Machines Corporation, declared in an unequivocal endorsement of the program, "We cannot build a wall around the United States and continue to improve and develop."[44] While the United States Chamber of Commerce blasted most New Deal programs, it adopted a resolution favoring the reciprocal trade agreement program.[45] In late October 1936, just days before the election, 200 business leaders, most of whom were Republicans and including former officials from the Coolidge and Hoover administrations, announced their enthusiastic endorsement of Hull's trade policies and pledged support for Roosevelt's reelection. A spokesman for the group warned that if the Republicans won and repealed it, "there would be a revolution among conservative businessmen."[46]

A survey of American newspapers in 1935 showed a large majority supported Hull's program, including quite a few Republican papers. In fact, some of the favorable papers criticized Hull for moving too slowly. The liberal weekly magazine the *Nation* even chastised the State Department for striving for agreements that gave the United States *too good* a deal. In a lead editorial, the magazine's editors reprimanded the American negotiators for increasing the already large balance of trade surplus that the United States had with Belgium and for employing tariff reciprocity "as a weapon to push down the defenses of debtor countries." While praising "Secretary Hull and those of his assistants who have worked conscientiously to bring about genuine tariff reductions," the editors regarded as a fundamental weakness in the deals concluded thus far the fact that "the United States has obviously obtained much greater concessions than it has granted." Unless the negotiators curbed their "nationalistic passions," the *Nation* warned, "there is real danger that the Administration's tariff program will fall of its own weight."[47]

From the opposite corner, a new weekly magazine, *Today*, the predecessor of *Newsweek*, became a major critic of the program's unconditional MFN approach and the "furtive" character of the negotiations. *Today*'s editor, FDR's disgruntled former confidant, Ray Moley, solicited critical articles from Hull's most outspoken opponents throughout 1935. In late November before its terms had even been released, Moley wrote a scathing column against the Canadian agreement, denouncing its secrecy as inconsistent "with the liberal protestations of an Administration devoted to the masses of the people." In trying "to depart so radically from the old days of special pleading before Congressional committees," Moley wrote, the Roosevelt administration was denying those who are affected by the agreement "their legitimate rights." Further, he said that in refusing to depart from the unconditional MFN principle, the State Department was not negotiating reciprocal bilateral agreements but rather granting "general tariff reductions" that would benefit "a horde of nondescript deadheads" who had paid nothing for the privilege. "These low-tariff policies are an integral part of a still more ominous policy of internationalism which is threatening the integrity and unity of the New Deal on every side," wrote the former leader of the Brain Trust. He cited "admirably clear" warnings on the "dangers of such internationalism" given by George Peek, whom Moley called "a victim in this Administration of a slow but relentless process of official extinction."

The column inspired an exchange of tart letters between the president and Moley, marking another stage in the termination of their relationship.[48]

Despite some opposition from within the party, the Republican National Convention adopted a platform that pledged to repeal the RTAA, calling it "futile and dangerous," and to maintain protection at "all times to defend the American farmer and the American wage earner" against commercially competitive imports. Condemning the "secret negotiations of reciprocal trade treaties," the platform pledged to "restore the principle of flexible tariffs in order to meet changing economic conditions."[49] Running against a popular president, GOP attacks on the trade program offered more hope than would opposition to other New Deal economic reforms, most of which were highly appreciated among the depressed electorate. The platform even endorsed Social Security, business regulation, and the right of labor to organize. With the Supreme Court having declared the Agriculture Adjustment Act unconstitutional in January,[50] the Republicans hoped to offer a better alternative to distraught farmers burdened with the potentially damaging effects of the Canadian trade agreement. The issue also offered an opportunity to harp on the excessive centralization of power by a "dictatorial" president.

The Democratic platform position on trade was a disappointment to Hull. Having been involved with party politics for decades, the secretary of state was a true believer in the importance of platform creeds. He worked diligently on a draft for the foreign policy section of the platform, which appraised the administration's trade agreements program as "the greatest single force in the world making for stable prosperity and peace."[51] But Hull's draft was largely ignored in favor of a more tepid endorsement of the program that added a commitment to "continue as in the past to give adequate protection to our farmers and manufacturers against unfair competition."[52] Assuming that the nationalists in his party had prevailed on the drafting committee, he called the protectionist language "Republican terminology almost word for word."[53]

The ultimate choice to head the GOP ticket in 1936 was Kansas governor Alfred M. Landon, the only incumbent Republican governor to win reelection in 1934. Landon was an amiable moderate expected to do well against Roosevelt. On trade, he had generally taken a progressive stance, even sending congratulations to the only Kansas Republican congressman to vote in opposition to the Smoot-Hawley bill in 1930. A month before the convention, Landon reportedly had wanted the Republican platform to endorse reciprocal trade agreements. But in an attempt to secure farm votes in the heat of the campaign, the GOP nominee promised more "cash benefits" than those provided under Roosevelt's agricultural program, even as he had been denouncing the president as a reckless spender. Following advice from the more conservative Old Guard faction of his party, Landon launched into an attack on Hull's reciprocal trade program. In particular, he opposed the unconditional MFN principle and the "star chamber" character of the negotiations. He argued that Hull's program undermined the protectionist system and "sold the American farmer down the river." [54] Proclaiming that he was not an isolationist, Landon said he favored more limited reciprocal negotiations, presumably like the horse-trading barter approach of George Peek, who was now advising Landon.

Hull had intended not to participate actively in the campaign, but Landon's accusations drew him out. He immediately challenged the remarks as "confused, inaccurate, and incoherent," claiming they were "shaped by the same interests that were behind the Smoot-Hawley tariff." In a speech given at the same venue as Landon's address two weeks before, Hull declared, "Governor Landon was right. The American farmer has been sold out. . . . The sellout took place during the Hoover administration and it was the Smoot-Hawleyites who did the work."[55] Plowing through specific rebuttals of every criticism made by Landon, Hull drew praise in a *New York Times* editorial the next day. The *Times* called Hull's remarks "most effective" and "certain to carry great conviction" with "concrete evidence" showing that the Republican candidate's accusations "were based upon inadequate information."[56] Roosevelt generally ignored Landon's campaign attacks no matter the issue, preferring to hail the benefits of his administration's domestic recovery policies and repeatedly to attack the tyranny of "economic royalists." But less than a month before the election, the president defended the benefits to both industry and agriculture contained in the Canadian agreement and pointed to the strong advantages provided US exporters in all the agreements signed to date. "But, my friends," he continued, "the increasing restoration of trade, of industry and of employment serves more than a mere economic end . . . . [It turns] us and other nations away from the paths of economic strife which lead to war and toward economic cooperation which lead to international peace."[57] In short, the program represented enlightened self-interest.

In the final analysis, the trade agreements program was not a deciding factor in the 1936 presidential election. The election was a referendum on

FDR and his New Deal experiments. As Jim Farley put it, "The only issue in the campaign was Franklin D. Roosevelt."[58] And the economic trends were solidly in his favor. Although the Depression would continue and in some respects get worse before the Second World War, 1936 was a vast improvement over 1932. Unemployment had been cut almost in half, with 6 million more people employed than in 1933; national income was up by more than 50 percent; and corporate profits and the stock market had moved light years ahead since Roosevelt entered the White House.[59] A New Deal electoral coalition grew in the traditional white Democratic South, built on the African-American abandonment of the party of Lincoln as the black population migrated to northern cities, and absorbed organized labor for the foreseeable future into the Democratic alliance. Though some were predicting a close race or even a Landon victory, Roosevelt won reelection in a landslide of seismic scale—28 million to 17 million in popular votes and 523 to 8 electoral votes. The congressional elections were equally impressive for the president's party. Building on the huge 1932 and 1934 victories, the Democratic caucus after the 1936 election held an 80-to-16 majority in the Senate and a 331-to-89 majority in the House.

While it may not have been a critical factor in the election, Hull declared the overwhelming victory an "unequivocal endorsement by the American people" of the president's foreign policy and, in particular, the trade reform program. In his hyperbolic fashion, when referring to the importance of trade in solving world problems, the secretary claimed that the program "has proved to be the most effective instrument for bringing about a revival of international trade, thereby stimulating general economic prosperity and affording an increasingly secure foundation for world peace." He promised to "go forward with this program in the same earnest, persistent, careful and cautious manner in which we have heretofore sought to advance this great undertaking."[60] Alf Landon also gave credit to the trade issue as an element contributing to the huge margin of his defeat and expressed regret over his decision to attack Hull's program. After the election the following year, Landon admitted that he had adopted this position "to fit the political situation," and that "it was not a position that really expressed [his] own personal views."[61]

But Hull remained cautious as he approached Congress to renew the president's negotiating authority under the RTAA. Protectionist sentiments were reigniting, especially in the farm and mining constituencies in the West, and isolationism was prevalent. In January 1935, the Senate had rejected Roosevelt's proposal to join the World Court, and in August, Congress overrode his attempt to gain discretion in applying neutrality legislation. Hull had been careful not to push tariff levels down too fast in the agreements reached during the first three years of the act. In a pragmatic retreat from his free-trade principles, he had even persuaded Japan to voluntarily reduce its textile exports to the United States in 1936. Most of the agreements had been reached with smaller economies; while American exports and trade balances were up in trade with nations with whom agreements were concluded, overall trade was still 40 percent below the pre-Depression level. Nevertheless, Hull declared that the trade program had helped to reduce unemployment from 26 percent when the RTAA went into effect to 16 percent in 1937. With the jobless rate remaining unacceptably high, he argued that the severe economic emergency demanded more time for the program to be successful. And as war clouds billowed over the European Continent and in the Pacific, he renewed his claim that new trade agreements were as important to the promotion of peace as they were to continuing the economic recovery. The limited impact that the agreements had produced in increasing import competition eased protectionist fears, and the peace prospects helped assuage isolationist opposition.[62] Despite a bitter debate in both chambers, with Democrats firmly in control and many opponents having been defeated, Congress easily adopted a three-year renewal of the RTAA by joint resolution on March 1, 1937.

THE BRITISH AGREEMENT

With deference to the intense criticism from farm groups that trade agreements benefited industrial interests over agriculture producers, the State Department began to seek negotiations with a major industrial nation and to avoid countries with predominantly agricultural economies. The United Kingdom became the primary target. Under Hull's leadership, however, the trade program, now more than ever, emphasized the broader goal of expanding world trade through a wider application of non-discriminatory MFN treatment over the promotion of specific, bilateral trade objectives. Hull had drawn his program based largely on nineteenth-century British trade agreements containing unconditional MFN provisions, which ironically the UK government had now abandoned. This goal ran counter to the British preferential trade policies increasingly pursued since 1931, including most importantly the imperial preferences of the Ottawa Agreements. These discriminatory preferences created a sterling bloc within the British Empire that denied access to American exports and restricted necessary raw materials otherwise available in the Dominions.

Agreements Britain had recently concluded with Argentina, Germany, Italy, and other countries were strictly designed to balance trade on a purely bilateral, barter basis, thus limiting commerce with other nations and obstructing the expansion of multinational trade. Early in 1936, Hull began lecturing the British ambassador in Washington, Sir Ronald Lindsay, on the importance of his program to international peace and prosperity. He cited the sacrifice made by the United States of vast quantities of American cotton exports when it rejected a barter arrangement with Germany similar to the current British agreements. In addition, he referred to the absence of a barter requirement in the US-Brazil agreement, an approach, Hull noted, which allowed Brazil to use the proceeds from exports to the United States, regardless of bilateral trade balances, to buy UK or other nations' exports and increase multilateral trade. He estimated that there was room for a $20 billion increase in international trade, which could provide employment for 12 to 14 million people and "would probably mark the difference between war and peace in Europe in the not distant future."[63]

The British were not moved by Hull's sermons, especially as they emanated from a senior official representing a country still maintaining prohibitive tariffs at the world's highest levels. Opposition to returning to non-discriminatory trade policies came principally from the British Treasury and Board of Trade, whose senior officials were skeptical of the likelihood that American protectionism would diminish. Neville Chamberlain, chancellor of the exchequer, was the son of imperialist MP Joseph Chamberlain, who as colonial secretary at the turn of the twentieth century had led the movement promoting imperial preferences and urged an end to British free-trade policies.

Yet while the chancellor opposed any compromise on colonial trade ties, the British foreign ministry was more open to accommodation with Hull. Like many officials and commentators on both sides of the Atlantic, Foreign Secretary Anthony Eden found Hull's strident lectures on the benefits of trade to world peace tiresome and unrealistic. After Germany remilitarized the Rhineland in March 1936, however, Eden was anxious to enhance the Anglo-American strategic relationship. When Hull proposed a joint declaration of commercial cooperation leading ultimately to non-discriminatory trade practices among non-Fascist economies, Eden responded favorably until overruled by Chamberlain. A disappointed Hull warned Lindsay that if Britain refused to cooperate with the United States economically, it could foster American "isolation in virtually every way in time of war."[64]

In September 1936, prospects for trade negotiations between the United States and Britain improved significantly when the two countries, along with France, reached a tripartite agreement to end the currency wars that had disrupted trade among them in the early 1930s. When Britain went off the gold standard in 1931, the pound dropped precipitously against the dollar, and the dollar fluctuated erratically, mainly downward, following FDR's abandonment of the gold standard in 1933. The French franc, remaining on the gold standard, was significantly overvalued until the United States and Britain accepted a 30 percent devaluation in the franc in conjunction with the tripartite stabilization agreement. The "beggar thy neighbor" currency movements, which had been the principal impediment to taking up Hull's tariff reform proposals at the London Economic Conference three years earlier—and which Roosevelt had refused to stabilize in his "bombshell" message—were now eliminated, at least for the time being. After the landslide victory returned FDR to the White House, another impediment had been removed.

In November, the two governments began exchanging lists of possible trade concessions as a basis for negotiations. On the day after Christmas, the British government gave notice to the State Department of its desire to initiate trade negotiations. This Yuletide gift to Hull was tempered, however, by the express caveat that the donor did not intend to surrender its imperial preferences. With the prospects of war looming in Europe as Germany accelerated its rearmament, along with the likelihood that American neutrality legislation adopted in 1935 could shut off access to the US market, the British considered their colonial Dominions the only certain supply source in the event that war broke out. Hull acquiesced but insisted that Britain must agree to reduce the scope of its colonial preferences. Prospects for an Anglo-American agreement grew brighter with this understanding but would have to wait for approval from the Commonwealth nations to modify the Ottawa commitments at the next Imperial Conference scheduled for the summer of 1937.

In late May, Neville Chamberlain was elevated to prime minister and immediately began pursuing an agreement with Hull and pressing Commonwealth leaders to accede to the necessary relaxation of imperial preferences. He would later become famous, or rather infamous, for his appeasement policy with Hitler, but at this point he surprisingly abandoned his father's imperial preference policies in order to seek economic appeasement with the United States. He found a strong ally in Canadian prime minister Mackenzie King in this effort, but King's support for modifying his country's preferences in the British market was contingent upon American willingness to renegotiate its 1935 pact with Canada for further concessions in opening the US market to Canadian agriculture exports. Hull ultimately agreed to the Canadian request, but demanded that the talks remain confidential until an agreement was reached with Britain that granted access for American farm exports to the UK.

The triangular negotiations that ensued with Britain and Canada proved to be the most troublesome the State Department had taken on under the RTAA. Strong opposition erupted on both sides of the Atlantic. Each side strenuously objected to the ambitious demands of the other as the negotiations dragged on for a year and more than once came close to breaking down. Finally, on November 17, 1938, Hull, fearing that the British were about to abandon the talks, signed agreements with both Britain and Canada in the White House in the presence of FDR. Hull believed that the agreement evidenced a reversal of Britain's "protectionist trend that had developed there in the previous eight years, and made major breaches in the preferential tariff wall erected around the British Empire in 1932."[65] Assistant Secretary of State Francis B. Sayre concluded that the British and Canadian agreements together provided "concessions on American farm products affecting *more than a quarter of a billion dollars'* worth of farm exports."[66] Chamberlain was also optimistic about the prospects for the agreement with the United States. He declared in the House of Commons that it "was not merely an attempt to come to a commercial agreement which . . . would be of great benefit to both countries, but I look upon it as an effort demonstrating the possibility of these two great countries working together on a subject which . . . may prove to be the forerunner of a policy of wider application."[67] Unfortunately, the ultimate effect of the agreement's rather modest trade benefits, however, was to be buried eight months after it went into effect when Hitler invaded Poland and Britain declared war on Germany.

Within weeks of the German attack, President Roosevelt called Congress into special session to take up revisions in the Neutrality Act enacted in 1935 and extended and enhanced in 1936 and 1937. Both the president and Secretary Hull had opposed this act, which embargoed the sale of US arms to belligerent nations in a declared war, but Roosevelt acquiesced and signed the bills into law due to the strong isolationist and non-interventionist sentiment then prevalent. Many Americans believed that profit-seeking bankers and arms merchants had drawn the United States into World War I and feared that a relaxation of the Neutrality Act would result in American troops returning to war in Europe. Following six weeks of bitter debate, FDR was able to persuade enough legislators to lift the embargo on sales to belligerent nations in early November, but the isolationists prevailed in requiring the sales to be on a "cash-and-carry" basis. No credit for arms sales, whether from government or private sources, was allowed, nor could American vessels transport the arms to the belligerent's ports. While the latter provision ensured that only Britain, whose navy dominated the Atlantic, would be able to make purchases under the guise of the "neutrality" authorization, the requirement of "cash only" transactions thwarted even sales to Britain, whose dollar and gold reserves were depleted within a few months.

10

The Anglo-American Special Relationship

I want to make it perfectly clear to you that it is the
furthest thing from my mind that we are attempting
in any way to ask you to trade the principle of imperial
preference as a consideration for Lend-Lease.[1]
>   —Franklin Roosevelt to Winston Churchill
>   February 11, 1942

The increasing threat of a new world war brought a different dimension to
the need for the president's trade agreement authority, which was due to
expire in 1940. Roosevelt's anxiety was revealed in a candid comment to his
close friend Secretary Morgenthau of the Treasury Department: "Henry,
these trade treaties are just too goddamned slow. The world is marching
too fast. They're just too slow."[2] Germany had built a broad network of barter agreements, orchestrated by Reichsbank president Dr. Hjalmar H. G.
Schacht, to supply raw materials for war production, including several in
South America, and the United States was being shut out of those markets
at a critical time. After the US-Brazil agreement, the administration began
to focus on negotiating with industrial nations, largely to stem the flow of
more politically sensitive agricultural imports. It was time now to shift the
focus back to Latin America, not only for the supply of raw materials but
also to diminish Hitler's economic influence in the Western Hemisphere.
Japanese expansive aggression throughout Asia made American access to
resources throughout the Western Hemisphere even more vital.

But US agriculture remained a serious political problem and presented the most daunting opposition to congressional renewal of the

RTAA. Following a new economic downturn rekindling the Depression in 1937–38, Democrats in the 1938 midterm elections lost a large number of the seats they had gained in the two previous elections. In the western states, party leaders blamed the trade program generally and the Canadian agreement in particular for the losses there. The National Grange, the oldest farm advocacy group in the nation, demanded an end to imports of foreign agriculture products the month before Congress took up the renewal. The Roosevelt administration estimated that about forty local and national organizations opposed continuing the trade program as it then existed.[3] Bipartisan opposition in the West was reflected in both the House and the Senate. Hull, a skilled vote counter, and Roosevelt, an intuitive judge of political sentiment, both feared the program would not survive in its present form. Nonetheless, Hull, against the advice of some of his friends in the Senate, refused to accept an amendment requiring Senate ratification of his agreements. Privately, FDR expressed grave concerns: "Hull is all wrapped up in this idea of reciprocal trade agreements. It is the one thing that he is interested in. But public sentiment is against them and I wish that Hull would not press the matter. He will be defeated, I think, and it will break his heart."[4] Despite his concern, the president gave the renewal his full-throated endorsement in his annual message to Congress in January 1940, and the House passed the resolution comfortably on a partisan vote.

In the Senate, a number of wavering Democrats wanted an amendment requiring some form of congressional approval to be imposed on the agreements. Senator Key Pittman, Foreign Relations Committee chairman and a Democratic protectionist, offered an amendment requiring Senate ratification, which failed on a close vote of 41 to 44. Pittman then joined Republicans in trying to kill the resolution, but the measure passed by 42 to 37 with fifteen Democrats joining all twenty of the Republicans who voted in opposition.[5] This proved to be the last contentious struggle over the renewal of the trade program during Hull's tenure at State.

LEND-LEASE

As Hitler's army blitzed its way through Europe, the Chamberlain government stumbled along with its policy of appeasement and the defiantly bellicose Winston Spencer Churchill became prime minister on May 10,

FIGURE 10.1 FDR presents to Secretary Hull the pen he used to extend the RTAA program in 1940 for three more years in the presence of (L to R) Secretary of Agriculture (and soon to be vice president) Henry Wallace; Senator Pat Harrison, chairman of the Senate Finance Committee; and Rep. Robert Doughton, chairman of the House Ways and Means Committee (Library of Congress)

1940. A few weeks later, the British Expeditionary Forces were compelled to evacuate nearly 340,000 British and French troops from the French port of Dunkirk in a miraculous retreat that left the bulk of Britain's existing armaments in the hands of the Germans. Churchill, who earlier, as first lord of the admiralty, had begun a private correspondence with Roosevelt, was now wooing the president intensely to help prevent the British Isles from becoming a vassal of Hitler's empire. Roosevelt was sympathetic, but his hands were tied by the isolationist flames in Congress, which were stoked by virulent radio addresses of popular aviator Charles A. Lindbergh— whom FDR believed was a closet Nazi—and Father Charles Coughlin, an anti-Semitic demagogue.

Another factor limiting Roosevelt's intervention on behalf of Britain was the presidential election of 1940; he decided to seek an unprecedented third term following the fall of France to the German forces. Fortunately for FDR and Britain, the GOP nominated an avowed internationalist, Wendell L. Willkie of Indiana, who had only recently been a Democrat before falling out with Roosevelt's New Deal domestic policies. The Republican National Convention passed over the better-known isolationist candidates, Senators Vandenberg and Robert A. Taft of Ohio, the eldest son of the former president and Supreme Court Chief Justice William Howard Taft, as well as the youthful New York prosecutor Thomas E. Dewey. The Republicans chose dark horse Willkie, a corporate lawyer with no prior experience in public office, based largely on his more realistic approach to the potential threat of war. But on June 19 while the convention was in session, Roosevelt enhanced his own bipartisan national security bona fides by appointing Henry Stimson, a former secretary of war and state in the Taft and Hoover administrations, respectively, as his new secretary of war and W. Frank Knox, one of TR's Rough Riders in Cuba and the 1936 Republican candidate for vice president, as his new secretary of the navy. Both Roosevelt and Willkie endorsed the adoption of a selective service draft, while promising not to send American boys to fight in a foreign war. Although Willkie refused to endorse a Roosevelt agreement with Churchill in August to trade over-aged American destroyers for military bases in British empirical territories in the Western Hemisphere without congressional approval, the GOP ticket made no issue of it. On Election Day, Willkie did substantially better in the popular vote count than had Landon in 1936, but FDR again won in a landslide of electoral votes.

This result cleared the path for the president to find another way to support the British in defending themselves now that the cash-and-carry approach was no longer viable. Following the Battle of Britain, in which the Royal Air Force defended against ruthless German air attacks throughout the summer and fall as a prelude to an intended land invasion, Churchill again appealed to Roosevelt for direct aid in the form of armaments. The president responded with a political masterstroke that avoided cash or credit payments for British war needs and maintained his "short-of-war" strategy to prevent a total fascist victory in Europe. In a December press conference he offered the simple analogy of lending a garden hose to a neighbor whose house was on fire and having the neighbor return it after the blaze was put out. In a famous fireside chat that followed, he said, "We must be the great arsenal of democracy . . . so that we and our children will be saved the agony and suffering of war which others have had to endure."[6] Since Britain remained in default on its war debts to the United States from World War I, the needed supplies would be provided this time without direct payments or loans. Rather, the Consideration for the war supplies would be negotiated in another form of compensation or repaid in kind. Roosevelt's proposal became popularly known as "Lend-Lease."

The president formally revealed the program in his annual message to Congress on January 6, 1941, announcing that he was sending the Lend-Lease Bill to the House, where it was entitled "An Act to Promote the Defense of the United States," and numbered with patriotic irony H.R. 1776. The bill faced significant opposition from isolationists and Anglophobes. Opposition from leading Republicans, including former president Hoover and Senator Arthur Vandenberg, also formed the America First Committee after the president entered the destroyers-for-bases agreement to protest any step potentially hindering America's own rearmament. Congress passed Lend-Lease in early March on a largely partisan vote in both Houses with Senator Taft leading a majority of Senate Republicans to vote no.

As contemplated by FDR, the legislation did not require Britain to pay for the aid in dollars or loans. Rather, the Act allowed "payment or repayment in kind or property, *or any other direct or indirect benefit which the President deems satisfactory*" [emphasis added].[7] With Hull and the State Department overseeing how the "indirect benefit," commonly referred to later as "the Consideration," would be defined after the hostilities ended, this provision would have a huge impact on postwar economic restructuring. Hull immediately seized on the language as leverage to eliminate the Commonwealth's imperial preferences in future trade negotiations— leverage he did not have in reaching the prewar bilateral trade agreement with Britain. Though Lend-Lease was now law, Congress still had to approve a $7 billion appropriation to fund the aid pursuant to a US-UK Mutual Aid Agreement yet to be negotiated. The State Department would seek to define the Consideration as a commitment to nondiscriminatory trade practices.

KEYNES

In May, the UK Treasury sent John Maynard Keynes to the United States as the personal representative of Chancellor of the Exchequer Sir Kingsley

FIGURE 10.2 Senators Robert Taft and Arthur Vandenberg, leaders of the GOP isolationists until after Pearl Harbor, when Vandenberg became a pro-trade internationalist often at odds with the Taft wing of the party (Library of Congress)

Wood in order to work out the aid agreement. The choice of Keynes as interlocutor was intriguing. A celebrated intellectual on both sides of the Atlantic, he possessed dazzling verbal dexterity but had no official government position. And while the brilliant economist may have possessed negotiating skills, in diplomatic interactions any skills he possessed were overshadowed by his penchant for witty, condescending sarcasm. His American counterparts often departed sessions with him impressed by his intellect but insulted and annoyed by his arrogance. Philosopher Bertrand Russell, who knew him as a colleague at Cambridge and in the Bloomsbury group of liberal intellectuals in London, wrote, "Keynes' intellect was the sharpest and clearest that I have ever known. When I argued with him, I felt that I took my life in my hands, and I seldom emerged without feeling something of a fool." Russell further observed of Keynes, "Insulting arguments darted out of him with the swiftness of an adder's tongue."[8]

The chancellor may have selected Keynes because his economic policies had much in common with Franklin Roosevelt's New Deal, which has often been referred to as "Keynesian." But principals among the American draftsmen of the New Deal seemed to resent the implication that FDR's economic policies derived from Keynes. Brain Trust member Rex Tugwell attributed what he called "the Keynesian myth" surrounding New Deal economics to FDR's favoring a "balanced economy rather than a balanced budget" and their corresponding views on the need to enhance purchasing power and increase price levels. According to Tugwell, Roosevelt "had arrived at these notions before he ever heard of Keynes . . . [and] never in his life had read anything Keynes wrote, except perhaps some newspaper pieces commenting on [Roosevelt's] own actions."[9] Another influence closer to the president was Marriner Eccles, a Salt Lake City banker whom Roosevelt appointed chairman of the Federal Reserve Board and who served throughout Roosevelt's presidency. Eccles had never read any of Keynes's work either and arrived at economic opinions that paralleled those of Keynes before he had ever heard of the British economist.

Yet Keynes no doubt did have an influence on the New Dealers, especially after the publication in 1936 of his seminal work, *The General Theory of Employment, Interest, and Money.* And prior to the London Economic Conference, Ray Moley had recommended Keynes's 1930 *Treatise on Money* to Governor James Cox, who was to chair the London currency negotiations, because Moley knew that Roosevelt had been influenced on the currency issue by ideas contained in this book, even if the president had not read it. In addition to proposing an end to the gold standard and urging the public management of currency exchange rates, Keynes's treatise called for a sharp drop in interest rates, price inflation, and public works programs to restore investment to a level that would exceed savings and lead to prosperity.

Though he had a generally unfavorable view of American politicians, Keynes had been impressed by a British press account of a 1932 FDR campaign speech calling for emergency relief and public works to restore purchasing power to Americans. In contrast to nearly universally negative European assessments of FDR's "Bombshell" message blocking currency stabilization at the London Conference, Keynes hailed it. In late December 1933, Keynes sent a letter to the president, published in the *New York Times,* expressing hope and praise for the American experiment embodied in the Hundred Days: "You have made yourself the trustee for those in every country who seek to mend the evils of our condition by reasoned experiment within the framework of the existing social system," Keynes wrote, adding, "If you succeed, new and bolder methods will be tried everywhere, and we may date the first chapter of a new economic era from your accession to office." He urged the American president to increase national purchasing power to stimulate output through deficit spending, writing, "Nothing else counts in comparison with this."[10]

With a letter of introduction from the president's friend and adviser, Harvard law professor Felix Frankfurter, Keynes first met with FDR in the White House on May 28, 1934. As a loyal Wilsonian, Roosevelt had not appreciated Keynes's criticism of the Versailles Treaty in his celebrated book, *The Economic Consequences of the Peace*, in which Keynes put down Wilson as a "blind and deaf Don Quixote" whose "thought and temperament were essentially theological not intellectual."[11] But after the meeting, in his tactful fashion, Roosevelt advised Frankfurter that they had had a "grand talk" and he liked Keynes "immensely."[12] To others he gave a less favorable and perhaps more candid assessment. He complained to Frances Perkins that Keynes had "left a whole rigamarole of figures" and said he "must be a mathematician rather than a political economist." Keynes returned the favor, telling Perkins after meeting FDR, that he found the president less "literate, economically speaking" than he had expected.[13]

Yet Roosevelt's intuitive approach to the political economy paralleled that of Keynes, even on trade policy. Keynes had always been an orthodox free-trader since his early years as a student and lecturer at Cambridge, where he served as secretary of the Cambridge University Free Trade Association. In his forties, as an increasingly outspoken and influential, if often controversial, economic commentator in 1923, Keynes attacked Conservative Party demands for protectionist policies with an unequivocal endorsement of free trade:

We must hold to free trade, in its widest interpretation, as an inflexible dogma, to which no exception is admitted, wherever the decision rests with us. We must hold to this even where we receive no reciprocity of treatment and even in those rare cases where by infringing it we could in fact obtain a direct economic advantage.

We should hold to free trade as a principle of international morals, and not merely as a doctrine of economic advantage.[14]

Keynes further declared, "If there is one thing Protection can*not* do, it is to cure unemployment. . . . The proposal to cure the present unemployment by a tariff on manufactured goods . . . is a gigantic fraud."[15]

To Keynes, however, as to Thomas Jefferson, consistency was no virtue. David Lloyd George, Liberal Party leader and prime minister from 1916 to 1922, described him as "mercurial and impulsive," observing that he "dashed at conclusions with acrobatic ease. It made things no better that he rushed into opposite conclusions with the same agility."[16] Lloyd George's appraisal seemed confirmed when in the early 1930s Keynes moved away from his liberal orthodoxy on free trade in an essay published in the *Yale Review*, entitled "National Self-Sufficiency," in which he concludes: "We do not wish . . . to be at the mercy of world forces working out . . . some uniform equilibrium according to the ideal principles of *laissez-faire* capitalism." Reaching a conclusion opposite to that of Cordell Hull, Keynes followed the rationale of Thomas Jefferson's retreat from free trade during the Napoleonic wars, writing, "I am inclined to the belief that . . . a greater measure of national self-sufficiency and economic isolation between countries than existed in 1914 may tend to serve the cause of peace, rather than otherwise. At any rate the age of economic internationalism was not particularly successful in avoiding war." Like Jefferson, as well as many New Dealers veering to economic nationalism to combat unemployment, Keynes had come to believe that goods should be "homespun whenever it is reasonably and conveniently possible."[17]

Keynes's first choice among several to reach full employment in Britain was to devalue sterling against gold in order to expand monetary policy, reversing the Bank of England's efforts to control inflation with an exchange rate pegged to gold at overvalued, prewar levels. In 1930, however, he did not think that there was any political likelihood that this remedy would be adopted. Hence, he proposed higher import tariffs and subsidies to industry to reduce unemployment. While he remained "frightfully afraid of protection as a long-term policy," he observed, "I am sure it is radically unsound, if you take a long enough view, but we cannot afford always to take long views. . . . [T]he question, in my opinion, is how far I am prepared to risk long-period disadvantages in order to get some help to the immediate position."[18] As he famously put it on another occasion, the "*long* run is a misleading guide to affairs. *In the long run* we are all dead."[19] His move to protection was "a question of a *choice* between alternatives," he wrote, "none of which are attractive in themselves. . . . [A] tariff is a crude departure from *laisser-faire* [*sic*], which we have to adopt because we have at present no better weapon in our hands."[20] To increase domestic employment in 1931, he suggested "import duties of 15 percent on all manufactured and semi-manufactured goods without exception, and of 5 percent on all foodstuffs and certain raw materials, whilst other raw materials would be exempt."[21]

Keynes withdrew his call for higher tariffs after the British government, in September 1931, suddenly abandoned the gold standard and the pound sterling began collapsing on the exchange markets. Rejoicing in the break from "our gold fetters," which he had been urging for years, Keynes explained, "Proposals for high tariffs have ceased to be urgent." But when Parliament began embarking on a protectionist path by passing a broad-based tariff in early 1932, Keynes did not object. In a 1932 radio broadcast, while noting that tariff protection "is a dangerous and expensive method of redressing a want of balance and security in a nation's economic life," Keynes remarked that "there are times when we cannot safely trust ourselves to the blindness of economic forces; and when no alternative weapons as efficacious as tariffs lie ready to our hand." In the same broadcast, however, he called most protectionist arguments "sophistries," and confirmed that he still thought

> a world wide system of tariffs [would] increase unemployment rather than diminish it, in the world as a whole. But I should now admit that if we put on a tariff at a time of severe unemployment it would be likely to shift on to other countries some part of our own burden of unemployment.[22]

To add further confusion to his message, Keynes also called the outcome of the just concluded Ottawa Imperial Conference, which adopted the system of discriminatory imperial tariff preferences, a stupidity that would be difficult to reverse. Later, however, he defended these preferences as a means of insulating the British economy within the sterling bloc from international market forces and from becoming a dependency of the United States.

Although limited with caveats, reservations, and apparent contradictions, Keynes's evolving pronouncements on the use of protectionist tariffs as an emergency tool to combat unemployment and to achieve economic recovery affected the political debate. According to economic historian Douglas A. Irwin, "Keynes's views had a profound impact on economic theory and policy and were perceived as weakening the case for free trade for decades."[23]

ARTICLE VII

Knowing what to expect from Hull's team at the State Department, Keynes attempted an end run around Hull when he arrived in Washington. He first arranged to meet with Treasury Secretary Henry Morgenthau, who was thought to be an Anglophile and less of a doctrinaire on trade than Hull. But Morgenthau was suspicious of Keynes's intentions, and the meeting went nowhere. Keynes reported on this meeting that he had "seldom struck anything stickier." Keynes then went to the top, arranging a meeting with President Roosevelt. Churchill had ordered Keynes to stonewall any financial commitments and limit compensation for the aid to vague military and political considerations and unspecified economic collaboration. Roosevelt, who generally favored vague commitments that allowed future wiggle room, agreed to Keynes's request that the Consideration not involve a money debt and "should not be such as to interfere with the economic and commercial relations between the countries or between either of them and other countries."[24]

Armed with this presumed presidential approval, Keynes arranged to meet with Assistant Secretary of State Dean G. Acheson, whom Hull had assigned to draft the aid agreement, and advised Acheson that the president had asked him to report their agreement to the State Department. Acheson would later wryly remark, "Keynes did not appear to think it unusual that I should receive instructions from the President via the British Embassy."[25] He believed that the conclusions from the White House meeting represented only Keynes's and not the president's views. A few days later, Keynes proposed a draft that included no obligation by the British to provide consideration for the aid other than returning such of the armaments provided under the Lend-Lease program as was practicable for them to return after the war and to "talk about other matters."[26]

Furious at Keynes's maneuver and proposal, Acheson called Keynes back to meet with him three weeks later on the day before Keynes was scheduled to return to England and presented him with the State Department's draft.

The agreement, a short document intended only to be a temporary skeleton basis for starting the aid shipments, had been approved by the president for discussion with the British government, Acheson said. Keynes read through the draft with few comments until he reached Article VII, which provided that the benefits to be received by the United States in return for the aid, as finally determined,

> shall be such as not to burden commerce between the two countries but to promote mutually advantageous economic relations between them and the betterment of world-wide economic relations; they shall provide against discrimination in either the United States of America or the United Kingdom against the importation of any product originating in the other country; and they shall provide for the formulation of measures for the achievement of these ends.[27]

Keynes, observing that the provision against discrimination raised "very serious considerations," asked whether it was intended to address imperial preferences, exchange controls, and other trade controls in the postwar period. Acheson affirmed that it did, but asserted that the article did not "impose unilateral obligations," rather only required the parties in the final settlement to review the matter and "work out to the best of their ability provisions which would obviate discriminatory and nationalistic practices and would lead instead to cooperative action in preventing such practices." Keynes became irate and responded with a lengthy argument that the British could not make such a commitment in good faith, that it would require an imperial conference for approval, that it contemplated a return to the gold standard, and that the nondiscriminatory MFN principle "saddled upon the future an ironclad formula from the Nineteenth Century." Acheson replied coldly that Keynes was taking "an extreme and unjustified position" and that the proposal made by Keynes that included no obligation in return for the aid "could not possibly be defended in this country." He added that "the British should realize that an effort of the magnitude of the lease-lend program on our part imposed upon them the obligation of continuing good will in working out plans for the future." Keynes said he would take the proposal back to London but noted that there were considerable differences of opinion in Britain as to future trade directions, including some who wanted to return to a free-trade policy; a middle group, including himself, who believed in the use of "control mechanisms" on imports and currency; and a third group that favored imperial policies.[28]

Thus began a six-month struggle to resolve the differences over the meaning of Article VII. Before leaving for London, Keynes wrote Acheson an apology for his "cavilling at the word 'discrimination'" and did not want it to be thought that he had overlooked the "excellence and magnanimity" of the offer embodied in the document as a whole. But in his inimitable style, he explained that his passionate response to the word was driven by its calling up "all the old lumber, most-favored-nation clause and the rest which was a notorious failure and made such a hash of the old world. . . . It is the clutch of the dead, or at least moribund, hand." Keynes, presumably referring to Smith's "invisible hand," declared that this "old lumber" would provide shelter for "all the unconstructive and truly reactionary people of both our countries." He concluded by asking Acheson to "forgive my vehemence which has deep causes in my hopes for the future. This is my subject. I know, or partly know, what I want. I know, and clearly know, what I fear."[29] Privately, however, Keynes was less diplomatic, referring to Article VII as one of the "lunatic proposals of Mr. Hull."[30]

Keynes was correct in assuming that the proposed language was, as Acheson later wrote, the "purest essence of Hull doctrine," designed to prohibit in the settlement "what Mr. Hull thought was evil," particularly trade discrimination.[31] But it was not only Hull in the State Department who held this view. Over the eight years that he had served as secretary, Hull had built a team of like-minded disciples of multilateral trade liberalism, including among others Acheson; Harry C. Hawkins, chief of State's Division of Commercial Policy and Trade Agreements; economic advisor Herbert Feis; Hull's chief lieutenant and speechwriter Leo Pasvolsky; and Undersecretary of State Sumner Welles, with whom Hull often clashed on nontrade matters. In fact, early drafts of Article VII, approved by Acheson and Welles while Hull was on health leave, specifically included the elimination of imperial preferences. Keynes was also mistaken in thinking that the State Department free-traders were in a world of their own without support from other departments and the president. Hull's views were shared, though without his intensity, by the secretaries of Commerce, Treasury, and Agriculture, as well as Henry Wallace, who became vice president after the 1940 election. While FDR was focused on other war-related priorities much of the time during the Article VII negotiations, he weighed in in favor of

Hull's approach when needed, albeit without the dogmatic resolution that Hull would have preferred.

THE ATLANTIC CHARTER

In August 1941, for the first time since each had become head of his respective government, the president met with Churchill secretly aboard war vessels in Placentia Bay off the coast of Newfoundland in what would become known as the Atlantic Conference. Roosevelt had been planning the meeting for months in order to discuss war aims. It was his intention to issue a joint declaration aimed at educating the American public as to what was at stake in the conflict and to generate public opinion against isolationists in Congress. Churchill also enthusiastically desired the meeting but with a more specific purpose in mind—tying the United States to the war effort. While the meeting began molding the intimate personal relationship between the two leaders that became vitally important to the future alliance and prosecution of the war, it also drew attention to the stark differences each leader represented in his historical outlook on world affairs and, in particular, on colonialism.

After several days of meetings, alternately on board the USS *Augusta*, a heavy cruiser carrying Roosevelt's delegation, and the HMS *Prince of Wales*, a battleship carrying Churchill and his entourage, the president and the prime minister issued an unsigned joint declaration, later dubbed the "Atlantic Charter," setting forth the guiding principles "on which they base their hopes for a better future" in the postwar world. They pledged no postwar territorial aggrandizement; no territorial changes made against the wishes of the people; self-determination, restoring self-government to those deprived of it by Hitler; access, on equal terms, to the trade and to the raw materials of the world as needed for economic prosperity; global cooperation to secure better economic and social conditions for all, including improved labor standards; assurance that, after ending Nazi tyranny, all men will be free from fear and want; freedom of the seas; and abandonment of the use of force and disarmament of aggressor nations, pending the establishment of a wider and permanent system of general security.[32]

The principle of equal access to trade proved the most difficult issue to resolve between the conflicting worldviews of the two statesmen. FDR's son Elliott, who attended the conference, later described the sparring between

FIGURE 10.3 FDR and Prime Minister Winston Churchill aboard the battleship HMS *Prince of Wales* on August 10, 1941, during the Atlantic Conference (Associated Press)

them over trade and British imperialism during a discussion after dinner over brandy and cigars. According to Elliott, his father told the prime minister that "after the war, one of the preconditions of any lasting peace will have to be the greatest possible freedom of trade. . . . No artificial barriers." FDR then came to the rub: "As few favored economic agreements as possible" would be permitted. Churchill tried to make a point about the British Empire trade agreements, but the president cut him off. "Yes," Roosevelt said, "Those Empire trade agreements are a case in point. It's because of them that the people of India and Africa, of all the colonial Near East and Far East, are still as backward as they are." In 1904, as a young Tory MP, Churchill had so strongly opposed Joe Chamberlain's proposals for imperial preferences that he dramatically bolted the Conservative Party over the issue and for twenty years joined the Liberal Party, which favored continuing Britain's nineteenth-century free-trade policies. But now, he suddenly became defensive on the issue. "Mr. President, England does not propose for a moment to lose its favored position among the British Dominions. The trade that has made England great shall continue, and under conditions prescribed by England's ministers." The president was not moved. He responded: "It is along in here somewhere that there is likely to be some disagreement between you, Winston, and me."

After accusing the British of following eighteenth-century policies in taking "wealth in raw materials out of a colonial country" and returning "nothing to the people of that country in consideration," FDR concluded: "I can't believe that we can fight a war against fascist slavery, and at the same time not work to free people all over the world from a backward colonial policy." In a snap response, Churchill declared, "There can be no tampering with the Empire's economic agreements. . . . They're the foundation of our greatness."[33] This was, however, not always Churchill's view, especially when he was a young free-trader concerned about the harm of higher tariffs on the working classes. In a speech he gave at the 1907 Imperial Conference as a Liberal MP serving as undersecretary of state for the colonies, Churchill said, "It is because we believe the principle of preference is positively injurious to the British Empire, and would create, not union, but discord, that we have resisted the [imperial preference] proposal."[34]

Undersecretary Welles, who accompanied the president during Hull's absence due to health treatments, urged Roosevelt to include outright "elimination of any discrimination" in the access to trade language, but Roosevelt preferred the less explicit requirement that access to trade be "without discrimination and on equal terms." Churchill insisted on language that allowed deference to the Ottawa Agreement preferences, arguing that the nondiscrimination commitment would require convening a conference of the Dominions for approval. This would take time that neither of the parties had, because Churchill wanted to begin the aid flow as soon as possible and Roosevelt wanted the declaration released promptly in order to begin using it to mobilize domestic support for his efforts on behalf of the Allied cause against Hitler. Against persistent opposition from Welles, the president finally gave in to Churchill and accepted the following language for the fourth paragraph describing the trade principle:

[The United States and the United Kingdom] will endeavor, with due respect for their existing obligations, to further the enjoyment by all States, great or small, victor or vanquished, of access, on equal terms, to the trade and to the raw materials of the world which are needed for their economic prosperity.[35]

Although the principle called for trade to be "on equal terms," it did not expressly prohibit "discrimination" and included the phrase urged by Churchill, "with due respect for their existing obligations," a loophole allowing the Ottawa preferences to survive.

In the understated style of his memoirs, Hull observed that he had been "keenly disappointed" in the trade principle in the charter's final form, pointing out that the phrase inserted by Churchill "deprived the article of virtually all significance."[36] He became determined to correct the problem in the Lend-Lease aid agreement. Negotiations dragged on for months following the Atlantic Conference, with Article VII presenting the major obstacle. In mid-October, the British finally offered a revised draft amending the proposal Acheson had given to Keynes at the end of July. Acheson, after only a glancing review, saw that "slippery words and phrases" had been added, robbing all meaning from the prohibition of trade discrimination.[37] The US ambassador to Britain, John G. Winant, later reported to Acheson that opposition to Article VII was political, "based on fear of a division in the Conservative Party" led by imperialist Tories, representing "a small but determined minority among Conservative membership of the Parliament."[38] This faction was emotionally and unalterably opposed to bartering the imperial preferences, and perhaps the Empire itself, in exchange for American military aid. Though they may have represented only a minority and Churchill claimed to be at best only lukewarm to their cause, the prime minister was unwilling to alienate any segment of his coalition in the House of Commons.

On December 2, Acheson presented to the new British ambassador in Washington, Lord Halifax (Edward Frederick Lindley Wood), a new draft, approved by the president, which accepted some of the British language, such as affirmation of the Atlantic Charter principles, but also proposed, through "agreed action" by the two countries, to eliminate "all forms of discriminatory treatment in international commerce, and to the reduction of tariffs and other trade barriers." Further, the new proposal invited "all other countries of like mind" to join in this agreed action, making it potentially a multilateral endeavor. Hull cabled Ambassador Winant in London to urge Churchill's speedy accession to the agreement, noting that with regard to the discrimination provision, "all that we ask is that the British sit down with us to work out the problems which lie ahead so that we may avoid substituting trade warfare in peacetime for the present wartime cooperation."[39] "Then began," in Acheson's words, "two months of blindman's bluff."[40]

With the Japanese attack on Pearl Harbor on December 7 and subsequent entrance of the United States into the war, the world changed for the negotiating parties. For the Americans, the need to arm and supply their own forces became more immediate, and aid under the Lend-Lease program to Britain had to be curtailed, at least for the short term. The British, pleased to have a new ally participating in the war as a belligerent rather than merely a supply source, assumed that the Lend-Lease program and its Consideration issue would be terminated or transformed. But within days of the attack, telegrams arrived in London from Washington with notification of Roosevelt's decision to continue Lend-Lease as the vehicle through which aid would be rendered and announcing the need to complete the aid agreement so that Congress would release the aid appropriation. Winant was not able to get through to Churchill to press the issue in London due to the prime minister's more pressing military concerns, and Hull urged FDR to take it up with Churchill during the conferences the two leaders held in Washington beginning on December 22, extending through mid-January 1942. The president later told Acheson that he tried to raise the Lend-Lease agreement several times during the visit, but was rebuffed by Churchill, citing more urgent matters.

In a confidential note to Lord Halifax, who at Hull's request had been urging his colleagues to resolve the Article VII issue, Churchill wrote on January 10:

> All this fussing about what is to happen after the war is premature at the present time, when we are probably a long way from any satisfactory conclusion. It is only the State Department which is pressing. . . . I told the President that the Imperial Preference would raise great difficulties in England if raised as a separate issue now but if raised as part of a large economic settlement, in which the United States would become a low tariff country, it would probably be easy to handle. He seemed to think this very sensible, and I am sure he felt, as I did, that we had better address our minds to the struggle on which the lives of our people depend. I should recommend you to stall any demand from the State Department with the usual diplomatic arts. . . . [W]ith every month that passes the fighting comradeship of the two countries as allies will grow, and the haggling about the lend-lease story will wane. After all, Lend-lease is practically superseded now.[41]

By the end of January, however, the "blindman's bluff," which had been central to Churchill's strategy, came to an end. Congressional hearings on the aid appropriation were scheduled for early February, and the administration would have to explain what was holding up the agreement. Roosevelt sent a note to Halifax that he "strongly hoped" the British would accept the latest American draft of Article VII because deferring the discrimination matter would leave "them in a much more difficult future economic situation." The British presumed the last phrase meant that generous Lend-Lease and postwar aid would become problematic and uncertain. Halifax cabled the message to London and again urged settlement of the issue on American terms.[42] At the same time, Hull cabled Winant, requesting that he explain the urgency of the matter to British foreign minister Anthony Eden and to Chancellor of the Exchequer Sir Kingsley Wood, noting that the Lend-Lease Act offered the only legislative authority for the United States to furnish aid to the Allies. "It is essential," Hull concluded, "that the provisions of this Act be followed and that the agreements contemplated and required by it be promptly made."[43]

In a tense meeting of Churchill's cabinet on February 2, Eden, against opposition from the chancellor, proposed accepting Article VII. The prime minister later told Winant that more than three-fourths of the cabinet opposed making Empire preference a part of the Lend-Lease settlement. One minister argued that the request to *eliminate* imperial preferences in exchange for the United States only *reducing* tariffs and other American trade barriers was unfair and would arouse passions giving rise to a demand for liberation from "American pluto-democracy."[44] On February 6, the cabinet finally reached a compromise that accepted Article VII, but with a reservation contained in interpretive notes that effectively exempted from the elimination of trade discrimination "special arrangements between members of the same commonwealth or federation such as the British Commonwealth or the United States of America and its possessions."[45] The latter reference alluded to American preferences in trade with the Philippines under US control since the Spanish-American War. When Halifax presented this response at the State Department the next day, Acheson rejected it out of hand.

Resolution of the impasse could now be accomplished only through the unique personal relationship developing between Roosevelt and Churchill. FDR, with assistance from Harry Hopkins, who since the death in 1936 of Louis Howe had become the president's closest personal adviser, drafted a telegram addressed "Personal for the Former Naval Person." That was a code name for Churchill, based on the common bond the two leaders had as, respectively, the former lord of the admiralty and former assistant secretary of the navy. As British economic historian L. S. Pressnell writes, FDR's cable represented "a brilliant weaving of clarification and of persuasion" in urging acceptance of Article VII as drafted by the State Department.[46] In the first paragraph the president said he wanted "to make it perfectly clear to you that it is the furthest thing from my mind that we are attempting in any way to ask you to trade the principle of imperial preference as a consideration for Lend-Lease." After expressing understanding of "the nice relationships your constitution requires . . . in dealing with the Dominions," he said, "All I am urging is an understanding with you that we are going to have a bold, forthright, and comprehensive discussion looking forward to the construction of what you so aptly call 'a free, fertile economic policy for the postwar world.'" He affirmed that the United States was not asking for a commitment in advance to abolish Empire preference, "and I can say that Article 7 does not contain any such commitment." Roosevelt said he realized that the British government "could not give now" such a commitment even if it wanted to, just as he "could not, on my part, make any commitment relative to a vital revision of our tariff policy." He urged the signing of the agreement based on his assurances without the exchange of notes, which might give a false impression "to our enemies," diluting the purpose of demonstrating "to the world the unity of the American and British people."[47]

Churchill read Roosevelt's message to the cabinet and recommended the execution of the agreement without the exchange of interpretive notes. Although the message did not differ in substance from the position conveyed by State Department diplomats previously, the president's assurances dispelled the notion that Hull's stridency was isolated among American economic policymakers. Even Maynard Keynes now favored acceptance. On February 23, the British signed the Mutual Aid Agreement containing the following language in Article VII:

> In the final determination of the benefits to be provided to the United States of America by the Government of the United Kingdom in return for aid furnished under the Act of Congress of March 11, 1941, the terms and conditions thereof shall be such as not to burden commerce between the two countries, but to promote mutually advantageous economic relations between them

and the betterment of world-wide economic relations. To that
end, they shall include provision for agreed action by the United
States of America and the United Kingdom, open to participation by all other countries of like mind, directed to the expansion,
by appropriate international and domestic measures, of production, employment, and the exchange and consumption of goods,
which are the material foundations of the liberty and welfare of
all peoples; to the elimination of all forms of discriminatory treatment in international commerce, and to the reduction of tariffs
and other trade barriers; and in general, to the attainment of all
the economic objectives set forth in the Joint Declaration made
on Aug. 12, 1941 [the Atlantic Charter], by the President of the
United States of America and the Prime Minister of the United
Kingdom.[48]

While the president's message cleared the logjam blocking settlement
of the Lend-Lease aid agreement, it clouded the meaning of Article VII,
which would be a critical element and a source of much friction in postwar
trade negotiations. While many in the State Department would persistently
cite the provision as a commitment to end the discriminatory imperial preferences, the British, equally inaccurately, recorded in their cabinet minutes
that Roosevelt had affirmed that there was no such commitment and that
these preferences "should be excluded from our discussions."[49]

BRETTON WOODS

As the war raged in Europe and the Pacific over the next three years, discussions and debates continued across the Atlantic among British and
American experts over a new international economic order for the postwar
world. Both sides accepted the need to address the two critical problems—
exchange rate instability and tariff barriers—that plagued the world economy and deepened conflict among nations during interwar years. While
agreeing in principle on this need, however, nationalistic bias as well as
competing political and economic interests precluded a common solution.
One thing was clear: The monetary issue had to be resolved first, because
eliminating trade barriers could not restore fair trade competition if currency manipulation continued to distort trade prices. As had been proven

in the 1930s, both high tariffs and currency depreciation offered effective alternatives in disrupting trade.

In Washington, the president assigned monetary issues to the Treasury Department. Just as negotiating jurisdiction had been divided at the London Economic Conference in 1933, Treasury held the monetary portfolio while State oversaw trade relations. Secretary Morgenthau assigned substantive details on the subject to his assistant and director of monetary research, Harry Dexter White, an economist in charge of Treasury's foreign affairs. Similarly in London, the British Treasury handled monetary matters, with policy planning and negotiations led by Maynard Keynes, who became Lord Keynes in June 1942. Morgenthau directed White to begin work on a stabilization plan in December 1941, while Keynes began developing a plan soon after returning from his Washington meetings on the Lend-Lease aid agreement earlier that fall. Except for the rumors that occasionally traveled across the ocean, they each worked independently without knowledge of what the other was doing.

Harry White had much in common with Keynes. Not only was he a disciple of Keynesian economics, but he also shared Keynes's acerbic wit and personality and was often rude, explosive, and arrogant in defending his point of view.[50] The plans they separately developed also had many common features, but key differences emerged from their efforts to promote their respective nationalistic interests in the new economic order. Until the First World War, British sterling had dominated the international financial market and continued to play an important role in the interwar years as the United States rose in eminence to become the world's creditor nation and the dollar began to eclipse the pound outside the sterling-controlled British Empire. Keynes knew that Britain would have severe balance-of-payment problems after the war and that sterling could not be restored to its prewar stature, but he hoped to maintain London's premier financial role and avoid a world economy totally dependent on the value of the dollar. White, on the other hand, wanted to make sure that exchange rates would be stabilized based on dollars or dollar-valued gold, most of the reserves of which America controlled. Morgenthau and White hoped to move the world financial center from London to Washington (not Wall Street) with the US dollar as the common exchange currency in the postwar world.

Keynes's plan, called "Proposals for an International Clearing Union," created a fund to finance balance-of-payments deficiencies and supervise exchange rates. The fund would use a new international currency he named "bancor," priced in gold, but not convertible into gold as under the gold standard. Member nations in the Union would be required to maintain an even balance-of-payments, so that countries with a surplus would need to take in more imports and those with a deficit could borrow from the fund to cover the deficiencies until they found new export markets. The United States and the United Kingdom would be the founding members of the Clearing Union and would agree on the initial bancor value of their currencies and bancor's value in gold. Although Keynes had not abandoned his bilateral, non-MFN approach to trade barter agreements, this monetary union would be multilateral. As new members came into the Union, agreements would be reached among the new and existing members fixing the value of the new members' currency in terms of bancor. These rates could not be changed without the approval of the governing board. Keynes explained that in joining the Union, members would be abandoning "that licence to promote indiscipline, disorder and bad-neighbourliness which, to the general disadvantage, they have been free to exercise hitherto."[51] Keynes's plan also proposed a second institution to finance reconstruction after the war and promote economic growth and development.

White's plan proposed establishing two new international organizations and for roughly the same purposes suggested by Keynes—an Inter-Allied International Stabilization Fund, as the instrument to stabilize foreign exchange rates, and an Inter-Allied Bank to finance economic reconstruction for Allied countries and to supply the short-term capital necessary to increase trade where such capital was not available at reasonable rates from private sources. The structure and procedures of the organizations differed between the two plans, however, as White's proposal made sure that the United States would control the decisions of the stabilization fund through votes allocated on the basis of contributions to the fund. And White's plan did *not* propose a new international currency. Morgenthau had suggested to White that his plan include an international currency before seeing Keynes's plan, although he may have heard about Keynes's bancor proposal through a leak or gossip. White would not consider it. "A 'trade dollar' or 'Demos' or 'Victor' (names suggested by FDR) or 'what-have-you' unit of currency supplementing the United States dollar, whether of the same or different value," White wrote to his boss, "would no more help foreign trade than would the adoption of a new flag." He added that the British pound had served as an international currency for many decades, but when it lost its stability, it lost its utility. "Only the United States dollar has any chance of serving in that capacity now." But if the United States were to propose the dollar as the unit of account, he said, it would draw opposition from "those countries who, out of reasons of national prestige or anticipated monetary loss, would prefer not to promote a broader use in international use of a currency unit of some other country."[52] White proposed that the multilateral stabilization rates be based on gold but with a fixed value denominated in dollars. He did offer a unit of account, named unitas, as a gold deposit receipt for members of the fund. But its value was also fixed in dollars and the unit seemed to have no purpose other than as a negotiating counter to bancor.

Keynes's plan was formally presented to the American side in September 1942, two months after White had informally given a draft of his plan to the British. Keynes, on seeing it, immediately expressed disdain for White's plan, calling it "quite hopeless," especially its reliance on gold as the reference for fixed exchange rates, which meant effectively returning to what Keynes considered the "barbarous relic" of the gold standard. Yet after some time, Keynes mellowed and hoped for compromise, believing he could convince White of the advantages of an international currency not tied to the dollar. He was encouraged that in White's plan "the line taken towards Hullism is extremely moderate" and that White had expressed disapproval of "hangovers from a Nineteenth Century economic creed" that found government "interference with trade and with capital and gold movements, etc., are harmful."[53] Extensive negotiations between each side's technicians on the competing plans took place over the next year. The British wanted to work out differences between the plans bilaterally before bringing in more participants, but the State Department did not want to give the appearance of an Anglo-Saxon conspired deal that would be offered "take it or leave it" to everyone else. The discussions were broadened to add other allies by mid-1943, including Canada and France, who offered their own plans, as well as the Russians and Chinese, who were consulted but less engaged.

The critical negotiations, however, continued to be between White and Keynes until they reached an agreement in late April 1944 to publish a joint statement outlining principles in establishing the stabilization fund, which the technical experts of the parties were prepared to recommend to their respective governments. A senior British official at the time commented on the unique process this agreement represented:

Usually, the politicians decided in the first place what courses of action they thought would commend popular approval in their countries, and then instructed the technicians to work out arrangements to implement these conclusions, but on this occasion the process had been reversed; the technicians were examining the problems together and attempting to reach solutions that appeared to them to be right on merits before submission to Cabinet Ministers.[54]

These principles largely followed White's plan, with few concessions to Keynes, in creating the International Monetary Fund (IMF), a name suggested by Keynes, and the International Bank for Reconstruction and Development, or World Bank. Morgenthau, with approval from the president, invited forty-four nations to a conference to agree on the details of the new organizations; the meeting was to be held in July at the picturesque Mount Washington Hotel resort at Bretton Woods, isolated in the White Mountains of New Hampshire. Although Morgenthau chaired the conference, Harry White effectively ran the discussions and got his way on most substantive issues.

After three weeks of often acrimonious talks, the participating countries reached agreements that largely conformed to American wishes. The conference established the IMF with contributions to the fund being made in gold or US dollars (25 percent) and national currencies (75 percent) in amounts allocated in quotas based on the size of each member's economy and reserves of gold or US dollars. Voting rights were to be proportional to the member's quota. The United States agreed to contribute $3 billion to the $8.8 billion total in the fund, thus holding more than a third of the votes. There would be no international currency. Members' currencies were given a fixed value essentially pegged to the dollar, which was valued at $35 per ounce of gold. Members agreed to maintain the value of their currencies within a 1 percent, plus or minus, range and could not depreciate their currency by more than 10 percent without IMF board approval. Countries with trade deficits could borrow from the fund to cover balance-of-payments problems, but, contrary to a proposal urged by Britain, creditor countries, such as the United States, were not required to import from debtors. The conference agreed to install the headquarters of both the IMF and the World Bank in Washington, rejecting Keynes's request to have at least one of the institutions located in London. New York was also rejected in order to limit the influence of the Wall Street tycoons, with whom Morgenthau and Roosevelt were often at odds.

As is obvious from the result, the Americans held all the leverage necessary to have their way at Bretton Woods. The United States controlled two-thirds of the world's gold supply and would likely remain in the postwar years the world's strongest economy. Perhaps more important, American loans and generosity would be needed by Britain and the other war-torn nations for rebuilding when the war ended. Morgenthau and White adroitly and persistently played the card of blaming Congress for their having to strike a tough bargain. Democratic strength was waning in Congress, as was the influence of the internationalists in both parties. It was indeed uncertain whether Congress would approve any agreement.

The New York bankers, concerned that the creation of new international financial institutions might interfere with their own business opportunities, were already lined up in opposition. As Keynes dithered over the statement of principles to be released before the conference, New York governor Thomas E. Dewey, the leading candidate for the 1944 Republican presidential nomination, was supporting measures backed by Wall Street to promote private, postwar reconstruction and stabilization loans. White urged quick British approval of the statement of principles to head off this effort. The bankers had even approached the British with the idea of a private loan to rebuild England after the war, apparently hoping to preempt Bretton Woods. Keynes rejected the idea, however, observing "we look gift horses in the mouth when they are of the breed offered by the New York bankers."[55] The political risks posed by Morgenthau and White would prove to be more than a bluff when the Bretton Woods agreements came up for approval by Congress the following year.

Likewise, Keynes would not find it easy to obtain ratification of the deal by the UK Parliament. At the closing dinner at Bretton Woods, the delegates had given Keynes a standing ovation, singing, "For He's a Jolly Good Fellow," as he left the room. On returning to London, he must have thought he was in a different world. Controversy surrounded him over the agreement, with criticism coming not just as anticipated from the Tory imperialists but also from those who maintained that Britain would need policy flexibility after the war to impose exchange controls, import restrictions, and bilateral balance-of-payments barter agreements. They argued that the IMF did not offer a sufficient credit facility to meet the needs anticipated in the coming years. A return to the gold standard at Bretton Woods made the restrictions on policy discretion in dealing with trade potentially disastrous. Though these criticisms mirrored many of his own past arguments,

Keynes dutifully defended the agreement, contending that the conference only addressed currency exchange policies and did not limit discretion in trade policy. Import restrictions and barter arrangements were unaffected by Bretton Woods. British negotiators would agree to abandon these policies in future trade negotiations only if offered "compensating advantages."

In October, Sir John Anderson, chancellor of the exchequer, summed up his government's views on Bretton Woods in realistic terms. Noting that the agreement was "a difficult document, inevitably long and technical" with "obscurities of language . . . which have led to misunderstanding and must be clarified," he cautioned that "the time for detailed exposition will come when the whole matter has to be debated by Parliament. . . . [I]f we find that the United States and other countries important in international trade and finance decide that it is acceptable to them, we must not reject it lightly."[56]

HULL RETIRES

During the final week of the Bretton Woods Conference, Secretary Hull announced that the United States, the United Kingdom, the Soviet Union, and China would meet the following month to discuss the formation of an international security organization. On August 21, 1944, Hull opened the conference at Dumbarton Oaks, the former Georgetown home of a State Department diplomat, and over the next six weeks, the four-party talks laid the foundation for the organization of the United Nations (UN), whose name FDR coined earlier to refer to the twenty-six Allied countries that had signed the Atlantic Charter in January 1942. Hoping to avoid the fate of the League of Nations after President Wilson failed to involve Congress in its formation, Hull was careful to consult with congressional leaders from both parties concerning the formation of such an organization.

Discussions regarding the organization had commenced soon after Hitler invaded Poland in September 1939, and Hull had been instrumental in obtaining passage in 1943 of a congressional resolution endorsing US participation. Hull even took care to consult with Roosevelt's 1944 Republican opponent, Thomas E. Dewey, and his foreign policy adviser, John Foster Dulles, after Dewey released a statement critical of the conference just before it began. Although he had led a highly partisan path for much of his political career, Hull was determined to maintain a nonpartisan policy on security affairs and to solidify bipartisan support for the creation of the United Nations.

Dumbarton Oaks represented the final act of Hull's nearly twelve years as secretary of state. The establishment of the United Nations in San Francisco the following year was a dream come true for internationalists like Hull, who had seen Wilson's League rejected only twenty-five years earlier. The secretary's respect in Congress proved instrumental in laying a credible political foundation for its ratification. When he advised the president at the end of September that he was exhausted and in such poor health that he would have to resign, Roosevelt urged him to stay on at least until the end of their third term the following January. Hull had been diagnosed with tuberculosis and diabetes in 1932. As his condition began deteriorating in 1939, he was forced to take extended leaves for months at a time for treatment and recuperation. Hull knew that his condition would not allow him to fulfill his responsibilities as secretary any longer. He agreed to stay only until after the election in November. When he turned seventy-three three days later, he began another period of rest and recovery, first in his apartment and then upon entering the Bethesda Naval Hospital for the next six months. In his letter accepting Hull's formal resignation, the president proposed, "When the organization of the United Nations is set up, I shall continue to pray that you as the Father of the United Nations may preside over its first session." In 1945, following Roosevelt's nomination, Hull received the Nobel Peace Prize for his record of achievement in promoting peace through international trade, the Good Neighbor policy, and the organization of the United Nations.

The Roosevelt-Hull relationship, however, was a complicated affair that often frustrated Hull. FDR's leadership style and habit of creating conflict among his subordinates continued to infuriate the secretary of state. The president began to favor the counsel of his family friend and protégé, Undersecretary of State Sumner Welles, over that of the secretary. Hull finally succeeded in forcing Welles's resignation, just as he had forced out Ray Moley and George Peek previously, by offering his resignation as an ultimatum. But even after Welles's departure, the president continued to shut Hull out of any military strategy discussions during the war and excluded him from the major allied conferences with Churchill and Joseph Stalin.

Part of the reason for Hull's exclusion resulted from his medical absences and the separation of military from foreign political affairs, but the president may have shunned him because he viewed as tiresome Hull's dogmatic, incessant, and often shrill appeals promoting trade as the cure for most world problems. Many in the administration viewed Hull as a plodding, predictable bore. For whatever reason, FDR often ignored Hull during the war years after Pearl Harbor, which wounded Hull's feelings. "I feel," Hull later wrote, "it is a serious mistake for a Secretary of State not to be present at important military meetings."[57] Dean Acheson, in memoirs published in 1969, observed that the "virtual exclusion of Secretary Hull from high-policy decisions during the war" led State under Hull to "become absorbed in platonic planning of a utopia, in a sort of mechanistic idealism." This detachment from "the practicalities of current problems and power relationships," Acheson observed, "accentuated the isolation of the Secretary and the Department in a land of dreams."[58] But this critical view of Hull's idealism—given in hindsight during the height of the Cold War—seems cynically overstated in reference to the State Department's organization of the UN and the pursuit of a world free of protectionist trade barriers.

No doubt, Hull's principal asset in his relationship with the president was the political sway he had over Congress and his popularity with the public, especially in the South, where Roosevelt was weakest. Hull was prominently mentioned as likely to have succeeded Roosevelt, had the president not decided to run for a third term in 1940. This asset was pivotal to winning the internecine struggles Hull fought to eliminate rivals to his authority in promoting his trade goals. Although the two men remained very cordial until the president's death in April 1945 and obviously shared a mutual empathy and respect for the talents and points of view of one another, Hull, with some justification, deeply resented being barred from the inner circle of White House advisers. Hull's confidant, Assistant Secretary of State Breckinridge Long, described in his diary Hull's state of mind after a meeting with him just before he finally resigned. He was "*not* a well man," Long wrote of his superior, "He was tired of intrigue . . . tired of being by-passed . . . tired of fighting battles which were not appreciated . . . and tired of service. . . . The end of a long career is at hand—ending not in satisfaction, as it should, but in bitterness."[59]

In retrospect, however, Hull's long career did end in satisfaction of his principal goal of laying the foundation for a multilateral trading system designed to promote peace and prosperity. With support from FDR often wavering but in the end holding firm, Hull succeeded in pursuing his trade agreements program through partisan congressional thickets, battles with New Deal rivals, and opposition from war allies. By the end of his nearly three terms as secretary, the State Department had negotiated twenty-eight reciprocal trade agreements, reducing average tariff rates from nearly 60 percent in 1932 to around 28 percent in 1945. And the RTAA had become more and more a bipartisan institution. Congress renewed the president's trade authority in 1943, though for only two years, with an overwhelming margin that included 145 House Republicans and 18 Senate Republicans voting in favor. By 1944, in stark contrast with tradition, the Republican Party platform even called for "a great extension of world trade" and pledged to "join with others in leadership in every cooperative effort to remove unnecessary and destructive barriers to international trade." The party no longer called for repeal of the RTAA but cautioned that protective tariffs "against foreign competition should be modified only by reciprocal bilateral trade agreements approved by Congress."[60] Before his death in 1955, Hull would live to see two Republican-controlled Congresses extend the program under a Republican president.

Fulfilling his dream first mentioned publicly in a 1916 congressional speech, he would also live to see the postwar creation of something close to the "international trade congress" that he proposed for formulating agreements "to promote fair and friendly trade relations among all the nations of the world," as manifested in the General Agreement on Tariffs and Trade (GATT). In a leading text describing the creation of the GATT, its authors conclude: "For almost single-handedly repositioning U.S. trade policy in the 1930s and inspiring the efforts at postwar planning during the 1940s, Hull was the most important individual responsible for what ultimately became the GATT."[61]

11

The Postwar Atlantic Alliance

How differently things appear in Washington than
in London, and how easy it is to misunderstand one
another's difficulties and the real purpose which lies
behind each one's way of solving them.[1]
—John Maynard Keynes
House of Lords, December 18, 1945

Soon after taking office following the death of Franklin Roosevelt in April
1945, President Harry S. Truman asked Assistant Secretary of State for
Economic Affairs William L. Clayton for a briefing on postwar plans for
international commercial relations. Clayton had been at State only since
the previous December but had been a valued adviser on economic and
trade issues in the Roosevelt administration since 1940. Clayton gave the
new president a detailed report on the Bretton Woods agreements, which
Congress had not yet ratified, and briefed him on upcoming trade negotiations while Truman listened carefully and took copious notes. In 1940,
Cordell Hull had listed Truman, then serving as a senator, among those he
feared might not vote for a clean renewal of the trade agreements program.
Truman did, however, vote to renew the program in the form desired by
Hull, as he always had. He claimed to have had a "particular interest" in
the idea of free trade ever since he led his high school debate team in arguing for the proposition of "Tariff for Revenue Only."[2] Like Hull, Truman
was a political liberal, an internationalist, and a reliable vote for most of
Roosevelt's New Deal programs.

After Clayton finished his exposition, Truman admitted, with characteristic humility and candor, "I don't know anything about these things. I certainly don't know what I'm doing about them. I need help."[3] Clayton received this confession and plea with the earnestness with which it was delivered, and the two men developed a bond of respect that would become critical to the fulfillment of Hull's international trade goals.

Will Clayton was tall, handsome, and debonair, with sharp, distinctive facial features as if chiseled by a classical Greek sculptor. In 1945, at sixty-five, his hair was silver-white and parted down the middle. Born in 1880 near Tupelo, Mississippi, on a cotton farm that his father lost to creditors in 1886, Clayton was forced to abandon his formal education in the eighth grade. At age twelve, after learning shorthand and teaching himself to type, he became a stenographer and court reporter in Jackson, Tennessee, where his father had moved the family after giving up the Tupelo farm. In addition to his court work, the young teenager typed for guests at the local hotel, which not only helped support his family but also introduced him to at least two people who later would be instrumental to his career. The first was William Jennings Bryan, then a Nebraska Democrat running for the US Senate. Bryan hired Clayton to type a political speech from which the young man learned his first lesson on the ills of high tariffs. He talked for days about Bryan's arguments attributing the South's dismal agriculture economy to protective tariffs. The second acquaintance was a cotton merchant who was so impressed with the talent and energy exhibited by Clayton that he hired him at the age of sixteen as his personal secretary and took him to the headquarters of his firm, the American Cotton Company, in New York City.

Clayton left the American Cotton Company in 1904 to start his own brokerage house with his brother-in-law in Oklahoma City, later moving it to Houston, Texas. Within twenty years, the new firm, Anderson, Clayton & Co., became the largest cotton merchant in the world and made its owners multimillionaires.[4] Clayton's success infuriated competitors, who claimed he was manipulating the market for his own benefit and spurred Congress to initiate four congressional investigations of his business practices between 1928 and 1936. In all of the investigations, recorded in 3,450 pages of testimony, Clayton appeared voluntarily and calmly explained in thorough detail how his business worked. The investigations vindicated him completely and left a favorable impression of him at the Capitol. Having been called "everything from a common gambler to an economic royalist," according to *Newsweek*, "he won a clean bill of health at each inquiry and was praised by congressmen for his business ethics."[5]

By the late 1920s, Will Clayton's influence began spreading beyond the cotton market to politics, particularly relating to agriculture and trade. Unlike businessmen who favored the Harding-Coolidge-Hoover hands-off approach to business, Clayton, a Wilsonian Democrat, believed that capitalism needed regulation. In a 1936 speech to the Harvard Business School Alumni Association, which drew praise from a *New York Times* editorial, Clayton chastised corporate tariff lobbies and monopolistic practices that curtail production, fix prices, and distort competition while seeking paternalistic government protection.[6] He vigorously opposed government intervention in the markets, however, especially efforts to manipulate the agricultural market, whether they came from Democrats or Republicans. For this reason he fell out with the Roosevelt administration in its first term over the National Industrial Recovery Act and the Agricultural Adjustment Administration. Clayton was a particularly bitter opponent of cutting production and "plowing-under" crops to raise prices. He even briefly joined the American Liberty League, a bipartisan anti-Roosevelt organization initiated by conservative Democrats, like Al Smith and John J. Raskob, and funded largely by the DuPont family.

Over the years Clayton served in the public arena, critics came to different conclusions about his political views depending upon the political perspective of the critic. From the left, in the words of the *Nation*, he was considered a "Southern reactionary."[7] From the right, isolationist Republicans referred to him as "a well-known one-worlder in do-gooder circles."[8] But the *American Magazine* probably rendered the most accurate description: "Will Clayton parts his hair right down the center, and his politics go the same way."[9] In his later years he revealed a notable interest in developing affordable housing for the poor and promoting world peace, but the most important political issue to Clayton was trade. He had been one of the 1,028 economists and businessmen who signed the public letter urging President Hoover to veto the Smoot-Hawley Tariff. When Alf Landon, the 1936 Republican nominee for president, blasted Hull's trade program and praised George Peek's economic nationalism, Clayton promptly came back to the Democratic fold and endorsed FDR's bid for reelection.

In 1940, Clayton took leave of his cotton brokerage and volunteered as one of the wealthy businessmen who served in the government for a "dollar a year" as needed to address economic emergencies arising from the threat of war. His work ranged from aiding Latin American nations seeking new markets following the Nazi occupation of continental Europe to heading the overseas procurement of critical defense materiel and managing the disposal of war surplus property. The Senate confirmed his appointment as assistant secretary of the Department of Commerce in July 1942, and a month after Cordell Hull retired, Roosevelt moved Clayton to the State Department as assistant secretary for economic affairs in December 1944. Long a disciple of Hull's free-trade philosophy and a true believer in the reciprocal trade agreements program, Clayton wrote to the former secretary who was then being treated at the Bethesda Naval Hospital: "The first letter I sign on State Department stationery is to you. . . . I want to assure you that your foreign policy is so thoroughly ingrained in my system that I shall always work and fight for it."[10] This assurance and Clayton's appointment proved to be especially critical to the furtherance of Hull's goals in view of the lack of attention, if not interest, given to trade by Hull's immediate successors, Edward R. Stettinius and James M. Byrnes.

RENEWAL OF THE TRADE AGREEMENTS PROGRAM

In one of his last messages to Congress, less than three weeks before his death, President Roosevelt on March 26, 1945, asked for a renewal of authority to negotiate trade agreements for three years. The existing authority was due to expire in June, and most of the authority under the original act, as extended through 1943, to reduce tariffs up to 50 percent of the 1934 rates had been exhausted. Under the twenty-eight agreements negotiated since 1934, rates had already been reduced from the Smoot-Hawley average levels of nearly 60 percent down to an average of below 30 percent. Under the new request, Roosevelt proposed a major change to allow reductions up to 50 percent of the rates in effect in 1945. If Congress agreed, the president would be allowed to take rates down to an average of less than 15 percent, which would be below the rates set during the Wilson administration in the Underwood Tariff. FDR justified this bold request as "essential to the substantial increase in our foreign trade, which is necessary for full employment and improved standards of living." He promised to pursue "the possibility also of reaching a common understanding with the friendly nations of the world on some of the other international trade problems that confront us." With this possibility fostered by the trade agreements legislation together with the Bretton Woods proposals and the organization of the United Nations, the president observed, "we shall have made a good beginning at creating a workable kit of tools for the new world of international cooperation to which we all look forward."[11]

There was more vocal support from the business community for the program than ever before and there appeared at first to be less partisan opposition. The GOP presidential nominees in the last three elections, Alf Landon, Wendell Willkie, and Thomas Dewey, had all endorsed Hull's trade program. In fact, when asked during the 1944 campaign to comment on the "Democrats' trade program," Dewey replied, "You mean the Republican reciprocal trade agreements program which Secretary Hull has been carrying out."[12] Dewey may have been referring to the reciprocity agreements authorized, but rarely implemented, in previous Republican-sponsored trade bills, but no more than five Republicans in either chamber had ever voted for Hull's program until 1943 when eighteen GOP senators voted to extend the program for only two years. With the war having diminished the popularity of isolationism, Republican support for protectionist interests now also seemed to be waning.

The economic planners in the State Department, acting upon political trends they perceived to be favoring more liberal trade, proposed to the president to go a step further and request authority to negotiate tariffs on a "horizontal," or across-the-board, multilateral approach rather than Hull's bilateral, item-by-item method. Roosevelt, however, was not so optimistic and stuck with the bilateral approach, fearing, as had Hull, a protectionist backlash if he went too far. The president's instincts were once again on target. Despite the growing acceptance of internationalism, public opinion polls at the time found that 61 percent of respondents opposed an increase in imports.[13] Congressman Robert L. Doughton (D-NC), chairman of the House Ways and Means Committee, warned that the absence of Hull, whom he considered a "tower of strength," and the resurgence of congressional determination to recapture its constitutional authority from the executive branch would weaken the chances for the renewal in the enhanced form. The chairman of the Senate Finance Committee, Walter F. George (D-GA), echoed the view reflected in his chamber that Congress wanted a return of its authority.[14] There had always been a minority of Democrats who would have opposed the trade program due to some protectionist interest in their district but found a reason to support it when Roosevelt characterized the measure a "must" among his list of legislative requests. With the absence of both Roosevelt and Hull to create the persuasive leverage to carry the proposal through both chambers, Truman's first test on Capitol Hill would prove to be a severe trial.

Soon after he took office, Truman met with his old friend, Speaker of the House Sam Rayburn (D-TX), Chairman Doughton, and other congressional leaders to convince them of the need to continue the Roosevelt-Hull trade policy. It was not a tough sell to Rayburn; the speaker had always been an ardent foe of protective tariffs, which he called "the most indefensible system that the world has ever known." In his first floor speech in the House, given in support of President Wilson's 1913 tariff bill only a few weeks after he was sworn into office, Rayburn blamed "Republican misrule" for the "wall of robbery" behind which the manufacturers had stood and "fattened their already swollen purse with more ill-gotten gain wrung from the horny hands of the toiling masses that have forever been ground under the heel of taxation with a relentless tread."[15]

As soon as the legislative process began, it became obvious that the extension debate would be a bitterly partisan battle. In stark contrast to Hull's practice of personal engagement in promoting the program, the new secretary of state Edward Stettinius pled that "pressing duties have crowded upon me" as he prepared for the San Francisco conference establishing the United Nations. He regretted that he could not appear personally before Ways and Means to advocate the renewal. Senior Republicans on the committee appeared outraged, arguing that Stettinius's written statement should not be admitted into the record until he "could come here and read it himself and be subject to cross-examination." The committee's ranking Republican, Harold Knutson of Minnesota, charged that Stettinius's failure to appear could give "the unfortunate impression that he has not enough confidence in the operation of the act to appear in its defense." In an extended tirade, Knutson demanded that Will Clayton, appearing on behalf of the secretary, put aside his prepared statement and commence the hearings with "a concession of complete failure" of the trade program to lift the economy to the standards achieved "under the Republican tariff system of the twenties." He said the justifications offered for the program in the past were nothing more than "scintillating fallacies, glittering generalities, [and] glistening absurdities."

When Knutson's turn came to question Clayton, he spent most of his allotted time quizzing Clayton about his cotton business practices in an attempt to show that Clayton was more interested in helping the Brazilian economy than that of the United States. The balance of Knutson's question-ing focused on defending the Republican protectionist system, which he said had "made America great and prosperous." Countering Cordell Hull's promise that the RTAA would promote peace, Knutson boasted that the trade program had failed to prevent World War II. Clayton's articulate and candid testimony in response to the congressman's charges exhibited the depth of his understanding of the issues and his remarkable patience.[16]

At the conclusion of the hearings, the committee narrowly defeated six-teen amendments that would have diluted or effectively gutted the program and favorably reported the measure to the floor by a vote of 14 to 11, with all Republicans and one Democrat opposed. This result was a major turna-round from the week before when both Knutson and Dean Acheson, who was now assistant secretary of state for congressional relations, believed the Republicans had the votes to defeat the bill in committee.[17] The debate on the bill on the House floor lasted three days, with Speaker Rayburn, according to the *New York Times*, repeatedly moving about "the floor, beaming with pleasure at being back again on the legislative firing line." Acheson called it a "dreary and wholly unrealistic debate," adding that "few of the claimed vir-tues of the bill were really true and none of the fancied dangers."[18] Chairman Doughton led the debate, targeting a multitude of amendments that had been rejected in committee, repeatedly moving to limit debate while the opposition leader Representative Knutson shouted: "Unfair." All of the amendments, which among other things would have given veto power to Congress over trade agreements and reduced or eliminated the negotiating authority, failed. Some fell short by fewer than twenty votes.

Fearing that the program might be terminated or gutted by amend-ment, President Truman issued a strong appeal in a letter to the speaker, who read it on the floor, declaring that the renewal and strengthening of the Trade Agreements Act was "of the first order of importance for the success of my administration." Speaker Rayburn introduced the letter by saying:

> If I were a wavering Democrat, with that assurance from this man (the President) who has caught the imagination of the people not only of the United States but of the world, I would hesitate not to comply with his first major request. If I were a Republican member of this House, realizing the tremendous responsibility that rests upon the shoulders of this man, with the world's great work ahead of him as well as of you and me, I would hesitate to throw anything

in his way that might impede his efforts to bring about world order
and peace and commerce.

In what the media called Truman's "greatest test thus far for his program in Congress," the bill finally passed comfortably, 239 to 153, with
thirty-three Republicans breaking ranks and joining the majority.[19]

In the Senate, Truman's old home, the Finance Committee posed a
nearly lethal threat by approving, on a 10-to-9 vote, Senator Robert Taft's
amendment to extend the act without any new authority to cut tariffs. Three
Democrats voted in favor. The bill was saved in a weeklong debate on the
floor, where the full Senate in a bipartisan effort restored the authority as
requested on a 47-to-33 vote and defeated all other amendments to restrict
or defeat the program. The final Senate vote passing the measure by 54 to
21, with fifteen Republicans voting aye and five Democrats opposed, gave
President Truman his first major victory. With its new grant of authority,
the State Department promised to "seek the widest possible agreement
among the Nations for common policies in the field of trade relations."[20] By
authorizing the reduction of the Smoot-Hawley tariff rates by as much as 75
percent, the New York Times editorial board declared, "Congress has taken
the most important step it has yet made toward making possible post-war
prosperity and world-wide economic cooperation."[21]

ARTICLE VII NEGOTIATIONS

Over the years following the 1942 signing of the Anglo-American Mutual
Aid Agreement implementing the Lend-Lease program, experts from both
sides of the Atlantic had conducted periodic consultations at the senior staff
level on the form and substance of postwar international economic relations
pursuant to the controversial Article VII of the Agreement and the principles of the Atlantic Charter. Harry Hawkins, first as head of the Division
of Commercial Policy and Trade Agreements and since 1944 minister-
counselor for economic affairs at the American Embassy in London, led
the State Department's team. Hugh Dalton, a Labor MP and president of
the Board of Trade, along with Lionel Charles Robbins and James Edward
Meade from the Economic Section of the War Cabinet Secretariat, principally represented the British. All were prominent academic economists—
Hawkins had formerly taught at the University of Virginia, Dalton and

Robbins[22] at the London School of Economics and Political Science (LSE), and Meade at Oxford and Cambridge—and all shared very similar views on the need for an international trade organization to govern commercial relations among nations after the war.

Meade, who in 1977 would receive the Nobel Prize in economics for work on international economic policy at LSE and Cambridge, produced a draft "Proposal for an International Commercial Union" in July 1942. This proposal, which was designed to work in parallel with Keynes's proposal for an International Clearing Union for monetary affairs, offered membership to any nation accepting the principles of nondiscrimination (with certain exceptions, including "a moderate degree of Imperial Preference") and the reduction of trade barriers favoring domestic over foreign products.[23] Based upon the Meade proposal, the Board of Trade produced a report that circulated through the staff levels of the appropriate British ministries and gained tentative approval for discussion purposes with the Americans in the autumn of 1943. In September and October, a UK delegation gathered in Washington for an informal exchange of ideas with their counterparts at the State and Treasury Departments. Representing the British Treasury, John Maynard Keynes met with Harry Dexter White at the US Treasury to discuss the monetary issues that would lead to the Bretton Woods Conference in 1944, while Robbins, Meade, and others from the Board of Trade met with Harry Hawkins and his staff at State on trade policy. The result of the consultations at State was a finding of significant compatibility on most issues, including the desire to form an international institution to facilitate the reduction of trade barriers, to limit the use of import quotas, and to focus on the means to ensure full employment when the war ended.

The two issues on which serious disagreement existed were the method to be used in conducting tariff negotiations and the issue of ending trade discrimination raised in Article VII. The British pushed for across-the-board tariff cuts negotiated at a multilateral conference with all parties participating in the negotiations. Although Hawkins was sympathetic to this approach—and Hull preferred it philosophically—FDR and the politically cautious Hull insisted on the bilateral, product-by-product approach that had been employed in the RTAA agreements. Hull favored a multilateral outcome imposed through the unconditional most-favored-nations clauses included in bilateral agreements negotiated simultaneously with one another. On the Article VII issue, the Americans insisted on targeting the Ottawa system of imperial preferences, the elimination of which they viewed as political consideration for the vast sums of money transferred to the British under Lend-Lease. Neither Robbins nor Meade liked the economics or the politics of the Commonwealth preference system. Robbins had "deplored" the system when it was introduced in the thirties. They found, however, "an element of dogmatism in the American case . . . difficult to swallow" and insisted that any step toward their elimination must be contingent on how far the United States was willing to go in reducing its high tariffs.[24]

Despite the generally positive tenor of the consultations, which had established a framework of common principles at least among the experts, the talks were not resumed for more than a year following the return of the British delegation to London. On hearing of the progress made in Washington, conservatives in the British War Cabinet staged a "revolt" against the discussions. Lord Beaverbrook (William Maxwell Aitken), an influential media tycoon and cabinet minister, whom Robbins called "the evil genius of British politics with his capricious enthusiasms and venomous hatreds—especially hatred of America and Americans,"[25] led the revolt with vehement support from Leopold S. Amery, the secretary of state for India. Both were diehard imperialists and economic nationalists committed to the preference system. Although Prime Minister Churchill was personally sympathetic to the liberal trade views of the experts and especially desired a strong partnership with America, he was preoccupied with the conduct of the war and acquiesced in Beaverbrook's insistence on putting a hold on further trade talks with Washington.

Disappointed and frustrated with the silent treatment they were receiving from London, the State Department officials continued their work in developing plans for a postwar trade regime throughout 1944. Dean Acheson, then assistant secretary for economic relations, appointed an inter-agency committee to draft optional proposals in furtherance of the Anglo-American expert discussions. In the fall of 1944, the group approved and presented to Acheson a memo entitled "Proposed Multilateral Convention on Commercial Policy."[26] The proposal called for a new 50 percent reduction in tariff rates with a 10 percent floor, the elimination of most tariff preferences and a reduction of the rest, limitations on subsidies, and the elimination of most import quotas but with a provision for an escape clause for temporary quotas permitted to safeguard against an import surge causing injury to a domestic industry. It also called for the creation of an international organization to supervise the implementation of these measures.

Acheson revealed a summary of this proposal in congressional testimony at the end of November and Harry Hawkins presented it to James Meade in December. Meade and the other British experts liked the proposal, seeing movement in it favorable to their point of view, but the senior cabinet response was largely negative or indifferent at best. Keynes, who had distanced himself from the trade talks, was also opposed. He remained skeptical that the United States would significantly reduce its tariffs and believed that Britain might need to utilize import restrictions and other measures proscribed in both the Meade and the State Department proposals after the war. Writing to the Board of Trade staff, Keynes said, "As you know, I am, I am afraid, a hopeless sceptic about this return to nineteenth century *laissez faire*, for which you and the State Department seem to have such a nostalgia."[27] Despite an appeal by President Roosevelt to Prime Minister Churchill to restart the Article VII discussions, the British continued to stall.

THE BRITISH LOAN

After Roosevelt's death and the surrender of Germany, President Truman met Churchill for the first time in July 1945 at the Potsdam Conference. He also met with Churchill's successor, Clement Richard Attlee, who led the Labour Party to a surprising victory over the Conservatives in an election concluded during the Potsdam meetings. Among the critical topics discussed at the conference was the Lend-Lease program. The British urged that the United States continue the Lend-Lease support after the war to aid in the disarmament and occupation of the defeated territories and in the huge financial requirements for the economic reconstruction of Europe. The Americans insisted that they had no legislative authority for using Lend-Lease funds beyond the conduct of actual military hostilities with Japan. After atomic bombs were dropped on Hiroshima and Nagasaki, and Japan subsequently notified its intent to surrender, President Truman shocked both Churchill and Attlee by announcing the discontinuance of Lend-Lease operations on August 21.[28] The news also shocked some American officials, especially Will Clayton, who learned of it while in London working on postwar financial relief and reconstruction. Many on both sides of the Atlantic believed that Roosevelt, had he been living, would have found a way to extend the program. Only eleven months before, at a meeting with Churchill in Quebec, Roosevelt had agreed to provide $3 billion in Lend-Lease aid to be used in nonmilitary industrial recovery for domestic and export purposes during a proposed "Stage II" Lend-Lease period between the projected German surrender and the ultimate defeat of Japan. Truman later acknowledged that his abrupt cancellation had been "a grave mistake,"[29] but under the restrictive legislative purposes of Lend-Lease, a new formulation for Anglo-American economic collaboration would in any event have been inevitable.

Unlike the United States whose industrial capacity received an enormous boost by the war, Britain had lost one-fifth of its national wealth due to the war with much of its industry devastated. Without the support of Lend-Lease, which had sustained the British people during the miseries of war, the UK did not have the resources to pay for critical food and energy imports. According to their estimates, the British were running a current account deficit of $5 billion and forecast a cumulative deficit over the next several years close to $6 billion, even with an "austere" import program.[30] Without reserves necessary to pay for vital imports, the standard of living was now likely to reach a new low, even worse than during wartime.

Many in Britain believed that there should be an acknowledgment of the sacrifices made by their nation while fighting a common enemy. After all, they had exhausted most of their foreign reserves during the three years of war prior to 1942 when the aid began. In addition to the roughly $20 billion of Lend-Lease aid, Britain had incurred another £4 billion ($16 billion) in debt with other allies and neutral countries in the war effort during the next three years.[31] Lord Keynes was among those who held the belief that Britain deserved this acknowledgment in the form of compensatory financial assistance. With characteristic hubris, Keynes immediately convinced his ministers to send him to Washington to make the case to his American friends for financial aid in the form of an outright grant or, if that did not work, at least an interest-free loan based on the principle of "equality of sacrifice." In asking for assistance of approximately $5 billion to $6 billion, Keynes and the British ambassador to the United States, the Earl of Halifax, intended to present statistics showing that Britain contributed considerably more, proportionately, than did the United States in defeating the Axis powers.[32] To the consternation of his British colleagues, particularly Lionel Robbins and James Meade, who had been conducting the commercial negotiations with the State Department, Keynes also planned to settle, on his own, the Article

VII issue concerning imperial preferences in establishing a nondiscriminatory multilateral trading system.[33]

Upon arriving in Washington in September, Keynes quickly realized that the prevailing public opinion on the American side of the Atlantic was not in line with his views as to which country had contributed the most in defeating Germany. A Gallup poll revealed that 60 percent of those participating in the survey opposed even a loan to Britain.[34] The predominant opinion of the US Congress, where any appropriation for aid or loans would have to be approved, was likewise unfavorable. Members of Congress from both parties had already expressed opposition to writing off Lend-Lease debts incurred for non-war supplies, such as prefabricated housing shipped to Britain after Germany surrendered.[35] After being dominated by the executive branch under FDR for the previous twelve years, Congress had become more jealous in the exercise of its prerogatives and would not be easily persuaded to defy public opinion. Instead of basing his request on the cause of "justice" in repaying Britain for its great sacrifice, Keynes's American friends persuaded him to focus on the needs of the future, not the comparative sacrifices of the past, to justify the loan. As Robbins observes in his memoirs, Keynes, with "his chameleon-like capacity for rapid adaptation to the colour of his environment,"[36] thereafter shifted his appeal to the American business interest in creating a multilateral trading system that promised to benefit the American economy. He argued that without US financial aid, Britain would have no choice but to continue its wartime restrictive trade policies and bilateral agreements focused on balance of payments. With sound financial footing made possible by continued American support, however, Britain could return, Keynes said, "at the earliest possible date to normal trade practices without discrimination and to increased freedom and liberality in commercial and tariff policies."[37] This shift in approach spawned an attack on Keynes in the English press, where the discussions were being closely followed, especially from Lord Beaverbrook, publisher of the *Daily Express* and *Evening Standard*.[38]

From mid-September until early December, negotiations on both the financial terms of the loan and commercial trade policy dragged on at an agonizing pace. While Lord Keynes continued to lead the financial negotiations, both the Americans[39] and his British colleagues objected to Keynes conducting the commercial negotiations on his own. These talks were largely taken over by Lionel Robbins and Sir Percivale Liesching from the UK Board of Trade, with Will Clayton and the new US secretary of treasury

Fred M. Vinson leading the American side. Clayton personally favored giving financial assistance to Britain, but he insisted that the aid be linked to trade concessions, especially the elimination of imperial preferences, which he deplored with a religious fervor at least equal to that of Cordell Hull. While the British persisted in trying to keep the loan negotiations separate from trade policy discussions, Clayton received repeated appeals from the business community and from Congress to hold firm to his position. The National Association of Manufacturers, for example, demanded that Congress not approve any assistance unless "the commitments the British make toward relaxing and eliminating discriminatory trade practices are definite, tangible, and practical from the standpoint of American industry." Similarly, the Special Committee on Post-War Economic Policy and Planning in the US House of Representatives recommended that "a prerequisite to the granting of large-scale loans to England should be the removal of discriminatory treatment, of quotas, exchange controls, and tariff preferences."[40]

Yet even those in the British delegation who had opposed the imperial preference system were not willing to be blackmailed into giving it up for financial aid without receiving major tariff concessions from the United States. As Robbins observed, "We were not prepared to sign away anything until we saw what we were to get in return."[41] The British remained highly skeptical that the Americans would enact tariff reductions sufficient to benefit UK industries. If it had not been for Smoot-Hawley and other protectionist American tariffs, the British argued, there would have been no need for the imperial preference system in the first place. "How do you expect us to do any horse trading (on tariffs)," Keynes told Secretary Vinson, "if the horse (Empire preferences) should be dead three months after these negotiations?"[42] Even if the State Department exercised the full authority to reduce tariffs by 50 percent below current rates, some rates on politically sensitive products would still be prohibitive to UK exports. The British also disliked the product-by-product, bilateral negotiations proposed by the Americans, instead favoring an across-the-board, multilateral framework, which they thought would more likely result in broad-range tariff cuts and would require them to staff fewer technical experts to reach satisfactory reductions. They were similarly wary of the "escape clause" provision, which permitted the temporary imposition of import quotas and other restrictions when imports caused serious injury to a domestic industry. The State Department, responding to political pressure from the Hill, had been including this provision in Hull's trade agreements since 1942. The fact that each of these aspects that the British found objectionable were offered by the Americans as necessary politically for congressional approval only intensified British anxiety.

In the end, the imperial preference issue was resolved with diplomatic ambiguity. Both sides agreed on the language contained in the State Department's "Proposals for Expansion of World Trade and Employment," which called for the United Nations to initiate an international conference on trade and employment for purposes of harmonizing policies and to create an international trade organization. The conference was to meet not later than the summer of 1946. For purposes of discussion at the conference, the "Proposals" outlined the structure and guiding principles of the international trade organization, including the following section on "Tariffs and Preferences":

> In light of the principles set forth in Article VII of the mutual aid agreements, members should enter into arrangements for the substantial reduction of tariffs and for the elimination of tariff preferences, action for the elimination of tariff preferences being taken in conjunction with adequate measures for the substantial reduction of barriers to world trade, as part of the mutually advantageous arrangements contemplated in this document.[43]

This language gave the Americans leave to claim that the British had committed to eliminate its imperial preferences but left the British a way out if they deemed the US tariff reductions not to be "adequate," "substantial," or "mutually advantageous."

In December, the president and Prime Minister Attlee announced the final settlement of the loan agreement for $3.75 billion at 2 percent interest; considering that the terms included an initial five-year interest-free grace period, however, the deal carried an effective rate of just over 1.6 percent interest on a fifty-five-year loan. Interest was to be waived altogether during any year in which British exports were insufficient to pay for imports at a minimal level. The Canadian government kicked in an additional $1.25 billion loan on similar terms to make the aggregate North American bailout total $5 billion. Additionally, Truman agreed to wipe out any further obligation by Britain to pay for Lend-Lease shipments made before the Japanese surrender—valued at over $20 billion—and granted ownership to Britain of the goods and capital assets transferred under Lend-Lease during the war. The Lend-Lease settlement also transferred ownership of assets received after the Japanese surrender at an undervalued, bargain price. Although the British approved the Proposals calling for an international trade organization and the possible negotiated end to discriminatory trade preferences in early November as consideration under Article VII of the Lend-Lease aid agreement,[44] the State Department publicly announced the Proposals simultaneously with the loan agreement, evidencing that the British had agreed to the trade concession on ending preferences as a condition of the loan. In a joint statement issued by Truman and Attlee announcing the loan agreement, the leaders noted the "common interest of their Governments in establishing a world trading and monetary system from which the trade of all countries can benefit and within which the trade of all countries can be conducted on a multilateral, non-discriminatory basis."[45]

PARLIAMENTARY DEBATE

The perception that Britain had abandoned the imperial preference system as a quid pro quo for the loan would no doubt aid the Truman administration in selling it to Congress, but this perception nearly killed it in the British Parliament. There could hardly have been a deeper schism within the Anglo-American alliance than that created by the perspective from which each side viewed the terms of this agreement. In Britain, many Members of Parliament, much of the media, and the public viewed the American loan as niggardly and inadequate, its conditions not only unrealistic but also an attack on British sovereignty. In the words of Conservative MP and former secretary of state for India Leopold Amery, "The American demand for the elimination of Empire Preference is a direct denial of the right of the British Empire to exist . . . an intolerable interference in our own domestic affairs." To deprive the Commonwealth of the support of trade preferences, Amery wrote, would allow each part of the Empire "to be swallowed separately, to become a field for American industrial exploitation, a tributary of American finance, and, in the end, an American dependency."[46] The United States made it even more difficult for the British by requiring Parliament to ratify the agreements on the loan, the Lend-Lease settlement, and Bretton Woods—*and* at the same time endorse the State Department Proposals on trade—by the end of the year, with only three weeks remaining. "I resent the indecent haste with which these most serious complex matters are thrust before us," declared Churchill, reflecting the view of many in the Conservative Party. "I make it a cause of complaint against the Government that they have let themselves be browbeaten in this matter of time."[47]

While the governing Labour Party had sufficient votes to approve the measure in the House of Commons with support from Liberal Party MPs, many Conservatives rallied passionately against it. A majority of the Tories, including opposition leader Churchill, abstained in the vote on approval. Actually, Churchill openly favored the loan outside of Parliament and told US ambassador John G. Winant that but for his partisan obligations he would have preferred to have been able to vote for the resolution.[48] But in a relatively short speech in the Commons debate, Churchill said he was "astonished that the United States should think it worthwhile to exact the equivalent of 1.62 percent interest from their debtor in the special circumstances in which we find ourselves" and thought it "a great pity" that the loan had been linked with the approval of Bretton Woods and the trade Proposals. He implied strongly that he could have gotten better terms than had the present government because relations with the United States, "as the last remaining haunt of capitalism," had deteriorated since the Labour Party had taken over with its "collectivist and totalitarian conceptions which underlie and animate Socialist policy." He urged Conservatives to abstain from voting on the resolution, so as to leave his party "unburdened with any responsibility for these proposals and at the same time keep our party free from any attitude of antagonism to the other great branch of the English-speaking world," observing that "any heavy vote by Conservative Members against the proposals would be specially injurious to our interests in America."[49]

Other opponents of the measure from both the right and the left in the Commons debate claimed that the United States was treating Britain, its main ally, as a defeated enemy in the war. None of them mentioned the American elimination of Britain's Lend-Lease obligations in the settlement, except to note: "Lend-Lease was passed in the United States as an 'Act for the defence of the United States.'" Robert J. G. Boothby, who led the opposition from the Conservative bench, argued that the new obligations would be impossible to meet, and the Bretton Woods Agreement "would mean the end of London as a financial centre." He predicted that ending the imperial preference would "involve the break-up of the British Empire." Urging his Conservative colleagues not to abstain but to join him in voting against approval, Boothby implored: "If the Tory Party ceases to believe in the Empire, and in the economic expansion and development of the Empire, it ceases to have any meaning in this country." Boothby chided the Labour Party's "Socialist Government [for leading] us back to international economic anarchy and to the economic system of the 19th century, the system of laissez faire capitalism, which crashed to destruction in 1929." The purpose of an agreement requiring nondiscriminatory trade principles, he claimed, "is to break up, prise open, the markets of the world for the benefit of the United States of America, who have an intense desire to get rid of their surplus products," and the only American imports Britain may be short of are "tobacco, cotton and films." It may be that the Labour Party had won a mandate in the election to nationalize industries, Boothby concluded, "but there is one mandate which His Majesty's Government never got from the people of this country, and that was to sell the British Empire for a packet of cigarettes."

Similarly, H. Norman Smith, a Labour backbencher, rose to challenge the leadership of his party. Referring to Hugh Dalton, now chancellor of the exchequer in the new Labour government and leader of the debate favoring approval of the American loan and its conditions, Smith argued that the chancellor did not win "votes in his agricultural villages by putting up posters, 'Vote for Dalton and Free Trade.'" He railed against the American conditions for the loan, particularly the proposal for an International Trade Organization (ITO) and Bretton Woods' International Monetary Fund. In 1944, Smith had published a book that included a warning against the dangers of Keynes's proposal at Bretton Woods "to set up a supra-national financial authority [the International Clearing Union, which evolved into the IMF] to which the sovereign national Governments would be subordinate." Smith called Keynes's plan "a device to impose on the world a hidden and irresponsible but all-powerful Government."[50] In the current debate, Smith gave significant attention to the International Trade Organization, which he said would prevent Britain from "developing our Socialist policy of bulk purchases of imports from the Dominions." Acceptance of this condition meant only "that the Labour Government in this country is going to appease American capitalism." Smith urged his colleagues to begin "the British war of independence against the domination of American capitalism" by voting against the proposals.[51]

In the House of Lords, the Conservatives had the power to block the resolution by effectively delaying the final approval beyond the December

31 deadline. Lord Keynes, who was being attacked by both the left and the right for having failed to obtain financial assistance as a grant-in-aid or at least on interest-free terms as he had promised before going to Washington, began writing his speech urging approval by the Lords on his return voyage to England. Though he remained a member of the Liberal Party, Keynes led the debate for the Labour government with his speech delivered the morning after he disembarked. Overnight, he had substantially rewritten the draft he had been preparing on the ship in order to address the rampant misunderstandings about the deal that he heard on his arrival. One reporter even asked Keynes if the rumor were true that he had made Britain the forty-ninth state of the United States of America. Exasperated, Keynes quipped, "No such luck."[52]

Keynes began his speech by observing "what a vast distance separates us here from the climate of Washington. . . . How differently things appear in Washington than in London, and how easy it is to misunderstand one another's difficulties." In a concise and articulate analysis that took up the entire morning, Keynes patiently explained the background behind the decisions leading to the terms of the loan and the rationale behind the Proposals for the International Trade Organization. "I shall never so long as I live," he said, "cease to regret that this is not an interest-free loan." He understood, however, "the fatal consequences" that would be ignited "if the [Truman] Administration were to offer us what Congress would reject." He emphasized the generous terms of the loan, especially in comparison to American loans granted to other allies, and the wiping out of any further obligations based upon the Lend-Lease aid during the war.

> Is it not putting our claim and legitimate expectations a little too high to regard these proposals, on top of Lend-Lease, anything but an act of unprecedented liberality? Has any country ever treated another country like this, in time of peace, for the purpose of rebuilding the other's strength and restoring its competitive position?

Turning to Bretton Woods and the Proposals on trade, which he called "the blue prints for long term commercial and currency policy," Keynes emphasized that they were "of the utmost importance in our relationship with the United States" and represented "the first elaborate and comprehensive attempt to combine the advantages of freedom of commerce with safeguards against the disastrous consequences of a laissez-faire system." Although throughout most of the preceding two decades he had opposed proposals for more liberal, multilateral trading schemes, whether they had emanated from what he had called the "lunatic proposals" of Cordell Hull or from his British colleagues on the Board of Trade, he now saw the Proposals as an effort to "implement the wisdom of Adam Smith" updated with the benefit of "modern experience and modern analysis." He saw the proposed international trade conference as a tremendous opportunity, now that "for the first time in modern history the United States is going to exert its full, powerful influence in the direction of reduction of tariffs, not only by itself but by all others." Keynes argued that the restoration of multilateral trade was in Britain's "prime interest" and represented a "system upon which British commerce essentially depends." Referring to the elimination of imperial preferences, he concluded: "This determination to make trade truly international and to avoid the establishment of economic blocs which limit and restrict commercial intercourse outside them, is plainly an essential condition of the world's best hope, an Anglo-American understanding, which brings us and others together in international institutions."[53]

Lord Beaverbrook, who gave the principal response to Keynes in opposition to the resolution, conceded that his side might be defeated, because "the Socialists and the bankers" were united behind the government in "a new phase in the development of the Socialist Party." His opposition was based entirely upon its effect on the Empire. He believed that the American loan was unnecessary as long as British needs could be supplied by the Dominions as in the past. Under the plan of Lord Keynes, whom Beaverbrook called "the finest living propagandist," America would supply the needs that had heretofore been provided by Britain's colonies. While acknowledging American generosity during the war, Beaverbrook admonished, "Let it be said and repeated with emphasis over and over again that the sterling bloc contributed more—a greater measure of financial help—to Britain than did the United States, including Lend-Lease and Mutual Aid." Now the government is proposing to eliminate imperial preference in exchange for a reduction in American tariffs. Thus, in exchange for "a little increase in the export of Scotch whisky, a trifling increase in suits for gentlemen," Beaverbrook noted, "we give them our Empire market." He concluded: "Destroy the sterling bloc . . . eliminate Imperial preference, and we throw away this Empire."[54]

In his book *Sterling-Dollar Diplomacy*, generally recognized as the most comprehensive and objective treatment of the postwar Anglo-American economic negotiations, author Richard N. Gardner concludes that opposition to the financial arrangement, which had been ominous, "collapsed after the unconvincing performance of Beaverbrook and the masterly statement of Keynes."[55] Virtually the entire British media, excepting Beaverbrook's papers, endorsed ratification, as did the general public as evidenced in subsequent polls.

In a January 11, 1946, cable to Secretary Byrnes describing the political state of play in London regarding bilateral financial and trade issues, Ambassador Winant included the following observance reflecting a commonly held view among Americans who had regularly dealt with Keynes:

> Recent events confirm importance of Keynes' role in art VII matters. From the signing of art VII we have believed that Keynes' active support and participation were more important than those of any other single person in UK. This may be said in full awareness of the lapses in his views on international trade in 1933 and 1941 and his occasional irritability and arrogance—aggravated by ill-health—in argument and negotiation. These defects are more than offset by the power and range of his mind which always bring him back from a partial to a comprehensive viewpoint that places economic issues in a world and not a mere national setting. Other economists among the UK team are more tactful in negotiating an agreement: None commands one-tenth of Keynes' influence in gaining acceptancy of the agreement in Great Britain.[56]

But success came at a great price. Keynes's efforts in negotiating the loan in Washington and securing its approval in the House of Lords proved to be the ultimate personal sacrifice for him. He had been seriously ill for years but continued working under great stress, against his doctor's warnings, while suffering a series of heart attacks in the process. While he shared a constructive camaraderie in working with many of his American counterparts, including Acheson and Clayton at State, he often clashed with others, especially Treasury Secretary Vinson, in endless daily and nightly negotiations with drafting sessions going into the wee hours of the morning. On returning to Britain, where he is widely revered as the most influential

FIGURE 11.1 Lord John Maynard Keynes and Lady Keynes, Lydia Lopokova, at the first meeting of the IMF in Savannah, Georgia, March 10, 1946, one month before his death (Associated Press)

economist of the twentieth century, he was vilified from all sides as he struggled to obtain approval of the only realistic option for his country's economic recovery.

One day in April 1946, Lionel Robbins picked up a newspaper and read the headline, "Loan Killed Keynes," and he knew at once that "the struggles and tensions of the preceding autumn in Washington" had taken its final toll on a colleague with whom he had often sparred, but whom he considered the most remarkable man he ever met.[57]

CONGRESSIONAL DEBATE

If approval of the loan conditions by the British Parliament seemed a near miracle, the prospects for US congressional approval of the loan were no less daunting. The mood in Congress, which reflected widespread public opinion, was not sympathetic to bailing Britain out of economic problems that most Americans failed to appreciate or at least greatly undervalued. Privately, some politicians recognized the potential merit of continuing the Anglo-American alliance in an uncertain postwar world, but publicly many of them objected to providing financial support simply to preserve the British Empire, especially as it was now under the control of the socialist-leaning Labour Party. And why lend money at little or no interest to a foreign country at a time when veterans were returning from war seeking employment and affordable housing? Reports on the debate in Parliament further aggravated the opposition by exposing what appeared to be an ungrateful British attitude and creating uncertainty that the loan would deliver on the promise of ending discriminatory trade practices against American exports. The reports brought disenchantment among supporters of the loan, and opponents began demanding new concessions.

In this atmosphere, President Truman submitted the loan to Congress in late January 1946, urging prompt approval based not upon the critical needs of its wartime ally but rather on the benefits it would bring to American producers. Truman concluded that the loan agreement would enable the United Kingdom to abolish its trade restrictions and "give wholehearted support to the [State Department's] Proposals for Expansion of World Trade and Employment . . . and to use its best endeavors in cooperation with the United States to bring to a successful conclusion international discussions based upon them."[58]

In hearings before the Senate Banking and Currency Committee, all administration officials remained strictly on message. Secretary Vinson declared, "The financial agreement is a sound investment in world peace and prosperity," which "will reap rich dividends" to American business by opening the "the markets of England and many other countries to our exporters." Acheson said that the agreement offered the "last, clear chance to restore world trade," and without it the British "would have to pull the Empire closer and closer together, and exclude us and every other country from this trade." According to Clayton, the loan would

> make it financially possible for Great Britain to remove the discriminations which now operate against American trade in all the markets of the sterling area, and the British Government agrees to remove them. . . . The approval of the financial agreement by the Congress will mean that the two largest trading countries have

decided not to get into an economic war, but to work together on a platform which is beneficial to them both, and to every other country in the world.

Commerce Secretary Henry A. Wallace offered similar views, touting the importance of the agreement "for expanding world trade, freeing it from hampering controls, and creating a peaceful world trading community."[59] Ironically, the manner in which the administration made its political case to Congress appeared to confirm the argument against the loan by opponents in the British Parliament—that is, ending imperial preferences would weaken the Empire and open colonial markets to the domination of American exports.

The Senate opposition, however, ignored the trade benefits promoted by the administration and focused mainly on whether Britain even needed a loan. Robert Taft, the leading Republican opponent, favored subsidizing American export production and engaging in bilateral barter agreements. Both of his alternatives would be barred under the rules of the proposed multilateral trading system, which he considered ill-advised intergovernmental interference with American trade. Following in part Lord Beaverbrook's analysis, Taft attempted to reduce the amount of financial assistance by two-thirds to $1.25 billion and to make it a gift, instead of a loan, arguing that that amount should be sufficient with aid provided by Britain's colonial possessions. Further, in view of its default on World War I debts, many believed that Britain was not likely to repay it anyway. While Taft's alternative did not gain traction, neither did the trade arguments offered by the administration. As the Senate hearings drew to a close, the *Economist*, which was following the issue closely for its British readers, reported that political interest had faded on the loan, with meager news stories about the trade benefits of the agreements being "relegated to the back pages of American newspapers." The magazine noted that an informal poll revealed that twenty-one senators (fifteen Democrats and six Republicans) favored approval and twenty opposed it, with the remainder yet wavering.[60] Besides Taft's proposal, others demanded securing the loan by British investments in the United States or that the loan be conditioned upon the permanent US possession of Britain's Atlantic military bases and American-built airfields in Great Britain. Any of these amendments, if passed, would have required renegotiation of the loan, which would have either killed it or at least delayed it for another year.

Surprisingly, the mood in the Senate began to shift favorably in late spring when the other dominant Republican voice in the upper body, Arthur Vandenberg, formally split with Taft and announced his support for the loan on the Senate floor. Vandenberg began by declaring that there were many things he did not like in the resolution and that Congress should have been consulted during the negotiation of the agreement that it was now being asked to underwrite. A converted isolationist, Vandenberg said the United States cannot sustain its prosperity by looking to markets only within its own borders: "These are not the pre-Pearl Harbor days, which are gone forever."

The Michigan senator favored the loan "as a matter of intelligent American self-interest," for both economic and strategic reasons. The United States, he noted, had "the greatest industrial capacity of any nation in the world," possessing "60 percent of the world's factory output," which would produce "great surpluses in both industry and agriculture." Twenty percent of the jobs in his state depended upon exports. With this loan, competitive world markets would be restored with up to three-quarters of all international trade being conducted in dollars or pounds sterling. Without it, Britain could not and would not be able to eliminate its restrictive trade practices, and Americans "would be thrust into a world of bilateral barter . . . linked with state regimentations which are the exact antithesis of every aspiration we Americans hold dear." He predicted that Russia and the "puppet premiers" controlled by the totalitarian regime in Moscow would continue the Soviet state-trading system, and Britain might be forced to join the trend without the proposed financial aid. Americans might then "confront a dominating surge of bloc arrangements and trade alliances, with all of their defensive and restrictive devices," potentially leading to new trade wars. He argued that the United States must "accept the economic as well as the moral leadership in a wandering world which must be stabilized just as necessarily for us as for others."[61]

The *Economist* gleefully reported that Vandenberg's last-minute decision to support the loan was "worth a dozen endorsements from more predictable sources" and came from "the foremost Republican spokesman on foreign affairs." The magazine noted that this senator's "voice reaches ears deaf to the pleadings of the Administration" and "his hostility might have signed [the resolution's] death-warrant." Instead, in supporting the loan with an appeal to self-interest and "the hardly veiled references to the danger of throwing Britain into the arms of an unnamed totalitarian Power," he was likely to draw a sympathetic response helpful to passage.[62]

Vandenberg's speech followed a number of other events that helped to move some of the undecided legislators into the plus column. In February, the Soviet leader, Joseph Stalin, made a rare and shocking public address in Moscow in which he called for rearming Russia in preparation for an inevitable war arising from the incompatibility between capitalism and communism. Less than a month later in Fulton, Missouri, Winston Churchill, after being warmly introduced by Harry Truman in the president's home state, gave his famous speech decrying the "iron curtain" that had descended across the European Continent encompassing the Soviet sphere of influence and, increasingly, imposing authoritarian control from Moscow. Churchill called for an alliance of Western democracies, and specifically an English-speaking union of Britain and the United States to emerge in response. At first, Churchill's speech was not well received by an American media and public wary of any alliance that might lead to another war. In the face of this public rejection, Truman falsely denied that he had any prior knowledge of the contents of Churchill's speech. As the Soviets continued to make threatening gestures to the West, however, the initial negative American reaction to Churchill's warning began to subside. Inside the Truman cabinet, some, including James Byrnes and Henry Wallace, continued to urge Truman to avoid confrontation with the Soviet Union while maintaining the hope of potential collaboration with this wartime ally in the postwar period. Strong approval of Churchill's message came from Undersecretary Acheson, however, along with the departing American ambassador and the chargé d'affaires to Moscow, W. Averell Harriman and George F. Kennan. Kennan's famous 8,000-word "Long Telegram" from Moscow in February of that year, which had been widely read in Washington political circles, warned that Soviet global goals were based upon ideology and historical Russian insecurity that would not be deterred except by a show of force.

On May 10, just three weeks after Vandenberg's endorsement, the Senate voted down nine amendments, including Taft's, which would have poisoned the loan, and authorized the package by a comfortable bipartisan margin of 46 to 34.

In the House Banking and Currency Committee hearings on the resolution, the administration continued its focus on the trade benefits in urging approval of the loan. During more than four weeks of testimony, the committee recorded statements and testimony from "about 70 organizations of businessmen, bankers, farmers, workers, civic, church, and peace groups"[63] in support of the financial agreements with a predominant focus on trade. Organized labor came out forcefully in favor of the resolution based on its trade implications. William Green, president of the American Federation of Labor, declared that the proposed International Trade Organization, which Britain had agreed to support under the loan agreement, "is of the greatest importance to the future world economy, for it would bring together world trade and world employment." Phillip Murray, president of the Congress of Industrial Organizations, noting that the ITO proposal included "the aim of building a code of fair trade practices based upon an expanding world economy," said the British loan was "an essential first step to an expanding world trade in which American labor has a vital stake." A spokesman for the Textile Workers Union of America advised the committee that even though "the textile industry in the United States in the past has at various times suffered as a result of the competition offered by the textile industry of Great Britain" and textile imports could threaten the higher wage and living standards prevailing in the American textile industry, his union, "along with all other labor organizations whose economic and political vision has been up to par, advocates that this country take every possible step to aid in the rehabilitation of the economy of Britain."[64]

On June 13, the committee reported the resolution to the floor with a strong majority vote urging passage in a twenty-five-page report based entirely on the administration's trade arguments. Citing Britain's commitment to end its discriminatory practices harming American exports and to support the American proposal for an international trade organization to reduce trade barriers and eliminate trade discrimination, the committee declared the agreement to be "a major part of the international economic policy of the United States."[65] The report also included the opposing minority views of four isolationist Republican members who predicted that the loan would "give impetus to Anglo-American imperialistic elements." According to these opponents, "Later the American people will be told this loan was an advance guaranty of American money, guns, and boys for all future British Empire needs or desires."[66]

By the time the House took up the floor debate on the resolution a month later, however, its proponents had moved beyond the administration's primary economic rationale for passage in favor of a strategy based on the growing Soviet threat. Majority Leader John W. McCormack (D-MA) began his speech by observing that the loan agreement was "purely a busi-ness arrangement in which both the United States and England have made and have received important economic concessions. . . . [A]ll considerations of sentiment and political cultural ties were ruled out of the discussions." A primary objective of the American negotiators had been carried out in the agreement by "the opening up of the trade of England and of the sterling area to all of the countries of the world on a fair and equitable basis" and "further developed in the proposals for an international trade organization which the British agreed to in principle." But, McCormack declared, "The approval of the financial agreement . . . has much deeper and broader impli-cations to us and to the rest of the world." He described the increasing dom-ination attempts emanating from Moscow as "challenging our civilization directly and other civilizations indirectly." The United States can either take its place in the world with "vision and courageous leadership," he said, "or we will go back again into provincialism and isolationism . . . leaving other countries and peoples the easy prey of totalitarianism."[67]

The two most important speeches came at the end of sixteen hours of debate spread over four days. Jesse P. Wolcott (R-MI), the ranking minority member of the Banking and Currency Committee, spoke candidly about the difficulty that he and others had gone through in understanding the issues involved in the agreement and said he shared the great concerns of many about its economic and political implications. He soon realized, however, that there were "consequences that transcended, important as it was, the dollars and cents consideration." In the final analysis, he concluded that the loan would prevent Britain from affiliating with the Russian sphere of economic and political influence. "Great Britain has already taken the first step to the left, let us grant that. . . . I do not want to be a party to pushing Great Britain over the brink into something worse than social-ism." Acknowledging the potential benefit of opening Europe and Asia to American exports, he concluded that the transcending benefit of the agree-ment was to "make it possible for us under a free-enterprise economy to prevent the spread of those forces which you and I and every American citizen should recognize are detrimental and destructive of the American way of life." Speaker Sam Rayburn gave the concluding speech, endorsing "every word" of Wolcott's address:

> World leadership is offered us today. The world around, good peo-ple want the United States of America, this great democracy, to

lead. Will we seize that leadership, or will we allow someone else to seize it? If we are not allied with the great British democracy, I fear somebody else will be, and God pity us when we have no ally across the Atlantic Ocean, and God pity them, too.[68]

According to John H. Crider of the *New York Times*, "Every member present in the House stood and joined in applauding the speaker as he returned to his seat." The House approved the resolution on a bipartisan vote of 219 to 155, including sixty-one Republicans in favor and thirty-two Democrats opposed.[69]

On December 28, 2006, the Labour government under Prime Minister Tony Blair made the final installment on the loan repayment to the US Treasury.[70]

12

The Birth of GATT

... a landmark in the history of international
economic relations. Never before have so many
nations combined in such a sustained effort to lower
barriers to trade. Never before have nations agreed
upon action, on tariffs and preferences, so extensive
in its coverage and so far-reaching in its effects.[1]
—President Harry S. Truman, announcing completion
of the General Agreement on Tariffs and Trade
October 29, 1947

Congressional approval of the Anglo-American financial agreement, signed in December 1945 by President Truman and Prime Minister Attlee, was a necessary precondition to any significant postwar trade negotiations. Whether Congress would grant approval was far from certain for another seven months. Yet, before the ink was dry on the signatures, State Department planners posted invitations to fifteen nations for a proposed March 1946 multilateral conference. Within a few weeks, fourteen invitees accepted— Australia, Belgium, Brazil, Canada, China, Cuba, Czechoslovakia, France, India, Luxembourg, the Netherlands, New Zealand, South Africa, and the United Kingdom. Only the Soviet Union ignored the invitation. After consulting the British and the Canadians, the Americans had selected this group representing over two-thirds of American trade to make up a "nuclear" core of major trading nations to reach a preliminary agreement on tariff reductions and multilateral principles for regulating tariff and nontariff trade barriers. The agreement reached among the nuclear group would later be presented for approval at an international conference among these and other nations wishing to participate in the new multilateral trading system.

SELECTIVE NUCLEAR-MULTILATERAL APPROACH IN TWO TRACKS

Negotiations for the preliminary agreement would be conducted under a new process, which the State Department, employing classic bureaucratic jargon, called "the selective nuclear-multilateral approach." In preliminary discussions held in July 1945, the Canadians had proposed this method of negotiations led by a small group of influential nations—which effectively became the model for multilateral trade negotiations for the remainder of the twentieth century—as a compromise between the strictly bilateral approach, which had been favored politically by FDR and Cordell Hull, and the broader multilateral approach that the British insisted upon. The Americans believed they were constricted by the requirements of the Reciprocal Trade Agreements Act specifically, and by political realities in Congress more generally, to negotiating bilaterally on select tariffs on an item-by-item basis.

The British wanted tariff reductions resolved through a multilateral convention at which all participating countries would agree to reduce all of their import duties by a certain percentage through horizontal, across-the-board cuts. The American side believed that it would "be very difficult to obtain approval by the American Congress for horizontal tariff reduction" and "would, in fact, be impossible" if the agreement had "to be presented as a treaty requiring the consent of two-thirds of the Senate" outside the provisions of the RTAA. The Canadians, who, like the British, feared that the American approach would be too time-consuming and too costly to staff, proposed that the bilateral negotiations be conducted within a small nuclear group to speed up the process with the tariff reductions agreed upon in the bilateral agreements to be generalized through a most-favored-nations clause to all members of the nuclear group. Other nations could join later but would have to accept the terms of the nuclear group agreement before negotiating their own concessions bilaterally with members of the preliminary meeting.

The United States accepted the Canadian compromise proposal and simply fit this negotiating method into the political confines of selective and bilateral tariff negotiations. The negotiations would thus be conducted bilaterally, sequenced in simultaneous round-robin talks within the nuclear group on selective, item-by-item tariff reductions. The entire nuclear group would then adopt the tariff reductions reached in the bilateral agreements on a multilateral MFN basis.[2]

In a confidential memorandum dated February 6, 1946, the State Department's Commercial Policy Division led by Winthrop G. Brown outlined its strategy for the preliminary meeting of the nuclear group. The principal purpose of the meeting would be to lay the groundwork for the adoption of "a code of commercial conduct" by all countries at a world trade conference convened by the United Nations. Negotiations would cover a range of issues affecting trade, including governmental trade barriers, cartels, and intergovernmental commodity agreements. The nuclear group would also establish a framework for building the "permanent international machinery" to manage these matters going forward. The commercial code and the management framework would follow the department's "Proposals for Expansion of World Trade and Employment" published on December 6, 1945, which emphasized "the close relationship between levels of trade and conditions of employment" and "also made clear the importance of domestic measures to maintain employment and the need for continuing international consultation on employment policies."

The purpose of the preliminary meeting would be to generate commitments on the department's proposals from this nuclear group of major trading nations that could be incorporated into a detailed international instrument to be called the "Charter of the International Trade Organization" (ITO). Like the Articles of Agreement of the IMF, this ITO Charter would include provisions dealing with the management of the organization, but would also include substantive commitments concerning the reduction in trade barriers and policies governing the international aspects of domestic employment policies in the member countries.

The Commercial Division's memorandum observed that an essential element of any undertaking to reduce trade barriers must involve actual tariff reductions. But since this process had to be conducted on a "selective, product-by-product basis," involving thousands of tariff items, the memorandum proposed negotiating the tariff reductions separately from the charter negotiations and simply including the resulting new tariff schedules in a protocol that could later be attached to the charter. The protocol would also include certain principles and rules from the charter related to trade barriers "designed to safeguard the value of the tariff concessions and which have customarily been included in trade agreements in the past." This protocol, including the tariff reductions, bindings against future increases, and the critical trade rules and principles (e.g., unconditional most-favored-nation treatment, nondiscriminatory treatment of imported and domestically produced goods, and limitations on use of import quotas), was intended to be enforceable independently of the ITO Charter in the event that ratification of the charter was delayed in the participating states. Thus, the negotiations would be divided into two tracks: one track dealing with the ITO Charter and a second track negotiating a protocol containing specific tariff reductions and the essential governing commercial principles for the trading system.[3]

It soon became obvious, however, that the prospect of beginning the nuclear negotiations in March was unrealistic. The participating nations needed significantly more time to prepare for the tariff negotiations, and Britain needed first to schedule a meeting to discuss the conference issues with its Empire Dominions. As Congress continued to drag its heels on approving the financial agreement, the British would not even consider a timetable until that precondition was met. In a resolution drafted by the US delegation and adopted by the Economic and Social Council of the United Nations at its first meeting in London on February 19, 1946, the council decided "to call an international conference on trade and employment in the latter part of 1946." The same resolution created a Preparatory Committee, consisting of the nuclear group of countries the State Department had invited to participate in the preliminary negotiations (with the addition of Chile, Norway, and Lebanon) to prepare a draft agenda. With a nod to the developing countries, the council requested that the Preparatory Committee "take into account the special conditions which prevail in countries whose manufacturing industry is still in its initial stages of development."[4]

In early April, Assistant Secretary Will Clayton and his director of the Office of International Trade Policy, Clair Wilcox, prepared a secret memorandum to President Truman proposing that the nuclear group tariff negotiations begin on September 15, a date subject to change only if Congress failed to approve or unduly delayed action on the British loan agreement. The Reciprocal Trade Agreements Act required the State Department to give ninety days' formal public notice of intention to negotiate trade agreements, including a list of the countries involved and the products on which US tariff concessions would be considered. The Clayton memorandum proposed that the notice go out and hearings be scheduled as soon as

Congress approved the British loan agreement. Clayton warned the president, however, that once the list is published, "minority interests will put strong pressure on the Administration for commitments that particular tariff rates will not be cut." He urged that all cabinet members be warned of the dangers of making any such commitments, as they "might easily defeat the objectives of the Trade Agreements Act, wreck the pending negotiations, and bring to nothing our *Proposals for Expansion of World Trade and Employment*."[5]

On April 12, President Truman approved the memorandum's proposal to inform the other governments of the proposed date to begin negotiations,[6] but that was before he talked the matter over with his old Senate colleague, Secretary of State Jimmy Byrnes. Byrnes saw nothing but political danger emanating from the publication of a broad list of potential trade concessions, many of which would have highly sensitive political consequences. Democratic prospects for maintaining control of Congress had dimmed, and Byrnes urged Truman to avoid adding the further risk posed by the tariff reductions. Word leaked to the press on April 14 that the president and Byrnes had decided to postpone the negotiations until after the November midterm elections.[7]

Clayton was livid about the postponement and sent Byrnes a list of reasons for maintaining the proposed schedule, including the following:

> Public opinion is prepared for action. We have enlisted the enthusiastic support of business, farm, labor, church, peace, and women's organizations for the Trade Agreements renewal, the British loan, and the Trade Proposals mainly on the ground that we planned to expand world trade. If we delay further, our friends will be discouraged and even resentful and we may lose their strong backing.[8]

Byrnes, who often expressed an arrogant disdain for political opinions that differed from his own, especially those of the career diplomats whom he once called "those little bastards at the State Department,"[9] ignored Clayton's appeal. Public notice of the products that would be subject to negotiated reductions was thus postponed until mid-November, and the tariff negotiations would not be scheduled until the spring of 1947. To maintain the momentum of the process, however, the State Department succeeded in convening a Preparatory Committee meeting of the nuclear countries, which avoided the public notice requirements of tariff negotiations.

Based largely on the proposals of December 1945, the selected countries began to discuss a draft prepared by the State Department of a "Suggested Charter" of the International Trade Organization in London on October 15 under the auspices of the United Nations. Eighteen countries participated in the meeting, formally called the Preparatory Committee for an International Conference on Trade and Employment, which lasted for six weeks and reached agreement on most of the provisions of the charter. Recognizing the relationship between full employment and high demand as a critical condition for the promotion of international trade, the participants first agreed to take appropriate domestic actions promoting high levels of employment in their respective economies. The committee agreed to limit the use of quantitative restrictions (import quotas), exchange controls, and export subsidies while establishing rules for state trading and tariff negotiations. They agreed to provide a procedure of limited exceptions from charter prohibitions on the use of protective measures to encourage the development of industries in underdeveloped countries. They also agreed on a chapter dealing with the organizational structure of the ITO.

The US delegation reported by cable to Will Clayton—recently promoted from assistant secretary to become the first undersecretary of state for economic affairs—that the new London draft was "a truly international document to which all delegates . . . have contributed." Claiming that it included the "essential principles of the American position," the report said that the charter was now "a better balanced and more complete document than the original American draft."[10]

In a confidential cable to Secretary Byrnes, the chair of the US delegation, Clair Wilcox, reported that the strongest opposition to the American efforts came from India and Australia, which, Wilcox said, "had two of the most effective delegations at the meeting." The Indians, Wilcox observed, "came with a chip on their shoulder," and regarded the proposals "as a document prepared by the U.S. and the U.K. to serve the interest of the highly industrialized countries by keeping the backward countries in a position of economic dependence." This perspective was understandable, expected even, given the context of India's other ongoing struggle. In less than ten months, India would finally achieve its long battle for political independence.

Wilcox noted that the British delegation was scrupulous "in its public statements of formal support" of the American positions, but in closed negotiations it "took a fairly independent line, supporting us on

FIGURE 12.1 President Truman (right) confers with his former Senate colleagues, Secretary of State James Byrnes (left) and Senator Arthur Vandenberg (center) (Harry S. Truman Presidential Library)

some issues, opposing us on others and acting as a mediator between us and our opponents on still others." Wilcox perceived that the UK commitments to the United States were "unpalatable to important segments of British opinion and the Government . . . is having to swim against a strong current of public sentiment." He concluded his report by observing that the program to which the Preparatory Committee had tentatively agreed was an American program that began in 1941 and 1942 with the Atlantic Charter and Article VII of the Lend-Lease agreements. Its success depended, most importantly, "upon the support that it receives within the United States."[11]

REPUBLICANS TAKE CONGRESS

Wilcox had good reason to worry about future American support for the program. President Truman's approval rating in the Gallup Poll had dropped almost to 32 percent just before the midterm elections,[12] and the Democrats suffered a resounding and humiliating defeat as the London meeting was taking place. Republicans took control of both Houses of Congress for the first time in fifteen years, and protectionists were in line to take the chairmanships of the committees with trade jurisdiction—Eugene D. Millikin (R-CO) to chair Senate Finance and Harold Knutson (R-MN) to head House Ways and Means.

In a lead editorial in the first issue following the election, the *Economist* asked, "Is this 1918 all over again?" In that year, the editors observed, the United States abandoned progressive policies and "turned its back on . . . its international obligations . . . to indulge in an orgy of prosperity and an almost complete abdication of government." With the high-tariff party back in charge, "the condition of an American low-tariff policy under which Britain agreed to abjure 'discriminatory practices' is unlikely to materialize."[13] Under the same rationale, the British Conservative Party, led by Churchill, opposed any move by the Labour government to compromise on the Ottawa preference system after the Republican takeover.

On election day, however, President Truman did not back down from approving the list of products on which concessions would be considered in tariff negotiations scheduled for the following April. The items included some of the most politically sensitive imports in the tariff schedule—dairy, meat, sugar, copper, wool, textiles, and shoes. The State Department memorandum to the president attaching the proposed items noted that the list was deliberately "bulky," without making any "effort to conceal the magnitude of the project." In order to get other countries to approve the trade principles in the charter, the memo declared, "it is essential that we grant tariff concessions to them which are substantial in extent and cover a wide range of items."[14] The reaction was immediate from the newly empowered Republican majority, who claimed the election was a repudiation of the Truman administration's trade program. Senator Hugh Butler (R-NE) wrote to Will Clayton that the negotiations should be suspended until the new Congress had time to write a new trade program, calling the attempt to use the negotiating authority of the RTAA, "previously wrested from a Democratic Congress, to destroy our system of tariff protection," was "a direct affront to the popular will expressed" in the election.[15]

In the House, Congressman Bertrand W. Gearhart (R-CA), serving as chairman of the Ways and Means Trade Subcommittee, warned about what "can happen at Geneva when 'the boys' of our State Department sit down with representatives of some 18 other nations and begin to barter—in secrecy—the economy of these United States":

> Are we going to stand idly by and permit this cunningly conceived, super-duper propaganda campaign to achieve its objective—the lulling of the American people into quiescence as the last vestige of the American protective-tariff system is wiped from our statute books?[16]

President Truman got a degree of revenge the following year as he helped to defeat Gearhart, a seven-term congressman who had run unopposed six times previously. While traveling through Gearhart's district on one of his famous whistle-stop tours in 1948, Truman told the farmers in California's Central Valley: "You have a terrible Congressman here. He has done everything he possibly could do to cut the throats of the farmer and the laboring man."[17] Gearhart, a lawyer and staunch conservative, lost in an upset to a cotton farmer inspired by Truman's speech to run for political office for the first time.

Congressman Gearhart was not the only political critic making wild charges against Clayton's delegation in Geneva. Three years before Senator Joseph R. McCarthy (R-WI) rose to national fame with unsubstantiated claims about communists employed in the State Department, Congressman Daniel A. Reed (R-NY) stated on the House floor: "I have reliable information that a substantial percent of [Clayton's] group are either Communists or Communist sympathizers or have had previous connections with Communist organizations." Citing the strict secrecy with which Clayton's negotiations were being conducted, Reed argued that "if our businessmen cannot be trusted and if the Congress cannot be trusted, why let these Communists and fellow travelers be in that group where they may be in position to warn Communists from other nations against the interests of this Nation?" Reed proposed a "Resolution creating a select committee to investigate the loyalty of certain assistants and advisers to the Undersecretary of State for Economic Affairs."[18]

Fortunately for Truman, Senator Arthur Vandenberg, an old friend from his days in the Senate, came to the rescue. Like Truman, Vandenberg had risen from a humble background to become one of the most respected leaders in the upper body and, as the new chairman of the Foreign Relations Committee, the senior GOP authority on foreign affairs. Responding to urgent appeals from Acheson and Clayton, Vandenberg joined with Senator Millikin in proposing a compromise to Truman. If the president would agree to submit the tariff reductions proposed in future trade agreement to the Tariff Commission for recommendations "as to the point beyond which reductions and concessions" could cause "injury to the domestic economy," the senators would not interfere with the trade negotiations authorized under the RTAA until 1948 when the program was up for renewal. The compromise also proposed that all trade agreements include an "escape clause" permitting the withdrawal or modification of trade concessions when surging imports caused or threatened serious injury to domestic industry.[19] Truman refused the first proposal requiring the Tariff Commission's "peril point" recommendations but went along with the second proposal on the escape clause requirement and issued an executive order to implement it. Cordell Hull had already included escape clauses in trade agreements since 1942, but allowing the Tariff Commission, an independent bipartisan agency, to be the fact finder on potential injuries to domestic industry was new to the process.

In a critically timed speech in early March at Baylor University in Waco, Texas, which the White House had announced would be a "major address," the president reiterated the importance of "reducing barriers to trade" and establishing "a code of good conduct in international trade" at the upcoming negotiations. While pledging to safeguard "domestic interests . . . in this process of expanding trade," he promised not "free trade but . . . freer trade." Warning those "who would seek to undermine this policy for partisan advantage and go back to the period of high tariffs and economic isolation . . . Take care! Times have changed. The temper of the people has changed. The slogans of 1930 or of 1896 are sadly out of date. Isolation, after two world wars, is a confession of mental and moral bankruptcy."[20] The editors of both the *New York Times* and the *Washington Post* praised the president's message, with the *Post* calling it "Persuasive and Timely."[21]

The compromise bought time for the State Department negotiators in conducting the next round of talks among the nuclear group nations until the 1948 presidential election, but it did not satisfy most of the senior Republican critics of the administration's trade policies. Robert Taft, the GOP's leader in the Senate on domestic issues; Harold Knutson, Ways and Means chairman; and Speaker of the House Joseph Martin (R-MA) were all constantly looking for opportunities to gut the program. At the same time, many progressive voices, such as the editors of the *Nation*, believed that the escape clause would "rob trade treaties of much of their value." While the compromise gave "temporary respite from the tariff-mongers," the *Nation* argued, the Republican congressmen attempting to sabotage the proposed international trade organization were living in a past era, listening only "to the bleating of protected constituents."[22]

In a move that tempered the volume of partisan opposition, Truman, after accepting the resignation of Secretary of State Byrnes, replaced him with General George C. Marshall, FDR's wartime chief of staff of the army. Marshall, who practiced the military tradition of strict nonpartisanship—he did not even vote—was highly respected on both sides of the political aisle and by the public at large. Although the general would be his third secretary of state in less than two years in the White House, Truman made a prudent choice. Senator Vandenberg rushed Marshall's nomination through his committee without even a hearing, and the full Senate confirmed him unanimously on the same day under a suspension of the rules. Within three weeks, the president's poll numbers jumped sixteen points to 48 percent favorable.[23]

THE TRUMAN DOCTRINE AND THE MARSHALL PLAN

As Undersecretary Clayton and his State Department team were preparing for the Geneva tariff negotiations set to begin in April 1947, the economic crisis in Europe was nearing a disastrous precipice. In a memorandum written on March 5 after returning from a visit to Europe where he had been inundated with requests for more US aid in country after country, Clayton warned of strategic dangers stemming from the economic crisis and threats of communist intervention directed by Moscow:

> The United States must take world leadership and quickly, to avert world disaster. . . . The evidence is indisputable that a systematic campaign is now being waged to destroy from within the integrity and independence of many nations. . . . Feeding on hunger, economic misery and frustration, some of these attacks have already been successful in some of the liberated countries, and there is now grave danger that they may be successful in others.[24]

During the last week of February, the British brought home the urgency of the crisis when they notified General Marshall that they could no longer afford to support the governments of Greece and Turkey and would have to withdraw military troops and aid to those countries in a matter of weeks. Greece was in the midst of a civil war and, in Acheson's words, "in the position of a semiconscious patient on the critical list whose relatives and physicians had been discussing whether his life could be saved."[25] Turkey was stronger but did not have the means to sustain an army vital to the defense of its border with Russia. In recent months the Soviets had begun to pose threats in the Balkans, Iran, northern Greece, and throughout the region. Before receiving the British withdrawal notification, Truman had asked Congress for $350 million for economic relief throughout war-torn Europe. Clearly, now, this sum would be grossly inadequate. On March 12, Truman delivered a historic message to a joint session of Congress in which he requested an additional $400 million in aid just for Greece and Turkey during the next year—at a time when both Houses of Congress were recommending billions of dollars in cuts to the president's budget.

The president laid out what became known as the Truman Doctrine after describing the threats, both military and political, to Greek and Turkish independence. Without mentioning the Soviet Union by name, Truman detailed the critical state of the region's economic deterioration and the dire consequences to the free world should these democracies fall to this unnamed foreign threat. Marking the heart of the doctrine US-assisted economic stability, he declared:

> I believe that it must be the policy of the United States to support free peoples who are resisting attempted subjugation by armed minorities or by outside pressures.
>
> I believe that we must assist free peoples to work out their own destinies in their own way.
>
> I believe that our help should be primarily through economic and financial aid which is essential to economic stability and orderly political processes.[26]

Despite substantial rhetorical opposition, Congress passed the Greek-Turkish Aid Act with an overwhelming margin two months later, again with critical support from Senator Vandenberg and opposition from Senator Taft.

In the meantime, Will Clayton returned to Europe in April to begin the Geneva tariff negotiations as he, Marshall, and Acheson began further consideration of the means of achieving economic recovery in Europe. At a six-week-long meeting in Moscow of the Council of Foreign Ministers of the Big Four (United States, Britain, France, and Russia), Marshall became convinced of Stalin's indifference to the European economic crisis, except as to the opportunities it provided for communist expansion. When he returned to Washington at the end of April, Marshall asked George Kennan to form a Policy Planning Staff within the State Department to come up with recommendations to address the threats arising from the European impoverishment and suffering. On May 8, Acheson delivered a speech to the Mississippi Delta Council at the request of the president, who later called it "the prologue to the Marshall Plan," in which the undersecretary described the need for further economic assistance for European recovery "to preserve our own freedoms and our own democratic institutions."[27]

Clayton—"to whom," according to the *New York Times*, "the President turns for advice on foreign economic matters to complement Marshall on foreign political matters"[28]—began drafting a second memorandum on the European crisis on his flight back to Washington from the ongoing Geneva tariff negotiations. Based largely on his own personal observations from recent European travels and meetings, Clayton began:

> It is by now obvious that we grossly underestimated the destruction to the European economy by the war. We . . . failed to take fully into account the effects of economic dislocation on production. . . . Europe is steadily deteriorating. . . . One political crisis after another merely denotes the existence of grave economic distress. Millions of people in the cities are slowly starving.

Clayton estimated the aggregate deficits of the major European countries at over $5 billion per year in providing an absolute minimum standard of living. "If it should be lowered," he predicted, "there will be revolution" and the "fast dwindling" reserves of gold and dollars in England and France would be depleted by the end of the year. Without prompt and substantial American aid, he wrote, "economic, social and political disintegration will overwhelm Europe." Clayton called for the president and the secretary of state to render "a strong spiritual appeal to the American people to sacrifice a little themselves, to draw in their own belts just a little in order to save

Europe from starvation and chaos . . . and at the same time to preserve for ourselves and our children the glorious heritage of a free America." He recommended a US grant of $6 billion or $7 billion in goods per year for three years to be distributed according to a plan to be designed by a "European economic federation," presaging by a decade the creation of the European Economic Community. "Europe cannot recover from this war and again become independent," he concluded, "if her economy continues to be divided into many small watertight compartments as it is today."[29]

To dramatic effect, Clayton delivered the memorandum to Acheson and General Marshall on May 27. The next day, Clayton, Acheson, and Kennan—the latter had just completed and delivered his own more cautious study on the subject[30]—met with Marshall and his special assistant, Charles E. ("Chip") Bohlen, among others, to discuss actions to be taken to address the crisis. In the meeting, Acheson found Clayton to be "one of the most powerful and persuasive advocates to whom I have listened," as Clayton spoke with "command of the subject and the depth of his conviction," corroborating his paper with details illustrating "the headlong disintegration of the highly complex industrial society of Europe."[31]

After the meeting, General Marshall asked Bohlen to draft a speech on the topic to be delivered on June 5 at a Harvard commencement ceremony at which Marshall was scheduled to receive an honorary degree. Bohlen drew heavily from the Clayton memorandum[32] and the Kennan report in preparing the short, but dynamic speech describing the desperate conditions, causes, and likely repercussions of the crisis. Marshall delivered the speech with Truman's approval, including this central message:

> The truth of the matter is that Europe's requirements for the next three or four years of foreign food and other essential products— principally from America—are so much greater than her present ability to pay that she must have substantial additional help, or face economic, social and political deterioration of a very grave character. . . . It is logical that the United States should do whatever it is able to do to assist in the return of normal economic health in the world, without which there can be no political stability and no assured peace. Our policy is directed not against any country or doctrine but against hunger, poverty, desperation and chaos. Its purpose should be the revival of a working economy in the world

so as to permit the emergence of political and social conditions in which free institutions can exist.[33]

Marshall's speech made public the Truman administration's shift in emphasis from a political or ideological focus to a strategy based upon achieving economic stability. As James Reston had reported in the *New York Times* on May 9, while the public debate had concerned the Truman Doctrine for the previous eight weeks, "the private talk among our officials has been about how the United States can help get industrial, democratic Europe on its feet as a unit strong enough to trade with the United States and block Soviet expansion."[34]

Clayton's job now involved turning Marshall's speech into the "Marshall Plan" while at the same time salvaging the Geneva negotiations, which had become threatened by economic collapse in Europe and trade politics in America.

WOOL

In a meeting with the president on April 3 before leaving for the Geneva talks, Will Clayton, along with Dean Acheson and Winthrop G. Brown (chief of State's Division of Commercial Policy), advised Truman of the "politically significant" concessions Clayton's delegation planned to offer, including tariff reductions on woolen and cotton textiles. Clayton said they were only planning to offer to bind (that is, freeze) the tariff on raw wool at its existing protective rate due to the political leverage wielded in Congress on behalf of domestic woolgrowers. He warned, however, he might have to offer to reduce wool tariffs in response to demands anticipated from other wool-exporting countries. Despite Clayton's further warnings that these recommendations were certain to attract "vociferous political protests from many well organized and powerful special interests throughout the country," Truman approved them. He assured Clayton of his resoluteness and welcomed the predicted protests, saying, "I am ready for it."[35]

The Geneva negotiations convened at the Palais des Nations, an imposing art deco structure built in the 1930s for the League of Nations on a hill overlooking majestic Lake Geneva surrounded by the snow-capped Alps. The United Nations took over the building as its Geneva headquarters only one year before the conference commenced. The atmosphere in Geneva is astonishing in the spring, and most of the delegates at the conference very likely expected to be able to enjoy the scenery and the mix of Swiss and Lyonnais cuisine as they waited for the heavy negotiations to begin. Normally, the parties in trade negotiations try to hold back their best offers until the other delegates reveal how far they might be willing to go with their own offers. The parties stay bunched together with few substantive offers in the beginning, cruising with the draft like cyclists in a Tour de France bicycle race, until one darts out, risking a break into the open and leading others to follow as the race becomes a race.

Breaking with tradition, Will Clayton darted early and laid out at the start what he considered was his best offer of American tariff concessions to the other nations' delegates. Believing his offer to be quite generous, Clayton chose this tactic in order to promote goodwill and, hopefully, to expedite the negotiating process. Representing not only the strongest economy in the world but also the principal organizer of the conference, expectations were very high for the opening American offer. The response from most of his counterparts to an offer Clayton thought very liberal, however, was disappointing. Considering the widely held view of the United States as the most protected market in the world, representatives of the other nations viewed the American proposals with a mixture of caution and cynicism. Most of them were starving for dollars to pay for urgently needed imports and teetering on the edge of financial disaster. Even though the generosity of Clayton's politically risky offer was unprecedented, the desperate hopes of the other delegates to gain better market access to the world's healthiest economy to survive the war were not easily satisfied.

The issue surrounding tariffs on raw wool best illustrates Clayton's dilemma. Wool became the single most important commodity under consideration at Geneva because of its economic importance within the British Commonwealth—especially to Australia, New Zealand, and South Africa—and the corresponding political importance of the Commonwealth to ending trade discrimination in a new international trade regime. Australia, with one of the most astute and highly engaged delegations at the conference, depended upon wool exports for nearly half of its export revenue, most of which was derived from US importers. During the war, both American and Commonwealth wool producers benefited hugely from the expanded, war-driven demand and market-enhancing government policies, including US price support programs and commodity cartels in the Commonwealth.

As demand diminished after the war, woolgrowers from every corner of the globe looked to the American market for salvation. Australia's sole reason for participating in Geneva was to gain better access to the American market through reduced wool tariffs. When they saw that Clayton was only offering to bind the US tariff at the current rate of 34 cents per pound, which was higher than Australian growers' costs of producing a pound of wool, the Australian delegation threatened to return to Canberra and thus spark a broad-scale retreat from the talks by the Commonwealth countries.

Clayton explained that a freeze on further tariff hikes was actually a significant concession in the current political environment, when powerful political interests were pushing rate increases in Congress. Indeed, as soon as he arrived in Geneva, Clayton received a cable informing him that the House Agriculture Committee reported out a bill imposing a 50 percent ad valorem "fee" on wool imports. A Senate measure supported by Truman to renew and enlarge price supports for raw wool was already progressing to the floor and had given Clayton hope that he might be able to offer a duty reduction at the conference if the legislation passed. When the House Committee added the import fee to the Senate bill, however, the Australians suspended negotiations and Clayton returned to Washington to find a way to keep the negotiations from falling apart. In a letter to a congressman, which was read to the House before the vote, Clayton warned that if this bill passed, "the moral leadership of the United States in world affairs will suffer a serious blow."[36] Ignoring this warning, however, the House voted 151 to 65 to pass the wool bill on May 23. A month later, Clayton appeared before a House-Senate conference committee and warned again of "the tragic consequences" the act would have on the Geneva conference. The conference committee nevertheless adopted a new version including both the price subsidies and the 50 percent import fee, and the Senate passed the Wool Act of 1947 with a bipartisan twelve-vote margin.

The head of the Australian delegation immediately notified the US delegation that "the U.S. Government should be aware that if this bill becomes law, every country concerned with the future of international trade will find it necessary to review its position. . . . I shall find it necessary to move that the present conference at Geneva be adjourned . . . in light of what appear to us to be substantially changed circumstances."[37] The acting head of the UK delegation, James R. C. Helmore, reinforced the Australian position, notifying Clair Wilcox that the enactment of this legislation would "shake the confidence in the ability of the US Govt to give effect to the policy of trade barriers reduction through a series of mutually advantageous agreements"—an explicit reference to the condition required to be met before the British had to begin eliminating imperial preferences. To make this point even more clearly, Helmore added the warning that allowing the wool bill to become law

> would constitute a serious setback to all the efforts made during the past several years towards the removal of trade barriers from the Atlantic Charter to the present Conference at Geneva and would endanger not only the tariff negotiations but also the negotiations in regard to the Charter for an International Trade Organization.[38]

On the day before the Senate voted, Truman called Clayton and Agriculture Secretary Clinton P. Anderson into his office to debate the case for and against vetoing the bill. Anderson, who favored the bill and opposed the veto, argued that the Geneva talks were going to fail anyway and the bill could help farmers compete with Australian wool imports. Politically, Anderson observed, signing the bill could make a difference for Truman in as many as eight Western farm states in the looming 1948 presidential election. Clayton countered that a veto was necessary in order to promote the broader foreign policy interests of the United States and to salvage the talks, allowing him to continue his efforts for success in Geneva.[39] The president ultimately endorsed Clayton's view, making the following observation in his veto message on June 26:

> The enactment of a law providing for additional barriers to the importation of wool at the very moment when this Government is taking the leading part in a United Nations Conference at Geneva called for the purpose of reducing trade barriers and of drafting a Charter for an International Trade Organization, in an effort to restore the world to economic peace, would be a tragic mistake. It would be a blow to our leadership in world affairs. It would be interpreted around the world as a first step on that same road to economic isolationism down which we and other countries traveled after the first World War with such disastrous consequences. I cannot approve such an action.[40]

The Senate lacked the votes to override the veto and six weeks later passed a wool price subsidy bill that the president approved. Truman would soon go a step further on the wool tariff issue, boldly granting Clayton's request to offer a 25 percent cut in wool tariffs in Geneva.

CRISIS IN THE ANGLO-AMERICAN ALLIANCE

With the wool issue resolved, Undersecretary Clayton, in a role described by the *New York Times* as "economic ambassador extraordinary,"[41] returned to Europe to revive the trade negotiations in Geneva with a stopover in London to explore methods of implementing Secretary Marshall's Harvard speech. At this stage, Marshall's message was only an idea, not a "plan" to solve the crisis. Within the State Department the "Marshall Plan" was being compared to a "flying saucer—nobody knows what it looks like, how big it is, in what direction it is moving, or whether it really exists."[42] In order to develop a viable plan that could be sold to Congress and the American public, Clayton intended to ask the Europeans for definitive statements on (1) what were the precise needs for Europe to get on her feet again, (2) how much of these needs could be provided from within Europe and how much had to come from outside, and (3) how long it would take to reach self-sufficiency.

In a meeting on July 1 with the British cabinet at the prime minister's residence at 10 Downing Street, Foreign Secretary Earnest Bevin, a former trade union leader who had served as labor minister in Churchill's coalition war cabinet, and Hugh Dalton, now chancellor of the exchequer, urged upon Undersecretary Clayton their belief that Britain's current financial crisis was fundamentally different from "the chronic troubles of Europe." The problems in the United Kingdom, they argued, were temporary and stemmed from its Empire obligations, the world dollar shortage, and a 40 percent increase in wholesale prices that had reduced the value of the American loan by a billion dollars. As a result of these problems, none of which had been anticipated when the parties negotiated the Anglo-American Financial Agreement, the loan "would be exhausted at the end of the year" at the present rate of drawings. Bevin and Dalton wanted a separate financial partnership with the United States—"something akin to Lend-Lease"—and were looking for "some temporary interim solution to enable the U.K. to play its part" in the economic recovery of continental Europe. The British Empire held stocks of commodities, such as rubber and wool, and could assist materially in rescuing the rest of Europe, Bevin argued. He said that they did not want to sacrifice the "little bit of dignity we have left" by going into the Marshall program without contributing as a partner in resolving the problem on the Continent. A senior British Treasury official expressed the fear of being lumped into a "European pool," in which Britain would be brought "down to the level of the lowest in Europe."

Clayton, however, gave them no hope for a separate deal, declaring that "no further piecemeal assistance was feasible for Europe." The Truman administration simply could not sell Congress and the American public on another interim arrangement for Britain outside of the European plan. Clayton also said that a firm plan for European economic integration would be necessary to convince Congress to approve further assistance. The British ministers, however, said they "did not contemplate going into a European Customs Union." Bevin questioned whether this type of economic integration among the European nations would, like the imperial preference system, violate the rules in the draft ITO Charter against trade discrimination. Clayton responded by pointing to the progress being made in the creation of an economic and customs union by Belgium, the Netherlands, and Luxembourg, which promoted free trade within the "Benelux" countries and set common tariffs for imports from countries outside the union. Clayton maintained that this customs union would not violate the ITO rules. He offered to "look into the matter jointly" with the UK delegation in Geneva to develop "something in the nature of special interim exceptions to nondiscrimination working gradually up to a Customs Union," which could reduce or eliminate tariffs for trade within Europe. The ultimate success of the Marshall aid was, after all, dependent upon the success of the multilateral trade negotiations to produce trade revenue and foreign exchange to supplant the need for American aid. The aid program and the trade talks in Geneva were mutually dependent initiatives. Clayton concluded that a firm plan for European economic integration would be necessary to convince Congress to provide additional financial assistance because US public opinion favored a "continental" approach to the trade and production problems of Europe. The British, however, continued to object to entering a European customs union because Great Britain "is not merely a European country but an international trader."[43]

On the subject of trade, James Helmore, vice chair of the British delegation in the Geneva negotiations, observed that "some people in the British Government felt that the U.K. would be better off to follow at this time a policy based on bilateral trade deals."[44] This idea was based upon the presumption that Britain held economic leverage with superior bargaining power in comparison with the rest of Europe and could obtain more favorable trade terms in bilateral deals with its suppliers than in the American-dominated multilateral context. Helmore's comment further confirmed the opinion of the American delegation in Geneva that the current British negotiators were not approaching the conference with the same collaborative spirit and good faith that their predecessors—in particular, James Meade, Sir Percival Liesching, and Lionel Robbins—had shown in the previous government. Wilcox and Hawkins had come to believe that Helmore had no intention of significantly modifying the imperial preference system and hoped that the wool tariff issue would give him an excuse for blaming the United States for wrecking the conference. Wilcox also expressed alarm concerning the stance of Sir Richard Stafford Cripps, president of the Board of Trade and chair of the British delegation in Geneva, who gave a speech on June 11 that Wilcox characterized in a cable to Clayton as "bitterly criticizing [the] US and disparaging importance [of the] tariff negotiations and ITO."[45]

Given the Labour Party's general disdain for imperialism, Clayton's team had reason to be surprised at the resolution with which their counterparts in the Labour government defended the imperial preference system. Since its inception in 1900, the Labour Party had strongly opposed protectionist policies, particularly Joseph Chamberlain's campaign for imperial preferences at that time.[46] In a speech broadcast early in 1940 explaining the Labour Party's reasons for supporting the war against Hitler's aggression in spite of Labour's hatred of war and distrust of the Conservative government under Neville Chamberlain, Labour leader Clement Attlee, while condemning German imperialism, challenged Britain's own arrogant and boastful colonialism, including "the Ottawa policy of economic imperialism." He cautioned:

If we . . . want to persuade others that we wish for a world free from imperialist domination, we must put ourselves right. . . . We must abandon any claim to special rights. . . . We must rid ourselves of any taint of imperialism. Only so can we put ourselves into a position to ask for a world organized on the democratic principle.[47]

Later, however, as deputy prime minister in Churchill's coalition government, Attlee changed his focus. Like Hugh Dalton, Stafford Cripps, and other Labour ministers in Churchill's government and *unlike* some of the Conservative ministers, Attlee favored multilateralism in trade relations and was supportive of the Anglo-American consultations seeking a multilateral postwar trade agreement. Throughout the three and a half years of devastating war, however, the Empire had provided a lifeline for survival and, without the Commonwealth, Britain's role as a world power would vanish after the war. Attlee was no longer so focused on ridding his country of the "taint of imperialism." In a paper he circulated to the cabinet in June 1943, he wrote:

> I take it to be a fundamental assumption that whatever post-war international organisation is established, it will be our aim to maintain the British Commonwealth as an international entity, recognized as such by foreign countries. . . . If we are to carry our full weight in the post-war world with the US and the USSR it can only be as a united British Commonwealth.[48]

Sir Stafford, whom the *Economist* called "beyond question, one of the ablest and most courageous members of the [Attlee] Government," also seemed to have shed some of his anti-colonialist views by the end of the war. Cripps was a complicated figure who often revealed seemingly contradictory political leanings. He had been a wealthy corporate lawyer, reportedly earning the equivalent of $200,000 a year, but gave it up in the 1930s because he grew tired of "taking large sums of money from one capitalist to give it to another capitalist." Politically, he was positioned at the extreme left of the Labour Party. In 1932, he helped found the Socialist League and was expelled from the Labour Party in 1939 for advocating unity with communists in forming an anti-Fascist popular front. Churchill, however, appointed him ambassador to the Soviet Union, due in part to Cripps's compatibility with Marxist economic views, and he later served in the coalition war cabinet as leader of the House of Commons and as minister of aircraft production.

Cripps's relationship with Churchill was strained more by Cripps's ascetic personality traits than their stark political differences. For health reasons, Cripps was a vegetarian, a nonsmoker, and a teetotaler, concerning which, Churchill observed, "He has all of the virtues I dislike and none of the vices I admire." The prime minister was also put off by Cripps's religious piety, once quipping, as Sir Stafford walked by, "There but for the grace of God goes God."[49]

Attlee also remarked upon Cripps's "deeply religious" beliefs, noting that as "a keen Socialist, his Christianity and socialism were the guiding forces of his life."[50] Attlee concluded that Cripps was an egotist, but had "the egoism of the altruist."[51] Cripps was readmitted to the Labour Party at the end of the war, having "lived down," according to the *Economist*, "some of the more fantastic prejudices that he used to parade in public."[52] Cripps had previously taken a leading role in the effort to negotiate India's independence from the Empire. Upon assuming his post in the new Labour government as president of the Board of Trade—considered the second highest economic post in the British government—he took ownership of the imperial preference system with a stubborn resistance to change that put the Tory imperialists to shame.

At a debate in the Commons held two weeks before the beginning of the Geneva conference, a critic of the trade negotiations asked Cripps, "Will [the Government's negotiators] go as far as elimination [of imperial preferences] if, in their opinion, they are getting a bargain which is worth it?" Despite the commitments made to negotiate an end to trade preferences in the Atlantic Charter, Article VII in the Mutual Aid Agreement for Lend-Lease, and in the Anglo-American Financial Agreement, Sir Stafford responded, "If the hon. Member is speaking of the elimination of all preferences, we do not see any prospect of anything of that sort happening."[53] Although there had always been a difference in views across the Atlantic on the actual meaning of the prior commitments as to the elimination of preferences, this definitive denial on the eve of the long-planned negotiations to address the issue appeared more than a political dodge of the question and was most revealing in forecasting the prospects for the conference.

A serious confrontation arose on July 12 in Clayton's first meeting with Cripps soon after they returned to Switzerland. The American minutes of the meeting described Cripps's attitude as being "marked by complete indifference bordering on open hostility toward the objectives of the Geneva Conference" and "manifested a complete reversal of the policy agreed to by the United Kingdom negotiators during the course of discussion which terminated in the conclusion of the Anglo-American loan agreement in 1945." On the issue of Empire preferences, Cripps argued "at great length" that no modification would be possible without prior approval of the Dominions and possessions affected and could not in any case be reduced or eliminated on short notice. British traders could not compete, he said, without the market advantages provided by the preferences until they had time to make modifications in production costs.

Adding further tension to the meeting, Clayton told Cripps that the tariff concessions offered thus far by the United Kingdom in the negotiations were "inconsequential" and amounted "to nothing more than token offers." While the United States had offered 50 percent reductions in tariff duties on nearly all products of importance in UK export trade to the United States, the British had made practically no offers worth considering in opening the UK market to American exports.

Sir Stafford replied that while statistically the British offers might be inconsequential, when considered from the point of view of the greater economic strength of the United States and the huge increase in American exports during the war, the UK offers compared favorably to American offers to Britain. If the United States was dissatisfied with the offers received from the United Kingdom, Cripps said, the only option to bring the offers in line with each other is for the United States to withdraw some of its offers, and he invited the United States to do so. The United Kingdom, Cripps said, has gone as far as it possibly can go.[54]

In the month that followed, the prospects of reaching a satisfactory conclusion to the tariff negotiations became more and more discouraging. Cripps and Helmore continued to maintain a stubborn insistence that each side had offered a fair balance under the circumstances and that the American negotiators should terminate the negotiations altogether and withdraw or reduce its offers if they desired a better balance and be satisfied with modest results.

Wilcox concluded in a memo to Clayton on August 6: "The vested interests that have been built up under the preferential system are strong, and the United Kingdom has shown no willingness to take the political risks involved in reducing or removing the protection afforded them by the preferences which they enjoy." At the same time, he said, American public opinion regards the Smoot-Hawley Tariff and the Ottawa imperial preference system as related parts of the abuses of interwar trade practices. The United States was offering to liquidate the Smoot-Hawley tariffs and return to rates below the Underwood Tariff enacted during the Wilson administration but could not succeed politically without "a front-page headline that says 'Empire Preference System Broken at Geneva.'" Without that headline, Wilcox wrote, "there is a grave danger that the whole trade program will end in defeat." He urged Clayton to advise Sir Stafford of the risks of a failure in Geneva, including "that the prospects of Congressional approval for additional aid under the Marshall Plan or otherwise, will be seriously impaired." Both governments must take action, Wilcox wrote, "to reestablish the mutual respect and confidence that are essential to our cooperation in the reconstruction of the western world."[55]

A different front-page headline appeared in the *New York Times* with a Geneva byline dated August 7, one day after Wilcox issued this memo to Clayton: "British Accused of Stalling in Tariff Parley at Geneva: Perils to Talks, Trade Pact with U.S. and ITO Are Laid to Their Refusal to Bargain Realistically on Empire Preference Cut." Citing "highly placed observers," the reporter wrote, "The persistent British refusal to bargain realistically on the reduction of Imperial preference tariffs is threatening to make a farce of the tariff bargaining part of the Geneva Trade Conference."[56] Obviously, this leak of what the reporter called "stalling and maneuvering [by the British negotiators] to avoid meeting the United States halfway on a tariff agreement," as London was pressing at the highest levels for US assistance in meeting Britain's short-run economic financial problems, was intended to embarrass Britain into a more flexible posture. It did not work.

After Sir Stafford candidly advised Clayton that it was politically impossible for his government to take any substantial action in eliminating preferences, the undersecretary sent an urgent, top-secret cable to the State Department listing four alternatives that were open to the United States in response:

1. Conclude an agreement based on current offers without substantial preference elimination;
2. Conclude an agreement without substantial preference elimination, but curtail US offers as Cripps had suggested;
3. Advise the British that negotiations would be discontinued without substantial action on preference elimination, advise the other delegations of the reasons for discontinuation of US-UK negotiations, and seek the best agreements possible with the others, preferably still on a multilateral basis; or
4. Adjourn tariff negotiations until after the Havana conference or indefinitely.

Clayton recommended the third alternative based largely on the promise he had given to Congress that the British would fulfill their commitment to end the preferences and break up the sterling bloc's discriminatory trading system. The other alternatives threatened the renewal of the trade agreement program and the progress made on the ITO Charter negotiations. He acknowledged that his recommendation also seriously risked jeopardizing success at the Havana conference and support for the Marshall proposals in the United States "with consequent broad political implications." Nevertheless, he believed that they must make a clear issue of the UK nonaction and face it "squarely." Cripps's use of political arguments as an excuse for no movement, he wrote, "bordered on a callous disregard of their commitment on preferences."[57]

Upon reviewing Clayton's four alternatives, President Truman rejected (1) and (4), and favored (2) over (3), as "the lesser of the two evils," on the recommendation of Robert A. Lovett, who had assumed the senior undersecretary position when Dean Acheson returned to the private sector on July 1. Lovett had worked closely with General Marshall during the war years while serving as an assistant secretary in the War Department, and his recommendation was driven more by the geopolitical issues concerning Europe than the purity of the Hull/Clayton ideals of trade liberalization. Due to the desperate financial dilemma and corresponding political problems the British were currently facing, Lovett explained, the Labor Cabinet was not likely to rein in Cripps and modify his stance on the preferences. The British had made it clear that they were prepared to violate any international obligations if essential to getting through this difficult period, and President Truman and General Marshall were attempting to help them avoid "irretrievable damage to their long-run position." Following Clayton's recommended alternative (3), the president felt, would be inconsistent with this effort and not likely result in an agreement.

Further, Lovett observed, Clayton's preferred alternative would "likely lead to strong resentment [from] the British public and considerable confusion and criticism in US," which would make congressional approval of additional assistance to Britain and Europe generally more difficult. On the broader geopolitical implications, Lovett wrote:

As you know, UK Govt now under intense pressure from left wing members Labor party to curtail sharply UK foreign commitments, reduce arm forces and to withdraw British forces from Greece and Italy. We are concerned over likelihood that USSR will exploit fully any such differences between US and UK just as they are now trying to capitalize on British weakness by increasing pressure throughout Eastern Europe and Near East.

He urged Clayton to grab the best agreement he could obtain and reserve some negotiating room "for use at a more propitious time by trimming our offers correspondingly." From the standpoint of congressional opinion, even a "thin agreement" would be better than none at this stage.[58]

Lovett's perceptive appraisal of the British crisis was impossible for Clayton to dispute. On July 15, the UK government had begun to comply with its obligation under the Anglo-American Financial Agreement to make the pound sterling convertible long before it had the capacity to do so. As a consequence, countries holding sterling effectively made a run on the bank for dollars at a time when Britain's current account deficit was rising to historic levels due to increasing import needs and minimal export production. With foreign currency rapidly depleting—Cripps predicted they would be out of dollars in early October—they were forced to suspend convertibility after only five weeks. Harold Wilson, a rising young MP and secretary for overseas trade, warned the other delegates at Geneva that Britain might have to use methods in the difficult times ahead that "may appear to be opposed to the principles and methods of the Draft [ITO] Charter" and would "find it necessary and desirable to have even closer economic co-operation with other countries of the Commonwealth."[59] Foreign Secretary Bevin even suggested forming a customs union within the Empire as a way to fit the imperial preferences into the exception to the ITO principle of nondiscrimination, which had been proposed by Will Clayton for Europe.

Opposition to American demands to eliminate the imperial preference system was growing in both of the main political parties in Britain. Opponents often cited the fact that the United States maintained preferences for Cuba and Puerto Rico and had just concluded, over Clayton's objection, a trade agreement with the Philippines extending its preferential tariffs for twenty years. Following the Republican takeover of Congress and Truman's reinforcement of the use of the "escape clause" to protect domestic industry in order to placate GOP demands, doubt grew in Parliament that Truman's liberal trade policies would survive. American tariff reductions were only authorized to last for three years under the RTAA (and that act was due to expire in 1948) while any reduction in preferences agreed to by the Commonwealth had no expiry date.

Despite the message from their superiors in the White House and the State Department urging the acceptance of a "thin" agreement, Clayton and Wilcox continued to push for more concessions on preferences. On September 15, Wilcox gave a long, pedagogic speech in Geneva to representatives of the Commonwealth countries analyzing the offers that had been made on preference reduction with detailed country-by-country statistics emphasizing their insignificance. He reiterated the multiple commitments the United Kingdom had made to eliminate imperial preferences in exchange for tariff reductions and observed with some exaggeration that the US proposals would reduce trade barriers to "the lowest average level of protection the United States has had in 40 years" and "reverse the international economic policy that the US has pursued for the past century and a half." Judged against the commitments made over the previous five years, "the prospective outcome at Geneva [based on current offers] will be one of failure." The political problem presented by this failure, he concluded, "is whether American people and American Congress will acquiesce in what may amount temporarily to a unilateral reduction of the US tariff . . . [and] to the provision of another 15 or 20 billion dollars of aid for Europe, when they can see no immediate gains for the US."

Not willing to accept failure, however, Wilcox announced that Clayton intended to make a new proposal to Cripps: The United States would accept current British offers on preferences for now but sought an agreement on a wider preference list, which after three years would be gradually eliminated over a period of ten years. Thus, a grace period would be allowed to get through the current financial crisis and would give the Commonwealth a total of thirteen years to adopt multilateral, nondiscriminatory trade practices.

It had become obvious by this time that the desire to keep the imperial preference system in place was far more important to the United Kingdom than to most of the members of the Commonwealth—many of whom, such as Canada, viewed increased trade with the United States more valuable than maintaining the preferential system within the British Empire. It was also clear that maintaining the Empire, or some semblance of it, weighed heavily upon the national pride of many British politicians following the catastrophic economic losses that the two world wars had inflicted upon London's international prestige. The American delegation hoped that by presenting their case to the Commonwealth before presenting the new proposal to Sir Stafford they might gain a tactical advantage in lobbying to change the British position on preferences, which Wilcox said was the "one remaining obstacle to the success of the Geneva meeting." He concluded his speech to the Commonwealth delegates by telling them: "The final decision on the success or failure of this program rests with you."[60]

Sir Stafford had read Wilcox's speech before Clayton met with him personally to present his proposal, which sought to eliminate preferences affecting one-third of the US prewar trade with the Dominions beginning three years from the date of the agreement at the rate of 10 percent of the preference margin per year until completely eliminated. Cripps said that he had carefully studied Wilcox's arguments but believed that the offers made thus far "had struck a balance" and any further preference reductions would have to be compensated for by further US tariff reductions. He said that he would present Clayton's present proposal to his cabinet with a recommendation that it *not* be accepted. Clayton responded that this would be interpreted in the United States as a repudiation of the UK commitment regarding preferences and asked to discuss the matter with Foreign Secretary Bevin.

Clayton and Lewis W. Douglas, the US ambassador to London, along with Sir Stafford, met with Bevin thereafter and made their respective cases to the foreign minister. Both Clayton and Douglas emphasized the critical political and economic importance of eliminating Empire preferences. Clayton said that he would be compelled to advise Secretary Marshall that Cripps's proposal was not acceptable for an agreement in Geneva and the whole matter would "undoubtedly seriously prejudice public opinion and Congressional action" favorable to British participation in the Marshall Plan. The ultimate success of the Marshall Plan was, after all, dependent upon success at Geneva in enhancing multilateral trade.

Douglas, who had been a member of Congress during the passage of the Smoot-Hawley Tariff Act and had opposed it, discussed the influence of that act on the creation of the Empire preference scheme in Ottawa in 1932. He advised Bevin that the American proposals being offered in Geneva added to the reductions of previous trade agreements reached since 1934, "wiped out" the Smoot-Hawley rates, and brought down tariffs to the lowest level since World War I, "so that the conditions which gave rise to the preference system no longer existed."

Bevin's private secretary summed up the meeting in his diary in one sentence: "A busy day in the Office, with Clayton and Douglas next door trying to blackmail E. B. and Cripps into dropping imperial preference under the threat of no help for Britain under the Marshall Plan."[61] Bevin, who shared Cripps's concerns about eliminating the preferences at a time when the economy was in such a precarious state, seemed moved by the Americans' arguments, or at least seriously troubled by the potential consequences to Britain of being left out of the Marshall aid. He noted that there were a great many people in the United Kingdom who thought that the best course for Britain in the present circumstances was "a policy of autarchy." He had always believed, however, that it was in Britain's best interest to return to multilateral trade as quickly as possible. In any case, he said, the British wanted to keep whatever commitment they had with the United States, "if it were at all possible to do so." He promised a prompt answer.[62]

The answer, which Cripps delivered to Clayton two days later, however, was again negative though a bit more conciliatory in tone, if not substance. Without adequate American concessions in return, Cripps said they could not commit to begin reducing preferences in three years in circumstances that then could not be foreseen. Cripps promised to negotiate further preference reductions against further American tariff concessions on a "mutually advantageous" basis and reaffirmed their commitment not to increase any preferences in the meantime.

The day after Clayton received the rejection, he and Ambassador Douglas left for Washington, and the *Christian Science Monitor* reported from London: "It is generally believed here, without definite proof," that Clayton has been bargaining aid for Britain "against Britain's pledge to start abolishing Empire trade preferences." The article observed that the British cabinet had rejected Clayton's preference proposal and reported for the first time that Washington considered the needs of France and Italy to be more urgent than UK needs. The American government believes "Britain can get through the winter with the dollar assets it now has." The *Monitor*'s report led with the question: "Is Great Britain 'at the end of the queue' for stopgap aid from the United States, and unlikely to receive any?"[63]

SETTLEMENT—THE GATT IS BORN

At this point with the two principal negotiators at loggerheads, a backchannel effort began to emerge around them. Both sides feared the consequences: a collapse of the alliance and, also, the wider political fallout that would inevitably endanger their respective strategic interests. Within

Clayton's delegation there was significant concern that a break-off in negotiations with Britain, even if justified against Cripps's obstinacy, would have
disastrous consequences, setting back American efforts for multilateral
tariff reduction for years. In a September 24 top-secret memo to Clayton,
Harry Hawkins and Winthrop Brown in London warned that the United
States in terminating negotiations with Britain would "appear to the world
as Uncle Shylock . . . exacting our pound of flesh," would "provide the
Russians with just the propaganda material they need," and "will end a joint
effort with our best friends in bitterness and disillusionment."[64]

Bevin was also deeply worried about the implications arising from the
discontinuance of Anglo-American negotiations if Secretary Marshall followed Clayton's advice. Bevin had the British ambassador to Washington
tell Marshall that the British were not closing the door to further proposals
and wanted to speak with Marshall before he made a decision. Prominent
members of the Commonwealth—including Canada, Australia, and India—
were also greatly concerned about the effects of a breakdown. Canadian
prime minister Mackenzie King cabled Prime Minister Attlee, urging that
every effort be made to avoid ending negotiations.

With encouragement from the Commonwealth representatives, James
Helmore and Winthrop Brown, the subordinate UK and US negotiators,
reached a tentative agreement that the United Kingdom would reduce the
preferences that it benefited from in the colonies by 25 percent if the United
States would agree to hold its domestic production of synthetic rubber to
25 percent of US consumption. Rubber exports from the British colonies
had been a valuable source of revenue until the wartime American production of synthetic rubber reduced demand for the colonial exports of the
naturally produced product. Although this agreement smacked of the type
of managed trade that Cordell Hull had set out to eliminate under his trade
program, Undersecretary Clayton reluctantly agreed to it.

The British cabinet, yet again, refused to go along with the preference
reduction in fear of political backlash in Westminster and in the colonies.
Helmore, the British negotiator of the deal, however, found his cabinet
ministers' rationale for refusal unconvincing and "strongly hinted" to his
American counterparts that they stand firm in insisting upon the colonial
concessions. The Canadian representatives also advised the Americans
to stand firm and, along with the Australians and Indian negotiators,
offered new bilateral concessions to improve the agreement and avoid a
breakdown.

FIGURE 12.2 British foreign secretary Earnest Bevin and Chancellor of the Exchequer
Sir Stafford Cripps (1949) (Library of Congress)

Within five days after the cabinet rejected the agreement, however, on
October 15 the British ambassador to Washington delivered to the State
Department a top-secret message from Bevin containing notification that
"His Majesty's Government have reconsidered . . . and have decided to
accept the United States proposal on the basis of making the proposed concession regarding Colonial Preferences in return for a United States concession regarding the rubber [production]."[65] Bevin's message effectively
brought the Geneva negotiations to conclusion.

The dollar value of the final British concession was small relative to the
total US exports as to which competitive British products enjoyed a preference advantage in the Commonwealth. The United Kingdom and Canada,
however, improved the deal by also agreeing to release each other from their
Ottawa obligation to maintain existing margins of preference so that future
negotiations with these major trading partners would be on nondiscriminatory terms. More important, the final concession on preferences made
possible the crucial settlement of six months of negotiations, involving 106

bilateral agreements that significantly reduced tariffs on a most-favored-nations basis among the twenty-three participating countries.

These countries, which together had been responsible for nearly three-quarters of world trade in 1938, also concluded an agreement on the major governing principles of the draft ITO Charter, based largely upon provisions included in Hull's previous reciprocal trade agreements. Together, the schedules of tariff concessions and the commercial policy principles included from the draft charter were named the General Agreement on Tariffs and Trade (GATT). Under the terms of an agreed Protocol of Provisional Application, the GATT would govern international trade relations among the contracting parties from January 1, 1948, until a critical mass of participating countries formally ratified the ITO Charter to be negotiated in Havana.

Acting Secretary of State Robert Lovett presented the agreement—with "pleasure" and, very likely, much relief—to President Truman for approval on October 24 with the observation that it "represents the most extensive action ever undertaken for the reduction of barriers to trade" and adding that it "has been concluded in the face of great difficulties."[66] In the summary analysis of the GATT terms released in the Department of State Bulletin, its author claimed: "Tariff preferences affecting a significant part of United States trade with countries in the British Commonwealth have been substantially reduced, and preferences on a considerable list of products which the United States exports to the various countries of the Commonwealth have been eliminated entirely."

On the other side of the Atlantic, as expected, British negotiators explained the agreement to their audience with an English spin on the ball. On October 29, Harold Wilson—now president of the Board of Trade after Sir Stafford Cripps was elevated to minister for economic affairs and subsequently to chancellor of the exchequer—told Parliament that the suggestion "made in certain quarters" that the agreement included

an overall reduction by some general formula of all Imperial preferences, including preferential margins which we enjoy either in our Colonial or Dominion markets . . . is quite inaccurate and misleading. . . . It is certainly untrue to suggest that the progress of these negotiations has in any way weakened the economic co-operation of the Commonwealth.[67]

Not everyone agreed with Wilson—especially the editors of the *Daily Express*, one of Lord Beaverbrook's newspapers, in an article headlined: "The Big Bad Bargain is sealed! The Big Black Pact is made! The citadel of Imperial Preference is breached."

The *Economist*, however, took a more positive view, while noting that the GATT "must be one of the longest and most complicated public documents ever issued and one of the hardest to comprehend." Even experts who had studied the agreement in detail "would be hard put to pronounce upon its significance" without reviewing its effect upon trade over the next few years, the journal observed. In contrast to the characterization in the *Daily Express*, the *Economist*'s editors declared that "though some reductions have been made in imperial preference, the 'citadel' is still substantially intact; 70 per cent of the imperial preferential rates are completely untouched and only 5 per cent of them eliminated." Of the foreign concessions, the London journal said, "by far the most important are those made by the United States," and concluded that the State Department seemed to be loosening its "theological" doctrine against "symbolic barriers" (i.e., imperial preferences).[68]

The reaction provoked by the GATT agreement among Republicans in Congress was predictable. Senator Edward V. Robertson (R-WY) called it "appeasement by tariff reduction," which would reduce wages and lower the standard of living in the United States. House Ways and Means Committee chairman Harold Knutson said the agreement had been negotiated behind "the iron curtain of secrecy . . . a travesty on the word democracy." Knutson blamed "the do-gooders and the bleeding hearts . . . [who are now] in the saddle, and they are not happy until they are playing Santa Claus to the peoples of other countries." Congressman Bertrand Gearhart charged that every concession obtained from other countries had "been conditioned upon the sacrifice of an American industry," and he specifically mentioned the synthetic rubber industry, the woolen industry, and the jewel and watch industry, as examples of the industries sacrificed.[69]

13

The Havana Charter

The Charter concluded at Havana is the best and most
practicable agreement for the purpose that can be
devised at this stage of our international relations.[1]
    —Will Clayton to General George Marshall
                        March 24, 1948

On October 15, 1947, the same day that British foreign secretary Ernest
Bevin released his message accepting the US proposal on imperial preferences, which effectively concluded the 1947 Geneva tariff negotiations
and established the GATT, Will Clayton formally concluded his official
government service. The timing of Clayton's resignation from the State
Department was not a coincidence.

The conclusion of the GATT negotiations and the preference
settlement—as unsatisfactory as the latter was to Clayton—finally brought
to an end a very difficult period of frustrating sixteen-hour workdays
and months of exhausting travel for Clayton, who had been essentially
volunteering his time to the public for the previous seven years. Now in
his late sixties, Clayton had been in poor health for much of the previous year, and his wife, Sue, had been hounding him for years to retire to
their home in Houston to a more relaxed lifestyle. The public reason he
gave for his resignation was his wife's health, but his friends at State and
in the White House knew that she had been seriously threatening him
with divorce if he did not resign. He had informed both General Marshall
and President Truman that he intended to leave office as soon as the

negotiations were resolved. Nevertheless, when he did officially resign, he agreed to remain on call as an adviser to Marshall on economic matters. He also agreed to head the US delegation at the Havana conference the following month to begin finalizing the Charter for the International Trade Organization (ITO).

Clayton's departure was widely lamented by officials who had been involved with the Geneva trade conference and the Marshall Plan talks in Paris. According to one reporter, the American and foreign officials following these meetings over the past critical months were "unanimous" in the opinion that Clayton had "been the greatest single force operating in the direction of bringing order out of the European economic chaos." A *New York Times* editorial hailed Clayton's "brilliantly successful labors in the Geneva Trade Conference" and called him "a symbol of American constructive energy and faith in the future." *Newsweek* covered Clayton's departure and the GATT conference in paired articles entitled "Good-by, Mr. Clayton" and "Freer Trade for the Free World," calling the agreement "a fitting climax" to his career as the "No. 1 architect of America's postwar foreign economic policy." The magazine observed that the British had given in to Clayton's "bold threats" to publicize their refusal to reduce the imperial preferences and praised the resulting agreement as being "basically on American terms" with the "free nations of the world" closing economic ranks with "lowered tariffs . . . established for two-thirds of the world's trade." In Paris, *Le Monde* called him the "champion of liberalism" and "one of the Americans who knew best European affairs . . . who brought to international discussions a spirit of wisdom and moderation."[2]

Not all of the media coverage of Clayton's tenure was favorable, however; the *Economist* was especially critical, as its editors assessed that "the harm he has done has greatly outweighed the good." The influential journal conceded, to Clayton's credit, that "he was one of the firmest advocates of the loan to Britain in 1945 and of large and immediate help for Europe in 1947." But oddly for a journal founded in 1843 on Adam Smith's principles of economic liberalism—specifically for the purpose of ridding Britain of the Corn Laws—the editors blamed Clayton for pushing "with such fervour" the twin fundamental economic policies "inherited from Mr. Cordell Hull": currency convertibility and nondiscrimination. They faulted Clayton for forcing "the premature attempt to make sterling convertible into dollars," under the terms of the American loan agreement, just as the British currency "was beginning to resume [its] function [as a medium of exchange] for a large part of the world." As to nondiscrimination, the editors condemned Clayton for being "impelled by the bogus doctrine that a preference, however small, is more noxious than a non-discriminating tariff, however high." This might be a valid point except that the agreement reached in Geneva between Clayton's team and the British negotiators involved historically huge reductions in US tariffs and comparatively minor reductions in imperial preferences. At the time they went to press with this criticism, the editors were not fully aware of the American concessions made in the agreement (which was not published until the following month), but their opinion of Clayton seemed to be based less on economic principles than on national bias fueled by what they cited as "indignation over the tactics that Mr. Clayton used to secure agreement."[3]

It is certainly true that the nondiscriminatory trade principles, which Clayton had indeed inherited from Cordell Hull, were deeply infused in the commercial policy provisions included in the GATT from the draft ITO Charter. The unconditional most-favored-nations (MFN) principle, requiring nondiscriminatory treatment among all the GATT contracting parties, is firmly established in Article I, the cornerstone of the agreement. Importantly, however, the agreement included significant exceptions for British Commonwealth imperial preferences, for colonial preferences of other countries and, for that matter, for the US preferences with Cuba and the Philippines. A national treatment standard also required nondiscriminatory treatment between imported and domestically produced goods with respect to internal taxation and regulation. Standards on anti-dumping and countervailing duties procedures, as well as safeguard measures under the escape clause and other measures, were provided to establish a code of nondiscriminatory practices for the contracting parties.[4] These principles were not new to the British; their experts had collaborated with the State Department in formulating the proposals for the charter in 1945, and afterward, at the successive drafting sessions at the Preparatory Committee conferences in London, New York, and Geneva. Hull had included similar provisions in trade agreements negotiated under the Reciprocal Trade Agreements Act, and the British had employed nondiscriminatory principles before retreating from free trade after the First World War.

ON TO HAVANA

The issues raised in the *Economist*'s criticisms of Clayton exposed the central problem confronting the State Department idealists trying to carry out the Hull agenda. Constructing a multilateral trading system would be a huge undertaking at any time, but dismantling world trade barriers seemed an improbable fantasy at a time when the economies of most countries were experiencing widespread and protracted unemployment, overvalued currencies, and severe trade deficits. Having been through the Depression and the Second World War, these desperate nations were trying to put millions of their citizens back to work, maintain the value of their currencies, and restore foreign reserves by protecting struggling domestic industries, arranging barter and preferential trade deals, imposing import quotas, and maintaining other wartime controls that violated the principles and many of the express provisions of the GATT and ITO Charter they were drafting.

The senior experts from the United States and the United Kingdom had collaborated with common objectives in 1942–43 as they began crafting the outline for a "Commercial Union" and a multilateral trade agreement in pursuit of the economic goals for the postwar world described in the Atlantic Charter. The devastating impact of the war on the world's economy made these plans less practicable. Most of the countries participating in the UN Preparatory Conferences, which led to the GATT agreement in Geneva and the ITO talks in Havana, did so either to avoid being left out of assistance programs such as the Marshall Plan or to avoid being excluded from any trade deal organized by the United States (the country with the largest import market in the world). Few were drawn to Havana because they shared, with Hull and Clayton, the belief that freer trade under uniform principles of fair-dealing set out in the draft ITO Charter would bring peace and prosperity to the world.

Fifty-six nations sent delegations to Havana to attend the United Nations Conference on Trade and Employment, which convened in the Cuban parliament building, the Capitolio Nacional, on November 21, 1947. This magnificent marble structure, with a central dome, was modeled after the US Capitol and the Panthéon in Paris and was constructed during the period of Cuba's "sugar boom" just before the 1929 crash. Its great hall was adorned with the world's second tallest indoor bronze statue, covered in twenty-two-carat gold leaf, and a twenty-five-carat diamond (once belonging to Tsar Nicholas II of Russia) was embedded in the center of the floor to mark the center of Havana. In this opulent setting, the stage was set for a grand celebratory occasion.

Havana, in its decadent pre-revolutionary days, was a well-known entertainment haven that offered visitors a wide variety of distractions and hedonistic temptations fueled by rum and centered on gambling and prostitution. However, Will Clayton (who did not even drink alcohol) and his delegation were intensely mission focused and planned grueling six-day workweeks with little time off even for the upcoming holidays. With the Havana meetings following only three weeks after the Geneva Conference, they hoped to expeditiously confirm the commercial policy principles, which had been adapted from the draft ITO Charter and were included in the GATT in Geneva to govern trade among the twenty-three signatory nations on a provisional basis from January 1, 1948, until the ITO Charter was formally adopted. Beyond those basic GATT principles, the charter provisions under negotiation in Havana involved much broader issues designed to promote international economic harmony with a focus on employment, economic development, foreign investment, restrictive business (anti-monopoly) practices, intergovernmental commodity agreements, and the institutional structure of the ITO.

The organizers' initial hope that the work of the Preparatory Committee in the three negotiating sessions conducted over the previous fourteen months would be merely reviewed, lightly polished, and promptly approved as a finished product by mid-January in Havana evaporated soon after their arrival in Cuba. According to an account by Clair Wilcox, vice chairman of the American delegation, the conference opened with a "chorus of denunciation" from representatives of thirty "undeveloped" nations. These delegates vehemently opposed the draft of the ITO Charter approved in Geneva, calling it one-sided, designed to serve only the interests of the great industrial powers, and holding no hope for the less developed states. These representatives offered 800 amendments to the draft, among which, Wilcox observed, "as many as two hundred . . . would have destroyed the very foundations of the enterprise." They challenged every specific commitment in the charter and attempted to reduce the ITO to a purely advisory organization. "With this beginning," Wilcox sighed, "the conference went to work."[5]

THE LATIN BLOC

During the first week, Clayton hosted a series of informal luncheons and dinners with Latin American delegations. The US team reported to Washington that nearly all of the Latin American delegation heads appeared to be friendly, and the Americans initially believed that understandings might be reached with them without great difficulty. A significant exception to this finding, however, was the Argentine delegation leader, Senator Diego Luis Molinari. An ardent nationalist and faithful lieutenant of President Juan Domingo Perón, Molinari began organizing an eighteen-nation Latin American voting bloc the first day of the conference with the obvious mission of burying the charter in Cuba. The mantra repeated endlessly from the bloc was that the charter was deliberately designed to stunt development in Latin countries. The US delegates reported in their diplomatic cables to Washington that the Latin American delegates were indifferent to European recovery and were resentful of any US agreement with Europe on trade policy. There may have been some jealousy mixed into this resentment sparked by the fact that, among the Latin nations in Havana, only Brazil, Chile, and Cuba had been invited to participate in the nuclear group in the earlier preparatory rounds. Only Brazil and Cuba gave general support to the ITO draft approved in Geneva.[6]

On the second day of the general debate, Clayton gave a speech responding to a challenge made by Ramon Beteta Quintana, chairman of the Mexican delegation. Beteta sought an amendment to the charter that would give less developed countries the right to impose import quotas and higher tariffs in order to protect their infant industries, without prior approval of the International Trade Organization. Beteta argued that the United States and other industrialized countries wanted to deny them this right to keep them in permanent economic subjugation. Clayton denied the charge by responding that "enlightened self-interest" causes the United States to favor other nations' industrialization because "our best customers have always been developed countries." Molinari, the Argentine chairman, also claimed that American prosperity had resulted from nineteenth-century protectionist policies employed during US industrialization and, therefore, less developed nations should be allowed a free hand in protecting their industries in the early stages of development.

Of course, both Beteta and Molinari were correct in citing the Hamiltonian argument for protecting infant industries and the predominance of protectionist policies in the robber baron era. They were simply following the argument made by conservative economist Henry C. Carey, favored by protectionist Whigs and later Republicans, that free trade was a British scheme to thwart American industrialization. But Clayton disputed the view that American industrialization derived from protectionism. "It would be more accurate," he explained, "to say that our development is the product of free trade among the forty-eight states." Clayton urged the conference to adopt the draft charter without "overloading it with a multiplicity of exceptions and escape clauses," warning that the United States could not accept "an instrument adopted in the name of economic cooperation which in fact, sanctioned economic conflict."[7]

Several days later, Molinari gave a sixty-nine-minute oration challenging Washington's leadership in reconstructing the world economy and social structure, as embodied by the charter. In particular, he argued that this charter forced the whole world to live "under the dollar sign" within "an international spider web of Shylocks squeezing the heart of hungry multitudes." In a demagogic appeal to the anti-capitalist segments of the less developed countries, he charged that the charter was an attempt by American capitalism, conceived in secret with the British during the Lend-Lease negotiations, to impose its economic system on a world that wanted socialism. The Argentine followed his speech with a long list of proposed amendments to the charter that would allow complete freedom to use import quotas and exchange controls and discriminate in how they are used against other nations, to establish preferential tariff systems, and to engage in state trading without ITO supervision of any kind.[8]

By the end of the first four weeks, the conference had accomplished very little in resolving the major divisions among the delegations. The most controversial issue—the question of using quantitative restrictions (QRs), including import quotas, for economic development—had not even been discussed in the charter proposals before the London Preparatory Conference in October 1946. Australia, India, Brazil, and Chile led the less developed countries' effort in London to add a special section on economic development to the charter as a primary objective of the ITO. This new section brought with it a number of new contentious issues.

In Geneva, with prompting from American business groups, the US delegation proposed a new article on standards for treatment of foreign investment, which the less developed countries insisted on filling with onerous restrictions and expropriation rights that were unfavorable to investors.

In Havana, the less developed countries reopened the investment issue with new proposals opposed by US business. Under the goal of promoting economic development, they also sought a broad exception to the prohibition of new tariff preferences for application within regional trade regimes using the imperial preference system as a model.

The most controversy, however, surrounded the demands for freedom to use QRs to promote economic development.[9] Under the draft charter approved in Geneva, less developed countries could not impose import quotas without ITO approval, except in very limited circumstances. When some less developed countries argued in Havana for the freedom to impose QRs on imports of luxury goods and imported products competitive with products of new domestic industries without prior ITO approval, the negotiations finally reached a stalemate.

On December 23, just before breaking for Christmas, Clair Wilcox (acting head of the US delegation in Clayton's absence) took the floor in great frustration. Despite holding a Swarthmore College professorship named for Joseph Wharton, one of the arch-protectionist robber barons of the Gilded Age, Wilcox, like Clayton, was a liberal trade idealist and a true believer in the Hull agenda. As a negotiator, he was a tireless and dedicated technician with a jovial personality. On extended leave from teaching, he enjoyed playing the diplomatic game and was confident that he played the game well. He was particularly fond of manipulating the media with well-placed leaks and aggressive attempts to control negative coverage. At times, however, his professorial confidence came across as pedantic and condescending, even arrogant.

On the day of his speech, the rotund, middle-aged economics professor ambled to the front of the room in his three-piece suit, much as he often did in his classroom at Swarthmore. The oration he proceeded to give to the "backward states" on quantitative restrictions became a blunt lecture as if to undergraduates, much in the vein of the ultimatum he gave in Geneva to the Commonwealth delegates on the subject of imperial preferences. He began by calling the proposed amendment allowing QRs on imports without limits "a prescription for economic anarchy":

> If this is to be the outcome of our negotiations here, I say that all our hopes for expanding trade, for raising standards of living, for promoting economic development, for achieving economic peace are doomed to failure. . . .

I must confess to a total inability to follow the logic of those who have argued here that we can expand trade by forbidding exporters to sell and importers to buy [through the use of QRs]. . . . So, too, with economic development. A reading of the verbatim record of these proceedings might lead one to the conclusion that an undeveloped country could achieve a rapid and far-reaching industrialization simply and solely by imposing quantitative restrictions on its trade. . . . New industries will not promise to succeed unless they have access to adequate markets. And they will not have access to adequate markets if everybody, everywhere, resorts to QR. QR does not open markets; it closes them. . . .

Several delegates . . . have referred to QR as a "weapon" and have said that the "weapon" is one of which they must not be deprived. The metaphor is all too appropriate. For a weapon is something that one uses in a war, and economic war will be the normal state of trade relations when everybody resorts to QR. . . .

The debate . . . seems to have proceeded on the assumption that the smaller countries and the weaker countries will be accorded complete freedom to employ QR while the larger and the stronger ones will voluntarily forego [*sic*] its use. This, I fear, is the sheerest phantasy.

My Government offered, in the Proposals which it published in December of 1945, to enter into an international agreement under which it would surrender its freedom to use QR for protective purposes. It maintained this offer at London. It maintained it at Geneva. It will maintain it at Havana. If this offer is accepted, no nation need fear that the United States will ever employ QR in ways that would be harmful to them. But if the offer is rejected, what then?[10]

Wilcox intended these remarks to warn of the consequences of indiscriminate economic warfare, but they were taken by the Latino delegates as hostile threats from an industrialized giant against the less developed world. This had the effect of only further galvanizing their position. In a confidential conversation with the American ambassador in Montevideo, the industry minister for Uruguay later attributed many subsequent difficulties at the conference to Wilcox's speech and the "unfriendly way in which it was delivered."[11]

By the end of December, it appeared to Wilcox that no agreement on the charter was likely to be obtained that would be satisfactory to the US delegation. He posed three alternatives for Clayton to consider in Washington: (1) try to get twenty-five to thirty countries to agree to a strong and satisfactory charter; (2) get general agreement on some of the chapters and sections, and adjourn consideration of the balance to a definite later date; or (3) accept a "skeleton" charter without substantive provisions that merely sets up a consultative body. Wilcox suggested that if the first alternative were adopted, congressional action could be taken in the 1948 session with a fifty-fifty chance of approval. However, this would require a maximum push from the top level at State, so he urged that General Marshall seek consultation with Senator Vandenberg. He said that if the second alternative were taken, he believed that most of the contracting parties of the GATT, except for three or four, would go along with it, but the adjournment would require waiting until 1949 to seek congressional approval.[12]

State Department officials in Washington saw the potential failure to produce an ITO Charter in Havana as a "severe diplomatic set-back" for the United States, a "loss of prestige" for the United Nations, and a "decided set-back" for free enterprise. An internal memorandum called the ITO project "the core of the post-war economic program" and "the very embodiment of economic liberalism in the international realm, adapted to present-day conditions." In the context of the Cold War, the memo observed that failure to produce an ITO charter at Havana would have serious consequences:

> The non-Russian world would be without a rudder in the international economic sea. . . . The Russians would be in a position to make heavy propaganda use of the Havana failure and would be in a better position to bring other countries under their economic or political influence.[13]

Clayton and Undersecretary Robert Lovett, in consultation with others at State, decided to continue to press for a strong and acceptable charter, staying in Havana as long as necessary to get agreement among a majority of countries representing at least three-quarters of world trade.

Clayton returned to Havana in early January with a new strategy. He ordered secret cables to be sent out to all of the US embassies in Latin America, urging American embassy diplomats to encourage their host governments to take a more constructive attitude toward American proposals at Havana. The embassy diplomats were instructed to explain the effects of failure at Havana and the residue of bitterness that could ensue in the upcoming Inter-American Conference in Bogotá, Colombia, where the goodwill of the United States might be important to the participating Latin American countries for financial assistance and trade. The cables provided the following background for use in discussion with local officials:

> There has been disconcerting absence [of] interest in supporting US positions or suggestions. [This] Absence particularly noticeable in view [of] practice [of] Latin American [Delegations] rushing to support one another even where issue is of no importance whatsoever [to] country giving support. Out of meetings certain Delegates have indicated instructions from their Govts to support Latin American positions generally.

The cables advised that the United States was "disturbed by the effect failure at Havana" would have on trade in Bogotá if an agreement was not reached on establishing rules for trade under the ITO. "Indeed," the cables emphasized, "Bogotá agenda item on trade left open pending conclusion [of the Havana] meeting." For those officials who needed diplomatic attention, each embassy was given intelligence about the stance taken by its host country's delegation.[14] Clayton and other State Department diplomats also approached Latin American embassy officials in Washington with similar outreach designed to influence the activities of the Havana delegations, which might otherwise be influenced by the Argentinian leadership of the Latin bloc in Havana.

By mid-February, an attitude of compromise began to emerge among the parties on both sides of the debate over using protectionist import quotas for purposes of economic development. In the end, the parties agreed that, as to commodities not included in trade agreements, the ITO would automatically approve import quotas imposed for economic development or reconstruction purposes under limited conditions. Among the conditions under which quotas would be permitted was the stipulation that the industry protected by the quota must be newly established during the war or recent postwar years (that is, between 1939 and 1948).[15] Another major concession made by Clayton and Wilcox was to permit, by a two-thirds majority vote of the ITO members, new regional preference agreements with discriminatory tariff systems to be formed, for a limited time, for the purpose of economic development among nations contiguous to one another or within the same economic region.[16]

THE BRITISH OBJECTIONS

The Latin bloc and other less developed nations seeking exceptions to nondiscriminatory most-favored-nations trade rules, however, were not the only impediment to success in Havana for US negotiators. Britain and other industrialized wartime allies presented their own obstacles to settlement. Like the British, the French also sought to remove or postpone restrictions on discrimination during their reconstruction and recovery period in order to deal with balance-of-payments crises. The British, French, Polish, Czech, and Chinese delegations all strongly opposed an American proposal to grant MFN status to the occupied territories of Germany and Japan.[17]

Another obstacle to settlement was American insistence on carving out agricultural trade from the prohibition on export subsidies and import quotas under the New Deal system of production controls and price-support schemes provided by the Agricultural Adjustment Act. This sticking point presented a major inconsistency in the principled US stance on trade liberalization in the industrial sector. The agriculture exception, which Congress and the Department of Agriculture forced on the State Department idealists, created embarrassing hurdles for the negotiators. The Latin American delegations "argued time and again" that the American reservation of the right to maintain agricultural import quotas without ITO approval, while insisting upon the prohibition of quotas for industrial imports, was patently unfair to less developed countries that were primarily exporters of agricultural products and importers of industrial products.

In an effort that anticipated Brazil's successful challenge to American cotton export subsidies in a 2004 dispute at the World Trade Organization, the Brazilian delegation in Havana proposed a ban on such subsidies without ITO approval. In a cable transmitted under Secretary Marshall's signature to the US Embassy in Rio de Janeiro, Marshall directed that the Brazilian government be advised that this proposal was not acceptable to the United States: "There is no prospect of US Congress accepting Charter which would subject to ITO approval . . . [the] right [of] US to use export subsidies." The British also opposed the United States on subsidies, but

Wilcox believed they were only doing so "in order to improve their bargaining position on discrimination."[18]

Wilcox and Clayton, when he was in Havana, worked incessantly in countless negotiating sessions to reach compromises on these objections that would be acceptable politically in Washington. By the last week in February, with most of the issues resolved, Clayton returned to Washington; Wilcox, nearing complete exhaustion, took the weekend off at a local beach for his first break in three intense months. When Wilcox returned from his respite, he called a meeting with the British, European, and other delegations who would be important to reaching final settlement. He reported to Washington that he "talked to these people like a football coach talks with his team before the last game of the season." He believed that every serious obstacle to concluding the agreement was settled and projected March 14 as a target for concluding the conference.[19]

As in the final settlement at the Geneva negotiations, however, serious objections came in from the same London officials who had nearly blocked the GATT agreement—Chancellor of the Exchequer Sir Stafford Cripps and president of the Board of Trade Harold Wilson. US ambassador Lewis Douglas cabled Clayton in Washington informing him of a meeting he had just had with Cripps and Wilson. In the meeting, they had notified Douglas that the new charter text, with the Havana compromises included, had "a number of most unsatisfactory features and it [was] very doubtful whether the United Kingdom [could] accept it." Cripps listed three main objections to the new draft: (1) the transitional period in which discriminatory trade would be permissible would not apply to Britain due to ambiguity in the language of the charter provision; (2) the concessions made to the less developed countries allowing quantitative restrictions for developmental purposes without ITO approval created a serious loophole, releasing all of the less developed countries from the import quota prohibition and enabling them to impose such restrictions as they themselves deemed necessary; and (3) the concession made to less developed countries to create new preferences for developmental purposes within an economic region among countries with common borders discriminated against members of the Commonwealth and Crown colonies on the sole grounds that they were simply not contiguous. Due to these objections, Cripps advised Douglas that it "would be politically impossible to present the charter to parliament." Cripps urged that the Havana conference be adjourned and reconvened in two or three months in order to settle these problems. Otherwise, the

British would have no choice but to refuse to sign the charter, a course of action Cripps professed to be reluctant to take.[20]

With palpable outrage, Wilcox immediately responded to these objections in a secret cable to Clayton in Washington. Expecting complete agreement on all outstanding issues within three or four days by over fifty countries, Wilcox advised Clayton that he believed the British were now simply making a "desperate attempt to extract additional concessions or prevent successful conclusion of negotiations." As to the objection regarding the transitional period that would allow for discriminatory trade practices, Wilcox noted that Clayton had negotiated this provision with the British, the Europeans, and the Commonwealth delegations in Havana with their full consent and no dissent from any delegation.

The second objection to import quotas for development purposes also involved a compromise negotiated by Clayton that had been approved by the British, the Commonwealth, Western Europe, Latin America, and all developing country delegations. The provisions of the compromise "related only to [a] minor part of trade not covered in agreements." He observed that this is the "one crucial compromise which will enable us to obtain almost complete agreement between developed and less developed countries here," which "may be [the] reason Cripps has singled it out for attack."

The third objection concerning the creation of new preferences, similar to the British imperial preference arrangement, was also drafted in full collaboration with the UK delegates. This article was designed to secure the adherence of Arab states and Central American countries whose trade, according to Wilcox, had "no great economic significance." When the British delegate presented Cripps's objections to the Commonwealth and European delegations the day before, Wilcox reported, "Australia and New Zealand flatly rejected UK position. Canada and South Africa remained silent. Europeans just smiled."

Noting that the British government had been publicly committed as a full partner of the United States in this project since the Atlantic Charter in 1941, Wilcox observed that it was "incredible" that they "would assume the responsibility of attempting to scuttle it at the eleventh hour." He then gave Clayton his opinion on their actions:

In my judgment, the present Government of the UK, while giving lip service to the principles of multilateral trade, really believes that Britain can never face free competition and must seek sheltered markets through preferential arrangements, discriminatory bilateral contracts, and barter deals. For that reason, it has never wanted the Charter to be adopted or the ITO to be set up. The UK delegates have not given the US delegation whole-hearted or effective support at London, Geneva, or Havana. The UK has apparently assumed that agreement, among so many countries, on so many vital issues, could not be obtained. Now that it is in hand they are seeking to destroy it. Fortunately they are too late.

Wilcox urged immediate rejection of Cripps's proposal to adjourn the conference for two or three months, stating simply, "The Havana steamroller cannot be stopped."[21]

And indeed, the steamroller did not stop, but it was definitely slowed to a near halt as negotiations and cable traffic between Washington, London, and Havana continued for another two weeks. One of the central points of debate revolved around which side was on the most precarious political ground for making concessions. In one cable, in preparation for a morning meeting to discuss the political risks with Cripps, Ambassador Douglas requested that the State Department "telegraph most urgently" their views on the importance of "US risks against British risks." Wilcox immediately responded that in Havana all the delegates knew that the British were the only remaining obstacle to completing the agreement. The Latin American delegates were insistent that the United States stand firm and offered their unanimous support. To accede to the British position would alienate most of the other delegates, who had already been complaining about Anglo-American collusion against their interests. Wilcox argued that it would be impossible to defend accepting the UK position in Washington with no quid pro quo. He warned that both the ITO Charter and the renewal of the trade agreements legislation, which was soon to expire, would be seriously endangered in Congress.[22]

In the final settlement, the British withdrew their objection to Clayton's compromise allowing the less developed countries to employ limited import quotas for development purposes. On the issue of new preferential arrangements for development purposes within certain economic regions, the United States, with approval from the Latin American and other delegates, agreed to add an interpretive note in the text stating that the ITO "need not interpret the term 'economic region' to require close geographical proximity if it is satisfied that a sufficient degree of economic integration exists between the countries concerned."[23] This note would, in theory, permit parts of the British Empire that were not contiguous to be considered within the same economic region in order to create new preferences under this provision. But as one commentator observed, in light of the lack of enthusiasm for such new preferences within the Commonwealth, "it amounted to little more than a political fig-leaf."[24] The most significant concession the US delegates granted to Britain in the final days of the conference was an option to continue discriminatory import restrictions for balance-of-payments purposes until March 1, 1952, thus extending the postwar transition period for implementing nondiscriminatory restrictions effectively for four years.

THE CONTROVERSIAL ISSUES FOR US BUSINESS

The Havana Charter was a long and complicated document that included six separate agreements, only one of which—representing about one-third of the charter—covered the GATT's commercial trade policy rules. The remaining chapters covered employment and economic activity, economic development and reconstruction, monopolies and restrictive business practices, intergovernmental commodity agreements, and the structure and functions of the newly formed UN agency, the ITO.[25] The most politically sensitive of these provisions in the United States involved (1) American concessions in the governance of the ITO, (2) the exceptions to the rules provided for purposes of balance-of-payments and economic development, (3) the security of foreign investment, and (4) the call for members to maintain full employment within their respective territories.

Regarding ITO governance, the charter granted each member country one vote in the Conference, the governing body composed of delegates from all the member states, in deliberations determining the Organization's policies. The US delegation had proposed a heavily weighted voting system based on the economic significance of each member's participation, similar to the voting system of the International Monetary Fund. This system would have given the United States more influence in the ITO decision-making process than the one-country one-vote system. Most of the important questions to be decided by the Conference, such as a waiver of obligations or an amendment to the charter, however, required a two-thirds majority vote to prevail; this minimized the possibility of the United States being outvoted on critical decisions. Further, the United States was guaranteed a permanent seat on the Executive Board of the Conference responsible for executing ITO policies. The Executive Board was to consist of representatives of eighteen member states, and eight of these board seats were to be reserved for member states "of chief economic importance" determined by their shares in international trade. The formula determining economic importance would assure that these seats would go—if they joined—to the United States, the United Kingdom, Canada, France, the Benelux customs union, India, China, and the Soviet Union. The Soviet Union was not expected to join since the Soviets had not participated in any of the conferences and its state-controlled media had repeatedly ridiculed the ITO project as a capitalist scheme to dominate the world.

Although the charter and the GATT firmly established for the first time in a multilateral agreement the principle of unconditional MFN tariff treatment (and the US delegation defeated a plethora of proposals for sweeping MFN exceptions), the United States, as previously discussed, made significant concessions that weakened the prohibition of discrimination as it applied to import quota restrictions when employed for purposes of economic development or balance-of-payments problems. These concessions would pose a major political hurdle for US ratification of the charter.

Another controversial provision that led to prolonged debate at the Conference and criticism from American business interests involved the security of foreign investment. While the charter acknowledged the "great value" of international investment "in promoting economic development and reconstruction, and consequent social progress," it provided that a member state has the right "to take any appropriate safeguards necessary to ensure that foreign investment is not used as a basis for interference in its internal affairs or national policies." The charter prohibited a member state from taking "unreasonable or unjustifiable action within its territory injurious to the rights or interests of nationals of other Members in the enterprise, skill, capital, arts or technology which they have supplied." But it only required the host member state to provide "just terms" as to ownership requirements of the investment and "adequate security for existing and future investments."[26] This language offered little certainty in the security of foreign investors from discriminatory treatment or arbitrary expropriation without adequate compensation by governments with home-turf advantages.

FULL EMPLOYMENT

In the first chapter following the statement of purposes and objectives, the charter laid out six articles addressing labor and unemployment. These provisions, which would ultimately ignite the most serious protest from the American business community, were directed at what many delegates considered the most ominous economic threat in the postwar world. These delegates argued that, at a foundational level, the avoidance of unemployment and underemployment is a necessary condition for achieving the objectives of the charter, including the expansion of international trade. Following the experience of the Great Depression, which brought a 25 percent unemployment rate to the United States and even higher rates in other parts of the world, a great fear arose in the last years of the war that bad times would soon return. Only the demands of war production ended the Depression and boosted domestic economies. As the Second World War drew to a close, the scaling back of wartime production was inevitable. At the same time, the US economy was being flooded with over 10 million soldiers and sailors returning from the war. Economists feared that the combination of shrinking war production and the influx of former military personnel looking for work as civilians could only bring disastrous economic results. Demobilization had already resulted in a US recession. The specter of mass unemployment in these years was on the minds of many of the delegates in Havana.

In the second week of the conference, the chairman of the Australian delegation, H. C. Coombs, gave a speech urging the other countries to take action to prevent unemployment that might arise because of what he called the "essentially unstable" nature of the US economy.[27]

In the United States, action to combat the risk of mass unemployment had begun several years earlier. President Roosevelt had addressed this threat in his annual address to Congress in January 1944, observing that "true individual freedom cannot exist without economic security and independence. . . . People who are hungry and out of a job are the stuff of which dictatorships are made." He called for a "Second Bill of Rights," an economic bill of rights, the first of which would be the "*right* to a useful and remunerative job in the industries or shops or farms or mines of the Nation (emphasis added)."[28] Roosevelt trumpeted the "economic bill of rights" in his campaign for a fourth term later that year on a Democratic platform that promised to "guarantee full employment and provide prosperity," along with peace and victory in the war.[29]

Both houses of Congress appointed Special Committees on Post-War Economic Policy and Planning. Senator Walter F. George (D-GA) chaired the Senate special committee, which included the Senate Republican leaders Robert Taft and Arthur Vandenberg, who in coalition with conservative Democrats on the committee held sway over the committee's direction. Chairman George's long record of opposing FDR's New Deal proposals had prompted the president to try, unsuccessfully, to defeat George in his 1938 reelection bid, an effort that George never forgave or forgot. The reports and proposals of the George Committee (as it became known) steered clear of the Keynesian formula of increased federal spending to create higher demand and more jobs, a formula that most of the economists in the Roosevelt administration now followed religiously and which underpinned the economic bill of rights. Although the George Committee actively competed with other committees in attempting to dominate the planning for the postwar economic agenda, it proposed no legislative recommendations for government-sponsored full employment.

Instead, a bill for the Full Employment Act of 1945, introduced on January 22, 1945, emanated from a report issued by the War Contracts Subcommittee of the Military Affairs Committee. Senator James E. Murray (D-MT), the principal sponsor of the bill, chaired this subcommittee, which also included Harry Truman before his elevation to vice president. Truman supported full employment legislation while on this subcommittee and later in the White House. Stephen Kemp Bailey, author of an excellent contemporary treatment of the political history of the Full Employment Act, describes Murray as a great anomaly in the Senate—one of the wealthiest men in the body, but "endowed with an unusually sensitive social conscience which in the last few years has developed into an almost messianic fervor for social justice."[30]

Joining Murray in guiding the bill through the upper chamber, Senator Robert Wagner (D-NY), chairman of both the Banking and Currency Committee and its Full Employment Subcommittee which obtained jurisdiction over the bill, was one of the most influential liberal members, especially on labor issues. In 1935, he authored the National Labor Relations Act, known as the Wagner Act. Despite considerable opposition from Taft and others on Wagner's subcommittee and the floor, the sponsors were able to maneuver the bill to passage by an overwhelming margin of 71 to 10.[31] Even Senators George, Taft, and Vandenberg voted in favor of the bill after a few floor amendments were adopted. The Senate-passed bill declared: "All

Americans able to work and seeking work are entitled to an opportunity for useful, remunerative, regular, and full-time employment." The measure included language ensuring that full employment would be implemented through "investment and expenditure" by the federal government if the private sector failed to produce sufficient jobs. With overtones reminiscent of five-year plans prevalent in socialist countries, the bill also ensured that national economic planning would play a critical role in the process.[32]

As the bill moved to the House, outside influences both for and against the bill began to emerge and strengthen. The Senate bill for "full employment" was supported by a range of groups, including both of the major labor organizations—the AFL and the CIO—the National Farmers Union, the Union for Democratic Action (predecessor of Americans for Democratic Action), the National Association for the Advancement of Colored People, and other progressive groups and liberal media (e.g., the *New Republic* and the *Nation*). Yet the conservative pro-business organizations coalesced into a much stronger force. The National Association of Manufacturers, national and local Chambers of Commerce, and the American Farm Bureau Federation came out in forceful opposition to the Senate bill. Conservative media and syndicated columnists with anti-FDR sympathies also weighed in heavily against the measure. Ray Moley, who entitled his weekly column for *Newsweek* on the subject "A Fool Employment Bill," wrote:

> What I am objecting to is the insincerity of enacting into law political slogans which mean either nothing or something which no one really wants. For "full employment," literally enforced, would mean the end of freedom for all classes of Americans.[33]

Another factor impacting the political popularity of the legislation grew from the 1944 publication of *The Road to Serfdom* by Friedrich von Hayek of the London School of Economics. This book, a bestseller on both sides of the Atlantic, became the conservative antidote to the increasingly popular theories that Lord Keynes proposed in his *General Theory of Employment, Interest, and Money*. Hayek made the case that state planning and government intervention, as envisioned in publicly guaranteed programs for full employment, ultimately led to totalitarian regimes like communism and fascism. *Reader's Digest*, in April 1945, published a twenty-page condensed version of his book, available from Book-of-the-Month Club for five cents a copy, and in the same year *Look* magazine even reproduced a cartoon version of the book originally published by General Motors Company in Detroit. Millions of Americans absorbed Hayek's message.

In the House, a conservative coalition of southern Democrats and Republicans took control of the bill in committee and produced a watered-down substitute of the Senate approach that some had labeled communistic. Despite a strong effort led by the liberal populist, Congressman Wright Patman (D-TX), to get a floor vote on the Senate version as an alternative, the House refused. And in mid-December 1945, the House passed the committee substitute, which included no right to work and no government-sponsored full employment. President Truman wrote to the House-Senate conference committee chairmen on December 20 to advise that a bill offering substantially less than the Senate version would not be acceptable. He followed this message with a radio address urging Americans to contact their representatives in Congress with essentially the same message. A month later, in his State of the Union Address, Truman again called for a strong full employment bill from the conference committee.

On February 6, however, the House overwhelmingly passed the "Employment Act of 1946" after it emerged from conference, and the Senate followed suit two days later. Though not as weak as the House substitute, the final version eliminated both the "right" of Americans to have a job and the goal of full employment. It also fudged on the Senate's Keynesian approach to public funding of job creation if private enterprise fell short and emphasized the need to maintain "purchasing power." This was a code phrase for containing inflation, a traditional bogeyman raised by political conservatives when opposing increased government spending. The Senate sponsors were not pleased with the result, but they supported it because they believed the language was broad enough to accomplish their goals. In the Act's Declaration of Policy, Congress gave responsibility to

> the Federal Government to use all practicable means . . . to coordinate and utilize all its plans, functions, and resources for the purpose of creating and maintaining, in a manner calculated to foster and promote free competitive enterprise and the general welfare, conditions under which there will be afforded useful employment opportunities, including self-employment, for those able, willing, and seeking to work, and to promote *maximum employment*, production, and purchasing power. [emphasis added][34]

In lieu of economic planning, the act required the president to submit an economic report at each regular session of Congress setting out the
levels of employment, production, and purchasing power in the United
States, along with economic trends, related government programs, and
legislative recommendations concerning the act's declaration of policy. To
assist and advise the president in fulfilling this obligation, the act created
the Council of Economic Advisers in the White House and the bipartisan
Joint Economic Committee in Congress (including both House and Senate
members) to oversee matters relating to the president's economic report.

It is important to recall the politics surrounding the full employment
issue here, especially as reflected in the enactment of the Employment Act
of 1946, because this issue weighed heavily on the minds of the US delegation as they negotiated the employment provisions contained in the Havana
Charter. As Clair Wilcox described it, "Trade policies advocated in the name
of 'full employment' may be unwise. But they are deeply rooted in the politics of other nations and they must be reckoned with."[35] Australia's Labor
government had introduced its own full employment legislation in 1945,
and its delegation in Havana led the fight for the most aggressive approach
to requiring affirmative action to expand employment. The UK delegation
also urged adoption of full employment measures in Havana and a separate
escape clause to permit limitations on imports causing unemployment and
balance-of-payments difficulties. They argued for the addition of language
to require countries with a trade surplus—a clear reference to the United
States—to increase imports from countries with declining employment and
trade deficits.

The British employment proposals had huge popular support at
home, encouraged as they were by the 1944 publication of William H.
Beveridge's influential book, *Full Employment in a Free Society*. Two years
earlier, Beveridge had published a report commissioned by the government
entitled *Social Insurance and Allied Services*, which became known as the
Beveridge Report and is credited with having inspired the welfare state programs enacted by the Labour government in the postwar years. Ironically,
Beveridge had been director of the LSE in 1931 when he and Lionel Robbins
recruited Friedrich von Hayek from the University of Vienna to bolster the
LSE economics faculty in its rivalry with Keynes at Cambridge University.

The US delegation, as a subordinate unit of the Roosevelt-Truman
administrations, was sympathetic to full employment policies but was reluctant to create new controversy for the charter by relitigating the politically

charged full employment issue to gain approval from a Congress controlled by Republicans following the 1946 election. It had been just over six
months since Congress had passed the conservative Taft-Hartley Act (the
Labor-Management Relations Act of 1947) overriding President Truman's
veto with significant southern Democratic support. Senator George made
the last speech in support of the bill before Senator Taft, the co-sponsor,
closed the debate. Observing that he had voted for the Wagner Act twelve
years before, George asserted that passing this bill, which severely restricted
the rights of labor organizations under the Wagner Act, was "one way to
break the stranglehold of the labor bosses." For its part, organized labor led
an expensive, but unsuccessful, campaign to defeat Taft-Hartley, which it
called the "slave labor" bill.[36]

The language adopted in the ITO Charter required each member state
to "take action to achieve and maintain full and productive employment
and large and steadily growing demand within its own territory," but left the
means of achieving this goal to the discretion of each member as "appropriate to its political, economic and social institutions." Some of the language used in the charter was taken directly from that already approved
by Congress in the Employment Act of 1946, such as the goal of providing
"useful employment opportunities for those able and willing to work" and
with no guarantee of a right to a job. Because of the common complaint
among leaders of conservative opinion that "full employment" was synonymous with "make-work" policies, the charter expressed a broader goal
of "full and *productive* employment" [emphasis added]. Clair Wilcox was
aware of the importance of describing this chapter of the charter in terms
that would be acceptable to an increasingly conservative Congress. Thus, he
stressed that the common slogan of "full employment," which he wrote was
"too deeply imbedded in popular psychology to be dislodged," really should
be understood to mean "industrial stability."

The final article in the employment chapter provided that members
recognize that employment measures "must take fully into account the
rights of workers under inter-governmental declarations, conventions and
agreements" and "that unfair labour conditions, particularly in production for export, create difficulties in international trade." Accordingly, each
member was required to "take whatever action may be appropriate and feasible to eliminate such conditions within its territory." Members who were
also part of the International Labor Organization (ILO) were required to
cooperate with that organization in implementing this chapter, and the ITO

was required to consult and cooperate with the ILO in all matters relating to labor standards.

During the course of negotiating this provision, a number of unsuccessful proposals were offered, including the encouragement of the adoption of social security legislation, specific obligations to provide equal pay for equal work, controls on the movement of migratory workers and protections for them against discrimination, and a US proposal condemning forced labor, which, according to Wilcox, drew no support from other delegates. While the charter's chapter on employment did not contain commitments to international action and conferred no new powers on any international agency for enforcing labor standards, the provision on labor standards required the ITO to consult and cooperate with the ILO to resolve any member's complaint against another for condoning unfair labor practices within its territory. Wilcox observed that it was possible that this article "might apply some leverage for the improvement of standards in countries where they are low."[37] In view of the development of GATT law in the dispute settlement process in the ensuing years, it is conceivable that this provision could have germinated into a body of law governing the relationship between trade and labor.

THE FINAL ACT

On March 24, 1948, the senior representatives for fifty-three of the fifty-six countries participating in the United Nations Conference on Trade and Employment in Cuba signed the final act, approving what became known as the Havana Charter, to be submitted to the participating countries for ratification. Only Poland—under Soviet influence—and Argentina refused to sign; Turkey signed at a later date. This day signified a landmark step in fulfilling the dream expressed in the Atlantic Charter and Article VII of the Lend-Lease Mutual Aid Agreement for a multilateral agreement to reduce trade barriers and bring an end to discriminatory trade practices that had proven so destructive to economic peace and world harmony in the interwar years. Not only did the Havana Charter reinforce the GATT rules that provisionally governed trade barriers and discriminatory practices until the charter was formally ratified, but it also attempted to address the broader goal of the Atlantic Charter "to bring about the fullest collaboration between all nations in the economic field with the object of securing, for all, improved labor standards, economic advancement and social secur-ity."[38] The State Department's press release announcing the signing of the final act stated that the main objective of the charter was to raise living standards throughout the world "by promoting the expansion of interna-tional trade on a basis of multilateralism and general nondiscrimination, by fostering the growth of production and employment, and by encouraging the economic development of backward areas."[39]

In his final remarks before signing the charter, Will Clayton observed that while each member state "will surrender some part of its freedom to take action that might prove harmful to others," he predicted that, if ratified and put into effect, this agreement "may prove the greatest step in history toward order and justice in economic relations, and a great expansion in production, distribution and consumption of goods throughout the world." Many delegates, including the British representative Stephen L. Holmes, paid tribute to the United States for having initiated the idea of the ITO and for having pushed the charter through to completion. Holmes cautioned,

FIGURE 13.1 Will Clayton with Clair Wilcox signing the ITO Charter in Havana on March 24, 1948 (Harry S. Truman Presidential Library)

however, that his government was less than satisfied with some of its provisions concerning preferences and the allowance of import quotas for development purposes. They would be watching closely, Holmes said, to ensure that the Commonwealth was treated fairly. Holmes also warned that, due to postwar balance-of-payments difficulties, his government would have to make full use of the exceptions to the rule of nondiscrimination.[40]

PART THREE

The Survival of the System

14

A New Economic Order?

It is my judgment that the ITO is no longer a practical
possibility.[1]
    —Secretary of State Acheson to President Truman
                 November 20, 1950

Exactly one year prior to the final act of the Havana Charter, an article
appeared on the front page of the *New York Times*, describing the American
business community's support for "the principles and objectives of the
Truman Administration's program for the Geneva Conference," which was
then scheduled to open the following month. The National Association of
Manufacturers (NAM), the United States Chamber of Commerce (USCC),
the International Chamber of Commerce (ICC), and the National Foreign
Trade Council (NFTC) were lead associations participating in the *Times*
survey. They all endorsed the objectives of the proposed ITO and expressed
hope that they would be able to support the final product. They believed
the principal issue confronting the negotiators to be the fundamental differences between the US concept of freer world trade "based upon maximum encouragement of free enterprise and competition, and the British
and European preference for socialization and cartelization." While many
businesses continued to favor high tariffs, the article noted that there was
"widespread agreement that the United States, as the world's greatest creditor, has a responsibility for leadership in attempting to free international
trade of needless barriers."[2]

To the extent that the *Times* article captured a true picture of the business perspective in 1947, a change of heart clearly occurred by the spring of 1948. As word arrived from Havana about the US concessions made to obtain the agreement of the less developed countries and the British Commonwealth participants, opposition began to grow among a new faction of critics who favored more liberal trade policy and objected to the charter for allowing too many exceptions to the principal free-trade rules. This faction, which would include all of the groups mentioned in the *Times* piece, came to be called the "perfectionists," who would, ironically, join forces with protectionist critics in opposition to the Havana Charter.[3] Dr. Elvin H. Killheffer of E. I. du Pont de Nemours & Company (a Chamber of Commerce representative who had been a private-sector adviser and a US delegate in Havana), speaking to a protectionist audience at a National Textile Seminar six weeks after the signing, called for Congress to reject the charter and begin again. He argued that "an entirely new group of negotiators would be necessary to eliminate much of the philosophy of government-planned economy and controls by the state," adding that "business and industry should be invited to write a preliminary draft before it is submitted to other nations." Another economist from the Cotton Textile Institute warned the same audience that the State Department was a peril to the US textile industry and should not even be administering the trade agreement program. In a later speech, Killheffer condemned the charter as a "vast invasion of the free enterprise principle," which "the people of the United States, who are engaged in the production of its wealth, still strongly believe in." When the Chamber came out against the charter, Clair Wilcox, who had an informant at the Chamber, wrote to Will Clayton that the decision "was dictated by Killheffer."[4]

Clayton and others in the Truman administration were seriously disturbed by the negative reports they were receiving from the business community. Indeed, they had faced similar protests surrounding the approvals of the Bretton Woods agreements, the British loan, and past renewals of the trade agreement program. But this year was markedly more threatening than the previous years when a Democratic Congress could be influenced by Hull carrying a "must have" FDR agenda. This year, the trade program was up for renewal in June for the first time under a Republican Congress, with Ways and Means chairman Harold Knutson (R-MN) having promised a bitter battle following what he called "the most sweeping tariff cuts in the history of the country" at Geneva. "When the full meaning of these tariff

cuts becomes apparent to the American public," Knutson said in a statement attacking the first tariff reductions under the GATT, "the reaction is
likely to prove . . . disconcerting to the 'do-gooders', who have traded us off
for very dubious and nebulous trade concessions that may never be realized."[5] As Clayton was preparing to sign the Havana Charter, Chairman
Knutson led the Ways and Means Committee in adopting a resolution, on a
party line vote, with this warning:

> Any action of the President or the Department of State prior to the
> consideration by Congress of the International Trade Organization,
> shall not, in so far as the Ways and Means Committee of the House
> of Representatives is concerned, be construed as a commitment
> by the United States to accept all or any of the provisions of the
> charter.[6]

Though the prospects did not look good for Truman and the Democrats
in the upcoming 1948 election, General Marshall and Clayton decided to
ask the president to wait until the next session of Congress to send the charter for approval.

THE TRADE AGREEMENTS EXTENSION ACT OF 1948

In late May and June, the battle over the renewal of the president's trade
authority was predictably brutal and ultimately unsatisfactory for the State
Department. The administration requested a three-year extension (the period normally granted since 1934), but instead, it received only a one-year
extension. This authority was further limited by the restriction that new
tariff concessions be reviewed by the bipartisan Tariff Commission before
being proposed in trade negotiations (a restriction previously demanded by
Senate Finance Committee chairman Millikin when the Republicans took
control in 1946, and which President Truman had refused). If the Tariff
Commission found that any of the proposed concessions threatened serious injury to domestic industry or impaired national defense (thus reaching "peril point" status), the commission must report this finding to the
president, who could still offer the proposal in the trade negotiations, but
would have to provide an explanation to Congress.[7]

The Truman administration objected to the new restrictions with full force led by General Marshall, who charged that this change in the program was a serious mistake. In a letter to the ranking Democrat on Ways and Means, R. L. Doughton, who read it on the House floor during the debate, Marshall said the trade agreements program had been a "cornerstone of our foreign economic policy for 14 years. Through it, we have exercised a significant part of our leadership in world economic affairs." He argued that the principle of the trade program was incorporated in the Economic Cooperation Act of 1948 (the Marshall Plan), which had just passed Congress the month before, and was dependent upon a great expansion in European production. This, in turn, depended upon markets enhanced by the lowering of trade barriers among all nations. According to Marshall, although this resolution extended the Trade Agreements Act for one year, "it does so with such crippling amendments that only a shadow of the original act is preserved while its substance is destroyed." It, in effect, "makes pure protection the sole criterion for tariff action and forbids the Tariff Commission from participating in the deliberations of the Trade Agreements Committee, in which, under the present system, other important aspects of the national interest are also taken into account." Under these circumstances, Marshall concluded the trade program would be "unworkable" and would be better served to expire than to be extended for another year under these amendments.

Congressman Doughton also brought into the debate supporting statements from a broad range of business and labor organizations seeking to maintain the trade program in its present form. The statement by James B. Carey, representing the Congress of Industrial Organizations (CIO), argued that the way to attain the "goal of full employment at a fair wage and full production is through international trade encouraged by reciprocal trade agreements." Carey called the Smoot-Hawley philosophy of high tariffs to eliminate foreign competition "fallacious." Doughton also offered the supporting views of the Chamber of Commerce, National Council of American Importers, National Foreign Trade Council, and other business associations. In fact, a Gallup Poll taken on May 12, 1948, showed 80 percent of voters in favor of the continuation of Hull's trade agreements program, with only 8 percent opposing such programs.[8]

The House passed the extension to the trade agreements program with the "crippling amendments" on a largely partisan vote with little concern for the objections raised by the secretary of state or those of anyone else.

In the Senate debate, however, the Republican leaders gave more attention to the substantive issues. Finance Committee chairman Millikin began the debate by reading the joint statement that he and Foreign Relations Committee chairman Vandenberg had made sixteen months before, soon after the Republicans had taken control. In the statement, they had urged President Truman (1) to include an "escape clause" in every trade agreement that the United States entered into thereafter, permitting the withdrawal or modification of tariff reductions in the event of certain import-caused injuries to the domestic economy, and (2) to require the Tariff Commission to review all proposed tariff reductions in future trade negotiations and make recommendations to the president as to the point beyond which reductions could be made without injury to the domestic economy (the "peril point" provision). Senator Millikin reminded his colleagues that President Truman had not accepted their suggestion regarding the role of the Tariff Commission in the "peril point" limitations on tariff proposals. He complained that even though the president had officially ordered the inclusion of escape clauses, he had hedged the escape procedures with so many conditions that they were ineffectual. This joint statement with Vandenberg, Millikin said, referred to the forthcoming negotiations scheduled in Geneva, and thus explained the essential rationale for the so-called crippling amendments and one-year limit to the extension of the trade agreement program:

> Remember, I am double-riveting the point that the proposed Charter, the Geneva Agreement, and the Trade Agreements Act, which we propose to amend, are so inextricably tied up together that they must have unified consideration, one over-all review, and we cannot have it until next year, because we do not have the proposed Charter before us, and will not have it until next year.[9]

THE VANDENBERG ASSESSMENT

Of all the congressional speeches given on trade during this postwar period, Senator Vandenberg's remarks on June 14, 1948, were the most candid and nonpartisan. These remarks are especially important because they document an early, objective perspective of the ITO from one of the most important foreign policy voices on Capitol Hill. He began by explaining that his support for the extension with its restrictions did not mean that he was abandoning his bipartisan approach to foreign policy or that he was "veering back toward an economic isolationism," where he had been before Pearl Harbor. He said he preferred an extension of three, or at least two, years, but since there were no agreements under consideration until after this year's election, the time period was academic under present circumstances.

Vandenberg said that he went along with Senator Millikin's peril point provision because it would allow the Tariff Commission only to make recommendations to the president. The president still would have the right to make the decision on tariff reductions, even if they would be perilous, as long as he explained the facts to Congress. Vandenberg said he would have opposed the provision if the final decision had been taken from the president and given solely to the Tariff Commission. He had, in fact, blocked a provision in the House bill, proposed by Ways and Means Trade Subcommittee chairman Bertrand W. Gearhart (R-CA), which would have granted a congressional veto on tariff rates in trade agreements. Though he had been one of the leading opponents of the original Reciprocal Trade Agreements Act (RTAA) in 1934, Vandenberg now declared, "The reciprocal trade agreement principle should be preserved unweakened. It is indispensable in today's world." Later in the speech he expounded on this point:

> If this formula gave Congress the last word in respect to rates, I would not support it. Tariff rate-making in Congress is an atrocity. It lacks any element of economic science or validity. I suspect the 10 Members of the Senate, including myself, who struggle [sic] through the 11 months that it took to write the last congressional Tariff Act [Smoot-Hawley], would join me in resigning before they would be willing to tackle another general congressional Tariff revision. . . . I happen to be one of those, Mr. President, who believes the reciprocal trade agreements practice is very necessary in this postwar world.

Senator Vandenberg summarized the importance of the International Trade Organization that he expected would be brought before Congress in 1949: "I doubt whether Members of the Senate fully appreciate the amazing extent of the so-called prospective ITO . . . which, after many, many months of preliminary effort, finally crystalized in the Charter. . . . The ITO Charter is almost as important in its scope and economic application as the Charter

of the United Nations is in the field of collective security. . . . We are talking about a fundamental reorganization of the economy of the earth." After
showcasing a sentence-by-sentence outline of the chapters of the charter
and giving it further effusive praise, he concluded, "If this is the pending
situation, and I believe it is, the pending extension proposal should pass."[10]
And it did.

Perhaps it was Senator Vandenberg's glowing assessment of the ITO
that influenced President Truman reluctantly to sign the one-year extension
of the Trade Agreements Act. Indeed, he signed, despite, according to the
Wall Street Journal, "widespread predictions from administration sources
that he would veto the measure" and Will Clayton's charge that the extension "was worse than none at all." In his signing statement, Truman noted
the "serious defects," "unwise changes," and "complicated, time-consuming,
and unnecessary procedure" in the extension, which he trusted would be
corrected next year, restoring the reciprocal trade agreements program as
one of high national policy and "as a fully effective instrument of permanent United States policy."[11]

1949

The odds were slim at this point, however, that Truman would even be
in the White House the following year. Several public opinion polls at
that time predicted that Truman would lose the 1948 presidential election by a wide margin to Governor Thomas E. Dewey of New York,[12] and
the Democrats were expected to lose even more seats in Congress. The
Democratic Party's pledge in the 1948 Democratic platform "to restore
the Reciprocal Trade Agreements program . . . crippled by the Republican
80th Congress," along with the platform's endorsement of the International
Trade Organization,[13] seemed doomed with the rest of the Democratic electoral hopes. With Truman's famous upset victory in November, however,
happy days appeared to be here again for the State Department idealists as
the Democrats regained control of both Houses of Congress.

As the new Congress began in 1949, the prospects for the ITO seemed
to improve right away. The *New York Times* reported on January 4 that
a special subcommittee of the House Foreign Affairs Committee had
"urged the incoming Congress to support the Charter as essential to
American bipartisan foreign policy." Although it noted that support from

the business community was mixed at best, the article concluded that the atmosphere appeared more favorable for ratification since the election. Revealing the tenor of the debate to come, however, the reporter observed that the opponents of the charter "denounced it as an example of collectivist thinking that would destroy or cripple private enterprise and lead to the domination of world trade by a sort of super-state and an international bureaucracy."[14]

Actually, the ITO supporters were forced to sail against multiple crosscurrents in the months ahead. Although a number of traditional protectionist interest groups, such as the American Tariff League,[15] had already joined in an odd alliance with the "perfectionists" and announced fierce opposition to the charter, it was quite true that the atmosphere for trade politics had improved in the new Congress. This improvement was most evident in the immediate turnaround on extending the Trade Agreements Act. Both Harold Knutson and Bertrand Gearhart, the leading protectionists in the House, were among those defeated in November, and Congressman Robert Doughton again became chairman of Ways and Means. Doughton introduced a bill on January 10 extending the program for the full three years from June 12, 1948, without the "crippling" peril point provision. The committee reported it out after six days of hearings, and the House passed it after one day of floor debate on February 9. The Senate Finance Committee also moved judiciously, holding more than two weeks of hearings after which they reported the House bill unchanged on a 7-to-6 partisan vote on March 11. Even so, the bill did not get to the Senate floor until September.

Two impediments prevented the trade initiatives from moving forward with due speed: conflicts emerged in scheduling priorities and opposition began to gain strength from an unexpected direction. At the close of the Havana conference in the spring of 1948, the Truman administration was focused on obtaining approval of the Marshall Plan. In 1949, the president's priority became ratification of the North Atlantic Treaty Organization (NATO). This shift in priorities was accompanied by a change in personnel in the State Department. At the end of 1948, General Marshall resigned as secretary of state for health reasons, and President Truman replaced him with Dean Acheson. Acheson supported the ITO ratification, but it was no longer a top priority. His attention was on NATO. President Truman submitted the Havana Charter to Congress on April 28, 1949,[16] where it languished for twelve months before the House began hearings on his recommendation of approval.

This NATO scheduling conflict might have provided an opportunity to draw attention to the strategic importance of the ITO, much as the Cold War had been used effectively to support the argument in Congress for the British Loan and the Marshall Plan. Indeed, on March 29, 1948, five days after returning from Havana, Clayton gave a speech in Detroit, declaring that America's world economic leadership would need to be backed by "overwhelming strength" against Russia. He cited the ITO as possibly "the greatest step in history toward order and justice in economic relations among members of the world community." He asserted that both the Marshall Plan and the ITO would be mighty contributions to world peace and prosperity.[17] Secretary Acheson made a similar argument, emphasizing "the interrelation of economics and politics" in a speech to the National Convention of the US Chamber of Commerce in Washington, DC, just days after Truman delivered the charter to Congress. "The obstruction of the Soviet Union, the aggressive conspiracy of the Communists of all countries, and the unexpectedly serious difficulties of reconstruction," he said, "prompted the United States to take additional measures." In that instance, he was referring to emergency aid to Greece and Turkey and the Marshall Plan, but he then used it as a segue to highlight the strategic importance of the ITO:

> The fabric of the world economy, of industry, finance, and commerce must be restored. But even that is not enough. We know that at its pre-war best, world production and world trade were not adequate to meet the basic needs of human society. We can be sure that the masses of people will no longer be satisfied with half a loaf. . . . An affirmative approach to the solution of world economic problems is an imperative need of our times. The United States Government has taken the lead in developing such an approach. . . . *The capstone of the economic structure we are seeking to erect is the charter of the International Trade Organization.* [emphasis supplied][18]

Even though Stalin had boycotted and been openly hostile to the Geneva and Havana conferences through his state-controlled media,[19] Acheson's argument never gained traction in soliciting support for ITO participation.

There was, in fact, a major new headwind trending against the ITO that was related to Cold War ideological struggles and the rise of socialist governments in the postwar era. This was the real and imagined conflict between free enterprise and socialistic planning that some opponents read into the charter. A special committee of the US Chamber of Commerce made an early judgment six weeks after the signing of the final act in Havana that "the present charter is not consistent with these principles [of free and competitive enterprise in world commerce] and the United States should withhold acceptance and seek renegotiation."[20] The board of directors of the NAM took a similar approach as they adopted a report that urged Congress to reject the Havana Charter, even as they observed that NAM had welcomed with high hopes the proposal to form an ITO. The report explained that the charter "makes the world safe for socialistic planning and makes it a very precarious place in which to function for privately conducted foreign trade; in particular it gives national economic planning the right-of-way over the requirements of an orderly world economy."[21]

The *Wall Street Journal* summed up the views of the "perfectionist" faction in an editorial published on August 9, 1948, which began by proclaiming that the purpose of the Havana Charter was "to create a world planning body, the International Trade Organization." The following are representative excerpts from the piece:

> Every declaration of the charter is subject to an exception, that there are exceptions to the exceptions and the grand climax is at the end where there appears a blanket exception which seems to say that no part of the charter is to be taken seriously anyway. All of this grows from an attempt, so it seems to us, to reconcile the irreconcilable, to cover in one place two things which are mutually antagonistic. The two things are unrestricted trade and something which is called "full employment." . . .
>
> "[F]ull employment" has come to have a special meaning. That special meaning is that not only shall there be jobs available in producing and exchanging things but that there shall be jobs available whether or not they contribute or are necessary to production and exchange; furthermore, the jobs are to be available under conditions of hours and wages that the product of the jobs may not be able to support. . . . "Full employment" . . . is an end in itself, to be attained regardless of the distortions practiced to attain it. . . .
>
> Then to protect this internal set-up, the managed economy must make rules against outside interference and these take the form of

quotas, tariffs, embargoes and a host of other devices all of which are the antithesis of unrestricted trade.

The framers of the International Trade Charter tried to compromise where no grounds for compromise existed. The result is a document which defies common understanding and common sense.[22]

If the *Journal* editorial seems hyperbolic, its overstatements pale in comparison to another critic's publication that makes the Havana Charter sound like the *Communist Manifesto*. In March 1949, Philip Cortney, a manufacturer active in international business, published a book entitled *The Economic Munich*, attacking the charter as a threat to "human freedom." Cortney, an internationalist, wrote that he "utterly" disliked finding himself among "isolationists, nationalists, high tariff minded people, with whom [he had] nothing in common" other than fighting the ITO Charter, but he explained that he was publishing this book "in defense of liberty." He wrote that the ideas and doctrines underlying many provisions of the charter were "the aftermath of Keynes' teachings, and, perhaps even more so, of its distortions by zealots, ignorants, clever politicians or 'do gooders.'" Ratifying this document would be giving an official endorsement to these "economic fallacies and theories," which, he said, supported "policies conducive to the destruction of our way of life" and "may prove to be the grave-diggers of our human liberties." Most of the book's chapters were reprints of articles Cortney had written in previous years. They ranged from his opinions about the cause of the Great Depression, to Lord Keynes's theories (which Cortney believed Keynes would have revised to conform to Cortney's views had he only lived longer), and the like. He gave very little attention to any provision in the charter other than two articles pertaining to the "full employment" provisions, about which he wrote: "The Charter implicitly takes sides in the fight between economic schools of thinking, between socialism and the individual competitive system, and proposes measures which will serve to spread economic fallacies and wrong policies, and, as a by-product, socialism or communism."[23]

The *New York Times*, which had strongly endorsed the Havana Charter on two separate occasions in recent months and printed a prompt letter to the editor from Cortney in rebuttal to the first endorsement, published a review by Will Clayton of *The Economic Munich* on March 20, 1949. In the review, Clayton wrote that he agreed with some of the author's economic views, but (like another reviewer's opinion in the *Washington Post*) he found Cortney's specific criticism of the "full employment" provision unclear and obscure. "The few pages devoted to the Charter present no description or analysis of any of its major provisions," Clayton argued, adding, "There are some 400 paragraphs in the Havana Charter, but Mr. Cortney confines his attention to two." Additionally, Clayton's review explained why some of Cortney's suggestions concerning the ITO Charter were politically unrealistic at best. Nevertheless, Cortney continued to be an outspoken influence against the charter in the public domain.[24]

As previously noted, Clayton was a highly successful, self-made businessman, who, judging by his record, knew more than most about the American free enterprise system. Clair Wilcox, the Joseph Wharton Professor of Political Economy at Swarthmore College, was also no slouch on the operation and benefits of the free market. They had been careful to ensure that the ITO employment provisions were consistent with existing US law and must have been surprised to learn from this criticism that the result of their negotiating efforts for the past two years was threatening the economic order of Western civilization. As might be expected, however, Clayton and Wilcox saw things from quite a different perspective. In fact, less than three months after the Havana conference concluded, Clayton gave a speech to the Economic Institute of the US Chamber in Washington, DC, warning that without the ITO, the United States "could not long remain an island of free enterprise in a sea of state-controlled international trade." He argued that there was a choice of two roads to take. One, under the ITO Charter, "leads in the direction of free enterprise and the preservation of democratic principles. The other road leads in the direction of Socialism and state trading."[25] Obviously, there was a tendency to exaggerate the danger of being drawn down the path to socialism on both sides of the argument.

Many of the business organizations favoring freer trade had endorsed the ITO concept but now urged rejection of the Havana Charter. The USCC, NAM, NFTC,[26] and others in the perfectionist faction were disappointed in the concessions made by the American delegation. Their views were reflected in brutal editorials denouncing the delegation's effort in the conservative business media. A *Fortune* magazine editorial called the charter "worthless," "all exceptions," and "one of the most hypocritical state documents of modern times." It criticized the three main purposes for which the charter granted exceptions permitting member nations to impose trade barriers that were otherwise proscribed by the rules: (1) to safeguard balance-of-payments, (2) to promote "full employment," and (3) to foster reconstruction and economic development. The editorial does not mention the limitations on the use of these exceptions. It only notes that the third "loophole" would be available to any country but the United States (because it had not suffered war destruction and was already developed). The piece concludes by conceding that the State Department "is in love with a great idea: that it is America's job to defend the notion of universality in trade." But this is not realistic, according to *Fortune*; "we should get control of our own protectionist groups and . . . make a bold *unilateral* offer, an offer of freer trade with those countries willing to accept our liberal-capitalist terms and negotiate away *all* forms of trade controls."[27]

In a later issue of *Fortune*, Michael A. Heilperin (an economist and adviser to the International Chamber of Commerce on ITO issues who attended both the Geneva and Havana conferences) offered an answer to the title of his article, "How the U.S. Lost the ITO Conferences." Heilperin acknowledged that the American negotiators were impeded by the number of exceptions and escape clauses with which they had been saddled in Washington. These were politically non-negotiable issues relating to agriculture, shipping, politically sensitive high-tariff items, and the US preferences for Cuba and the Philippines. These carve-outs made it hard for the negotiators to maintain the purity of their position when demanding concessions from others. But, according to Heilperin,

> by and by our bargaining position was destroyed by the excessive eagerness of our negotiators to reach a wide agreement on a charter and their insufficient stubbornness when it came to defending basic principles. In Geneva and in Havana the generally accepted view was that the U.S. delegates were so anxious to get a charter that they would, in the end, accept all those changes in that document that would prove indispensable for obtaining its general acceptance.[28]

As business opposition grew with the informal alliance of protectionists and perfectionists, Clayton began putting together his own business lobby to seek congressional approval. The National Council of American Importers had already become the first national foreign trade group to endorse the charter in December. Even though the importers recognized that there were "imperfections" in the charter, the council felt the world had more to gain than lose by accepting it, and they urged Congress to approve it as soon as possible. The council leader regarded the chances of acceptance by the new Congress to be "pretty good" following Truman's reelection, and he characterized the charges that the ITO would lead to a "super-state" as "bunk."[29]

The word against the charter, however, was growing in the business community, and Clayton was getting a lot of rejections in his pleas for additional support. Ultimately, he was able to enlist William L. Batt, a Philadelphia industrialist, to lead the lobbying effort. Clayton had been associated with Batt while they both worked on war production and procurement issues as "dollar a year men" in the early 1940s. During the three months before the president presented the charter to Congress, Clayton and Batt worked long hours (and at their own considerable expense) building a committee of 124 members, including a broad range of business, banking, industry, civic, and labor leaders, along with educators and publishers from fifty-three cities and twenty-eight states. Batt, as chairman, and Clayton, as vice chairman, announced the formation of the Committee for the International Trade Organization on May 2, with special emphasis on combating the public impression that "business as a whole" was opposed to the charter. "In and around New York," Batt said, "of those expressing an opinion, most businessmen are against it. When you get out into the country, it has enormously more support," particularly from labor and agriculture. He cited the endorsements of the CIO and the Farm Bureau Federation as examples.[30]

The CIO endorsement, announced on February 27 in its official publication, *Economic Outlook*, also endorsed the European Recovery Program embodied in the Marshall Plan and an expanded Reciprocal Trade Agreements program. *Outlook* called these three steps "the tripod of U.S. economic policy." An article in the *Christian Science Monitor* depicted this CIO publication as one of two "propaganda broadsides" exchanged in a publicity campaign being waged by labor and business interests over participation in the ITO—the business broadside being Philip Cortney's *The Economic Munich*. In addition to some of Cortney's comments mentioned above, the article repeats some of Cortney's anti-labor opinions. For instance, it points out Cortney's placement of blame on the British Labour government for flaws in the charter, and his argument for the necessity of halting wage increases.

The *Monitor* quoted the CIO report's depiction of charter opponents, who were complaining about the charter's alleged invasion of free competitive enterprise, as "huge corporations, which were associated with German cartels before the war, and which are now under indictment for violations of the Sherman Antitrust Act." The CIO reported that the concentration of economic power was becoming more intense, with fewer firms controlling more of the production of American industrial products. The *Outlook* said that no fewer than 2.5 million nonagricultural American jobs were "directly dependent" on US export trade in 1947, a threefold increase from 1939. American labor also benefited from imports, it said, and limiting imports of many raw materials would result in reduced industrial production, unemployment, and higher prices. The CIO study concluded that reducing tariffs would not result in flooding the United States with cheap foreign goods, "since our competitive strength is due to the efficiency of American labor and industry in relation to abundant natural resources and a larger domestic market."[31]

Another important endorsement came in mid-June when the Committee for Economic Development (CED) urged ratification of all of the provisions of the charter but the two investment articles. The committee charged that these provisions had a "blank check" vagueness that obligated the United States to aid "backward areas" financially and otherwise, without enforceable protection against arbitrary and discriminatory actions by the host foreign governments. The CED was an independent organization of business leaders and educators created to study national economic policy and make policy recommendations. The men leading the group were heads of some of the most prominent companies in the United States, such as Continental Inc. and the General Electric Company, but their appraisal was less than effusive. They called it a "multitude of compromises" and said that even without the investment articles, the charter remained imperfect. Still, they acknowledged that "the committee feels it is a better document than none at all."[32]

In addition to the work of organizing the pro-charter lobby, much effort went into refuting the perfectionists' criticism. Will Clayton was constantly debating the criticism in person and in letters. In Clayton's papers at the Truman Library, there are many boxes of Clayton's correspondence seeking members for the Batt Committee. Many were honored to accept, but quite a few declined for ideological reasons. Mario Giannini, president of the Bank of America, for example, declined, writing that he thought the charter should be revised to give "broader recognition to the part that free enterprise can play," that "the 'world-planning' emphasis should be altered," and he objected to having a chapter on employment in a charter laying down rules for international trade. The president of the Houston Oil Company of Texas also declined with a similar complaint, saying that "an organization whose signatory members were dominated by socialist-dominated or other autocratic governments" could not be expected to "give but slender support to our free enterprise system."[33]

Most of the heavy lifting in promoting the charter was handled by Clair Wilcox. In January 1949, Wilcox published his book, *A Charter for World Trade*, explaining and defending each of the charter's provisions and giving the background from which they had evolved. In a short, but highly favorable, review in the *Washington Post*, the reviewer wrote that "Dr. Wilcox sometimes sees the new charter as the be-all and end-all of world recovery. But he is frank enough to say that some of its provisions are compromises which are far from ideal, and makes a powerful case for the charter as a long-range instrument for prosperity and peace." The reviewer went on to predict that the book would be the authoritative source material for the important congressional debate expected "in a few weeks."[34]

The reviewer's estimate as to when the congressional debate would begin turned out to be exceedingly optimistic, and the public debate continued for more than a year leading up to congressional hearings. In one article, Wilcox addressed a number of the criticisms directed at the charter. He conceded that some of the charter's provisions were "weaker than they should be, and its exceptions are open to abuse." Of the six most important exceptions, however, he said three were insisted upon by the United States and three were included to meet the needs of countries with balance-of-payments difficulties and countries in the process of economic development. The exceptions adopted at the insistence of the US negotiators were (1) the "escape clause" permitting suspension of tariff concessions when an import surge threatens injury to domestic producers, (2) import quotas on agricultural products and agricultural export subsidies, and (3) national security exceptions. The other three important exceptions related to (1) the use of import quotas by countries threatened with a serious loss of monetary reserves, (2) the use of quotas and preferences necessary to establish new industries in less developed countries, and (3) the creation of customs unions, such as the one planned to create a European common market. Unlike the exceptions required by the United States, the other exceptions, according to Wilcox, were subject to numerous preconditions and were more limited in scope and in duration. If anything, Wilcox implied, the charter was more one-sided in favor of the United States.[35]

SENATE DEBATE ON EXTENDING THE TRADE PROGRAM

The end of summer approached without any congressional activity on the ITO and with no floor action in the Senate on extending the Trade Agreements Act, which had officially expired on June 12. State Department trade policy officials were getting nervous about ongoing trade negotiations. The second round of GATT tariff negotiations following Geneva had already commenced several months before in Annecy, France, and the US negotiators, while continuing to hammer out new tariff agreements, could not be sure whether they would be able to honor them. Moreover, a new currency crisis forced the United Kingdom to devalue the pound sterling by 30 percent and to seek alternatives involving bilateral barter arrangements for commodity transactions (including a proposed grain deal with the Soviet Union) in the absence of applicable rules under the ITO. The State Department was in a quandary as to whether to attempt to invoke the unratified ITO rules and administrative procedure to deal with the crisis. They feared that if they invoked the ITO rules and procedures to respond, they would merely give ammunition to congressional critics who had accused them of trying to put the charter into effect without congressional approval.[36] Finally, on September 7, Senator Walter F. George (D-GA), chairman of the Senate Finance Committee, was able to get the extension bill to the Senate floor, citing both the British currency crisis and the Annecy GATT negotiations, which now included thirty-three countries, up from the original twenty-three Contracting Parties of the GATT.

Senator George emphasized the urgency of continuing the program when he observed, "Every day that passes without passage of this bill adds credence to the fears of foreign countries that we preach world cooperation, but do not intend to make it real in terms of concrete performance." After reviewing the success of the program over the previous fifteen years, he declared that never during this time had the "country been swamped by imports." Anticipating that a peril point amendment would be offered again, he added, "I believe the peril-point report is totally unnecessary, that the computation it calls for cannot be done with scientific accuracy, and that the requirement that it be done is heavily slanted toward the protec-tionist, and only the protectionist, aspect of the trade agreement program." George went further to say that the amendment would defeat the main pur-pose of the act and would be "a reactionary move which will only further aggravate the very serious international economic and political problems which confront us in the months ahead."[37]

Much of the six-day debate on the bill concerned the floor amendment that Senator Millikin had, unsurprisingly, offered to restore the peril point provision to keep European imports from destroying "the American pay-roll." In view of this rationale, Senate Majority Leader Scott W. Lucas (D-IL) raised the question of why is it "that every great labor organization, which undoubtedly has the laboring man as much at heart as does the Senator from Colorado, has definitely gone on record approving the reciprocal trade program?" Millikin mentioned a few unions that had endorsed his amendment but was unable to satisfy Lucas concerning the bulk of organ-ized labor, represented by the American Federation of Labor (AFL) and the CIO, whose leadership, Lucas noted, had testified before the Ways and Means Committee in support of the House bill now before the Senate.[38] Indeed, the Ways and Means Committee Report recorded that, in addi-tion to the business organizations supporting the extension (including the USCC and the NFTC), both the AFL and CIO favored renewal. The CIO, in the following testimony, had specifically addressed the charge that lower tariffs would produce a flood of goods produced in unfair competition with American labor:

> The number of American workers affected by reduced tariffs is very limited, whereas, all workers as consumers are injured by high tariffs. . . . Wages of American workers in industries which are typically high protected industries are lower than the wages of the industries with little or no tariff protection. . . . A sharp reduc-tion in American foreign trade would reverberate throughout the whole domestic economy and would make it impossible to main-tain full employment in this country.[39]

Senator George introduced into the record correspondence from numerous progressive, religious, and labor organizations that had specifically opposed the peril point amendment, including Americans for Democratic Action, the League of Women Voters of the United States, Young Women's

Christian Organization, National Council of Jewish Women, National Farmers' Union, National Women's Trade Union League, Textile Workers Union of America (CIO), and United Textile Workers (AFL).[40]

The long debate on the Millikin amendment prompted harsh partisan rhetoric. Even Senator Vandenberg's support of the amendment was significantly stronger and more partisan than it had been in 1948. Besides Senator Millikin, however, the most militant foe of extending the trade program was Senator Robert Taft, who called it "a complete abandonment of the legislative power of Congress with relation to the levying of tariffs." He claimed that he had no desire to return to congressional tariff making, which had developed the "log-rolling" process of trading votes for higher tariffs between different parts of the country. He favored giving authority to the Tariff Commission to both fix the rates and lower them when they found that "actual reductions offered by other countries [would] substantially reduce the tariffs on American goods into those countries." He opposed the current program in the present act because it "[would give] the President arbitrary power to destroy American industry." Taft argued that the State Department was so "anxious to please certain nations and . . . to get them in a state of mind in which they [would] cooperate with us in other respects" that it appeared "to have no hesitation in sacrificing American industries." Even if the peril point amendment were to pass, Taft said he was inclined to vote against the bill as he had done in the past. The amendment was ultimately defeated by a vote of 43 to 38.[41]

During the course of this debate in the Senate, there were several offhand comments about the pending status of congressional approval of the ITO. Interestingly, at one point, Senator George advised that he thought the ITO matter had been "submitted to the Senate as a treaty sometime in April or May." Senator Millikin then interjected that he had understood that it was *not* submitted as a treaty and demanded an accurate answer, pointing out that it was "a rather important fact in connection with the whole business." If it had been submitted as a treaty, ratification would require a two-thirds favorable vote in the Senate. After seeking advice from a senior State Department official, Senator George confirmed that the ITO Charter had been submitted for approval by joint resolution of both Houses and not as a treaty.

George further mentioned that he had been informed that the administration "hoped the ITO agreement might also be considered this session." He added, however, that he was not committed for or against the ITO

Charter as a whole. George said he thought that he "would not support" the investment provisions and there might also be other parts he would oppose. Later in the debate, Senator Millikin chastised the Truman administration for trying to sell the ITO "as the final solution of all the difficulties of world trade" while simultaneously "[keeping] it buried" for over a year before submitting it to Congress at a time when the Foreign Affairs Committee was swamped and could not get to it. Millikin drew the conclusion "that there has been a great loss of confidence in what will happen to ITO when it does get before the Congress."[42]

As President Truman signed the Trade Agreements Extension Act into law on September 26, he urged prompt action by Congress to approve the ITO Charter to provide "the firmest assurance to the world that the United States recognizes its position of world economic leadership, and is prepared to do its share in reestablishing world economic relations on a sound competitive basis for the mutual well-being of all peoples."[43]

ITO HEARINGS

It would be another seven months, however, before any formal action began in Congress on the consideration of the ITO Charter. In the months leading up to the hearings, the public debate continued to rage as opposition hardened from domestic industries fearing increased competition. Others continued to attack the charter as "socialistic" and its supporters as "'world planners' of either starry-eyed or sinister variety."[44] The State Department supporters were fighting an uphill battle to overcome an increasingly relentless ideological assault. During this time, Winthrop Brown (director of the Office of International Trade Policy) gave a speech entitled "Why Private Business Should Support the ITO" before the Synthetic Organic Chemical Manufacturers Association (whose spokesman was the persistent charter opponent Elvin Killheffer). Brown's speech began with a simple answer:

> You should support it because you are believers in the private-enterprise system and in the United States. You have a great stake in the private-enterprise system and in the prosperity of the United States. . . . For the ITO Charter is essentially a limitation upon the power of governments to use these restrictive and controlling devices. . . . This is important, and I want to repeat it. The Charter

gives no new powers to governments to interfere with business. It limits the powers which governments now have and which they are using to interfere with business.[45]

Will Clayton also weighed in, firing off a letter from Houston to the editor of the *Washington Post* in response to a *Post* editorial that urged a deferral of the decision on the ITO. Given that the charter contained so many "so-called" transitional and permanent exemptions, the editors wrote that it was "premature to press for action on a plan that is based on future hopes rather than immediate accomplishment." The case for deferral was also strengthened, the editors said, by the "sharp differences of opinion among business groups, trade and civic organizations." Clayton responded, "May I remind you that the charter was completed two years ago; that it took more than three years and several international conferences to reach agreement on it." After all this labor and waiting, he wrote, further postponement would likely lead the fifty-odd other countries involved to conclude that there would be no ITO. Clayton admitted that the charter included "certain exemptions and escapes but far from giving any nation any rights it does not already have, it has secured agreement on many vital principles of multilateral trade." As to the surprising suggestion that action should be postponed because there were conflicting views about the ITO, he asked, "Have there not always been conflicting views in the United States on international trade?" He suggested that the Reciprocal Trade Agreements Act of 1934 never would have been passed, or renewed, "if its consideration by the Congress had been deferred until opinion about it had ceased to be divided."[46]

On April 19, 1950, almost one year after the president submitted the ITO Charter to Congress, the House Committee on Foreign Affairs began hearings lasting fifteen days on House Joint Resolution 236. This resolution, if adopted, would authorize participation by the United States in the ITO. After more than two years of public discourse over the issues presented by the charter, there was not much new ground to be covered in the approximately 800 pages of testimony, written statements, tables, and charts compiled by the committee. By far, most of the business, civic, and labor groups represented at the hearings supported US participation in the ITO, even though most supporters acknowledged imperfections in the charter. Still, the unique coalition of traditional protectionists and influential perfectionists represented among the opponents was formidable.

The Truman administration, led by Secretary of State Dean Acheson, performed ably in making the case that approval was vital to maintaining US leadership in the world economy, enhancing US interests in international trade, and preserving the free enterprise system at the beginning of the Cold War. But Truman's team lacked the popular influence on Capitol Hill that had been carried by Cordell Hull in promoting trade initiatives under FDR. Indeed, at the time of these hearings, Acheson had become a controversial target for Republican anti-communist attacks. For instance, he was blamed for "losing China" following the communist civil war victory in 1949. The charges by Senator Joseph R. McCarthy (R-WI) and others that communists were being harbored in the State Department led to numerous calls for Acheson's dismissal as a "bad security risk." Senator Millikin even accused Acheson of violating the bipartisan foreign policy principle by not consulting Republican senators before asking Congress for action on the ITO Charter. Millikin promised strenuous resistance to the "highly controversial" charter in the Senate.[47]

Another factor that may have weakened the effectiveness of the administration's presentation was the absence of Will Clayton. The former undersecretary, who had been instrumental in initiating and negotiating the charter, enjoyed considerable popularity and respect on Capitol Hill. He was a particularly effective communicator in presenting complex and controversial testimony. Indeed, Clayton's exhausting pursuit of support for the charter came at a personal price that likely prevented his participation in the hearings. After promising his wife a life of retirement, his persistent involvement with the charter finally contributed to her filing for divorce in April 1949. The divorce was granted the next month, but the status did not last long. The couple remarried in August, and Will, thereafter, seldom left her side.[48]

One valuable advantage that the ITO proponents had on their side was the effective support provided by two junior GOP members on the committee—Congressmen James G. Fulton of Pennsylvania and Jacob K. Javits of New York. Both Fulton and Javits had attended the GATT negotiations in Geneva and served as members of the US delegation in Havana. They had participated in the conference sessions, working committees, and delegation meetings. In October 1948, they submitted a 120-page report on the conference to the Foreign Affairs Committee, including a thorough appraisal of the charter and its provisions. The report concluded with a strong endorsement of the efforts of the US negotiators in Havana, who were, according to the report, "determined to bring about a charter that would conduce to the preservation and the strengthening of private enterprise in the United States." This was not an easy task, according to Fulton and Javits, who observed that the US delegates were "not entirely isolated" in this approach at Havana, but their stance "about private enterprise often put [the United States] in the minority." The report offered the following basis for its favorable appraisal of the charter:

> The requirement is not for a charter that will clear up all the problems and erase all the differences but for a charter that will provide a framework for easing the problems that arise from the differences. A charter that eliminates all the difficulties is manifestly impossible. This Nation must appraise the charter with a realistic recognition that it necessarily represents a formula for bringing divergent interests and viewpoints together—not a formula for dictating to countries or intervening in their domestic institutions. . . . The crux is not how this proposed charter compares to the perfect formula but how it compares to the situation that will obtain if the charter does not go into effect.[49]

The efforts of Fulton and Javits did not end with their report. Throughout the fifteen days of hearings, they doggedly pursued the anti-ITO witnesses, displaying their years of legal experience with skillful cross-examinations. Some of the Democrats on the committee may have been as supportive of the charter as Fulton and Javits, but none showed their level of passion or persistence. Indeed, Fulton and Javits seemed to be dividing their time in a tag-team effort, exhaustively covering all the opposing witnesses while carrying out their other respective congressional responsibilities. Their independence from the position taken by other Republicans on the committee was striking and presaged both of their future careers in the liberal, progressive wing of the GOP. "We believe that the ITO charter merits a place above party consideration," they explained. "It is not perfect, but is probably the best obtainable under existing world conditions, and this country's interests will be better served by this trade charter than by none at all."[50]

As previously noted, the opposition included traditional protectionists, who appeared to be emerging from a twenty-year coma induced by the trauma of fallout from Smoot-Hawley and tranquilized by the lack of import competition during the Depression and World War II. The protectionist groups testifying at the hearings included the American Tariff League, the Wage Earners' Protective League, and a new group called the National Labor-Management Council on Foreign Trade Policy, which represented unions and management from about a dozen industries concerned with protecting their markets from foreign producers. Several other import-sensitive industries weighed in independently, such as the Organic Chemical Manufacturers Association, represented by Elvin H. Killheffer, whose opposition derived from protectionist interests but often employed perfectionist rhetoric. The arguments against the ITO presented by the protectionists at the hearings did not differ markedly from those made by their predecessors during the Gilded Age—that is, low wages in other countries are the main "comparative advantage" of foreign imports and allowing them to compete with unprotected domestic industries would simply lower the American standard of living. The ITO was not only unnecessary, one protectionist argued, but it was not "anything more than an expression of pious intentions."[51]

The second faction of opponents—the laissez-faire perfectionists wary of any governmental interference in the marketplace—were actually more threatening to the approval of the charter than their odd bedfellows in the opposition camp. The protectionists alone could not likely have succeeded in defeating the ITO at this point in history, following the widely discredited period of protectionist dominance crowned by the Smoot-Hawley debacle and its aftermath. But the perfectionists brought into the picture an entirely new dimension: Here was a group that had supported freer trade now joining the protectionists in opposing a move toward a more liberal trade regime. With both free-traders and protectionists opposed, doubts were being raised as to where the charter's imperfections might lead. Was it really taking the United States down a path to socialism? At the very least, the group muddied the water so that there was no clear answer going forward. Hull and his disciples at State who had labored in the trenches for over fifteen years to get to this point must have been pulling their hair out with this unexpected development.

In his testimony at the hearings, perfectionist Earl O. Shreve, former president of the USCC, explained that the Chamber's "first and most obvious objection" was that the charter "attempts to solve too many economic problems in too great detail." The Chamber supported the original proposals released in December 1945 when the British Loan was announced. But as it went through the various conferences, each succeeding draft was expanded and, in their view, got worse: "more far-reaching, more complex, and more unwieldy." The main criticisms of the charter presented by the Chamber's interdepartmental committee were these:

1. The exceptions and escapes were so numerous as to subordinate and obscure the general objectives of nondiscriminatory multilateral trade.
2. The charter failed to eliminate or mitigate the discriminatory system of preferential tariffs and even created an opportunity to establish new preferences.
3. There was "grave danger in concessions provided in the charter to the philosophy of state planning, control, and trading."
4. Foreign investment provisions of the charter failed to provide positive incentive to a flow of American capital to less developed nations.
5. The United States was placed at a disadvantage in having only one vote, particularly in light of the ambiguity in the drafting of the provisions, which would be subject to further interpretation by the ITO in which the United States would likely be outvoted.

The central complaint of the USCC, as echoed in the objections of most of the perfectionists, was the charter's "excessive acceptance of economic planning." Shreve stated that it was impossible to escape the conclusion that the underlying philosophy of many of the charter's provisions was the assumption of "various nations" that it was "their right and duty to intervene in the competitive trading mechanisms." The United States was "the last great champion of the free enterprise system," he said, adding, "We should defend and advance our ideals rather than compromise them." He mentioned several articles in the charter under the chapters affecting employment, economic development, and the use of quantitative restrictions that he said could not be carried out without surrendering principles of free enterprise. He urged renegotiating the charter with a restriction on the number of subjects covered in order to eliminate "world planning and controlling attempts to solve every conceivable problem." He specifically questioned "whether there is a real need for . . . dealing with economic development and reconstruction." During the questioning period of his testimony, Shreve proposed that the renegotiation should be carried out by the International Chamber of Commerce wherein the delegates would all be businessmen who, he implied, would be more "competent" to understand "the everyday actuality of business . . . to reach conclusions that are going to work from a commercial point of view."[52]

In what appeared to have been a team production, the representatives of the other perfectionist opponents took nearly an identical ideological approach in their attacks. Lee H. Bristol, representing the National Association of Manufacturers, called the Havana Charter "dangerous," representing "a victory of state socialism over private enterprise and of economic nationalism over the principles of good international economic relations." He pointed to the employment provisions as laying down "the obligation upon each member to plan governmentally its economic life," and he observed that the Truman administration "was actually denied that right in 1945–46 when the much-debated pro-planning Murray bill [the Senate's Full Employment Act of 1945] was replaced by the Employment Act of 1946 in which planning powers of the Government [were] made quite minor." Bristol argued that the socialistic countries attached much importance to the employment provisions, "which the United States delegates should never have accepted."[53]

Gaylord C. Whipple, chairman of the International Trade Committee of the Illinois Manufacturers Association, was more specific about his objections to the charter's employment and labor provisions. In response to one question from Congressman Fulton, Whipple said, "I do not think we should tie up imports with any labor situations in any country. I do not think anybody should be permitted to tell us what to do with our production." Fulton asked him if he agreed with the provision in the Atlantic Charter in which Roosevelt and Churchill aspired "to bring about the fullest collaboration between all nations in the economic field, with the object of securing for all improved labor standards, economic advancement, and social security." Whipple responded, "I do not approve of including labor specifications in anything having to do with our contact with foreign nations."[54]

Testimony given by the chairman of the National Foreign Trade Council (NFTC), R. F. Loree, offered one of the most comprehensive statements on the charter, providing nearly all negative analysis, on practically every provision in the document. The NFTC opposition was a particular disappointment to the State Department idealists; this council, formed in 1914, was the oldest pro-trade association in the nation. Like the other perfectionist opponents, the NFTC complained about the exceptions granted to the nondiscriminatory trade rules and gave special attention to the employment provisions. According to Loree,

> The Havana Charter imposes an obligation on the United States to take action to achieve and maintain full employment not only within this country, but in all other member countries. . . . This obligation to cooperate in achieving full employment in all member countries might require the United States, during periods of decline in business activity, to participate in programs involving the manipulation of money and credit and heavy Government deficit spending, thus setting in motion dangerous inflationary forces in this country.

Repeating the common theme from this faction of opponents, the NFTC's formal statement predicted that these employment provisions would lead "inexorably" to transforming "the free-enterprise system of this country into a system of planned economy, with consequent initiative-destroying regimentation, reduction in productive output and standards of living, and threat to the free institutions and liberties of the American people."[55]

Naturally, there were numerous challenges to the line of opposition presented by both the protectionists and the perfectionists. The senior Democrats on the committee, including Chairman John Kee of West Virginia, let it be known through courteous questioning that they welcomed and were sympathetic to the testimony of the business groups but were unconvinced by what they perceived as threats raised by the charter. Kee was an ITO supporter but did not attend many of the hearings due to illness. The second-ranking Democrat on the Ways and Means Committee, Congressman Jere Cooper (D-TN), who had served as a US delegate and congressional adviser in Havana, was the final witness at the hearings and gave a ringing endorsement of the charter—an important signal from his influential committee.

The most persistent congressional combatants against the charter opponents, however, were the liberal Republican congressmen Fulton and Javits. They could always be counted on to provide supportive questions for proponents of the charter and stiff cross-examination of the opponents. During Lee Bristol's NAM testimony, Javits introduced into the record several independent studies refuting Bristol's conclusions and supporting acceptance of the charter, including the newly published study by the

Brookings Institution, written by William Adams Brown Jr. This 557-page book offered the most comprehensive and objective appraisal of the GATT and the ITO Charter published to date.[56]

Brown's book specifically addressed the criticisms emanating from what he termed "extreme interpretations of the Charter." These interpretations predicted that the ITO would, for example, direct the US government to interfere with private enterprise, interfere with US employment policy, and promote the creation of an international WPA (the New Deal's Works Project Administration that created public jobs for the unemployed). "None of these interpretations," Brown wrote, "is borne out by the text of the document. . . . [T]he Organization would have no power to coerce the United States into taking positive action of any sort." He specifically declared that there was no basis for fears that the employment provisions would allow international interference with US domestic policy, or that "anything in the charter would create an international bureaucracy imposing its will upon this country." Brown observed that the charter simply laid down a code of international conduct in which free enterprise and state trading countries could advance toward a multilateral, nondiscriminatory system of trade.[57]

Brown's views on the employment provisions were consistent with the official US government position, as reflected in Clair Wilcox's analysis of the charter and the statement presented to the Foreign Affairs Committee by Maurice J. Tobin, Truman's secretary of labor. Wilcox made sure that the language used in the charter matched the commitment stated in the Employment Act of 1946, to provide "useful employment opportunities for those able and willing to work." Wilcox declared, "The *Charter* itself contains no commitment to international action and confers no new powers on any international agency." Secretary Tobin wrote that the charter's employment provisions were

> fully in keeping with our own domestic policy of maintaining a high and productive level of employment as set forth in the Employment Act of 1946. . . . The Charter preserves our right to seek full employment with the minimum of Government intervention that we ourselves determine to be wise. . . . [W]e would not be agreeing to any planning that we ourselves do not find to be necessary. . . . We would remain free to devise our own policies and programs.[58]

One of the most effective witnesses testifying in support of the charter was Stanley H. Ruttenberg, the chief economist and director of education and research for the CIO. Ruttenberg described the CIO's support for the ITO as a necessary step in providing intergovernmental standards to promote the purposes of the United Nations in the economic sphere and establishing a sound foundation for peace and the enhancement of world prosperity. He asserted that the CIO and its international unions were actively fostering the principles and practices of democracy, free trade-unionism, and rising living standards through contacts with trade unions from other countries. In March, the CIO and the AFL had joined in the London formation of the International Confederation of Free Trade Unions (ICFTU), comprising unions representing roughly 50 million workers from fifty-three countries. One of the major points in the constitution of the ICFTU adopted in London states:

> We reject the narrow nationalism which leads to the protection of national markets by high tariff walls and other trade restrictions. The resulting limitation of the international exchange of goods and services, and the consequent inaccessibility of raw material sources, have made it impossible to realize a rational sharing out of work among nations. The solution lies in creating ever-broadening areas of international economic cooperation.

The CIO had its own representative as a member of the US delegation at Havana who had reported on the intense efforts to find "practicable, working solutions" to the countless problems arising in article after article in the charter. Considering the alternative of returning to the disastrous prewar trade practices, Ruttenberg said the CIO believed that the substance of the charter's "rules for the conduct of world trade is sound." The CIO supported negotiating tariff rates downward, reductions in preferences, and "the all-important escape clause."

On the employment chapter, Ruttenberg criticized the charter for failing to provide an obligation for ITO members to actually maintain full employment rather than simply to take measures "designed" to achieve full employment. Thus, organized labor criticized the employment chapter for not doing what the business critics blamed it for doing. The charter provisions on employment and labor standards, argued the CIO, provided even less of an obligation to maintain full employment than did the Employment Act of 1946. According to Ruttenberg,

> The vagueness of the provision in the charter will not satisfy American labor that it has won any victory in achieving its provisions; our battle to achieve full employment will still have to be carried on at home through measures that are more specifically spelled out. We are interested in results, not intentions.

Nevertheless, Ruttenberg said the CIO understood the importance of the provisions, "vague as they are," in allaying the internationally prevalent fears of another US depression. "The specter of the unemployment of the 1930s, and the fear that it may rise again," Ruttenberg said, was also on the mind of every trade-unionist in the United States. Many union members believed, based on this fear, that trade should be restricted, but the CIO believed the more promising approach was "to take all possible positive steps to expand trade, and to underpin that trade with the demand and purchasing power engendered by full employment" in the United States and other countries. "If we fail to attain the goals of full employment and production," he said, "the whole underpinning of our concept of increased foreign trade is jeopardized and thus our whole foreign policy."

The CIO also found fault with the charter's article on labor standards. The CIO's consistent position had been that a specific code of minimum fair labor standards be established to underpin the work of an international trade organization. The charter recognized "that unfair labor conditions, particularly in production for export, create difficulties in international trade, and, accordingly, each Member shall take whatever action may be appropriate and feasible to eliminate such conditions with its territory." The CIO felt that this recognition of principle was important, but that more could have been provided to enhance its implementation.

Ruttenberg noted that the charter's employment provisions were being attacked by the same interests that attacked the concept of the Employment Act. "The bogeys of State control and socialism have again been raised," he said, observing that in 1945 and 1946 "the fear was voiced that we were legislating ourselves into socialism." Now the critics charged that other nations were pushing the United States to socialism with this agreement. As each nation was free to choose its own method of reaching the full employment goal, however, Ruttenberg said, "this charge is at best frivolous."[59]

THE DENOUEMENT

When the hearings concluded on May 12, the number of witnesses who had spoken in favor of US participation in the ITO more than doubled the number of opposing witnesses. Although lacking the intense fervor and overriding influence of the Hull era, the administration had made an effective case in hailing the ITO as the "capstone of the economic structure"[60] of the postwar foreign policy focused on full recovery and prosperity in the free world—a structure that included the Bretton Woods agreements, the Marshall Plan, and the United Nations. The private-sector supporters from business, labor, and agriculture also established a firm rationale for accepting the charter, even while acknowledging its imperfections. In the House, there appeared to be significant support among the Democratic leadership for joining the ITO, and there was an important level of support among progressive Republicans like Fulton and Javits, who had taken a strong interest in the charter. Most of the rank-and-file members in both parties, however, knew very little about the charter and had no apparent interest in it. Nonetheless, media appraisals anticipated that the House would act on it in a matter of weeks.[61] On the Senate side, the prospects seemed worse. Senator Millikin was actively seeking an opportunity to attack the charter, and the Democratic chairmen on the Finance Committee, Walter George, and the Foreign Affairs Committee, Thomas T. Connally (D-TX), were, at best, unenthusiastic about taking it up.

Just six weeks after the ITO hearings concluded, an event occurred that changed everything. On the evening of June 24, 1950, as he was spending the weekend at home in Independence, Missouri, President Truman received notification that the North Korean People's Army had crossed the 38th parallel in a surprise attack against the Republic of Korea. Within days, the president committed US troops to defending the South Koreans under a UN Security Council resolution that passed at a time when the Soviets were boycotting the Security Council and thus could not veto the resolution. For the first three months, news from the war was devastating as the North Koreans overwhelmed the unprepared and outnumbered US and Republic of Korea (ROK) forces and occupied most of the Korean Peninsula. In mid-September, fortunes turned against the North Koreans, following the famous US counterattack involving a daring amphibious landing at Inchon and a successful counterinvasion north across the 38th parallel. Despite predictions by commanding General Douglas MacArthur that US troops would be home by Christmas, fortunes dramatically turned again in late November when an estimated 260,000 Chinese troops crossed the Yalu River to join the fight to defend North Korea.

Adding to the turmoil emanating from the war, and frustrating the pursuit of other policies on President Truman's agenda, the Democrats suffered a serious setback in the November midterm elections. Joe McCarthy, who was nearing his high-water mark with effective lies and distortions that attacked the State Department for harboring communists, blamed the "Korean death trap" on Acheson and Truman. McCarthy vowed, successfully, to defeat two of Truman's strongest allies on trade issues in the Senate, Majority Leader Scott Lucas and Millard Tydings of Maryland. One tactic he used effectively against Tydings was to circulate fake photographs of Tydings talking with Earl Browder, head of the Communist Party. The Democrats retained control of both Houses, but their margin in the House was cut from seventeen to twelve, and in the Senate from twelve to two. Sadly, Truman was also losing his reliable Republican friend and bipartisan foreign policy ally, Arthur Vandenberg, to lung cancer.[62]

Reports from trade interests following the Republican gains in the election predicted not only the "death" of the ITO Charter but also a curtailment of Marshall Plan aid. Noting that many "business executives have disliked the charter from its inception," the trade groups reportedly predicted "that chances of favorable consideration of the charter next year are practically nil." Conservative southern Democrats were expected to line up with Republicans against the measure. Most believed that the Trade Agreements Act would survive and be renewed in 1951. "A serious upset in world trade would result" if it was abandoned, according to the comments from the political trade community. An expansion of the program would be "tough," however, and it would not be surprising "if Republicans fought to have 'peril point' legislation incorporated in any extension."[63]

On November 20, 1950, Secretary Acheson sent a secret memorandum to the president urging an expedited decision on the legislative program for the next Congress regarding the trade agreements program and the ITO Charter. He reminded the president that the ITO hearings had been held in the House Foreign Affairs Committee but that no action would be taken on the matter in the present congressional session. Chairman Kee had written Truman earlier advising that the committee would have to postpone action on it until next year due to the press of emergency business. He emphasized the urgency of the decision with the observation that the US trade program had been both a symbol of American leadership in world economic improvement and "a test of the willingness of the United States to do its part in making that improvement possible." Trade expansion, he wrote, is indispensable in "our total effort to create strength and unity in the free world."

It was vital, the memorandum continued, to "face the legislative problems" confronting the administration in the next Congress in order to obtain two things essential to keeping the trade program going: (1) authority to continue the process of reducing trade barriers, and (2) authority to participate with other countries in establishing an international forum for the discussion and settlement of trade problems and disputes. The first would be provided by the renewal of the RTAA in some form. The second would have been provided by the Havana Charter; however, he advised:

> It is my judgment that the ITO is no longer a practical possibility. Reintroduction of the ITO Charter in the next Congress would mean either rejection of the Charter outright or an indefinite delay in getting it established. Either of these results would be damaging to our foreign policy.

Acheson said the need for a trade organization with a permanent secretariat was a matter of urgency. The principal trade agreement concluded by the United States to date was the GATT, which was only provisional and did not create an organization with an executive board. There were now thirty-three contracting parties participating in the GATT negotiations transpiring in Torquay, England, and about forty would be participating at their conclusion. Without an administrative structure, he wrote, "there is real danger that the General Agreement may become unworkable." He urged dropping the ITO and instead advocated obtaining the necessary legislative changes and authority to make the GATT an international organization, as a specialized agency of the United Nations. If this could be accomplished, all of the functions of the ITO could be implemented in one way or another. The purposes of the full employment chapter, according to Acheson, were now being carried out through the UN Economic and Social Council. The economic development and reconstruction chapter was being fulfilled through a new Truman program designed to drive industrialization in developing countries threatened by Soviet influence and intervention. The commercial policy chapter was already incorporated in the GATT. The restrictive business practice (anti-trust) provisions and the rules for commodity agreements could be added to the GATT later.

Acheson also predicted that the proposal to make the GATT a permanent organization to perform these functions would likely be "supported, with conviction," by those who support the Trade Agreements Act in order to strengthen the program. He also had reason to believe that some of the influential groups which had opposed the ITO, such as the National Foreign Trade Council and some members of Congress, would support an expansion of the GATT if the ITO were to be withdrawn. Nevertheless, he anticipated "a major battle in Congress" on the renewal of the RTAA. In order "to float the program over the shoals" of protectionist opposition unimpaired, the proposal "must be presented as necessary to the achievement . . . of strengthening the free world through an expanding world economy."[64]

President Truman read the memorandum and sent Acheson word to raise the matter at the cabinet meeting scheduled for the next day. When Acheson brought it up at the meeting, he explained that he was taking this method of getting a cabinet-level discussion rather than initiating a lower-level interdepartmental clearance process to reduce the possibility of public exposure at this point. After some discussion, the president asked for an expression of views from all members. All of the cabinet present concurred with Acheson's recommendations. Confidential notices of the president's decision went out immediately to the US delegation in Torquay and, on December 4, to thirty-eight US diplomatic posts. It was officially announced on December 6 that while the proposed ITO Charter "should not be resubmitted to Congress, Congress should be asked to consider legislation which will make American participation in the General Agreement more effective." The official explanation for the decision was this: "The many serious problems now facing our Congress and the legislatures of other countries require that we concentrate on the trade programs that are most urgently needed and will most quickly produce concrete results." The administration would ask Congress to strengthen the GATT by providing for administration machinery, including a small permanent staff, to approve legislation to simplify customs procedure to comply with the GATT, and to extend the RTAA scheduled to expire in six months.[65]

A PROVISIONAL NEW ECONOMIC ORDER

Acheson's idea of elevating the GATT into an international organization with an administrative secretariat approved by Congress got no traction. The following June, Congress passed the Trade Agreement Extension Act of 1951 with a Senate amendment expressly clarifying that the act's extension "is not to be construed as approval or disapproval by Congress of the General Agreement on Tariff[s] and Trade."[66] The GATT remained effectively in an unbaptized, nebulous status as an executive agreement among "Contracting Parties" (thirty-nine nations in 1951), whose collective actions and decisions were not self-executing under US law. In other words, any trade barriers eliminated in GATT negotiations had to be either preapproved by Congress under, for example, the RTAA or ratified later through implementing legislation. This requirement would also have applied to ITO decisions, but the ITO Charter was more comprehensive and included provisions for an administrative staff. Since the GATT was only intended to be used on a provisional basis until the ITO was ratified, it suffered from a number of functional defects that would need to be addressed over time.

Despite these defects, the GATT's evolutionary adaptations over the next five decades, before it was replaced by the World Trade Organization (WTO) in 1995, proved to be more than adequate to establish a liberal multilateral trade regime in a world accustomed to economic warfare and chaos. In the early days, Eric Wyndham White, a British economist who served as the innovative first executive secretary (later first director-general) of the GATT, used the staff of the Interim Commission for the International Trade Organization for administrative support. This Interim Commission had been formed soon after the final act in Havana to make organizing arrangements for the ITO. Over the next few years, White created a more formal administrative structure and a dispute settlement system. In fulfilling its primary function, the GATT, between 1947 and 1994, orchestrated eight rounds of multilateral trade negotiations to make huge reductions in tariffs and nontariff trade barriers. The last of these, the Uruguay Round, created the WTO, a full-fledged international organization with administrative structure and a sophisticated dispute settlement body. The WTO agreement includes the entire 1947 GATT text, which was based fundamentally upon principles espoused by Adam Smith and modeled after the reciprocal trade agreements of Cordell Hull.

15

Labor's Love Is Lost

The Congress must move quickly and decisively to
slow the massive flood of imports into the U.S. market
which are sweeping away jobs and industries in
wholesale lots. . . . [T]he concept of "free trade versus
protectionism" which dominated the thinking and
actions of the thirties and forties is badly out of phase
with the vastly changed world of the seventies. . . .
[T]he game is being rigged in favor of the overseas
producer and the multinational corporations.[1]
—I. W. Abel, President,
United Steelworkers of America,
Chairman, AFL-CIO Economic Policy Committee
May 17, 1973

Lessons can be drawn from the political struggles surrounding the creation
of the liberal trading system that are helpful in addressing current anxieties
over trade and broader anti-globalization tensions. Before drawing conclusions, however, it is important to review the evolutionary political movements of the two major combatants in the battle over trade policy—business
and labor—in the aftermath of the abandonment of the International Trade
Organization.

The stillbirth of the Havana Charter and the ITO has been attributed to
several different maladies. Most prominent among these are (1) the conflicting priorities presented by the Cold War, (2) the sharp move to the political

right in the US Congress as the influence of the successors of Cordell Hull and Will Clayton waned, and (3) the objections of US business groups to the concessions in the charter accepted by US negotiators.[2]

The increasing gravity and corresponding impact of the Cold War was certainly a major impediment to the approval of the ITO, if not the primary reason it failed. The preeminence of this threat had not fully emerged when the Bretton Woods institutions and the United Nations were created in 1944 and 1945. But over the next three years the territorial expansion of Soviet domination began to overwhelm the congressional agenda and affected both the negotiations and the approval process for the ITO Charter. Had the charter been ready for congressional review in 1945, or even 1946, the political climate would have been much more favorable for its approval as the vital third leg—"the capstone of the economic structure"—of postwar institutions. The efforts by Dean Acheson, Will Clayton, and others in the administration to emphasize the importance of stability of trade relations under the ITO in promoting peace through economic strength in the free world were largely ignored.

By the time of the final act in Havana in March 1948, the priorities of the Truman administration and the Acheson State Department (which was simultaneously fending off the attacks of McCarthyism) had shifted markedly to building a collective national security infrastructure founded upon the Marshall Plan and NATO to contain Soviet expansion. During the first GATT negotiations in the summer of 1947, the president signed legislation unifying the nation's armed services under the new Department of Defense and creating both the Central Intelligence Agency and the National Security Council. In June 1950, just after the conclusion of the much-delayed congressional hearings on the charter, this security priority exploded with deadly force on the Korean Peninsula as the Cold War suddenly turned hot. By the end of the year, following the intervention of the Chinese People's Voluntary Army, which forced the long retreat of US and Republic of Korea forces, President Truman simply withdrew the Havana Charter from consideration by Congress.

The resurgence of conservative politics and economic nationalism in the post-Roosevelt era was also a contributing factor leading to the demise of the ITO. The strength of this political shift was significantly reflected in the strong Republican gains in the 1946 and 1950 midterm elections but also in the rising influence of southern Democrats. These southerners, many of whom had never supported FDR's New Deal policies, began moving away from their traditional support for liberal trade policies after Cordell Hull retired. Protectionism appeared to be making a political comeback after having been dethroned for two decades by the excesses of Smoot-Hawley and the successful efforts of Roosevelt and Hull to liberalize trade. The renewal of the Trade Agreement Act in 1951 was indicative of the state of play in trade politics in the final segment of Truman's presidency. Even in a protectionist revival, there was little interest in completely abandoning Hull's trade agreement program and returning to the log-rolling days of congressional tariff-making. Congress easily passed the RTAA extension with a bipartisan majority, *but* for only two years *and* with an enhanced escape clause provision and a restoration of Senator Millikin's "crippling" peril point restrictions. To the frustration of the State Department, Congress also expressly refused to endorse the GATT and, contrary to the spirit of GATT principles, expanded opportunities for US import quotas for agriculture.

Yet, even acknowledging the significant conflicts presented by the Cold War and the postwar protectionist revival in Congress, the matter that ultimately tipped the scales in blocking ITO approval was the strident opposition of the avowed "perfectionist" business interests. Had these business interests joined the other pro-trade business groups, including the business lobby organized by Will Clayton, along with most labor organizations in supporting acceptance of the charter, it seems likely that Congress would have found time in its schedule to approve it. After all, even with the protectionist revival, there was now a bipartisan majority in favor of Hull's trade program. The opposition of the perfectionists confounded the politicians who would otherwise have been a part of this majority in approving the ITO.

As we have seen, the perfectionists raised a number of objections to the compromises accepted by the United States during the course of the Havana negotiations. According to their testimony in the hearings, the perfectionists wanted the charter renegotiated—this time led by businessmen who were "competent" in commercial transactions. They wanted stronger protections for foreign investment, no employment or labor provisions, no concessions for economic development or reconstruction, an end to all preferences discriminating against American business interests, and voting control for the United States in the ITO decision process.

While admitting that the charter was not perfect, the US negotiators argued that the exceptions to the charter's rules provided for economic development, and severe balance-of-payments problems were accepted mainly on a temporary, transitional basis. These exceptions were vital to the less developed countries and to industrialized countries still recovering from the destruction of the war. The United States had also insisted on exceptions that benefited its own interests—agriculture, for instance—and could not reasonably demand acceptance of these exceptions favoring American political interests and refuse exceptions vital to others. It was important for strategic purposes in the Cold War context that a broad-based, critical mass of member states join the ITO, including developing countries as well as industrialized allies, many of which had elected socialist governments and could possibly be drawn into the Soviet orbit. In any case, no action was permitted by these exceptions that countries could not already do. Without the ITO and the GATT, there were *no* binding rules at all, and renegotiation of the charter made no practical sense to anyone familiar with the issues and the negotiating process.

THE PERFECTIONISTS AND ADAM SMITH

It was obvious from the repetitive arguments coming from the perfectionist camp—in the public debate, the congressional hearings, and the editorials in the pro-business media—that the primary source of their opposition came from the charter's provisions on labor and employment. The perfectionists did not care for the provisions relating to economic development and reconstruction either, but their main grievance involved the full employment goals of the charter.

Following a popular theory of the period, the perfectionists claimed that these provisions promoted state economic planning that would somehow displace the free enterprise system. The widely circulated *Reader's Digest* condensed version of Friedrich Hayek's *Road to Serfdom* warned that socialists "believed that our economic life should be 'consciously directed,' that we should substitute 'economic planning' for the competitive system." Predicting that these socialist trends would lead straight to "abhorred tyranny," Hayek observed that many dictators, including Benito Mussolini, "began as socialists and ended as fascists or Nazis."[3]

One leading business representative, however, called this theory "bunk," and the independent Brookings analysis written by William Brown declared that it was based upon an "extreme" interpretation of the charter, not borne out by its text. But regardless of whether the theory presented a plausible threat, the perfectionists' unrelenting opposition to the goal of full employment put them squarely at odds with American labor and the working-class interests in the economically depressed parts of the world. According to the CIO representative in the ITO hearings quoted in the previous chapter, most labor organizations at the time were strongly in favor of "all possible positive steps to expand trade" in the charter, but "the whole underpinning of [labor's] concept of increased foreign trade [was] jeopardized" without the goals of full employment.

Once again, as with the conflicting interests described by Adam Smith in 1776, the moneyed special interests had pitted themselves against the interests of the common laborer. Smith based his approach to the political economy on the simple observation quoted in the introduction of his book: "To promote the interest of one little order of men in one country," he wrote, "it hurts the interest of all other orders of men in that country, and of all men in all other countries."

Except during times of war, this conflict has been central to the politics of trade since the commencement of the first government of the United States that followed soon after Smith published those words. Alexander Hamilton's *Report on Manufactures* made the case to Congress for a government-business partnership with a full complement of protectionist tariffs, public subsidies, and even theft of foreign technology to establish an industrial foundation for the new country. In contrast, Thomas Jefferson submitted to Congress his *Report on Commerce*, which followed the sentiments of Smith in urging the natural right of freer trade in order to better the condition of mankind who labor in the earth. Jefferson also urged reciprocal trade negotiations with countries to eliminate trade restrictions, but this idea was largely precluded by the Napoleonic Wars. Following the War of 1812, Henry Clay continued Hamilton's struggle to industrialize through government protection until Andrew Jackson and his followers, defending the populist interests of the common man, put the country back on a liberal trade path after the crisis caused by the Tariff of Abominations—the most protectionist tariffs in American history.

The conflict continued in the post–Civil War era of the robber tariff barons, which carried the struggle into the most politically corrupt period in American history. Gilded Age politicians claimed to be standing up for American labor as they maintained an inconsistent hodgepodge of protectionist tariffs created through the log-rolling congressional process, effectively owned and managed by protected industries. As Grover Cleveland noted in the Great Tariff Debate of 1888, less than 15 percent of manufacturing workers were employed in protected industries. Like all farmers and workers whose industries were not protected, these protected workers, whose wages remained low, paid higher prices for necessities while the tariff profits flowing from government trade policies went straight into the pockets of their employers. In fact, it was during this time of extreme income inequality, low wages, and poor working conditions that the American labor movement emerged in the midst of the most violent labor conflicts in history.

During the Progressive Era that followed, Woodrow Wilson, the often aloof academic, became the champion of the working class on trade politics. His administration brought US tariffs down to the lowest level since the Civil War and implemented significant labor and other progressive reforms. AFL president Samuel Gompers, who until his death in 1924 maintained a neutral position on trade protection versus free trade within his organization, became Wilson's friend and political supporter. Concerning Wilson's 1913 tariff reform legislation, Gompers wrote favorably in the official AFL magazine that the Underwood tariff reductions would not necessarily result in lower wages, because wage reductions, he argued, are "the result of the deliberately conceived and carefully executed plan of employers to retain tariff protection."[4]

In the 1920s, Warren Harding brought back the "normalcy" of Republican trade protectionism, and Calvin Coolidge unleashed business from Wilson's regulatory reforms, thus renewing the Hamiltonian partnership with big business. Herbert Hoover crowned this business-government partnership by signing the Smoot-Hawley Tariff Act and received much of the blame for failing to prevent the massive unemployment that accompanied the Great Depression. In the 1930s, Franklin Roosevelt became a "traitor to his class," as the defender of the working man (the "forgotten man") with the New Deal and began the transformation to a new liberal trade order with the appointment of Cordell Hull as his secretary of state. As the political evolution continued to confirm in the American context Adam Smith's depiction of the economic class conflict in trade between the working class and the wealthy business interests, the US labor movement gradually joined the struggle on the side of freer trade.

William Green, the successor to Samuel Gompers as AFL president, continued the neutrality policy on trade until the 1940s, when labor leaders began testifying in support of Hull's reciprocal trade agreements program. In 1928, however, several AFL-affiliated unions whose industries were affected by imports (e.g., the glass bottle blowers, shoe workers, and potters) under the leadership of Matthew Woll, an AFL vice president, formed the Wage Earners' Protective Conference to seek increased tariff protection. This group grew to thirteen unions, accounting for less than 10 percent of AFL membership, but it did not include the most prominent unions, such as the United Mine Workers, the Ladies' Garment Workers, and the Textile Workers.

The Textile Workers opposed the tariff protection provided to the manufacturers mainly because of the industry's anti-union tactics. "If the protective tariff meant high wages, then the textile workers would be the highest paid in the United States," argued Textile Workers president Thomas McMahon. "We know the frauds that are being committed in our industry upon the American public insofar as the clothes we wear are concerned, and we know the greater fraud that is being perpetrated upon the workers when the words appear in large type in the newspapers that the protective tariff means high wages."[5]

Although the AFL was nonpartisan, its executive council endorsed the Democratic ticket in every election after William Jennings Bryan was nominated in 1896, except two. In 1924, the council endorsed the Progressive Party candidate, Senator Robert La Follette, and endorsed neither Democrat Al Smith nor Republican Herbert Hoover in 1928. The council's refusal to endorse Al Smith was reportedly due to the influence of Matthew Woll, the father of the Wage Earners' Protective Conference. Woll wanted to keep his options open during the 1928 campaign because he was considered a possible labor secretary in Hoover's future cabinet. Woll's group even supported the Smoot-Hawley Tariff Act, which led some to assume that the AFL endorsed the bill, but the larger organization remained steadfastly neutral. Some contemporary critics viewed the efforts of Woll and the Protective Conference as "class collaboration" in cooperating with management's call for protection and damaging to the goals of the labor movement in improving working conditions.[6]

The Congress of Industrial Organizations (CIO) was formed in 1938 under the leadership of John L. Lewis, president of the United Mine Workers, to organize workers largely in mass-production industries, as opposed to the AFL's predominant membership of craft trades of skilled workers. From its beginning, the CIO supported the trade program and tariff reductions. In a Senate hearing on the 1949 extension of the program, the statement of CIO secretary-treasurer James B. Carey explained the group's support:

> The number of American workers [adversely] affected by reduced tariff is very limited, whereas all workers as consumers are injured by high tariffs. . . . [W]ages . . . in industries which are typically high protected industries are lower than the wages in the industries with little or no protection. . . . A sharp reduction in American foreign trade would reverberate throughout the whole domestic economy and would make it impossible to maintain full employment in this country.[7]

The AFL representative also "unequivocally" supported the RTAA extension but with the caveat that its members might oppose certain tariff reductions, particularly on imports produced under poor labor standards that threatened American labor standards.[8]

Arguably, it is the absence of rules promoting fair labor standards in the international trade regime of the GATT, and later in the WTO, that has been the driving force behind trade protests to this day. The labor and employment provisions of the ITO Charter, which were adamantly opposed by the pro-trade perfectionists, could have potentially evolved into the missing link between trade and labor standards. Likewise, the full employment goals in the ITO context could have aided in the promotion and development of a more effective trade adjustment assistance program to safeguard workers from unemployment resulting from liberal trade policies. Instead, liberal trade norms have become entrenched in the accepted economic order of the GATT without the ITO labor and employment goals upon which organized labor conditioned its pro-trade position.

EISENHOWER ON TRADE

The election of General Dwight D. Eisenhower to the presidency in 1952 began a period of increasing bipartisan support for the new liberal trade order created under Roosevelt and Truman. Like most senior military officers during his time, Eisenhower had previously kept his political views largely to himself and eschewed any interest in running for office. In June 1952, however, he announced himself a moderate Republican and accepted a draft to run for president. As the former supreme commander of the Allied Forces in Europe and later of NATO, Eisenhower was moved to seek the office because the leading Republican candidate was Senator Robert Taft, whose isolationist views Eisenhower believed were unfit for the Cold War era. Unlike much of the GOP Old Guard led by Taft, Eisenhower was an internationalist who believed in the importance of collective security agreements supported by the economic security of expanded trade. Eisenhower became the first Republican president to support a more open trade policy in the United States.

After the election, in which the popular general won comfortably and Republicans retook control of Congress with slim majorities in both Houses, however, the new president was soon confronted with serious opposition within his party on trade. He later wrote in his memoirs that "a few even hoped we could restore the Smoot-Hawley Tariff Act, a move which I knew would be ruinous." Believing that expanded international trade was vital to sustaining the free economic system and to preventing the expansion of communism in the Third World, Eisenhower considered the extension of the trade agreements program "of utmost importance to [the US] economy and to the conduct of [US] foreign relations."[9] His call for "trade-not-aid" recognized both the strategic importance of trade to economic development in blocking Soviet expansion and the limits of American generosity.

At Eisenhower's request, the Republican-led Congress reluctantly extended the Trade Act in 1953 but for only one year and conditioned upon the president's commitment not to participate in any new GATT negotiations until receiving trade policy recommendations from a Legislative-Executive Commission on Foreign Economic Policies that he agreed to create. Eisenhower appointed Clarence B. Randall, chairman of Inland Steel Corporation, to chair the commission. At a time when imported steel was not a major problem for the American steel industry, Randall was a known proponent of liberal trade policies and was able to drive the commission to produce a mainly pro-trade report.

One of the commissioners, United Steelworkers of America president David J. McDonald, who strongly supported the commission's proposal to lower tariffs, became one of the first labor leaders to propose amending the trade program. He argued for the provision of government-sponsored adjustment assistance to workers and communities negatively affected by increased imports and for the requirement of labor standards in international trade to combat unfair competition. The commission rejected the proposal for adjustment assistance, but accepted, in part, McDonald's labor standard proposal, stating: "Our negotiators should simply make clear that no tariff concessions will be granted on products made by workers receiving wages which are substandard in the exporting country."[10] There were also strong dissenting views from some of the ten commissioners from Congress, including the able, Old Guard protectionist Senator Eugene Millikin. In the end, however, election year politics and protectionist control of the congressional trade committees prevented anything more than another one-year extension in 1954.

The midterm elections returned control of both Houses of Congress to the Democrats (where it would remain for the next forty years) under the pro-trade sympathies of the new Senate Majority Leader Lyndon Baines Johnson (LBJ) (D-TX) and his mentor, House Speaker Sam Rayburn. Yet even in this more receptive environment, the president experienced only meager success on his trade agenda in Congress. Eisenhower, schooled for decades in the efficiencies of military command, disliked the constant

FIGURE 15.1 President Eisenhower, Senate Majority Leader Lyndon Johnson, and Secretary of State John Foster Dulles at a bipartisan White House luncheon seeking a more receptive political environment for trade (1955) (Library of Congress)

give-and-take required for effective engagement with the power centers in both political parties in Congress. He grew frustrated with their instinctive, whiggish jealousy in opposing proposals from the White House and proved more willing to compromise than battle with opponents in his own party to push his agenda. Eisenhower claimed satisfaction when Congress gave him a three-year extension on his trade authority, but this extension limited tariff reductions to 15 percent of the 1955 rates in increments spread over three years. The extension also expanded the escape clause provisions and gave the president broad discretionary authority to impose quotas on imports that potentially threatened domestic industries vital to national security.

THE ORGANIZATION FOR TRADE COOPERATION (OTC)

In an effort to strengthen the GATT, the president requested congressional approval of membership in a new Organization for Trade Cooperation (OTC) proposed in Geneva talks in April 1955. Following the idea suggested by Dean Acheson after the abandonment of the ITO, the OTC would provide the administrative organization to administer the GATT's trade rules, sponsor trade negotiations, and facilitate consultation on trade disputes. In his message requesting approval, Eisenhower praised the accomplishments of the GATT, which by this time included thirty-five countries representing 80 percent of the world's trade, and touted the importance of the OTC to the "free world." Ways and Means Committee chairman Jere Cooper (D-TN) immediately introduced legislation authorizing US membership, but Congress took no action on the measure in 1955. The president continued to urge its approval over the next year, including in his 1956 State of the Union address, as strong protectionist forces lined up against it.

When the Ways and Means Committee held hearings on Chairman Cooper's resolution to approve the OTC (HR 5550) in the first two weeks of March, Secretary of State John Foster Dulles warned that US refusal to participate in the OTC would have "grave consequences" in the current era when economic issues had moved to the forefront of the Cold War. This second attempt to form an international trade organization, which had much more modest goals than the first attempt with the ITO, appeared to have much less opposition. The OTC was intended primarily to provide an administrative arm to facilitate the GATT's commercial policy rules and, therefore, omitted the ITO's controversial provisions on full employment and labor standards, investment, anti-trust, and other broader issues. This time, the spokesman for the US Council of the International Chamber of Commerce, which had opposed the ITO, supported OTC membership, testifying that the "GATT is the most important agreement ever concluded for dealing with barriers to international trade." All of the agriculture associations, including the conservative Farm Bureau, along with such liberal groups as the Americans for Democratic Action and the League of Women Voters, endorsed the OTC.

After the merger of the AFL-CIO in 1955, the executive council under the leadership of George Meany announced a policy calling for gradual lowering of trade barriers. The council, however, also proposed an adjustment assistance program to safeguard workers adversely affected by trade liberalization and demanded that fair labor standards throughout the world underlie international trade.[11] Stanley Ruttenberg, representing the newly merged AFL-CIO, testified that the federation "wholeheartedly supports" US membership in the OTC, arguing that the United States had more to gain than to lose from a review of international restrictive trade practices. He continued to emphasize, however, that "the AFL-CIO firmly believes that the failure to establish and maintain at least minimum labor standards in an exporting country should be a valid cause for withdrawal of U.S. tariff concessions."

There remained strong opposition from the traditional protectionist groups led by the American Tariff League and the American Textile Manufacturers Institute (ATMI). Their supporters in Congress maintained that approval of the OTC would be interpreted as constituting approval of the GATT even though its provisions had never been submitted to Congress. They argued that joining the OTC would commit the United States to further tariff reductions and transfer Congress's authority over foreign commerce to an international organization. The OTC would become, they added, a "permanent international bureaucracy susceptible to use as a powerful propaganda agency directed against the essential protection of U.S. industry."

Although the Ways and Means Committee favorably reported the resolution approving the OTC on a vote of 17 to 7 with amendments addressing the issues raised by opponents, no action was taken by the House. Majority Leader John W. McCormack (D-MA) said on July 8 that it would be useless to bring it to a vote because it would be defeated. He noted that Republican counts revealed a 2-to-1 margin against it in the GOP caucus, and he knew that there were significant numbers of Democrats opposed as well. With the textile industry opposed, many of the southeastern and New England representatives would follow the views of ATMI unless the president brought strong pressure to the contrary. Although the president warned Minority Leader Joseph Martin (R-MA) that he would refuse requests for political endorsements from members not supporting his OTC proposal, he dropped the matter from his list of legislative priorities soon after making this threat.[12]

LABOR BEGINS ITS RETREAT

Near the end of Eisenhower's second term, organized labor began to redefine its traditional support of liberal trade policies. In August 1959, four key textile and apparel unions—the Textile Workers Union, the International Ladies Garment Workers Union, the Amalgamated Clothing Workers of America, and the United Hatters, Cap and Millinery Workers International Union, all of which had long supported trade expansion—submitted a proposal calling for quota restrictions on imported goods produced under substandard labor conditions. The executive council of the AFL-CIO responded by adopting a resolution calling for legislation imposing such a safeguard. The council noted that the federation had endorsed the Marshall Plan and other programs offering assistance to develop and rebuild the economies of foreign nations, but many nations had failed to give their workers a fair share of the fruits of economic growth and raise their living standards. This failure was threatening the stability of US industries.

The resolution contended that the United States had become "a major target" for exported goods that had been produced under "substandard wages and working conditions." It also cast blame on a "small group of domestic profiteers" seeking to enrich themselves by importing "sweatshop conditions from abroad." The worst examples involved apparel imports from Japan and Hong Kong being sold at one-third the price charged by domestic producers. In addition to textiles and apparel, concern was rising over increasing imports of automobiles, cameras, electronic equipment, and other products, which added to the fear of a flood of subsidized exports from communist countries.[13]

The textile industry had always been at the forefront of protection seekers; it even succeeded in getting Cordell Hull to negotiate a "voluntary" export quota agreement with Japan in 1937 to reduce the surging Japanese textile exports before the war. In 1955, when Japan entered the GATT and began receiving MFN tariff benefits, the US textile industry sought import quotas under the Agricultural Adjustment Act directed at apparel imports made with cotton, an agricultural product. This effort resulted in another "gentlemen's agreement" to restrain Japanese apparel exports, but the result did not satisfy the textile manufacturers. ATMI continued to oppose extending trade authority for Eisenhower and approving US membership in the OTC.

At that time, however, the textile workers' unions largely opposed the protectionist politics of the textile manufacturers, whose harsh anti-union activities, low wages, and poor working conditions ignited constant labor-management conflicts. With these labor unions in 1959 joining in the anti-trade political attack spearheaded by the textile industry management—the largest employer in the manufacturing sector—politicians took notice. As the first American industry spawned during the industrial revolution,

FIGURE 15.2 President-elect John F. Kennedy with Arthur Goldberg, special counsel to AFL-CIO to become Secretary of Labor, and AFL-CIO president George Meany at Kennedy's Georgetown home (1960) (Associated Press)

textiles represented a crucial economic and political force up and down the eastern seaboard from New England to Georgia. In the presidential election of 1960, the nominees from both parties, Senator John F. Kennedy and Vice President Richard M. Nixon, favored expanded trade policies with the explicit caveat that special priority be given to preserving the textile and apparel industries. According to Kennedy, who hailed from New England where the American textile industry began and continued to thrive, these industries were "peculiarly susceptible to competitive pressure from imports."[14]

THE TRADE EXPANSION ACT

While trade was not a top priority for him when he first entered the White House, President Kennedy became an ardent believer in the importance of expanded trade during the first year of his administration. In back-to-back speeches to the National Association of Manufacturers and the AFL-CIO on December 6 and 7, 1961, he urged that the Reciprocal Trade Agreements Act, which was due to expire in six months, "not be simply renewed—it must be replaced . . . [with] a new and bold instrument of American trade policy."[15] This new initiative was needed, he argued, if the West is to lead the world economy, the United States is to stay ahead of the revolutionary changes taking place throughout the world, and US exports are to retain and expand their status in the world market. The bold instrument he proposed was the Trade Expansion Act of 1962 (TEA), initially drafted by the State Department, delegating authority to the president to reduce 1962 tariff levels by 50 percent over five years and to eliminate tariffs that were no higher than 5 percent.[16] To expedite the process, negotiators would be authorized for the first time to cut tariffs across the board, using the "linear" method of reductions, previously proposed by the British, without being limited to the cumbersome product-by-product reciprocal method favored for political reasons by Cordell Hull. The fight to pass this trade expansion bill became the administration's leading legislative initiative for 1962.

Kennedy was primarily interested in expanding trade with Western Europe in order to enhance the strength of the North Atlantic alliance in containing Soviet expansion. "The two great Atlantic markets will either grow together or they will grow apart," he told Congress in his 1962 State of the Union address. "That decision will either mark the beginning of a new chapter in the alliance of free nations—or a threat to the growth of Western unity."[17] The prominent journalist Joseph Kraft dubbed this argument "the Grand Design,"[18] referring to the common pursuit across the Atlantic of economic, political, and military defense against communism. Will Clayton and Christian A. Herter, Eisenhower's secretary of state serving after the death of John Foster Dulles, jointly endorsed the concept with a bipartisan proposal to form a US-European trade partnership.

To encourage Britain to join the six continental European countries that in 1957 had formed the Common Market, formally called the European Economic Community (EEC), and to encourage the EEC to accept Britain, the State Department proposed eliminating tariffs on products in which the United States and the EEC produced 80 percent of world trade. To reach 80 percent in most products, the United Kingdom would need to join the EEC. French president Charles De Gaulle, however, had other ideas and vetoed Britain's membership during his lifetime under the pretense of preventing US hegemony from infiltrating the EEC via the Anglo-American special relationship.

In addition to the unprecedented negotiating authority in both breadth and flexibility of coverage and the five-year term of authority, the bill also largely eliminated the "peril point" provisions. The measure only required the president to consider Tariff Commission advice as to the impact that tariff reduction proposals might have on US industry, agriculture, and labor. The bill also made import relief under the escape clause provision of the RTAA significantly harder to obtain, by requiring domestic industries to prove that imports benefiting from tariff concessions were causing or threatening "serious" injury in idling production facilities, reducing reasonable profit levels, and causing unemployment or underemployment.

To gain the support of labor, the bill included for the first time a program providing trade adjustment assistance (TAA) for workers and industries seriously injured or threatened with serious injury by import competition resulting from trade agreement concessions. David McDonald of the Steel Workers Union had unsuccessfully proposed this program in Eisenhower's Randall Commission to provide federal financial assistance, retraining, and relocation allowances for affected workers and firms. Many Republicans opposed the program as just another step toward socialism, but free-trade proponents favored it as an alternative to the use of the escape clause to reinstate protectionist tariffs and import quotas.

In his testimony supporting the TEA before the Ways and Means Committee, AFL-CIO president George Meany noted that the labor movement had supported gradual liberalization of trade as reflected in Cordell Hull's trade program for more than a quarter of a century. His organization supported the bold new expansion of the program reflected in President Kennedy's bill because, he said, "the time has come for a fundamental revision of our country's trade policy." The delegates to a recent AFL-CIO convention had passed a resolution calling for a program very similar to that in the TEA. Even unions under the greatest pressure from imports, he noted, such as the textile unions, rose to support the resolution. Meany admitted that "imports can and do cause unemployment in some industries," but the labor movement supports trade expansion because, he argued, "we, and the Nation, as a whole, will gain far more than we lose." However, he added conditions for labor's support:

> A trade adjustment assistance program is absolutely essential to a successful foreign trade policy, and, as we have said repeatedly, it is indispensable to our support of that policy. Trade adjustment assistance is based on the broad moral principle that if the Government adopts certain policies designed to promote the welfare and security of the Nation as a whole, it has an obligation to extend effective remedies to those who are penalized by those policies.

Meany also urged the adoption of a procedure to be established in the GATT to hear complaints of unfair competition caused by violations of international fair labor standards. He suggested that substantive actions by the GATT might be possible, but the moral effect of airing this type of complaint in front of the GATT as a whole "might well be decisive." He recommended that the bill provide that improvement of labor standards be a key consideration in tariff negotiations and "that establishment of international machinery to improve fair labor standards in world trade should be a major objective of the United States."[19] This proposal would have been a more feasible proposition if the labor and employment provisions of the ITO had been included in the GATT, but it was not viable at this stage without the ITO foundation.

In addition to the major labor organizations, Kennedy was also able to gain the support of the leading industrial opponent of trade expansion, the textile manufacturers, *and* the textile unions. The politically powerful industry had worked throughout the 1950s to establish a formal quota system to protect itself from growing competition in the postwar years. On becoming president, Kennedy responded to their demands by appointing Governor Luther H. Hodges of North Carolina—a former textile millworker and ultimately a textile industry executive—to be secretary of commerce and chairman of an interagency group to come up with solutions to textile industry problems. In the meantime, the House Informal Textile Committee (later known and hereinafter referred to as the Textile Caucus), led by the influential chairman of the Armed Services Committee, Congressman Carl Vinson (D-GA), was threatening to oppose any further delegation of trade authority unless textile import quotas were enacted. In May 1961, Kennedy proposed a seven-point plan to aid the industry. A principal commitment contained in the plan was to initiate GATT negotiations in Geneva to produce a more comprehensive multilateral voluntary restraint agreement limiting textile exports to the United States. A short-term agreement was concluded in July, followed by a long-term agreement in February 1962, which froze cotton textile imports for two years at the current level with only a 5 percent annual increase permitted thereafter. This result pleased Vinson, most of the other members of the Textile Caucus, the industry lobbyists, and the textile unions. Though some congressmen from textile districts would vote against the TEA, the textile interests—including the labor unions—largely withdrew their opposition to the bill.

SPECIAL TRADE REPRESENTATIVE (STR)

One of the most significant changes to US trade policy introduced in the TEA to mollify opposition in Congress included the termination of the leading role of the State Department in the management of trade negotiations. In the years following the retirement of Cordell Hull and Will Clayton, Congress grew increasingly annoyed with what it perceived as the high-handed approach assumed by the State Department in trade policy management. Many members of Congress, being hounded by constituent business interests on import competition, considered the State Department bureaucrats unresponsive to their concerns and took offense at what they deemed a self-righteous attitude emanating from State in determining which trade policies were in the best national interests of the country. Undersecretary of State for Economic Affairs George W. Ball underscored the rationale for congressional contempt when he boasted in his memoirs that he intentionally appeared before textile groups "dressed in a British-made suit, a British-made shirt, shoes made for [him] in Hong Kong, and a French necktie." He wrote that he reveled in their criticism of him, taking it as "heartwarming" praise.[20]

Cold War priorities controlled the Department's agenda during the Eisenhower years, and, under Kennedy, Secretary of State Dean Rusk and Undersecretary Ball were both free-trade advocates with a primary focus on enhancing the economic strength of the Western alliance and rebuilding Japan as a strong ally in the East. Adding to congressional discontent, inter-agency jealousies and rival policy priorities coming from the Departments of Agriculture, Commerce, Treasury, and Labor were a constant menace to State's supremacy over trade policy decisions.

In the final analysis, it was Congressman Wilbur D. Mills (D-AK) who forced an end to the State Department's dominance over trade policy that had begun with Cordell Hull. Mills, a brilliant Harvard-trained lawyer and politically savvy power broker, served as chairman of the Ways and Means Committee from 1958 to 1974. He was an expert on all the substantive issues within the committee's jurisdiction—especially tax, Social Security, and later Medicare—and was a pro-trade liberal. Highly respected on both sides of the political aisle, he was, most importantly, an expert in moving compli-cated and controversial legislation out of his committee and through pas-sage on the House floor. Part of his power came from the fact that since the days Cordell Hull first served on Ways and Means in 1911, the Democrats on the committee served as the "committee on committees," controlling all House committee assignments for Democrats. Additionally, under Mills's leadership, Ways and Means was limited to twenty-five members and had no subcommittees, which effectively gave dominating control to a chair-man who knew how to listen and lead the members to support his agenda.

Expressing the collective will of Congress regarding the role played by State, Mills later explained, "I was sick about how the State Department had been trading away our economic advantages for political advantages." On another occasion, he complained about the enormous authority granted in the TEA and about who was going to administer the authority. "Nobody trusts the Commerce Department because they're too stupid," he said, "and nobody trusts the State Department because they're always giving it away to foreigners."[21] He met with the president and proposed an amend-ment requiring the appointment of a special trade representative (STR),

FIGURE 15.3 Representative Wilbur Mills, the powerful chairman of the Ways and Means Committee (1971) (Library of Congress)

confirmed by the Senate, to manage trade negotiations from within the Executive Office of the President in the place of the State Department. He said he would not take the bill to the floor without this provision. Kennedy had favored continuing State's leading role, hoping to isolate the White House from politically risky trade policy decisions, but he reluctantly agreed to Mills's condition.

Congress made other significant adjustments to the bill during the nine-month legislative process that made the unprecedented delegation of presidential trade authority more palatable. It provided for a legislative veto, by majority vote in both the House and Senate, over any presidential decision against escape clause relief recommended by the Tariff Commission. It also added two members from each House, representing each political party, to the official US delegation in the upcoming GATT negotiations. In the past, congressional representatives had only attended as observers. Under the TEA, Congress could be an integral player in the negotiations in contrast to the outside advisory role it previously had with the State Department's negotiating team.

With these changes, the TEA passed easily in both Houses with over-whelming Democratic majorities and a minority of Republicans in favor. In a White House signing ceremony on October 11, 1962 (only three days before U-2 reconnaissance photographs discovered the Soviet missile construction sites in Cuba that led to the Cuban Missile Crisis, the dark-est moment of the Cold War), President Kennedy explained the strategic importance of the legislation:

> By means of agreements authorized by the act, we can move for-ward to partnership with the nations of the Atlantic Community. Together with the Common Market, we account for 90 percent of the free world's trade in industrial products. Together we make up—and I think this is most important in this vital period—the greatest aggregation of economic power in the history of the world.... A vital expanding economy in the free world is a strong counter to the threat of the world Communist movement. This act is, therefore, an important new weapon to advance the cause of freedom.[22]

Among the legislators and others attending the signing whom the pres-ident thanked for assisting in moving the bill through the process, Kennedy singled out George Meany (incidentally, a fervent anti-communist) for hav-ing been "of great importance to the passage of this bill." In fact, the AFL-CIO's involvement in the passage of the TEA represented the high-water mark for organized labor's support for trade expansion legislation.

THE KENNEDY ROUND

The GATT tariff negotiations authorized by the TEA became known as the Kennedy Round from the beginning of the negotiations in early 1963 in honor of its principal promoter and in memory of JFK's trade legacy after his assassination. Kennedy's successor, President Lyndon Johnson, was a devoted free-trade proponent but was preoccupied during most of the Round with enacting civil rights legislation and his Great Society programs and with prosecuting the Vietnam War. The Round concluded at practically the last minute before the TEA authority expired in June 1967, after four years of difficult and frustrating give-and-take with the Europeans, which nearly resulted in failure for the Round. The negotiators for the major industrialized countries—the United States, the six EEC member states, the United Kingdom, and Japan—agreed to reduce average tariffs by 35 to 39 percent on industrial products. These reductions, representing three-quarters of all world trade in those products, brought the overall average import tariff down to 10 percent in each of these countries, marking a dramatic decline in the role of tariffs as a significant barrier to trade in the free world.[23] Johnson hailed the effort as the most successful trade negotiations in history.

But tariffs were now proving not to be the most significant impediment to trade liberalization. Since its accession to the GATT in 1955, Japan had effectively remained a closed market to foreign imports through an elaborate set of nontariff barriers—import quotas, nontransparent customs and manufacturing standards regulations, and discriminatory taxes. The EEC adopted its Common Agricultural Policy in 1962, which, like US agricultural policy, was replete with nontariff restrictions that were highly discriminatory against imports. One of the principal goals of the Kennedy Round for American negotiators was to open markets for American farm exports to Europe and all exports to Japan. The fact that US negotiators came home with only lower tariffs and no progress on these goals created a strong political backlash against the Round.

Politicians again blamed the State Department for sacrificing domestic economic interests in exchange for its strategic political priorities. Although the negotiations were now led by the STR out of the White House, Kennedy had appointed, as the first STR, Christian A. Herter, a former secretary of state and a true believer in the State Department's religious fervor for free trade and a strong Atlantic partnership. Further, Kennedy directed that all negotiations with Europe, including trade, be coordinated through Undersecretary of State George Ball.

The TEA, like the RTAA before it, only authorized tariff reductions; it did not include any authority to negotiate nontariff barriers. Separate legislation would be required to negotiate nontariff modifications. This restriction, however, did not keep the negotiators from discussing nontariff barriers altogether. In one case the American negotiators agreed to harmonize US anti-dumping practices with a new international anti-dumping code negotiated during the Kennedy Round that potentially modified the provisions of a US anti-dumping statute adopted by Congress in 1921. They justified this agreement under the president's constitutional authority to conduct foreign affairs and argued that the new code was consistent with US law. In another important instance, in exchange for EEC tariff concessions, US negotiators promised to obtain from Congress the repeal of the controversial "American Selling Price" (ASP) customs valuation system enacted in 1922 to protect the American chemical industry. The ASP system required that US tariffs on imported chemicals be calculated based on the selling price of comparable American-produced chemicals rather than the actual import price. If the ASP was twice the actual price of the import, for example, US customs would double the tariff, resulting in a much higher price for the imported chemicals. Neither of these concessions went down well with Congress, which passed a resolution declaring that the negotiated anti-dumping code would be enforceable only to the extent that it was consistent with the 1921 statute and refused to repeal the ASP statute.

Adding to the political fallout from the tariff reductions opening the US market to competitive imports and the increasing problems posed by nontariff barriers to US exports, the remedies provided in the TEA to aid domestic workers and producers harmed by imports were not working. The adjustment assistance program that George Meany had deemed "indispensable" to labor's support for passage of the TEA proved to be useless during the first five years after its enactment. The Tariff Commission from 1963 to 1968 denied all thirteen petitions filed for trade adjustment assistance, six of which were filed by labor unions. Ten out of the thirteen cases were rejected unanimously by the commissioners. Three additional petitions were withdrawn before the commissioners even voted on them. In 1969, the commission began approving some of the petitions, but the meager awards were inadequate to cover relocation costs and came too late to be beneficial.

Likewise, the commission gave even worse treatment to petitions filed under the escape clause remedy with the TEA's tighter criteria required for receiving tariff or quota relief. None of the twelve escape clause petitions filed from 1963 to 1968 claiming injuries from import surges caused by trade concessions got a single favorable vote from any of the commissioners.[24]

CONGRESS REACTS

By 1967, protectionist pressures for relief were mounting to a degree not seen since the 1920s. For the first time in the twentieth century, the US merchandise trade surplus had begun to evaporate. By 1971, when the final stage of Kennedy Round tariff concessions were phased in, the era of US trade deficits officially began and, with the exception of only two years, has continued to this day. The trade deficit was not solely produced by the Kennedy Round concessions—inflationary spending on the Vietnam War, the increasingly over-valued dollar, increased consumer demand for imports, higher cost of expanding energy imports, and nontariff barriers blocking US exports all contributed to the deficit—but much of the political blame was assigned to the Kennedy Round negotiators.

Even before the results were fully available, Congressman John H. Dent (D-PA), chairman of the Subcommittee on Labor of the House Committee on Education and Labor, called the Kennedy Round a "sellout," declaring it "a time bomb loosed against the American economy."[25] Dent, who had been a severe critic of the TEA and the round from the beginning, introduced a bill amending the Fair Labor Standards Act (FLSA), authorizing the president to impose tariffs or quotas on imported goods produced abroad under labor standards below those required under the FLSA and which threatened the employment of US workers producing competitive domestic products. The bill attracted strong bipartisan support as Dent initiated lengthy hearings on the measure in his Labor Subcommittee.

The first witness Dent called to testify was George Baldanzi, president of the United Textile Workers of America. Baldanzi observed that he had testified on behalf of President Kennedy's trade expansion program in 1962, confirming that his union "could agree to the abolition of all restrictive tariffs if a world-wide system of equitable [labor] standards were established." In pursuit of the goal of expanded reciprocal trade, however, he emphasized that American workers must "not be called upon to underwrite the exploitation of workers in other parts of the world." The United Textile Workers of America, he said, intends to do all it can to see that the millions who work in the textile industry "are not sacrificed on the unsupportable ground that America's present trade policy furthers its foreign policy." He argued that current trade policy "foolishly" subsidizes the "greed of entrepreneurs" profiting from the low-wage countries "who couldn't care less about raising the standards of those they exploit." Since no worldwide system of enforceable labor standards had been created, textile workers could only be saved by "an industrywide import control program based on quotas by country and category."[26]

Chairman Dent heartily endorsed Baldanzi's criticisms of the State Department policy priorities, as he underlined the fact that Undersecretary of State George Ball was "an early advocate of the Common Market." Implying that Ball cared more about building up the strength and unity of Europe than preserving American employment, Dent added that the undersecretary "is publicly on record . . . with the statement that textiles is one of the industries that is expendable" under the theory of free trade. Dent posited that the free-trade philosophy was "the most destructive force set loose in the world." He praised Baldanzi's retreat from his prior support of expanded trade:

> You seem to recognize for the first time in factual language our two chief exports from the United States are jobs, and money, and our two chief imports are unemployment and poverty appropriations.[27]

The House passed Dent's bill with an overwhelming roll-call vote of 340 to 29, but the Senate never considered it.[28] Both the Senate and the House were preoccupied by this time with a plethora of protectionist quota bills that were reaching a crisis stage and threatened to "turn the clock back . . . all the way to the Smoot-Hawley Tariff Act of 1930," according to William A. Roth, who succeeded Christian Herter as STR following Herter's death in December 1966. More than forty bills were introduced in both Houses to impose quotas on imports in anticipation of the competition spurred by the Kennedy Round tariff concessions. Ninety of the 100 senators and more than half of the House members ultimately signed on to sponsor at least one of the quotas, which together covered a wide range of products from textiles, watches, petroleum, meat, dairy products, and zinc, to mink furs and baseball gloves. A major addition to the list was a proposed quota on steel imports, which had recently increased to take an 11 percent share of the total US steel market.[29]

The reentry of steel into the battle was particularly significant because for much of the twentieth century, this sector had abandoned its protectionist legacy from the robber baron era and adopted a free-trade strategy in order to capture more of the export market. However, as exports began to fall due to discriminatory nontariff barriers imposed in foreign markets and steel imports increased with the aid of foreign subsidies, the U.S. Steel Corporation and the American Iron and Steel Institute led a retreat from the free market and sought government protection.

As in the case of the textile workers, the steel workers joined the protectionist lobbying effort led by the management leaders with whom they were normally at war over wage and benefit issues. I. W. Abel, president of the United Steelworkers of America, said that while his union was "fully committed to free world trade," it sought government assistance to eliminate the unfair trade practices of foreign producers dumping their surplus steel in the US market at "distress" prices and exploiting labor abroad to undermine American steel markets.

President Johnson came out strongly against the quota proposals, declaring they "must not become law and they are not going to become law as long as I am President." He drew valuable support from Chairman Wilbur Mills, who had sponsored several of the quota bills himself only to ensure that he could control them in his committee. Instead of import quotas, including the ones he sponsored, Mills favored negotiating "orderly marketing agreements," imposing "voluntary" export restraints, with the exporting countries. Opposition also came from liberal Senate Republicans led by Senators Charles H. Percy (R-IL) and Jacob Javits (R-NY), who attacked the "logrolling" tactics that had been rejected thirty years before and were now being used to obtain support for a wide variety of quotas. Javits urged the formation of a business-labor "emergency coalition" to fight protectionism. The *New York Times* also weighed in with an editorial urging defeat of what it referred to as a "protectionist binge by Congress" to hold the line for the "liberal trade policy that has served this country well."

Secretary of State Dean Rusk and three other cabinet officers headed an administration counterattack in testimony before the Senate Finance Committee as it considered the quota legislation. Citing diplomatic protests received from global trading partners from around the world, including a threatening note of "serious concern" from the British Embassy, Rusk warned that the legislation would destroy the advantages gained from the Kennedy Round by provoking massive retaliation against US exports and cause severe damage to the national economy and to foreign relations. The proposed quotas seriously undermined and were in direct contravention of the nondiscrimination requirements provided as a fundamental tenet of the GATT.

Senator Russell B. Long (D-LA), chairman of the Finance Committee, complained in his opening statement about foreign restrictions blocking US exports and argued it was "time someone began to show a little concern for our own people." He warned that the United States risked being a "patsy" to the rest of the world if it did not erect nontariff barriers to counter those of other nations. "Try explaining to a U.S. textile worker who just lost his job because of rising imports," Long quipped, "that it's all in the national interest."[30]

In the end, none of the quota bills made it to passage with Johnson's veto threat effectively stymying the effort as to any single quota. Senate Minority Leader Everett M. Dirksen (R-IL) proposed lumping all of the quotas into an omnibus quota bill and attaching it as an amendment to Johnson's high-priority Social Security bill, but the president let it be known that he would even veto the Social Security bill if Dirksen persisted and was successful. While the pro-trade forces were able to block the quotas, they were unable to advance the TEA program. At the end of May 1968, Johnson proposed extending negotiating authority under the TEA to 1970 and modifying the requirements of the adjustment assistance program to make it easier for industries and workers injured by trade concessions to obtain relief.

Chairman Mills held nineteen days of hearings on the proposal in the Ways and Means Committee with testimony from over 300 witnesses. The steel industry spokesman said that management and the United Steelworkers were "of one mind as to the seriousness of the problem of imports of pig iron and steel mill products into the United States," and in calling for reasonable import quotas. Likewise, George Baldanzi of the United Textile Workers called for textile quotas, declaring, "The AFL-CIO cannot ignore the fact that rising imports have disrupted some domestic markets and . . . have imposed severe hardships on thousands of American workers."[31]

At a time when President Johnson had suddenly become a lame duck following his March announcement that he would not accept another nomination for president and was deeply involved in trying to end the war in Vietnam, Congress took no action on his proposal to extend the TEA or any final action to impose protectionist quotas during the remainder of his term of office.

THE MILLS BILL AND BURKE-HARTKE

For several years following the Kennedy Round, the liberal trading order was overcome by a period of neo-mercantilism. In a comprehensive, influential article published in *Foreign Policy*, Harald B. Malmgren, who served as a senior trade official for several Democratic and Republican presidents, wrote: "Today, we are seeing a resurgence of mercantilism, whereby governments meet domestic economic demands with conscious policies of manipulation, passing the costs of these policies onto other countries." Malmgren cited the EEC's Common Agricultural Policy as one "mercantilist machine" designed to decrease imports, stimulate domestic farm production, and increase exports. Another example he offered was the series of quantitative "import restrictions inconsistent with the GATT" imposed by Japan, which by 1970 had the third largest GDP in the world. He also cited the sudden and sharp rise in protectionist sentiment in Congress following the Kennedy Round, which Malmgren called "the greatest trade liberalization effort in history."[32]

Although President Richard M. Nixon, like Eisenhower, leaned in favor of more liberal trade policies, he was certainly no free-trade idealist. In fact, he seemed largely agnostic to the virtues of trade. Trade policy issues were low on his list of priorities except as to their effect on domestic politics and on his broader strategic foreign policy goals in dealing with the Soviet Union and China. As part of his "Southern strategy," orchestrated by South Carolina political strategist Harry S. Dent in the 1968 presidential campaign, Nixon had pledged to restrict textile imports beyond the restraints implemented during the Kennedy-Johnson years. Despite significant opposition within his own administration, the president tried to fulfill his promise to the textile industry during his first two years by approaching Japan and other textile exporting countries in an effort to obtain "orderly marketing agreements" that would result in "voluntary" restraints on their textile exports. When Japan resisted, the president encouraged Wilbur Mills to introduce an import quota bill in order to enhance his negotiators' leverage with the exporting countries. As a practical matter, it made little difference to domestic producers whether it was an import quota or an export quota that limited competition from foreign-produced textiles, but the voluntary export restraints in orderly marketing agreements were preferable because they were permissible under the GATT while import quotas, generally, were not.

In a distinct departure from nearly three decades of progressive trade liberalization, not to mention an abrupt retreat from his own liberal trade views, Chairman Mills introduced a bill in April 1970 that would renew the TEA negotiating authority until 1973 and relax the requirements for escape clause import relief and adjustment assistance, but which also slapped import quotas on textiles and shoes. Following extensive hearings, the Ways and Means Committee during closed mark-up sessions expanded the Mills Bill, officially named the Trade Bill of 1970, to empower the Tariff Commission to recommend quotas for *any* industry threatened by imports and to compel the president to accept the recommendations unless he found them to be contrary to the national interest. Despite bitter opposition from free-traders, the bill passed the House by a comfortable margin on November 19, 1970.[33] With little time left before the end of the term in the Senate, Russell Long attached the quota provisions from the Mills Bill to the Social Security bill in his committee, but a Senate filibuster prevented consideration by the full Senate.

It was never clear whether Nixon would have signed or vetoed the Mills Bill had it passed both Houses. Commerce Secretary Maurice Stans strongly favored the bill, while the State Department and STR opposed it, but the president kept his own counsel as the issue soon subsided. Bilateral export restraint agreements were reached on textiles over the next year with most textile and apparel exporting countries, including Japan, Hong Kong, Taiwan, and South Korea. In the meantime, however, the administration's trade policy became more chaotic and unpredictable.

In August 1971, Nixon addressed the nation to announce a "New Economic Policy," later called the "Nixon shock," urged by his new treasury secretary, the brashly nationalistic John B. Connally, recently Democratic governor of Texas and formerly an LBJ protégé. In the face of rising unemployment, inflation, trade deficits, and an overvalued dollar and looming balance-of-payments crisis, Nixon—now famously proclaiming himself to be a Keynesian—suspended the convertibility of dollars into gold, imposed a surtax of 10 percent on imports, and instituted a wage and price freeze for the first time since World War II.[34] Although these actions had a direct impact on trade policy, the president did not consult either STR or State before announcing them. The 10 percent surtax was removed and the dollar devalued by the end of 1971, but the Nixon shock was followed by another devaluation of the dollar in 1973. Nixon's actions effectively ended the Bretton Woods fixed exchange rate system and ushered in the current floating rate system.[35]

Paul A. Samuelson, a genuine Keynesian and the Massachusetts Institute of Technology economics professor who wrote the economics textbook used by most students of my generation, opined that the 1960s and 1970s represented a Freudian age where anxieties of "nameless dreads" dominated the subconscious minds of ordinary citizens. "In every walk of American life," he wrote, "there is great uneasiness over foreign competition." The days of the 1950s, when everyone seemed to have accepted belief in the benefits of liberal trade, he observed, are gone forever, replaced with "the mushrooming of protectionism." Yet, even "if the most dire pessimists are correct in their belief that much of existing American industry can be preserved in its present form only by universal protective quotas," he concluded, ". . . it is a pitiful delusion to believe that such measures will enhance rather than lower the real standard of living of the American people."[36]

The Nixon Shock and the near success of the quota restrictions in the Mills Bill spawned an even more protectionist bill, the Foreign Trade and Investment Act, introduced by two steadfast labor supporters, Congressman James A. Burke (D-MA) and Senator R. Vance Hartke (D-IN). The Burke-Hartke Bill, as it became known, was drafted by the AFL-CIO and provided not only for protectionist import restrictions with a radical expansion of mandatory import quotas but also, for the first time, a major effort to regulate the foreign investments of US-based manufacturers and eliminate tax incentives for moving manufacturing abroad and exporting American jobs.

The economic policy committee of the AFL-CIO had denounced the role of US investment abroad in American job losses in a major report released in February 1970, which stated that the federation's traditional support for the "orderly" expansion of trade did not include the "promotion of private greed at public expense or the undercutting of United States wages and labor standards." The report cited the skyrocketing rise of investments by US companies in foreign subsidiaries and the spread of American multinational corporations as a major cause of the deterioration of the US position in world trade.[37] In testimony before the Senate subcommittee on international trade, a senior union official observed that the AFL-CIO had been "all out for a liberal trade policy" until 1969 when it became obvious that liberal trade policy was jeopardizing workers by creating stiff competition from abroad and "a lot of that stiff competition abroad [was] from American multinational companies." He argued that US multinationals were shutting down American production and exporting technology, capital, and jobs abroad, to export back to the United States goods that previously had been produced by American workers.[38]

Burke-Hartke made the multinational corporation a primary target in its attack on trade by eliminating tax credits for foreign taxes paid on foreign-sourced income from "runaway plants" and requiring that US taxes be paid on a current basis rather than being deferred until the earnings were repatriated to the United States. The bill also created an onerous regulatory framework to manage the transfer of capital and technology beyond the US border. While Burke-Hartke never received formal consideration, it remained a major source of heated debate during consideration of trade legislation for years. The issues arising from the corporate tax incentives for "runaway plants" and the exportation of jobs by multinational corporations—which, in the 1970s, organized labor labeled "a modern day dinosaur which eats the jobs of American workers"[39]—remain at least as inflammatory today as they were nearly fifty years ago.

THE TRADE REFORM ACT OF 1973

Nearly six years after the TEA trade negotiating authority expired in June 1967 and following the collapse of two legislative efforts to restore this authority, the Nixon administration proposed to Congress on April 10 the Trade Reform Act of 1973 (TRA), the most expansive request for negotiating power in US history to reduce or eliminate *all* tariff and *nontariff* trade barriers. Administration officials believed the timing had improved for this proposal as unemployment rates had dropped below 5 percent and the United States was returning to a marginal trade surplus in 1973 following the first two years of trade deficits since the Gilded Age.

To enhance his chances, President Nixon reached out to labor leaders hoping to gain their support for his trade bill by moving a step toward the Burke-Hartke Bill's provisions on the "runaway plant" issue. On the same day the president submitted the trade bill to Congress, the administration also proposed removing the "artificial incentives" of foreign investment by taxing the earnings of US companies that operate plants abroad through a subsidiary on a current basis if the foreign-earned income derived more than 25 percent of its receipts from goods exported to the US market and was subject to a foreign income tax less than 80 percent of the US corporate tax rate.[40]

On behalf of the AFL-CIO, George Meany rejected the administration's overture and reaffirmed the federation's unequivocal support for Burke-Hartke.[41] But the pro-business lobbies, while generally supportive of the new trade bill, turned out in force to defeat the administration's multinational tax reform proposals. The National Association of Manufacturers, the Chamber of Commerce, and an organization representing over sixty of the largest US multinational corporations—the Emergency Committee for American Trade (ECAT) formed in 1967 to combat the growing protectionist trend in Congress—prepared for a showdown with labor on Capitol Hill. In the beginning, there was much sympathy in Congress for the AFL-CIO tax proposals. Why, many thought, should the United States indefinitely defer taxing income from "runaway plants" operating in foreign tax havens and exporting goods previously produced by American workers to the United States, while any losses from those plants were allowed as a deduction from present US income taxes? Chairman Mills, who favored an approach closer to Burke-Hartke than the Nixon proposal, initially insisted that the multinational tax reform provisions be included in the trade bill.

Donald M. Kendall—chairman of PepsiCo, personal friend of President Nixon, and a beneficiary of Nixon's détente policy with the acclaimed Pepsi-for-vodka trade deal with the Soviet Union—made the case for the multinationals as chairman of ECAT. He led the argument that foreign investment is important to strengthening US domestic employment by expanding export sales and called the administration's tax proposals "unacceptable." Without manufacturing investments in foreign markets, many American manufacturers would not have been able to expand or maintain their share of sales in those markets. Tax inducements were not the motivation for investing abroad, he argued, but without them many US companies would abdicate the market to foreign investors from other nations.[42] Despite the initial support it received on the tax proposals, labor's lobbying efforts were no match for the leverage brought to the battle by big business; labor was simply outgunned and lost the battle. The Ways and Means Committee quietly dropped the multinational tax reforms from consideration during its executive mark-up sessions.

Although the climate for new trade negotiations had improved since the protectionist backlash that followed the Kennedy Round, it was far from certain that Congress would approve the delegation of negotiating authority that the president requested. By the time the trade hearings began on May 9, Washington was absorbed with the constant revelations concerning the abuse of power coming from the Nixon White House in the growing Watergate scandal. On April 30, Nixon's first televised speech on Watergate was piped in to a Chamber of Commerce reception I attended at the Sheraton Park Hotel for the Georgia congressional delegation and their staff. To a stunned audience, the president announced the forced resignations of chief of staff Bob Haldeman, chief domestic policy adviser John Ehrlichman, White House counsel John Dean, and Attorney General Richard Kleindeinst.

I attended the Georgia Chamber reception as a member of the staff of Congressman Phil M. Landrum (D-GA), but I was in the process of moving to the Ways and Means staff to work on the trade bill. At the reception, Stoney Cooks, the administrative assistant for civil rights icon and then freshman congressman Andrew J. Young (D-GA), introduced me to his boss, telling him that I was a member of the Ways and Means staff. Young immediately reacted: "I want you to tell your chairman that the people need tax reform this year, they don't need a trade bill pushed on them. Tell him to give the people tax reform!" I responded out of respect for Young that I would convey the message, while knowing that I would not dare approach Mills with a suggestion to change the priorities of his committee. In any event, Mills already knew well the sentiments expressed by Young that were held by many members of Congress. As the committee began to take up the trade bill, just after conducting thirty-five days of hearings on tax reform, the chairman assessed the temperature of his membership: "Most of us feel [the president's] got to have [trade] discretion," but added, "The mood in Congress is not good for getting a trade bill. . . . It's a bad time to ask for presidential discretion."[43]

As the committee heard twenty-four days of testimony from senior administration officials, special interests, and a wide variety of public witnesses on trade policy and revised the bill over the summer and fall in executive session, the experience for me was one of intense education in the politics of trade. Unlike today, when the Ways and Means trade staff has a wealth of depth in personnel, which is divided by party affiliation, the committee's only full-time trade staffer in 1973 was Harry Lamar, an experienced, tough, and very able trade economist. I came to work for Lamar as a twenty-five-year-old recent law school graduate with the naïve perspective of a starry-eyed internationalist, steeped in the ideals of free trade. I soon received a rude awakening from an intense forced-feeding of political realism. One of my jobs was to summarize the hearing testimony for the committee—a laborious task, but one that gave me a better understanding of the complex interests affected by trade policy. Even more illuminating in the political education I received from this job was the task of attending the committee's executive mark-up sessions with Lamar to take down the amendments debated and adopted by the membership, which we would later draft, with the aid of legislative counsel, into the bill to be reported to the House floor.

In reviewing my notes and journal from this period, I find an interesting contrast in the political divisions on trade then with the debates on trade twenty years later when I served as a member of Congress during consideration of the implementing legislation for the North American Free Trade Agreement and the World Trade Organization. The main difference was that under Mills's leadership, partisanship was negligible and there were hardly any significant ideological battles between the few high protectionists and the even fewer free-traders on the committee. My congressman, Mr. Landrum, who was then serving as chairman of the Textile Caucus, would get into personal arguments on the virtues of preserving the textile industry with another southern Democrat, Sam M. Gibbons of Florida, an outspoken liberal trade partisan, but they were both strong supporters of the main purposes of the bill. Of the ten Republicans on the committee, Congressman Barber B. Conable (R-NY) was the most effective in moving the administration's bill through the process and one of the most competent members on the committee.

By far, however, the chairman was the most critical player in the process. Mills conducted the committee like a symphony orchestra, leading each instrument section through the movements to its finale on the House floor. Without any exception that I noticed, all twenty-five members looked to him for general direction and with obvious respect. He always asked the most relevant and incisive questions of the witnesses, the substance of which reflected his interest in expanding trade but with an eye to preserving the strength of American industry within the rules of the GATT. Yet, in the summer of 1973, he began to slow down due to back pain that led to surgery for a degenerative disc, which limited his time on the committee and slowed down the process.[44] Actually, some of his friends thought he had begun to lose his mind when he made a brief, quixotic run for the Democratic nomination for president in 1972. "Wilbur, why would you want to run for president," they asked, "and give up all this power?" One of his friends, James Burke, the third-ranking Democrat on Ways and Means, however, thought the Mills candidacy was a good idea and even ran Mills's campaign.

Burke, the House sponsor of the Burke-Hartke Bill, was the most entertaining member of the committee—always diligent, persistent, bombastic, and especially funny. His speeches were replete with populist clichés—for example, he frequently referred to "fat cats crying all the way to the bank," and told Harvard professors to "step down from their ivy covered campus with the beautifully flowing grasses above the scenic Charles [River] to the teeming tenements of Roxbury." He also often repeated himself. Sam Gibbons told him once that he should number his speeches and just refer to them by their number so he wouldn't have to deliver them over and over.

Burke attempted to incorporate parts of Burke-Hartke into the bill by proposing amendments in committee that would have required quotas to be maintained at *current* import levels. These quota proposals were actually a compromise from the more protectionist Burke-Hartke quotas that clawed back imports to the average of the 1965–69 levels. Yet the amendments attracted only seven favorable votes. The AFL-CIO subsequently dropped further efforts to improve the bill, seeking only to kill it in the hope of reviving Burke-Hartke. With this shift in strategy, Burke adopted a new refrain in the executive mark-up sessions and repeated it often in his inimitable Boston brogue:

> You people can do anything you want to this bill. You won't get any argument from me. I don't give two hurrahs about what happens to the damn thing. I'm just sitting back and watching it all. You can amend it from here to doomsday. It doesn't bother me. But I'm warning you when this bill gets to the floor I'm blowing the whistle. There's going to be tough sledding ahead when it gets to the floor. I'm telling you.[45]

ADJUSTMENT ASSISTANCE

There was not complete unity among labor organizations in the approach taken to Nixon's TRA and Burke-Hartke. Leonard Woodcock, president of the United Automobile Workers (UAW), testified on the TRA before Ways and Means that his union "still supports liberal international trade policies," but trade liberalization must be accompanied by measures to protect workers against "victimization." This stipulation required, "above all, an adequate program of adjustment assistance" and a provision "requiring fair labor standards in international trade." The UAW (which had disaffiliated from the AFL-CIO in 1968 following disagreements between George Meany and Walter Reuther, Woodcock's predecessor) opposed the protectionist quotas in Burke-Hartke. Woodcock argued, "We think [the quotas] would lead to a retaliatory trade war to the detriment of this and all the other involved countries." The UAW did, however, support the elimination of tax incentives for foreign investment by US multinationals provided in Burke-Hartke, which incentives, Woodcock observed, worked to the "detriment of American jobs." Woodcock maintained that he had "a substantial faith in the workings of a free market system," but he urged the committee to rein in the multinationals "to give capitalism a human face."[46]

Two days after Woodcock's testimony, I. W. Abel, president of the United Steel Workers Union and chairman of the Economic Policy Committee of the AFL-CIO, appeared before the committee in the absence of George Meany, who was ill. In response to a committee member's question, Abel offered an explanation for the opposition of the UAW to Burke-Hartke. He said the UAW "happens to have a great number of their members employed in the country's largest multinational corporations," including, he mentioned, the largest multinational in the world, General Motors. When asked about other large labor organizations that might agree with the UAW, Abel said that there were some unions that were removed from the threat of foreign competition and had not taken the time to analyze fully the overall impact of the problem. He assumed that they were "still operating under the age-old theory in the United States that we have all had of being great free traders."[47] He did not mention that the UAW supported Burke-Hartke's repeal of the tax incentives favoring multinational corporations nor that the rationale given by Woodcock for opposing the import quota provisions was to avoid retaliatory trade wars.

Besides their differences on the import quotas imposed in Burke-Hartke, the UAW and the AFL-CIO also diverged on the importance of adjustment assistance to the trade bill. Much like the approach previously taken by Meany for the federation in 1962, Woodcock insisted that an effective trade adjustment assistance program was critical to the UAW's support for the TRA. The AFL-CIO position, however, had shifted somewhat over the previous decade as reflected in the statement of Andrew J. Biemiller, the federation's director of legislation, in hearings a year earlier before the House Foreign Affairs Subcommittee on Foreign Economic Policy: "Trade adjustment assistance as a meaningful answer to jobs lost from imports is an idea whose time has passed. No amount of patchwork on this idea can solve the nation's need for new foreign trade and investment policies in 1972."[48] Two things prompted this view: one, the poor record of successful adjustment assistance petitions filed since the enactment of the TEA; and two, the shift in strategy reflected in the Burke-Hartke proposals to impose protective import quotas and to prevent job losses caused by multinational corporations through tax reform.

There was also a wide difference of opinion on adjustment assistance within the executive branch. In order to attract broader support for more liberal trade policies and to ward off more protectionist alternatives, the State and Labor Departments, along with STR, strongly favored the TAA program and argued for less restrictive qualifications for approval. The Office of Management and Budget, Commerce Department, and Treasury Secretary George P. Shultz, however, were skeptical of both of these rationales. Shultz argued against distinguishing people who lost their jobs because of trade from those who were laid off for other reasons, such as automation. The White House reached a compromise among the competing agencies that essentially accepted the Schultz position. The administration's bill proposed continuing the program with slightly better benefits and less restrictive qualifications, but only until comprehensive unemployment insurance legislation could be enacted in which TAA would be lumped in with other jobless benefits and turned over to the states for funding and administration.

The Shultz approach gained very little traction in the committee or in the Republican caucus. The administration had difficulty even finding anyone willing to introduce its proposal to overhaul unemployment compensation. A permanent TAA program with more liberal benefits and less restrictive qualifying requirements had strong bipartisan support. Even the Chamber of Commerce supported a program similar to that proposed by the UAW over the administration's proposal, which business groups opposed because it increased unemployment benefits funded by employers. The committee's TAA program was to be funded out of US customs revenue. Even so, there were political conservatives from both parties who continued to oppose adjustment assistance. Phil Landrum (co-author of the Landrum-Griffin Act of 1959, which had been vigorously opposed by labor unions), often spoke of TAA "as nothing more than glorified welfare." But he was in the distinct minority and supported the final committee bill with enhanced TAA.[49]

Some labor unions were still not satisfied. Speaking for the AFL-CIO, I. W. Abel concluded, "Adjustment assistance at best is burial insurance, not a jobs program." Referring to Meany's endorsement of the TEA being conditioned upon an effective adjustment assistance program, he said the ten-year record of the program amounted to a broken promise and "a rip-off." Although Abel criticized the Shultz proposal to repeal TAA and replace it with general unemployment insurance, the AFL-CIO was silent on endorsing the committee's amendments because its leaders were committed to defeating the whole bill in favor of Burke-Hartke.[50] Every time the subject of adjustment assistance came up in committee, James Burke, in accord with his labor loyalties, would remove the cigar from his mouth and say: "It's a cruel hoax. It's a cruel hoax!"[51]

JACKSON-VANIK

In view of the complicated role that Cold War issues played in US trade policy decisions throughout the postwar period, it is not surprising, though a little ironic, that the efforts of President Nixon and his national security adviser (soon to be secretary of state), Henry A. Kissinger, to promote détente with the Soviet Union ignited the most controversial issue in the bill. On October 18, 1972, three weeks prior to Nixon's reelection and following on the heels of an epic US-Soviet summit in May and the signing of the treaties on Anti-Ballistic Missiles and Strategic Arms Limitation, officials of the two superpowers signed a trade agreement in which the United States agreed to grant most-favored-nation status and Exim Bank credits to the Soviet Union. Since 1951, imports from most communist countries had been denied MFN status and were subject to the exorbitant Smoot-Hawley tariff rates. In a separate agreement the Soviets agreed to repay the balance of their World War II Lend-Lease debts of $722 million. The bulk of the debt payments were deferred until and conditioned upon MFN being granted. The MFN commitment, of course, could only be fulfilled by an act of Congress, and the administration included it in the TRA proposal.

Two weeks before the trade agreement was even signed, Senator Henry M. (Scoop) Jackson (D-WA)—a military hawk who had run for the Democratic presidential nomination in 1972 and planned to do so again in 1976—introduced legislation, co-sponsored by over seventy senators, to deny MFN status to any nonmarket economy (communist) country that prohibited emigration or imposed more than a nominal tax on persons desiring to emigrate. Congressman Charles A. Vanik (D-OH), a senior member of Ways and Means, introduced the same measure in the House in January 1973, with 60 percent of the House signing on as co-sponsors.

The language was aimed at aiding Soviet Jews seeking to emigrate to Israel who were being blocked from doing so by a prohibitive education tax, the "diploma tax," among other impediments. When the president proposed the MFN provisions as part of his trade reform proposal, Vanik offered Jackson's measure as an amendment, endorsed by Chairman Mills, to the TRA. The resulting Jackson-Vanik (sometimes called Jackson-Mills-Vanik to give it more heft) amendment was bitterly opposed by Nixon and Kissinger, who saw it as a major impediment to their diplomatic strategy.

The political dynamics over the Jackson-Vanik amendment were both intense and complicated. First, there was vigorous debate within the executive branch, with Secretary of State Kissinger seeking to delay action on the bill until the anti-Soviet provisions were eliminated and Treasury Secretary Shultz, STR William D. Eberle, and the president's Assistant for International Economic Affairs Peter M. Flanigan all urging Nixon to consent to moving the bill forward. Kissinger argued for delay and hoped to be able to weaken or eliminate Jackson-Vanik because he felt détente was too important and too fragile to endure a bitter House debate over human rights. The economic advisers believed that the trade bill was too important to the nation's economy to jeopardize it with further delay. New GATT negotiations were being initiated in Tokyo, and support for the trade bill could evaporate over time. Indeed, after Ways and Means approved its bill in early October, organized labor's opposition became more unified as the UAW joined the AFL-CIO in opposing the TRA. Labor's best strategy at this point was to delay action and lobby for more opponents. George Meany, an avowed anti-communist, considered détente "appeasement . . . pure and simple . . . a give away in search of profits for our corporations through a combination of American capital and Soviet slave labor."[52] Meany was a natural ally of Jackson-Vanik supporters for many reasons, including delaying the vote on the TRA as long as possible. Nixon ultimately consented to moving forward with a floor vote but indicated to House Speaker Carl B. Albert (D-OK) that he would veto the bill if it came to him with the anti-Soviet provisions.[53]

Kissinger admitted in his memoirs that his "ignorance of the subject [of international trade] was encyclopedic,"[54] and the same might be said of his lack of appreciation for the political priorities of Congress. While Kissinger succeeded in getting action postponed in both the House and the Senate, bipartisan support for the amendment remained unshakable throughout the process. A floor amendment offered by Congressman Conable to delete the Jackson-Vanik amendment from the bill failed by a three-to-one margin. Support for the amendment continued well past the end of the Cold War. The MFN restrictions prescribed by Jackson-Vanik had to be repealed before the United States granted permanent, unconditional MFN status to both China (2000) and Russia (2012) when they joined the WTO.

The presence of the amendment actually improved the strength of support for passage of the TRA bill, which passed by a slightly smaller margin of 272 to 140 than the vote to delete the Jackson-Vanik amendment failed by. Labor's opposition was not strong enough to defeat the bill, but its influence was obvious among Democrats. For the first time, a majority of Democrats voted against a major trade authorization bill, 121 to 112, while an overwhelming majority of Republicans, 160 to 19, voted for it.[55]

For many of the same reasons that delayed a vote in the House, the TRA languished in the Senate, almost to the point of death, before passing 77 to 4 one year after the House action. Responding to organized labor's continued opposition in favor of Burke-Hartke, Senator Hartke was one of the four votes against the bill. After months of discussions, Senator Jackson and Secretary Kissinger announced a compromise on the Jackson-Vanik amendment that allowed the president to grant temporary MFN treatment to the Soviet Union upon receiving assurances that the country was proceeding to grant freedom of emigration to its citizens. This compromise was sufficient to get the bill out of the Finance Committee and approved by the full Senate on December 13, 1974, but a month later the Soviets rejected the terms of the compromise and backed away from the 1972 trade agreement.[56]

FAST-TRACK AND "LIBERAL PROTECTIONISM"

Final passage of the TRA—renamed the Trade Act of 1974—marked an important new cornerstone for American participation and leadership in the liberal world trading system. In expanding negotiating authority to cover nontariff barriers, increasing congressional oversight and private sector input, and providing broader access to enhanced trade remedies, the act was a significant departure from the RTAA and the TEA and laid the foundation for US trade policy in the modern era.

In the Trade Act, ultimately signed by President Gerald R. Ford on January 3, 1975, Congress delegated authority to the president for five years to eliminate tariffs on goods with rates of 5 percent or less and to reduce higher rates by up to 60 percent. The president had asked for unlimited authority for five years to raise and lower tariffs and authority to eliminate or modify certain nontariff barriers (for example, the American Selling Price system of customs valuation) without further ratification by Congress. As to any other legislative modifications relating to nontariff barriers, Nixon originally requested authority to change laws as he saw necessary in negotiations, subject only to a subsequent veto by either House of Congress. Harry Lamar, after first seeing this proposal, told the STR general counsel John Jackson, the international trade law expert who drafted it, "You must have rocks in your head if you think Congress will approve this." Lamar was right, of course; Ways and Means did scale back the requested open-ended delegation but still granted liberal tariff authority and accepted the congressional veto approach on nontariff barrier modifications. The Senate, however, did not.

In the Senate, the bill confronted the skeptical leadership of the Finance Committee, Chairman Long, and the chairman of the Subcommittee on International Trade, Senator Herman Talmadge (D-GA). Having inherited the fervent southern populism of their fathers, Huey Long and Eugene Talmadge, they had grown cynical about the benefits of liberal trade to their agricultural constituencies and had little faith in the promises of the State Department and STR in heralding new export opportunities in the European market. Soon after the bill was introduced in the House, Kissinger called for a New Atlantic Charter, in which trade policy would be linked to continued US military security in Europe, but the Europeans rejected the linkage if it meant opening their markets to US agricultural exports. In his opening statement at the Finance Committee hearings on the bill, Chairman Long said, "The bloom is off the rose of 'Atlantic partnership.' . . . I still desire an 'open, nondiscriminatory, and fair world economic system,' but I am tired of the United States being the 'least favored nation' in a world which is full of discrimination. . . . [T]rade legislation comes before committee bearing a heavy burden."[57]

Senator Talmadge previously had the image of the quiet, tobacco-chewing farmers' senator often overshadowed by his Georgia colleague, Senator Richard B. Russell (D-GA), but he had recently burnished that image by becoming a media celebrity as one of the most effective inquisitors in the televised Watergate Committee hearings. Talmadge objected vigorously to the authority granted to the president to modify statutory law relating to nontariff barriers, even if subject to a congressional veto. The

Finance Committee thus changed the role of Congress to an affirmative approval process that ensured more legislative collaboration in the negotiation process. Under this procedure, Congress would have to be notified three months before an agreement was signed, allowing consultations with the Ways and Means and Finance Committees as to the final agreement and implementing legislation. Congressional approval would also involve preliminary collaboration between the committees in both Houses in drafting the bill for an up-or-down vote, with no possibility of amendments, within a fixed time schedule. The procedure adopted and approved in the final bill later began to be called "fast-track authority," until it was changed in 1998 to a more euphemistically appealing name, "trade promotion authority."

Having been introduced at the end of a six-year period of "neo-mercantilism," when organized labor was in full opposition and the United States was experiencing its first trade deficits of the twentieth century, the delegation of negotiating authority in the Trade Act of 1974 was remarkably liberal. The authority to reduce tariffs by 60 percent was the highest ever granted, and the average tariffs were already lower than they had been since Jefferson's first term as president. The fast-track authority to reduce and eliminate nontariff barriers was also unprecedented. It is notable that during the twenty-one months it took to pass the bill, the country experienced the trauma of Watergate and watched as their president resigned from office to avoid being impeached for abusing the power he already possessed. It may have helped that Gerald Ford, liked and respected on both sides of the aisle, occupied the Oval Office when the final vote was taken on the last day of the Ninety-Third Congress. It also helped politically when Russell Long amended the bill to elevate STR to cabinet rank in order to insulate trade a bit more from the foreign policy preferences of the State Department. But the most important political advantages included in the legislation were the trade remedy enhancements, some of which had been considered protectionist during Cordell Hull's tenure.

One trade journalist characterized the bill—with its liberal negotiating authority and protectionist-leaning trade remedies—a hybrid policy of "liberal protectionism."[58] The final act gave the president authority to impose an import surcharge of up to 15 percent and in some cases import quotas for a period up to 150 days in order to deal with "large and serious balance-of-payments deficits" or to prevent "an imminent and significant depreciation of the dollar." The trade remedy provisions offered a significant improvement to import-injured domestic companies and workers over the TEA remedies. To authorize adjustment assistance or an escape clause safeguard measure under the TEA, the import-caused injuries—such as loss of jobs and business profits—had to be linked to a negotiated tariff concession, and imports had to be the "major" cause of the injury. To qualify for adjustment assistance under the Trade Act of 1974, workers, businesses, and communities were now only required to show that imports contributed "importantly" to the injury and need not link it to a trade concession. The act also dramatically increased the TAA benefits. Similarly, the new law relaxed the eligibility qualifications for escape clause relief from the TEA provisions. The new escape clause provision required no link to previous tariff concessions, and imports now needed only to be a "substantial" cause of injury (slightly more stringent than contributing "importantly" for TAA purposes). The Tariff Commission (renamed the International Trade Commission [ITC] due to the increasing importance of nontariff impediments to trade) was the fact-finder in these cases and made recommendations to the president for action or inaction. Based on a positive ITC finding, the president was authorized to impose a number of optional escape clause remedies, including raising tariffs by up to 50 percent, imposing limited quotas, or negotiating orderly market agreements. The president continued to have the discretion to reject the ITC recommendations if he found that doing so was in the national interest, but his determination could be overturned by congressional veto.

These remedies for injuries caused by surges in imports were accompanied by the act's strengthening of remedies for injuries caused by "unfair trade practices." As proposed by the AFL-CIO in Burke-Hartke, the act tightened the procedures in anti-dumping and countervailing duty (anti-subsidy) cases by imposing strict time limits on the decision process and adding the right of court review when administrative decisions went against the petitioner. Most significantly, Section 301 of the act authorized the president to take "all appropriate and feasible" actions (normally, withdrawing trade concessions, raising tariffs, or imposing quotas) to enforce the rights of the United States under any trade agreement or to respond to any foreign practice that is "unjustifiable, unreasonable, or discriminatory and burdens or restricts United States commerce." This broad authority to retaliate against foreign governments violating international trade law overhauled and strengthened a similar TEA provision. The TEA retaliation provision had largely been ignored in the 1960s, for which Russell Long and others in Congress gave the executive branch a tongue-lashing and devised this new remedy. Although controversial, unilateral US actions under Section 301 came to be an effective tool of last resort in the arsenal of available remedies before the dispute resolution process matured under the WTO. Congress not only has kept this tool in force as a possible threat but has expanded it over the years.

Interestingly, Congress came closer to formally approving the GATT in this legislation than ever before. Section 121 specifically authorizes the annual appropriation of "such sums as may be necessary for the payment by the United States of its share of the expenses of the Contracting Parties to the General Agreement on Tariffs and Trade." But just to clarify, the section adds: "This authorization does not imply approval or disapproval by the Congress of all articles of the [GATT]." In order to promote "the development of an open, nondiscriminatory, and fair world economic system," Congress directed the president to seek a number of revisions in the GATT, including "the adoption of international fair labor standards and of public petition and confrontation procedures in the GATT." This proposal, when added to the adjustment assistance improvements adopted in the act, seemed to respond precisely to the conditions proposed by George Meany when testifying for the AFL-CIO in favor of trade expansion in 1962. Although these provisions came too late to move organized labor from its unwavering devotion to Burke-Hartke as the exclusive approach to trade in 1973, labor drew very few followers down this path.

Indeed, even some of the standard industry opponents to trade, textiles in particular, did not fight the bill. On December 20, 1973, the United States completed negotiations with other GATT countries and signed the Multifiber Arrangement in Geneva, which established a multilateral agreement governing textile quotas for the next four years, covering manufactured products made from cotton, wool, man-made fibers, or blends. This agreement provided textiles a predictably stable market for a period ultimately extended for thirty more years. The Trade Act also exempted textile products, along with certain steel products and a few other import-sensitive sectors, from the duty-free preferences the act granted to developing countries pursuant to a GATT agreement on the Generalized System of Preferences. As a result, ATMI, representing the textile industry, endorsed the Trade Act of 1974 in early December just before the Senate voted on it.

On final passage of the House-Senate conference bill, the Senate maintained its overwhelming vote for it with only four senators opposed. One of the four, Senator Hartke, speaking for the organized labor position, declared: "It is my belief that the present trade bill continues worn-out economic philosophy, and it is an element which is driving us fast down the highway toward the destruction of the western economic system." In the House, the Democratic vote in favor increased considerably over the previous year. Only a few stuck with labor to the end in the final vote, which passed the act by a vote of 323 to 36.[59]

The Trade Act of 1974, with its expansive authority to reduce trade barriers further and its provisions emboldening the trade remedy protections, established the fundamental framework within which the United States has continued to participate in the world trading system created in 1947. The Tokyo Round of GATT negotiations, authorized by this act and conducted between 1973 and 1979, reduced tariffs again by nearly 40 percent among the eighty-five Contracting Parties, from an average of 10.4 to 6.4 percent for industrial products among the major industrialized countries. The tariff reductions even included some reductions on agricultural imports. More important than the tariff actions, the Tokyo Round addressed nontariff barriers effectively for the first time. The negotiators reached agreements on nine separate "codes"—obligating only the countries signing on to each code in "a la carte" choices—addressing nontariff problems affecting trade, such as customs valuation (as in the American Selling Price issue), import licensing, government procurement, and the application of trade remedies for anti-dumping and countervailing duties. The Tokyo Round also adopted four understandings applicable to all Contracting Parties, including a declaration on trade measures taken for balance-of-payments purposes and a codification of the practices and procedures developed for dispute settlement. In the WTO Agreement signed twenty years after the act passed, all of these measures were adopted (*verbatim* in some cases) with few exceptions and some additions, along with the 1947 provisions of the GATT, as a "single package" obligating all WTO member states.

In July 1979, Congress passed the Trade Agreements Act of 1979, which implemented into US law the major nontariff agreements reached in the Tokyo Round, with votes of 395 to 7 in the House and 90 to 4 in the Senate. These tremendous margins were driven significantly by the political skills of Robert S. Strauss, STR under President Jimmy Carter and the first STR to hold office with the increased prestige of the newly named Office of the United States Trade Representative (USTR). In addition to his perceptive political insights and keen persuasive talents, the Texas Democrat and former national chairman of the Democratic Party had a close working relationship with his president and with the congressional leadership from both parties. He had an early bias for the free-trade politics of FDR, Sam Rayburn, and LBJ but was also keenly aware of the political need to respond to congressional constituencies.

In the final analysis, it is this blend mixing the benefits of liberal trade ideals with (at least potentially) effective fair trade remedies that has maintained American leadership in the world economic order. The issues do not change very much from age to age, and the ideals and the remedies are never perfected, but the political struggle continues.

16

Advancing Worker Rights beyond the WTO

Adam Smith, at the same time as he was writing
about the invisible hand, he was also writing about
that moral sense—that human ecology—that allows a
market to work. . . . It has to do also with our politics
and our culture, and when that starts eroding it
inhibits economic growth as well.[1]

—Senator Barack Obama
2008 Presidential Campaign

The labor protests attacking the current liberal trade order do have a point. It is certainly true that the current international trading system suffers from a serious birth defect resulting from business objections to the Havana Charter of the International Trade Organization. Among the myriad causes for populist complaints against an excess of corporate-lobbyist influence in trade, some are quite legitimate. For example, as in the issues raised in the Havana debates on investor protections urged by American business interests, US investors have overreached in demanding the private legal right to sue host countries to block regulations adopted to protect public health and environmental safety. Pharmaceutical companies have also successfully demanded excessive patent protections that make vital drug treatment inaccessible to the poor in developing countries. And as previously discussed in Chapter 14, business "perfectionists" effectively blocked the adoption of the Havana Charter in large part because of its provisions promoting full employment and fair labor standards. Unlike the proposed ITO's stipulated commitment to eliminate unfair labor conditions, the GATT only permitted importing countries to prohibit imports made by prison labor.

In the early 1950s, the United States proposed amending the GATT to address the issue of substandard labor conditions using language similar to that in the ITO Charter but failed to obtain the necessary consensus of other contracting parties.[2] Over the succeeding decades, it became increasingly apparent that including fair labor standards in the GATT and later WTO agreements might have offered a solution to many of the labor protests threatening the system today.

During the Uruguay Round, which concluded in 1994 with the adoption of the WTO, the United States and other developed countries again raised the issue of labor conditions, but once more without success. Their negotiators failed even to establish a committee to study the link between trade and labor standards. Congress had mandated that respect for workers' rights be among the Uruguay Round's objectives. In submitting the proposed implementing legislation to Congress, the Clinton administration committed to continue its efforts to place labor rights on the WTO agenda. Two years later at the first WTO Ministerial Conference in Singapore, the members agreed to a declaration promoting "internationally recognized core labor standards," but concluded that the "International Labor Organization (ILO) is the competent body to set and deal with these standards." The consensus declaration specifically stated: "We reject the use of labor standards for protectionist purposes, and agree that the comparative advantage of countries, particularly low-wage developing countries, must in no way be put into question."[3]

NORTH AMERICAN FREE TRADE AGREEMENT (NAFTA)

With the continued exclusion of labor issues from the GATT/WTO agenda, the United States has sought to address worker rights and environmental protection in other venues—bilateral and regional trade agreements. Interestingly, the most troublesome issue in the Anglo-American relationship in forming the nondiscriminatory international trading order—the British Commonwealth's imperial preference arrangements—has now been all but forgotten in the multilateral system that condones, and even encourages, bilateral and regional free trade agreements among WTO members. The significance of the imperial preferences diminished largely due to the effect of postwar inflation. When prices rose, preferences, which were based on specific tariffs set by weight (ten cents per pound, for example), and not ad valorem currency value, became insignificant when prices went up and the preference margins stayed low. Although the US negotiators, following the philosophy of Cordell Hull and Will Clayton, abhorred discriminatory tariffs, the GATT specifically permitted them for customs unions and free-trade areas, primarily to promote the economic unification of Europe after the war. Clair Wilcox, the senior GATT/ITO negotiator under Will Clayton, explained the apparent inconsistency: "A customs union is conducive to the expansion of trade on a basis of multilateralism and non-discrimination; a preferential system is not."[4] In other words, customs unions and free-trade areas may be discriminatory, but they expand free trade and encourage other countries to join in lowering trade barriers on a multilateral basis. Wilcox, Clayton, and, previously, Cordell Hull argued that the imperial preferential system was intended to restrict trade by walling off competition from nations outside the system. Free-trade agreements within the WTO came to be favored under the concept called "competitive liberalism," which encouraged other countries to do the same.

Regardless of the rationale, the loophole for free-trade agreements provided by Article XXIV of the GATT for customs unions and free-trade areas has been significantly expanded in recent decades. The bilateral and regional free-trade agreements provide a ready vehicle to fill in deficiencies of the WTO, in particular the labor rights deficiency. One year before the creation of the WTO, the United States, Canada, and Mexico formed the North American Free Trade Agreement (NAFTA), commencing in 1994, to strengthen the economic unity of North America. NAFTA has been controversial from the beginning mainly because of the economic disparity of Mexico as a developing country compared to its wealthy developed partners to the north.

As a member of Congress, I voted for NAFTA in 1993, primarily because the economic interests in my congressional district mainly favored it, led by farmers, who wanted to export more, and textile fabric producers, who were better able to compete with Asian imports under its terms. I also believed that strengthening the economic relationship with Mexico and Canada favored US strategic interests in the world political economy. Of course, not all of my constituents agreed with me. One apparel manufacturer—a John Birch Society follower who opposed any government intervention in private commerce except protection for his business against foreign competition—protested outside my office in Washington demanding I vote against NAFTA. Many of my colleagues also disagreed with me, as 60 percent of the Democrats in the House voted against NAFTA under the leadership of Majority Leader Richard A. Gephardt (D-MO) and Majority Whip David E. Bonior (D-MI), men I greatly respect but disagreed with on many trade issues.

Since its inception, NAFTA has been the political poster child and scapegoat for all the alleged ill-effects of international trade. The agreement has been constantly attacked by organized labor supporters and anti-establishment crusaders, like Ralph Nader, on the left and by ultra-nationalists, including presidential candidates Pat Buchanan and Ross Perot, on the right. As this book is focused on the politics of trade, I will largely defer to others on the economic implications of NAFTA, except to note that independent analyses from the US International Trade Commission and the Congressional Budget Office have found that NAFTA has "had a small, but positive, effect on the overall U.S. economy."[5] This result is exactly as predicted by most economists at the time of the vote on NAFTA in 1993. In an unusual convergence of opinion, 300 economists, including conservative monetarists, like Milton Friedman, and liberal Keynesians, like Paul Samuelson, wrote President Clinton with an appeal supporting NAFTA while debunking the exaggerated political claims on both sides of the debate. Paul Krugman, then at the Massachusetts Institute of Technology, called the agreement "economically trivial" for the US economy, but supported it in part to aid the political strength of the free-market reformers in Mexico. In the late 1980s, Mexico began moving from statist economic policies with nationalized industries and trade protectionism to a more open economy. Krugman and others correctly predicted that the agreement would enhance the Mexican middle class and reduce pressures on illegal immigration. Describing the debate, Krugman observed, "The anti-NAFTA people are telling malicious whoppers. The pro-NAFTA side is telling little white lies."[6]

No doubt some jobs have been lost to Mexico as a result of the agreement, just as some industries and American workers have benefited from it.[7] Other factors, besides NAFTA, have also played an important role in the North American economy and job displacement during this period, including the collapse of the Mexican peso after NAFTA became effective and the technological advances in production automation. In any case, the US unemployment rate gradually dropped to a thirty-year low of 4.1 percent in the five years after NAFTA went into effect.[8] I remember seeing a front-page story in my local Athens, Georgia, newspaper at that time about job losses resulting from the closing of a local blue jeans factory, which company management blamed on NAFTA. Several pages into the same paper, however, appeared an article about the expansion of another local textile-related factory whose management could not find enough workers in the same labor market to fill its new jobs. Suffice to say, as the economists predicted, neither the glowing predictions of NAFTA proponents nor the dire, "giant sucking sound" of millions of jobs moving south forecast by Ross Perot ever materialized.

During his campaign for a second term in 1992, President George H. W. Bush, whose administration negotiated NAFTA, criticized his opponent, Governor Bill Clinton, for refusing to take a position on the agreement, after having previously endorsed its negotiations in 1991. With organized labor and environmental groups attacking the deal as it was being finalized, Clinton said he wanted to study the completed product before supporting it. In the last month before the election, Clinton said he favored NAFTA, but not without adding provisions to enhance labor and environmental standards in Mexico. In December 1992, one month after his defeat, President Bush quickly signed the agreement without any labor and environment provisions, which made it more difficult for Clinton to add changes to the text of the agreement. Within two months after his inauguration, however, the Clinton administration initiated talks with the Mexicans and over the next five months produced side agreements on labor and environment with both countries.

The main issue in these negotiations revolved around the US demand that each country be able to invoke sanctions against either of the other countries upon failure to enforce its own labor and environmental laws. Canada was the most opposed to this demand, which nearly wrecked the negotiations. The issue was finally resolved with an agreement to create two tri-national Commissions for Environmental Cooperation and for Labor Cooperation to monitor compliance with environmental and labor laws, respectively. Among other things, the commissions would have the power to develop minimum standards and, in the case of the United States and Mexico, would have dispute resolution authority. If disputes could not be resolved within the commissions, an arbitration panel would be established with the power to impose limited trade sanctions and monetary penalties up to $20 million if a country fails to enforce its laws. In the case of a complaint against Canada, however, Canada's court system would have to enforce any penalties. Apart from the labor side agreement, President Carlos Salinas de Gortari of Mexico offered to take steps to raise minimum wages in Mexico.

The response from American labor supporters in Congress was immediate. Majority Leader Dick Gephardt, who had run for the 1988 Democratic presidential nomination on a pro-labor, anti-trade platform, announced that the "side agreements fall short in important respects. . . . I cannot support the agreement as it stands." AFL-CIO president Lane Kirkland explained: "The side agreements would relegate worker rights and the environment to commissions with no real enforcement mechanisms, no power to impose trade sanctions and no effective remedies."[9] In truth, because the side agreements were not an integral part of the agreement with the same enforcement power as the commercial dispute settlement provisions, the NAFTA labor provisions were only a modest first step and proved largely ineffective.

US-CAMBODIA TEXTILE AGREEMENT

I was serving as USTR's textile ambassador when the next opportunity, after NAFTA, arose to advance labor standards in US trade relations. This occasion involved textile trade with Cambodia, which was not yet a member of the WTO and thus beyond its jurisdiction. After twenty years of brutal chaos, Cambodia emerged from the wilderness in 1996. This period included the three-year genocidal rule of the Khmer Rouge that killed 2 million people (one-quarter of the population), followed by civil war and misrule under the domination of Vietnam, and a period of violent political turmoil after the Vietnamese withdrew. To encourage development and bring the country into the twentieth century, the United States signed a comprehensive trade agreement with Cambodia in October 1996. The following year President Clinton designated Cambodia a Least-Developed Beneficiary Developing Country under the US Generalized System of Preferences (GSP) program.

The GSP program, first authorized in the Trade Act of 1974, granted duty-free status or preferential tariffs on certain imports (e.g., not including politically import-sensitive products like textiles and apparel) from developing countries and additional special trade preferences for the poorest countries designated as "least developed." This nonreciprocal, discriminatory treatment favoring developing and least developed countries was authorized as an exception to MFN requirements of the GATT during the Tokyo Round in 1979. Industrialized countries that adopted GSP programs established their own criteria and conditions for granting the preferences. Under the US program, Congress required the president to take a number of criteria into account before selecting beneficiary countries—for example, whether the country provided adequate and effective protection of intellectual property rights. Most important to the present discussion, the president, since 1984, must consider whether the recipient country "has taken or is taking steps to afford workers . . . internationally recognized worker rights."[10] Prior to designating Cambodia a beneficiary country under its GSP program, the United States required the government to recognize worker rights by replacing its existing communist-style labor law with a labor code meeting international standards, which the Cambodian National Assembly did with strict supervision and aid from the US Department of Labor and labor rights nongovernmental organizations (NGOs).

Unfortunately, in a country with no history of labor-management regulation and without the necessary training and enforcement resources, a strong labor law did little to improve working conditions. The American Embassy in Phnom Penh frequently received reports of labor rights violations in garment factories, including unsafe working conditions, mistreatment of workers by management, forced overtime work, arbitrary firing of shop stewards and union representatives, corruption of labor inspectors, late payment or underpayment of salaries, and management interference with shop steward elections. In June 1998, the AFL-CIO and a coalition of human rights, labor, academic, and religious groups formed an organization to fight for workers' rights in international trade, now called the International Labor Rights Fund, which filed petitions with USTR to suspend Cambodia from the GSP program for failing to meet the worker rights eligibility criteria.

As the labor petitions were being filed, the American textile industry began loudly demanding protection from surging Cambodian imports. In the two years following the signing of the trade agreement, Cambodia's economic development was exploding with new foreign investment, predominantly in the industrial sector always first to develop in poor countries—garment manufacturing. Cambodian garment factories increased in this short period from 25 to 114, employing 72,000 workers, with pending new investment approvals that would more than double those numbers. Apparel exports to the United States went from $2.4 million in 1996 to $308 million in 1998, representing approximately 75 percent of Cambodia's total apparel production. For a country with pervasive unemployment and per capita annual income estimated at $252, this new investment and production had a powerful effect on job creation, especially for women with few other job prospects.

As USTR's chief textile negotiator, I was primarily responsible for coming up with a solution to address the US textile industry's demands and the labor issues in a manner that would not block the progress that Cambodia was making in emerging from its tragic recent history. My concern for Cambodia went back to 1970 when my then future wife and I marched in the student protests at our university against the Nixon/Kissinger invasion of Cambodia during the Vietnam War, at the time of the student massacre at a similar protest at Kent State University. The initial secret bombings and ultimate US invasion of Cambodia ordered by President Nixon destabilized the country, which led to civil war and the disastrous takeover by Pol Pot and the genocidal Khmer Rouge.

As always, our negotiations with Cambodia over textile issues drew the attention of a multitude of competing interests and involved strategic foreign policy priorities. As to the latter, it was in our strategic interest for Cambodia to have a sound economy and stable, democratic political system after years of chaos and communist control.

Of the two principal competing interests, American importers and retailers were on the side of continuing with no trade restrictions on Cambodia, which provided them a new source of apparel beyond the textile exporting members of the WTO. The WTO member producers were limited by the complex quota system of the Multi-Fiber Arrangement until 2005 when quotas were mandated to be eliminated under the Uruguay Round agreements. The US domestic textile industry, naturally, represented the protectionist interests desiring to scale back or at least control the fast-growing Cambodian imports. Although much of the US textile industry was located in the Southeast and was traditionally fiercely anti-union, organized labor joined with the industry's protectionist positions on most trade issues. The main textile workers' union affiliated with the AFL-CIO, the Union of Needletrades, Industrial and Textile Employees (UNITE), represented 250,000 textile workers. American consumers, along with retail business owners, were the beneficiaries of the trade position of the importers and far outnumbered the voters within the textile community

of management, workers, and others directly benefiting from textile protectionist policies. Nevertheless, the political powers in Washington have
historically favored textile industries and workers over the less organized
consumer interests.

Even though US textile and apparel manufacturing had been declining
since at least the 1970s, the textile industry remained the largest employer
in the US manufacturing sector in 1999, providing jobs for nearly 1.3 million workers, not counting wool and cotton growers and other suppliers.
It is not surprising that the Congressional Textile Caucus, of which I was a
member in the early 1990s, has been one of the strongest political forces on
trade issues on Capitol Hill. Textile and apparel firms were the dominant
employers at this time in rural regions of the Southeast (representing, for
example, 30 percent of North Carolina's total employment), but these firms
were also a significant source of employment in California and metropol-
itan regions in New England and the Mid-Atlantic, including Manhattan's
garment district. At the time we were negotiating with Cambodia, the textile industry came under a huge onslaught of competitive imports during
the Asian financial crisis beginning in 1997 when ten major textile exporting countries devalued their currencies by nearly 40 percent. The US textile
and apparel industry lost 121,000 jobs, an 8.9 percent decline, from July
1998 to July 1999.[11] It should not be surprising that currency manipulation
has become a top issue in the trade debate.

In coming up with a negotiating stance in dealing with Cambodia, my
interagency delegation took all of the competing interests under consideration. Along with my colleague at the Commerce Department, Troy Cribb,
who chaired the interagency Committee for the Implementation of Textile
Agreements (CITA) and on whom I relied for technical information on
import statistics and other support, I held several meetings with representatives of each interest group that might be impacted. While we often heard
from lobbyists for these interests separately, as they usually preferred, my
preference was to bring them all in together in a public meeting so they all
could hear unfiltered the opposing positions that we were receiving.

Besides participants from the Department of Commerce, our delegation consisted of representatives from the Departments of State, Labor,
Treasury, and US Customs. In most cases, State and Treasury representatives
favored more liberal trade, although in this case the State representative
favored protection and Treasury relied on Customs, then under Treasury,
to represent its interest. The Commerce and Labor representatives generally

favored a more protectionist approach, because of their ties, respectively, to domestic industry and organized labor. Representing USTR as a part of the Executive Office of the President, I was tasked with leading the delegation in developing its proposals and ensuring that the president's views were foremost in the position we agreed to present.

One thing was certain; President Clinton favored including labor standards in trade agreements. He had frequently mentioned the importance of labor in trade in public remarks, including his most recent State of the Union address. Even without this presidential preference, I was personally determined to make this a priority in the negotiations and had decided to try a new approach to reaching this goal. At the suggestion of Assistant USTR Jon Rosenbaum, who was working on the AFL-CIO petition to deny GSP benefits to Cambodia because of its labor record, we decided for the first time in a trade agreement to propose offering trade benefits for labor law enforcement instead of punitive sanctions for enforcement failures—in other words "a carrot and not a stick" for encouragement. When I consulted with the USTR, Ambassador Charlene Barshefsky, about this approach, she said, "Go for it."

Recognizing that one of the main impediments to enforcing labor standards in Cambodia was the lack of training and resources in this poorest of developing countries, I decided to try bringing in assistance from the International Labor Organization (ILO) to provide training and to establish an objective, independent monitoring program to review Cambodia's labor practices. The ILO, a unique tripartite organization giving voice to workers, employers, and governments in enhancing workers' rights, was formed, along with the League of Nations, under the Versailles Treaty ending World War I in 1919. Samuel Gompers, then head of the AFL, chaired the commission that wrote its constitution. Although the Republican-controlled US Senate blocked approval of the treaty, the United States under President Franklin Roosevelt joined the ILO in 1934, the same year that Cordell Hull began his reciprocal trade agreement program that ultimately led to the creation of the GATT.

The membership of the ILO, however, also included the WTO developing countries that were adamantly opposed to any connection between trade and labor standards. For this reason, I was concerned about objections that might be raised to the ILO's participation in our proposal that tied labor rights enforcement to trade benefits. During my next trip to the WTO, I quietly arranged a meeting with senior staff at the ILO headquarters in Geneva to explore the possibility of engaging them in our labor proposal with Cambodia. Fortunately, they were already operating in the region from their office in Bangkok, Thailand, and agreed to take on the project. Deputy Undersecretary Andrew Samet of the Labor Department would later serve an instrumental role in obtaining funding to support the ILO program.

Another factor favoring our cause in reaching a sound agreement on labor standards was my Cambodian counterpart in the negotiations, Minister of Commerce Cham Prasidh. As soon as I met him in our first round of talks in December 1998, I knew that he was smart, transparently honest, and seemed motivated by a determination to lift his country out of its impoverished state. I had been wary at first because I thought his official ties to Prime Minister Hun Sen might present difficulties. Hun Sen had a questionable reputation as an undemocratic strongman, who maintained power through force with little regard for human rights and election results. Hun Sen had lost the sight in one eye as a jungle fighter for the Khmer Rouge forces in the beginning of Pol Pot's takeover; he had fled to Vietnam and came back to Cambodia with the Vietnamese invasion in 1979. By the time the Vietnamese left ten years later, Hun had become prime minister and has managed to hold on to power for most of the period since then. Cham Prasidh had been Hun Sen's loyal secretary for years and obviously owed his senior ministerial office to the prime minister.

Cham was a near fatal victim of the "killing fields" ordered by Pol Pot to kill all government officials and educated people. The Khmer Rouge killed Cham's father, a mid-level government official; Cham's mother; and more than seventy other members of his family. Pol Pot's forces threatened to kill Cham because he wore glasses, which they perceived as bourgeois symbols of education and literacy. Cham convinced his oppressors into believing his glasses were so thick they were for blindness and not for reading. Cham and his sister were the only members of his family to survive the massacre, and they spent three years being "re-educated" as they worked in the fields until the Vietnamese took control.

When Cham arrived with his delegation in Washington for our first negotiating session, he demonstrated to me that his principal goal was to bring his country out of the barbarism and minefields of the past. In both the first session and the final meeting in Phnom Penh, we negotiated over quota numbers and product categories, but not significantly over the enforcement of labor standards that our side demanded. I believed Cham was genuine and sincere in wanting Cambodia to become known as a place where workers were well treated, not a country whose economy thrived on ruthless sweatshops. In Phnom Penh, he took me and Kenneth Quinn, the US ambassador to Cambodia, to meet with the prime minister at his home. There, Hun Sen told me that he knew that other developing countries were criticizing him for accepting the labor provisions in our agreement, but he concurred with Cham Prasidh that this stipulation was important for Cambodia's industrial development in the modern world.

Cham also told me that Cambodia's neighboring developing countries were complaining to him about our labor provisions and advising against accepting them. His American consultants and advisers, who represented US retailers sourcing in Cambodia and lobbyists for US importers, were all adamant in opposing these provisions and in expressing their opposition to our delegation and to Cham and his subordinates. The American Apparel Manufacturers Association, which represented US manufacturers who also imported apparel, had developed their own voluntary code for labor standards in their foreign factories, but they opposed a government-enforced code that might restrict their sourcing options. The US textile industry thought the labor provisions were a good idea, but its representatives were mainly concerned about ensuring that the agreement imposed sufficient new import quotas. Our delegation listened to all of the interested parties' concerns, but we were determined to include labor rights enforcement in the agreement.

Because it was the AFL-CIO's petition to deny GSP benefits for labor abuses that initiated the labor discussions in the negotiations—and, quite frankly, we wanted their support for our efforts—I was in frequent contact with UNITE as we prepared our proposal, including their leadership in New York: President Jay Mazur, chief policy adviser Mark Levinson, and legal adviser Mark Barenburg. Their main concern was that the requirements be substantive and definitive. They wanted us to avoid using the traditional vague requirement that Cambodia "take steps" to provide labor rights. They even proposed language for the provision, drafted by Mark Barenburg, who was on the Columbia Law School faculty. I found his language too much of an overreach into Cambodia's sovereign authority for the post-imperial age, even as an opening bargain position.

The language we proposed, and Minister Cham accepted, committed the Cambodian government to the effective enforcement of existing labor law and the promotion of the general labor rights as embodied in Cambodia's strict labor code. The government also agreed to support the implementation of a training program to improve working conditions in the textile and apparel sector, including internationally recognized core labor standards, through Cambodian labor law. Though not included in the signed agreement because the ILO was not a party to it, the Cambodians agreed that this program would be implemented through the ILO, which would also monitor enforcement of the labor law once the arrangements were finalized.[12]

The three-year agreement established import quotas on twelve apparel categories with annual growth rates of 6 percent for most categories. These quotas pleased the US textile industry but were liberal enough to satisfy Cambodia. As an incentive (i.e., the "carrot") to encourage higher labor standards, we agreed to increase all of the quotas by an additional 14 percent each year the US government determined that working conditions in the Cambodia textile and apparel sector "substantially comply" with the Cambodia labor law and the core labor standards. The process for setting up the ILO monitoring program suffered from bureaucratic delays and did not get started until the second year of the agreement. The monitoring process was performed the first year, however, by US embassy staff, who visited twenty-six of Cambodia's garment factories (representing 15 percent of the factories) from August to November 1999 and conducted numerous interviews with government, management, workers, and unions.

The embassy's report included a mix of both positive and negative findings but concluded that labor conditions did not yet "substantially comply" with Cambodian law. The Cambodian government had, however, made significant improvements in a short period of time, including facilitating union registration, improving health and safety conditions in factories, ratifying twelve ILO conventions, and issuing declarations to factories clarifying the labor code and demanding compliance to qualify for export licenses. The report found Cambodia to be in compliance with core labor standards on child labor (often a problem in developing countries), minimum wage, forced labor, and nondiscrimination. On the negative side, the report found widespread involuntary overtime and weekend work abuses, insufficient resources devoted to labor code enforcement, and freedom of association and collective bargaining irregularities. The Ministry of Labor had successfully mediated seventy-seven labor disputes, including forty-two strikes, in garment factories, but generally viewed its role as a neutral mediator rather than a labor rights enforcer. The most significant reason for the weak enforcement report was attributed to lack of training and resources and to the fact that unions were poorly organized, untrained, and undisciplined.

Before deciding on our response, the Commerce Department issued a Public Request for Comment on the quota bonus decision. Without seeing the embassy report, the importers and retailers urged us to give the full 14 percent, based upon their view that Cambodia was in full compliance with the labor law. UNITE, on the other hand, demanded that we give no bonus. Neither UNITE nor the AFL-CIO has a presence in Cambodia. UNITE based its recommendation upon a report attached to its comment prepared by the Free Trade Union of Workers of the Kingdom of Cambodia. This report cited a number of incidents of alleged labor violations that occurred during the first five months of the year before some of the government's compliance actions had become effective. It must be noted that this union, which was registered by the minister of labor near the time we signed the agreement, was the only union in Cambodia affiliated with a political party, and it happened to be the main opposition party to Hun Sen's governing Cambodian People's Party.

Based upon the embassy's analysis—which was the only thorough and objective report we had on the question of Cambodia's compliance with its labor code on the date set for our decision in the agreement, December 1, 1999—we had to deliver a negative decision to the Cambodians. This date happened to transpire when both Cham Prasidh and I were in Seattle attending the tumultuous WTO conference. Cambodia was then only a prospective member; Cham was in Seattle as an official observer.

The two of us met for dinner in a Japanese restaurant, where I gave him the unwanted news. I told him that our delegation sincerely believed that his government had made a good-faith effort at compliance and had made many improvements in Cambodian labor conditions over the first year, but that more needed to be done to meet the standard set in the agreement. In order to acknowledge the improvements they had made, however, I told him that we were considering a quota increase for a smaller percentage this year in recognition of their good-faith efforts and to continue the program. Cham did not hide his disappointment. He argued that we had agreed to reward their efforts with "a real carrot, not a virtual carrot," as he characterized our decision. He said they believed that they had met the standard and did not want a partial reward.

When I returned to Washington, I wrote Minister Cham confirming our decision, attaching the embassy's report, and advising him that we intended to increase his quotas by 5 percent as soon as the ILO program was in place to encourage Cambodia to continue to expand its efforts.

I learned from completing my first trade agreement after joining USTR in 1998 that, as in politics, it is impossible to make all the competing interests happy with trade negotiations, especially in the politically charged textile sector. Therefore, I revised my approach to setting negotiating goals for trade agreements; from then on my goal was not to try to please all of the interest groups but to try to make all of them only moderately unhappy. From the sound of the reactions we received following the reaction to the final Cambodia agreement, we appeared to have succeeded in making all of the interests unhappy, and some were immoderately so.

Labor's reaction was immediate. In the first sentence of a letter to me when our decision was made public, Jay Mazur wrote: "Your proposal to give Cambodia a 5% increase in their quota greatly disturbs me." He continued: "Gross violations of Cambodian labor law remain unaddressed. . . . I still believe countries should be rewarded in the international trading system for observing and enforcing core labor standards along with basic human rights. But to increase Cambodia's quota would undercut the very incentives the agreement was designed to encourage."[13] In a long telephone conversation with Mazur on Christmas Eve from my farm in Georgia, I explained to him that we believed the Cambodians were trying in good faith to improve labor conditions and had made significant progress in enforcing their labor code without adequate resources to fully meet the standard we set. If we completely ignored what they had accomplished, they would likely heed the advice of American importers and abandon the labor rights program.

As to the views of the American importers, their lobbyists disliked both the quotas and the labor provisions in the agreement and completely ignored our 5 percent quota bonus. A February 28, 2000, article in the *Wall Street Journal* essentially lays out the position of the US importers and retailers. A lobbyist for the importers' association took the reporter on a tour of apparel factories in Cambodia and apparently supplied her with ample misinformation for the story to support the importers' side of the argument. The reporter rhetorically asked: "Can trade policy be used to improve the lives of workers in poor countries?" She then offers an answer to her question:

The [Cambodia textile] trade deal clearly has made a difference in the lives of the thousands of women who make knit shirts for the Limited and blue jeans for the Gap. But the story doesn't stop there. It's a far more complicated tale that raises questions not only about the best means of helping poor nations, but also about the motives of those in the U.S. who advocate labor rights abroad. As yet, the Cambodians haven't gotten any increase in their apparel quota. Despite the improved conditions, American labor unions have blocked any quota change.

The reporter writes in some detail about the improvements in labor conditions spurred by the agreement and quotes Ambassador Barshefsky and me praising the Cambodian improvements. But the reporter states that we refused a quota increase (disregarding the 5 percent increase) because, she alleges, "The input from UNITE was just about the only outside view Clinton administration officials considered when making their quota decision." Significantly, she gives no value to the objective factory review rendered by the embassy, which we primarily relied upon, and dismisses the US Labor Department participation as "one bureaucrat" sent to review progress.[14]

When the ILO program was up and running in May 2000, we officially granted Cambodia the promised 5 percent quota bonus. In September 2000, the United States added an additional 4 percent for a total of 9 percent (plus the agreed annual increase of 6 percent) in increased quotas after the Cambodians exhibited progress in four areas of labor rights compliance. The US importers, the Cambodian garment manufacturers, and Minister Cham Prasidh still grumbled that the United States was continuing to short-change the Cambodians for their efforts. While the US textile industry opposed any boost in the quotas, organized labor began to praise the program by the end of 2000 and offered support for the US government's actions in creating and carrying out the agreement. "The government of Cambodia has been good in this," said one AFL-CIO official; "they have demonstrated a sincere effort to respond to U.S. concerns." Another labor official acknowledged that while Cambodia had not yet reached the level of substantial compliance, "there has been improvement," he said. "A balance has to be struck between rewarding progress but using the leverage we have to help workers gain more rights. . . . We can support the additional quota if it's used to help the workers, not just reward companies."[15]

In the final analysis, the precedent-setting US-Cambodia Textile Agreement of 1999 produced remarkably positive results for years. In

January 2002, Ambassador Robert B. Zoellick, the first USTR in President George W. Bush's administration, renewed the agreement with the labor provisions and ILO participation for three more years, calling the renewal "an excellent example of the way trade agreements lead to economic growth and promote a greater respect for workers' rights." The 9 percent quota bonus was continued even though some of the same problems remained, and the 14 percent potential increase was raised to 18 percent.[16]

In 2004, the final year of the agreement, many observers raised concerns about the growing threat of China as the end of the quota system, scheduled for 2005, came closer. Many textile-producing developing countries, whose trade ministers had complained about quotas for years, now saw them as guaranteeing the countries a market share as the quotas contained China, the 800-pound gorilla among apparel producers. Cambodia by this time had developed a reputation with buyers and consumers as a producer with high labor standards and began to rely on this factor to give it a competitive edge. The president of the Global Fairness Initiative urged Western retailers and consumers to continue buying Cambodian apparel, writing in a December 2004 *Washington Post* op-ed:

> The Cambodian Labor compliance program is one of the most successful and widely regarded innovations in trade-related partnerships. Industry, government, unions and civil society are unanimous in their praise.[17]

Even after the agreement ended and Cambodia joined the WTO in 2004, and with the termination of the Multi-Fiber Arrangement quotas the following year, Cham Prasidh said, "We are extending our labor standards beyond the end of the quotas because we know that is why we continue to have buyers. If we didn't respect the unions and the labor standards, we would be killing the goose that lays the golden eggs." His colleague Roland Eng, Cambodian ambassador to the United States in 1999 and in charge of development issues in 2005, agreed: "The labor program in the textile industry is more important to Cambodia than any other development program because we know the wages go directly to Cambodian workers and raise their standard of living."

The higher labor standards provided a valuable incentive for Levi Strauss, the Gap, and Abercrombie & Fitch, among other international retailers and apparel producers, to source in Cambodia. The Gap, the largest

FIGURE 16.1 The author and Cambodian commerce minister Cham Prasidh sign the US–Cambodia Textile Agreement in Phnom Penh (January 1999)

buyer of Cambodian garments in 2005, assured Cambodians that they would continue to buy from them as long as they followed the ILO special labor program created pursuant to the 1999 textile agreement. Minister Cham concluded that the benefits of the agreement had gone beyond anyone's expectation.[18]

From January 2005 to November 2006, the ILO increased the number of factories monitored in Cambodia from 50 to 212 and reported compliance rates of 80 percent in the five major standards it uses to assess labor conditions.[19] The ILO program was jointly funded by the United States (70 percent), the Cambodian government (15 percent), and the Cambodian Garment Manufacturers Association (15 percent). In an issue brief prepared by the Carnegie Endowment for International Peace, the author recommends the US-Cambodian model for other trade agreements, observing:

> The striking improvements in working conditions and compliance with law that have been achieved in [the Cambodian garment manufacturing] sector suggest that this has been one of the most successful and cost-effective programs to promote worker rights abroad that the US Government has ever funded.[20]

SEATTLE

The issue of labor rights was raised again formally at the WTO at the 1999 Ministerial Conference in Seattle (previously discussed in the Introduction) at a time when organized labor, and others discontented with the effects of globalization, mounted the largest and loudest public protest in the United States since the 1960s. Foremost among the labor voices demanding attention was the very angry John J. Sweeney. The normally mild-mannered and unflappable president of the AFL-CIO, which then included 13 million members from sixty-eight unions, came to Seattle with a sense of betrayal. Representing a significant segment of the political base of support for the Democratic Party, he had opposed but tolerated President Bill Clinton's pro-trade policies over the previous seven years. Sweeney had even tried to work with the administration in preparation for the Seattle Ministerial. Serving on the President's Advisory Committee for Trade Policy and Negotiations with thirty-four other industry and labor leaders, Sweeney was persuaded by Clinton to sign a letter of endorsement for the US objectives in Seattle after the White House agreed to call for a WTO Working Group on Trade and Labor. The proposed working group was to analyze and report on a number of labor issues, which would be considered at the next ministerial meeting. In view of the unrelenting opposition by many WTO members from the developing world to including workers' rights in any trade negotiations, it was seen as an important first step toward injecting the issue into the international trade regime.

As soon as the letter was published, however, administration officials began downplaying the significance of the labor proposal, knowing that it would be a nonstarter with a significant portion of developing countries if viewed as a "first step" to creating enforceable labor standards in trade agreements. USTR officials presented it in a much less threatening manner to their WTO counterparts. The USTR talking points for use in discussing the working group on trade and labor included this suggested comment: "Let there be no doubt—we are not seeking to create a protectionist Trojan Horse. Nor are we engaged in promoting a conspiracy to undermine comparative advantage."

One of the more outspoken members of the president's advisory committee, Thomas J. Donohue, chief executive of the US Chamber of Commerce, however, went much further in denying the significance of the proposal. A *Washington Post* article, which reported that Donohue had lobbied Sweeney to endorse the letter, quoted Donohue saying, "The negotiation of an agreement has nothing to do with these [trade and labor working group] studies." He later expanded upon the extent of his disdain: "Environment and labor standards won't be tied to trade even if the U.S. stands on its head and spits wooden nickels. The Chamber won't let it happen, and the rest of the world won't let it happen."[21] Obviously, the chamber's position, as expressed by Donohue, had not progressed beyond where it was in 1950.

Sharp criticism came quickly from the ranks of Sweeney's constituency union leaders, who expressed shock that Sweeney had given such an endorsement. One Teamsters official said, "When we get to Seattle, we will be opposing the WTO. This letter is not our position."[22]

By the time he arrived in Seattle, Sweeney had other reasons to think that his support for the administration's trade objectives had been a grave mistake. On November 15, the administration announced that it had reached an agreement with China necessary to China's accession to the WTO. The American labor establishment vehemently opposed China's membership in the WTO. Sweeney immediately issued a statement mocking Clinton's stated desire to "put a human face on the global economy"[23] at Seattle while making a deal with China, a country Sweeney called a "rogue nation that decorates itself with human rights abuses as if they were medals of honor." Not mincing words, he continued:

At a time when WTO rules protecting workers' and human rights and the environment are yet unwritten, this agreement undermines that possibility and squanders a chance for the WTO to achieve the legitimacy it and other international institutions lack among people around the world.[24]

Sweeney was also infuriated by the notice given to him by administration officials on the eve of the conference that the United States would support an initiative to grant duty-free access for "essentially all products" from the least developed countries. Despite assurances that this broad language would not include textile products from Bangladesh, a least developed WTO member and a leading apparel supplier to the United States, Sweeney refused to be taken in again. As one Sweeney subordinate observed, "John went out on limb for them with that letter of endorsement, and they sawed it off on him."[25] Revealing his sense of betrayal and frustration, the normally calm Sweeney lost his temper with Congressman Sander (Sandy) M. Levin (D-MI), a longtime labor ally, when Levin suggested to him in Seattle that things would be much better when the Democratic Party took back control of the US House of Representatives.

President Clinton promptly tried to calm the storm by empathizing with labor protesters in a newspaper interview given by telephone from San Francisco as the demonstration overwhelmed Seattle. Anyone who knew Bill Clinton and his political style would not be surprised at his embracing the right of protesters to be heard and included in the trade process—particularly those from the labor and environmental base of his party. But to the shock of almost everyone, including everyone on his own trade delegation, he embraced much more than that in the interview. In what appeared to be an ad libbed stream of consciousness, he said:

> What we ought to do first of all is to adopt the United States' position on having a working group on labor within the WTO, and then that working group should develop these core labor standards, and then they ought to be a part of every trade agreement, and *ultimately I would favor a system in which sanctions would come for violating any provision of a trade agreement.* [emphasis added][26]

Clinton's startling endorsement of trade sanctions for labor violations was naturally praised by labor leaders but was received like a hand grenade by practically all of the trade delegates. Stunned, one labor leader enthusiastically gushed, "We have never had this kind of reaction from any government agency before, especially the White House. It's movement forward."[27]

In a speech given on November 30 before the labor protest march began, John Sweeney had demanded that the WTO "incorporate rules to enforce workers' rights and environmental and consumer protections" before beginning a new round of trade negotiations. The next day, Sweeney welcomed the president's statement and credited Clinton with having "instantly understood that the terms of the debate over trade have changed."[28]

But Deputy Prime Minister Supachai Panitchpakdi of Thailand, who had been selected to succeed Mike Moore as the next WTO director general, told a news conference that Clinton had confirmed the worst suspicions of developing countries that labor standards were simply a pretext for new trade barriers. Another diplomat predicted that if such sanctions were formalized as a US proposal, "you'll see dozens of developing country ministers lining up at their hotel desks to check out of Seattle."[29] The EU delegation had supported the labor working group proposal but reacted promptly to the Clinton interview by confirming unequivocally that it opposed linking trade sanctions to labor standards. Within the EU, France and Germany led most of the northern European countries for a strong position favoring labor, supporting the inclusion of what they called a "social clause" in trade agreements. Britain, the Netherlands, Spain, and Greece, however, opposed the labor working group in the US proposal.

The US delegation had been assuring trade representatives from developing nations that the working group proposal was not a hidden agenda for new trade restrictions. In the words of one delegation source, as reported by Reuters, "It cut the legs right out from under U.S." The official response given by an unnamed "senior Washington aide" was unavoidably feeble: "He (the president) was expressing an ultimate goal, not an immediate negotiating objective in the WTO."[30]

The issue of the *Seattle Post-Intelligencer* containing the front-page story of Clinton's interview appeared at the door of most delegates' hotel rooms on the morning of December 1, when the streets between the major hotels and the conference center had finally been cleared of demonstrators and the official meetings were able to begin in earnest. The collective official position of most delegates professed that neither the protests nor Clinton's statement had had a significant impact on the negotiations. "We are very much on track substantively," declared the USTR, Ambassador Charlene Barshefsky, for example.[31] However, the negotiations had at least been frustrated with a critical delay and undeniably knocked off balance. There were now only three days left to close the wide gaps separating the United States and the European Union on agriculture subsidies and the other complex interests of the WTO membership.

One of the US goals at Seattle and in the anticipated new round of trade negotiations was to address the concerns of "civil society," a euphemism for those politically disaffected by trade, by offering several proposals to put a "human face" on the global economy. In addition to the WTO Working Group on Trade and Labor, the US delegation pushed to make the WTO "more open and more accessible" by allowing more input from NGOs and strengthening the WTO's institutional relationship with the ILO and the UN Environmental Program. Central to the US position in Seattle was the proposal to launch a new trade round focused on agriculture, services, and

industrial tariffs to be concluded within three years. By far, the most important piece of the US agenda was agriculture, for which it sought to eliminate
export subsidies, reduce tariffs and trade-distorting domestic support programs, and ensure market access for bio-engineered products.

The EU proposed a much broader agenda for Seattle, which the US
delegation argued amounted to negotiations about "anything but agriculture."[32] The Europeans wanted an agenda that deemphasized agriculture to
avoid a negative impact on its politically sensitive Common Agricultural
Policy. Under NGO scrutiny similar to that in the United States, the EU
underlined the need to address the concerns of its civil society and, with
strong reservations from a number of its member states, endorsed the formation of a working "forum" on labor rights. The EU proposal was intended
to be less objectionable than the US proposal to developing countries by
including the ILO in the forum and confirming European opposition to
"sanctions-based approaches" and protectionist limitations on the comparative advantage of low-wage countries. It also proposed an initiative calling
for the elimination of tariffs and quotas on "essentially all" imports from
the least developed countries. It insisted on the elimination of "peak tariffs"
exemplified by the high US tariffs on textile fabrics.

The developing countries were led by a group that referred to themselves as the "Like-Minded Group," then principally India, Pakistan, Egypt,
and Malaysia. Even when India and Pakistan were threatening each other
with nuclear war on their common border, they remained "like-minded"
in Geneva on trade against the rich countries. The primary demand of the
like-minded developing countries involved better market access for their
all-important textiles exports, and they took an unbending hard-line position against labor rights. Foreseeing the proposals of both the United States
and the EU on labor as leading to new barriers to the markets of developed
countries, they remained adamantly opposed. One developing country official insisted that they would not consider labor standards as a potential
bargaining chip for any of their textile demands.

"Developing countries feel somewhat cheated," said Stuart Harbinson,
Hong Kong's representative to the WTO, the week before Seattle. Then serving as the chairman of the International Textile and Clothing Bureau (ITCB),
an organization of textile exporting nations, Harbinson led the bitter refrain
against sluggish progress in eliminating textile quotas. The implementation
of this part of the Uruguay Round agreements was especially slow in the
United States. "It will be difficult to begin a meaningful round of new trade

negotiations while the developing countries feel that the anticipated benefits of the Uruguay Round have not been felt," he said. "All the rhetoric from developed countries about trade and labor standards will be seen as hollow and lacking credibility. There could be no better way to raise living standards and labor standards in developing countries around the world than for industrial countries to open their doors to imports."[33] The ITCB countries demanded elimination of at least 50 percent of the quotas by January 1, 2002.

In the lead-up to Seattle, the EU began sending positive signals responding to these demands; but their accommodating signals were risk-free, as one trade official observed, because "there is not a chance" the United States would agree to expedite its quota reductions, especially in the year preceding a presidential election. Pakistan's ambassador to the WTO told me that he knew the EU's favorable stand on faster quota reductions was simply "a tactical ploy," but said, "Let us call their bluff." A senior diplomat from Portugal, one of the EU's top textile producers, confirmed this ploy when he urged me not to move to the European position.[34]

Opposition to the US proposal on labor became increasingly insurmountable following President Clinton's call for linking trade sanctions to labor rights. Four-fifths of the 135 members of the WTO in 1999 were developing countries that collectively were demanding more influence in the consensus-driven WTO decisions previously dominated by the United States and the EU. The US labor proposal had become their prime target. The American negotiators began to back off their call for a labor working group within the WTO and hinted that it might accept an EU proposal for a joint forum consisting of the ILO, the WTO, and other international organizations like the World Bank and the International Monetary Fund. This forum would examine the relationship between trade and labor, excluding "any issue relating to trade sanctions," and report its findings at the next ministerial conference. But the "Like-Minded Group" would not consider it. "We will block consensus on every issue if the United States proposal goes ahead," the Pakistani trade minister threatened. "We will explode the meeting."[35]

The Indian WTO ambassador, Srinivasan Narayanan, who was considered one of the toughest negotiators in Geneva, took an equally obstinate line. He later explained to me that trade is a highly politicized issue in India. He said that when he loses a dispute or negotiating advantage, it is highly publicized in the Indian press, while "no publicity is given to the dispute settlement cases that India wins." In Geneva he is considered most difficult, he said, but in India he is often criticized for being "too soft." "There is a broad convergence of interests among developing countries in theory," he said, "but not in practice except for labor issues."[36] This "like-minded" position simply will not allow labor rules to be used for protectionist purposes. After Seattle, India's commerce secretary said at a WTO meeting of senior officials in Geneva that "consistent with our well-known approach, I will avoid talking about [labor standards] while in the WTO building."[37]

On the final day, the ministerial conference simply folded and the delegates left Seattle with no declaration establishing a new trade round, no resolution of the agriculture issue or any other matter scheduled for discussion, and no foreseeable hope for labor standards to be a part of WTO agreements.

Regardless of one's point of view, the weeklong "Battle in Seattle" offered a panoramic snapshot of the international politics of trade at the end of the twentieth century. The carnival of competing interests represented by the protesters, NGOs, business lobbyists, politicians, and official delegates all together offered a complex set of conflicts that essentially overloaded the WTO's limited political system. The protests from the "civil society" were a loud, boisterous sideshow to the ultimately fatal competing domestic interests of the WTO member states. The developed countries were stymied over such issues as agriculture, intellectual property, and anti-dumping. The developing nations' demands for enhanced market access were blocked as they refused to discuss labor standards. Yet the protests exposed a nerve of public dissatisfaction with some of the effects of globalization, a pulse so strong that it could no longer be ignored by politicians in a democratic world.

Seattle also exposed the institutional shortcomings of the WTO as a political decision-making body. Can complex multilateral negotiations be ruled by a consensus of now 164 member states in a trade regime no longer dictated by the demands of the most powerful members? These questions along with the entry of China into the WTO two years later and the labor and environmental issues so prominent at Seattle were thus pushed into the twenty-first century.

ADVANCING THE LIBERAL ORDER BEYOND THE WORLD TRADE ORGANIZATION (WTO)

One thing became very clear after Seattle: labor standards were not going to become an institutional part of the liberal world trade order governed by the WTO. Indeed, WTO multilateral negotiating rounds designed to reach consensus on settling other difficult issues may have become a thing of the past after the Uruguay Round. The Doha Round began in 2001 three months after the 9/11 attack—a tragedy that brought the WTO members together in a unified effort to exhibit world order—but ended after more than a decade, punting on the big issues that divided the developed and developing worlds. Doha did finally produce the Trade Facilitation Agreement, which adds significant value to the system in addressing technical trade barriers, and the WTO has since expanded the Information Technology Agreement. The WTO most importantly continues to perform a crucial role in resolving trade disputes and establishing a body of international trade rules to guide the member states. Negotiations that involve political conflicts over labor, environment, enhanced market access, and ending agricultural subsidies, however, have reached a dead end for now. As in NAFTA and the Cambodia Textiles Agreement, attempts at progress on the broad multilateral front have moved to more narrowly focused forums.

In the year following the implementation of the Cambodia agreement, President Clinton and King Abdullah II met for the signing of the US-Jordan Free Trade Agreement (FTA) in October 2000. As in the Cambodia pact, the Jordan FTA included strong labor provisions in the body of the agreement, not in side letters as were added to NAFTA. Unlike the Cambodia agreement, which primarily dealt with quotas authorized under existing law, the Jordan agreement involved tariff modifications that had to be approved by Congress. President Clinton did not have "fast-track" negotiating authority, which had expired in 1994, making the approval process for trade agreements more difficult.

The Jordan agreement's labor provisions offered substantial improvements over the NAFTA side agreements, improvements that Democrats generally favored and many Republicans opposed. Principally, the workers' rights provisions covered a broader list of labor standards than were covered under the NAFTA side letter, and the Jordan agreement's labor provisions were covered by the same dispute settlement procedure as commercial disputes. A major complaint about the NAFTA side letter on labor was that its dispute settlement procedure had proven to be largely ineffective. In the Jordan agreement, if a dispute was not resolved satisfactorily under the dispute procedure, either party could take "any appropriate and commensurate measure," including trade sanctions. In the Cambodia agreement, the incentive for complying with labor standards was the "carrot" of expanded quotas. The incentive in the Jordan agreement was a "stick" of potential sanctions that could reduce market access if tariff concessions in the agreement were withdrawn.

Based largely on the popularity of the late King Hussein's legacy of moderation and cooperation in the Middle East conflict, which his son, King Abdullah II, was continuing, the Senate followed the House in easily approving the Jordan agreement on September 28, 2001, during President George W. Bush's first year in office and less than three weeks after the 9/11 attack. Despite the strategic importance of Jordan and the popularity of its king, the labor provisions in the agreement raised considerable controversy among some members. Conservatives argued that trade agreements should not include workers' rights and environmental protection. Senator Phil Gramm (R-TX), for example, alleged that the agreement infringed upon US sovereignty by limiting Congress from legislating new labor and environmental rules. Gramm warned that he would oppose any effort to use the Jordan FTA as a model for future trade agreements.

President Bush's USTR, Robert Zoellick, resolved the sanctions debate before Congress approved the agreement by exchanging identical letters with Jordan's ambassador to Washington that pledged to settle any disputes under the agreement without resorting to its dispute settlement procedures and without "blocking trade." This exchange of letters satisfied the Republican majority, but Congressman Sandy Levin, the ranking Democrat on the trade subcommittee of the House Ways and Means Committee, called the letter exchange "a step backwards for future constructive action on trade."[38] Levin's assessment proved to be accurate over the next five years, during a period of high partisan tension over trade with a complete reversal of the traditional stance taken on trade by each of the political parties.

Following the 1994 midterm elections, when the Republicans took control of the House for the first time in forty years and many pro-trade moderate Democrats (me included) lost their seats, trade legislation was vitally dependent upon GOP votes for passage. Although both President Clinton and the Republican leadership desired approval of fast-track negotiating authority, the Republicans refused to provide labor and environmental objectives satisfactory to Clinton and most Democrats. House Speaker Newt Gingrich, despite Clinton's objections, brought a fast-track proposal to the floor in September 1998 only to watch it fail in order to embarrass the president. It was not until four years later during the Bush presidency that Congress ended an eight-year fast-track hiatus and granted the president trade negotiating authority (this time, euphemistically, renamed "Trade Promotion Authority").

Even with a Republican majority, trade authorization was not easy to obtain. While the GOP had moved light years from its traditional protectionist stance, there remained in its caucus a stubborn contingent of right-wing isolationists and many protectionist members representing influential steel or textile constituencies. Another impediment to attracting favorable trade votes was the chief sponsor of the authorization bill, Ways and Means chairman William (Bill) M. Thomas (R-CA), a hot-tempered autocrat with a personality ill-suited to winning friends and influencing votes. Thomas was smart, however, and shrewd enough to know that he needed some Democratic votes to pass his bill. Yet he completely bypassed the minority leadership on the committee—Congressmen Charles B. Rangel (D-NY), Robert T. Matsui (D-CA), and Sander Levin (D-MI), all of whom were favorable to trade under the right conditions. One commentator observed that Thomas treated Rangel, the senior Democrat, "like a car-park attendant."[39] Thomas simply ignored Rangel and sought co-sponsorships from three more junior pro-trade Democrats—moderates who consented to vague negotiating objectives on labor and environment.

Thomas introduced the bill under the misleading title, "The Bipartisan Trade Promotion Authority Act of 2001." In December 2001, the bill passed the House by a vote of 215–214, with only twenty-one Democrats in favor, after the leadership held open the vote for a highly unusual extra twenty minutes. This additional time allowed Majority Whip Tom (the "Hammer") DeLay (R-TX) to perform his enhanced-level arm-twisting and President Bush to sign a letter to a North Carolina congressman committing to further protections on textiles over the objections of Chairman Thomas. When the measure came back from the Senate the following year with an expansion of the Trade Adjustment Assistance program, the final vote on the conference agreement picked up four more favorable Democratic votes and lost an equal number of Republicans.

Under the new authority, President Bush over the next four years completed negotiations and managed to pass seven new free-trade agreements involving twelve countries—Australia, Chile, Singapore, Morocco, Bahrain, Oman, and, under the Dominican Republic–Central American Free Trade Agreement (DR-CAFTA), Costa Rica, El Salvador, Guatemala, Honduras, Nicaragua, and the Dominican Republic. The labor provisions in these agreements were weaker than those in the original Jordan FTA, before it was weakened by Ambassador Zoellick's exchange of letters with the Jordanian ambassador. The Bush FTAs also placed a $15 million limit on monetary penalties in labor disputes, which many considered too low to be effective, while placing no such limits on commercial disputes.

THE MAY 10TH AGREEMENT

The political environment on the Hill shifted dramatically after the 2006 midterm elections, when the Democrats gained a sweeping victory, taking control of both Houses of Congress again for the first time since 1994. Many trade advocates feared that this turnover, in which many free-trade proponents were among the thirty seats lost by Republicans and were replaced by Democrats who had run anti-trade campaigns, did not bode well for the future of trade policy. When the new Congress convened, however, the incoming chairman of the Finance Committee, Senator Max Baucus (D-MT), published an op-ed in the *Wall Street Journal* calling for a renewal of fast-track authority, which was due to expire in six months. With the renewal, Baucus called for an aggressive trade policy "with better trade enforcement capability and better environmental and labor provisions," along with a significantly expanded Trade Adjustment Assistance program. On the day the Baucus piece appeared, US Chamber of Commerce president Tom Donohue expressed a willingness to talk about "those issues" in a fast-track renewal, but warned, "The devil is in the details." He indicated opposition to an AFL-CIO proposal to include ILO labor standards in trade agreements that would be subject to dispute resolution and sanctions.[40]

On the House side, Charlie Rangel became chairman of Ways and Means, a committee on which he had served for thirty-two years. A New York liberal representing a district centered in Harlem since 1970, Rangel became a major target by Republicans during the 2006 campaign, who cited the customary threat that his chairmanship of the committee would bring back the "tax and spend" policies of the past if the GOP failed to maintain control of the House. Vice President Dick Cheney even suggested in one insulting putdown that Congressman Rangel "doesn't understand how the economy works." Upon assuming the chairmanship, Rangel promptly made trade reform a priority with the hope of attracting a true bipartisan coalition. The new chairman's record on trade had been mixed in the past; for example, he voted against NAFTA but was a primary sponsor of the Trade and Development Act of 2000, which promoted preferential trade with countries in sub-Saharan Africa and the Caribbean Basin. Trade policy now offered him an opportunity to leave a legacy during his tenure as chairman. "I'm 76," he explained, "and I can't afford the luxury just to gridlock." Unlike his predecessor, Bill Thomas, who retired in 2006, Rangel had the desire and the personality to bring members of both parties into the reform effort. Even the conservative *Weekly Standard* described him as "the Democrat best positioned to salvage a free trade agenda—should he wish to and should his caucus not stamp out such efforts."[41]

Rangel's principal partner on trade reform in the House was Sandy Levin, chair of the Ways and Means Subcommittee on Trade. A bright and innovative legislator representing, since 1982, a Detroit suburban district significantly populated by families of autoworkers, Levin had always maintained an appreciation for the benefits of expanded trade but with a firm pro-labor perspective. He was amenable to extending the president's negotiating authority but only after addressing the effects of trade on US workers. "The [Bush] Administration's policy," Levin argued, "has been far too

FIGURE 16.2 Chairman of the House Ways and Means Committee Charlie Rangel (left) and Subcommittee on Trade chairman Sander Levin, authors of the May 10th Agreement (Associated Press)

passive in enforcing trade agreements, in breaking down unfair barriers to U.S. products, and in establishing rules that raise standards of living in the U.S. and around the globe." Before extending fast-track negotiating authority for future agreements, Levin demanded that the three pending trade agreements with Peru, Colombia, and Panama be renegotiated and that a tougher stance be taken on auto policies in current trade negotiations with South Korea.[42]

In order to have a true bipartisan trade policy that could gain majority approval, Baucus, Rangel, and Levin needed a buy-in from the Bush administration and from the GOP ranking leadership of the trade committees, Congressman Jim McCrery (R-LA) and Senator Charles Grassley (R-IA). Neither party had the votes to succeed alone anymore. On February 14, at a hearing of the full Ways and Means Committee on trade policy with the USTR, Ambassador Susan C. Schwab, Chairman Rangel welcomed the chief US negotiator in his opening remarks at the hearing by telling her, "I want to be your new best friend." Noting that the recent thinking on trade policy had been "polarized," he pointed out that the Chamber of Commerce has "never seen a trade agreement they didn't like, and labor hasn't seen one they did like." The perception giving trade a bad name was, he said, "that negotiations only concern the multi-national corporations, while the victims of globalization believe they're denied the attention they deserve." He concluded that this perception could only be corrected by making "certain that agreements before this committee will be considered in a very bipartisan way."[43]

Levin was more specific in his opening statement: "We strongly favor expanded trade," but "it is time to craft a new trade policy for this new era of globalization." Amending the pending Latin America FTAs offered "an excellent opportunity," he argued, to begin "a real partnership between this Administration and the new [Democratic] majority to rebuild the bipartisan foundation for trade." Levin declared that the agreements must include the five core ILO standards, which must be enforceable like other provisions in the agreement.[44]

While McCrery and Grassley acknowledged that they had little choice but to accept stronger protections for labor and environment in the FTAs to obtain approval of the pending agreements and a renewal of fast track, Schwab stalled in offering any compromise offers. Congressman Paul Ryan (R-WI), among other GOP members of the committee, objected to adding ILO standards in the agreement because the United States had not ratified all of the ILO conventions. Ryan warned against overreaching in making labor demands of trading partners, and administration officials raised concerns that these provisions could force a rewrite of US labor laws.[45]

At the same time, dissension arose within the Democratic Caucus as organized labor expressed concern about Rangel's firmness in withstanding Republican opposition to enforceable ILO standards. Levin publicly expressed his unequivocal demand that ILO standards be added to the pending FTAs; Rangel had not. Some in organized labor feared that Rangel was too eager to prove that he could put together a bipartisan deal. Steelworkers president Leo Gerard warned that "free-trade" Republicans had been replaced by "fair-trade" Democrats in the previous elections, and his union would be looking for primary opponents to run against members moving away from that position. Unions and environmental groups alike expressed opposition to *any* extension of fast-track authority. Thirty-nine of the forty-two freshman Democrats requested a meeting with Rangel and Levin to develop a new model for trade policy that Democratic members could support. Leaders of the pro-trade New Democrat Coalition also met with Rangel and Levin and expressed support for the effort to find a bipartisan solution.

Despite the disagreements within his own party, Levin by mid-March reached his own conclusion on the vote count: "I don't think [the Bush administration has] the votes for an FTA that doesn't have international labor standards and environmental standards."[46] By the end of March, Rangel and Levin produced "A New Trade Policy for America," endorsed by Speaker Nancy Pelosi (D-CA), that covered the waterfront of Democratic trade policies, including workers' rights and environmental protection, and establishing a balance between the demands of the pharmaceutical lobby and promoting access to generic medicines in developing countries. While all of these policies had been resisted by the Bush administration, Ambassador Schwab welcomed the proposal as "another step in what has been a good-faith effort in a continuing dialogue by all sides." The AFL-CIO also praised the Democratic proposals as an improvement of the pending FTAs and the negotiations with South Korea. Rangel conceded that while "everyone is pretty upbeat about this," some members from "the extremes" of each party will oppose trade deals. "There's going to be a coalition vote for trade with moderates in both parties in support," he predicted.[47]

A major divide remained within the Democratic Party between members of the party from the industrial heartland who tended to oppose trade and those in more high-tech urban regions or those in pro-trade agricultural districts who were more inclined to favor trade. A higher percentage of Democratic members on Ways and Means were pro-trade than in the caucus as a whole. Representative Marcy Kaptor (D-OH), a persistent trade critic, emphasized the strong influence of Wall Street on Sandy Levin's committee, and said, "I hope he'll be able to stand up for Main Street, but I don't know." She also pointed to the fact that Rangel was from New York and Pelosi from San Francisco, questioning whether they could appreciate the different outlook on the global economy from the rust belt. Rangel and Levin lobbied members for their new policy with an emphasis on the creation of new programs to help displaced workers in the global economy, like expanded education and training programs. Seventy-one Democratic members signed a letter endorsing the new trade policy.[48]

On May 10, 2007, after six weeks of continued negotiations following the release of the new Democratic trade policy, the Bush administration and the leadership of the House announced they had reached agreement on "a fundamental shift in U.S. trade policy." The announcement was essentially a Democratic victory as the agreement tracked the new trade policy announced by Ways and Means on March 27 on all principles. The agreement provided a template for renegotiating the pending agreements and for use in future trade deals. On labor, the bipartisan agreement accepted Levin's requirement that trade agreements include enforceable obligations that countries must adopt and maintain in their laws and that countries practice the five basic internationally recognized labor principles, as stated in the 1998 ILO Declaration on Fundamental Principles and Rights at Work: (1) freedom of association, (2) recognition of the right to collective bargaining, (3) elimination of all forms of forced or compulsory labor, (4) abolition of child labor and prohibition of the worst forms of child labor, and (5) elimination of discrimination in respect of employment and occupation.

These principles are based on the 1998 ILO Declaration, and since the United States was already obligated to and in compliance with this declaration, the Republican objection that adding ILO standards to trade agreements might force modifications in US labor laws did not apply. Finally, the May 10th Agreement requires that labor violations under trade agreements must occur in a manner affecting trade or investment between the parties to fall under the enforcement provisions. When labor violations occur, however, the disputes are subject to the same settlement procedures and the same enforcement penalties as any other dispute arising under the trade agreements (for example, the same as commercial or environmental disputes). The bipartisan agreement also addressed environmental protections (requiring the parties to implement the obligations of seven multilateral environmental agreements), intellectual property provisions to improve access to generic medicines, services, investment, and other issues.[49] For the present discussion, however, the focus here is on labor issues.

The significance of the May 10th Agreement is obvious when compared to the record of US trade agreements since the Havana Charter and its labor provisions were abandoned in 1950. Except for the eligibility criteria in GSP and other preference agreements, which after 1984 required recipient countries to be "taking steps" to afford workers internationally recognized worker rights, labor protections were not included in the body of a trade agreement until the US-Cambodia Textile Agreement in 1999. Neither the Israel FTA of 1985, nor the Canadian FTA in 1987 mentioned labor. NAFTA added side agreements on labor and the environment in 1994, but the dispute provisions were considered ineffective in practice. The 2001 Jordan agreement contained stronger labor provisions, but an exchange of letters between the Bush administration and the Jordanian Embassy essentially defanged these protections. The seven FTAs negotiated under the Bush administration before the May 10th Agreement contained weak labor protections with limited penalties for violations.

Of the three FTAs pending on May 10, only the Peru FTA, formally called the United States–Peru Trade Promotion Agreement (PTPA), was ready for approval by Congress.[50] The original agreement had been signed in April 2006, and the United States and Peru signed amendments to the PTPA on June 25, 2007, to reflect changes required by the May 10th Agreement. The Peruvian Congress ratified those changes two days later, and in a joint press statement, Speaker Pelosi, Majority Leader Steny Hoyer, Rangel, and Levin trumpeted this as "an historic accomplishment."[51] Congressmen Rangel and Levin, leading a bipartisan delegation, traveled to Lima to work with the Peruvian government on implementation of the new labor provisions. Completion of these changes, carried out by "supreme decrees" issued in the fall, held up action in their committee, but the Senate Finance Committee commenced hearings on September 11.

One of the first witnesses in the Finance Committee hearing, AFL-CIO policy director Thea M. Lee, praised the new provisions on workers' rights and the environment negotiated by Chairman Rangel and Subcommittee

chairman Levin in the May 10th bipartisan agreement. Lee said these provisions "represent significant progress in crucial areas that we have fought
to achieve for many years" and would provide a "starting point" for future
efforts in enforcing protections for workers in the global economy. While
the May 10th template represents progress, she said, "it is by no means a
complete fix appropriate for any country or any situation." Because of conflicting views among the federation's unions, the AFL-CIO would neither
endorse nor oppose the PTPA, but would "vigorously oppose the FTAs with
Colombia and Korea and any renewal of the current fast track authority."
She applauded the efforts that went into improving the PTPA, "marking a
substantial step forward toward a trade model that will benefit the working people of both countries," but concluded that "the May 10th agreement
represents the tip of the iceberg in addressing what is wrong in our trade
policy." She listed problems needing reform beyond worker rights, such as
investor-state dispute provisions, currency manipulation, an unfair and
imbalanced tax code, and inconsistent enforcement of trade law remedies.[52]

Rangel passed the agreement out of his committee on a unanimous
voice vote without even holding a hearing on it. Despite substantial opposition from labor and other anti-trade organizations, the implementing legislation for PTPA passed easily in the House with a comfortable bipartisan
majority, after the passage of an enhanced Trade Adjustment Assistance
program—a priority sequence required by Speaker Pelosi. The Speaker's
leadership down this path avoided the protectionist label, demonstrated
moderation to the business community, and showed concern for those
negatively affected by trade. It nevertheless drew strong objections from
many among her caucus and from some labor sectors. Teamsters president
James P. Hoffa protested, "We believe the leadership is wrong and we continue to fight them." Voting for the agreement were 109 Democrats and 176
Republicans, while 116 Democrats and 18 Republicans voted against it.

The nearly equal split among Democrats can be explained largely by the
different perspectives of those members representing the industrial regions
of the Northeast and Midwest and those representing agricultural districts
or high-tech constituencies along the East and West Coasts. But apart from
these distinctions, trade was a risky, hot political topic, and the easier vote
(especially if not needed for passage) was in the anti-column, especially
after the heavy criticisms of the Bush trade policies remained foremost
in voters' memories from the 2006 elections. Although the yea votes did
not quite reach a majority in the Democratic Caucus, they represented a

fivefold increase over the positive Democratic numbers in the vote for the so-called Bipartisan Trade Promotion Authority in 2002.[53]

In the far more pro-trade Senate, the Peru trade agreement received overwhelming approval, on December 4, 2007, with a 77-to-18 vote, including twenty-nine Democrats and nearly all Republicans voting in favor. Senator Baucus called the vote a "very significant" breakthrough for trade, while Senator Bernie Sanders (I-VT), one of seventeen senators caucusing with Democrats who voted no, said that one of the major reasons that "the gap between the rich and the poor is growing wider is in fact due to our disastrous, unfettered trade policy."

None of the five senators who were then running for the 2008 presidential nomination bothered to leave the campaign trail to participate in the Peru Agreement vote. By this time, a month before the Iowa caucuses, however, they all had announced where they stood on it. John S. McCain (R-AZ), Hillary Rodham Clinton (D-NY), and Barack H. Obama (D-IL) all announced that they were for it. Joseph R. Biden (D-DE) and Christopher J. Dodd (D-CT) were against it. Former senator John Edwards (D-NC), then also a top-tier candidate, was firmly against it, saying: "Like the failed free trade agreements before it, the Peru agreement puts the interests of the big multinational corporations first, ahead of the interests of American workers and communities."[54]

LABOR AND THE TRANS-PACIFIC STRATEGIC ECONOMIC PARTNERSHIP AGREEMENT (TPP)

The presidential election season that began in 2007, just as the financial crisis leading to the Great Recession was emerging, offered more than the usual variety of populist, anti-trade candidates. A poll released in September offers one explanation for the candidacy of Republican populists: an estimated 59 percent of likely GOP primary voters viewed foreign trade as being bad for the US economy.[55] The eleven candidates running in the Republican primaries included former Arkansas governor Mike Huckabee from the religious right (questioning evolution and favoring constitutional bans on abortion and same-sex marriage), who railed against the corporate greed behind shipping jobs overseas, NAFTA, and free trade in general. Surprisingly, Huckabee won the Iowa Republican caucus and five states on Super Tuesday with that message. Congressman Ron Paul, a libertarian

Republican from Texas, opposed any foreign entanglements and had voted for withdrawing from the WTO and against other trade agreements. Paul did not gain many delegates but had strong financial support from a dedicated group of followers. He remained in the race against Senator John McCain (R-AZ) longer than any other Republican candidate.

Of the eight candidates in the Democratic primaries, John Edwards led the major candidates with his populist campaign emphasizing the divide between what he called the "two Americas"—that is, the rich America and the working-class America. A wealthy personal injury attorney and the son of a textile millworker, Edwards had experienced both "Americas," apparently neither of which led him to appreciate the benefits of trade. He was not the king of the populist anti-trade Democrats in the campaign, however; that title would have to belong to Congressman Dennis Kucinich of Ohio. Before he dropped out of the race, he promised at every debate that one of his first acts as president would be to "cancel" US membership in both NAFTA and the WTO, as if he were canceling membership in the Book-of-the-Month Club.

The top Democratic candidates, Obama and Clinton, were both economic centrists who favored liberal trade but weighed in with more populist views during the campaign. These views advanced as they battled over Edwards's share of the labor vote (importantly, the United Steelworkers, which had endorsed Edwards) after he folded his campaign.[56] Even though neither of them held elective office in 1993 when NAFTA passed, they both claimed to have been against it from the beginning. This position was a bit harder for Clinton to establish since her husband signed the agreement into law while she was First Lady. Her surrogates spread the word that she tried to talk her husband into opposing it while running against President George H. W. Bush in 1992.[57] In fairness, obviously, the Democratic presidential primary often necessarily becomes a contest for the labor vote; both candidates promised to review and revise all prior trade agreements for their effects on American workers, as did the 2004 nominee, Senator John Kerry, an avid free-trader.

In any case, the two Democratic candidates ultimately held the same stance on most trade issues. They both had voted against DR-CAFTA, both supported the Peru FTA and opposed the Colombia, Panama, and Korean FTAs under existing conditions. They both proposed eliminating tax incentives for outsourcing jobs and promised to name China a currency manipulator, among other aggressive legal actions they pledged to take against

China for a variety of alleged unfair trade practices. On the Chinese currency issue, they both supported treating the undervalued yuan as a subsidy subject to countervailing duties. Senator Clinton went even further, promising to consider raising tariffs on Chinese imports by 27.5 percent to equal the percentage that the yuan was undervalued, according to an outdated estimate. And, finally, both said they would renegotiate NAFTA to add stronger labor and environment protections and better enforcement mechanisms. They bolstered their bargaining position with the threat of opting out of the agreement if Mexico and Canada refused to renegotiate.[58]

After he finally clinched the nomination, Senator Obama continued to press these positions in the general election campaign against Senator John McCain.[59] Upon sealing the Republican nomination in March, McCain said in a victory speech that he would "leave it to my opponents to argue that we should abrogate trade treaties and pretend the global economy will go away, and Americans can secure our future by trading and investing only among ourselves." Characterized by his campaign as an "unabashed free-trader," McCain, even in the rust belt states, strongly defended his vote for NAFTA, which he said had "created millions of jobs" and was "a benefit to our country." He also bluntly declared several times that the manufacturing jobs that have been lost will not return. In their final presidential debate on October 15, McCain blasted Obama's opposition to the pending Colombia and Korea FTAs, Obama's votes for trade-distorting farm subsidies, and Obama's call for the "unilateral" renegotiation of NAFTA.[60]

By the time of his inauguration on January 20, 2009, however, President Barack Obama's allegiance to his campaign trade policies had been overwhelmed by more pressing economic priorities. With American job losses rising to 8 million from the Great Recession and threatening an economic depression, the new administration focused its attention on reviving the Keynesian stimulus policies begun under President Bush in 2008. Equally demanding of his time and political capital was the president's drive for healthcare reform that culminated in the signing of the Affordable Care Act in March 2010.

Rather than attempting to reopen NAFTA during the first foreign trip of his presidency across the border to Canada in February 2009, Obama assured Prime Minister Stephen Harper that he wanted "to grow trade, not contract it." Two months later, following a summit meeting Obama held with the leaders of Mexico and Canada in Trinidad, the newly confirmed USTR, Ronald "Ron" Kirk, announced to the press that the leaders were "all of the mind we should look for opportunities to strengthen NAFTA [labor and environmental protections] . . . [but] don't believe we have to reopen the agreement now." Thea Lee of the AFL-CIO responded that she would have preferred a more certain expression of their labor concerns but understood the need to begin with a nonconfrontational approach.[61]

Repeating the view of many trade observers during Obama's first year in office, Finance Committee chairman Senator Max Baucus complained on November 10, 2009, that the administration "lacked a comprehensive trade agenda, and that absence is palpable." Surprisingly, this void began to be filled within a matter of days after Baucus's comment during an official eight-day presidential excursion to Asia. Before arriving in Singapore for a meeting of the Asia-Pacific Economic Cooperation forum (APEC), Obama dubbed himself "America's first Pacific president" because of his Hawaiian birth and pledged to start negotiations for possible membership in a little-known free-trade agreement known as the Trans-Pacific Strategic Economic Partnership Agreement (TPP).[62] At this time, the TPP included only four small countries—Brunei Darussalam, Chile, New Zealand, and Singapore—but potentially could become much larger with other APEC members and was being expanded at a time when another China-led Asian trading block was being formed that would exclude and discriminate against the United States.

Over the next seven years, highly partisan trade battles transpired over passage of the Bush-negotiated Colombia, Panama, and Korea FTAs of 2006; the adjustment assistance program; and even continuance of the fifty-year-old GSP program, which Senator Jeff Sessions (R-AL) had blocked to protect an Alabama sleeping bag company. All the while, Obama's principal trade policy, TPP, grew at a snail's pace to a culmination of the agreement in his last year in office on February 4, 2016. At the signing, the TPP members included twelve Asia-Pacific countries with both economic and strategic importance to the United States, including Australia, Brunei, Canada, Chile, Japan, Malaysia, Mexico, New Zealand, Peru, Singapore, and Vietnam, which together with the United States comprise 40 percent of the world's GDP and one-third of world trade. If approved by Congress, it would be the largest FTA in which the United States participates. An open agreement in terms of size and geo-political significance, it is designed to integrate the United States into the Asia-Pacific region with new trade rules and disciplines on a range of thirty chapters of issues, many of which are not found in previous FTAs or the WTO.

Most significantly, the TPP made important expansions on the protections of the rights of workers beyond the May 10th Agreement that had provided the historic benchmark for the last four free-trade agreements approved by Congress. As in the May 10th Agreement, the TPP obligates its members to conform to the rights and principles of the 1998 ILO Declaration (as previously listed). For the first time defined within the body of an FTA explicitly as a labor right, the TPP further requires members to adopt and maintain laws and practices governing "acceptable conditions of work": minimum wages, hours of work, and occupational safety and health regulations. The TPP also adds new ILO labor protections in the Export Processing Zones (EPZs), a long-neglected labor-intensive assembly sector, which employed transient workers in Malaysia, Mexico, Singapore, and Vietnam. This protection is also intended for possible future new members with EPZs, such as Indonesia and the Philippines. The World Bank estimates that there are thousands of such zones in Asia with lax labor standards assembling products for export.

In the developing countries with the weakest labor law standards, the United States negotiated bilateral Labor Consistency Plans in the case of Brunei and Malaysia to lay out legal and institutional reforms to shape capacity and political initiative. For Vietnam the agreement was more rigorous and was called the Plan for Enforcement of Trade and Labor Relations. Union activity in Vietnam is currently heavily influenced by the Communist Party, and workers have limited rights to form trade unions and organize strikes. Both Malaysia and Vietnam pledged to seek technical assistance in capacity building and obtain independent monitoring from the ILO (much like the successful Cambodia Textile Agreement) for five years to improve its labor law and practices to form independent labor unions and organize workers across enterprises, sectors, and regions. If Vietnam fails to comply within this period, the United States may withhold further tariff reductions otherwise due under the TPP, subject to possible review by a dispute panel. Vietnam's commitments under the five-year plan are also subject to review by an independent Labor Expert Committee that is required to submit periodic reports containing findings and recommendations on labor conditions in Vietnam.

Although the labor terms of TPP were the strongest of any trade agreement in history, AFL-CIO president Richard Trumka panned it as too weak as soon as it was released. He argued that it would provide incentives for businesses to move US jobs to TPP countries with poor labor conditions, like Brunei, Malaysia, Vietnam, and Mexico. Oddly, the first three of these countries would have the most closely monitored labor reforms of the TPP, and Mexico would now finally have its weak NAFTA labor side letter renegotiated with stronger, more effective labor provisions. The AFL-CIO was obviously moving the goalpost. Some members of Congress also took up Trumka's cause and complained with prejudgments that these developing countries would not be able to meet their labor obligations.[63]

Another view given to the Democrats on the Ways and Means Committee came from Steve Charnovitz, on the Law Faculty at George Washington University, where he has taught international trade and worker rights for over thirty years. He opened his statement simply: "The Labour chapter of the Trans-Pacific Partnership (TPP) is the most progressive set of labor obligations ever to be negotiated in a free trade agreement." Throughout his statement he makes the case affirming the USTR claim that "TPP has the strongest protections for workers of any trade agreement in history [not just in US FTAs]." Charnovitz concluded his statement with this observation:

> The moral arc of labor rights has influenced world trade for over a century and the new TPP labor chapter makes a signal contribution toward governing the social dimension of global markets. This important labor chapter provides one more reason for the US Congress to enact TPP implementing legislation.[64]

The TPP was the most comprehensive trade deal ever negotiated between developed and developing countries. It set a broad and high standard of "competitive liberalism" for future FTAs within the Doha-stalled WTO and reached the highest level yet on worker rights and environmental protection in the world trading system. Yet it was not perfect in the eyes of many trade opponents in the United States. Although the TPP participants released a declaration concurrently with the TPP agreement reaffirming IMF commitments against currency manipulation to gain unfair trade competitive advantages, the declaration did not provide any new enforcement mechanisms, as many members of Congress had advocated. Congressman Sandy Levin and others also charged that the intellectual property provisions in TPP backed off the positive steps taken under the May 10th Agreement promoting public health, by caving in to "Big Pharma's" excessive demands for patent protection and denying generic medicines to developing countries.[65]

The most robust blowback against TPP, however, came from the presidential election year politics of 2016. Only one year before, in 2015, the president won passage of fast-track/trade promotion authority to complete negotiations of TPP, which had not come easy, but seemed a breeze in comparison to the headwinds of the summer of 2016. Until October 2015, Hillary Clinton said she was still reviewing the deal although she was "worried" that it benefited drug companies and did not adequately deal with currency manipulation. When she did come out against TPP that month, she was met with a sharp degree of cynicism from her primary opponents, Senator Bernie Sanders of Vermont and former Maryland governor Martin O'Malley, both of whom had always opposed it and would not let anyone forget that she had once called TPP the "gold standard" of trade agreements before her political epiphany turned her against it.[66]

Undaunted, President Obama pressed ahead even though he faced heckling and delegates waving anti-TPP signs during his keynote speech at the Democratic convention. On August 12, USTR sent the agreement to Congress for consideration under the fast-track legislation to be considered during the lame-duck session after the election. The president said he was not concerned that both presidential candidates were opposed to TPP. He planned to put together the same bipartisan coalition that passed his negotiating authority in 2015 after the election. Both House Speaker Paul Ryan (R-WS) and Senate Majority Leader Mitch McConnell (R-KY), however, said that there were not enough votes to pass it and they would not bring it up. This did not pacify labor. Leo Gerard, president of the United Steelworkers, said he wouldn't be surprised if the TPP came up during the lame-duck session. "I wouldn't trust Mitch McConnell or Paul Ryan as far as I could throw them," Gerard said. "It's important that we be vigilant."[67]

And finally, Republican presidential nominee Donald Trump promised to withdraw from TPP, NAFTA, and many other "disastrous" trade agreements if he was elected to the White House. But no one seriously believed that could happen.

Conclusion

Donald Trump, the Forgotten Man, and the Liberal Economic Order

The forgotten man will never be forgotten again.
> —President-Elect Donald J. Trump
> November 9, 2016

In the months following the 2016 US presidential election, ominous clouds again rise over the liberal world trade order founded seventy years ago. Before the creation of the current rules-based system implementing the principles of Adam Smith, Americans struggled through nearly two centuries of economic uncertainty under the dominance of the visible hand of mainly protectionist trade politics. Among the products of this dominance was the war-threatening nullification crisis, the corrupt logrolling system of prohibitive tariffs during the robber baron era, Smoot-Hawley, and the ensuing trade wars of the interwar years, to name only some of the most egregious periods. As the system finally came into existence in the postwar years, the same destructive political forces buried the Havana Charter containing the foundation for labor rights in trade agreements and a potential solution to the most prominent cause of the protests threatening the system today.

Over the decades since its birth, the world trading system has endured periodic bouts with neo-mercantilism, but it has always survived with balanced legislative remedies such as those provided in the Trade Act of 1974 and its successors. Many presidential candidates, including several who were successful, have espoused populist, anti-trade positions in the campaign only to adopt pro-trade policies once settled in the White House. In the recent election, however, the visible hand has returned with a new and potentially fatal abandon.

PRESIDENT TRUMP—THE TRANSACTIONAL BUSINESSMAN

In late June 2016, Republican presidential candidate Donald J. Trump offered one of the most specific policy statements of his entire campaign— an aggressive seven-point plan on trade policy. Departing from his norm of tweet-sized policy pronouncements, the candidate, in a surprisingly thorough and legalistic plan, trashed existing trade agreements and threatened economic sanctions against many nations, friend and foe alike, but predominantly targeting China and Mexico. Yet even after his election five months later, it was still uncertain where a President Trump would land on trade policy, as he veered away from some of his hard-line positions on other issues. Despite his harsh anti-trade campaign rhetoric blaming at least the last five previous presidents, along with Democratic candidate Hillary R. Clinton, for the "ruinous" trade policies of the past, Trump's private businesses had frequently exploited the global supply chain guaranteed by liberal trade policies, sourcing generous quantities of imports from within the two countries he most often blasted in the campaign. In post-election interviews he softened some of the rhetoric on issues that his supporters had raucously cheered at campaign rallies, leading some GOP leaders to hope that his brash oratorical promises were not all intended to be taken *too* seriously.

During his first week in the Oval Office, however, President Trump dramatically demonstrated his intent to follow through with his severe rhetoric on trade. Among a series of executive orders signed in those first days of his administration, the president directed the Office of United States Trade Representative (USTR) to withdraw the United States as a signatory to the Trans-Pacific Partnership (TPP) agreement reached with eleven Pacific nations during the Obama administration and to "permanently" withdraw from any further TPP negotiations. He declared that it was the intention of his administration "to deal directly with individual countries on a one-on-one (or bilateral) basis in negotiating future trade deals." He further directed USTR to begin pursuing "bilateral trade negotiations to promote

American industry, protect American workers, and raise American wages."[1] In an action not legally required to withdraw from the TPP, this public notice gave the president a reality television moment to hold up before the cameras a large portfolio framing the short, six-sentence memo to USTR with his notable, expansive signature emblazoned at the bottom proving that he was indeed on the path to fulfill his promise.

He also demonstrated his resolve to renegotiate the North American Free Trade Agreement (NAFTA) by arranging to meet the following week with the leaders of Canada and Mexico in Washington to begin trade discussions. President Enrique Peña Nieto, however, canceled his visit to the meeting when Trump repeated his prior demand that Mexico pay for a multibillion-dollar wall to be built on the US-Mexico border to prevent illegal immigration into the United States. Matters got worse when the president's press secretary, Sean M. Spicer, explained that the Trump administration would make Mexico pay for the wall by imposing a 20 percent border tax on all imports from Mexico. This proposition drew protests

FIGURE C.1 President Trump, with then chief of staff Reince Preibus (center) and trade adviser Peter Navarro (right), displays Executive Order directing USTR to exit TPP and move to bilateral from multilateral negotiations (Getty Images)

from Congress, business and consumer interests, and trade experts who recognized that this border tax—even if the president had the authority to impose it unilaterally, which was questionable—would ultimately have to be paid by US consumers, not Mexicans. The proposal was quickly withdrawn, when White House chief of staff Reinhold R. "Reince" Priebus told the press that it was just one of "a buffet of options" being considered. One other buffet option, which candidate Trump listed in his seven-point plan on trade, was to formally withdraw from NAFTA if he did not get his way in the renegotiation. This option had also been in the 2008 campaign plans of both Hillary Clinton and Barack Obama.

A critical question immediately comes to mind from these early decisions to terminate regional, multilateral trade agreements and direct USTR to engage only in country-by-country trade agreements. Is this the beginning of the end of Cordell Hull's dream of a rule-based liberal economic order, promoting peace and stability through a multilateral trading system to settle disputes and reduce discriminatory trade barriers?

Trump's background in private business traces a path of deals exhibiting his approach to most decision making. It is often said that he has a "transactional," rather than a strategic, perspective. He is a shrewd businessman who makes decisions quickly—some say impulsively—based on his assessment of the transaction at hand, viewing his goals in every deal as a zero-sum game. One side wins and the other side necessarily loses. Generally, the businessman's goals are narrowly focused on the maximization of monetary profit, whether for immediate or long-term gain. Within the bounds of fiduciary responsibilities, and legal and ethical rules, this focus is appropriate to satisfy shareholders, business partners, and personal needs. Every tool, from economic dominance to filing bankruptcy, can be employed to maximize leverage for winning or preserving profit. In a private trade transaction it is understandable that the businessman may often be able to bring greater leverage to a one-on-one, bilateral transaction with a party of fewer resources than would be possible in trying to reach agreement with multiple parties of diverse interests and more combined resources. In the political economy with hundreds of state actors, however, history has shown that the nondiscriminatory multilateral system promoted by Cordell Hull is more likely to promote and sustain economic stability and broader strategic security goals.

As we have seen, in the 1930s Cordell Hull was able to establish the unconditional nondiscriminatory most-favored-nations foundation of his reciprocal trade program. He did so only by defeating the efforts of others in the Roosevelt administration—Ray Moley and George Peek, in particular—who preferred bilateral, "horse-trading" barter agreements for the same fundamental reasons the current president and some of his aides want to abandon multilateral agreements now. The goals for Hull's trade agreements and those of his successors in the postwar creation of the international trading system were far broader than ensuring a mercantilist favorable balance of trade. The State Department received severe criticism from within both political parties for its perceived neglect of American business interests in the late 1950s and 1960s. The negotiators were accused of favoring too heavily the strategic goals of building an economic alliance among free-market countries and enhancing the NATO alliance. In hindsight, it is difficult to find fault with this strategy in view of the role these goals played in ultimately winning the Cold War, especially as safeguards were enhanced to aid import-sensitive domestic manufacturers. Even after the Cold War ended, the strategy of maintaining strong alliances among nations with common economic interests has enjoyed overwhelming support among foreign policy experts.

AMERICA FIRST

In the first months of his tenure, President Trump has taken bold steps to abandon, almost ostentatiously, America's leadership roles in the world—leadership that began a century before Trump took office as World War I devastated the European economy and power centers. It is with some irony that Trump has been marking this withdrawal from world leadership and abandoning international engagement under the guiding catchphrase "America First," as his party continues to criticize the Obama administration for "leading from behind." Every politician is naturally expected to give the highest priority to his or her own country in foreign policy decision making, but the "America First" slogan in the context used by Trump is an appeal to a heightened degree of economic nationalism and is blind to other national priorities. Likewise, it was in this narrow focus that noninterventionists—mainly ultra-nationalists and isolationists (including some prominent anti-Semitic Nazi sympathizers)—assumed this slogan in demanding neutrality in the 1930s before the Japanese attacked Pearl Harbor. FDR and Cordell Hull were in a constant conflict with this America

First group in their effort—driven by long-term American interests—to provide aid to Britain and other allies against the Hitler onslaught before devising the Lend-Lease aid program.

In the postwar period it was not purely charitable interests that inspired the Marshall Plan to provide food and reconstruction aid to Europe. It was rather the "enlightened self-interest" of informed American states-men that supported the appropriation of $130 billion in current dollars to save Europe. Businessman Will Clayton and Cold Warrior George Kennan wrote the memos upon which General George Marshall based his 1947 speech that sparked that plan. President Truman, faced with a tough reelec-tion, nevertheless proposed the Marshall Plan to Congress, and Republican senator Arthur Vandenberg, a former isolationist, helped to pass it through the GOP-controlled Congress. It was also these same informed, "self-interested" American statesmen who encouraged the formation of a united Europe after the war for both security and economic purposes. It seems highly unlikely that a Marshall Plan could prevail in the current *uninformed* self-interested "America First" environment.

President Trump, quite apart from his businessman's transactional approach to trade, seems to give little weight to the broader strategic goals in trade negotiations. He seems unaware of them and shows little apparent interest in learning about them. Regardless of the reason for his disinterest, he rejects the traditional diplomatic approach to promoting long-standing US alliances. American statesmen since the beginning of the postwar era have played an important role in encouraging European unification, including Britain, for both economic and national secur-ity reasons. Carelessly abandoning these objectives, President Trump applauds the British vote to exit the European Union (Brexit) and glee-fully predicts that other members will follow. While he has pined for an alliance with the brutal, authoritarian leadership of Russia to fight radical Islamic terrorists, President Trump simultaneously exposes doubts about the US commitment to defend its allies in NATO, an organization he often called "obsolete" before becoming president and even later refused to com-mit consistently to its fundamental collective defense obligation in Article Five of the Treaty. The Trump administration thus not only jeopardizes the international trading system, but his team's policies pose a threat to every institution designed after the Second World War to prevent the likelihood of a return of catastrophic world war and world depression. Allies, such as Canada and Germany, have said publicly the Trump policies mark the end of an era. The Canadian foreign affairs minister told Parliament that their friends to the south had obviously decided "to shrug off the burden of world leadership."[2]

Among the team with whom President Trump surrounded himself in the White House to reinforce and inspire his populist, America First nationalism against the liberal trade order, first and foremost (at least until his departure after less than nine months in office) was his senior counselor and chief strategist (and formerly CEO of the Trump campaign) Stephen K. Bannon. Although Bannon may no longer be the "second most powerful man in the world," as *Time* magazine called him in a cover story just three weeks after the inauguration, his philosophy still seems to reign over the critical decisions in the Oval Office. His official role as chief strategist has ended and his direct influence may not have lasted any longer than that of Ray Moley in the Roosevelt administration after *Time* did a very similar cover story on Moley (see Chapter 8), but Bannon's philosophy (though not exactly what Plato had in mind for his ideal philosopher king) has certainly ruled in the early stages of the Trump administration. And his nationalist spirit remains solidly with the president.

Born and reared in the working class, but with Hollywood wealth, an Ivy League degree, and Goldman Sachs on his resume, Bannon is not exactly one of the forgotten men. Yet his disdain for Wall Street (developed from his own experience there), economic populism (i.e., xenophobic anti-globalization), and ethnic (white Christian) nationalism is simpatico with Trump's base supporters and obviously appeals to the president. Bannon's philosophy is identical to that of the ultra-nationalist party leaders seeking power in Europe. Ultra-right Europeans view Trump's election ratifying the Trump-Bannon ideology as a spectacle, in political terms, approaching the Second Coming of Christ, even though it did not inspire them to victory in their own elections in 2017.

Bannon's nationalist imprint was highly visible in the president's dark hyperboles spread throughout Trump's America First–themed inaugural address. Even former president George W. Bush, whose unilateralist foreign policy reached its own bold heights, was heard to say after that speech, "That was some weird shit."[3] The former chief strategist also was behind the president's ill-conceived, hastily executed "travel ban" and the drafting of the TPP withdrawal memo to USTR. In the campaign and early days of the Trump presidency, Bannon did not utter many statements for public dissemination; his views are well known, however, from his time as chief of the far right ("platform for the alt-right," he calls it) Breitbart News website and its radio shows. Not surprisingly, he was vocal in supporting Brexit and other nationalist efforts to break up the EU, opposing immigration, promoting what he calls the Judeo-Christian West's war with radical Islam, and pronouncing skepticism of multilateral trade agreements. In the TPP withdrawal directive, he is the author of the language directing that USTR trade negotiations in the future be "directly with individual countries on a one-on-one (or bilateral) basis." After the Brexit vote and Trump's victory, Bannon was quoted as declaring, "This is only the top of the first inning." As head of Breitbart.com, in November 2013, Bannon compared himself to Lenin, declaring, "I want to bring everything crashing down, and destroy all of today's establishment."

Bannon confirmed his Leninist aspiration in an email to the *Washington Post*, writing, "What we are witnessing is the birth of a new political order." It is quite apparent that he does not intend to include in the "new political order" the liberal trading system supported by a bipartisan consensus at least since Eisenhower. In his first public outing one month after the inauguration, appearing with Reince Priebus at the annual Conservative Political Action Conference (CPAC), Bannon reconfirmed the administration's priority for the "deconstruction of the administrative state" along with its foundation of taxes, regulations, and trade agreements. The intent of his appearance at CPAC seemed mainly to be a victory lap taunting anti-Trump detractors among the traditional Republicans in the audience and the "corporatist, globalist media" (which he called the "opposition party" and Trump has dubbed the "enemy of the people"), whom he observed, "are adamantly opposed to an economic nationalist agenda like Donald Trump has." He made clear his threatening view of the current rules-based trade order by declaring that Trump's announced TPP withdrawal was "one of the most pivotal moments in modern American history."[4]

Bannon is often said to be a voracious reader of history, but he must have missed the part about the twentieth-century devastation caused by the First and Second World Wars sparked by fierce nationalism. Bannon is an arch-nationalist who despises the European Union because it dilutes national identity and sovereignty; he wants to see it collapse and fail. Naturally, these views being prominently displayed in the White House after at least sixty years of the uninterrupted, vitally important US-EU alliance are quite disturbing to the European leadership. "Anyone who would support a more assertive national identity in Europe has not read their history," commented David O'Sullivan, EU ambassador to Washington. Before he joined the Trump campaign, Bannon hosted a victory celebration on his Breitbart radio show for the UK Independence Party leader, Nigel Farage, the day after the Brexit victory in June 2016. "The European Union project has failed," Farage declared. "It is doomed, I'm pleased to say." Bannon responded, "It's a great accomplishment. Congratulations."[5]

Before his ouster, there were several times in the topsy-turvy early months of the Trump administration, when it appeared to the outside world that Bannon might be losing favor for the moment in his war with the moderates (Democrats, Bannon calls them) in gaining access to the Oval Office. In the beginning, the president in an unprecedented move gave Bannon, a political adviser with no national security experience, a permanent seat on the National Security Council (NSC). But at a time when press leaks reported that Bannon and Jared Kushner, the president's son-in-law and adviser, were feuding and the president had to warn them to stop, Bannon was removed from the NSC and appeared to be on the way out. Then, the president turned his favor back to Bannon's preferred inward-looking "America First" nationalism, snubbing world leaders and international cooperation again as he dramatically rejected the voluntary Paris Agreement on climate change with a declaration that he was elected to represent "Pittsburgh not Paris." Trump's decision ignored the counsel of the White House moderates and Secretary of State Rex Tillerson. The true lesson here is that Trump's instincts are aligned with Bannon's, regardless of Bannon's presence or his personal standing in the White House court of advisers. This lesson is not a good one for the institutions that have ensured peace and prosperity to the world for the past seventy years.

At an event in Washington in mid-May 2017, I heard a senior policy assistant to Bannon explain the Trump policy process, which he repeatedly referred to as MAGA (Making America Great Again). He said you could not get this explanation from the news media, which he described as "80 percent fallacious." The approach Trump's senior staff take is "neither right-wing nor left-wing; it is not ideological at all," he said; "it is based on the Trump brand: namely, excellence." To understand this, he said, it helps to read Trump's book, *The Art of the Deal*, which teaches that "in any and all negotiations, you cannot be wedded to the deal; you have to be willing to walk away from any deal that is not excellent for you." And, he said, you cannot be patient, nor have a strategic focus. "You must reject all of the establishment foundations of the last twenty-five years." I assume, though he did not say this specifically, that he would also urge rejection of the foundations of the last seventy years as well. He said that President Trump was a "preternatural instinctual actor" who makes decisions on impulse and his impulsive instinct "was always right." He described the attributes and functions of all of the principal staff members, which I won't detail here, except to note that he said Jared Kushner's function was "to see the vision of his father-in-law, and then make it happen."

The White House insider who provided this description of the Trump policy process asked that his background remarks remain anonymous and he resigned his position soon after Bannon departed. His description is broadly confirmed in a contemporary lead article of the *Economist*, under the heading, "The impulsiveness and shallowness of America's president threaten the economy as well as the rule of law." The magazine, which had just interviewed Trump, writes that the president's "displays of dominance, his need to be the centre of attention and his impetuousness have a whiff of Henry VIII about them." The article continues that Trump's plan for the economy "treats orthodoxy, accuracy and consistency as if they were simply to be negotiated away in a series of earth-shattering deals."[6]

THE TRUMP TRADE TEAM

The team supporting the president in creating the new political order for trade are Secretary of Commerce Wilbur Ross, director of the newly created Office of Trade and Manufacturing Policy Peter Navarro, and the United States Trade Representative Robert Lighthizer. As senior policy advisers to the Trump campaign in September 2016, Ross, a billionaire private equity investor, and Navarro, an economics professor at the University of California–Irvine business school, issued a highly partisan report, "Scoring the Trump Economic Plan," in rebuttal to the conclusion reached in the nonpartisan, though "supply-side" analysis by the Tax Foundation of Trump's tax plan. The Tax Foundation report predicted that Trump's plan would cost $2.6 trillion in revenue losses to the US Treasury. The Ross-Navarro report called the Tax Foundation report "incomplete and highly misleading," because it isolates the tax cuts from revenue offsets they predict will come from Trump's "synergistic suite of trade, regulatory, and energy policy reforms."

On the trade piece, Ross and Navarro argue that Trump's "tough, smart" negotiators will renegotiate every one of the "poorly negotiated trade deals," dating "back to at least 1993," coinciding with the Bill Clinton presidency. These renegotiations will be conducted according to the "Trump Trade Doctrine," which they defined as ensuring that "any deal must increase the GDP growth rate, decrease the trade deficit, and strengthen the US manufacturing base." The deals to be renegotiated include not only NAFTA and other regional and bilateral free-trade agreements completed under Presidents Clinton, George H. W. Bush, and George W. Bush, but also the multilateral WTO agreement. Ross and Navarro propose that the WTO be amended to favor and give more control to the United States based upon its leverage as the largest importer, third-largest exporter, and currently with the largest economy in the world. They boldly forecast that the Trump Trade Doctrine will eliminate the US trade deficit of $500 billion, end offshoring of American jobs, and rebuild America's manufacturing base. Suffice to say, it will take more than "smart, tough" negotiators to pull off this miraculous trifecta, but they do not stop there with bold predictions.

In addition to the increased revenue projected to be derived from regulatory and energy reforms, the report predicts that Trump's trade policies alone will produce $2.44 trillion in revenues to offset the revenue loss from the proposed tax cut. The president called Navarro " a visionary economist" when he selected him to serve as the White House inside guru on trade policy, but more realistic experts would describe this paper as offering only visions, if not delusions, of grandeur.

Navarro explained his approach to eliminating the trade deficit to the *Wall Street Journal* in terms that would be familiar to the eighteenth-century mercantilists and to the Germans during the interwar years under Hitler's fiercely nationalistic Minister of Economics H. H. G. Schacht, who negotiated bilateral barter agreements. It is the very approach Cordell Hull fought against in the 1930s when establishing the nondiscriminatory MFN trade program. "Any country we have significant trade deficit with needs to work with us on a product-by-product and sector-by-sector level," Navarro declared, "to reduce that deficit over a specified period of time." This simple formula might seem reasonable in a government-controlled, nonmarket economy ruled by national socialism or communism, but it is less than practical in a market-driven economy. Trade agreements are about balancing the legal rules of trade; they are not intended to change the economics of supply and demand. Navarro, following Trump's political instincts, seems most interested in trying to exploit the trade deficit for political gain, regardless of its economic relevance to the US economy.

Navarro disregards the effect of the "global supply chain" in weighing the significance of trade deficits in both Mexico and China. For example, Apple iPhones are assembled in China using parts from suppliers around the world. The value added by Chinese workers in assembling foreign-made components, including US inputs, is small relative to the total value of the product. Under the rules of origin for customs valuation, however, the full value of the iPhone imported into the United States is treated as originating from China, thus inflating the size of the US trade deficit. A 2010 study estimated that, in 2009, China exported 11.3 million iPhones to the United States at a total export value at $2 billion. The study estimated that 96.4 percent of the value of each unit was attributed to foreign suppliers, but under standard trade data, China would be credited with a $1.9 billion surplus for the iPhone trade. A joint study by the Organisation for Economic Co-operation and Development (OECD) and the WTO estimated that in 2011 over 40 percent of China's manufactured exports comprised foreign imports.[7]

As to the trade war with China that some critics say will follow Trump's trade policies, including a threatened 45 percent tariff on Chinese imports, Ross and Navarro naively expect "that China's leaders will quickly understand they are facing strength on the trade issue in Trump rather than the kind of weakness on trade that has characterized the Obama-Clinton years . . . and [will] rein in their [China's] mercantilist impulses."[8] In a profile of Navarro, the *Economist* calls him a "China-bashing eccentric," who once supported free trade and is now part of the "populist insurgency" in the White House with his own mercantilist views and "dodgy economics" about the trade deficit. Despite his prediction that China would back down from a trade war with the forceful Trump, Navarro wrote a book more than a decade ago forecasting *The Coming China Wars*. He now promises "a seismic and transformative shift in trade policy."[9]

Recently at a conference luncheon, I was seated next to a very senior and respected trade diplomat who had served in several administrations, the last being that of President George W. Bush. He was asked by someone else if he would be interested in going back to USTR and working with Bob Lighthizer, with whom he had worked during the Reagan presidency. The diplomat quickly answered, "Not as long as Peter Navarro is in charge of trade in the White House."

Like Bannon, Navarro has had ups and downs in the strength of his influence with the president in struggles with White House moderates. The strength of Navarro's influence depends largely upon how often the occasion arises when President Trump finds it politically advantageous to attack trade deficits with Mexico or China.

Secretary Wilbur Ross also brings an interesting background to the president's populist inner circle on trade. Known as the "king of bankruptcy," Ross became an ally of Trump by saving him from personal bankruptcy while Ross was representing investors in the doomed Trump Taj Mahal Casino in Atlantic City. Since then, Ross has netted billions of dollars as a "vulture investor" buying bankrupt or deeply distressed companies and saving them by cutting jobs and benefits and selling them for a profit—in some cases shipping American jobs to other countries. An analysis by Reuters disclosed that Ross sent 2,700 American jobs offshore by relocating production of companies he had taken control of since 2004. He claims to be pro-trade and has moved production to Mexico to reduce labor costs and take advantage of NAFTA supply chain opportunities in several of his investments.

Ross also lobbied for the Dominican Republic–Central American Free Trade Agreement (DR-CAFTA), another trade agreement Trump now denounces. Two of his biggest investments were made in the most protected of US industries—textiles and steel. While taking advantage of the high tariff and import quota protections afforded these industries, he sold the steel conglomerate he created to an Indian billionaire. In 2003, Ross acquired the assets of North Carolina–based Burlington Industries, which had been the world's largest textile manufacturer with 80,000 employees, but was then in bankruptcy. He also bought the assets of another bankrupt North Carolina textile giant, Cone Mills, in 2004, and combined the two into a new company, International Textile Group (ITG). ITG sold off many of the assets and moved much of the production to Asia and Latin America. In announcing the sale of ITG to a new private equity group in October 2016, the company press release observed that it then employed "approximately 4,800 people worldwide with operations in the United States, Mexico and China."

But now Ross has converted to the Trump populist position on trade, and some predict he will have a leading, if not *the* leading role on trade negotiations due to his close relationship with the president. But the Commerce Department's broad jurisdiction beyond trade functions make this takeover of the legislative authority granted USTR as improbable now as it has been when similar takeovers have been tried under previous administrations. It is also unclear how significant the roles of others close to Trump will be in the reconfiguration of trade policy decision making. The president appointed his son-in-law, Jared Kushner, as a senior adviser with a potentially unlimited portfolio. In the early days of the administration, Kushner, as the president's personal emissary, has met with a number of foreign officials, including those within the NAFTA partnership.[10] His meetings with Russians, of course, have gotten a lot more attention and are very likely to seriously limit his other meetings and activities.

The central figure on the trade team, despite the attention given to others during his long confirmation process, is, as an institutional matter, the president's pick for USTR, Robert E. Lighthizer. An affable and highly competent trade lawyer-lobbyist, Lighthizer is arguably the most qualified of any of Trump's initial cabinet appointees in terms of direct experience and specialized talent. If the president is serious about dismantling the established liberal trade order and replacing it with a nationalistic, protectionist regime prepared for the trade wars to follow, he has chosen a master technician ready and possibly willing to lead the effort.

After a substantial tenure on Capitol Hill as chief counsel and staff director on the Senate Finance Committee under Chairman Bob Dole (R-KS), Lighthizer served for several years as deputy USTR under President Ronald Reagan. During his presidency, Reagan normally talked like a free-trader but often walked like a protectionist, and Lighthizer often led the march. At a time when Japan was the most threatening trade ogre to American industry—the role now played by China—Reagan bashed Japan with every protectionist tool in the USTR arsenal.

Much later, in private practice on the protectionist side, Lighthizer testified before the House Ways and Means Trade Subcommittee in 2007 that the United States was being treated unfairly in the WTO dispute settlement system. He called the system "fundamentally flawed" with "rogue" WTO panel and Appellate Body decisions exceeding their mandate and engaging in "judicial activism," a term no doubt employed to conjure up memories among conservatives of the US Supreme Court under Chief Justice Earl Warren. He charged that these decisions were "gutting our trade laws," citing two instances when WTO decisions ultimately prompted legislation eliminating US anti-dumping provisions that had given excessive advantages to US domestic industry. The Manufacturers Alliance for Productivity and Innovation, however, disputed Lighthizer's analysis with a study showing that over the previous five years the United States had "benefited substantially from its participation in WTO disputes, having prevailed in twice as many disputes as it lost."[11]

In a March 2008 op-ed piece in the *New York Times*, Lighthizer scolded the then presumptive Republican presidential nominee Senator John McCain for citing his unbridled support for free trade to "prove his bona fides as a conservative." Lighthizer correctly noted that conservatives from Alexander Hamilton, who, Lighthizer wrote, "could be considered the founder of American conservatism," to former senator Jesse Helms (R-NC) have opposed free trade. President Reagan, "the personification of modern conservatism," according to Lighthizer, "often broke with free-trade dogma." From his own experience, Lighthizer reminded McCain that Reagan, despite his "open-markets rhetoric," restricted imports of automobiles, steel, sugar, textiles, and motorcycles (to protect Harley-Davidson); and Reagan "made Japanese imports more expensive" by forcing Japan to increase the value of the yen. Lighthizer declared that free trade is not the mantra of conservatives; it is rather the ideal of "liberal elites," like Senator Ted Kennedy (D-MA), who embraced it "with a passion that makes Robespierre seem prudent."[12]

McCain has a long memory and did not forget this scolding when Lighthizer came up for confirmation nine years later. He and Senator Ben Sasse (R-NE) sent a long public letter to Lighthizer in a similarly scolding tone announcing their opposition to his nomination because of his "vocal advocacy for protectionist shifts in our trade policies, the Administration's ongoing, incoherent, and inconsistent trade message," and his "skepticism of NAFTA." They declared, "America deserves a USTR who will renegotiate NAFTA in order to build on its successes, not as a pretext for unraveling it."[13]

Three years after his op-ed on McCain, Lighthizer had better luck when he chose to enter the fray supporting the budding Donald Trump presidential campaign in 2012. In an op-ed in the *Washington Times*, Lighthizer praised Trump for his anti-China protectionist rhetoric that was then being criticized within the GOP. A potential Trump campaign would at least focus attention on China's abusive trade practices, Lighthizer predicted, and thus "will have done a service to both the Republican Party and the country."[14] As a top lobbyist for the steel industry and lead counsel for the U.S. Steel Corporation in trade litigation, Lighthizer's personal views on China and the WTO offered a legalistic version of Trump's visceral reactions to trade questions.

During the presidency of Barack Obama, Lighthizer admonished USTR to stop wringing its hands and hoping for the best and urged aggressive and imaginative action to address the US-China trade deficit. The hand-wringing characterization of Obama's USTR was not substantiated in the record. Obama filed twenty-five WTO cases during his two terms, including sixteen against China; all of these that had been decided by the end of his second term had been won or settled favorably. The aggressive new actions Lighthizer proposed included some that had been rejected by the George W. Bush and Obama administrations as not sanctioned under the GATT/WTO agreements.

Defending the aggressive approach, Lighthizer observed, "WTO commitments are not religious obligations." He argued:

> The point is that an unthinking, simplistic and slavish dedication to the mantra of "WTO-consistency" . . . makes very little sense, and is plainly *not* dictated by our international obligations. Indeed, derogation may be the only way to force change in the system.

At the time he made this statement—seven years before he would become USTR—he stated explicitly, "I am not advocating that the United States leave the WTO system—that body is too important to us and the global trading system."[15] A serious question arises, however, considering his lack of commitment to WTO obligations: Will he be willing to chuck the system that has effectively provided a rules-based, liberal trade order since 1948 now that he is a member of a team determined to upend the political order under the slogan of America First?

Whatever path he takes, organized labor seems to think it will be the right one. United Steelworkers president Leo Gerard, for example, wrote a letter sent to all senators before the confirmation vote calling Lighthizer "a man of great integrity" and adding:

> At this critical juncture, both businesses and workers have lost confidence in the execution of trade policy that has been designed more to advance foreign policy goals and Wall Street's interests than balancing these competing demands . . . ensuring that we can both engage in further liberalization while advancing our own economic interests and values.[16]

With strong bipartisan support, Lighthizer was overwhelmingly confirmed over McCain's objection.

Even before he was confirmed by the Senate to lead USTR, his influence was obvious in "The President's Trade Policy Agenda for 2017," publicly submitted to Congress by USTR, as required by statute, on March 1, 2017. This document declares: "It is time for a more aggressive approach. . . . [I]t is time for a new trade policy that defends American sovereignty." The new agenda adopts Lighthizer's view, and some of his same words, expressed in 2010 that WTO commitments are not "religious obligations." The agenda explains that "if a WTO dispute settlement panel—or the WTO Appellate Body—rules against the United States, such a ruling does not automatically lead to a change in US law or practice . . . [and] the Trump Administration will aggressively defend American sovereignty over trade policy." The agenda promises that the Trump administration "will act aggressively as needed" to combat unfair trade practices through US trade remedies, such as Section 301 of the Trade Act of 1974, "when the WTO adopts interpretations of WTO agreements that undermine the ability of the United States" to employ these remedies.[17]

I was among the majority of Members of Congress in 1994 who voted for the Uruguay Round implementing legislation that created the WTO and vividly remember insisting with others that the legislation make clear that WTO commitments and dispute decisions would not impact our national sovereignty and would not be binding on federal or state law.[18] The WTO dispute settlement system, which is arguably the most effective international legal forum in world history, is based entirely on voluntary participation and compliance. When a decision goes against the United States and would require a legislative change for compliance, Congress can ignore the decision if it so chooses. That was what Congress did when Brazil won a WTO decision holding US cotton subsidies to be in violation of WTO obligations. The winning side is authorized under WTO agreements to retaliate against the offending side by withdrawing trade concessions, for example, raising tariffs against the member refusing to comply. In an unusual outcome in the Brazil cotton case, the United States ultimately reached a monetary settlement favoring Brazilian farmers and retained the "illegal" subsidies for its cotton farmers.

Since 1995, the WTO has handled over 500 disputes in a manner that has enhanced the rules-based trade system and thus maintained global economic stability. On balance, these WTO decisions have been highly favorable to US interests. Prior to this system, the old GATT dispute process had serious weaknesses that made it less useful to the establishment of trade rules limiting unfair trade practices. As I recall as a Ways and Means staff assistant at the time, Congress enacted Section 301 of the Trade Act of 1974, in response to this legal vacuum, as a mechanism for unilateral enforcement by the United States of fair trade practices. Among the strong motivations for creating a new dispute system under the WTO was the ineffectiveness of the GATT system for settling disputes, mixed with the criticisms against erratic unilateral US actions under Section 301. After 1995, Section 301 has continued to be used for certain limited purposes, but expansion of its use as a vigilante-style, unilateral preference to the WTO dispute process (as arguably contemplated under the Lighthizer/ Trump agenda) poses serious risks of retaliation and trade wars in a Wild West–based environment.

The initial reactions to Trump's 2017 Trade Agenda following its release have been mixed. Naturally, the traditional protectionists have responded positively. The American Alliance for Manufacturing, a partnership between import-sensitive domestic manufacturers and the United Steelworkers Union, praised it, observing that the WTO dispute system fails to respect "long-standing recognition of the legitimacy of trade remedies." The reaction on Capitol Hill, however, has been wary at best from trade leadership of both parties. Congressman Richard Neal (D-MA), the ranking Democrat on Ways and Means, agreed that the WTO dispute system deserves some criticism, but said "it sounds like the Administration is considering a far too drastic response. We need to fix the problems with the current international trading system, not scrap the system altogether."[19]

Congressman Kevin Brady (R-TX), chairman of Ways and Means, issued a statement agreeing with Trump's effort to make a better deal for American workers, but defended the WTO:

> I strongly believe that our current trade agreements—including the WTO—have been successful for Americans because these agreements establish a firm rule of law to hold our competitors in check and open markets for us to sell our goods, services, and farm products. However, I agree with President Trump that we should improve our trade agreements to make them better serve American workers.[20]

With this degree of bipartisan support for the WTO in the House it seems unlikely that the president would dump that organization as he has the Paris Climate Agreement, TPP, and other multilateral international agreements. Under the Uruguay Round Agreements Act, any member of the Senate or House may introduce a joint resolution to revoke congressional approval of the WTO agreements once every five years. Representative Ron Paul (R-TX) introduced one in 2000 and Representative Paul and Representative Bernie Sanders (I-VT) tried again in 2005. Neither resolution got many votes. Embarrassingly to me as a Georgian, however, even though only 20 percent of the House voted in favor of the 2005 resolution, a bipartisan majority of the Georgia delegation voted to revoke the WTO.[21] This was clearly a political throwaway vote. Even if the resolution had passed both Houses (and the Senate has never even considered such a resolution), every president since the GATT/WTO has existed, except possibly the present one, would have vetoed it, requiring a two-thirds vote in both houses to override. The point here is that despite the political rhetoric emanating from the White House, there remains a strong base of political support for the WTO system under the clouds currently hanging over the system.

Nevertheless, as this book goes to press, Ambassador Lighthizer continues to make the case that the WTO dispute settlement process has failed to enforce adequately US rights or has imposed obligations not agreed to in the WTO agreements. As a result, USTR is having to consider "a more muscular kind of an approach" by using Section 301 of the Trade Act of 1974 to enforce its rights. Will this lead to the destruction of Cordell Hull's rule-based multilateral system? My friends who remain at senior levels at USTR caution patience. They say that when I write the next edition of this book, I will be describing the "pragmatic" solutions that the Lighthizer team derived to solve the system's problems.

POTENTIAL REVIVAL OF A MEGA-REGIONAL BILATERAL FREE TRADE AGREEMENT (FTA)

President Trump and his trade team, with its focus on bilateral negotiations targeting trade deficits, had to go through a learning process concerning the European Union in the early months of the administration. In an interview with the *Times* of London before the inauguration, president-elect Trump said he thought that "Brexit is going to end up being a great thing." He predicted that other countries would follow Britain's lead in leaving the EU. "People, countries want their own identity, and the UK wanted its own identity. . . . I believe others will leave." Trump revealed that he was inviting British prime minister Theresa May to visit him "right after" he gets in the White House and that he wants to secure a trade agreement between the two countries immediately. The rush to move Britain to the head of the bilateral trade agreement queue probably had something to do with President Obama's argument against Brexit before the referendum that if it passed, Britain would be at the back of the queue for a US agreement. Trump obviously saw this as another opportunity to prove his predecessor wrong. It also was in this interview that Trump criticized German chancellor Angela Merkel's immigration policies and called NATO obsolete. Merkel responded that Europe would obviously have to fend for itself during the new era in Washington. "We Europeans have our fate in our own hands," she said.[22]

The president soon learned that as long as the United Kingdom remained in the EU and had not officially "Brexited," which would take at least another two years, Britain could not enter into a bilateral trade agreement with the United States. This result was equally embarrassing for Boris Johnson, the British foreign secretary, who had been a proponent of Brexit when he was mayor of London and criticized Obama's intervention in the referendum. He bragged that Britain would be "first in line" for a deal after talking with Trump's advisers in January.

When things did not work out with Britain, the president tried to initiate bilateral trade talks with Germany when Chancellor Merkel visited Washington. According to Peter Navarro, the $65 billion US trade deficit with Germany is "one of the most difficult" trade issues facing the United States. According to her cabinet colleagues, when she returned Merkel briefed them on what she said were "very basic misunderstandings" by President Trump on the "fundamentals" of the EU and trade. "Ten times Trump asked her if he could negotiate a trade deal with Germany. Every time she replied, 'You can't do a trade deal with Germany, only the EU,' " a senior German politician was quoted. On the eleventh refusal, Trump said, "Oh, we'll do a deal with Europe then."[23] Since 2013, the United States and the European Union have been negotiating a "comprehensive and high-standard" free-trade agreement called the Transatlantic Trade and Investment Partnership (T-TIP). The fifteenth and latest round of T-TIP negotiations was completed in October 2016, and both sides have been on pause since the Trump election, standing by for the next move. In trade parlance this is a "mega-regional" FTA, like the TPP, but it can pass for a bilateral trade negotiation to satisfy the Trump/Bannon rule, because it only involves two teams of negotiators, though covering twenty-nine countries until Brexit is completed. It is safe to say, there is much leverage on the side of the one superpower that Trump leads, but this is a far more complex negotiation than a Trump Tower real estate deal. Both Bob Lighthizer and Wilbur Ross have expressed interest in exploring ways to reduce barriers to US exports to Europe (and thus the trade deficit) and EU trade commissioner Cecilia Malmström also favors trade engagement with the United States whether involving T-TIP or not.

Political support for a transatlantic trade partnership has always been high on both sides of the Atlantic, but many sensitive issues remain outstanding. Although both the United States and the EU maintain high levels of domestic protection in worker rights and the environment, and T-TIP could set a high bar to improve world standards in the trade context, public opposition is significant in other areas. Protesters in Brussels, the EU political center, opposing, for example, US exports of genetically modified organisms (GMOs), invasion of data privacy, and potential investor dispute system abuses, are fond of painting "STOP TAFTA" graffiti (grafting the unpopularity of NAFTA onto T-TIP) all over the European capital. T-TIP was never especially popular in the European Parliament, which does not have a lot of power but is close to the pulse of the civil society. One may logically assume that even if the Trump team decides to reengage on T-TIP, the president's high level of unpopularity in Europe may have even weakened the enthusiasm of the EU Commission for the project at least for the time being.

NAFTA RENEGOTIATION

For at least eighteen months candidate Trump repeatedly claimed that NAFTA is a "disaster" and "the worst trade deal in history anywhere," but this was campaign hyperbole for demagogic appeal, not fact-based analysis. After becoming president, he continued to repeat the claim, but has not had a consistent position on what to do about it. After the early row over who was going to pay for the "wall," resulting in President Peña Nieto's cancellation of a meeting to discuss renegotiation, there was a period of radio silence between the capitals, as the Mexicans began to weigh the possibility of leaving NAFTA.[24]

In the meantime, then White House National Trade Council director Peter Navarro announced that the administration would make the reduction of US bilateral trade deficits its top policy focus. He noted the potential national security risks from the commercial behavior of its major trading partners, including China and Germany, suggesting a "strategic rival intent on hegemony in Asia and perhaps world hegemony." He argued that the administration would seek "to reclaim all of the supply chain and manufacturing capabilities that would otherwise exist if the playing field were level." Navarro was disdainful of the majority of economists who have criticized his obsession with bilateral trade deficits but offered few specifics on how the administration intended to reduce them.[25]

At the end of March, President Trump signed an executive order requiring a "systematic evaluation" of all bilateral trade deficits and all trade agreements, including NAFTA and the WTO, to determine the impact of these agreements and whether there have been violations or abuses, and what actions need to be taken with respect to them. The president put Secretary Wilbur Ross in charge of the evaluation, and Ross attempted to explain the project to the press assembled in the White House Briefing Room the day before the signing. Like Navarro, Ross focused on the bilateral trade deficits because that is where the president directed his focus. But of the countries with whom the United States has the top ten largest deficits, only two were involved in US FTAs, but all were in the WTO—China ($347 billion), Japan ($69 billion), Germany ($65 billion), Mexico ($63 billion), Ireland ($36 billion), Vietnam ($32 billion), Italy ($28.5 billion), S. Korea ($28 billion), Malaysia ($25 billion), and India ($24 billion).

Frankly, Ross showed surprisingly little understanding of the nondiscrimination principle that is the cornerstone of the GATT/WTO system, saying,

> The President has talked a lot about [reciprocity]; namely if we have a country that has big trade barriers against us, we should logically have similar trade barriers against them. . . . The only problem is, the World Trade Organization has what's called a "most favored nation clause," meaning that of all the countries with whom we do not have a free-trade agreement, we must charge the same tariff

on the same item to those countries as we charge to the others. So that's a significant impediment toward getting to anything like a reciprocal agreement.

As noted earlier, Navarro and Ross wrote a paper during the campaign calling for fundamental amendments to the WTO agreements based on the leverage held by the United States as the number-one importer in the world, the number-three exporter, and having a trade deficit that equals the cumulative surplus of the rest of the world. Citing this leverage again to the press, Ross said, "I wouldn't dismiss the potential for seeking modification"[26]— a very troubling proposition for those concerned about maintaining the liberal world trade order and the economic stability developed after the Second World War. For anyone with an understanding of the complexities of the negotiating history of the GATT/WTO system, or even of the history of the more recent Doha Round, it also seems an extremely improbable proposition.

Secretary Ross also confirmed that the trade agreement evaluation that he would be leading would necessarily include NAFTA, which was also back in the news the week he explained the new executive order. According to an eight-page draft letter under Acting USTR Stephen Vaughn's unsigned signature block, the legally required ninety-day notice was ready to be given to Congress that President Trump intends to renegotiate NAFTA. No longer calling it a "disaster"—the letter only demanded "swift action" to deal with the "persistent U.S. trade deficit in goods trade with Canada and Mexico"— the letter mainly suggested modest changes to NAFTA and did not even threaten to drop out if the proposals were not accepted.

The letter further adopted the TPP enforceable labor and environment standards and other high-standard TPP provisions, such as digital trade.[27] At the end of its term, the Obama administration viewed the TPP as the promised renegotiation of NAFTA because it included both Mexico and Canada, and the TPP included the provisions (strong, enforceable labor and environment standards, etc.) it wanted for NAFTA. But Mexico and Canada got more in the exchange with the TPP (market access in Japan and other Asia markets, for example) than they may get in a Trump renegotiation without the other TPP partners.

Less than a month after the draft letter with the modest changes was released on the Hill, however, the president had a mood change again. Three days before the 100th day of his presidency was to occur, Trump decided he would announce on that day that he was withdrawing the United States from NAFTA at the end of a required six-month notice period. In fact, the one-hundred-day mark seemed to have more to do with changing the president's mind than anything having to do with NAFTA. Up to that point, he had won no legislative victories, just a few back-of-the-envelope tax reform proposals and a lot of executive orders reversing Obama executive orders—nothing to support his claim that his administration had accomplished more than any president in history at this point, with the possible exception of FDR during the Great Depression. On trade, he had floated some protectionist measures on steel and softwood lumber with Canada and had initiated a new order to collect past-due trade penalties, but he had completely backed off his promise to name China a currency manipulator. By now announcing that he had decided not to renegotiate but to withdraw from NAFTA, the president would at least chalk up one victory for his campaign promises within the first one hundred days.

This proposed announcement, however, proved to be highly unpopular among most of the president's advisers, including the secretaries of State (Rex Tillerson), Commerce (Wilbur Ross), and Agriculture (Sonny Perdue), and the influential moderates, Jared Kushner and Gary Cohn, director of the National Economic Council. On the other hand, the protectionist "America First" faction, Peter Navarro and Steve Bannon (who had pen ready to mark NAFTA off the "to do" list on his office wall), cheered the decision. As word of the decision spread further from the White House, more opposition poured in from Congress, agriculture associations, and business groups. Ultimately, President Trump changed his mind again, claiming that he decided not to sign the NAFTA withdrawal letter after receiving phone calls from the leaders of Mexico and Canada. In a *Washington Post* interview, Trump explained: "In one way, I like the termination. In the other way, I like them—a lot, both of them. We have a very good relationship. . . . They called me up, they said, 'Could we try negotiating?' I said, 'Absolutely, yes.' If we can't come to a satisfactory conclusion, we'll terminate NAFTA."[28]

Many commentators and diplomats have expressed the opinion that tactics like this appear to be some kind of bluff maneuver to increase his leverage in negotiations. One conservative columnist writes of this particular incident: "To the contrary, chest-thumping followed by swift retreat trains adversaries and partners to disregard his threats. As many Americans have, other countries come to regard him as a feckless blowhard."[29]

In his interview with the *Economist*, Trump insisted, "I was all set to terminate, you know? . . . this wasn't a game I was playing . . . I wasn't playing chess or poker or anything else." He continued to insist that he only agreed to continue to negotiate "out of respect" for his NAFTA counterparts. "It would've been very disrespectful to Mexico and Canada had I said, 'I will not.'"

When the *Economist* asked if he was imagining a "pretty big renegotiation," Trump responded, "Big isn't a good enough word. Massive." The *Economist*, knowing that it was a favorite Trump word, asked, "Huge?" Trump responded, "It's got to be. . . . Otherwise we're terminating NAFTA." Trump said the $63 billion trade deficit (which he rounded up to $70 billion in the interview) would have to be dropped to zero, not immediately, but "over an extended period of time" to "become at least fair."[30] It might be debatable whether a bilateral trade deficit is "unfair," depending upon the level of nontariff barriers maintained by the parties in an otherwise free-trade agreement. But, according to C. Fred Bergsten, senior economic adviser to several previous administrations of both political parties,

> Most economists agree that the most effective, perhaps the only, policy initiative that would reduce the US current account deficit on a lasting basis would be a reduction in the US budget deficit, which would simultaneously reduce domestic absorption and the demand for foreign capital to finance it—especially with the economy near full employment as is now the case. By contrast, further increases in the budget deficit, perhaps driven by tax cuts as proposed by the Trump administration, would increase the external deficit whatever NAFTA or other trade partners might do.[31]

The Mexican government offered essentially a corresponding explanation for the cause of the US trade deficit in its response to the Commerce Department's request for comments following the president's executive order to review all trade agreements. It observed that it was the low domestic savings rate and persistent federal budget deficit that contributed to the US aggregate trade deficit. "In 2015," it noted, "the US Gross Savings as a percentage of GDP was 19%, significantly below the average of East Asia & Pacific countries (36%), the European Union (22%), and OECD members (22%). Moreover, the US has been running budget deficits for the past 15 years, with an annual average deficit of 4.2% of GDP." It further argued that the US trade deficit with Mexico is explained mainly by the way "NAFTA has enhanced regional competitiveness, increasing the regional value-added goods produced in North America. In fact, US value-added accounts for 40% of Mexico's exports of final goods to the US."[32] Like the effect of the global supply chain in China and elsewhere, reducing the trade deficit requires dismantling of comprehensive systems of division of labor. It is often said that automobiles produced in North America cross the border about eight times before they are completed.

Within a few days after his confirmation, USTR Lighthizer sent formal notification to the congressional leadership of the administration's intent to renegotiate NAFTA, which began the ninety days of consultations with Congress before negotiations formally began on August 16, 2017. Lighthizer's letter, less than a page and a half, was much shorter than the draft letter leaked in late March and revealed few details on proposed modifications. He noted, "Many chapters are outdated and do not reflect modern standards," and told reporters afterward that he was looking to improve and update the agreement, not to scrap it. In updating the agreement, he included the labor and environment upgrades, presumably from the TPP agreement, as he criticized the NAFTA provisions on those matters as being treated as an "afterthought." With all the uncertain rhetoric that has surrounded the administration's trade policy during the first six months, there is something to be said for having a "tough, smart" negotiator in place when the talks commence. "We should build on what has worked in NAFTA but change and improve what has not," Lighthizer concluded; "our hope is that we will end up with a structure that is similar to what we have now. If that proves to be impossible, we will move in another direction."[33]

As this book goes to press, the NAFTA renegotiations have finished their third round with Ambassador Lighthizer and the Canadian and Mexican negotiators expressing cautious optimism, while Secretary Ross and President Trump continue to threaten termination of the agreement in what appears to be a kind of "good cop, bad cop" approach to trade negotiations, which is both unconventional and unpromising.

THE FORGOTTEN MAN

On the White House webpage, President Trump defines America First in the trade context to mean reversing the liberal trade policies of all of his predecessors after Herbert Hoover, which policies he claims "put the interests of insiders and the Washington elite over the hard-working men and women of this country." Paradoxically, this populist assertion is obviously intended to draw attention to the administration's other campaign slogan, the "forgotten man," which also came to prominence in the 1930s during the first Franklin Roosevelt campaign when it was used to support polar opposite economic policies from those of the Trump campaign. Apart from his populist trade pronouncements, however, Trump has proposed, for example, significant tax cuts for corporations and the top 1 percent, elimination of worker protections, repeal of the Affordable Care Act, the nomination of a labor secretary (who later withdrew) opposed to overtime pay and the minimum wage, dismantling consumer financial protection, and deregulation of banks and businesses on a scale not seen since Calvin Coolidge. These proposals seem more likely to benefit only "insiders and Washington elites" and to increase the inequality between the privileged elites and the "forgotten" workingman. The most likely result of Trump's trade policy proposals is not to raise the wages for the forgotten man but rather to raise the price of imported goods and the forgotten man's cost of living.

In the 1932 election, Franklin Roosevelt also made the "forgotten man" the focus of his campaign speeches. But unlike Trump, FDR opposed Smoot-Hawley trade protectionism and directed his New Deal programs to address the plight of the working class and against abusive excesses of the wealthy during the Harding-Coolidge-Hoover years preceding the Great Depression. Raised among the aristocratic elites of the Hudson River Valley, Roosevelt, as president, became known as "a traitor to his class."

There can be no doubt that President Trump's populist campaign rhetoric contributed to his high percentage of blue-collar votes—the highest received by any Republican presidential candidate since Ronald Reagan. His initial actions on the TPP and his rhetoric on NAFTA following his inauguration have been well received by organized labor and pro-labor, anti-trade Democrats in Congress. Without mentioning the president's name, AFL-CIO president Richard Trumka, a strong Hillary Clinton supporter during the campaign, welcomed Trump's announcement of the US withdrawal from the TPP and the reopening of NAFTA as "an important first step toward a trade policy that works for working people." Senator Bernie Sanders, the runner-up for the 2016 Democratic presidential nomination, who for years has campaigned against these and other trade deals, declared: "Now is the time to develop a new trade policy that helps working families, not just multinational corporations. If President Trump is serious about a new policy to help American workers, then I would be delighted to work with him."[34] Weighed against other Trump policies and actions impacting working families, however, it is not likely that Trump will find many endorsements from progressives for the new political order conceived by Trump and his former chief strategist Bannon.

In an op-ed column in the *Washington Post* entitled "Why Trump's con can't last forever," Katrina vanden Heuvel, editor of the liberal/progressive weekly the *Nation*, writes: "Trump has shown himself a master at populist stunts," which "provide red meat to his movement." But his proposed tax cuts and deregulation, she argues, "will shaft the very people Trump promises to help." She predicts, "It won't be long before working people catch on to Trump's game." Since its founding at the beginning of the robber baron era in 1865, the *Nation* fervently opposed protectionism due to its impact on the cost of living for the working class and its contribution to the highest level of income inequality in history attained at the peak of the protectionist era. Its editors endorsed Senator Sanders in the 2016 Democratic primary with a long rationale that barely mentioned his effort to "undo the corporate-defined trade regime" by opposing the TPP.[35] The week after Trump's victory, while participating in a conference panel that I moderated on the new administration's likely trade policies, vanden Heuvel observed: "Trade has become a proxy for ethnic-right populism," indicating a distinction from the progressive anti-trade position.

In tracing the long historical narrative of trade politics, one finds the progressive position weighing heavily in favor of the rules-based liberal order and against nationalistic protectionism. As a foundation point, in *The Wealth of Nations,* the enlightened Adam Smith explains the principle that labor is the source from which a nation derives its necessities; improvements in the division of labor determines its productivity; and the free ability to trade for the benefit of workers to share in the wealth of their labor is a product of natural law. From the era of the politically corrupt Gilded Age, progressives have viewed trade protection as a tool that crooked politicians used to line their own pockets and those of the narrow special interests the politicians were protecting, while making life more costly for the general public. All the while, the working class and organized labor generally opposed protection and favored freer trade to keep prices down. Samuel Gompers believed unions should employ their energy fighting the bosses for fair wages, not pressing the government for higher tariffs that enriched only the bosses. As we have seen, these positions remained constant with strong support from progressive political and labor organizations through the postwar years during the creation of GATT and the liberal order. In the 1950s and 1960s organized labor remained supportive and became more involved in proposing stronger labor standards in trade agreements and trade adjustment assistance for workers adversely affected by trade. It was not until the late sixties and early seventies that the labor and progressive movements began moving away from liberal trade as opposition to multinational corporations moving jobs abroad became an overriding issue.

In the early seventies, labor supported the Burke-Hartke Bill, which proposed, along with protectionist import quotas, the elimination of tax incentives for foreign subsidiaries of multinational corporations to export jobs abroad. The bill would have eliminated both the tax credits for foreign income taxes paid and the indefinite deferral of US taxes until the foreign income was repatriated to the United States. Burke-Hartke was never formally even taken up, but the issue of "runaway plants" and "offshoring" always remained, especially in election years. Business lobbyists have always been able to defeat reform efforts aimed at limiting even the currently unlimited deferral of tax on foreign profits. In 2004, President Bush's chairman of the White House Council of Economic Advisers, Gregory Mankiw, made the mistake of saying, "Outsourcing is just a new way of doing international trade. . . . More things are tradable than were tradable in the past and that's a good thing." He immediately received a barrage of bipartisan condemnation from every direction. Even President Bush seemed to disown Mankiw's rationale for shipping jobs overseas at a time when he affirmed that the country needs "to make sure there are more jobs at home."[36]

The issue again drew even more prominent attention in the 2016 election with Trump's populist campaign against multinationals moving jobs beyond the border with promises to raise tariffs by 35 to 45 percent on imports manufactured in "runaway plants" or otherwise outsourced facilities. It is difficult to imagine how such discriminatory tariffs could be structured in a way that would be constitutional under US law, much less sustainable under the WTO agreements. It would be possible, however, to eliminate the tax incentives for moving manufacturing abroad as has been proposed in the past, but the Trump tax plans have not offered such proposals. Under Trump's campaign tax plan, in fact, the option to defer US corporate taxes would end, but the tax on corporate foreign income would only be 10 percent, while he proposed to reduce tax on domestic corporate income to 15 percent and foreign tax credits would continue. Thus, the tax incentive to manufacture abroad would remain in effect. Without structural changes affecting the tax or financial advantages of outsourcing, no amount of browbeating corporate executives will have any lasting impact on keeping jobs from being exported. Even Trump's much-touted "reversal" of the Carrier Corporation's decision to move "1,100 jobs" from Indiana has turned out to be a farce.

The issue of maintaining fair wages in trade is also a critical part of the debate but has always been subject to confusion and demagoguery. During the final American period of high protection, excessive tariff levels were justified to neutralize the "pauper" wages of countries with competing imports in an effort to "scientifically" equalize the "cost of production" with imports produced in low-wage countries. Yet classical economists pointed out that low wages are the vital "comparative advantage" that developing countries have in a fair trade system. Unless the wages are below a "fair remuneration" or "living wage" in the exporting country, comparatively low wages are expected in countries where the cost of living is also comparatively low. In a hearing before a congressional committee in 2006, Thea Lee, public policy director for the AFL-CIO, testified that a human rights petition the federation had filed against China "did not challenge China's right to compete in the global economy on the basis of low wages. It is natural for a developing country with an excess supply of poorly educated rural workers to have low wages. . . . The AFL-CIO challenge was specifically targeted to the *incremental* cost advantage that comes from the brutal and undemocratic repression of workers' human rights."[37]

At the beginning of the Great Recession several liberal economists who had previously been "take-no-prisoners" free-traders, holding that everyone always benefited under free trade, began to back off a bit. Both Paul Krugman and Alan S. Blinder, for example, who for years had pushed a free-trade agenda from a Democratic point of view, suddenly concluded that in the current environment more jobs were becoming "highly offshorable" in Blinder's words. Krugman also decided for the first time that the wages of unskilled Americans in labor-intensive jobs were being adversely impacted by imports from low-wage countries. Neither Blinder nor Krugman, however, believes that these revelations called for a protectionist response; rather, they urge a stronger safety net to deal with the

fallout and better education and training to prepare for competitive production skills. Higher-educated workers benefit from trade, while the less-
educated potentially lose their jobs to offshoring or have their pay squeezed,
adding to the inequality of income that derives mainly from forces outside
of trade. These economists and others are calling not for protection, but for
a New Deal for globalization that focuses on education and tax reform that
addresses income inequality, reform that does not resemble the education
and tax reforms proposed to date by the Trump administration.[38]

When Trump came into office, the Great Recession was over; the US
economy was effectively at full employment and had one of the top three
average employee wage rates (slightly behind Switzerland and Luxembourg)
among all major world economies.[39] President Trump, nevertheless, promised to "make America great again" with an old approach—one that favored
walls and called for protectionism. At every opportunity in major international economic conferences since his inauguration, the president has
directed his administration to reject the postwar custom of officially condemning protectionism. In joint declarations at the Group of 20, the Group
of 7, the OECD, and the Asia-Pacific Economic Cooperation (APEC),
US delegates have refused these now traditional condemnations, creating
waves and rifts everywhere US diplomats meet. Treasury Secretary Steven
Mnuchin at the G-20 meeting explained: "I understand what the president's
desire is and his policies . . . and we couldn't be happier with the outcome."[40]

To prove that he intends to move on his protectionist threats, President
Trump has already taken action that could lead to protective tariffs on steel
and/or aluminum imports based upon a rarely used national security provision, Section 232 of the Trade Expansion Act of 1962. This action has drawn
bipartisan protests in Congress, raising concerns about retaliation from
other nations and objections from domestic industries that use steel and
aluminum in manufacturing.[41] Contrary to his overall free-trade approach,
President George W. Bush raised steel tariffs based on a safeguard justification early in his first term to fulfill a campaign promise made in steel-
producing swing states that helped him win the presidency, but promptly
withdrew them after an adverse WTO ruling. Perhaps President Trump is
just setting up an opportunity to defy an anticipated similar WTO ruling. If
he follows through with his protectionist vows, however, he may soon learn
the economic risks that often accompany trade retaliation.

Finally, in considering the effect of Trump's trade policies on the
forgotten man, it is important to come back to the fundamental flaw in

the system: the lack of labor standards in the multilateral trading order. The negotiators of the twelve nations participating in the TPP, building on work done by others in previous FTAs and especially on the May 10th Agreement fostered by Charlie Rangel and Sandy Levin in 2007, produced labor provisions tailored to be enforceable in all participating countries, including Vietnam, with no history of legitimate worker rights. TPP opponents argued that the labor standards would not be enforced, but in the countries of most concern regarding working conditions, the agreement included labor action plans that had to be completed before the country could access any trade benefits. The Obama administration argued that the TPP labor standards were the strongest of any FTA in history and would allow the United States to write the rules of the road in the Asia-Pacific region for the twenty-first century. As previously discussed, many other issues were covered in the TPP, some for the first time in a multilateral FTA; there were some areas that would require improvement in the future, but overall it represented a major contribution to the architecture of the world trading system. Organized labor had been struggling to include enforceable labor standards in trade agreements at least since the early 1950s. With strong labor standards now being included in a mega-regional FTA—initially accounting for over one-third of world GDP and destined to expand with other nations in the region—the rejection of the agreement by organized labor was a major disappointment.

Although the TPP countries covered a large world market, most economic studies predicted only modest increases in imports from low-wage countries to the United States.[42] A significant basis for labor's opposition to the TPP came from the agreement's failure to prohibit currency manipulation. Robert E. Scott, senior economist and director of trade research at the labor-affiliated think tank the Economic Policy Institute, ridiculed Trump, who had cited Scott's research nearly twenty times during the campaign, for boasting that his smart negotiators would bring back jobs with great trade deals. Scott said Trump had missed the simple truth that the entire trade negotiation process "has been fundamentally captured by corporate interests. The idea that a billionaire who promises to cut taxes and regulations on corporations would negotiate better bargains for American workers is simply absurd." Scott blamed two decades of currency manipulation by twenty countries, led by China and in collusion with multinational corporations, for being "largely responsible for the loss of more than five million U.S. manufacturing jobs."[43] Scott is correct that currency manipulation has been a problem in the past and that it should be monitored and regulated, but it is not the most pressing issue at the moment.

During the Asian financial crisis of the late 1990s, many countries devalued their currencies, but China held firm to its peg to the US dollar at the time and did not devalue. Later, until 2005, China maintained the peg as its currency became undervalued and came under severe criticism from the United States and Europe. It responded by gradually allowing its currency to appreciate by 35.3 percent against the dollar. Yet, as its economy has slowed down since 2015, China has had to support its own currency (the RMB or yuan) to keep it from depreciating. In April 2016, China agreed to language in a G-20 meeting communiqué stating that members would "avoid competitive devaluation and not target the exchange rate for competitive purposes."[44] The International Monetary Fund in July 2016 stated that the RMB "was broadly in line with fundamentals." Trump reneged on his campaign promise to name China a currency manipulator after a few months in office. In the president's interview with the *Economist*, Treasury Secretary Mnuchin explained to the reporter that China stopped manipulating its currency as soon as Trump got elected.[45] Mnuchin must not have been keeping up with the currency markets before the election, or maybe he thought the *Economist* wasn't.

With the termination of the Trans-Pacific Partnership and the collapse of its comprehensive and high standards agreement, flawed as it may have been, what do the nationalist and populist victors have to celebrate? An end to imports from low-wage developing countries? An end to exporting jobs to countries with poor labor standards? An end to imports from countries with poor environmental standards? An end to currency manipulation? Perhaps the president's "smart, tough negotiators" can bring back fair trade with protectionist tariffs and trade surpluses under eleven bilateral trade agreements with all of the former TPP participants.

On November 15, 2016, a week after the election, I picked up a *China Daily USA*, the Chinese government's English-language newspaper, in the airport in Washington, DC. On the editorial page above the fold was a large cartoon depicting President Obama diving off the bow of a large container ship named "TPP" stuck in the desert surrounded by cactus, sand dunes, and cattle skulls. A long editorial described Beijing's relief that "TPP is looking ever less likely to materialize by the day. After all, the trade grouping has been essentially . . . meant to counter China's economic influence in the Asia-Pacific." The piece described Chinese President Xi Jinping and

President Trump's phone call exchanging good wishes for the "Trump era." The writer suggested that the "incoming administration should realize that the more open, inclusive Regional Comprehensive Economic Partnership (RCEP) will turn out to be a far more efficient vehicle for advancing US interests [than the TPP and urged the US to join] . . . and become involved from the rule-making stage."[46]

The RCEP is a multilateral FTA, including the ten Southeast Asian members of ASEAN (Association of Southeast Asian Nations) and six nations with which they have trade agreements—Australia, China, India, Japan, New Zealand, and South Korea. Seven of these countries also participated in the TPP. The *China Daily* editorial mentioned the RCEP "rule-making stage"—the concept of that term is narrowly defined in comparison with TPP rule-making. Under China's leadership, rules covering intellectual property rights, investment, state-owned enterprises, and labor and environmental protection are expected to be less extensive or nonexistent, or effectively not enforceable, compared with rules in the TPP. The current ASEAN trade agreements are less comprehensive than the proposed TPP, even in terms of trade liberalization. Regardless of whether the United States decides to join RCEP—which seems doubtful under the Trump affinity for bilateral agreements, among many other better reasons—withdrawing from TPP has the effect of abandoning what would have been a significant and influential step forward on worker's rights in the Asia-Pacific region and beyond.

Strategically, the demise of the TPP was a major win for China. As President Trump withdraws the United States from the world leadership roles built over the last century, President Xi Jinping is attempting to transform his nation into a global leader based on a strong economy, a strong defense, and an extensive application of soft power. For several years, Xi has been calling for fulfilling the "Chinese dream of a great rejuvenation of the Chinese nation," recalling a time during the Ming Dynasty when China was the most powerful nation on Earth. His plans include the construction of a land-based Silk Road Economic Belt and the Maritime Silk Road tying Asia to Europe, the Middle East, and Africa (known in a characteristically Chinese expression, as "One Belt, One Road") running along the path of the historic Silk Road and the maritime voyages of Admiral Zheng He in the early fifteenth century (referenced in the Preface). The One Belt, One Road project is not just a transportation project. China is committing more than $1 trillion for infrastructure projects in over sixty countries, spreading its soft power to win friends and expand its orbit of influence, presumably to "Make China Great Again."

Like the Ming emperors who withdrew behind the Great Wall, keeping barbarians from entering the Middle Kingdom and allowing Admiral Zheng's great ships to rot in the docks, the Trump administration is building its own walls to withstand intrusion by foreign barbarians and is withdrawing from world leadership masked by the illusion of America First and economic nationalism. Three days before the Trump inauguration, President Xi appeared for the first time to reach out to the global elites with a free-trade message at the World Economic Forum in Davos, Switzerland, as if to offer himself in a debut role as the new champion of the liberal world economic order.

In a live broadcast on August 24, 1941, Prime Minister Winston Churchill announced to the world his previously undisclosed conference with President Franklin Roosevelt held on warships in the Atlantic Ocean two weeks earlier. It was a tragic and treacherous time. Churchill described in lengthy, brutal detail how the "whole of Europe has been wrecked and trampled down by the mechanical weapons and barbaric fury of the Nazis." He also described the "carnage, ruin and corruption" wrought by Japanese military factions in China and throughout Asia emulating "the style of Hitler and Mussolini." And this, he said, is just the beginning: "Famine and pestilence have yet to follow in the ruts of Hitler's tanks." The meeting between Churchill and Roosevelt was symbolic, he said, to demonstrate "the deep underlying unities which stir and, at decisive moments, rule the English-speaking peoples throughout the world." He suggested the meeting also symbolizes "the marshalling of the good forces of the world against the evil forces which are now so formidable and triumphant and which have cast their cruel spell over the whole of Europe and a large part of Asia."

Even though the United States was not in the war at this point, FDR had a distinct interest in its outcome and Churchill, of course, wanted to give him any opportunity to be involved. As discussed more fully in Chapter 10, Roosevelt's principal goal at the conference was to prepare a declaration of war aims to help him explain to the American people why the Allies were fighting the war. These included the goal of providing the freedom of self-government, improved labor standards, freedom from fear and want, and other basic human rights suppressed under fascist tyranny. The postwar goals also included a new trade order with access on equal terms to world trade needed for economic prosperity. Churchill declared in his broadcast that unlike the mistake made after the First World War, all countries would be guaranteed access to trade and the world's resources; even Germany would not be punished with additional trade barriers.[47]

Less than four months after Churchill's broadcast, the United States entered the Second World War. The sacrifices and successes of the Allied forces during the war made the pledges of freedom in the Atlantic Charter come true at least in the noncommunist world. Much is owed to the soldiers and statesmen who preserved security and established the liberal economic order conceived in that prescient document. Some of us, who were born soon after the suffering subsided and the sacrifices made, do not seem to appreciate the importance of continuing the role of American leadership in sustaining the liberal economic order created when only the United States had the economic strength and strategic interest to build it and now alone has both the economic strength and a vested interest to maintain it.

Notes

INTRODUCTION

1. Smith, *An Inquiry into the Nature and Causes of the Wealth of Nations*, 374, 548.

2. Kim Murphy, "Echoes of Another Era Fill Streets of Seattle," *Los Angeles Times*, December 1, 1999; David Postman, "WTO in Seattle: Everyone Has an Agenda, Including the Turtles," *Seattle Times*, November 28, 1999.

3. Helen Jung, "French Farmer Basks in Limelight of Anti-Trade Movement," *Seattle Times*, November 28, 1999; Robert L. Jamieson Jr., "French Farmer Bové Takes His Beef to McDonald's," *Seattle Post-Intelligencer*, November 30, 1999; Thomas Sancton, "Super Fries Saboteur," *Time*, December 6, 1999.

4. Appellate Body Report, *United States—Import Prohibition of Certain Shrimp and Shrimp Products*, WT/DS58/AB/R (October 12, 1998).

5. Ibid.

6. CNN, *Earth Matters*, October 18, 1998, Transcript # 98101800V25.

7. John Sweeney, "Making the Global Economy Work for Working Families: Beyond the WTO," *Remarks at the National Press Club Ballroom*, November 19, 1999 (copy in author's papers at Richard B. Russell Library for Political Research and Studies, The University of Georgia Libraries, Athens, Georgia).

8. Sam Howe Verhovek and Steven Greenhouse, "Seattle Is under Curfew after Disruptions," *New York Times*, December 1, 1999.

9. Jonathan Peterson, Evelyn Iritani, and Kim Murphy, "Protest, Chaos Delay World Trade Summit," *Los Angeles Times*, December 1, 1999.

10. "Bogus Arguments against the World Trade Organization," *Slate Magazine*, November 23, 1999.

11. "Clueless in Seattle," *Economist*, December 3, 1999.

12. "Street Violence, Protests Delay Opening of WTO Conference," *CNN Today*, November 30, 1999, Transcript # 99113006V13.

13. Thomas L. Friedman, "Senseless in Seattle," *New York Times*, December 1, 1999.

14. *Economist*, December 3, 1999, *supra* note 11.

15. "Members of Congress Push Own Agenda for WTO Talks," National Journal's *Congress Daily*, December 2, 1999.

16. Sarah Lyall, "Internationally, Embarrassment for U.S.," *New York Times*, December 2, 1999.

17. John Burgess and Steve Pearlstein, "Protests Delay WTO Opening," *Washington Post*, December 1, 1999.

18. David E. Sanger and Joseph Kahn, "A Chaotic Intersection of Tear Gas and Trade Talks," *New York Times*, December 1, 1999.

19. *Washington Post*, December 1, 1999, *supra* note 17.

20. Michael Paulson, "Clinton Takes Strong Stand on Labor Rights," *Seattle Post-Intelligencer*, December 1, 1999.

21. Smith, 12.

22. Ibid.

23. Journeymen Tailors, London Act, 1720, (7 Geo. 1 St. 1) C A P. XIII.

24. Journeymen Tailors, London Act Amendment, 1768, (8 Geo. 3) C A P. XVII.

25. Smith, 59.

26. Ibid.

27. Combination of Workmen Act, 1796, (36 Geo. 3) C A P. CXI.

28. Hitchcock, *Down and Out in Eighteenth-Century London*, 10.

29. Smith, 76.

30. Ibid., 65–66.

31. Ibid., 72.

32. Ibid., 61–62.

33. Ibid., 65.

34. Ibid., 394.

35. Ibid., 396.

36. Ibid., 549.

37. Otteson, ed., *Adam Smith: Selected Philosophical Writings*, 230.

38. Smith, 382–383.

39. Ibid., 70.

40. Locke, *Locke's Two Treatises of Civil Government*, 305.

41. Smith, 306.

42. Ibid., 435.

43. Ibid., 399.

44. "Introducing Big Government," *Economist*, December 23, 1999.

45. Smith, 10.

46. Ibid., 70.

47. Ibid., 13.

48. Ibid., 399.

49. Ibid., 309.

50. Ibid., 407.

51. Ibid.

52. Ibid.

53. Ibid.

54. Ibid., 410.

55. Ibid., 409.

56. Ibid., 410–411.

57. Ibid., 411.

58. Ibid., 413.

59. Ibid., 414.

60. Ibid., 413.

61. Hague, *William Pitt the Younger*, 161.

62. 1 Parl. Reg. (1801) 249–250.

63. Hague, 196.

64. Buxton, *Finance and Politics: An Historical Study 1789–1885*, 65.

65. Pickering and Tyrrell, *The People's Bread: A History of the Anti-Corn Law League*, 2.

66. 69 Parl. Deb. (3d ser.) (1845) 386–387.

67. 69 Parl. Deb. (3d ser.) (1845) 390.

68. 87 Parl. Deb. (3d ser.) (1846) 1055.

69. Mill, *Principles of Political Economy*, vol. 2, 569.

70. Monypenny and Buckle, *The Life of Benjamin Disraeli: Earl of Beaconsfield*, vol. 3, 241.

71. Manchester, *The Last Lion: Winston Spencer Churchill: Visions of Glory 1874–1932*, 353.

72. Rabushka, *From Adam Smith to the Wealth of America*, 112; Jastram, *The Golden Constant: The English and American Experience: 1560–1976*, 32–33.

73. Smith, 620.

74. Wood, *The Americanization of Benjamin Franklin*, 88; Isaacson, *Benjamin Franklin: An American Life*, 196.

75. Smith, Introduction by D. D. Raphael, xix; Isaacson, 260–261.

76. Smith, 519.

CHAPTER 1

1. Alexander Hamilton, "The Continentalist, No. V, April 18, 1782," in Frisch, *Selected Writings and Speeches of Alexander Hamilton*, 55.

2. Interview with Ambassador Peter Allgeier, Deputy US Trade Representative, Geneva, July 19, 2007.

3. Young, *A History of the American Protective System*, 14.

4. Eckes, *Opening America's Market: U.S. Foreign Trade Policy since 1776*, 2.

5. James Madison to Thomas Jefferson, March 18, 1786, *Papers of James Madison* vol. 8, 500–501; Bowen, *Miracle at Philadelphia: The Story of the Constitutional Convention May to September 1787*, 10.

6. Richard Henry Lee to George Mason, May 15, 1787, *Papers of George Mason* vol. 3, 876 (Robert Rutland, ed., 1970).

7. William Hill, "Protective Purpose of the Tariff Act of 1789," *Journal of Political Economy* 2, no. 1 (December 1893): 54–76.

8. Hamilton, *The Report on Manufactures*, in *The Reports of Alexander Hamilton*, ed. Cooke.

9. Ibid., 137–138.

10. Ibid., 139.

11. Ibid., 140.

12. Ibid., 142.

13. Ibid., 166.

14. Ibid., 167. Interestingly, this point seems to indicate a change of heart by Hamilton from four years earlier while urging support for broad taxing authority to the federal government in *The Federalist Papers*. In *Federalist* 35, he argued that limiting the authority to import duties alone would tempt Congress to impose "exorbitant duties," giving the manufacturing classes "a premature monopoly of the markets." *The Federalist Papers*, 212. His position in 1787 might be explained by his bias favoring the New York merchant and financial class, which then thrived on imports, or simply by his desire to make the strongest argument he could for ratification in New York.

15. Hamilton, *Report*, 168.

16. Ibid., 171–172; Chernow, *Alexander Hamilton*, 378–379.

17. Hamilton, *Report*, 204.

18. Ibid., 175–176.

19. Chernow, 372.

20. Passaic County Historical Society, Gledhill Collection, SEUM, box 2, prospectus for the Society for Establishing Useful Manufactures, April 29, 1791, as quoted in Chernow, 373.

21. Chernow, 386–387.

22. Jefferson to Washington, September 9, 1792, in Jefferson, *Writings*, 994. As will be seen, this is not to say that Jefferson and Madison were always averse to protective trade measures, especially against Great Britain. Madison authored the Tariff Act of 1789, the object of which was in part to protect American manufactures. Ironically, Tench Coxe, the young writer who helped supply Madison with information about British trade and the protectionist rationale for the bill when he was guiding it through Congress, later served as Hamilton's assistant secretary and helped him write the *Report on Manufactures*. See Baxter, *Henry Clay and the American System*, 18–19.

23. Hamilton, *Report*, 131.

24. Chernow, 375.

25. Schlesinger, *The Age of Jackson*, 9–10.

26. "Speeches in the Federal Convention," *Works of Alexander Hamilton*, vol. 1, 401.

27. Hamilton to Robert Morris, 1780, *Works of Alexander Hamilton*, vol. 3, 338.

28. See Chapters 3 and 4.

29. Jefferson, *Notes on the State of Virginia*, *Writings*, 290–291.

30. Jefferson, *A Summary View of the Rights of British America*, *Writings*, 108.

31. On the subjects of money and commerce, Jefferson recommended: "Smith's Wealth of Nations is the best book to be read," Jefferson to John Norvell, June 14, 1807, *Writings*, 1176.

32. 4 Annals of Cong. 1297 (1793).

33. Jefferson, *Report on the Privileges and Restrictions on the Commerce of the United States in Foreign Countries*, *Writings*, 446.

34. Meacham, *Thomas Jefferson: The Art of Power*, 352.

35. Jefferson, *Report on Commerce*, *Writings*, 448.

36. Letter from Hamilton to Edward Carrington, May 26, 1792, in Schlesinger, *History of U.S. Political Parties*, vol. 1, 277.

37. Gallatin to Thomas Jefferson, December 18, 1807, in *The Thomas Jefferson Papers, Series 1. General Correspondence. 1651–1827*, image 164, http://memory.loc

.gov/cgiin/ampage?collId=mtj1&fileName=mtj1page040.db&recNum=163 (accessed September 30, 2011).

38. Jefferson to Major Joseph Eggleston, March 7, 1808, as quoted in Malone, *Jefferson and His Time*, vol. 5, 483.

39. Meacham, 432.

40. Jefferson to Lafayette, February 24, 1809, in *The Thomas Jefferson Papers*, as quoted in Meacham, 431.

41. Jefferson to Benjamin Austin, January 9, 1816, in *The Thomas Jefferson Papers, Series 1. General Correspondence. 1651–1827*, image 737, http://memory.loc.gov/cgi-bin/amp age?collId=mtj1&fileName=mtj1page048.db&recNum=736 (accessed September 30, 2011).

42. Jefferson, *Notes, Writings*, 290.

43. Malone, *Jefferson and His Time*, vol. 5, 629.

44. The report proposed amendments essentially (1) prohibiting any trade embargo lasting over 60 days; (2) requiring a two-thirds congressional majority for declaration of war, admission of a new state, or interdiction of foreign commerce; (3) removing the three-fifths representation advantage of the South; (4) limiting future presidents to one term; and (5) requiring each president to be from a different state than his predecessor. Dwight, *History of the Hartford Convention*, 377–378; Banner, *To the Hartford Convention*, 341–342.

45. Baxter, 17.

46. 33 Parl. Deb. (1st ser.) (1816) 1099.

47. 28 Annals of Cong. 256 (1815).

48. Baxter, 20.

49. 42 Annals of Cong. 1963 (1824).

50. 42 Annals of Cong. 1970 (1824).

51. 42 Annals of Cong. 1978 (1824).

52. 42 Annals of Cong. 1976 (1824).

53. 42 Annals of Cong. 1992 (1824).

54. 42 Annals of Cong. 1920 (1824).

55. 42 Annals of Cong. 1979 (1824).

56. Remini, *Daniel Webster*, 221–222.

57. 42 Annals of Cong. 2043 (1824).

58. 42 Annals of Cong. 2034 (1824).

59. 42 Annals of Cong. 2054 (1824).

60. Baxter, 29.

61. Ibid., 32.

CHAPTER 2

1. Robert J. Walker, Report from the Secretary of the Treasury, December 8, 1845, Taussig, *State Papers and Speeches on the Tariff*, 227.

2. Ellis, *American Creation*, 170.

3. Ibid., 175.

4. Lin-Manuel Miranda, *Hamilton*, Act II, Scene 8; the play is based on Chernow, *Alexander Hamilton*.

5. Witcover, *Party of the People: A History of the Democrats*, 120.

6. Brant, *The Fourth President: A Life of James Madison*, 597.

7. Andrew Jackson to William Lewis, February 14, 1825, Bassett, *Correspondence of Andrew Jackson*, vol. 3, 276, quoted in Brands, *Andrew Jackson*, 388.

8. Remini, *John Quincy Adams*, 113.

9. *Papers of John C. Calhoun*, vol. 10, 480.

10. Ibid., 531.

11. Brands, 434.

12. 6 Reg. Deb. 50 (1830).

13. 6 Reg. Deb. 69 (1830).

14. 6 Reg. Deb. 49 (1830).

15. Adams, *Memoirs*, vol. 10, 43; Remini, *Daniel Webster*, 298.

16. 6 Reg. Deb. 80 (1830).

17. Brands, 445–446; Bartlett, *John C. Calhoun*, 168.

18. Bartlett, 182.

19. Gallatin, "Memorial of the Committee of the Free Trade Convention," Taussig, *State Papers and Speeches on the Tariff*, 108.

20. 8 Reg. Deb. 267 (1832).

21. *Memoirs of John Quincy Adams*, ed. Charles Francis Adams, vol. 8, 446.

22. Brands, 475.

23. Ibid., 477.

24. Bartlett, 192–193.

25. 9 Reg. Deb. 539 (1833).

26. 9 Reg. Deb. 587 (1833).

27. Bartlett, 381.

28. Ibid., 384.

29. 9 Reg. Deb. 741 (1832).

30. Bartlett, 84.

31. Schlesinger, *Age of Jackson*, 12.

32. Ibid., 316.

33. Jackson, Bank Veto Message, July 10, 1832, Schlesinger, *History of U.S. Political Parties*, vol. 1, 543.

34. Biddle to Henry Clay, August 1, 1832, in *The Correspondence of Nicholas Biddle Dealing with National Affairs*, ed. Reginald McGrane (Boston: Houghton Mifflin, 1919), 196.

35. 8 Reg. Deb. 1240 (1833).

36. Webster to Nicholas Biddle, December 21, 1833, in Nicholas Biddle, *The Correspondence of Nicholas Biddle Dealing with National Affairs*, 218, quoted in Schlesinger, *The Age of Jackson*, 84.

37. Schlesinger, *The Age of Jackson*, 84.

38. Cohn, *The Fabulous Democrats*, 40.

39. Ibid., 51.

40. Baxter, *Henry Clay and the American System*, 181.

41. Cong. Globe, 29th Cong., 1st Sess. 1022 (1846).

42. Cong. Globe, 30th Cong., 2d Sess. 9 (1848).

43. Johnson and Porter, *National Party Platforms*, 26.

CHAPTER 3

1. Foner, *Mark Twain: Social Critic*, 97.

2. Taussig, *The Tariff History of the United States*, 115.

3. Witcover, *Party of the People: A History of the Democrats*, 201–202.

4. Schlesinger, *History of U.S. Political Parties*, vol. 2, 1241.

5. Lincoln, Republican: 180 electoral/1,866,000 popular (39.8 percent); Douglas, Democratic (northern): 12 electoral/1,383,000 popular (29.5 percent); Breckinridge, Democratic (southern): 72 electoral/848,000 popular (18.1 percent); Bell, Constitutional Union: 39 electoral/593,000 popular (12.6 percent).

6. Donald, *Lincoln*, 110.

7. "Fragments on the Tariff," Lincoln, *Speeches and Writings: 1832–1858*, 149–158.

8. Boritt, *Lincoln and the Economics of the American Dream*, 118.

9. Ibid., 132.

10. AL to Edward Wallace, May 12, 1860, Lincoln, *Speeches and Writings 1859–1865*, 156.

11. Sandburg, *Abraham Lincoln: The War Years*, vol. 1, 50.

12. Freehling and Simpson, ed., *Secession Debated: Georgia's Showdown in 1860*, 38.

13. Tarbell, 10–11.

14. Taussig, *The Tariff History of the United States*, 165.

15. A typical example noted by Ida Tarbell was a 20 percent tariff added for wood-screws by Senator James Simmons of Rhode Island, who was thereafter known as "Wood-Screw" Simmons. At the time of its passage there was only one small producer of wood-screws in the United States, located in Providence, Rhode Island. Tarbell, 7. In an unrelated matter a year later, Senator "Wood-Screw" resigned his office after the Senate Judiciary Committee reported that it had enough evidence to expel him from the Senate for corruption in an influence-peddling scandal.

16. Tarbell, 15.

17. Taussig, *The Tariff History of the United States*, 166–167.

18. Stanwood, *American Tariff Controversies in the Nineteenth Century*, 153.

19. Ibid., 149.

20. Cong. Globe, 40th Cong., 3rd Sess. 1508–09 (1869); Tarbell, 48.

21. Taussig, *The Tariff History of the United States*, 221.

22. "Plan of the 'Wharton School of Finance and Economy' of the University of Pennsylvania, May, 1881," in *Education of Business Men, An Address before the American Bankers Association, September 3, 1890*, by Edmond J. James, Published by William B. Greene, Secretary, 1891, 34.

23. Cong. Globe, 41st Cong., 2d Sess., 2018 (1870).

24. Stanwood, 196–197; *National Party Platforms: 1840–1972*, compiled by Johnson and Porter, 50.

25. Tarbell, 95.

26. Ibid., 97.

27. Stanwood, 202–203.

28. Tarbell, 101.

29. 14 Cong. Rec. 8–9 (1882).

30. Taussig, *The Tariff History of the United* States, 249.

31. Tarbell, 131.

32. *Bulletin Wool Manufacturers*, vol. xiii, 94, as quoted in Taussig, *The Tariff History of the United States*, 249, fn.1.

CHAPTER 4

1. 19 Cong. Rec. 4,405 (1888).
2. *Official Proceedings of the Republican National Convention Held at Chicago, June 3–6, 1884,* 92.
3. Johnson and Porter, *National Party Platforms 1840–1972,* 66.
4. See "James G. Blaine, Acceptance Letter, July 15, 1884," Schlesinger, *History of U.S. Political Parties,* vol. 2, 1460–1469.
5. 17 Cong. Rec. 113 (1885).
6. 18 Cong. Rec. 7 (1887).
7. *Public Opinion* 26, no. 25 (June 22, 1899): 771.
8. 19 Cong. Rec. 9–11 (1888).
9. Reitano, *The Tariff Question in the Gilded Age—The Great Debate of 1888,* 11.
10. Ibid., 19.
11. 19 Cong. Rec. 3,058 (1888).
12. 19 Cong. Rec. 3,059 (1888).
13. 19 Cong. Rec. 3,060, 3,063 (1888).
14. 19 Cong. Rec. 3,063 (1888).
15. Ibid.
16. 19 Cong. Rec. 3,064 (1888).
17. 19 Cong. Rec. 3,065 (1888).
18. 19 Cong. Rec. 3,069, 3,071 (1888).
19. Andrew Carnegie, "Wealth," *North American Review* 148, no. 391 (1889): 653–664, http://www.jstor.org/stable/25101798.
20. Reitano, 103.
21. Ibid.
22. Ibid., 98–99.
23. Caro, *The Years of Lyndon Johnson: Master of the Senate,* 34.
24. Jerome L. Sternstein, "Corruption in the Gilded Age Senate: Nelson W. Aldrich and the Sugar Trust," *Capitol Studies* 6, no. 1 (Spring 1978): 13–37; "Senator Aldrich and Sugar—The Republican Tariff Leader Owned by the Trust Indebted to It for Financial Aid," *New York Times,* June 20, 1894.
25. Johnson and Porter, ed., *National Party Platforms: 1840–1972,* 76–78.
26. Ibid., 80.
27. Tarbell, *The Tariff in Our Times,* 175.
28. Ibid., 177.
29. Krass, *Carnegie,* 238.
30. Reitano, 123.
31. Tarbell, 188.
32. Thomas B. Reed, "Rules of the House of Representatives," *Century Magazine* 15 (March 1889): 795, quoted in Gould, *Grand Old Party: A History of the Republicans,* 106.
33. Tarbell, 312.
34. Gould, 109.
35. Krass, 256.
36. Brodsky, *Grover Cleveland,* 280.
37. Joseph Nimmo Jr., "The Views of the Majority," *American Economist,* January 5, 1894; Tarbell, 218, 220.

38. 26 Cong. Rec. 7712 (1894).

39. Kyvig, *Explicit and Authentic Acts: Amending the U.S. Constitution, 1776–1995*, 195–196.

40. 157 U.S. 429 (1895) and 158 U.S. 601 (1895).

41. *Springer v. United States*, 102 U.S. 586 (1881).

42. *Pollock*, 157 U.S. at 563–564.

43. *Hylton v. U.S.*, 3 Dallas (3 U.S.) 171 (1796).

44. 157 U.S. at 596, 607.

45. Id., at 608, 652.

46. 158 U.S. at 695.

47. David G. Farrelly, "Justice Harlan's Dissent in the Pollock Case," *Southern California Law Review* 24 (1950–1951): 175, 177–180.

48. 158 U.S. 564 (1985)

49. 156 U.S. 1 (1895).

50. 163 U.S. 537 (1896).

51. *Augusta Chronicle, St. Louis Post-Dispatch,* and *New York World* quoted in Kyvig, 199.

52. Leinwand, *William Jennings Bryan: An Uncertain Trumpet*, 31–32.

53. William Jennings Bryan, "Cross of Gold Speech," delivered at the Democratic National Convention, Chicago, IL, July 9, 1896, http://teachingamericanhistory.org/library/index.asp?document=163.

54. Thomas, *The War Lovers*, 141, 223.

55. Beatty, *Age of Betrayal: The Triumph of Money in America, 1865–1900*, 367.

56. Phillips, *William McKinley*, 116.

57. Richardson, *A Compilation of the Messages and Papers of the Presidents 1789–1897*, vol. 10, 1920, 393–397.

58. "Mr. Roosevelt Is Now the President," *New York Times*, September 15, 1901.

59. Goodwin, *The Bully Pulpit*, 280.

CHAPTER 5

1. *Des Moines Register and Leader*, March 2, 1912, as quoted in Link, *Wilson: The Road to the White House*, 397.

2. Upton Sinclair, *The Jungle*, 193.

3. Ibid., ix.

4. Ibid., 275.

5. Goodwin, *Bully Pulpit*, 339.

6. "Ida M. Tarbell's Activities Include Every Interest of the People," *Washington Times*, June 24, 1910.

7. Morison, *The Letters of Theodore Roosevelt*, vol. 1, 504, as quoted in Buchanan, *The Great Betrayal*, 232.

8. Gould, *The Presidency of Theodore Roosevelt*, 25.

9. Goodwin, 309.

10. Roosevelt to Joseph B. Bishop, April 27, 1903, in *The Letters of Theodore Roosevelt*, vol. 3, 471, quoted in Goodwin, 133.

11. Josephson, *The President Makers: The Culture of Politics and Leadership in an Age of Enlightenment, 1896–1919*, 150, 125.

12. Foner, *Mark Twain: Social Critic*, 97–98.

13. 42 Cong. Rec. 1349 (1908).

14. "Address of President Roosevelt on the occasion of the laying of the corner stone of the Pilgrim memorial monument" in Provincetown, MA, on August 20, 1907 (Washington, DC: US Government Printing Office, 1907).

15. Roosevelt to Lyman Abbott, January 11, 1905, in *The Letters of Theodore Roosevelt*, vol. 4, 1100.

16. Tarbell, 296.

17. Krass, *Carnegie*, 479.

18. Tarbell, 258–261.

19. Goodwin, 591.

20. Ibid., 586.

21. Ibid., 592.

22. Tarbell, 310.

23. Mowry, *Theodore Roosevelt and the Progressive Movement*, 247, 248.

24. Kyvig, 201–208.

25. William Howard, Taft, "Tariff Speech," September 17, 1909, in Schlesinger, *History of U.S. Political Parties*, vol. 3, 2181.

26. Caro, 49.

27. Tarbell, 326.

28. Tarbell, vii; Goodwin, 630.

29. Gould, *Grand Old Party*, 178.

30. Roosevelt, *The New Nationalism*, 3–33.

31. Mowry, *Theodore Roosevelt and the Progressive Movement*, 144.

32. "Roosevelt Expounds New Nationalism," *New York Tribune*, September 1, 1910; La Forte, "Theodore Roosevelt's Osawatomie Speech," *Kansas Historical Quarterly* 32, no. 2 (Summer 1966): 187–200.

33. "G. Fred Williams Assails Wilson," *New York Times*, March 23, 1912.

34. The accuracy of this remark is challenged in Berg, *Wilson*, 347–350, and Mark E. Benbow, "Birth of a Quotation: Woodrow Wilson and 'Like Writing History with Lightning,'" *Journal of the Gilded Age and the Progressive Era* 9, no. 4 (October 2010): 509–533.

35. Diamond, *The Economic Thought of Woodrow Wilson*, 23.

36. W. Elliot Brownlee, "Wilson's Reform of Economic Structure: Progressive Liberalism and the Corporation," in Cooper, *Reconsidering Woodrow Wilson: Progressivism, Internationalism, War, and Peace*, 60.

37. Ibid.

38. *Woodrow Wilson: Essential Writings and Speeches of the Scholar-President*, Mario R. Dinunzio, ed., 323.

39. Woodrow Wilson, "The Tariff Make-Believe," *North American Review* 190, no. 647 (October 1909): 535–556, http://www.jstor.org/stable/25106485.

40. *Harper's Weekly*, May 15, 1909, 4, as quoted in Startt, *Woodrow Wilson and the Press: Prelude to the Presidency*, 59.

41. Berg, *Wilson*, 190.

42. "No Doubt Where Wilson Stands on the Tariff," *New York Times*, August 3, 1912.

43. "Gov. Wilson Derides Protection Maxims," *New York Times*, January 4, 1912.

44. "Democrats End Feuds at Jackson Banquet," *Washington Post*, January 9, 1912.

45. Witcover, *Party of the People: A History of the Democrats*, 306.

46. *Official Report of the Proceedings of the Democratic National Convention*, 131.

47. Johnson and Porter, *National Party Platforms: 1840–1972*, 168–169.

48. Wilson, *The New Freedom: A Call for the Emancipation of the Generous Energies of a People*, 18. www.gutenberg.org/files/14811/14811-h/14811-h.htm.

49. Ibid., 19.

50. *Rocky Mountain News*, October 8, 1912, as quoted in Link, 514.

51. Buchanan, *The Great Betrayal*, 235.

52. Wilson, *The New Freedom: A Call for the Emancipation of the Generous Energies of a People*, 43.

53. Ibid., 49.

54. Quoted in Lyle W. Cooper, "The Tariff and Organized Labor," *American Economic Review* 20, no. 2 (June, 1930): 212, fn. 6.

55. Robert D. Leiter, "Organized Labor and the Tariff," *Southern Economic Journal* 28, no. 1 (July 1961): 56, 62.

56. 50 Cong. Rec. 3 (1913).

57. "President's Visit Nettles Senators," *New York Times*, April 8, 1913.

58. 50 Cong. Rec. 130 (1913).

59. Hull, *The Memoirs of Cordell Hull*, vol. 1, 71.

60. Brands, *Woodrow Wilson*, 33.

61. 50 Cong. Rec. 1804 (1913).

62. Burns, *The Workshop of Democracy*, 386–387.

63. Berg, *Wilson*, 314.

64. Taussig, *The Tariff History of the United States*, 419.

65. "Wilson Signs New Tariff Law," *New York Times*, October 4, 1913.

66. Cooper, *Reconsidering Woodrow Wilson: Progressivism, Internationalism, War, and Peace*, 12.

67. Diamond, *The Economic Thought of Woodrow Wilson*, 100.

68. Ibid., 100, 102, 103.

69. Brandeis, *Other People's Money—and How the Bankers Use It* (first published as a series of articles in *Harper's Weekly* in 1913–14, and published as a book in 1914).

70. Kaufman, *Efficiency and Expansion: Foreign Trade Organization in the Wilson Administration, 1913–1921*, 73.

71. 55 Cong. Rec. 104 (1917).

72. 56 Cong. Rec. 680 (1918).

73. Revenue Act of 1916, ch. 463, 39 Stat. 756 (1916).

74. Revenue Act of 1918, ch. 18, 40 Stat. 1057 (1919).

75. Roy G. and Gladys C. Blakey, "The Revenue Act of 1918," *American Economic Review* 9, no. 2 (June 1919): 213–243.

76. "Full Text of President Wilson's Address to the Houses of Congress in Joint Session," *New York Times*, May 28, 1918.

77. Caro, *Master of the Senate*, 52.

78. Ibid., 39.

79. Dean, *Warren G. Harding*, 30.

80. 60 Cong. Rec. 4498–99 (1921).

CHAPTER 6

1. 71 Cong. Rec. 3549, 3547 (1929).
2. "Harding Deplores Growth of Factions and Strikes at Klan," *New York Times*, May 18, 1923.
3. "Harding Outlines Policies He Favors," *New York Times*, November 5, 1920.
4. 60 Cong. Rec. 4534 (1921).
5. Taussig, *The Tariff History of the United States*, 452.
6. 61 Cong. Rec. 3478 (1921).
7. 62 Cong. Rec. 5763 (1922).
8. Taussig, *The Tariff History*, 453; Irwin, *Peddling Protectionism: Smoot-Hawley and the Great Depression*, 105.
9. Jaan Pennar, "Richard Cobden and Cordell Hull: A Comparative Study of the Commercial Policies of Nineteenth-Century England and Contemporary United States" (Ph.D. dissertation, Princeton University, 1954), 146–147.
10. "Tariff Bill Signed; Ships Speed to Port to Beat High Tariffs," *New York Times*, September 22, 1922.
11. 62 Cong. Rec. 38 (1921–1922).
12. Ibid.
13. Taussig, *The Tariff History*, 480.
14. 65 Cong. Rec. 97 (1923).
15. "Topics of the Times," *New York Times*, September 12, 1930.
16. Keynes, *The End of Laissez-Faire: The Economic Consequences of the Peace*, 24, 36, 44.
17. Gould, *Grand Old Party: A History of the Republicans*, 242.
18. Kenkel, *Progressives and Protection*, 175.
19. Ferrell, *The Presidency of Calvin Coolidge*, 72.
20. Mellon, *Taxation: The People's Business*, 13, 16.
21. Stephen A. Schuker, "American Foreign Policy," in Haynes, *Calvin Coolidge and the Coolidge Era: Essays on the History of the 1920s*, 297.
22. 70 Cong. Rec. 20 (1928).
23. Alter, *The Defining Moment: FDR's Hundred Days and the Triumph of Hope*, 45.
24. McCoy, *Calvin Coolidge: The Quiet President*, 390.
25. Alter, 77.
26. Johnson and Porter, *National Party Platforms: 1840–1972*, 272.
27. Ibid., 280, 282.
28. Gould, *Grand Old Party: A History of the Republicans*, 249.
29. *New Republic* 58 (March 20, 1929), 126; 59 (June 12, 1929), 88, quoted in Hicks, *Republican Ascendancy: 1921–1933*, 216.
30. Hoover, *The Memoirs of Herbert Hoover: The Cabinet and the Presidency 1920–1933*, 223.
31. 71 Cong. Rec. 42 (1929).
32. 71 Cong. Rec. 43 (1929).
33. For a comprehensive treatment of the legislative process and history of this act, see Schattschneider, *Politics, Pressures, and the Tariff: A Study of Free Private Enterprise in Pressure Politics, as Shown in the 1929–1930 Revision of the Tariff*; and Irwin, *Peddling Protectionism: Smoot-Hawley and the Great Depression*.

34. 71 Cong. Rec. 1068 (1929).

35. Schattschneider, 145.

36. Taussig, *The Tariff History*, 492.

37. 71 Cong. Rec. 1068 (1929).

38. Tariff Readjustment—1929, Report to Accompany H.R. 2667, H.R. Rep. No. 7, at 8 (1929).

39. Irwin, 36.

40. Tariff Readjustment—1929, H.R. Rep. No. 7, at 11 (1929).

41. Robert D. Leiter, "Organized Labor and the Tariff," *Southern Economic Journal* 28, no. 1 (1961): 56–57; however, President Hoover wrote in his memoirs that among the groups urging him to approve the final bill was the American Federation of Labor. Hoover, *Memoirs*, 296.

42. Schattschneider, 40.

43. Cordell Hull, Minority Views, Tariff Readjustment—1929, H.R. Rep. No. 7, pt. 2, at 1–8 (1929).

44. Irwin, 42.

45. Taussig, *The Tariff History*, 496.

46. Smoot survived a challenged to his eligibility to serve in the Senate in 1904, based on the claim that he could not swear to uphold the Constitution of the United States while serving in leadership of an organization that sanctioned the violation of polygamy prohibition laws.

47. "An Exceptional Senator," *American Economist* 75, no. 24 (June 12, 1925): 188.

48. Merrill, *Reed Smoot: Apostle in Politics*, 332.

49. Irwin, 50, 52.

50. 71 Cong. Rec. 5335 (1929); Irwin, 54.

51. 72 Cong. Rec. 5414–5420, 5491–5495, 5520 (1930); Merrill, 166–171.

52. Taussig, *The Tariff History*, 498.

53. "Senate Surrenders to House in Vote on Tariff Amendments," *Washington Post*, May 20, 1930.

54. Hoover, 296.

55. "Senate, by Two Votes Margin, Passes Tariff," *Washington Post*, June 14, 1930.

56. M. Colleen Callahan, Judith A. McDonald, and Anthony P. O'Brien, "Who Voted for Smoot-Hawley?" *Journal of Economic History* 54, no. 3 (September 1994): 683–690, at 686.

57. 72 Cong. Rec. 10789–90 (1930).

58. 72 Cong. Rec. 10760 (1930).

59. "1,028 Economists Ask Hoover to Veto Pending Tariff Bill," *New York Times*, May 5, 1930.

60. Burner, *Herbert Hoover: A Public Life*, 298.

61. Hoover, 296.

62. Hoover, 299. Hoover writes that his administration changed the tariff rates under the flexible tariff provision about seventy-five times, "mostly downward" in the last two years of his term and that more "would have been changed but for the depression trade war." However, according to Douglas A. Irwin, from June 18, 1930, to November 30, 1933, only fifty-seven Tariff Commission investigations were conducted under the flexible tariff provisions under which twenty-six resulted in presidential decisions to decrease rates of duty and twenty-three to increase rates and eight left rates unchanged. Irwin, *Peddling Protectionism*, 97, fn23.

63. Steel, *Walter Lippmann and the American Century*, 287–288.

64. Leuchtenburg, *Herbert Hoover*, 91–92.

65. Taussig, *The Tariff History*, 500.

66. Irwin, 105–108.

67. Jones, *Tariff Retaliation: Repercussions of the Hawley-Smoot Bill*, 2.

68. Jones, 35–53, 75, 112–140, 211; Gordon and Wilcox, *Monetarist Interpretations of the Great Depression*, 105–107; Percy Wells Bidwell, "The New American Tariff: Europe's Answer," *Foreign Affairs*, 1930, 13–26.

69. Destler, *American Trade Politics*, 11–12, citing US Department of Commerce, Bureau of the Census, *Historical Statistics of the United States: Colonial Times to 1970, Part 2* (Washington, DC: US Department of Commerce, 1975), 884.

70. See Irwin, 101–225; Makinen, "The Smoot-Hawley Tariff and the Great Depression of 1929–1933," *CRS Report for Congress* (June 10, 1994); for protectionist perspectives on the Smoot-Hawley Tariff and the Great Depression, see Reed Smoot, "Our Tariff and the Depression," *Current History*, November 1931, 173–181; Buchanan, *The Great Betrayal*, 240–252; Eckes, *Opening America's Market: U.S. Foreign Trade Policy since 1776*, 100–139.

71. "The Free Trade Accord; Excerpts from the Free Trade Debate between Gore and Perot," *New York Times*, November 10, 1993.

72. 75 Cong. Rec. 3,504–12 (1932); Hull, *Memoirs*, vol. 1, 146.

73. Pastor, *Congress and the Politics of U.S. Foreign Economic Policy: 1929–1976*, 84.

CHAPTER 7

1. 42 Cong. Rec. 10,653–54 (1916).

2. Smith, *FDR*, 87–88.

3. Hull, *The Memoirs of Cordell Hull*, vol. 1, 69.

4. Smith, *xiv*.

5. Hull, 4.

6. *Pollock v. Farmer's Loan and Trust*, 157 U.S. 429 (1895).

7. Alter, *The Defining Moment: FDR's Hundred Days and the Triumph of Hope*, 18.

8. 42 Cong. Rec. 3,519–21 (1908).

9. Hull, 66.

10. Ibid., 82.

11. Daniels, *The Wilson Era: Years of War and After*, 253.

12. Brands, *Traitor to His Class*, 97.

13. Smith, 181.

14. Eleanor, Roosevelt, *This Is My Story*, 192.

15. Lash, *Eleanor and Franklin*, 178.

16. http://fdrlibrary.wordpress.com/tag/1924/.

17. "Scenes and Foibles of the Convention," *New York Times*, July 10, 1924.

18. Perkins, *The Roosevelt I Knew*, 10–12.

19. Alter, 63–65.

20. "Democrats Move to Hold Conference for Party Reforms," *New York Times*, March 9, 1925.

21. Franklin D. Roosevelt, "Is There a Jefferson on the Horizon," *New York Evening World*, December 3, 1925, reprinted in *American Mercury*, September 1945, 277–281.

22. Hull, 130–131.

23. Ibid., 142.

24. Schlesinger, *The Age of Roosevelt,* vol. 1, *The Crisis of the Old Order: 1919–1933,* 277.

25. Ibid.

26. "Roosevelt Opposed to League Entry; Also against Cancelling the War Debts," *New York Times,* February 3, 1932.

27. Roosevelt, *The Public Papers and Addresses of Franklin D. Roosevelt,* vol. 1, *The Genesis of the New Deal, 1928–1932,* Samuel I. Rosenman, ed., 624–627.

28. Hull, 147–148; Moley, *After Seven Years,* 11.

29. Roosevelt, *Public Papers,* vol. 1, 645–646.

30. "Text of Ex-Governor Smith's Announcement of His Willingness to Be Democratic Candidate," *New York Times,* February 8, 1932.

31. "Aggressive Address of Ex-Gov. Smith Features Meeting of Nation's Democrats," *New York Times,* April 14, 1932.

32. Alter, 98.

33. Johnson and Porter, *National Party Platforms: 1840–1972,* 331–333.

34. Alter, 109.

35. Roosevelt, *Public Papers,* vol. 1, 647–659.

CHAPTER 8

1. "Text of Radio Broadcast by Raymond Moley on Prospects of World Economic and Monetary Conference May 20, 1933," Appendix E, Moley, *After Seven Years,* 414.

2. "The Candidacy of Franklin D. Roosevelt," *New York Herald Tribune,* January 8, 1932, quoted in Steel, *Walter Lippmann and the American Century,* 291–292.

3. Schlesinger, *The Age of Roosevelt,* vol. 1, *The Crisis of the Old Order: 1919–1933,* 291, 149; Alter, *The Defining Moment,* 80–82.

4. Moley, 23.

5. Tugwell, *The Democratic Roosevelt: A Biography of Franklin D. Roosevelt,* 231.

6. Ibid, 411.

7. Roosevelt, *Public Papers,* vol. 1, 665.

8. Moley, 47–48.

9. Ibid., 51.

10. Roosevelt, *Public Papers,* vol. 1, 767, 769.

11. Oscar G. Villard, "The Pot and the Kettle," *Nation,* November 2, 1932, 418.

12. "Hoover Attack Sweeping," *New York Times,* November 1, 1932; "President Draws 13 Minutes of Cheering: Says Churches and School Houses Would Rot," *Washington Post,* November 1, 1932.

13. Roosevelt, *Public Papers,* vol. 1, 836, 853–854.

14. Anne O'Hare McCormick, "The Two Men at the Big Moment," *New York Times Magazine,* November 6, 1932.

15. Smith, *FDR,* 286.

16. *New Republic,* November 16, 1932.

17. Moley, 81.

18. Hull, *Memoirs,* 155.

19. Ibid., 156–157.

20. Morgan, *FDR: A Biography,* 371.

21. Moley, 112.

22. Ibid., 114.

23. Ibid., 115–116.

24. Lindsay Rogers to George F. Milton, February 2, 1933, Milton Papers, Library of Congress, quoted in Butler, *Cautious Visionary*, 20.

25. Perkins, *The Roosevelt I Knew*, 11, 141.

26. Roosevelt, *Public Papers*, vol. 2, 11–16.

27. Henry F. Ashurst, *A Many-Colored Toga: The Diary of Henry Fountain Ashurst*, 333, ed., George Sparks (Tucson: University of Arizona Press, 1962), as quoted in G. Dunne, *Hugo Black and the Judicial Revolution*, 148.

28. Caro, *Master of the Senate*, 355.

29. "A Week of Great Events," *Wall Street Journal*, March 13, 1933.

30. "Couch and Coach," *Time*, May 8, 1933, 11.

31. Moley, 190.

32. Ibid., 189.

33. Cohen, *Nothing to Fear*, 242–243.

34. Moley, 24.

35. Cohen, 245.

36. Brands, *Traitor to His Class*, 346.

37. *Schechter Poultry Corp. v. United States*, 295 U.S. 495 (1935).

38. Perkins, 252–253.

39. Hull, 196–199.

40. Moley, 159.

41. "State Department Memorandum on United States Monetary and Economic Policy," April 3, 1933, in Nixon, ed., *FDR and Foreign Affairs*, vol. 1, 35–37.

42. Walter Lippmann, "Today and Tomorrow," *New York Herald Tribune*, April 18, 1933, quoted in Smith, 328.

43. Keynes, *Essays in Persuasion*, 208.

44. Moley, 160.

45. "Hull Tells Powers No 'Club' Was Sought in Our New Monetary Legislation Moves," *New York Times*, April 23, 1933.

46. Moley, 198.

47. Butler, *Cautious Visionary*, 41.

48. Dallek, Robert, *Franklin D. Roosevelt and American Foreign Policy, 1932–1945*, 42.

49. Moley, 208–209.

50. Ibid.

51. Hull, 249.

52. Moley, 217.

53. Rexford G. Tugwell, "Notes from a New Deal Diary," May 31, 1933, quoted in Leuchtenburg, *Franklin D. Roosevelt and the New Deal 1932–1940*, 200.

54. *Foreign Relations of the United States* (hereafter *FRUS*) *1933*, vol. I, 923–924.

55. Hull, 252.

56. Moley, 193,

57. *FRUS 1933*, vol. I, 633–634.

58. Orville H. Bullitt, *For the President: Personal and Secret*, 35.

59. Hull, 255.

60. Ibid., 254.

61. Ibid., 256–257.

62. Tugwell, *The Democratic* Roosevelt, 316.

63. Moley, 227.

64. "Vacillation Is Observed in Our London Program," *New York Times*, June 25, 1933.

65. Hull, 260.

66. Moley, 241.

67. Ibid., 250.

68. Ibid., 257.

69. Memorandum of George F. Milton-Hull conversation, October 13, 1933, Milton Papers, Box 17, as quoted in Butler, 61; see also Hull, 261.

70. Roosevelt, *Public Papers*, vol. 2, 264.

71. Moley, 262.

72. See Appendix G in Moley, 419–421.

73. Moley to FDR, July 4, 1933, *FRUS 1933*, vol. I, 680.

74. Butler, 69.

75. Ibid., 70–71.

76. Nixon, 298–300.

77. Hull, 267.

78. Ibid., 268; Butler, 79.

79. "Moley Takes Reins in Drive at Crime," *New York Times*, August 5, 1933.

80. "Books of the Times: Political Autobiography, the Parting Gallery and Record," *New York Times*, September 20, 1939.

81. Tugwell, 238.

82. Alter, 323.

83. http://www.webcitation.org/query?url=http%3A%2F%2Fwww.presidency.ucsb.edu%2Fws%2Findex.php%3Fpid%3D2482&date=2011-12-25.

84. Brands, 372.

CHAPTER 9

1. Hull, *The Memoirs of Cordell Hull*, vol. 1, 375.

2. Ibid., 308.

3. Ibid., 319.

4. Butler, *Cautious Visionary*, 87.

5. Hull, 321.

6. Ibid., 324.

7. Ibid., 329.

8. Nixon, *Franklin D. Roosevelt and Foreign Affairs*, vol. 1, 560.

9. Butler, 90.

10. "Friendship for US Grows at Parley," *New York Times*, December 10, 1933.

11. 78 Cong. Rec. 3,579–80 (1934).

12. "Tariff Bill Voted by Senate, 57 to 33; Adjournment Dims," *New York Times*, June 5, 1934.

13. 78 Cong. Rec. 5,262–70 (1934).

14. Schatz, "Cordell Hull and the Struggle for the Reciprocal Trade Agreements Program, 1932–1940," 109–110.

15. Scheslinger, *The Age of Roosevelt*, vol. 2, 254.

16. For example, *Field v. Clark*, 143 U.S. 649 (1892); *Hampton & Company v. United States*, 276 U.S. 394 (1928).

17. 299 U.S. 304 (1936).

18. Ibid., at 320.

19. Rothgeb, *U.S. Trade Policy: Balancing Economic Dreams and Political Realities*, 44.

20. Hull, 357.

21. Ibid., 370.

22. "H. I. Stimson Urges Tariff Authority for the President," *New York Times*, April 30, 1934; Stimson and Bundy, *On Active Service in Peace and War*, 298–299.

23. Schlesinger, *Age of Roosevelt*, vol. 2, 58.

24. Sayre, *The Way Forward: The American Trade Agreements Program*, 100.

25. Fite, *George N. Peek and the Fight for Farm Parity*, 276.

26. Sayre, 205–206.

27. Fite, 276.

28. Hull, 370.

29. Ibid., 372.

30. Dallek, *Franklin D. Roosevelt and American Foreign Policy, 1932–1945*, 92.

31. While the first trade agreement concluded after the RTAA was signed into law was a preferential agreement with Cuba, negotiations on that agreement began before Roosevelt sent the trade agreements bill to Congress and its terms were not part of Hull's MFN trade program.

32. Hull, 373–374.

33. Butler, 119.

34. "Divided Counsels," *New York Times*, May 13, 1935.

35. "Mr. Hull and Mr. Peek," *Washington Post*, September 21, 1934.

36. Fite, 278–279.

37. "Sane Nationalism or Fatuous Internationalism—Which Shall It Be?" *Washington Herald*, November 26, 1935.

38. Fite, 281–285.

39. Schlesinger, *The Age of Roosevelt*, vol. 2, 259.

40. Schatz, 234.

41. Hoover, *Addresses upon the American Road, 1933–1938*, 155.

42. "Wisconsin Appeal Is Made by Borah," *New York Times*, April 7, 1936.

43. "Vandenberg Urges a 'Coalition' Vote," *New York Times*, June 1, 1936.

44. "Watson Appeals for World Trade," *New York Times*, January 27, 1935.

45. "Chamber Denounces Plans of New Deal but Advisers of President Uphold Him," *New York Times*, May 3, 1935; "Views of C. of C. on NRA," *New York Times*, May 3, 1935.

46. "200 Trade Leaders Back New Deal Aims; Republicans Join in Praise of Tariff Policy," *New York Times*, October 29, 1936.

47. Editorial, *Nation*, March 13, 1935, 289; "One Year of Tariff Reciprocity," *Nation*, June 26, 1935, 731.

48. Raymond Moley, "Open Covenants, Limited," *Today*, November 23, 1935, 12–13; Moley, 321–330.

49. Johnson and Porter, *National Party Platforms, 1840–1972*, 368; "Republican Shift on Tariff Is Urged," *New York Times*, April 11, 1936; "Money and Tariff Platform Issues," *New York Times*, June 5, 1936.

50. *United States v. Butler*, 297 U.S. 1 (1936).

51. Nixon, *Franklin D. Roosevelt and Foreign Affairs*, vol. 3, 326–329.

52. Johnson and Porter, 363.

53. Hull, 486.

54. "Gov. Landon's Address on the Reciprocal Trade Program," *New York Times*, September 25, 1936.

55. "Hull Sees Trade Rebuilt by Reciprocity Treaties; Says Old Tariff Ruined It," *New York Times*, October 8, 1936.

56. "Hull's Address Upholding Foreign Trade Policy," *New York Times*, October 8, 1936; "Mr. Hull's Reply," *New York Times*, October 8, 1936.

57. "Roosevelt Praises Pacts," *New York Times*, October 10, 1936.

58. Schlesinger, *The Age of Roosevelt,* vol. 3, 578.

59. Ibid., 571.

60. "Hull Holds Vote Backs Trade Pacts," *New York Times*, November 5, 1936.

61. Schlesinger, *The Age of Roosevelt,* vol. 3, 612–613.

62. Rothgeb, *U.S. Trade Policy: Balancing Economic Dreams and Political Realities*, 47–48.

63. Hull, 521.

64. Schatz, 283.

65. Hull, 530.

66. Sayre, 150.

67. "Text of Leading Passages in Chamberlain Speech," *New York Times*, July 27, 1938.

CHAPTER 10

1. *FRUS* 1942, vol. I, 535.

2. Blum, *From the Morgenthau Diaries: Years of Crisis, 1928–1938*, 524.

3. "Trade Pacts Safe, Officials Declare," *New York Times*, December 17, 1939.

4. Ickes, *Secret Diary of Harold L. Ickes*, vol. 3, 68.

5. 86 Cong. Rec. 4,105 (1940); Pastor, 97.

6. Roosevelt, *Public Papers and Addresses*, 1940 volume: *War—And Aid to Democracies*, 607–608, 643.

7. An Act to Promote the Defense of the United States, Pub. L. No. 11, §3(b), 55 Stat. 32 (1941).

8. Skidelsky, *Keynes: The Return of the Master*, 57; Woods, *A Changing of the Guard: Anglo-American Relations, 1941–1946*, 27.

9. Tugwell, *The Democratic Roosevelt*, 374.

10. "From Keynes to Roosevelt: Our Recovery Plan Assayed," *New York Times*, December 31, 1933.

11. Keynes, *The End of Laissez-Faire: The Economics Consequences of the Peace*, 87.

12. Schlesinger, *The Age of Roosevelt,* vol. 3, 406.

13. Perkins, 225–226.

14. Keynes, *The Collected Writings of John Maynard Keynes*, vol. 17, 451.

15. Keynes, *Collected Writings*, vol. 19, 151–152.

16. George, *War Memoirs*, 410.

17. John Maynard Keynes, "National Self-Sufficiency," *Yale Review* 22, no. 4 (June 1933): 755–769; Keynes, *Collected Writings*, vol. 21, 233–246.

18. Keynes, *Collected Writings*, vol. 20, 120.

19. Skidelsky, 80; Keynes, *Collected Writings*, vol. 4, 65.

20. Keynes, *Collected Writings*, vol. 20, 494–495.

21. Keynes, *Essays in Persuasion*, 278.

22. Keynes, *Collected Writings*, vol. 21, 204–210.

23. Irwin, *Against the Tide*, 189.

24. *FRUS* 1941, vol. III, 7.

25. Acheson, *Present at the Creation*, 29.

26. *FRUS* 1941, vol. III, 12.

27. Ibid., 15.

28. Ibid., 11–13.

29. Ibid., 16–17.

30. Harrod, *The Life of John Maynard Keynes*, 512.

31. Acheson, 29.

32. http://avalon.law.yale.edu/wwii/atlantic.asp.

33. Roosevelt, *As He Saw It*, 35–37.

34. Churchill, *Liberalism and the Social Problem*, 54.

35. http://avalon.law.yale.edu/wwii/atlantic.asp.

36. Hull, vol. 2, 975.

37. Acheson, 31.

38. *FRUS* 1942, vol. I, 528.

39. *FRUS* 1941, vol. III, 49.

40. Acheson, 32.

41. Pressnell, *External Economic Policy since the War*, Vol. 1, 50–51.

42. Ibid., 54.

43. *FRUS* 1942, vol. I, 527.

44. Pressnell, 52.

45. *FRUS* 1942, vol. I, 531.

46. Pressnell, 57.

47. *FRUS* 1942, vol. I, 535–536.

48. http://avalon.law.yale.edu/wwii/angam42.asp.

49. Pressnell, 59.

50. Unlike Keynes, however, it must be noted that White was a Soviet sympathizer and later believed to be a Soviet informant based upon the testimony of former communist spy Whittaker Chambers and others before the House Special Committee on Un-American Activities. Except for his efforts to promote easy terms for Soviet participation in the Bretton Woods agreements, however, this sympathy did not appear to affect his nationalistic approach in negotiating the agreement. And in the end, the Soviets refused to ratify the Bretton Woods agreements. For an account of the investigation of White's alleged espionage activities, see Steil, *The Battle of Bretton Woods*, 317–329.

51. Van Dormael, *Bretton Woods: Birth of a Monetary System*, 37.

52. Ibid., 46.

53. Steil, *The Battle of Bretton Woods*, 159–160.

54. Van Dormael, 108.

55. Ibid., 121.

56. Ibid., 266.

57. Hull, 1110.

58. Acheson, 88.

59. Israel, *The War Diary of Breckinridge Long*, 386–388.

60. Johnson and Porter, 411.

61. Irwin, Mavroidis, and Sykes, *The Genesis of the GATT*, 12.

CHAPTER 11

1. 138 Parl. Deb., H.L. (1945) 777 (U.K.).

2. Truman, *Memoirs*, vol. 1, 153, 156.

3. Fossedal, *Our Finest Hour: Will Clayton, the Marshall Plan, and the Triumph of Democracy*, 152.

4. For more extensive treatment of the path of Clayton's business success, see Fossedal, 15–46, and Garwood, *Will Clayton: A Short Biography*, 43–95.

5. "What's Clayton Doing," *Newsweek*, March 27, 1944, 64.

6. "Clayton's Talk to Harvard Men on Business Evils and the Remedies," *New York Times*, September 17, 1936; "A Case for Capitalism," *New York Times*, September 20, 1936.

7. "The War Surplus Bill," *Nation*, August 26, 1944, 228.

8. Congressman Paul Shafer (R-MI), quoted in *Time*, January 27, 1947, 21.

9. *American Magazine*, May 1945, 134.

10. Fossedal, 136.

11. *1945 Extension of Reciprocal Trade Agreements Act: Hearings on H.R. 2652 Superseded by H.R. 3240 before the H. Committee on Ways and Means*, 79th Cong. 2–4 (1945); Pastor, *Congress and the Politics of U.S. Foreign Economic Policy: 1929–1976*, 95; Lansing Warren, "Roosevelt Seeks Powers to Slash Tariffs 50%," *New York Times*, March 27, 1945.

12. Richard L. Strout, "Senate Faces Showdown on Reciprocal Tariffs," *Christian Science Monitor*, June 12, 1945.

13. Zeiler, *Free Trade Free World: The Advent of GATT*, 46.

14. John H. Crider, "Opposition Grows over Trade Pacts," *New York Times*, February 24, 1945.

15. 50 Cong. Rec. 1247–49 (1913).

16. *1945 RTAA Extention Hearings*, 5–46, *supra* note 11.

17. Frederick R. Barkley, "Trade Act Passed by Ways and Means," *New York Times*, May 17, 1945; "Trade Agreements," *Washington Post*, May 18, 1945; Acheson, *Present at the Creation*, 106.

18. Acheson, 107.

19. William S. White, "House, after Truman Plea, Votes Tariff Bill, 239–153," *New York Times*, May 27, 1945.

20. Robert C. Albright, "Senate Sends Trade Act to Truman Unchanged," *New York Times*, June 21, 1945.

21. "A Victory for World Trade," *New York Times*, June 20, 1945; see also "President Signs Bill to Extend Reciprocal Trade Act Three Years," *New York Times*, July 6, 1945.

22. It was my great fortune to have attended Lord Robbins's famous lectures on international economic theory and history at the London School of Economics in 1977, which contributed significantly to my interest in the topic of this book.

23. Irwin, Mavroidis, and Sykes, *The Genesis of the GATT*, 29, 213–221.

24. Robbins, *Autobiography of an Economist*, 201–203.

25. Ibid., 204.

26. See reprint in Irwin, Mavroidis, and Sykes, 239–244.

27. Harrod, *The Life of John Maynard Keynes*, 567.

28. *FRUS* 1946, vol. VI, 109.

29. Acheson, 122.

30. *FRUS* 1945, vol. VI, 126–127.

31. Harrod, 606.

32. John H. Crider, "British Base Plea for Aid on Justice over War's Costs," *New York Times*, September 21, 1945.

33. Robbins, 204.

34. Quoted in Gardner, *Sterling-Dollar Diplomacy*, 194, citing the *Chicago Daily News*, October 10, 1945.

35. Bert Andrews, "Truman Stirs Bi-Party Row on War Debts," *New York Herald-Tribune*, September 1, 1945.

36. Robbins, 206.

37. Gardner, 191.

38. *FRUS* 1945, vol. VI, 134.

39. *FRUS* 1945, vol. VI, 110, 117.

40. "British Warned U.S. Will Act if Trade Barriers Continue," *Journal of Commerce*, October 29, 1945, quoted in Gardner, 197–198; Special Comm. on Postwar Economic Policy and Planning, *Economic Reconstruction in Europe*, H.R. Rep. No. 79-1205, at 29 (1945).

41. Robbins, 203.

42. John H. Crider, "Proposals on British Loan Go to the London Cabinet," *New York Times*, October 26, 1945.

43. "Proposals for Expansion of World Trade and Employment," State Dept. Publication No. 2411 (December 1945), 12; reprinted in Dep't St. Bull. XIII, No. 337 (December 9, 1945), 913–929.

44. James B. Reston, "Britain's Cabinet Approves U.S. View on World Trade," *New York Times*, November 7, 1945; John H. Crider, "New Hope Held Out on Loan to Britain," *New York Times*, November 22, 1945.

45. "Conclusion of Anglo-American Financial and Trade Negotiations," Dep't St. Bull. XIII. No. 337 (December 9, 1945), 905.

46. Amery, *The Washington Loan Agreements*, xi, xv.

47. 417 Parl. Deb., H.C. (1945) 714–715 (U.K.).

48. *FRUS* 1945, vol. VI, 199.

49. 417 Parl. Deb., H.C. (1945) 713–728 (U.K.).

50. Smith, *Politics of Plenty*, 74.

51. 417 Parl. Deb., H.C. (1945) 455–471 (U.K.).

52. Harrod, 617.

53. 138 Parl. Deb., H.L. (1945) 777–795 (U.K.).

54. Ibid., 857–870.

55. Gardner, 235.

56. *FRUS* 1945, vol. VI, 202.

57. Robbins, 193 and 211.

58. H.R. Doc. No. 79-429; Dep't St. Bull. XIV, No. 345 (February 10, 1946), 183–184, 216.

59. S. Rep. No. 79-1144, at 12 (1946); John H. Crider, "Vinson Calls Loan to Britain a 'Must,' " *New York Times*, March 6, 1946.

60. "The Loan Hearings," *Economist*, March 23, 1946, vol. 150, 455.

61. 92 Cong. Rec. 4079–4082 (1946).

62. "Delaying the Loan," *Economist*, April 27, 1946, vol. 150, 669.

63. Comm. on Banking and Currency, H.R. Rep. No. 79-2289, at 18 (1946).

64. *Anglo-American Financial Agreement: Hearings on H.J. Res. 311 and S.J. Res. 138, before the Comm. on Banking and Currency,* 79th Cong. 335–336, 338–339, 521–522 (1946).

65. Comm. on Banking and Currency, H.R. Rep. No. 79-2289, at 1, 12.

66. Ibid., at 31.

67. 92 Cong. Rec. 8823–8824 (1946).

68. Ibid., 8913–8915.

69. John H. Crider, "Nonpartisan Vote," *New York Times*, July 14, 1946.

70. Philip Thornton, "Britain Pays Off Final Installment of US Loan—after 61 Years," *Independent*, December 28, 2006.

CHAPTER 12

1. "Statement by the President on the General Agreement on Tariffs and Trade," October 29, 1947, *Public Papers of the Presidents of the United States* (Pub. Papers), (Washington, DC: Government Printing Office, 1947), 480.

2. *FRUS* 1945, vol. VI, 61–76, quotations from 62, 72, and 75.

3. *FRUS* 1946, vol. I, 1280–90, quotations from 1280, 1281, and 1283.

4. Ibid., 1291–1292.

5. Ibid., 1307.

6. Ibid., 1312.

7. Ibid., 1313.

8. Ibid., 1312.

9. Robertson, *Sly and Able: A Political Biography of James F. Byrnes,* 443.

10. *FRUS* 1946, vol. I, 1359.

11. Ibid., 1360–1366.

12. McCullough, *Truman*, 520.

13. "The Republicans Return," *Economist* 151 (November 9, 1946): 737–738.

14. *FRUS* 1946, vol. I, 1350, 1352, 1354.

15. Quoted in Irwin, Mavroidis, and Sykes, 81.

16. 93 Cong. Rec. House 773 (1947).

17. "The Congress: Face of the Victor," *Time*, November 15, 1948.

18. 93 Cong. Rec. House 5630 (1947).

19. 93 Cong. Rec. 912 (1947); see also three favorable editorials on the compromise printed in the *Congressional Record* from *New York Times*, February 1, 1947; *New York Herald Tribune*, February 8, 194; and *Washington Post*, February 8, 1947, 93 Cong. Rec. 912–13 (1947).

20. "Peace, Freedom, and World Trade: Address by the President," Dep't St. Bull. 16 (March 16, 1947), 481–485.

21. "Mr. Truman at Waco," *New York Times*, March 7, 1947; "Persuasive and Timely," *Washington Post*, March 7, 1947.

22. "G.O.P. Saboteurs," *Nation*, February 15, 1947, 171–172.

23. "The Presidency: Marked Change," *Time*, February 10, 1947; McCullough, *Truman*, 532–536.

24. Garwood, 116–117.

25. Acheson, 221.

26. Felix Belair Jr., "Truman Acts to Save Nations from Red Rule," *New York Times*, March 12, 1947; "Recommendations on Greece and Turkey: Message of the President to the Congress," 16 Dep't St. Bull. (Supp., May 4, 1947), 831.

27. Acheson, 228–229.

28. Lester Markel, "Truman, as the Crucial Third Year Opens," *New York Times*, March 16, 1947.

29. *FRUS* 1947, vol. III, 230–232.

30. Ibid., 223–230.

31. Acheson, 231; see also, *FRUS* 1947, vol. III, 234–235.

32. See comparison of language from Clayton's memo and the Marshall speech in Fossedal, 228–229.

33. "The Address of Secretary Marshall at Harvard," *New York Times*, June 6, 1945; *FRUS* 1947, vol. III, 237–239.

34. James Reston, "Administration Now Shifts Its Emphasis on Foreign Aid," *New York Times*, May 9, 1947.

35. *FRUS* 1947, vol. I, 913–915.

36. Ibid., 948–950; "Beyond the Truman Doctrine," *New York Times*, May 24, 1947.

37. *FRUS* 1947, vol. I, 956.

38. Ibid., 957.

39. Zeiler, 94–103; Fossedal, 237–238.

40. Harry S. Truman, "Veto of the Wool Act," June 26, 1947, Gerhard Peters and John T. Woolley, *The American Presidency Project*, http://www.presidency.ucsb.edu/ws/?pid=12683.

41. "Economic Ambassador," *New York Times*, October 16, 1947.

42. *FRUS* 1947, vol. III, 239.

43. Ibid., 268–287.

44. Ibid., 275.

45. *FRUS* 1947, vol. I, 953–955.

46. For a thorough discussion of the Attlee government and the Labour Party in dealing with imperial preferences in the first GATT negotiations, see Richard Toye, "The Attlee Government, the Imperial Preference System and the Creation of the GATT," *English Historical Review* 118, no. 478 (September 2003): 912–939; see also Richard Toye, *The Labour Party and the Planned Economy: 1931–1951*, Chapter 7, 156–184.

47. Attlee, *As It Happened*, 154.

48. Bullock, *Ernest Bevin: Foreign Secretary: 1945–1951*, 64–65.

49. "Cripps Once Called England's Most Dangerous Revolutionary," *New York World-Telegram*, February 20, 1942; Schneer, *Ministers at War: Winston Churchill and His War Cabinet*, 117.

50. Attlee, 279.

51. Bullock, 87.

52. "No Motive Power," *Economist* September 20, 1947, vol. 153, 465.

53. 435 Parl. Deb., H.C. Deb. (1947) 892 (U.K.).

54. *FRUS* 1947, vol. 1, 964–966.

55. Ibid., 974–977.

56. Michael L. Hoffman, "British Accused of Stalling in Tariff Parley at Geneva," *New York Times*, August 8, 1947.

57. *FRUS* 1947, vol. I, 977–979.

58. Ibid., 980–982.

59. Second Session of the Preparatory Committee of the United Nations Conference on Trade and Employment, Plenary Meetings, Verbatim Report, Sixth Meeting, August 23, 1947, E/PC/T/PV.2/6, p. 31; Gardner, 357.

60. *FRUS* 1947, vol. I, 983–993.

61. Bullock, 462.

62. *FRUS* 1947, vol. I, 993–996.

63. Saville R. Davis, "Britons Sobered by Hint U.S. Stopgap Aid Unlikely," *Christian Science Monitor*, September 26, 1947.

64. *FRUS* 1947, vol. I, 997.

65. Ibid., 1014.

66. Ibid., 1015.

67. 443 Parl. Deb. H.C. (1947) col. 874 (UK).

68. "Tariffs and Trade" and "Trade under the New Tariff," *Economist* November 22, 1947, vol. 153, 827–828, 848–850.

69. 93 Cong. Rec. 10674, 11482 (1947).

CHAPTER 13

1. *FRUS* 1948, vol. I, 900.

2. Michael G. Hoffman, "Europe Will Feel Loss," *New York Times*, October 15, 1947; Felix Belair Jr., "Clayton Resigns U.S. Economic Post," *New York Times*, October 15, 1947; "Economic Ambassador," *New York Times*, October 16, 1947; Bertram D. Hulen, "Clayton Agrees to Stay on Call," *New York Times*, October 16, 1947; "Freer Trade for the Free World," "Good-by, Mr. Clayton," *Newsweek*, October 27, 1947, 23; *Le Monde*, October 17, 1947, as quoted in Garwood, *Will Clayton: A Short Biography*, 31.

3. "Mr. Clayton Goes," *Economist* October 18, 1947, vol. 153, 630–631.

4. For a thorough discussion of the GATT provisions, their negotiation history, and legal significance see Dam, *The GATT: Law and International Economic Organization*; Jackson, *World Trade and the Law of GATT*; Irwin, Mavroidis, and Sykes, *The Genesis of the GATT*.

5. Wilcox, *A Charter for World Trade*, 47–48.

6. *FRUS* 1948, vol. I, 804, fn. 3, 818, fn. 3, 830–831.

7. Russell Porter, "Clayton Warns ITO on 'Diluted' Rules," *New York Times*, November 28, 1947.

8. Russell Porter, "Argentina Rejects Draft ITO Charter," *New York Times*, December 3, 1947.

9. Russell Porter, "Fight for Quotas Pushed in Havana," *New York Times*, December 21, 1947.

10. Dep't St. Bull. 18, No. 445 (January 11, 1948), 39–42.

11. *FRUS* 1948, vol. I, 837.

12. Ibid., 824.

13. Ibid., 825.

14. Ibid., 829–833.

15. Article 13, 7 (a) (i), Havana Charter for the International Trade Organization, reprinted in Wilcox, *A Charter for World Trade*, 239.

16. Ibid., Article 15, in Wilcox, 243–245.

17. *FRUS* 1948, vol. I, 855–858.

18. Ibid., 840, 848–850.

19. Ibid., 872–874.

20. Ibid., 869–872.

21. Ibid., 875–879.

22. Ibid., 881–883.

23. Ibid., 882.

24. Richard Toye, "Developing Multilateralism: The Havana Charter and the Fight for the International Trade Organization, 1947–1948," *International History Review* 25, no. 2 (June 2003): 299.

25. For a comprehensive review and analysis of the ITO Charter provisions, see Wilcox, *A Charter for World Trade*, and Brown, *The United States and the Restoration of World Trade: An Analysis and Appraisal of the ITO Charter and the General Agreement on Tariffs and Trade*.

26. Articles 11 and 12, Havana Charter, in Wilcox, 236–237.

27. Russell Porter, "Argentina Rejects Draft ITO Charter: Havana Delegate Lashes Out at U.S. Economy and Offers Crippling Amendments," *New York Times*, December 3, 1947.

28. "Franklin D. Roosevelt State of the Union Message," January 11, 1944, reprinted in Schlesinger, *History of U.S. Political Parties*, Vol. 3, *1910–1945: From Square Deal to New Deal*, 2054.

29. "Democratic Platform of 1944," Johnson and Porter, *National Party Platforms: 1840–1972*, 402.

30. Bailey, *Congress Makes a Law: The Story behind the Employment Act of 1946*, 38–39; another valuable and more recent analysis of the legislative process behind the act is found in Wasem, *Tackling Unemployment: The Legislative Dynamics of the Employment Act of 1946*.

31. 91 Cong. Rec. 9153 (1945).

32. Full Employment Bill of 1945, S. 380, 79th Cong. (1945), as passed in the Senate, September 28, 1945, and referred in the House of Representatives to the Committee on Expenditures in the Executive Departments on October 1, 1945.

33. Raymond Moley, "A Fool Employment Bill," *Newsweek*, June 18, 1945.

34. 92 Cong. Rec. 975 (1946).

35. Wilcox, 133.

36. William S. White, "Bill Curbing Labor Becomes Law as Senate Overrides Veto, 68–25; Unions to Fight for Quick Repeal," *New York Times*, June 23, 1947; "National Affairs: Barrel No. 2," *Time*, June 23, 1947.

37. Havana Charter, Chapter II, Articles 2–7, Wilcox, 131–139, 232–234; see also Brown, *The United States and the Restoration of World Trade*, 93–96; Russell Porter, "ITO Group Finishes Employment Study," *New York Times*, January 10, 1948.

38. http://avalon.law.yale.edu/wwii/atlantic.asp.

39. "Completion of ITO Charter Hailed as Hope for Troubled World," Dep't. St. Bull. 18, No. 457 (April 4, 1948), 441.

40. Russell Porter, "Clayton Acclaims Cooperation in ITO," *New York Times*, March 24, 1948.

CHAPTER 14

1. *FRUS* 1950, vol. I, 783.

2. Russell Porter, "Business Backs U.S. in Stand on Trade," *New York Times*, March 24, 1947.

3. For an excellent contemporary account of the business opposition to the ITO Charter, see Diebold, *The End of the ITO*.

4. Herbert Koshetz, "Ask Sharp Revision of Charter of ITO," *New York Times*, May 13, 1948; "U.S. Chamber Group Opposes Approval of ITO Charter by Government," *Wall Street Journal*, May 10, 1948; Dryden, *Trade Warriors: USTR and the American Crusade for Free Trade*, 25–29.

5. "Knutson Indicates GOP to Seek Revised Reciprocal Trade Act," *Christian Science Monitor*, November 19, 1947.

6. "Support for the ITO," *New York Times*, December 22, 1948.

7. H.R. 6556, 80th Cong. (1948).

8. 94 Cong. Rec. 6504–05 (1948).

9. 94 Cong. Rec. 8032–35 (1948).

10. 94 Cong. Rec. 8049–51 (1948).

11. "Truman Signs One-Year Extension of Trade Agreements Act but Points to 'Serious Defects' in Amendments," *Wall Street Journal*, June 28, 1948; Harry S. Truman: "Statement by the President upon Signing the Trade Agreements Extension Act," June 26, 1948. Online by Gerhard Peters and John T. Woolley, *The American Presidency Project*, http://www.presidency.ucsb.edu/ws/?pid=12943.

12. McCullough, *Truman*, 657.

13. Johnson and Porter, *National Party Platforms: 1840–1972*, 431–432.

14. Russell Porter, "Better U.S. Prospects Now Seen for Ratification of Trade Charter," *New York Times*, January 4, 1949.

15. "Tariff League Hits Proposed ITO Charter," *Washington Post*, October 28, 1948; "Demands Congress Reject ITO Charter," *New York Times*, October 28, 1948.

16. 95 Cong. Rec. 5234–35 (1949); H.J. Res. 236, 81st Cong. (1949).

17. "Clayton Says U.S. Must Keep Strong," *New York Times*, March 30, 1948.

18. "Economic Policy and the ITO Charter," address by Secretary Acheson (delivered May 3, 1949), Dep't St. Bull. 20 (May 15, 1949), 623–624.

19. See, for example, Soviet media excerpts and remarks of representatives of Soviet Union on the ITO cited in Membership and Participation by the United States in the International Trade Organization: Hearings on H.J. Res. 236 Before the H. Comm. on Foreign Affairs, 81st Cong. 53–63 (1950) (Documentation submitted by Department of State of remarks made by representatives of the Soviet Union on the ITO).

20. "U.S. Urged to Stay Charter Approval," *New York Times*, May 10, 1948; see also "Faults of Havana Trade Charter Exceed Merits, Says U.S. Chamber," *Wall Street Journal*, August 15, 1949.

21. "ITO Charter Fought by NAM on 6 Points," *New York Times*, March 31, 1949.

22. "Reconciling Opposites," *Wall Street Journal*, August 9, 1948.

23. Cortney, *The Economic Munich: The I.T.O. Charter: Inflation or Liberty: The 1929 Lesson*, ix–xi, 17, 34.

24. W. L. Clayton, "Economic Pitfalls: *The Economic Munich*. By Philip Cortney," *New York Times*, March 20, 1949; "Support for the ITO," *New York Times*, December 22, 1948; Letters to the Times, "International Trade Charter: The Instrument Signed at Havana Is Criticized as Restricting Trade," letter from Philip Cortney, December 29, 1948, *New York Times*, January 4, 1949; "For Freedom of Trade," *New York Times*, January 10, 1949; Morris Katz, "Trade Charter Assailed as Threat to Freedom: *The Economic Munich*, by Philip Cortney," *Washington Post*, September 25, 1949; George Ericson, "Is Trade Charter Open Door to Freer Trade?" *Christian Science Monitor*, June 11, 1949; "Ratification of ITO Charter Assailed as Threat to Trade," *Washington Post*, October 12, 1949.

25. "Why and How We Came to Find Ourselves at the Havana Conference," address by William L. Clayton, Adviser to the Secretary of State, delivered June 15, 1948, Dep't St. Bull. 18 (June 27, 1948), 826.

26. "Export Group Asks Ban on ITO Charter," *New York Times*, January 26, 1949.

27. "The ITO Charter," *Fortune Magazine*, July 1949, 61–62.

28. "How the U.S. Lost the ITO Conferences," *Fortune*, September 1949, 81.

29. "Import Unit Backs Adherence to ITO," *New York Times*, December 21, 1948.

30. "Group Formed to Ratify ITO Charter," *Washington Post*, May 3, 1949; "Committee Set Up to Promote ITO," *New York Times*, May 3, 1949.

31. Harlan Trott, "U.S. Participation in ITO Stirs Capital Controversy," *Christian Science Monitor*, March 1, 1949; "World Trade Plea Made by CIO Organ," *New York Times*, February 28, 1949.

32. Brendan M. Jones, "CED Favors Most of Trade Charter," *New York Times*, June 12, 1949.

33. L. M. Giannini to W. L. Clayton, March 16, 1949; George A. Hill Jr. to W. L. Clayton, March 15, 1949, William L. Clayton Papers, Harry S. Truman Presidential Library.

34. Ferdinand Kuhn Jr., "A Strong Case Is Made for ITO Charter: A Charter for World Trade, by Clair Wilcox," *Washington Post*, January 30, 1949.

35. Clair Wilcox, "Why the International Trade Organization?" *Annals of the American Academy of Political and Social Science*, 264, World Government (July 1949): 70–72, http://www.jstor.org/stable/1028090.

36. Michael L. Hoffman, "U.S. Embarrassed at Tariff Parley," *New York Times*, August 1, 1949.

37. 95 Cong. Rec. 12615–19 (1949).

38. 95 Cong. Rec. 12632–33 (1949).

39. H.R. Rep. No. 81–19, at 8 (1949).

40. 95 Cong. Rec. 12872 (1949).

41. 95 Cong. Rec. 12631–34, 12759–63, 12925 (1949); H. Walton Cloke, "Taft Fears 'Power' in Trade Pact Bill," *New York Times*, September 10, 1949.

42. 95 Cong. Rec. 12620, 12632 (1949).

43. Harry S. Truman: "Statement by the President upon Signing the Trade Agreements Extension Act of 1949," September 26, 1949. Online by Gerhard Peters and John T. Woolley, *The American Presidency Project*, http://www.presidency.ucsb.edu/ws/?pid=13313.

44. Brendan M. Jones, "Opposition Grows to I.T.O. Charter," *New York Times*, January 22, 1950.

45. Winthrop G. Brown, "Why Private Business Should Support the ITO: A Definite Code of Rules for International Trade," *Vital Speeches of the Day* 16, no. 9 (February 1950): 279–280.

46. "Acheson's Plea for ITO," *Washington Post*, April 21, 1950; W. L. Clayton, "A Communication: Clayton Urges ITO Charter Approval," *Washington Post*, May 2, 1950.

47. Charles E. Egan, "Acheson Accused of Ignoring G.O.P.," *New York Times*, April 22, 1950.

48. Fossedal, *Our Finest Hour*, 259–260.

49. James G. Fulton and Jacob K. Javits, Committee on Foreign Affairs, 80th Cong., Rep. on the International Trade Organization: An Appraisal of the Havana Charter in Relation to United States Foreign Policy, with a Definitive Study of Its Provisions, at 56–57 (Comm. Print 1948).

50. "U.S. Support of ITO Charter Urged in House Unit Report," *Washington Post*, October 28, 1948.

51. Membership and Participation by the United States in the International Trade Organization: Hearings on H.J. Res. 236 Before the H. Comm. on Foreign Affairs, 81st Cong. 172 (1950) (testimony of O. R. Strackbein, chairman, National Labor-Management Council on Foreign Trade Policy).

52. Membership and Participation by the United States in the International Trade Organization: Hearings on H.J. Res. 236 Before the H. Comm. on Foreign Affairs, 81st Cong. 172 (1950), 407, 409–410, 425, 427, 429, 431–432 (testimony of Earl O. Shreve, United States Chamber of Commerce).

53. Membership and Participation by the United States in the International Trade Organization: Hearings on H.J. Res. 236 Before the H. Comm. on Foreign Affairs, 81st Cong. 172 (1950), 561, 562, 565, 568 (testimony of Lee H. Bristol, representing The National Association of Manufacturers); "ITO Charter Supported and Opposed, in Hearing before House Committee," *Wall Street Journal*, May 12, 1950.

54. Membership and Participation by the United States in the International Trade Organization: Hearings on H.J. Res. 236 Before the H. Comm. on Foreign Affairs, 81st Cong. 172 (1950), 499, 506, 507 (testimony of Gaylord C. Whipple, chairman, International Trade Committee, Illinois Manufacturers Association).

55. Membership and Participation by the United States in the International Trade Organization: Hearings on H.J. Res. 236 Before the H. Comm. on Foreign Affairs, 81st Cong. 172 (1950), 177, 192, 259 (testimony of R. F. Loree, chairman, National Foreign Trade Council).

56. Membership and Participation by the United States in the International Trade Organization: Hearings on H.J. Res. 236 Before the H. Comm. on Foreign Affairs, 81st Cong. 172 (1950), 592 (statement submitted by Hon. Jacob K. Javits).

57. Brown, *The United States and the Restoration of World Trade: An Analysis and Appraisal of the ITO Charter and the General Agreement on Tariffs and Trade*, 371–372; "Brookings Report for Joining I.T.O.," *New York Times*, April 24, 1950.

58. Wilcox, *A Charter for World Trade*, 135–136; Membership and Participation by the United States in the International Trade Organization: Hearings on H.J. Res. 236 before the H. Comm. on Foreign Affairs, 81st Cong. 482–83 (1950) (statement of Maurice J. Tobin, Secretary of Labor).

59. Membership and Participation by the United States in the International Trade Organization: Hearings on H.J. Res. 236 before the H. Comm. on Foreign Affairs, 81st Cong. 172 (1950), 269–273 (statement of Stanley H. Ruttenberg, director of the Department of Education and Research, CIO).

60. Acheson, "Economic Policy and the ITO Charter," *supra* note 18.

61. "Hoffman Appeals for US to Join I.T.O.," *New York Times*, May 13, 1950.

62. McCullough, *Truman*, 813–814.

63. Thomas F. Conroy, "Revival Forecast of 'Peril Point' Bill," *New York Times*, November 12, 1950.

64. *FRUS* 1950, vol. I, 782–786.

65. Ibid., 786–788; "Future Administration of GATT" (Released to the press December 6), Dep't St. Bull. 23, No. 598 (December 18, 1950), 977, https://archive.org/details/departmentofstat2350unit; "Truman Backs Plan on I.T.O. Substitute," *New York Times*, December 8, 1950.

66. "Trade Agreements Extension Act of 1951," Conference Report to Accompany H.R. 1612, Rep. No. 82–537, at 4 (1951).

CHAPTER 15

1. *Trade Reform: Hearings on H.R. 6767 before the H. Comm. on Ways and Means*, 93d Cong. 1210, 1212 (1973) (statement of I. W. Abel, chairman of AFL-CIO Economic Policy Committee).

2. See, e.g., Zeiler, *Free Trade, Free World: The Advent of GATT*, 180–189; Diebold, "The End of the ITO," *Essays in International Finance*, No. 16, October 1952, published by the International Finance Section of the Department of Economics and Social Institutions in Princeton University; and Toye, "Developing Multilateralism: The Havana Charter and the Fight for the International Trade Organization, 1947–1948, *International History Review* 25, no. 2 (June 2003): 282–305.

3. Friedrich, Hayek, "The Road to Serfdom: A Condensation from the Book," *Reader's Digest*, April 1945, 2.

4. Quoted in Lyle W. Cooper, "The Tariff and Organized Labor," *American Economic Review* 20, no. 2 (June 1930): 212, fn. 4.

5. Ibid., 215, fn. 16.

6. Ibid., 222–223, fn. 32.

7. *Extension of Reciprocal Trade Agreements Act: Hearings on H.R. 1211 before the S. Comm. on Finance*, 81st Cong., 627–28 (1949) (statement of James G. Carey, secretary-treasurer, CIO, presented by Stanley H. Ruttenberg, director of Research and Education, CIO).

8. *Extension of Reciprocal Trade Agreements Act: Hearings on H.R. 1211 before the S. Comm. on Finance*, 81st Cong., 675–77 (statement of Walter J. Mason, national legislative representative, AFL).

9. Eisenhower, *Mandate for Change, 1953–1956*, 195, 208.

10. US Commission on Foreign Economic Policy, Report to the President and the Congress, H.R. Doc. No. 83–290, at 53–64 (1954).

11. Robert D. Leiter, "Organized Labor and the Tariff," *Southern Economic Journal* 28, no. 1 (July 1961): 58.

12. "Trade Organization," *CQ Almanac 1956*, 12th ed., 09-485-09-488 (Washington, DC: Congressional Quarterly, 1957); Kaufman, *Trade and*

Aid: Eisenhower's Foreign Economic Policy 1953–1961, 75; see also George Bronz, "An International Trade Organization: The Second Attempt," *Harvard Law Review* 69 (1956): 440–482.

13. A. H. Raskin, "Union Chiefs Seek Quotas for 'Sweatshop' Imports," *New York Times*, August 17, 1959.

14. Brandis, *The Making of Textile Trade Policy: 1935–1981*, 17.

15. Quoted in Pastor, *Congress and the Politics of U.S. Foreign Economy Policy: 1929–1976*, 107.

16. Trade Expansion Act of 1962, Pub. L. No. 87–794, 76 Stat. 872 (1962).

17. Schlesinger, *A Thousand Days*, 847.

18. Kraft, *The Grand Design: From Common Market to Atlantic Partnership* .

19. *Trade Expansion Act of 1962: Hearings on H.R. 9900 before the H. Comm. on Ways and Means*, 87th Cong. 1145–52 (1962) (statement of George Meany, president of AFL-CIO).

20. Ball, *The Past Has Another Pattern: Memoirs*, 190–191.

21. Lewis, *Office of the United States Trade Representative: America's Frontline Trade Officials*, 13.

22. John F. Kennedy, "Remarks upon Signing the Trade Expansion Act," October 11, 1962. Online by Gerhard Peters and John T. Woolley, *The American Presidency Project*. http://www.presidency.uscb.edu/ws/?pid=8946.

23. Despite this achievement, as one critic observes, "30 percent of the dutiable imports of the major participants were left untouched by tariff reductions . . . so in the Kennedy Round the across-the-board principle was seriously compromised." Dam, *The GATT: Law and International Economic Organization*, 77. For an excellent discussion of the political dynamics involved in the negotiation of the Kennedy Round, see Dryden, *Trade Warriors*, 61–113.

24. Frank V. Fowlkes, "Economic Report/Administrative Escape Valves Relieve Pressures of Imports on Domestic Industries," *National Journal*, July 24, 1971, 1548, cited in Pastor, *Congress and the Politics of U.S. Foreign Economic Policy: 1929–1976*, 117–118.

25. 113 Cong. Rec. 16,526–27 (1967).

26. *Impact of Imports on American Industry and Employment: Hearings on H.R. 478 and H.R. 479 before the General Subcomm. on Labor of the H. Comm. on Education and Labor*, 90th Cong., 4–22 (1967) (statement of George Baldanzi, president of United Textile Workers of America).

27. Ibid., 22–24.

28. "Low-Wage Imports," *CQ Almanac 1967*, 23rd ed., 07-816-07-817 (Washington, DC: Congressional Quarterly, 1968), http://library.cqpress.com.proxy-remote.galib.uga .edu/cqalmanac/cqal67-1312932.

29. "Roth Stresses the Perils of Retaliation," *New York Times*, October 6, 1967; Edwin L. Dale Jr., "Congress's Drive for Import Quotas," *New York Times*, November 2, 1967.

30. "U.S. Industries Seek Protection Legislation," *CQ Almanac 1967*, 23rd ed., 07-810-07-816 (Washington, DC: Congressional Quarterly, 1968), http://library.cqpress .com.proxy-remote.galib.uga.edu/cqalmanac/cqal67-1312924; John D. Morris, "4 in Cabinet Condemn Bills Asking Stiff Import Quotas," *New York Times*, October 19, 1967; "Again, the Protectionists," *New York Times*, November 2, 1967; Gerd Wilcke, "Protectionist Moves in Congress Assailed," *New York Times*, November 2, 1967.

31. "Trade Expansion, Protectionist Moves Both Blocked," *CQ Almanac 1968*, 24th ed., 08-729-8-736 (Washington, DC: Congressional Quarterly, 1969), http://library.cqpress.com.proxy-remote.galib.uga.edu/cqalmanac/cqal68-1282185.

32. Harald B. Malmgren, "Coming Trade Wars? (Neo-Mercantilism and Foreign Policy)," *Foreign Policy*, no. 1 (Winter 1970–71): 115–143.

33. "Trade Bill Foes Lose Hard Fight on Amendments," *Wall Street Journal*, November 19, 1970; "House Approves a Controversial Trade Measure," *Wall Street Journal*, November 20, 1970.

34. Richard Nixon: "Address to the Nation Outlining a New Economic Policy: 'The Challenge of Peace,'" August 15, 1971. Online by Gerhard Peters and John T. Woolley, *The American Presidency Project*, http://www.presidency.ucsb.edu/ws/?pid=3115.

35. "U.S. Devalues Dollar 10% by Raising Price of Gold; Japan Agrees to Let the Yen Float," *Wall Street Journal*, February 13, 1973.

36. Paul A. Samuelson, "Freud, Fear and Foreign Trade," *New York Times*, July 30, 1972.

37. Damon Stetson, "Labor Report Calls for Revised World Trade Policy," *New York Times*, February 22, 1970.

38. *Multinational Corporations: Hearings before the Subcomm. on International Trade of the S. Comm. on Finance*, 93d Cong. 299–300, 302 (1973) (statement of Andrew Biemiller, director of legislation, AFL-CIO).

39. Richard S. Frank, "Washington Pressures/Multinationals Mobilize to Preserve Favorable Tax Status on Overseas Income," *National Journal*, July 14, 1973, 1019–1028.

40. "Presidential Statement to Congress: Nixon's Trade Reform: New Tariff Adjustment Powers Asked," *CQ Almanac 1973*, 29th ed., 42-A-47-A (Washington, DC: Congressional Quarterly, 1974); see also *Prepared Statements of Administration Witnesses Submitted to the Comm. on Ways and Means at Public Hearings Beginning on May 9, 1973 and Other Materials Relating to the Administration Proposal Entitled the "Trade Reform Act of 1973" (H.R. 6767)*, 93d Cong. 118–20 (1973) (statement of George P. Shultz, Secretary of the Treasury).

41. Brendan Jones, "Business Lauds, Assails Trade Plan; Meany Scores Bill," *New York Times*, April 12, 1973.

42. "House Passes Trade Act; USSR Denied Tariff Concessions," *CQ Almanac 1973*, 29th ed., 833–845.

43. *CDJ Journal*, May 13, 1973; Donald Johnson, "Congress Putting Democracy Back into Foreign Trade Policy," *Atlanta Journal*, December 15, 1973, 2-A.

44. Mills told his friends that the pain was so great that he would have to retire after this term if it persisted. It must be noted that he was forced to retire the following year due to a serious alcohol problem he developed in attempting to alleviate the pain. The decisive incident, which resulted in an embarrassing end to his career, involved an exotic dancer—stage-named Fanne Foxe, the "Argentine Firecracker"—who one night while in a car with Mills in Washington jumped out of the car and into the Tidal Basin across from the Jefferson Memorial. See Stephen Green and Margot Hornblower, "Mills Admits Being Present during Tidal Basin Scuffle," *Washington Post*, October 11, 1974.

45. From *CDJ Journal*, September 6 and 13, 1973.

46. *Trade Reform: Hearings on H.R. 6767 before the H. Comm. on Ways & Means*, 93d Cong. 849, 851, 880, 887 (1973) (statement of Leonard Woodcock, president,

International Union, United Automobile, Aerospace & Agricultural Implement Workers of America [UAW]).

47. Ibid., 1269 (statement of I. W. Abel, chairman, Economic Policy Committee, AFL-CIO).

48. Richard S. Frank, "Trade Report/Administration Torn between Domestic, Overseas Interests in Drafting Trade Bill," *National Journal*, January 13, 1973, 50.

49. *CDJ Journal*, July 18, 1973; Landrum was not always on the conservative side. He authored the Economic Opportunity Act of 1964, for example, a key part of LBJ's "War on Poverty" legislation; see also Charles Culhane, "Labor Report/ Labor Readies Stronger Jobless-Pay Plan, Rejects Version Offered with Nixon Trade Bill," *National Journal*, June 9, 1973, 821–830.

50. *Trade Reform: Hearings on H.R. 6767 before the H. Comm. on Ways & Means*, 93d Cong. 1217–1218 (1973) (statement of I. W. Abel, chairman, Economic Policy Committee, AFL-CIO); see also Charles Culhane, "Trade Report/ Labor Shifts Tactics on Administration Bill, Seeks Concessions on Imports, Multinationals," *National Journal Reports*, July 28, 1973, 1091–1098.

51. See, e.g., Burke's questioning of the former director of the Office of Trade Adjustment Assistance, Department of Commerce, in *Trade Reform: Hearings on H.R. 6767 before the H. Comm. on Ways & Means*, 93d Cong. 1195–1202 (1973) (Statement of Andrew L. Gray).

52. Stern, *Water's Edge: Domestic Politics and the Making of American Foreign Policy*, 132–133.

53. Edwin L. Dale Jr., "Foreign Trade Bill: Nixon Accepts Risks," *New York Times*, December 15, 1973; Richard S. Frank, "Trade Report/Administration's Reform Bill Threatened by Dispute over Relations with Russia," *National Journal Reports*, November 24, 1973, 1741–1752; Ed Townsend, "Labor Leaders Oppose Nixon Trade-Reform Bill," *Christian Science Monitor*, October 26, 1973.

54. Kissinger, *White House Years*, 330.

55. "House Passes Trade Act; USSR Denied Tariff Concessions," *CQ Almanac 1973*, 29th ed., 833–845.

56. Richard M. Weintraub, "Senate Panel Set to Clear Trade Measure," *Washington Post*, November 20, 1974; Spencer Rich, "Senate Votes Long-Stalled Bill on Trade," *Washington Post*, December 14, 1974; Ewin L. Dale Jr., "Senate Approves Trade Bill Giving Benefit to Soviet," *New York Times*, December 14, 1974.

57. Quoted in Pastor, 166–167.

58. Brendan Jones, "U.S. Trade Policy Faces an Airing in Congress," *New York Times*, July 5, 1973.

59. "Congress Clears Trade Bill on Final Day," *CQ Almanac 1974*, 30th ed., 553–562.

CHAPTER 16

1. David Leonhardt, "Theory and Morality in the New Economy," *New York Times*, August 23, 2009.

2. See proposed language quoted in Janelle M. Diller and David A. Levy, Note, "Child Labor, Trade and Investment: Toward the Harmonization of International Law," *American Journal of International Law* 91 (1997): 663, 685–686.

3. Singapore WTO Ministerial Declaration, adopted December 13, 1996, https://www.wto.org/english/thewto_e/minist_e/min96_e/wtodec_e.htm.

4. Wilcox, *A Charter for World Trade*, 71.

5. US International Trade Commission, "The Impact of the North American Free Trade Agreement on the U.S. Economy and Industries: A Three Year Review," Publication 3045, June 1997; US International Trade Commission, "The Impact of Trade Agreements: Effect of the Tokyo Round, U.S.-Israel FTA, U.S.-Canada FTA, NAFTA, and the Uruguay Round on the U.S. Economy," Publication 3621, August 2003; and Congressional Budget Office of the United States, "The Effects of NAFTA on U.S.-Mexican Trade and GDP," *A CBO Paper*, May 2003, p. xiv, as cited in M. Angeles Villarreal and Ian Fergusson, "NAFTA at 20: Overview and Trade Effects," *CRS Report*, No. R42965, April 28, 2014.

6. Sylvia Nasar, "A Primer: Why Economists Favor Free-Trade Agreement," *New York Times*, September 17, 1993.

7. See, for example, Robert E. Scott, *Heading South: U.S.-Mexico Trade and Job Displacement under NAFTA*, Economic Policy Institute, May 3, 2011; Hufbauer and Schott, *NAFTA Revisited: Achievements and Challenges* .

8. Bureau of Labor Statistics, US Department of Labor, "Lowest Unemployment Rates in Decades at End of 1999," *Economics Daily*, March 29, 2000, https://www.bls.gov/opub/ted/2000/mar/wk4/art03.htm (visited March 16, 2017).

9. Keith Bradsher, "3 Nations Resolve Issues Holding Up Trade Pact Vote," *New York Times*, August 14, 1993; "Congress Oks North American Trade Pact," *Congressional Quarterly Almanac*, 103rd Congress, 1st Session, 1993, vol. 49, 173.

10. 19 U.S.C. §2462(c)(7); this eligibility criteria, in similar form, also applies to the Caribbean, Andean, and sub-Saharan Africa trade preference programs first enacted in 1983, 1991, and 2000, respectively; see Alisa DiCaprio, "Are Labor Provisions Protectionist? Evidence from Nine Labor-Augmented U.S. Trade Arrangements," *Comparative Labor Law and Policy Journal* 26 (2004): 1–32.

11. See William A. Amponash and Victor O. Boadu, "Crisis in the U.S. Textile and Apparel Industry: Is It Caused by Trade Agreements and Asian Currency Meltdowns?" May 2002, http://cnas.tamu.edu/confsummaries/AMPONSAHT.pdf; Dickerson, *Textiles and Apparel in the Global Economy*; National Employment, Hours, and Earnings, Series Catalog: Series ID: ees32230001, Bureau of Labor Statistics Data (extracted August 25, 1999).

12. For a discussion of the development of the Cambodian ILO program, see Kevin Kolben, "Trade, Monitoring, and the ILO: Working to Improve Conditions in Cambodia's Garment Factories," *Yale Human Rights & Development Law Journal* 7 (2004): 79–107.

13. Jay Mazur to C. Donald Johnson, December 21, 1999, published in Regina Abrami, "Worker Rights and Global Trade: The U.S.-Cambodia Bilateral Textile Trade Agreement," HBS Case No. N1-703-034, p. 27, Exhibit 12, March 31, 2003 (Boston: Harvard Business School Publishing, 2003).

14. Helene Cooper, "Dropped Stitches: A Trade Deal Helps Cambodian Workers, But Payoff Is Withheld—U.S. Commitment to Raise Apparel Import Quotas Is Unraveled by a Union—Empty-Handed in Seattle," *Wall Street Journal*, February 28, 2000.

15. "Cambodia Unlikely to Get Full Hike of Labor-Linked Textile Quotas," *Inside US Trade*, December 15, 2000.

16. "U.S.-Cambodian Textile Agreement Links Increasing Trade with Improving Workers," USTR Press Release, January 7, 2002, www.ustr.gov; "Problems Persist at

Cambodian Factories but Child Labor, Harassment Rare, ILO Finds," *International Trade Reporter*, BNA Inc., 19, no. 17 (April 25, 2002): 750.

17. Karen A. Tramontano, "Stitching Up Global Labor Rights," *Washington Post*, December 11, 2004; "Where Free Trade Hurts: Thirty Million Jobs Could Disappear with the End of Apparel Quotas," Asian Cover Story, *BusinessWeek online*, December 15, 2003.

18. Elizabeth Becker, "Cambodia's Garment Makers Hold Off a Vast Chinese Challenge," *New York Times*, May 12, 2005.

19. International Labor Organization, "17th Synthesis Report on Working Conditions in Cambodia's Garment Sector," November 31, 2006, cited by Gene Sperling in "Finding a New Consensus on Trade and Globalization," prepared testimony before the House Committee on Ways and Means, January 30, 2007.

20. Sandra Polaski, "Central America and the U.S. Face Challenge—and Chance for Historic Breakthrough—on Workers' Rights," Carnegie Endowment for International Peace Issue Brief: Trade, Equity, and Development Project, February 2003; see also Sandra Polaski, "Combining Global and Local Forces: The Case for Labor Rights in Cambodia," *World Development*, May 2006.

21. John Burgess, "AFL-CIO Backs Agenda for WTO," *Washington Post*, October 29, 1999; Margot Hornblower, "The Battle in Seattle," *Time*, December 6, 1999.

22. James Cox, "AFL-CIO Backs Global Trade Talks," *USA Today*, October 29, 1999.

23. "Troubling Signs of New Isolationism," transcript of Pres. Clinton's White House News Conference Criticizing Senate's Rejection of Nuclear Test Ban Treaty, *New York Times*, October 15, 1999.

24. "Statement by AFL-CIO President John Sweeney on China and the WTO," AFL-CIO Press Release, November 15, 1999.

25. Mary McGrory, "Labor's Battle in Seattle," *Washington Post*, December 2, 1999.

26. Michael Paulson, "Clinton Takes Strong Stand on Labor Rights," *Seattle Post-Intelligencer*, December 1, 1999.

27. Ibid.

28. "Remarks by John J. Sweeney, President of the AFL-CIO, March and Rally against WTO Global Injustice," Seattle, Washington, November 30, 1999 (printed remarks released by AFL-CIO are maintained in author's papers at Richard B. Russell Library for Political Research and Studies, University of Georgia Libraries, Athens, Georgia); Joel Connelly, "Clinton Implores WTO to Open Itself Up," *Seattle Post-Intelligencer*, December 2, 1999.

29. Robert Evans, "US Seen Pushing for Trade-Labor Sanctions," Reuters News Service, December 1, 1999.

30. Anton Entous, "Clinton Stuns Own Negotiators with Labor Stance," Reuters News Service, December 3, 1999; Guy de Jonquieres and Mark Suzman, "Clinton Tries to Soothe Fears over Labour Rights," *Financial Times*, December 2, 1999.

31. "New Trade Round Looks Likely Despite Lack of Progress," *National Journal's Congress Daily*, December 2, 1999.

32. "In Parenthesis," *Economist*, November 13, 1999, 78.

33. Scott Malone, "U.S., Asian Officials Face Off on Quota," *Women's Wear Daily*, November 23, 1999.

34. Author's notes, December 1, 1999.

35. Steven Greenhouse and Joseph Kahn, "U.S. Effort to Add Labor Standards to Agenda Fails," *New York Times*, December 3, 1999; Edwina Gibbs, "Poorer Nations Stand Firm over Labor at WTO," Reuters News Service, December 3, 1999.

36. Interview with Ambassador Srinivasan Narayanan in Geneva, July 4, 2001.

37. Statement by Mr. Prabir Sengupta, Commerce secretary, Government of India at the informal General Council meeting of the WTO on June 25, 2001.

38. See generally, "Jordan-U.S. Free Trade Agreement: Labor Issues," Congressional Research Service Report for Congress, RS20968, updated July 15, 2003.

39. Steven Pearlstein, "An Opportunity on Trade," *Washington Post*, March 28, 2007.

40. Max Baucus, "A Democratic Trade Agenda," *Wall Street Journal*, January 4, 2007; Rossella Brevetti, "Sen. Baucus Urges TPA Renewal with Labor, Enforcement Improvements," *International Trade Daily*, BNA Monitoring Service, January 5, 2007.

41. Robin Toner, "After Many Years, It's Rangel's Turn at the Helm," *New York Times*, January 8, 2007; *Weekly Standard*, quoted in Robert McMahon, "Backgrounder: The 110th Congress—Democrats and Trade," *Council on Foreign Relations*, January 4, 2007.

42. Rossella Brevetti, "Rep. Rangel Seeks Bipartisan Plan to Renew Trade Promotion Authority," *International Trade Daily*, BNA Monitoring Service, January 31, 2007; Jutta Hennig, "Rangel Signals Possible Limited Fast-Track Renewal for Doha Round," *Inside US Trade*, February 2, 2007.

43. "Congress and Administration Must Be Partners in Promoting Trade," House Committee on Ways and Means Press Release, February 14, 2007.

44. "Levin Opening Statement at Ways and Means Committee Hearing on U.S. Trade Agenda," Office of Congressman Sander Levin Press Release, February 14, 2007.

45. Jutta Hennig, "Effort on FTA Labor Deal Stalled, Rangel Seeks Meeting with Schwab," *Inside U.S. Trade*, February 16, 2007; Steven R. Weisman, "G.O.P. Shift Is Seen on Trade," *New York Times*, March 6, 2007.

46. Jutta Hennig, "Schwab Offers Proposal to Advance Lagging FTA Labor Talks," *Inside U.S. Trade*, February 23, 2007; "Freshmen to Meet to Discuss Trade Future; New Dems Back Rangel," *Inside U.S. Trade*, March 16, 2007; "Levin Signals No Change in FTA Labor Talks; Some See New Proposal," *Inside U.S. Trade*, March 16, 2007.

47. "A New Trade Policy for America," House Ways and Means Committee Press Release, March 27, 2007; Steven R. Weisman, "Break Seen in Logjam over Trade," *New York Times*, March 28, 2007.

48. Robin Toner, "For Democrats, New Challenge in Age-Old Rift," *New York Times*, May 8, 2007.

49. Steven R. Weisman, "Bush and Democrats in Accord on Trade Deals," *New York Times*, May 11, 2007; "Congress and Administration Announce New Trade Policy," Press Release Issued Jointly by House Ways and Means Committee, Hon. Charles B. Rangel, Chairman, and Hon. Jim McCrery, Ranking Member, May 10, 2007; "Bipartisan Trade Deal," Office of the US Trade Representative, May 2007, www.ustr.gov.

50. The Colombia agreement was on hold because of unprosecuted violence and murder committed against Colombian union leaders; the Panama agreement was held up because a politician indicted for murdering a US soldier was elected leader of the Panamanian parliament; and the Korean agreement was stalled due to market access issues concerning American automobile and beef exports. All three contained the labor and environment provisions required by the May 10th agreement and were approved by Congress in 2011.

51. Statement issued by offices of House Speaker Pelosi, Majority Leader Hoyer, and Ways and Means Committee on June 29, 2007.

52. Thea Mei Lee, "Testimony before the Senate Finance Committee on the U.S.-Peru Trade Promotion Agreement," September 11, 2007; "Ways and Means Hearing on Peru FTA in Doubt as Senate Presses Forward," and "AFL-CIO Questions Provisions in U.S.-Peru Deal, Takes No Position on FTA," *Inside U.S. Trade*, September 14, 2007.

53. "House Ways and Means Committee Backs Draft Legislation on Peru FTA by Voice Vote," *International Trade Daily*, BNA Monitoring Service, September 26, 2007; Jamie Strawbridge, "Bush Sends Final Peru FTA Bill to Congress; Pelosi Links FTA to TAA," *Inside U.S. Trade*, September 28, 2007; Victoria McGrane, "Pelosi Seeks Middle Road on Trade," *Politico*, November 6, 2007; Steven R. Weisman, "Democrats Divided as House Passes Peru Trade Bill," *New York Times*, November 8, 2007; see official vote tabulation by Clerk of the House of Representatives, http://clerk.house.gov/evs/2007/roll1060.xml.

54. Steven R. Weisman, "Senate Approves Peru Trade Deal," *New York Times*, December 5, 2007; https://www.senate.gov/legislative/LIS/roll_call_lists/roll_call_vote_cfm.cfm?congress=110&session=1&vote=00413; "Edwards Opposes U.S.-Peru FTA, Saying It Puts Business over Workers," *International Trade Daily*, BNA Monitoring Service, October 31, 2007.

55. John Harwood, "Republicans Grow Skeptical on Free Trade," *Wall Street Journal*, October 4, 2007; NBC/Wall Street Journal GOP Primary Voters Survey taken September 28–30, 2007.

56. "Trading Down: On Economics, Mr. Obama Goes Populist," *Washington Post*, February 17, 2008.

57. David Leonhardt, "The Politics of Trade in Ohio," *New York Times*, February 27, 2008.

58. "Obamanomics: Hope and Fear," and "Dr. Obama's Patent Economic Medicine," *Economist*, March 1, 2008, 14–15, 31–32; "As Pennsylvania Primary Nears, Clinton, Obama Target China Trade," *Inside U.S.-China Trade*, April 16, 2008; "President Bush Says Clinton, Obama Seeking Political Gain in Blasting NAFTA," *International Trade Daily*, BNA Monitoring Service, February 29, 2008.

59. In the interest of full disclosure, I note that I served on the Obama campaign's very large trade advisory committee. I was generally an inactive participant other than joining in conference calls and agreeing to serve as a surrogate in a trade debate to be held in Atlanta. The event was canceled due to the failure of the McCain campaign to produce an opposing surrogate.

60. Gary G. Yerkey, "U.S. Would Have to 'Pay' Canada, Mexico with Trade Concessions to Reopen NAFTA," *WTO Reporter*, BNA Monitoring Service, March 6, 2008; Elisabeth Bumiller, "Pro-Nafta, McCain Delivers Bad News to Ohio Audience," *New York Times*, April 23, 2008; "McCain Blasts Obama on Colombia FTA, NAFTA, Ethanol at Final Debate," *Inside U.S. Trade*, October 17, 2008.

61. Sheryl Gay Stolberg, "Obama Makes Overtures to Canada's Leader," *New York Times*, February 20, 2009; Brian Knowlton, "Obama Doesn't Plan to Reopen Nafta Talks," *New York Times*, April 21, 2009.

62. "Baucus Says Obama Administration Lacks Comprehensive Trade Agenda," *Inside U.S. Trade*, November 11, 2009; Andrew Higgins and Anne E. Kornblut, "On Trip to Seal Ties with Asia, Trade Policy Threatens Rift," *Washington Post*, November 15, 2009.

63. "The Trans-Pacific Partnership (TPP): Key Provisions and Issues for Congress," *CRS Report*, R44489, June 14, 2016, 61.

64. Steve Charnovitz, "Remarks Submitted to the Committee on Ways and Means Democrats, January 2016, https://democrats-waysandmeans.house.gov/sites/democrats.waysandmeans.house.gov/files/documents/Labor%20Forum%20Remarks%20-%20Steve%20Charnovitz.pdf; see also Cathleen Cimino-Isaacs, "Labor Standards in the TPP," *Peterson Institute for International Economics Briefing 16–4* (2016) Chapter 4, 41–65.

65. Rep. Sandy Levin, "Is TPP the Most Progressive Trade Agreement in History? Not If You Need Access to Affordable Medicines," *The Blog: Huffington Post*, May 28, 2016, 380.

66. Sam Frizell, "Hillary Clinton Opposes Trans-Pacific Partnership," *Time*, October 7, 2015.

67. Len Bracken, "Obama Undaunted, Presses Ahead for TPP Vote," *International Trade Daily*, Bloomberg BNA, July 30, 2016; Erik Wasson and Danielle Bernstein, "TPP Doesn't 'Have the Votes,' Ryan Says," *International Trade Reporter*, Bloomberg BNA, August 8, 2016; Michael Rose, "AFL-CIO to Continue Pressure to Defeat TPP after Election," *International Trade Reporter*, Bloomberg BNA, August 11, 2016.

CONCLUSION

1. Tessa Berenson, "Donald Trump Details Plan to Rewrite Global Trade Rules," *Time*, June 28, 2016; Memorandum on Withdrawal of the United States from the Trans-Pacific Partnership Negotiations and Agreement, *Federal Register* 82 (January 23, 2017): 8497.

2. Ian Austen, "Canada Will Pursue a More Robust Global Role, Minister Says," *New York Times*, June 6, 2017.

3. Yashar Ali, "What George W. Bush Really Thought of Donald Trump's Inauguration," *New York* magazine, March 29, 2017, quoting three people who were present.

4. See, e.g., Ronald Radosh, "Steve Bannon, Trump's Top Guy, Told Me He Was 'A Leninist' Who Wants to 'Destroy the State,'" *Daily Beast*, August 22, 2016; Ishaan Tharoor, "Today's WorldView," *Washington Post*, January 30, 2017; Frances Stead Sellers and David A. Fahrenthold, "'Why Even Let 'Em In?' Understanding Bannon's Worldview and the Policies that Follow," *Washington Post*, January 31, 2017; David Ignatius, "For Bannon, the Game Has Only Just Begun," *Washington Post*, January 31, 2017; Eduardo Porter, "Trump and Trade: Extreme Tactics in Search of a Point," *New York Times*, January 31, 2017; David Von Drehle, "The Second Most Powerful Man in the World?" *Time*, February 13, 2017, 24–31; Philip Rucker, "Bannon: Trump Administration Is in Unending Battle for 'Deconstruction of the Administrative State,'" *Washington Post*, February 23, 2017.

5. Michael Crowley, "The Man Who Wants to Unmake the West," *Politico*, March/April 2017.

6. "Courting Trouble," *Economist*, May 13, 2017, 9.

7. Wayne M. Morrison, "China-U.S. Trade Issues," *Congressional Research Service*, RL33536, March 6, 2017, 13–14.

8. Peter Navarro and Wilbur Ross, "Scoring the Trump Economic Plan: Trade, Regulatory, & Energy Policy Impacts," https://assets.donaldjtrump.com/Trump_Economic_Plan.pdf; Steven Mufson, "Meet Mr. 'Death by China,' Trump's Inside Man

on Trade," *Washington Post*, February 17, 2017; Bob Davis, "To Reduce Trade Deficit, White House Wants Partners to Buy American," *Wall Street Journal*, March 8, 2017.

9. "Free-Trader Turned Game-Changer," *Economist*, January 21, 2017.

10. "International Textile Group Acquired by Platinum Equity," *PR Newswire*, October 24, 2016, http://www.prnewswire.com/news-releases/international-textile-group-acquired-by-platinum-equity-300349833.html; Alan Rappeport and Emmarie Huetteman, "Wilbur Ross Vows to Push Trump's Trade Agenda, Starting with Nafta," *New York Times*, January 18, 2017; Nick Timiraos, Andrew Browne, and John W. Miller, "Cabinet Pick Wilbur Ross Has Used Trade to His Benefit," *Wall Street Journal*, November 29, 2016; John W. Miller, "Donald Trump to Name Wilbur Ross as Commerce Secretary, Transition Official Says," *Wall Street Journal*, December 1, 2016; Azam Ahmed and Elisabeth Malkin, "For Commerce Pick Wilbur Ross, 'Inherently Bad' Deals Paid Off," *New York Times*, February 25, 2017; Len Bracken, "Trade Policy: Team Trump to Share Power in Trade Policy," *Bloomberg BNA: International Trade Daily*, February 24, 2017.

11. "Study Rebuts Claim of U.S. Disadvantage in Dispute Settlement," *Inside US-China Trade*, May 14, 2008.

12. Robert E. Lighthizer, "Grand Old Protectionists," *New York Times*, March 6, 2008.

13. "Sasse and McCain Announce Opposition to President's Nominee for Trade Representative," *United States Senate News Release*, May 10, 2017.

14. Robert E. Lighthizer, "Lighthizer: Donald Trump Is No Liberal on Trade," *Washington Times*, May 9, 2011.

15. Robert E. Lighthizer, Testimony before the U.S.-China Economic and Security Review Commission: Evaluating China's Role in the World Trade Organization over the Past Decade, June 9, 2010.

16. Leo W. Gerard, international president, United Steelworkers to United States Senate, May 10, 2017; Megan Cassella, "McCain and Sasse's Opposition Is Likely Not Enough," *POLITICO's Morning Trade*, May 11, 2017.

17. The 2017 Trade Policy Agenda and 2016 Annual Report, Office of the United States Trade Representative, Exec. Office of the President, March 1, 2017, 1–7.

18. Uruguay Round Agreements Act, Pub. L. No. 103–165, § 102 (a) and (b), 19 U.S.C. §3512 (a) and (b).

19. Brian Flood, "Some Push for Tough Approach with WTO, Others Urge Caution," *WTO Reporter, Bloomberg BNA*, March 3, 2017.

20. Weston Williams, "Trump Administration Says US May Defy WTO Rulings: What Does That Mean?" *Christian Science Monitor*, March 2, 2017.

21. 109 Cong. Rec. H4318 (2005); "Congress Sidesteps Five-Year Debate on Costs, Benefits of WTO Membership," *World Trade Online*, June 23, 2010.

22. Michael Gove and Oliver Wright, "Donald Trump: I'll Do a Deal with Britain," *Times*, January 17, 2017; David Charter, Tom Parfitt, and Bruno Waterfield, "Trump: Broadside Stuns Europe," *Times*, January 18, 2017.

23. James Dean, Bruno Waterfield, and Oliver Wright, "Trump Puts EU Ahead of Britain in Trade Queue," *Times*, April 23, 2017; Dalibor Rohac, "Trade Chief's Policies Could Be Disastrous for Eurozone," *Hill*, March 9, 2017.

24. Elisabeth Malkin, "Facing Trump, Mexicans Think the Unthinkable: Leaving Nafta," *New York Times*, January 24, 2017.

25. Nick Timiraos, "Trump Adviser Peter Navarro: Trade Deficits Endanger U.S. National Security," *Wall Street Journal,* March 6, 2017.

26. "Press Briefing by Secretary of Commerce Wilbur Ross on an Executive Order on Trade Agreement Violations and Abuses," White House Office of the Press Secretary, March 30, 2017 (posted April 28, 2017).

27. Bob Davis and William Mauldin, "Trump Administration Signals It Would Seek Mostly Modest Changes to Nafta," *Wall Street Journal*, March 30, 2017; Adam Behsudi and Doug Palmer, "Trump's NAFTA Goals a Small Shift From Obama Policies," *PolitcoPro.com*, March 29, 2017.

28. Ashley Parker, Philip Rucker, Damian Paletta, and Karen DeYoung, " 'I Was All Set to Terminate': Inside Trump's Sudden Shift on NAFTA," *Washington Post*, April 27, 2017; Damian Paletta and Todd C. Frankel, "Trump Says No Plan to Pull Out of NAFTA 'at this Time,' " April 27, 2017.

29. Jennifer Rubin, "NAFTA: Another Stunt, Another Hasty Retreat for Trump," *Washington Post*, April 27, 2017.

30. "Transcript: Interview with Donald Trump," *Economist,* May 11, 2017.

31. C. Fred Bergsten, "Policy Brief 17-23: Trade Balances and the NAFTA Renegotiation," Peterson Institute for International Economics, June 2017.

32. Kenneth Smith Ramos, Minister, Trade and NAFTA Office, Embassy of Mexico, Government of Mexico Response to USDOC And USTR Request for Comments on Significant Trade Deficits, April 17, 2017. www.regulations.gov docket number DOC 2017-0003.

33. Ana Swanson, "Wonkblog: Trump Administration Formally Launches NAFTA Renegotiation," *Washington Post*, May 18, 2017; Andrew Mayeda and Billy House, "U.S. Seeks to Shift Trade Tides as It Kicks Off NAFTA Overhaul," *International Trade Daily, Bloomberg BNA*, May 19, 2017; Rossella Brevetti, "Trade Czar Says NAFTA Negotiating Objectives Coming," *International Trade Daily, Bloomberg BNA,* May 19, 2017; Letters from R. E. Lighthizer to House/Senate Leadership, May 18, 2017.

34. David Weigel, "Sanders, Joined by Rust Belt Democrats, Praises Trump for Nixing TPP," *Washington Post,* January 23, 2017.

35. Katrina vanden Heuvel, "Why Trump's Con Can't Last Forever," *Washington Post*, January 24, 2017; "Bernie Sanders for President," *Nation*, January 14, 2016.

36. John Cassidy, "Winners and Losers: The Truth about Free Trade," *New Yorker*, August 2, 2004, 26.

37. Thea Lee, "On Human Rights in China: Improving or Deteriorating Conditions," Hearing before the Subcommittee on Africa, Global Human Rights, and International Operations to Examine the Status of Human Rights in the People's Republic of China; Committee on International Relations. House, April 19, 2006, quoted in Gene B. Sperling, "Finding a New Consensus on Trade and Globalization," Prepared Testimony before the House Committee on Ways and Means, January 30, 2007; see also Steve Charnovitz, "The Influence of International Labour Standards on the World Trading Regime: A Historical Overview," *International Labour Review* 126, no. 5 (September–October 1987): 565–584.

38. Paul Krugman, "Trouble with Trade," *New York Times*, December 28, 2007; "Krugman's Conundrum," *Economist*, April 19, 2008, 92; "Beyond Doha: Freer Trade Is under Threat—But Not for the Usual Reasons," *Economist*, October 11, 2008, 30–33; David Wessel and Bob Davis, "Pain from Free Trade Spurs Second Thoughts: Mr. Blinder's Shift Spotlights Warnings of Deeper Downside," *Wall Street Journal*, March

28, 2007; Kenneth F. Scheve and Matthew J. Slaughter, "A New Deal for Globalization," *Foreign Affairs*, July–August 2007.

39. $59,691—2015 average US annual wages for a full-time equivalent employee measured in US dollars at market exchange rates, http://data.oecd.org/earnwage/average-wage.htm (accessed on June 26, 2017).

40. Damian Paletta, "New Rifts Emerge as Trump Administration Rejects Free Trade Statement at G-20 Meeting," *Washington Post*, March 18, 2017.

41. Chad Bown, "Trump's Threat of Steel Tariffs Heralds Big Changes in Trade Policy," *Washington Post*, April 21, 2017; William Mauldin, "Trump's Steel-Tariff Threat Faces Resistance from Lawmakers," *Wall Street Journal*, June 23, 2017.

42. James K. Jackson, "The Trans-Pacific Partnership: Analysis of Economic Studies," *Congressional Research Service*, R44551, June 30, 2016.

43. Robert E. Scott, "Why Is President Obama Making One Last Push for the TPP?" *Working Economics Blog:* Economic Policy Institute, August 23, 2016, http://www.epi.org/blog/why-is-president-obama-making-one-last-push-for-the-tpp/; Robert E. Scott, "Currency Manipulation and Manufacturing Job Loss," Economic Policy Institute, July 21, 2016, Epi.org/111038.

44. International Monetary Fund, *Communiqué: G20 Finance Ministers and Central Bank Governors Meeting,* April 15, 2016, https://www.imf.org/en/News/Articles/2015/09/28/04/51/cm041616.

45. "Transcript: Interview with Donald Trump," *Economist,* May 11, 2017.

46. "Both the US and China Deserve Better than TPP," *China Daily USA*, November 15, 2016.

47. "Prime Minister Winston Churchill's Broadcast to the World about the Meeting with President Roosevelt," *British Library of Information*, August 24, 1941, https://www.ibiblio.org/pha/timeline/410824awp.html.

Bibliography

Acheson, Dean. *Present at the Creation. My Years in the State Department*. New York: Norton, 1969.

Adams, John Quincy. *Memoirs of John Quincy Adams*. Edited by Charles Francis Adams, vol. 8. Philadelphia: J. B. Lippincott, 1876.

Alter, Jonathan. *The Defining Moment: FDR's Hundred Days and the Triumph of Hope*. New York: Simon & Schuster, 2006.

Amery, L. S. *The Washington Loan Agreements*. London: MacDonald, 1946.

Andreano, Ralph, ed. *The Economic Impact of the American Civil War*. Cambridge: Schenkman, 1967.

Attlee, C. R. *As It Happened*. New York: Viking Press, 1954.

Bailey, Stephen Kemp. *Congress Makes a Law: The Story behind the Employment Act of 1946*. New York: Columbia University Press, 1950.

Baker, Ray Stannard, and William E. Dodd, eds. *The Public Papers of Woodrow Wilson*, 6 vols. New York: Harper & Brothers, 1925–1927.

Ball, George W. *The Past Has Another Pattern: Memoirs*. New York: W. W. Norton, 1982.

Banner, James M., Jr. *To the Hartford Convention: The Federalists and the Origins of Party Politics in Massachusetts, 1789–1815*. New York: Alfred A. Knopf, 1970.

Bartlett, Irving H. *John C. Calhoun: A Biography*. New York: W. W. Norton, 1993.

Bassett, John Spencer, ed. *Correspondence of Andrew Jackson*. Vol. 3, *1820–1828*. Washington, DC: Carnegie Institution of Washington, 1928.

Baxter, Maurice G. *Henry Clay and the American System*. Lexington: University Press of Kentucky, 1995.

Beatty, Jack. *The Age of Betrayal: The Triumph of Money in America, 1865–1900*. New York: Alfred A. Knopf, 2007.

Berg, A. Scott. *Wilson*. New York: G. P. Putnam's Sons, 2013.

Blum, John Morton. *From the Morgenthau Diaries: Years of Crisis, 1928–1938*. Boston: Houghton Mifflin, 1959.

Boritt, G. S. *Lincoln and the Economics of the American Dream*. Memphis, TN: Memphis State University Press, 1978.

Bowen, Catherine Drinker. *Miracle at Philadelphia: The Story of the Constitutional Convention, May to September 1787*. Boston: Little, Brown, 1966.

Brandeis, Louis D. *Other People's Money—and How the Bankers Use It*. New York: Frederick A. Stokes, 1914.

Brandis, R. Buford. *The Making of Textile Trade Policy: 1935–1981*. Washington, DC: American Textile Manufacturers Institute, 1982.

Brands, H. W. *Andrew Jackson: His Life and Times*. New York: Doubleday, 2005.

Brands, H. W. *T. R.: The Last Romantic*. New York: Basic Books, 1997.

Brands, H. W. *Traitor to His Class: The Privileged Life and Radical Presidency of Franklin Delano Roosevelt*. New York: Doubleday, 2008.

Brands, H. W. *Woodrow Wilson*. New York: Times Books/Henry Holt, 2003.

Brant, Irving. *The Fourth President: A Life of James Madison*. New York: Bobbs-Merrill, 1970.

Brodsky, Alyn. *Grover Cleveland: A Study in Character*. New York: St. Martin's Press, 2000.

Brown, William Adams, Jr. *The United States and the Restoration of World Trade: An Analysis and Appraisal of the ITO Charter and the General Agreement on Tariffs and Trade*. Washington, DC: Brookings Institution/Menasha, WI: George Banta, 1950.

Buchanan, Patrick J. *The Great Betrayal: How American Sovereignty and Social Justice Are Being Sacrificed to the Gods of the Global Economy*. New York: Little, Brown, 1998.

Bullitt, Orville H., ed., *For the President: Personal and Secret: Correspondence between Franklin D. Roosevelt and William C. Bullitt*. Boston: Houghton Mifflin, 1972.

Bullock, Alan. *Ernest Bevin: Foreign Secretary: 1945–1951*. New York: W. W. Norton, 1983.

Burner, David. *Herbert Hoover: A Public Life*. New York: Alfred A. Knopf, 1979.

Burns, James MacGregor. *The Workshop of Democracy*. New York: Alfred A. Knopf, 1985.

Butler, Michael A. *Cautious Visionary: Cordell Hull and Trade Reform, 1933–1937*. Kent, OH: Kent State University Press, 1998.

Buxton, Sydney. *Finance and Politics: An Historical Study, 1789–1885*. New York: A. M. Kelley, 1888.

Calhoun, John C. *The Papers of John C. Calhoun*. Vol. 10, *1825–1829*. Edited by Clyde N. Wilson and W. Edwin Hemphill. Columbia: University of South Carolina Press, 1977.

Capaldi, Nicholas. *John Stuart Mill: A Biography*. New York: Cambridge University Press, 2004.

Carnegie, Andrew. "Wealth." *North American Review* 148, no. 391 (1889): 653–664, http://www.jstor.org/stable/25101798.

Caro, Robert A. *The Years of Lyndon Johnson: Master of the Senate*. New York: Alfred A. Knopf, 2002.

Cashman, Sean Dennis. *America in the Age of the Titans: The Progressive Era and World War I*. New York: New York University Press, 1988.

Chace, James. *Acheson: The Secretary of State Who Created the American World*. New York: Simon & Schuster, 1998.

Chang, Ha-Joon. *Bad Samaritans: The Myth of Free Trade and the Secret History of Capitalism*. New York: Bloomsbury Press, 2008.

Chernow, Ron. *Alexander Hamilton*. New York: Penguin Press, 2004.

Church, R. A. *The Great Victorian Boom: 1850–1873*. London: Macmillan Press, 1975.

Churchill, Winston S. *Liberalism and the Social Problem: A Collection of Early Speeches as a Member of Parliament*. Rockville, MD: Arc Manor, 2007.

Clements, Kendrick A., and Eric A. Cheezum, *Woodrow Wilson*. Washington, DC: CQ Press, 2003.

Cobden, Richard. *Speeches on Free Trade*. London: Macmillan, 1903.

Cohen, Adam. *Nothing to Fear: FDR's Inner Circle and the Hundred Days that Created Modern America*. New York: Penguin Press, 2009.

Cohn, David L. *Picking America's Pockets: The Story of the Costs and Consequences of Our Tariff Policy*. New York: Harper & Brothers, 1936.

Cohn, David L. *The Fabulous Democrats: A History of the Democratic Party in Text and Pictures*. New York: G. P. Putnam's Sons, 1956.

Cooper, John Milton, Jr., ed. *Reconsidering Woodrow Wilson: Progressivism, Internationalism, War, and Peace*. Washington, DC: Woodrow Wilson Center Press and Baltimore: Johns Hopkins University Press, 2008.

Cortney, Philip. *The Economic Munich: The I.T.O. Charter: Inflation or Liberty: The 1929 Lesson*. New York: Philosophical Library, 1949.

Dallek, Robert. *Franklin D. Roosevelt and American Foreign Policy, 1932–1945*. New York: Oxford University Press, 1995, 1979.

Dam, Kenneth W. *The GATT: Law and International Economic Organization*. Chicago: University of Chicago Press, 1970.

Daniels, Josephus. *The Wilson Era: Years of War and After*. Chapel Hill: University of North Carolina Press, 1946.

Dean, John W. *Warren G. Harding*. New York: Times Books/Henry Holt, 2004.

Destler, I. M. *American Trade Politics*. Washington, DC: Institute for International Economics, 2005.

Democratic National Convention. *Official Report of the Proceedings of the Democratic National Convention*. Chicago: Peterson Linotyping Co., 1912.

Democratic National Convention. *Official Proceedings of the National Democratic Convention, June 27, 28, 29, 1876*. St. Louis: Woodward, Tiernan & Hale, 1876.

Diamond, William. *The Economic Thought of Woodrow Wilson*. Baltimore: Johns Hopkins University Press, 1943.

Dickerson, Kitty G. *Textiles and Apparel in the Global Economy*. Upper Saddle River, NJ: Prentice-Hall, 1999.

Diebold, William, Jr. "The End of the ITO." *Essays in International Finance*, No. 16, October 1952. Princeton, NJ: International Finance Section of the Department of Economics and Social Institutions in Princeton University, 1952.

Dobson, John M. *Politics in the Gilded Age: A New Perspective on Reform*. New York: Praeger, 1972.

Donald, David Herbert. *Lincoln*. New York: Simon & Schuster, 1995.

Dryden, Steve. *Trade Warriors: USTR and the American Crusade for Free Trade*. New York: Oxford University Press, 1995.

Dunne, Gerald T. *Hugo Black and the Judicial Revolution*. New York: Simon and Schuster, 1977.

Dwight, Theodore. *History of the Hartford Convention*. New York: N. & J. White, 1883.

Eckes, Alfred E., Jr. *Opening America's Market: U.S. Foreign Trade Policy since 1776*. Chapel Hill: University of North Carolina Press, 1995.

Eisenhower, Dwight D. *Mandate for Change, 1953–1956*. Garden City, NY: Doubleday, 1963.

Ellis, Joseph J. *American Creation: Triumphs and Tragedies at the Founding of the Republic*. New York: Alfred A. Knopf, 2007.

Ellis, Joseph J. *American Sphinx: The Character of Thomas Jefferson*. New York: Alfred A. Knopf, 1996.

Ferrell, Robert H. *The Presidency of Calvin Coolidge*. Lawrence: University Press of Kansas, 1998.

Fite, Gilbert C. *George N. Peek and the Fight for Farm Parity*. Norman: University of Oklahoma Press, 1954.

Foner, Philip S. *Mark Twain: Social Critic*. New York: International, 1958.

Foreign Relations of the United States. 1933, vol. I; 1941, vol. III; 1942, vol. I; 1945, vol. VI; 1946, vol.VI; 1947, vols. I & III; 1948, vol. I. Washington, DC: US Government Printing Office, 1950, 1959, 1960, 1969, 1969, 1973, 1972, 1976, 1977, respectively.

Fossedal, Gregory A. *Our Finest Hour: Will Clayton, the Marshall Plan, and the Triumph of Democracy*. Stanford, CA: Hoover Institution Press, 1993.

Fowler, Dorothy G. *John Coit Spooner: Defender of Presidents*. New York: University Publishers, 1961.

Freehling, William W., and Craig M. Simpson, eds. *Secession Debated: Georgia's Showdown in 1860*. New York: Oxford University Press, 1992.

Frisch, Morton J., ed. *Selected Writings and Speeches of Alexander Hamilton*. Washington, DC: American Enterprise Institute for Public Policy Research, 1985.

Gardner, Richard N. *Sterling-Dollar Diplomacy: The Origins and the Prospects of Our International Economic Order*. London: McGraw-Hill, 1956.

Garwood, Ellen Clayton. *Will Clayton: A Short Biography*. Austin: University of Texas Press, 1958.

George, David Lloyd. *War Memoirs*. London: Oldhams Press, 1938.

Goodwin, Doris Kearns. *The Bully Pulpit: Theodore Roosevelt, William Howard Taft, and the Golden Age of Journalism*. New York: Simon & Schuster, 2013.

Gordon, Robert J., and James A. Wilcox. *Monetarist Interpretations of the Great Depression*. Boston: Martinus Nijhoff, 1981.

Gould, Lewis L. *Grand Old Party: A History of the Republicans*. New York: Random House, 2003.

Gould, Lewis L. *The Presidency of Theodore Roosevelt*. Lawrence: University Press of Kansas, 1991.

Hague, William. *William Pitt the Younger*. New York: Alfred A. Knopf, 2005.

Hamilton, Alexander. *The Reports of Alexander Hamilton*. Edited by Jacob E. Cooke. New York: Harper Torchbooks, 1964.

Hamilton, Alexander. *The Works of Alexander Hamilton*. Edited by Henry Cabot Lodge, vols. 1 and 2. New York: G. P. Putnam's Sons, 1904.

Hamilton, Alexander, James Madison, and John Jay. *The Federalist Papers*. New York: New American Library, 1961.

Harrod, R. F. *The Life of John Maynard Keynes*. New York: Harcourt, Brace, 1951.

Haynes, John Earl, ed. *Calvin Coolidge and the Coolidge Era: Essays on the History of the 1920s*. Hanover, NH: University Press of New England, 1998.

Hicks, John D. *Republican Ascendancy: 1921–1933*. New York: Harper & Brothers, 1960.

Hirst, F. W. *From Adam Smith to Philip Snowden: A History of Free Trade in Great Britain*. New York: Adelphi, 1925.

Hitchcock, Tim. *Down and Out in Eighteenth-Century London*. New York: Palgrave, 2005.

Hofstadter, Richard. *The Age of Reform: From Bryan to F.D.R.* New York: Alfred A. Knopf, 1955.

Hoover, Herbert. *Addresses upon the American Road: 1933–1938*. New York: Charles Scribner's Sons, 1938.

Hoover, Herbert. *The Memoirs of Herbert Hoover: The Cabinet and the Presidency, 1920–1933*. New York: Macmillan, 1952.

Hufbauer, Gary Clyde, and Jeffrey J. Schott. *NAFTA Revisited: Achievements and Challenges*. Washington, DC: Institute for International Economics, 2005.

Hull, Cordell. *The Memoirs of Cordell Hull*, Vols. 1–2. New York: Macmillan, 1948.

Ickes, Harold. *The Secret Diary of Harold L. Ickes*. Vol. 3, *The Lowering Clouds: 1939–1941*. New York: Simon and Schuster, 1954.

Irwin, Douglas A. *Against the Tide: An Intellectual History of Free Trade*. Princeton, NJ: Princeton University Press, 1996.

Irwin, Douglas A. *Peddling Protectionism: Smoot-Hawley and the Great Depression*. Princeton, NJ: Princeton University Press, 2011.

Irwin, Douglas A., Petros C. Mavroidis, and Alan O. Sykes. *The Genesis of the GATT*. New York: Cambridge University Press, 2008.

Isaacson, Walter. *Benjamin Franklin: An American Life*. New York: Simon & Schuster, 2003.

Isaacson, Walter. *The Wise Men: Six Friends and the World They Made*. New York: Touchstone, 1986.

Israel, Fred L., ed. *The War Diary of Breckinridge Long*. Lincoln: University of Nebraska Press, 1966.

Jackson, John H. *World Trade and the Law of GATT*. Indianapolis: Bobbs-Merrill, 1969.

Jastram, Roy W. *The Golden Constant: The English and American Experience 1560–1976*. New York: John Wiley, 1977.

Jefferson, Thomas. *Thomas Jefferson: Writings*. Notes and Contents Selected by Merrill D. Peterson. New York: Library of America, 1984.

Johnson, Donald Bruce, and Kirk H. Porter, eds. *National Party Platforms: 1840–1972*. Chicago: University of Illinois Press, 1973.

Jones, Joseph M., Jr. *Tariff Retaliation: Repercussions of the Hawley-Smoot Bill*. Philadelphia: University of Pennsylvania Press, 1934.

Josephson, Matthew. *The President Makers: The Culture of Politics and Leadership in an Age of Enlightenment, 1896–1919*. New York: Harcourt Brace, 1940.

Kaufman, Burton I. *Efficiency and Expansion: Foreign Trade Organization in the Wilson Administration, 1913–1921*. Westport, CT: Greenwood Press, 1974.

Kaufman, Burton I. *Trade and Aid: Eisenhower's Foreign Economic Policy, 1953–1961*. Baltimore: Johns Hopkins University Press, 1982.

Kehl, James A. *Boss Rule in the Gilded Age: Matt Quay of Pennsylvania*. Pittsburgh: University of Pittsburgh Press, 1981.

Kenkel, Joseph K. *Progressives and Protection: The Search for a Tariff Policy 1866–1936*. Lanham, MD: University Press of America, 1983.

Kennedy, David M. *Freedom from Fear: The American People in Depression and War, 1929–1945*. New York: Oxford University Press, 2005.

Keynes, John Maynard. *The Collected Writings of John Maynard Keynes*, vols. 17–21. London: Macmillan, 1977–89.

Keynes, John Maynard. *The End of Laissez-Faire: The Economic Consequences of the Peace*. Amherst: Prometheus Books, 2004.

Keynes, John Maynard. *Essays in Persuasion*. London: Macmillan, 1931.

Kissinger, Henry. *White House Years*. Boston: Little, Brown, 1979.

Kraft, Joseph. *The Grand Design: From Common Market to Atlantic Partnership.* New York: Harper & Brothers, 1962.

Krass, Peter. *Carnegie.* Hoboken, NJ: John Wiley, 2002.

Kyvig, David E. *Explicit and Authentic Acts: Amending the U.S. Constitution, 1776–1995.* Lawrence: University Press of Kansas, 1996.

Lash, Joseph P. *Eleanor and Franklin.* New York: W. W. Norton, 1971.

Leinwand, Gerald. *William Jennings Bryan: An Uncertain Trumpet.* Lanham, MD: Rowman & Littlefield, 2007.

Leiter, Robert D. "Organized Labor and the Tariff." *Southern Economic Journal* 28, no. 1 (1961): 55–65.

Leuchtenburg, William E. *Franklin D. Roosevelt and the New Deal, 1932–1940.* New York: Harper & Row, 1963.

Leuchtenburg, William E. *Herbert Hoover.* New York: Times Books/Henry Holt, 2009.

Lewis, Charles. *Office of the United States Trade Representative: America's Frontline Trade Officials.* Washington DC: Center for Public Integrity, 1990.

Lincoln, Abraham. *Speeches and Writings, 1832–1858.* New York: Library of America, 1989.

Lincoln, Abraham. *Speeches and Writings, 1859–1865.* New York: Library of America, 1989.

Lincoln, Abraham. *The Speeches of Abraham Lincoln: Including Inaugurals and Proclamations.* New York: Lincoln Centenary Association, 1908.

Link, Arthur S. *Wilson: The Road to the White House.* Princeton, NJ: Princeton University Press, 1947.

Link, Arthur S. *Woodrow Wilson: A Brief Biography.* Cleveland: World Publishing, 1963.

Locke, John. Peter Laslett ed. *Locke's Two Treatises of Civil Government*, 2nd ed. Cambridge: Cambridge University Press, 1967.

Madison, James. William Thomas Hutchinson, William M. E. Rachal, and Robert Allen Rutland, ed. *The Papers of James Madison*, Vol. 8. Chicago: University of Chicago Press, 1962.

Malone, Dumas. *Jefferson and His Time.* Vol. 5, *Jefferson the President: Second Term, 1805–1809.* Boston: Little, Brown, 1974.

Manchester, William. *The Last Lion: Winston Spencer Churchill: Visions of Glory, 1874–1932.* Boston: Little, Brown, 1983.

Mason, George. Robert A. Rutland, ed. *The Papers of George Mason, 1725-1792*, Vol. 3. Chapel Hill: University of North Carolina Press, 1970.

McCoy, Donald R. *Calvin Coolidge: The Quiet President.* Lawrence: University Press of Kansas, 1988.

McCullough, David. *Truman.* New York: Simon & Schuster, 1992.

McGrane, Reginald, ed. *The Correspondence of Nicholas Biddle Dealing with National Affairs.* Boston: Houghton Mifflin, 1919.

Meacham, Jon. *Thomas Jefferson: The Art of Power.* New York: Random House, 2012.

Mellon, Andrew W. *Taxation: The People's Business.* New York: Macmillan, 1924.

Merrill, Milton R. *Reed Smoot: Apostle in Politics.* Logan: Utah State University Press, 1990.

Merrill, Samuel Horace, and Marion Galbraith Merrill. *The Republican Command: 1897–1913.* Lexington: University Press of Kentucky, 1971.

Mill, John Stuart. *Principles of Political Economy.* New York: Oxford University Press, 1994.

Malone, Dumas. *Jefferson and His Time*. Vol. 5, *Jefferson the President: Second Term, 1805–1809*. Boston: Little, Brown, 1974.

Moley, Raymond. *After Seven Years*. New York: Harper & Brothers, 1939.

Monypenny, William Favelle, and George Earle Buckle. *The Life of Benjamin Disraeli: Earl of Beaconsfield*, vol. 3. New York: McMillan, 1929.

Morgan, Kenneth O., ed. *The Oxford Illustrated History of Great Britain*. Oxford: Oxford University Press, 1988.

Morgan, H. Wayne. *From Hayes to McKinley: National Party Politics, 1877–1896*. Syracuse, NY: Syracuse University Press, 1969.

Morgan, Ted. *FDR: A Biography*. New York: Simon & Schuster, 1985.

Morison, Elting E., ed. *The Letters of Theodore Roosevelt*, 8 vols. Cambridge, MA: Harvard University Press, 1951.

Morris, Edmund. *Theodore Rex*. New York: Random House, 2001.

Mowry, George E. *Theodore Roosevelt and the Progressive Movement*. Madison: University of Wisconsin, 1946.

Murray, Robert K. *The Harding Era: Warren G. Harding and His Administration*. Minneapolis: University of Minnesota Press, 1969.

National Association of Wool Manufacturers. *Bulletin of the National Association of Wool Manufacturers, January 1883 to December 1883*. Boston: National Association of Wool Manufacturers, 1883.

Nevins, Allan, ed. *Letters of Grover Cleveland: 1850–1908*. Boston: Houghton Mifflin, 1933.

Nixon, Edgar B., ed. *Franklin D. Roosevelt and Foreign Affairs*. Vol. 1, *January 1933–February 1934*. Vol. 3, *September 1935–January 1937*. Cambridge: Belknap Press of Harvard University Press, 1969.

Otteson, James R., ed. *Adam Smith: Selected Philosophical Writings*. Exeter: Imprint Academic, 2004.

Pastor, Robert A. *Congress and the Politics of U.S. Foreign Economic Policy: 1929–1976*. Berkeley: University of California Press, 1980.

Paterson, Thomas G. *American Foreign Policy: A History/Since 1900*. 2nd ed. Lexington, MA: D. C. Heath, 1928.

Perkins, Frances. *The Roosevelt I Knew*. New York: Viking Press, 1946.

Phillips, Kevin. *Wealth and Democracy: A Political History of the American Rich*. New York: Broadway Books, 2002.

Phillips, Kevin. *William McKinley*. New York: Times Books, 2003.

Pickering, Paul A., and Alex Tyrrell. *The People's Bread: A History of the Anti-Corn Law League*. London: Leicester University Press, 2000.

Pressnell, L. S. *External Economic Policy since the War*. Vol. 1, *The Post-War Financial Settlement*. London: Her Majesty's Stationery Office, 1987.

Rabushka, Alvin. *From Adam Smith to the Wealth of America*. New Brunswick, NJ: Transaction Books, 1985.

Reitano, Joanne. *The Tariff Question in the Gilded Age—The Great Debate of 1888*. University Park: Pennsylvania State University Press, 1994.

Remini, Robert V. *Daniel Webster: The Man and His Time*. New York: W. W. Norton, 1997.

Remini, Robert V. *John Quincy Adams*. New York: Times Books, 2002.

Republican National Convention. *Proceedings of the Republican National Convention, Held at Chicago, May 16, 17, 18, 1860*. Albany: Weed, Parsons, 1860.

Republican National Convention. *Official Proceedings of the Republican National Convention Held at Chicago, June 3–6, 1884*. Minneapolis: Charles Johnson, 1903.

Robbins, Lionel Charles. *Autobiography of an Economist*. London: Macmillan, 1971.

Robertson, David. *Sly and Able: A Political Biography of James F. Byrnes*. New York: W. W. Norton, 1994.

Roosevelt, Eleanor. *This Is My Story*. New York: Harper & Brothers, 1937.

Roosevelt, Elliott. *As He Saw It*. New York: Duell, Sloan and Pearce, 1946.

Roosevelt, Franklin D. *The Public Papers and Addresses of Franklin D. Roosevelt*. Edited by Samuel I. Rosenman, 13 vols. New York: Random House, Macmillan, Harper & Brothers, 1938–1950.

Roosevelt, Theodore. *The Letters of Theodore Roosevelt*. Cambridge, MA: Harvard University Press, 1951–1954.

Roosevelt, Theodore. *The New Nationalism*. New York: Outlook, 1910.

Rothgeb, John M., Jr. *U.S. Trade Policy: Balancing Economic Dreams and Political Realities*. Washington, DC: CQ Press, 2001.

Sandburg, Carl. *Abraham Lincoln: The War Years*, Vol. 1. New York: Harcourt, Brace, 1939.

Sayre, Francis Bowes. *The Way Forward: The American Trade Agreements Program*. New York: Macmillan, 1939.

Schattschneider, E. E. *Politics, Pressures and the Tariff: A Study of Free Private Enterprise in Pressure Politics, as Shown in the 1929-1930 Revision of the Tariff*. New York: Prentice-Hall, 1935.

Schatz, Arthur W. "Cordell Hull and the Struggle for the Reciprocal Trade Agreements Program, 1932-1940." PhD Thesis, University of Oregon, 1965.

Schlesinger, Arthur M., Jr. *The Age of Jackson*. Boston: Little, Brown, 1945.

Schlesinger, Arthur M., Jr. *The Age of Roosevelt*. Vol. 1, *The Crisis of the Old Order: 1919-1933*. Boston: Houghton Mifflin, 1957.

Schlesinger, Arthur M., Jr. *The Age of Roosevelt*. Vol. 2, *The Coming of the New Deal*. Boston: Houghton Mifflin, 1959.

Schlesinger, Arthur M., Jr. *The Age of Roosevelt*. Vol. 3, *The Politics of Upheaval*. Boston: Houghton Mifflin, 1960.

Schlesinger, Arthur M., Jr., ed. *History of U.S. Political Parties*. Vol. 1, *1789-1860: From Faction to Parties*. New York: Chelsea House, 1973.

Schlesinger, Arthur M., Jr., ed. *History of U.S. Political Parties*. Vol. 2, *1860-1910: The Gilded Age of Politics*. New York: Chelsea House, 1973.

Schlesinger, Arthur M., Jr., ed. *History of U.S. Political Parties*. Vol. 3, *1910-1945: From Square Deal to New Deal*. New York: Chelsea House, 1973.

Schlesinger, Arthur M., Jr., ed. *History of U.S. Political Parties*. Vol. 4, *1945-1972: The Politics of Change*. New York: Chelsea House, 1973.

Schlesinger, Arthur M., Jr. *A Thousand Days: John F. Kennedy in the White House*. Boston: Houghton Mifflin, 1965.

Schneer, Jonathan. *Ministers at War: Winston Churchill and His War Cabinet*. New York: Basic Books, 2014.

Sievers, Harry J. *Benjamin Harrison*. New York: Bobbs-Merrill, 1968.

Sinclair, Upton. *The Jungle*. Norwalk, CT: Heritage Press, 1965.

Skidelsky, Robert. *Keynes: The Return of the Master*. New York: Public Affairs, 2009.

Smith, Adam. *An Inquiry into the Nature and Causes of the the Wealth of Nations*. Introduction by D. D. Raphael. New York: Everyman's Library, 1990.

Smith, Henry Norman. *The Politics of Plenty*. London: George Allen and Unwin, 1944.

Smith, Jean Edward. *FDR*. New York: Random House, 2007.

Stanwood, Edward. *American Tariff Controversies in the Nineteenth Century*, vol. 2. New York: Russell & Russell, 1967.

Startt, James D. *Woodrow Wilson and the Press: Prelude to the Presidency*. New York: Palgrave Macmillan, 2004.

Steil, Benn. *The Battle of Bretton Woods: John Maynard Keynes, Harry Dexter White, and the Making of a New World Order*. Princeton, NJ: Princeton University Press, 2013.

Stern, Paula. *Water's Edge: Domestic Politics and the Making of American Foreign Policy*. Westport, CT: Greenwood Press, 1979.

Stimson, Henry L., and McGeorge Bundy. *On Active Service in Peace and War*. New York: Harper & Brothers, 1948.

Strouse, Jean. *Morgan: American Financier*. New York: Random House, 1999.

Tarbell, Ida M. *The Tariff in Our Times*. New York: Macmillan, 1911.

Taussig, F. W. *The Tariff History of the United States*. New York: G. P. Putnam's Sons, 1931.

Taussig, F. W., ed. *State Papers and Speeches on the Tariff*. Clifton, NJ: Augustus M. Kelley, 1972.

Thomas, Evan. *The War Lovers: Roosevelt, Lodge, Hearst, and the Rush to Empire, 1898*. New York: Little, Brown, 2010.

Truman, Harry S. *Memoirs*. Vol. 1, *Year of Decisions*. New York: Doubleday, 1955.

Tugwell, Rexford G. *The Democratic Roosevelt: A Biography of Franklin D. Roosevelt*. Garden City, NY: Doubleday, 1957.

Van Dormael, Armand. *Bretton Woods: Birth of a Monetary System*. New York: Holmes & Meier, 1978.

Ware, Alan. *The Democratic Party Heads North: 1877–1962*. Cambridge: Cambridge University Press, 2006.

Wasem, Ruth Ellen. *Tackling Unemployment: The Legislative Dynamics of the Employment Act of 1946*. Kalamazoo, MI: W. E. Upjohn Institute for Employment Research, 2013.

Webster, Daniel. *Great Speeches and Orations of Daniel Webster*. Edited by Edwin P. Whipple. Littleton, CO: Fred B. Rothman, 1993.

Webster, Daniel. *The Works of Daniel Webster*, vol. 3. Boston: Little, Brown, 1853.

Wilcox, Clair. *A Charter for World Trade*. New York: Macmillan, 1949.

Wilson, Woodrow. *The New Freedom: A Call for the Emancipation of the Generous Energies of a People*. New York: Doubleday, Page, 1913. www.gutenberg.org/files/14811/14811-h/14811-h.htm.

Wilson, Woodrow. *Woodrow Wilson: Essential Writings and Speeches of the Scholar-President*. Edited by Mario R. Dinunzio. New York: New York University Press, 2006.

Witcover, Jules. *Party of the People: A History of the Democrats*. New York: Random House, 2003.

Wolf, Martin. *Why Globalization Works*. New Haven, CT: Yale University Press, 2004.

Wood, Gordon S. *The Americanization of Benjamin Franklin*. New York: Penguin Press, 2004.

Woods, Randall Bennett. *A Changing of the Guard: Anglo-American Relations, 1941–1946*. Chapel Hill: University of North Carolina Press, 1990.

Young, Andrew W. *A History of the American Protective System, and Its Effects upon the Several Branches of Domestic Industry*. New York: John J. Reed, 1860.

Zeiler, Thomas W. *Free Trade, Free World: The Advent of GATT*. Chapel Hill: University of North Carolina Press, 1999.

About the Author

C. Donald Johnson is Director Emeritus of the Dean Rusk International Law Center at the University of Georgia School of Law, where he was on the faculty for eleven years and taught international trade law in China and Geneva. Previously, he was a partner at a major law firm in Washington, DC, where he specialized in international trade law. From 1998 through 2000, as an ambassador in the Office of United States Trade Representative, he served as the chief textile negotiator during the negotiation of the US–China WTO Accession Agreement and the precedent-setting Cambodia Textile Agreement. From 1993 to 1995, he represented the 10th District of Georgia as a member of Congress, where he focused on national security and international economic policy, including NAFTA and the WTO implementing legislation. Johnson also served in the Georgia State Senate from 1987 to 1992, where he was chairman of the Appropriations Committee. He served on the trade staff of the US House of Representatives Ways and Means Committee during consideration of the Trade Act of 1974. He holds a BA in history and JD from the University of Georgia and a Master of Laws degree from the London School of Economics.

Index

Note: Photographs are indicated by an italic page number. Entries pertaining to endnotes are indicated by an italic "*n*" followed by the note number.

AAA. *See* Agricultural Adjustment Act
    (AAA) (1933)
Abdullah II, King of Jordan, 511–512
Abel, I. W., 440, 465, 475, 476–477
Abercrombie & Fitch, 502
Acheson, Dean G., 334, 368, 405
    Article VII negotiations, 323–324
    drafting of Article VII, 294–296,
        300, 302
    GATT negotiations, 357, 437–439
    on Hull, 312
    ITO Charter debates in US, 413, 426,
        436–439, 441, 450
    Marshall Plan, 355–356
    postwar loan to British, 336
    renewal (1945) of RTAA, 320
    secretary of state appointment of, 412
    on threat of Soviet Union, 339, 354
Adams, John, 63, 65, 163
Adams, John Quincy, 56, 65–67, 72–74, 78
Adam Smith and history of US trade politics,
    introduction
    government's role, 15–16, 19–21
    impact of British free-trade era, 28–30
    impact on American trade policy, 30–31
    the invisible hand, 16–19, 41–43, 296, 486
    mercantilism in Enlightenment age, 10,
        11–16, 17
    Smith's legacy in nineteenth century
        Britain, 21–28

Wealth of Nations and working class, 8,
    9–10, 14, 20–21, 29
Affordable Care Act (2010), 523
AFL-CIO
    criticism of TPP, 525–526, 559
    human rights petition against China, 557
    International Labor Rights Fund and, 492
    opposition to job loss due to multinational
        corporations foreign investments, 469
    proposes quota restrictions, 452
    at Seattle WTO meeting, 4–5, 504
    support for Burke-Hartke bill, 470, 474, 477,
        478–479
    support for labor provisions in trade
        agreements, 451, 491, 492, 495, 497, 501
    support for Rangel/Levin trade policy, 517
    support for TEA, 456, 460
After Seven Years (Moley), 255
Age of Betrayal (Beatty), 133
Age of Discovery, 14
Age of Roosevelt, The (Schlesinger), 270
Agricultural Adjustment Act (AAA) (1933),
    236, 242, 247, 254, 258, 275, 315, 388, 453
agricultural industry and tariffs/trade, 174–175,
    178, 186–187, 190–191, 195, 198, 228–229,
    240–241, 263–264, 273, 276–277, 282, 285,
    388, 480, 507–508
Agricultural Marketing Act (1929), 190–191
AISI. *See* American Iron and Steel
    Institute (AISI)

Aitken, William Maxwell, 323, 326, 333–334, 337, 376
Aldrich, Nelson W.
  as chair of National Monetary Commission, 167
  influence as congressional protectionist, 106, 119–120, 140, 141
  lobbyist shares congressional office space with, 134
  McKinley Tariff and, 122–123
  Payne-Aldrich Tariff Act and, 144–148, 150, 154–155
Amalgamated Association of Iron and Steel Workers, 124, 160–161
Amalgamated Clothing Workers of America, 452
American Alliance for Manufacturing, 545
American Apparel Manufacturers Association, 497
American Farm Bureau Federation, 396
American Federation of Labor (AFL). *See also* AFL-CIO; *specific leaders*
  joins ICFTU, 433
  positions on tariffs/trade, 194, 445–446
  support for NIRA, 238
  support for proposed ITO, 340, 396
  support for renewal of RTAA, 422
  support for Wilson, 160
American Individualism (Hoover), 190
American Iron and Steel Association, 115, 121
American Iron and Steel Institute (AISI), 101, 464
American Liberty League, 315
American Magazine, The, 138
American Party. *See* Know-Nothing Party
American Revolution, 36–38
Americans for Democratic Action, 396, 422–423. *See also* Union for Democratic Action
American Sugar Refinery Company, 120
American System and early trade protectionism, 35–60, 64–67, 120. *See also* Clay, Henry
  overview, 35–36
  Embargo Act and War of 1812, 49–53
  emergence of Clay's vision of, 53–60
  Hamilton and protectionism, 39–45, 48–49, 568n14
  Jefferson and economic nationalism, 45–49
  during J.Q. Adams's presidency, 64–68
  lack of support for, 85
  trade oppression in colonies and chaos in confederation, 36–39

American Tariff League, 412, 427, 451
American Textile Manufacturers Institute (ATMI), 451–452, 453, 483
American Tin Plate Association, 111, 123
American Tobacco Company, 209
Amery, Leopold, 329–330
Anderson, Clinton P., 360
Anderson, John, 310
Anglo-American Mutual Aid Agreement (1942), 288, 303–304, 321–329. *See also* Lend-Lease program
Anglo-American special relationship, 284–313
  overview, 284–285
  Article VII negotiations, 294–297, 300, 301–304
  Atlantic Charter, 297–304
  Bretton Woods, 304–310
  Keynes influence on, 288–297, 303, 305
  Lend-Lease program, 285–297, 300, 301–304
Anti-Corn Law League, 24–27, 29–30
anti-dumping standards, 379, 461–462, 465, 482, 484, 510, 541
anti-globalization views, 1–8, 45. *See also* Battle in Seattle protests (1999)
Aranha, Oswaldo, 271
Arthur, Chester A., 104–105
Art of the Deal, The (Trump), 536
ASEAN (Association of Southeast Asian Nations), 560–561
Asia-Pacific Economic Cooperation forum (APEC), 524
Atlantic Charter, 297–304, 380, 400–401, 430, 562–563
Atlantic alliance. *See* postwar Atlantic alliance
ATMI. *See* American Textile Manufacturers Institute (ATMI)
Attlee, Clement Richard, 324, 328, 343, 363–364, 365
Australia, and GATT negotiations, 358–360, 373

Bagehot, Walter, 154
Bailey, Stephen Kemp, 395
Baker, Ray Stannard, 137–138, 144, 154
Baldanzi, George, 463–464
Ball, George W., 457–458, 461, 463–464
Bangladesh, and garment industry, 505
banking system, in US, 166–169, 231, 235, 236
Bank of England, 166, 292
Bank of the United States, 45, 62, 64, 80–82, 83, 85, 166
Bannon, Stephen K., 534–536, 539, 551
Barbour, Philip P., 58
Barenburg, Mark, 497
Barshefsky, Charlene, 495, 501, 507

Bartlett, Irving H., 73
Batt, William L., 418
Battle in Seattle (film), 5
Battle in Seattle protests (1999), 1–8, 506
Baucus, Max, 514, 516, 521, 524
Baxter, Maurice G., 55, 79
Beard, Charles A., 270
Beatty, Jack, 133
Beaverbrook, Lord. *See* Aitken, William
    Maxwell
Becker, George, 5
Beer-Wine Revenue Act (1933), 236
Bell, John, 89
Bergsten, C. Fred, 552
Berle, Adolf A., Jr., 226
Bessemer process, for steel, 99
Beteta Quintana, Ramon, 382–383
Bethlehem Steel Company, 100–101
Beveridge, William H., 398
Bevin, Earnest B., 361–362, 369, 371–374,
    374, 377
Biddle, Nicholas, 81, 82
Biemiller, Andrew J., 475
Birth of a Nation, The (film), 153
Bismarck, Otto von, 27
Black, Hugo L., 198, 238, 239
Blaine, James G., 103, 109–110
Blair, Tony, 342
Blinder, Alan S., 557
Bohlen, Charles E. "Chip," 356
"The Bombshell" message (FDR), 251–254, 281,
    290–291
Bonior, David, 6
Boothby, Robert J. G., 330–331
Borah, William E., 196, 199, 261–262, 274
Boritt, G. S., 91
boss system, in states, 119, 155, 214. *See also*
    Tammany Hall
Bové, José, 2, 5
Bowers, Claude, 218
Brady, Kevin, 545
Brain Trust. *See* FDR's Brain Trust
Brandeis, Louis D., 158, 167–168, 189, 239
Brands, H. W., 164, 238–239
Brazil
    ITO Charter negotiations, 388–389
    WTO decision on US cotton subsidies as
        violation, 544
Breckinridge, John C., 89
Breitbart News, 535
Bretton Woods, 304–310, 314–315, 317–318,
    329–331, 332, 435, 441, 468
Brexit, 533, 535–536, 546–547
Bright, John, 24–25, 31

Bristol, Lee H., 430
British East India Company, 14, 15, 17, 37
Brookings Institution, trade study,
    431–432, 444
Brougham, Henry, 54–55
Browder, Earl, 436
Brown, Henry, 129–130
Brown, John, 88
Brown, William Adams, Jr., 431–432, 444
Brown, Winthrop G., 345, 357, 373, 424
Brunei, bilateral trade agreement with US, 525
Bryan, William Jennings "the Great
    Commoner," 128, 131–132, 152–153, 156–157,
    158, 170, 213, 315
Buchanan, James, 87–88, 93
Buchanan, Pat, 489
Bullitt, William C., 247
Bull Moose Party. *See* Progressive Party
Burke, Edmund, 152, 153–154
Burke, James A., 469, 473–474, 477
Burlington Industries, 540
Bush, George H. W., 490
Bush, George W., 230, 523, 543
    FTAs with weak labor provisions, 511–514,
        516–517, 519–520, 524
    on outsourcing of jobs, 556
    renewal of US-Cambodia Textile
        Agreement, 502
    steel tariffs and WTO rulings, 558
    on Trump's inaugural address, 534
business and labor, trade policy debates,
    440–485. *See also specific labor unions*
    overview, 440–447
    congressional debates, 462–466
    Eisenhower and trade, 447–450
    fast track and "liberal protectionism," 479–485
    GATT payments and Multifiber
        Arrangement, 483
    Jackson-Vanik amendment, 477–479
    Kennedy Round, GATT, 460–464
    Mills and Burke-Hartke bills, proposed,
        466–470, 474–479, 483, 556
    Organization for Trade Cooperation (OTC),
        proposed, 450–452
    perfectionists and Adam Smith, 443–447
    Special Trade Representative, 457–460
    Trade Adjustment Assistance, 448–449,
        455–456, 462, 474–477, 482
    Trade Expansion Act, 454–462, 466–468,
        470, 481–482
    trade quotas and, 452–454
    Trade Reform Act, 470–475, 478–485
Butler, Hugh, 350
Butler, Michael A., 253

Buxton, Sydney, 24
Byrnes, James M., 317, 339, 347, *349*, 353

Calhoun, John C., *70*
    debate with Jackson, 64
    on Force Bill, 76–77, 79
    as leader of southern free-traders, 65
    as vice-president, 65–66, 68–69, 70–73, 76
    as Whig, 82
Cambodia
    comprehensive trade agreement with US
        (1996), 491–492
    establishment of labor code of international
        standards, 492, 495–500, 502–503
    Free Trade Union of Workers report, 499
    garment exports to US, 492–493
    GSP program and, 491–492
    Khmer Rouge in, 491, 493, 496
    labor dispute mediation by Ministry of
        Labor, 498–499
    US-Cambodia Textile Agreement (1999),
        491–503, 511, 519
    US invasion of, 493
    as WTO member, 502
Cambodian Garment Manufacturers
        Association, 503
Canada
    GATT negotiations, 344–345, 370, 373, 374
    NAFTA and, 488, 490–491
    Ottawa Agreements, 202, 272–273,
        279–280, 293
    postwar loan to British, 328
    renegotiation of NAFTA, 548–553
    TPP and, 550
    trade negotiations with US during 1930s,
        279–283
Cannon, Joseph G., 141, 144–148, 211
Cardozo, Benjamin, 239
Carey, Henry C., 31, 90, 383
Carey, James B., 408, 447
Carnegie, Andrew, 100, 118, 123, 124, 142,
        143, 151
Carnegie Endowment for International Peace,
        503–504
Carnegie Steel Company, 124
Caro, Robert, 172
Carrier Corporation, 556
Carter, Jimmy, 484
Cather, Willa, 138
CED (Committee for Economic
        Development), 419
Central Intelligence Agency (CIA), 441
Chamberlain, Joseph, 28, 280, 363

Chamberlain, Neville, 250, 252, 280–282,
        285–286, 363
Cham Prasidh, 496–499, 501–503, *503*
Charnovitz, Steve, 526
Charter for World Trade, A (Wilcox), 420
Chase, Salmon P., 91, 94
chemicals industry and tariffs/trade, 170–171,
        178, 462
Cheney, Dick, 514
Chernow, Ron, 43, 45
child labor, 44–45, 53, 136, 150, 171, 217
China
    accession to WTO, 505
    Asian trading block, proposed, 524
    concerns about currency manipulation by,
        522–523, 559–560
    garment industry, 502
    iPhone exports, 538–539
    during Korean War, 441
    One Belt, One Road project, 561–562
    RCEP and, 560–561
Churchill, Winston S., *298. See also* Anglo-
        American special relationship; postwar
        Atlantic alliance
    appointment of Cripps, 364–365
    Article VII negotiations, 294, 324
    Atlantic Charter, 31, 297–304, 562–563
    correspondence with FDR, 285–286
    "iron curtain" speech, 339
    on Sinclair's book, 137
    trade views of, 28
    US loan to British and, 329–330
CITA (Committee for the Implementation of
        Textile Agreements), 494
Civil War and robber barons, 85
    overview, 85–86
    events leading to, 86–92
    Lincoln as distracted protectionist, 90–92
    postwar special interest
        protectionism, 96–102
    Republican Congress and high
        tariffs, 92–96
    slavery issues as paramount, 86–90
    Tariff Commission reforms, 102–107
Clark, Champ, 152, 155–157, 163, 208
Clay, Henry, *54*, 444
    Compromise Tariff (1833), 78–79
    Force Bill and, 78
    as presidential candidate, 73–75, 83
    as proponent of American System of trade,
        53–60, 64–67, 79–80, 85
    as secretary of state, 65–66
    as senator, 73, 76

as craftsman of compromises on slavery
    issues, 86
Clayton, William L., 334, *401*
    background of, 315–316
    endorsement of US-European trade
        partnership, 455
    GATT negotiations, 346–347, 353–354, 355,
        357–361, 362, 365–376, 378–379
    ITO Charter debates in US, 406–407, 413,
        417–419, 425, 441, 442
    ITO Charter negotiations, 377–378, 380,
        382–389, 401
    Marshall Plan, 355–356, 361–362, 533
    postwar loan to British negotiations, 324,
        326–327, 336–337
    renewal of RTAA (1945), 319–320
    review of *The Economic Munich*, 415–416
    in State Department under Truman, 314–317
    Trade Agreements Act extension debates
        (1948), 411
Clayton Antitrust Act (1914), 166
Cleveland, Grover, 109–114, 118, 120–122, 124,
    126–127, 131–133, 210, 445
Clinton, Bill, 8, 522. *See also* North American
    Free Trade Agreement (NAFTA)
    attempts to place labor rights on WTO
        agenda, 487, 495
    calls for WTO Working Group on Trade
        and Labor, 504, 507–508
    campaign statements on NAFTA, 490
    statements regarding Seattle WTO meeting,
        7, 506–507
    trade agreements with Mexico, 490
    trade negotiations with Cambodia, 501
    trade negotiations with Jordan, 511–512
Clinton, Hillary Rodham, 521, 522–523, 527, 531
Cobden, Richard, 24–26, 31
Cohn, Gary, 551
Coinage Act (1873), 103, 125–126
Cold War, impact on trade policy, 440–442, 458
Collier Tariff Bill (1932), 203–204
collusion by employers to restrict wages, 12–13
Coming China Wars, The (Navarro), 539
Committee for Economic Development
    (CED), 419
Committee for the Implementation of Textile
    Agreements (CITA), 494
Committee on Trade Agreements, 263
comparative advantage (Ricardo), 181, 557
competitive liberalism concept, 488, 526
Compromise of 1850, 86
Compromise Tariff (1833), 78–79
Conable, Barber B., 473, 478–479

Cone Mills, 540
Congressional Budget Office, 489
Congressional Textile Caucus, 457, 473, 494
Congress of Industrial Organizations (CIO).
        See also AFL-CIO
    joins ICFTU, 433
    positions on tariffs/trade, 408, 446–447
    support for proposed ITO, 340, 396, 418–419
    support for renewal of RTAA, 422
Connally, John B., 468
Connally, Thomas T., 435
Constitutional Convention (1787), 38–39, 62
Constitutional Union Party, 89–90
Cooks, Stoney, 472
Coolidge, Calvin, 174, 183–187, 188–189, 192,
    235, 445
Coombs, H. C., 394
Cooper, Jere, 431, 450
Cooper, John Milton, Jr., 166
Copper Act (1869), 98–99
copper industry and tariffs/trade, 98–99, 106
"corporate greed," revolt against, 5
corporate taxes, 556
Cortney, Philip, 415–416, 418
Costa, Arthur Souza, *271*
cotton industry and tariffs/trade, 29, 53, 57, 58, 64
Coughlin, Charles, 286
Council of Economic Advisers, 398
Couzens, James J., 185
Cox, James M., 174, 214, 245, 247
Crane, Stephen, 138
Crawford, William, 56, 65
Crédit Mobilier scandal (1872), 102–103, 109
Cribb, Troy, 494
Crider, John H., 342
Cripps, Richard Stafford, 363–368, 371–373, *374*,
    375, 389–391
"Cross of Gold" speech (Bryan), 132
Crowther, William, 270
Cuban-American Treaty (1903), 257
Culbertson, William S., 180, 182–183
Cummins, Albert B., 141, 165
currency manipulation, 304–305, 494, 522–523,
    526–527, 559–560
currency stabilization, 248–252, 281, 304–310

Dallas, Alexander, 55
Dalton, Hugh, 321–322, 331, 361–362
Daniels, Josephus, 207, 213
Debs, Eugene V., 157–158, 160
Declaration of Independence, 37–38
Declaration on Fundamental Principles and
    Rights at Work (ILO), 518–519, 525

De Gaulle, Charles, 455
DeLay, Thomas D. "Tom", 513
Democratic National Committee, 215, 219, 220
Democratic Party. *See also specific leaders and candidates*
    division of party control during 1800s, 84, 123–124
    during Great Depression, 278
    protectionist wing of, 103, 108–109, 114
    trade/tax/tariff platforms during 1800s, 79–84, 89, 91, 103, 120–121
    weakening of due to Kansas-Nebraska Act, 87–88, 89
Dent, Harry S., Sr., 467
Dent, John H., 463–464
developing countries
    current views on protectionism, 35–36, 44–45
    GSP program, 491–492, 519
    ITO Charter negotiations and, 382–388, 389–392
    US negotiated bilateral trade agreements with labor provisions, 525
    WTO country opposition to labor rights enforcement tied to trade benefits, 495, 504, 506–510
Dewey, Thomas E., 287, 309, 318, 411
Dingley, Nelson, 133
Dirksen, Everett M., 466
Disraeli, Benjamin, 25–26, 27
Dodd, Christopher J., 521
Dolan, Mike, 2
Dominican Republic-Central American Free Trade Agreement (DR-CAFTA), 514–515, 522, 540
Donald, David Herbert, 90
Donohue, Thomas J., 504–505, 514
Doughton, Robert L., *286,* 318–320, 408
Douglas, Lewis W., 241, 371–372, 374, 389, 391, 412
Douglas, Stephen, 72, 86, 87–88, 89
DR-CAFTA. *See* Dominican Republic-Central American Free Trade Agreement (DR-CAFTA)
Dred Scott case (1857), 87, 130, 131
Duer, William, 43–44
Dulles, John Foster, *449,* 450, 455
dumping, 28, 54–55, 99, 178, 264. *See also* anti-dumping standards

Early, Jubal, 95
Earth Island Institute, 4
Eberle, William D., 478

ECAT (Emergency Committee for American Trade), 470–471
Eccles, Marriner, 290
Economic Consequences of the Peace, The (Keynes), 291
Economic Cooperation Act (1948). *See* Marshall Plan
economic inequality, 116, 118. *See also* wages of workers; working classes, in US
Economic Munich, The (Cortney), 415–416
economic nationalism. *See also* American System of trade; *Report on Commerce* (Jefferson); *specific individual proponents of*
    era of dominance in US trade policy, 36
    Jefferson and, 45–49, 63–64
    Keynes on, 292
    Peek's appeals to FDR for, 267
    in post-Roosevelt era, 441
    in Trump's America First agenda, 532–546, 553
    during War of 1812, 51
Economic Policy Institute, 559
Eden, Anthony, 280–281, 302
Edwards, John, 521, 522
EEC. *See* European Economic Community (EEC)
Eighteenth Amendment, 223
Eisenhower, Dwight D., 447–453, *449,* 458
Ellis, Joseph, 62
Embargo Act (1807), 49–53
Emergency Agricultural Tariff Act (1921), 174–175
Emergency Banking Act (1933), 235
Emergency Committee for American Trade (ECAT), 470–471
Emergency Tariff Act (1921), 178
Employment Act (1946), 397–399, 430, 432, 433–434
End of Laissez-Faire, The (Keynes), 183–184
Eng, Roland, 502
England's Treasure by Foreign Trade (Munn), 17
escape clauses
    in proposed ITO Charter, 398, 417, 420
    in RTAA extensions, 442, 450
    in TEA, 455, 462, 482
    in trade agreements, 323–324, 327–328, 352–353, 369, 379, 383, 409
Esserman, Sue, 7
European Economic Community (EEC), 455, 461, 467

European Union (EU)
  agenda at WTO/Seattle conference, 508, 509
  Brexit, 533, 535–536, 546–547
  Common Agricultural Policy, 461, 467, 508
  mixed country views on tying labor rights
    to trade sanctions, 507
  T-TIP and, 547–548
Export-Import Bank of Washington, 264–265,
    267–270
Export Processing Zones (EPZs), under
    TPP, 525

Fair Labor Standards Act (FLSA) (1938),
    239, 463
Farage, Nigel, 536
Farley, James A., 220, 223, 227, 229–230,
    233, 278
Farm Bureau Federation, 418
FDR and Cordell Hull, 207–224
  during 1920s, 214–219
  overview, 207
  contrasting commonalities of, 208–214
  presidential nomination (1932), 219–224
FDR's Brain Trust, 225–255. See also Berle,
    Adolf A., Jr.; Moley, Raymond; Tugwell,
    Rexford G.
  overview, 225–226
  "The Bombshell" message, 251–254, 281,
    290–291
  first hundred days, 233–239
  presidency and Hull as secretary of state,
    229–233
  privy council and New Deal, 226–229
  World Economic Conference, London, 231,
    239–255, 281
Federal Deposit Insurance Corporation
    (FDIC), 236
Federal Farm Board, 190–191
Federal Reserve Act (1913), 168
Federal Reserve System/Board, 166–169, 177,
    186, 202
Federal Securities Act (1933), 236
Federal Trade Commission (FTC), 166,
    184, 236
Feis, Herbert, 296
Ferrell, Robert H., 184
Field, Stephen, 129
Fifth Amendment, 87
Fillmore, Millard, 87
First Continental Congress (1774), 37
Flanigan, Peter M., 478
FLSA. See Fair Labor Standards Act
    (FLSA) (1938)

Force Bill (1833), 75–79
Ford, Gerald R., 479–480, 481
Ford, Henry, 186, 199
Fordney, Joseph W., 179–181
Fordney-McCumber Tariff Act (1922), 178–183,
    194–195, 215, 273
the "forgotten man" slogan, 221–222, 553–560
Forkan, Patricia, 3
Fort Hill Address (Calhoun), 73
Foster, Frank K., 160
Foster, James P., 121
Frankfurter, Felix, 291
Franklin, Benjamin, 30, 37
Free Silver movement, 125–127, 132, 133
Free Trade Club of New York, 154
Free Trade Union of Workers of the Kingdom
    of Cambodia report, 499
Fremont, John, 87
Friedman, Milton, 489
Friedman, Thomas L., 6
FTC. See Federal Trade Commission (FTC)
Full Employment Act (1945), proposed, 395–396
Full Employment in a Free Society
    (Beveridge), 398
Fuller, Melville, 129
Fulton, James G., 426–427, 431–432

Gallatin, Albert, 49–50, 74, 177
Gap, 502–503
Gardner, Richard N., 334
Garfield, James A., 103–104
garment industry and tariffs/trade, 492–494,
    498, 500–501
Garner, John N., 194, 196, 199, 223–224
Gearhart, Bertrand W., 350–351, 376, 410, 412
General Agreement on Tariffs and Trade
    (GATT), 343–376. See also ITO Charter
    (1948);
    most-favored-nation (MFN) principle;
    World Trade Organization (WTO);
    specific member countries
  accomplishments of, 439
  Annecy Round, 421
  Article XX, trade restrictions, 3–4
  congressional Republicans and, 349–353
  crisis in Anglo-American alliance and,
    361–372
  discriminatory tariffs for customs unions
    and free-trade areas, 488
  dispute resolution system, 544
  Kennedy Round, 460–464, 465
  lack of fair labor standards in, 447, 456,
    486–487

General Agreement on Tariffs
and Trade (GATT) (*cont.*)
OTC proposal and, 450–452
selective nuclear-multilateral negotiation
approach, 344–349
settlement and approval of (1945), 343–344,
372–376
Tokyo Round, 484, 492
Truman Doctrine, Marshall Plan and, 343,
347, 349–350, 352, 353–357, 360–361,
367–368, 371–372
wool tariffs and, 357–361, 363
General Motors Company, 199, 396–397
*General Theory of Employment, Interest, and
Money, The* (Keynes), 290, 396
George, David Lloyd, 292
George, Walter F., 318, 395, 399, 421–424, 435
Gephardt, Richard A., 489, 491
Gerard, James W., 214
Gerard, Leo W., 517, 527, 543
Giannini, Mario, 419–420
Gibbons, Sam M., 202, 473–474
Gilded Age of protectionism, 108–135
overview, 102–103, 108–109, 136, 555
Cleveland and tariff reform, 109–114
election of 1888, 120–122
failure of reforms of 1893, 125–128
Great Tariff Debate of 1888, 114–120
income tax and, 128–131
McKinley and Dingley tariff, 131–135
McKinley tariff and fallout of, 122–124
Gingrich, Newt, 512
Gladstone, William, 24, 26, 27, 28–30, 31, 154,
211, 240
Glass-Steagall Banking Act (1933), 236
Global Fairness Initiative, 502
Goldberg, Arthur, *453*
gold standard, 132, 133, 240–241, 243, 247, 249,
281, 307
Gompers, Samuel, 160–161, *161*, 194, 445,
495, 555
Gore, Al, 202–203
Gorman, Arthur P., 127–128
Gramm, Phil, 512
Grant, Ulysses S., 102, 104
Grassley, Charles, 516
Great Britain. *See* United Kingdom (UK)
Great Depression, 201–203, 223, 226–227,
278, 394
Great Recession (2008), 230, 523, 557
Great Tariff Debate (1888), 114–120, 445
Greek-Turkish Aid Act (1948), 354
Green, William, 194, 340, 446
Grundy, Joseph R., 197–198

GSP. *See* US Generalized System of Preferences
(GSP) program

Halifax, Lord. *See* Wood, Edward F. L.
Hamilton (musical), 62–63
Hamilton, Alexander, 38, *40*, 53. *See also*
American System of trade
on Bank of the United States, 62, 166
on cost of embargo on Britain, 48–49
as founder of American conservatism, 542
as founding father of protectionism, 39–45,
63–64, 568n14
Report on Manufactures, 39–45, 63,
444, 568n22
statue of, 176–177
on trade policy, 35
Hamiltonian government-business partnership.
See also American System of trade; *Report
on Manufactures* (Hamilton); *specific
individual proponents of*
during 1920s, 445
Carnegie and, 100, 118
FDR and, 237–238
Federal Reserve System/Board and, 177
infant industry theory, 44–45, 53, 56, 64, 112,
382–383
monopolies and trusts during Gilded Age,
119–120
Republican Party and, 89
robber tariff barons and, 100–101
TR New Nationalism and, 158–159
Whig Party and, 82
Hanna, Mark, 132–133, 140
Harbinson, Stuart, 508–509
Harding, Warren G., 174, 176–177, 180–183, 186,
188, 215, 445
Harlan, John Marshall, 130
Harriman, W. Averell, 339
Harrison, Benjamin, 82, 84, 120–122, 123, 124
Harrison, Pat, *286*
Hartford Convention (1814), 52, 569n44
Hartke, R. Vance, 469, 479, 483–484
Harvey, George, 155
Haugen, Gilbert N., 186–187
Havana Charter. *See* ITO Charter (1948)
Havemeyer, Henry O., 114
Hawkins, Harry C., 296, 321–324, 363, 373
Hawley, Willis C., *191*, 193, 195–196,
199–200, 204
Hayek, Friedrich von, 396–397, 398, 443
Hayes, John L., 97–98, 105, 107
Hayes, Rutherford B., 130
Hayne, Robert Y., 70–72
Hearst, William Randolph, 133, 216, 221

Heilperin, Michael A., 417–418
Helmore, James R. C., 359–360, 363, 366, 373
Herter, Christian A., 455, 461, 464
Hewitt, Abram S., 123–124
History of the American People
    (Wilson), 152
Hitler, Adolf, 268, 282, 285–286, 297, 299,
    538, 562
Hodges, Luther H., 457
Hoffa, James P. "Jimmy", 5, 520
Holmes, Oliver Wendell, Jr., 226
Holmes, Stephen L., 401–402
Hoover, Herbert, 214, 226, 234, 445
    criticism of McNary-Haugen bill, 186
    as critic of FDR trade policies, 274
    European war debts, 230–231
    flexible tariff authority provision,
        199–201, 577n62
    foreign policy of, 235
    objections to Smoot-Hawley provisions,
        195–197, 203–204
    opposition to Lend-Lease, 288
    presidential campaigns, 228–229
    rugged individualism approach, 236–237
    as secretary of commerce, 182
    signs Smoot-Hawley Tariff Act, 9
    as the "wonder boy," 187–192
Hoovervilles, 229
Hopkins, Harry, 302–303
House, Edward, 188
Houston, David F., 164–165
Howe, Louis
    collaboration with Hull, 215, 219, 222–223,
        227, 251, 257
    as political adviser to FDR, 214, 215–217, 224,
        229–230, 302
Hoyer, Steny, 519
Huckabee, Mike, 521
Hughes, Charles Evans, 257, 266
Hull, Cordell, 165, 216, 271, 286, 445. *See also*
    FDR and Cordell Hull
    on Atlantic Charter, 300
    Brain Trust and, 227–228
    drafting of RTAA, 262–263
    efforts with multilateral trading system,
        263–279, 322
    formation of UN, 310–311
    on imperial preference system, 488
    income tax proposal, 146, 163–164
    legacy of, 31, 311–313, 317, 379, 439, 531–532
    Lend-Lease and, 288, 296
    opposition to Fordney-McCumber bill,
        194–195
    plans to roll back Smoot-Hawley, 203

receives Nobel Peace Prize, 311
    role at Pan-American Conference, 257–259
    role at World Economic Conference,
        London, 239–255
    as secretary of state, 231–233, 235, 239–256,
        263–272
Hume, David, 11, 30
Hun Sen, 496–497, 499
Huskisson, William, 23, 64

ICC. *See* International Chamber of
    Commerce (ICC)
ILO. *See* International Labor
    Organization (ILO)
IMF. *See* International Monetary Fund (IMF)
income tax, 128–131, 146, 150, 163–165, 171, 212
India
    British East India Company and, 14, 17, 37
    GATT negotiations, 348, 373
    opposition to WTO labor rights
        enforcement tied to trade benefits, 508,
        509–510
Industrial League of Pennsylvania, 101, 104
infant industry theory, 44–45, 53, 56, 64, 112,
    382–383
inheritance tax, 150
Inquiries Concerning Human Understanding
    (Hume), 11
intellectual property protection, 526
Interim Commission for the International
    Trade Organization, 439
International Longshore and Warehouse
    Union, 4
International Brotherhood of Teamsters, 5,
    505, 520
International Chamber of Commerce (ICC),
    405, 429–430, 451
International Clearing Union. *See*
    International Monetary Fund (IMF)
International Confederation of Free Trade
    Unions (ICFTU), 433
International Labor Organization (ILO)
    Declaration on Fundamental Principles and
        Rights at Work, 518–519, 525
    EU proposal for labor forum and,
        507–508, 509
    proposals to tie labor standards to trade
        agreements, 514, 516–517
    proposed employment provisions in ITO
        and, 399–400
    provides training/monitoring in Cambodia,
        495–496, 497–503
    WTO member consensus on role with labor
        standards, 487

International Labor Rights Fund, 492
International Ladies Garment Workers
    Union, 452
International Monetary Fund (IMF), 308–310,
    331, 332, 392, 509, 526, 560
International Textile and Clothing Bureau
    (ITCB), 508–509
International Textile Group (ITG), 540
International Trade Organization
    (ITO),proposal, 305–306, 322, 331–335,
    340, 392. *See also* ITO Charter (1948);
    specific member countries
interposition doctrine, 73
investigative journalism, 137–138
the invisible hand (Smith), 16–19, 41–43,
    296, 486
iPhone trade, 538–539
iron industry and tariffs/trade, 39, 67, 74, 95,
    101, 123, 145, 197, 273
Irwin, Douglas A., 193, 294
ITC. *See* US International Trade
    Commission (ITC)
ITO Charter (1948), 377–402, 442–443. *See
    also* General Agreement on Tariffs and
    Trade (GATT)
    overview, 377–379
    approval of, 400–402
    British objections to exceptions requests,
        388–392
    delegations to, 380–381
    full employment policies, 394–400
    governance provisions, 392–393
    Latin American voting bloc, 382–388
    quantitative restrictions (QRs) debates,
        383–387, 389–392
    security of foreign investment, 393

Jackson, Andrew, *75. See also* Jacksonian
    democracy and free trade
    Battle of New Orleans, 52
    legacy of, 85, 444
    as president, 68–69, 72, 73–76
    as presidential candidate, 56, 65–67
    on tariffs, 69–70
    vetoes renewal of Bank charter, 80–82, 166
Jackson, Henry M. "Scoop," 477–479
Jacksonian democracy and free
        trade, 61–84
    overview, 61–65
    events leading to Nullification
        Crisis, 68–74
    Force Bill and Tariff of 1833, 75–79
    free trade and Democratic Party, 79–84

presidential election of 1824, 65–66
Tariff of Abominations (1828), 66–69,
    72, 75, 82
Japan, and US trade policy, 461, 467, 542
Jarrett, John, 160–161
Jasinowski, Jerry, 6
Javits, Jacob K., 426–427, 431–432, 465
Jay Treaty (1795), 265
Jefferson, Thomas, 46, 162, 292
    agrarian utopia concept, 40
    on Bank of the United States, 62
    economic nationalism and, 45–51, 63–64
    Kentucky and Virginia Resolutions,
        51–52, 73
    as mentor to J.Q. Adams, 65
    Report on Commerce, 47–48, 63, 444
    views on protectionism, 44
    writes Declaration of Independence,
        30, 37–38
Jefferson and Hamilton (Bowers), 218
Jim Crow segregation, 153
Johnson, Andrew, 95, 97, 98–99
Johnson, Boris, 547
Johnson, C. Donald, 503
    arranges for ILO training/monitoring in
        Cambodia, 495–501
    attends Robbins's lectures
        in London, 585n22
    Augusta Chronicle, on candidacy of, 131
    goals of negotiations, 500
    issue brief on success of US-Cambodian
        trade agreement, 503
    as member of Congress, 488–489, 494, 512, 544
    as member of Congressional Textile
        Caucus, 494
    Obama campaign trade advisory committee
        and, 601n59
    as pro-trade Democrat, 8
    responsibility for Cambodian trade
        negotiations, 493–503, 511, 519
    as trade staff member for Ways and Means,
        471–473
    as USTR textile ambassador, 491–503
    votes for NAFTA, 488–489
Johnson, Hiram W., 261
Johnson, Lyndon B., 166, 449–450, *449*, 460,
    465–466
Jones, Joseph, 201–202
Jordan, Free Trade Agreement with US (2000),
    511–514
J. P. Morgan and Company, 209
Judge (magazine), 118–119
Jungle, The (Sinclair), 136–137

Kansas-Nebraska Act (1854), 86–87, 89
Kaptor, Marcy, 518
Kee, John, 431, 436–437
Kelley, William "Pig Iron," 106, 116–117
Kellogg-Briand Pact (1928), 259
Kendall, Donald M., 471
Kennan, George F., 339, 355–356, 533
Kennedy, John F., 453, 454–457, 458, 459–462
Kennedy, Ted, 542
Kentucky and Virginia Resolutions (Jefferson
    and Madison), 52, 73
Keppler, Joseph, 119
Kerry, John, 522
Keynes, John Maynard, 314, 335
    Bretton Woods, 305–310
    The End of Laissez-Faire, 183–184
    on FDR's "The Bombshell" message, 252
    The General Theory of Employment, Interest,
        and Money, 290, 396
    on gold standard, 241
    influence on Anglo-American special
        relationship, 288–297, 303, 305
    meetings with FDR, 291, 294
    "National Self-Sufficiency," 292
    Proposals for the International
        Trade Organization, 305–306, 322,
        331–335
    references to A. Smith, 333
    as skeptic of laissez faire, 324, 332–333
    Treatise on Money, 290
    on US loan to British, 325–326
Kieran, James M., 226
Killheffer, Elvin H., 406, 427
King, Mackenzie, 273, 282
Kirk, Ronald "Ron," 523–524
Kirkland, Lane, 491
Kissinger, Henry A., 477–479, 480
Knights of Labor, 161
Know-Nothing Party, 87
Knox, W. Frank, 287
Knutson, Harold, 319–320, 350, 352, 376,
    406–407, 412
Korean War, 435–436, 441
Kraft, Joseph, 455
Krock, Arthur, 249
Krugman, Paul, 5–6, 489, 557
Kucinich, Dennis, 522
Kushner, Jared, 536, 537, 540–541, 551

Labor Consistency Plans, 525
labor law, 217, 220, 238. See also specific laws
Labor-Management Relations Act. See
    Taft-Hartley Act (1947)

labor rights. See worker rights
labor unions. See also business and labor, trade
        policy debates; specific unions
    efforts to prohibit in Great Britain, 12–13
    history of neutrality on trade issues,
        160–161, 446
    opposition to fast-track authority, 517
    opposition to Taft-Hartley Act, 399
    rejection of TPP, 559
    strikes, 124, 130–131
    trade liberalization and, 4–5, 7
    wages vs. tariffs platform, 555
La Follette, Robert, 142, 145, 149, 151, 157, 164, 179
La Follette, Robert M., Jr., 198
La Guardia, Fiorello, 185
Lamar, Harry, 472, 480
Lamont, Thomas, 200, 274
Lamy, Pascal, 7
Landon, Alfred M., 276–278, 318
Landrum, Phil M., 472–473, 476
Latin America. See Pan-American Conference,
        Uruguay (1933); specific countries
Lawrence, Abbott, 72
League of Nations, 173, 214–215, 221
League of Women Voters of the United States,
    422–423
least developed countries
    GSP program, 491–492, 519
    US duty-free access to all products
        from, 505
Lee, Richard Henry, 38–39
Lee, Thea M., 519–520, 524, 557
Lend-Lease program, 285–297, 300, 301–304,
    324–326, 328–331
Lenin, Vladimir, 535
Leuchtenburg, William E., 201
Levin, Sander M. "Sandy," 506, 512, 513, 515–
    520, 515, 526
Levinson, Mark, 497
Levi Strauss, 502
Lewis, John L., 446–447
liberal protectionism. See Trade Reform Act
    (TRA) (1973)
Liesching, Percivale, 326–327, 363
Lighthizer, Robert E., 537, 541–544, 546,
    547–548, 552–553
Lincoln, Abraham, 89, 90–92, 149
Lindbergh, Charles A., 286
Lindsay, Ronald, 280–281
Lippmann, Walter, 201, 214, 225, 241, 252
List, Friedrich, 31
Locke, John, 16–17
Lodge, Henry Cabot, 145, 173, 177, 182, 188

logrolling, 191–193, 197, 465
London Economic Conference. *See* World
    Economic Conference, London
Long, Breckinridge, 312
Long, Russell B., 465–466, 468, 480–481
"Long Telegram" (Kennan), 339
Longworth, Nicholas, 196
Loree, R. F., 430–431
Lovett, Robert A., 368–369, 375, 386
Lowell, Francis, 55
Lucas, Scott W., 422, 436

MacArthur, Douglas, 435–436
MacDonald, Ramsey, 242–243, 250
Madison, James, 77
    on Bank of the United States, 62, 64, 166
    Kentucky and Virginia Resolutions,
        51–52, 73
    on politics of trade, 38
    as president, 55–56, 64, 166
    proposes embargo on France/Britain, 48–49
    views on protectionism, 44, 568n22
MAGA (Making American Great Again), 536.
    See also Trump Trade Doctrine, impacts
    on liberal economic order
Malaysia, bilateral trade agreement with
    US, 525
Malmgren, Harald B., 466–467
Malmström, Cecilia, 548
Malone, Dumas, 50–51
Manchester School, 24, 153–154, 194
Mankiw, Gregory, 556
Manufacturers Alliance for Productivity and
    Innovation, 541
Marshall, George C., 353–357, 368, 373, 388–389,
    407–408, 412, 533
Marshall Plan, 353–357, 361–362, 367–368, 371–
    372, 408, 413, 418, 435, 441, 533
Martin, Joseph, 352
Marvin, Thomas O., 182–183
Matsui, Robert T., 513
May, Theresa, 546
May 10th Agreement "A New Trade Policy for
    America" (2007), 514–521, 558, 600n49
Mazur, Jay, 5, 497, 500
McAdoo, William G, 169
McCain, John S., 159, 521, 522–523, 541–542, 543
McCarthy, Joseph R., 351, 426, 436
McClure, Samuel S., 138
McClure's Magazine, 137–138
McConnell, Mitch, 527
McCormack, John W., 340–341, 451–452
McCrery, Jim, 516

McCumber, Porter J., 179–181
McDonald, David J., 448–449, 455
McKinley, William, 106, 108, 115, 118, 122–124,
    131–135
McMahon, Thomas, 446
McMillin, Benton, 128, 146, 209–210
McNary, Charles L., 186–187, 273
Meacham, Jon, 50
Meade, James Edward, 321–324, 363
Meany, George, 451, 453, 456, 460, 462, 470,
    478, 483
meat packaging industry and tariffs/trade,
    136–137
Mellon, Andrew, 176–177, 185, 186
Mencken, H. L., 225
mercantilism, in Enlightenment age, 10, 11–16
Merkel, Angela, 547
Mexico
    NAFTA and, 488–490
    renegotiation of NAFTA, 548–553
    TPP and, 550
military-industrial complex, 101
Mill, James, 31
Mill, John Stuart, 27, 31, 118
Millikin, Eugene D., 350, 409–410, 422–424,
    426, 435, 449
Mills, Ogden, 230, 274
Mills, Roger, 115–116
Mills, Wilbur D., 458–468, 459, 471–473, 478,
    596n44
Milton, George Fort, 233
mining industry and tariffs/trade, 98–99,
    100, 101
Miranda, Lin-Manuel, 62–63
Missouri Compromise (1820), 86, 87
Mnuchin, Steven, 558, 560
Moley, Raymond
    After Seven Years, 255
    as assistant secretary of state, 232–233, 235,
        237–238, 240, 242, 244–255, 290, 534
    as editor of *Today/Newsweek*, 275–276, 396
    as member of Brain Trust, 222, 224, 225,
        226–230,
    views on bilateral trade, 532
Molinari, Diego Luis, 382–383
money trust. *See* Wall Street "money trust"
monopolies, 113–114, 115, 141, 148, 159, 211
Monroe, James, 56, 65–66
Morgan, John Pierpont, 100, 138, 142, 151, 156,
    166–167
Morgenthau, Henry, 294, 305–309
Morrill, Justin S., 92–95, 102, 106, 115–116
Morrison, William R., 111

most-favored-nation (MFN) principle,
    265–277, 279–283, 295–296, 345,
    379, 388, 477–479, 549. *See also*
    General Agreement on Tariffs and
    Trade (GATT)
Mowry, George E., 150
muckrakers, use of term, 138–139
Mugwumps, use of term, 109
multilateral trading system under RTAA,
    emergence of, 256–283. *See also* General
    Agreement on Tariffs and Trade (GATT);
    International Trade Organization (ITO),
    proposal
  overview, 256
  MFN treatment and British agreements,
    279–283
  MFN treatment and RTAA, 265–277
  Pan-American Conference, Uruguay,
    257–260, 268–271
  Peek and Tariff Commission, 263–272
  presidential election (1936), 272–279
  Reciprocal Trade Agreements Act (RTAA),
    260–266, 268–269, 276, 278–279, 282,
    284–285
multinational corporations and job
    loss, 559
Munn, Thomas, 17
Murphy, Charles Francis, 214
Murray, James E., 395
Murray, Phillip, 340
"My Experience with, and Views upon, the
    Tariff" (Carnegie), 142

Nader, Ralph, 489
NAFTA. *See* North American Free Trade
    Agreement (NAFTA)
Narayanan, Srinivasan, 509–510
Nation, The (magazine), opposition to
    protectionism, 554–555
National Association for the Advancement of
    Colored People (NAACP), 396
National Association of Manufacturers
    (NAM), 141, 327, 396, 405, 414, 416, 430,
    470–471
National Association of Wool Manufacturers,
    97–98, 134
National Council of American Importers, 408,
    417–418
National Council of Jewish Women, 423
National Farmers Union, 396, 423
National Foreign Trade Council (NFTC), 405,
    408, 416, 422, 430–431, 438
National Grange, 190–191, 285

National Industrial Recovery Act
    (NIRA) (1933), 237–239, 242,
    254, 258, 315
National Labor-Management Council on
    Foreign Trade Policy, 427
National Labor Relations Act (1935), 239
National Monetary Commission, 167
National Security Council (NSC), 441
"National Self-Sufficiency" (Keynes), 292
National Women's Trade Union League, 423
NATO. *See* North Atlantic Treaty
    Organization (NATO)
natural justice, 16–17, 21, 30
Navarro, Peter, *530*, 537–539, 547, 548–549, 551
Neal, Richard, 545
neo-mercantilism, 466–470, 481, 528–529
Neutrality Act (1935), 282–283
Nevins, Allan, 201
New Deal, 222, 226–229, 233–242, 248, 251–252,
    260, 277–278, 290, 292, 314, 394–395
New Democrat Coalition, 517
new economic order, during Truman years,
    405–439. *See also* business and labor,
    trade policy debates
  overview, 405–407
  GATT negotiations, 437–439
  ITO Charter debates, 406, 410–421, 423–
    424, 426, 432, 436–439, 441
  ITO hearings, 424–439
  legacy of GATT, 438–439
  Trade Agreements Act extension debates,
    407–411, 421–424, 436–439, 442
  Vandenberg assessment of extension,
    409–411
New Freedom reforms. *See* Wilson, Woodrow
New Nationalism (TR), 148–151, 158–159
"New Trade Policy for America, A" (2007),
    514–521. *See also* May 10 Agreement
NFTC. *See* National Foreign Trade
    Council (NFTC)
Nineteenth Amendment, 215
NIRA. *See* National Industrial Recovery Act
    (NIRA) (1933)
Nixon, Richard M., 255, 454, 467–468,
    470–471, 477–478, 480, 493
Nobel Prize, 311, 322
nondiscriminatory trade principles. *See*
    General Agreement on Tariffs and Trade
    (GATT); most-favored-nation (MFN)
    principle
Non-Intercourse Act (1809), 51
Norris, George W., 184
North, Frederick, 37

North American Free Trade Agreement
(NAFTA), 473
   labor side agreements, 487–491, 511, 519
   Al Gore-Ross Perot debate over, 202–203
   Trump calls for renegotiation of, 522–524,
      530–531, 538, 542, 547, 548–553, 554
North Atlantic Treaty Organization (NATO),
   412, 441, 454–455, 532, 533
Notes on the State of Virginia (Jefferson),
   45–47, 50
Nullification Crisis (1832–33), 75–82

Obama, Barack H.
   on Adam Smith, 486
   on Brexit and trade with Britain, 546–547
   files WTO disputes, 542–543
   Great Recession and, 230
   as presidential candidate, 159, 521, 522–524,
      527, 531
   on TPP, 550, 559
Office of the United States Trade
   Representative (USTR), 484, 491–495,
   504, 527, 529–530
offshoring of jobs. *See* outsourcing of jobs
O'Malley, Martin, 527
Organic Chemical Manufacturers
   Association, 427
Organization for Economic Cooperation and
   Development (OECD), 539
O'Sullivan, David, 535–536
Other People's Money (Brandeis), 167–168
outsourcing of jobs, 469–471, 555–557

Paine, Thomas, 37
Pakistan, opposition to WTO labor rights
   provisions, 508, 509
Palmer, A. Mitchell, 223
Pan-American Conference, Uruguay (1933),
   257–260, 268–271
Panic
   of 1857, 88
   of 1893, 126, 132
   of 1907, 166–167
Panitchpakdi, Supachai, 506
Paris Agreement, 536
Pasvolsky, Leo, 296
Patman, Wright, 397
Paul, Ron, 521–522, 545–546
Payne, Sereno E., 145
Payne-Aldrich Tariff Act (1909), 144–148, 150,
   154–155
*Peddling Protection: Smoot-Hawley and the
   Great Depression* (Irwin), 193

Peek, George N., 263–272, 274, 275, 532
Peel, Robert, 24, 25–26, 28–30, 166
Pelosi, Nancy, 517, 518, 519–520
Peña Nieto, Enrique, 530–531, 548
Percy, Charles H., 465
Perdue, Sonny, 551
perfectionists. *See also* business and labor,
      trade policy debates; *specific individuals*
   Adam Smith and, 443–447
   during ITO debates, 406, 412, 414–417, 425,
      428–431, 442, 443–447
Perkins, Francis, 217, 233
Peron, Juan Domingo, 382
Perot, Ross, 202–203, 489, 490
Peru, Trade Promotion Agreement with US,
   519–521
Phillips, William, 233, 267
Pierce, Franklin, 85, 87
Pinchot, Gifford, 149, 150
Pitt, William (the Younger), 22–23
Pittman, Key D., 228, 245, 248, 252, 285
Plessy v. Ferguson (1896), 131
Polk, James K., 83–84, 91, 101
Pollock v. Farmers' Loan and Trust (1895),
   128–131, 146
Pol Pot, 493, 496
Populist Party, 127
postwar Atlantic alliance, 314–342
   overview, 314–317
   Article VII negotiations, 321–324
   negotiations over British loan, 324–329
   Parliamentary debate and approval of loan
      from US, 329–335
   renewal of RTAA, 317–321
   US congressional approval of loan, 335–342,
      346–347
Potsdam Conference, 324
Pou, Edward, 212
Preibus, Reinhold R. "Reince," 530, 531, 535
Pressnell, L. S., 303
Principles of Political Economy (Mill), 27
Progressive era and trade reform, 136–175
   overview, 136–138
   election of 1912, 157–161
   Federal Reserve System and trade
      expansion, 166–169
   impact of WW I on trade, 169–172
   New Freedom reforms, 158–159, 161–169
   New Nationalism and, 148–151, 158–159
   TR/Taft and tariff legislation, 138–151
   Underwood tariff of 1913, 161–165, 170
   W. Wilson as free trader, 152–157
   W. Wilson's final years, 172–175, 178

Progressive Party, 151
Prohibition, 171, 189, 219–220, 223, 236
Puck (magazine), 123
  "Bosses of the Senate" cartoon, 119
  "Et tu, Andy!" cartoon, *143*
  "Our Robber Barons" cartoon, *125*
Pujo, Arsène P., 167–168
Pure Food and Drug Act (1906), 137

Quay, Matthew, 121, 127
Quinn, Kenneth, 497

Raleigh, Walter, 14
Rand, Ayn, 9
Randall, Clarence B., 448
Randall, Samuel J., 103
Randolph, John, 64
Rangel, Charles B., 513, 514–520, *515*
Raskob, John J., 219, 315
Rayburn, Sam, 319–321, 341–342, 449
RCEP. *See* Regional Comprehensive Economic
  Partnership (RCEP)
Reader's Digest, condensed *Road to Serfdom,*
  396, 443
Reagan, Ronald, 185, 541, 542
Reciprocal Trade Agreements Act (RTAA)
  (1934), 260–266, 268–269, 276, 278–279,
  282, 284–285, 317–321, 344, 346, 407–411,
  421–424, 436–439, 442, 447, 448–450.
  See also Trade Expansion
  Act (TEA) (1962)
reciprocity treaties, 85, 134–135, 140–141,
  150–151
Redfield, William C., 168–169
Reed, Daniel A., 351
Reed, David, 197
Reed, Thomas Brackett, 118, 122
Regional Comprehensive Economic
  Partnership (RCEP), 560–561
Reitano, Joanne, 114
Remini, Robert V., 59, 67, 77
Report on Commerce (Jefferson), 47–48, 63,
  444, 568*n*33, 35
Report on Manufactures (Hamilton), 39–45, 63,
  444, 567*n*8–18, 22–23
Republican League, 121
Republican Party. *See also specific leaders and*
  candidates
  formation of, 86–87
  New Nationalism and, 148–151
  protectionist platform during 1800s, 89,
    102–103, 108–109, 114, 120–121
Reston, James, 357

Revenue Acts
  of 1916, 171
  of 1918, 171
  of 1921, 185
  of 1926, 185
Ricardo, David, 31, 181
Road to Serfdom, The (Hayek), 396–397, 443
robber barons. *See* Civil War and robber
  tariff barons
Robbins, Lionel Charles, 321–323, 325–327, 335,
  363, 398
Robertson, Edward V., 376
Rockefeller, John D., 100, 138, 151
Rogers, Will, 236
Roosevelt, Eleanor, 209, 215–217, 221
Roosevelt, Elliott, 297–298
Roosevelt, Franklin D. (FDR), 166, 188,
  234, 271, 286, 298, 445. *See also* Anglo-
  American special relationship; Atlantic
  Charter; FDR and Cordell Hull; FDR's
  Brain Trust; multilateral trading system,
  emergence of; New Deal
  Atlantic Charter, 297–304, 562–563
  calls for economic bill of rights, 394
  correspondence with Churchill, 285–286
  as governor, 190
  legacy of, 31
  meetings with Keynes, 291, 294
  presidential appointments by, 229–233
  proposal for renewal of RTAA, 317–318
  reelections of, 277–278, 286–287
  as assistant secretary of Navy, 165, 214
  Stage II for Lend-Lease, 324–325
  as vice-presidential candidate, 174
  on working classes as "forgotten man," 221–222
Roosevelt, Theodore (TR), *139,* 173, 208, 211.
  See also Progressive era and trade reform
  New Nationalism and, 149–151, 158–159
  as president, 135, 137–142
  as presidential candidate in 1912, 157–161
  reeducation on trade politics, 138–142
  on Sinclair's book, 137
Roper, Daniel C., 264
Rosenbaum, Jon, 495
Rosenman, Samuel I., 224, 226
Ross, Wilbur, 537–540, 547–551, 553
Roth, William A., 464
Rove, Karl, 133
RTAA. *See* Reciprocal Trade Agreements Act
  (RTAA) (1934)
rubber industry and tariffs/trade, 373–374, 376
rugged individualism concept. *See* Hoover,
  Herbert

runaway plants. *See* outsourcing of jobs
Rusk, Dean, 458, 465
Russell, Bertrand, 289
Russell, Richard B., 480
Ruttenberg, Stanley H., 433–434, 451
Ryan, Paul, 516–517, 527

Saavedra Lamas, Carlos, 258–260
Salinas de Gortari, Carlos, 491
Samet, Andrew, 496
Samuelson, Paul A., 468–469, 489
Sanders, Bernie, 521, 527, 545–546, 555
Sasse, Ben, 542
Sayre, Francis B., 282
Schacht, Hjalmar H. G., 268, 284, 538
Schattschneider, E. E., 192, 194
Schlesinger, Arthur, Jr., 45, 80, 81, 220–221, 270
Schwab, Susan C., 516, 517
Scott, Robert E., 559
Seattle Machinists Union, 4
Seattle WTO Ministerial Conference (1999).
    See World Trade Organization (WTO);
    Battle in Seattle protests (1999)
SEUM (Society for Establishing Useful
    Manufactures), 43–44
Seventeenth Amendment, 119, 214
Sherman, John, 94–95, 102, 106
Sherman Anti-Trust Act (1890), 131, 161
Sherman Silver Purchase Act (1890), 126
Shreve, Earl O., 428–429
Shultz, George P., 475–478
Simmons, Furnifold M., 165
Sinclair, Upton, 136–137
Sixteenth Amendment, 131, 163
slavery, 86–90
Sloan, Alfred P., 199
Smith, Adam, 118. *See also* Adam Smith and
    history of US trade politics, introduction
    engraving of, *10*
    H. Clay, critic of, 58
    influence on GATT principles, 439
    Jacksonian democracy and, 80
    on labor, 555
    Obama on, 486
    perfectionists and, 443–447
    quotations of, 1, 11, 12–16, 17, 18
    relations with B. Franklin, 30
    on trade restrictions, 19–21
    The Wealth of Nations, 8, 9–11, 14, 15–16,
        17–18, 21, 30, 40, 153, 555
Smith, Alfred E., 189, 214, 216–217, 219–220,
    222, 315, 446
Smith, H. Norman, 331

Smith, James, Jr. "Sugar Jim," 155
Smith, Jean Edward, 208
Smoot, Reed O., 145, 176, *191*, 196–200,
    204, 577n46
Smoot-Hawley during 1920s, 176–204
    introductory overview, 176–177
    Collier Tariff Bill (1932),vetoed, 204
    Coolidge prosperity, 183–187, 192
    flexible tariff authority provision, 180–183,
        191, 197, 198–200, 577n62
    Fordney-McCumber Tariff Act (1922),
        178–183, 194–195
    Hoover the "wonder boy," 187–190
    McNary-Haugen Act, vetoed, 186–187, 189,
        190–191
    Smoot-Hawley Tariff Act (1930), 190–204
Smoot-Hawley Tariff Act (1930), 9, 190–204,
    221, 223, 262, 272–273
smuggling, 22, 50, 95–96
Social Insurance and Allied Services
    (Beveridge), 398
Socialist League, 364
Society for Establishing Useful Manufactures
    (SEUM), 43–44
South Carolina Exposition and Protest
    (Calhoun), 68–69, 70–71, 73, 75
Soviet Union
    Churchill's "iron curtain" speech on, 339
    as nonparticipant in GATT negotiations,
        343, 393
    proposed MFN treatment for, 477–479
    US postwar concerns regarding, 341,
        353–355, 357, 413
Special Trade Representative (STR),
    457–461, 468, 475, 480, 481. *See also*
    Office of the United States Trade
    Representative (USTR)
Spicer, Sean M., 530–531
Stalin, Josef, 339, 355
Standard Oil Company, 138, 209
Stans, Maurice, 468
steel industry and tariffs/trade, 99–101, 106,
    123–124, 273, 464–465, 483, 558
Steffens, Lincoln, 137, 154
Sterling-Dollar Diplomacy (Gardner), 334
Stettinius, Edward R., 317, 319
Stevens, Thaddeus, 95, 97, 98
Stimson, Henry, 200, 264, 274, 287
Stowe, Harriet Beecher, 88
Strauss, Robert S., 484–485
Strong, Caleb, 52
sugar industry and tariffs/trade, 66, 120, 123,
    127, 155, 163, 164

Sumner, William Graham, 142
Swank, James M., 121
Sweeney, John J., 4–5, 504–506

TAA. *See* Trade Adjustment
    Assistance (TAA)
Taft, Robert A., 287, *289*
    GATT negotiations, 352
    opposition to British loan, 337, 339
    opposition to Lend-Lease, 288
    opposition to Trade Agreements extension,
        321, 423
    opposition to Truman Doctrine, 354
    as presidential candidate, 448
    votes for Wagner Act, 395
Taft, William Howard, *139*, 142, 144–151,
    157–161, 174
Taft-Hartley Act (1947), 398
Talmadge, Herman, 480–481
Tammany Hall, 156–157, 189, 214, 216
Tarbell, Ida Minerva, *107*
    declines position on US Tariff
        Commission, 170
    on impact of tariffs on wages, 143–144
    on Thaddeus Stevens's protectionist
        views, 95
    as journalist for *McClure's Magazine*,
        137–138, 154
    on robber tariff barons, 121
    support for Hoover, 189
    on T. Roosevelt's views on tariff reform,
        141–142
    on tariff bills, 106–107, 123, 141–143,
        145, 571*n*15
    The Tariff in Our Times, 95, 142–143
Tariff Acts
    of 1789, 39
    of 1816, 55
    of 1824, 56, 67
    of 1842, 83
    of 1846, 84, 90–91
    of 1857, 88, 97
    of 1861, 92–93, 94–96
    of 1864, 93, 97
    of 1883, 102–107
    of 1890, 122–124, 126, 132, 134
    of 1894, 125–128, 133
    of 1897, 133–134, 141, 143–144, 145
    of 1909, 144–148, 150, 154–155
    of 1913, 163–165, 170, 178–179
    of 1921, 178
    of 1922, 178–180, 262, 273
    of 1930, 9, 190–204, 221, 223, 262, 272–273

tariff for revenue only concept, 127, 165, 314.
    See also Democratic Party; Jacksonian
    democracy and free trade
Tariff History of the United States, The
    (Taussig), 192
Tariff in Our Times, The
    (Tarbell), 95, 142–143
Tariff of Abominations (1828), 66–69, 72, 75,
    82, 444
Taussig, Charles W., 227
Taussig, Frank W.
    appointment to US Tariff Commission,
        170, 178
    on Copper Act, 99
    on flexible tariff authority, 181–182
    on growth of tariffs during Civil War,
        93–95, 96
    on Hawley-Smoot Act, 198
    on Smoot, 196
    on Tariff Act of 1883, 106
    Tariff History of the United States, The, 192
    on Underwood Tariff, 165
Taxation: The People's Business (Mellon), 185
Tax Foundation report, 537–538
Taylor, Zachary, 84
TEA. *See* Trade Expansion Act (TEA) (1962)
textile industry and tariffs/trade, 340, 446,
        452–454, 456–457, 463–464, 468, 483,
        492–494, 498, 501
Textile Workers Union of America (CIO), 340,
        423, 446, 452
Theory of Moral Sentiments, The (Smith), 11
Thomas, William M. "Bill," 513, 515
Thoughts and Details on Scarcity (Burke), 153
Thurman, Allen G., 121–122
Tillerson, Rex, 536, 551
Tobin, Maurice J., 432
Toombs, Robert A., 93
TPP. *See* Trans-Pacific Strategic Economic
        Partnership Agreement (TPP)
TRA. *See* Trade Reform Act of 1973 (TRA)
Trade Act of 1974, 479–484, 491–492, 528,
        544, 546. *See also* Trade Reform Act of
        1973 (TRA)
Trade Adjustment Assistance (TAA), 448–449,
        455–456, 462, 474–477, 482, 513, 514,
        520, 524
Trade Agreements Act (1979), 484–485
Trade and Development Act (2000), 514–515
Trade Expansion Act (TEA) (1962), 454–462,
        466–468, 470, 481–482, 558
Trade Reform Act of 1973 (TRA), 470–475,
        478–485. *See also* Trade Act of 1974

Transatlantic Trade and Investment
  Partnership (T-TIP), 547–548
Trans-Pacific Strategic Economic Partnership
  Agreement (TPP), 521–529, 534–535, 550,
  554–555, 558–561
Treadway, Allen T., 261
Treatise of Human Nature, The (Hume), 11
Treatise on Money (Keynes), 290
Treaty of Ghent (1815), 53, 74
Truman, Harry S., 349. *See also* new economic
  order, during Truman years; postwar
  Atlantic alliance
  GATT negotiations, 343, 347, 349–350, 352,
    353–357, 360–361, 368
  Korean War, 435–436, 441
  labor legislation and, 397, 399
  Lend-Lease termination, 324
  Marshall Plan, 353–357, 533
  NATO ratification, 412–413
  political capital of, 351
  postwar loan to British, 324–325,
    328–329, 336
  re-election of, 411
  relations with Soviet Union, 339
  reliance on Clayton for trade advice, 314–315
  renewal of RTAA, 319, 320–321
  as senator, 395
  signs Trade Agreements Extension Act,
    411, 424
Truman Doctrine, 354–357
Trumka, Richard, 525–526, 554
Trump, Donald J., 527, 530
Trump Trade Doctrine, impacts on liberal
  economic order, 528–563
  overview, 526–527
  America First slogan, 532–546, 553
  the "forgotten man" slogan, 553–563
  NAFTA renegotiation, 522–524, 530–531,
    538, 542, 547, 548–553, 554
  potential for mega-regional bilateral FTAs,
    546–548
  tenets of trade doctrine, 537–539, 543–546
  Trump as transactional businessman,
    529–532
trusts, 113–114, 115, 138, 158–159
T-TIP (Transatlantic Trade and Investment
  Partnership), 547–548
Tugwell, Rexford G.
  on Hull, 227, 246, 264
  on Keynesian myth on New Deal, 290
  as member of Brain Trust, 226–229, 238,
    240, 242, 246, 248, 255
Twain, Mark, 85, 141

Twenty-first Amendment, 236
Tydings, Millard, 436
Tyler, John, 78, 82–83

UAW. *See* United Automobile Workers (UAW)
Uncle Tom's Cabin (Stowe), 88
Underwood, Oscar W., 152, 155, 163–165, 208
Union for Democratic Action, 396. *See also*
  Americans for Democratic Action
Union of Needletrades, Industrial and Textile
  Employees (UNITE), 493–494, 497,
  499, 501
Union Pacific Railroad, 102–103, 109
United Automobile Workers (UAW),
  474–475, 478
United Hatters, Cap and Millinery Workers
  International Union, 452
United Kingdom (UK). *See also* Anglo-
  American special relationship; postwar
  Atlantic alliance; *specific leaders*
  Brexit, 533, 535–536, 546–547
  Coercive Acts (1774), 37
  Corn Laws, 23, 24–27, 30, 56, 64
  currency crisis, 421
  EEC and, 455
  history of labor law in, 12–14
  impact of free-trade era, 28–30
  imperial preference system, 241, 243,
    279–282, 288, 293, 296, 298–304, 322–323,
    325–333, 363, 365–376, 487–488
  Navigation Acts, 19–20, 26
  Ottawa Agreements, 202, 272–273,
    279–280, 293
  protection of textile technology, 43
  Royal Navy, 51
  Smith's legacy in nineteenth century, 21–28
  standard of living of working classes,
    12, 29–30
  Tea Act Crisis (1773), 37
  trade negotiations with US during 1930s,
    279–283
  trade policies with colonial North America,
    36–38, 48, 54, 85
  US postwar loan to, 324–326, 328–330,
    335–342, 346–347
  WW II and, 286–287, 325
United Mine Workers, 446–447
United Nations (UN). *See also* ITO
  Charter (1948)
  Conference on Trade and Employment
    (1947), 380
  Economic and Social Council, 346, 437
  Environment Program, 507

formation of, 310–311, 317–318, 435, 441
Geneva headquarters, 357–358
Security Council, 435
United States (US). *See also* Anglo-American
    special relationship; *specific presidents,
    congressmen, eras, and legislation*
    early state regulation of trade/tariffs, 38
    joins ILO, 495
    manufacturing output (1926–29), 185–186
    regulation of shrimp imports, 3–4
    treaty of reciprocity with Great Britain, 85
United States Chamber of Commerce (USCC)
    on NIRA codes, 238
    positions on tariffs/trade, 179, 274, 405, 408,
        414, 416, 422, 428–429, 470–471, 476, 516
    on proposed WTO Working Group on
        Trade and Labor, 504–505
*United States v. Curtiss-Wright Export
    Corporation* (1936), 262
United Steelworkers, 465, 517, 545
United Textile Workers of America (AFL), 423,
    463, 466
University of Pennsylvania, Wharton School of
    Finance and Economy, 101–102
Uruguay Round Agreements Act (1994),
    545–546
US-Cambodia Textile Agreement (1999), 491–
    503, 511, 519
USCC. *See* United States Chamber of
    Commerce (USCC)
US Congress
    regulation of foreign commerce, 39
    senate as "Millionaire's Club," 119
    tax increases during Civil War, 94
US Constitution. *See also specific amendments*
    constitutional amendment on income tax,
        146–147
    general welfare clause, 44
    on status of slaves, 86, 87
    Webster on, 77
US Customs Service, 197–198
US Generalized System of Preferences (GSP)
    program, 483, 491–492, 495, 497, 519, 524
US International Trade Commission (ITC),
    482, 489
US-Jordan Free Trade Agreement (2000),
    511–514
US Justice Department, anti-trust case against
    U.S. Steel, 151
US–Peru Trade Promotion Agreement (2006),
    519–521
U.S. Steel Corporation, 100, 138, 142, 151,
    464, 542

US Supreme Court
    on congressional authority in trade
        negotiations, 262
    on constitutionality of child labor, 171
    Dred Scott case, 87, 131
    on income tax, 128–131, 146
    on NIRA provisions as
        unconstitutional, 239
    on unconstitutionality of AAA, 275
    viewed as tool of vested corporate interests,
        130–131
US Tariff Commission. *See also* US
    International Trade Commission (ITC)
    appointments to, 170
    denial of TAA petitions, 462
    flexible tariff authority, 180–183, 191
    formation of and reforms, 102–107, 147
    during Kennedy administration, 455
    role with peril point limitations, 407–410,
        423, 442
    RTAA requirement for president to
        consult, 263
    testimony by W. Wilson, 154
    during Truman administration, 352
USTR. *See* Office of the United States Trade
    Representative (USTR)

Van Buren, Martin, 80
Vandenberg, Arthur H., 287, 289, 349, 436
    appointment to Special Committees
        on Post-War Economic Policy and
        Planning, 395
    GATT negotiations, 352–353
    Marshall Plan, 533
    opposition to Lend-Lease, 288
    opposition to RTAA, 261–262
    on Ottawa Agreements, 274
    support for postwar loan to British,
        338–339
    support for Truman Doctrine, 354
    Trade Agreements Act extension debates,
        409–411, 423
vanden Heuvel, Katrina, 554–555
Vanik, Charles A., 477–479
Vaughn, Stephen, 550
Versailles Treaty, 172–173, 291, 495
Victoria, Queen, 25
Victory Liberty Bond Act (1919), 171
Vietnam, Plan for Enforcement of Trade and
    Labor Relations, 525
Vinson, Carl, 457
Vinson, Fred M., 326–327, 334, 336
voter fraud schemes, 121

Wage Earners' Protective League, 427, 446
wages of workers
    employer collusion and, 12–13
    Smith on, 13–14, 17
    Tarbell on impact of tariffs on, 143–144
    trade debates and, 557
    US ranking after Great Recession, 558, 605n39
Wagner, Robert F., 239, 395–396
Wagner Act. *See* National Labor Relations
    Act (1935)
Walker, Robert J., 61, 83
Wallace, George C., 108
Wallace, Henry A., 264, 273, *286*, 296, 337, 339
Wall Street "money trust," 166–168, 233–234
Walsh, Thomas J., 228
Wanamaker, John, 121
War of 1812, 49–53, 63
Warren, Harris, 201
Washington, George, 163, 265
Watergate scandal, 471, 481
Watson, Thomas J., 274
Wealth of Nations, The (Smith), 8, 9–11, 14,
    15–16, 17–18, 21, 30, 40, 153, 555
Webb-Pomerene Act (1918), 168–169
Webster, Daniel, 55, 58–59, 67, 70–72,
    77–78, 80–81
Welles, Sumner, 296, 299, 311
Wells, David A., 96–97, 98–99
Wharton, Deborah Fisher, 101
Wharton, Joseph, 100–102, 103–104, 140
Whig Party, 82–84, 85, 86–87, 90, 91
Whipple, Gaylord C., 430
White, Edward Douglass, 129
White, Harry Dexter, 305–309, 322, 584n50
White, William Allen, 137
Why Quit Our Own (Peek and Crowther), 270
Wilcox, Clair, *401*
    A Charter for World Trade, 420
    on customs unions and free-trade areas, 488
    GATT negotiations, 346, 348–349, 363, 366–
    367, 370–371
    ITO Charter debates in US, 406, 416,
    420–421, 432
    ITO Charter negotiations, 381, 384–391, 398,
    399–400
Willkie, Wendell L., 287, 318
Wilson, Harold, 369, 375–376, 389
Wilson, William L., 126–128, 133
Wilson, Woodrow, *158*, *162*, 177, 190, 208, 212,
    213, 445. *See also* Progressive era and
    trade reform
    final years of, 172–175, 178
    as free trader, 152–157

History of the American People, 152
    legacy of, 31
    on monopoly, 136
    New Freedom reforms, 158–159, 161–169
    during WW I, 169–172, 187–188, 213
Wilson-Gorman Tariff Act (1894), 125–128, 133
Winant, John G., 300, 334
Wolcott, Jesse P., 341
Woll, Matthew, 446
Wood, Edward F. L., 300, 301–302, 325
Wood, Fernando, 103
Wood, Kingsley, 288–289
Woodcock, Leonard, 474–475
Wool Act (1947), vetoed, 359–360
Wool and Woolens Act (1867), 97–98
Wool Manufacturers' Association, 105, 107
wool/woolens industries and tariffs/trade,
    97–98, 106, 107, 113, 134, 163, 357–361
worker rights. *See* worker rights, beyond
    WTO; *specific labor laws*
worker rights, beyond WTO, 486–527
    overview, 486–487
    Bush FTAs with weak labor protections,
    511–514, 516–517, 519–520, 524
    Labor Consistency Plans, 525
    May 10th Agreement "A New Trade Policy
    for America" (2007), 514–521, 558, 600n50
    NAFTA and labor side agreements,
    487–491, 511, 519
    regional free-trade agreements, 488
    TPP and labor, 521–527, 558–561
    US-Cambodia Textile Agreement (1999),
    491–503, 511, 519
    US-Jordan Free Trade Agreement (2000),
    511–514
working classes, in US
    as FDR's "forgotten man," 221–222
    as Donald Trump's "forgotten man," 553–560
    progressive income tax, 163–164
    standard of living, 148
    Tarbell on wages, 143–144
    tariff debates and effects on, 116, 123–124
    working conditions, 118, 136–137
World Bank, 308, 509, 525
World Economic Conference, London, 231,
    239–255, 281
World Trade Organization (WTO). *See also*
    worker rights, beyond WTO
    Agreement provisions, 484
    competitive liberalism concept, 488, 526
    congressional critics of, 6
    dispute resolution, 511
    dispute resolution system, 3, 541, 544–546

Doha Round, 511
Information Technology Agreement, 511
Krugman on leftist views of, 5–6
lack of fair labor standards in, 447, 487
Multi-Fiber Arrangement, 493, 502
OECD joint study on China's manufactured
  exports, 539
Seattle Ministerial Conference (1999), 1–8,
  504–510
Trade Facilitation Agreement, 511
Trump renegotiation of, proposed, 538
Uruguay Round, 487, 493, 508–509
US disputes against China under Obama,
  542–543

US five-year renewal cycle, 545–546
Working Group on Trade and Labor,
  proposed, 504–507, 509
World War I, 28, 169–172, 213
World War II, 31, 286, 325

Xi Jinping, 560–562

Young, Andrew J., 472
Young Women's Christian Organization,
  422–423

Zheng He, 561–562
Zoellick, Robert B., 502, 512, 514